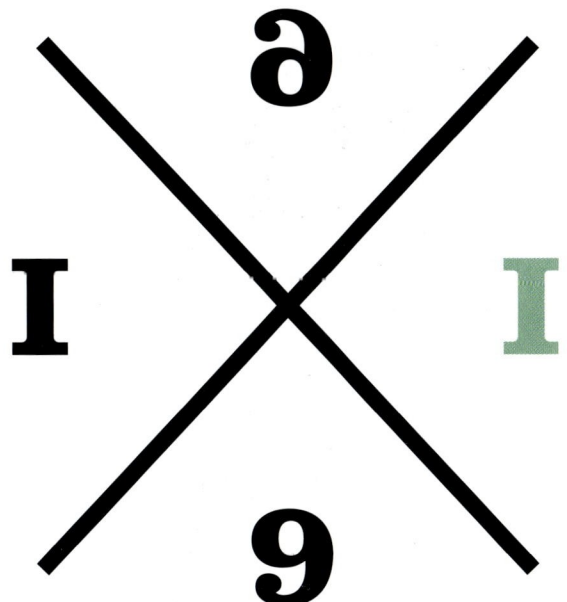

americanillustration o**19**
NINETEEN

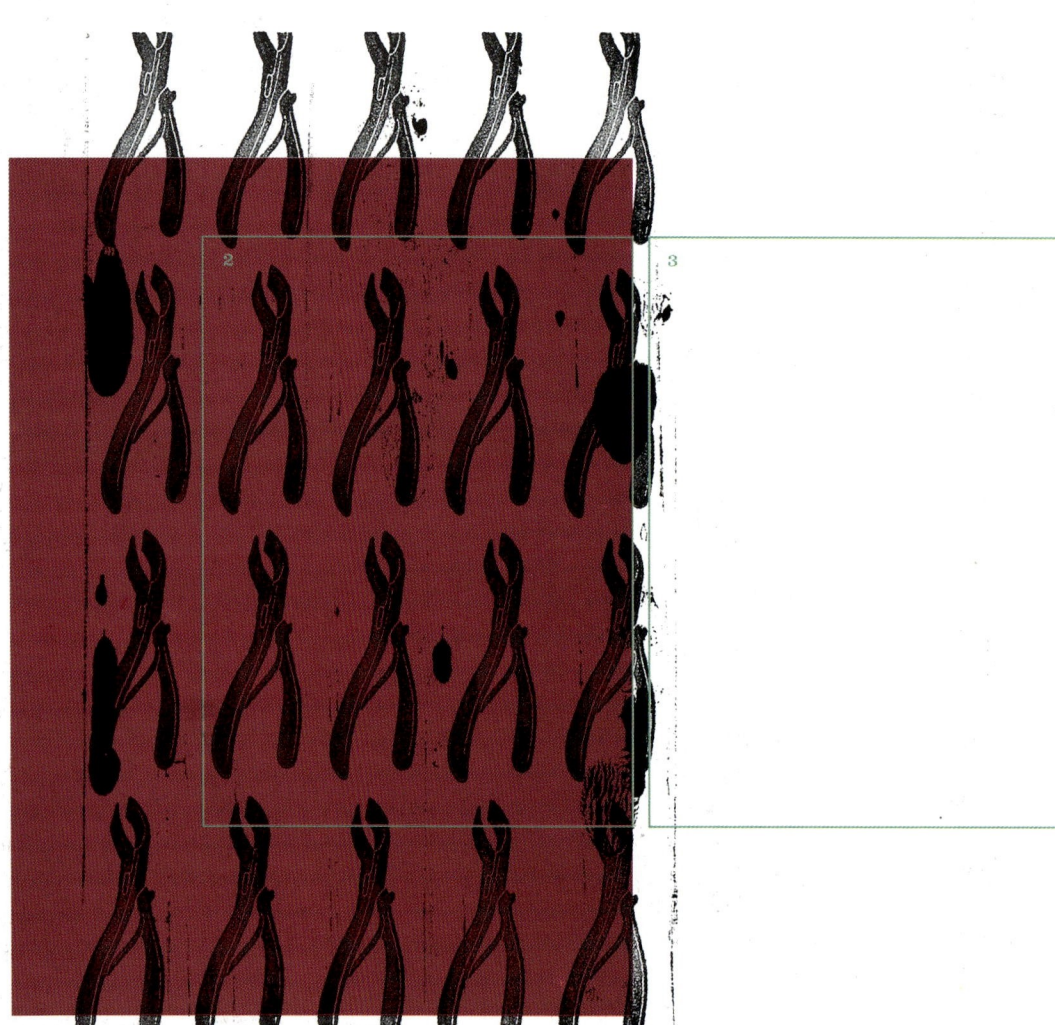

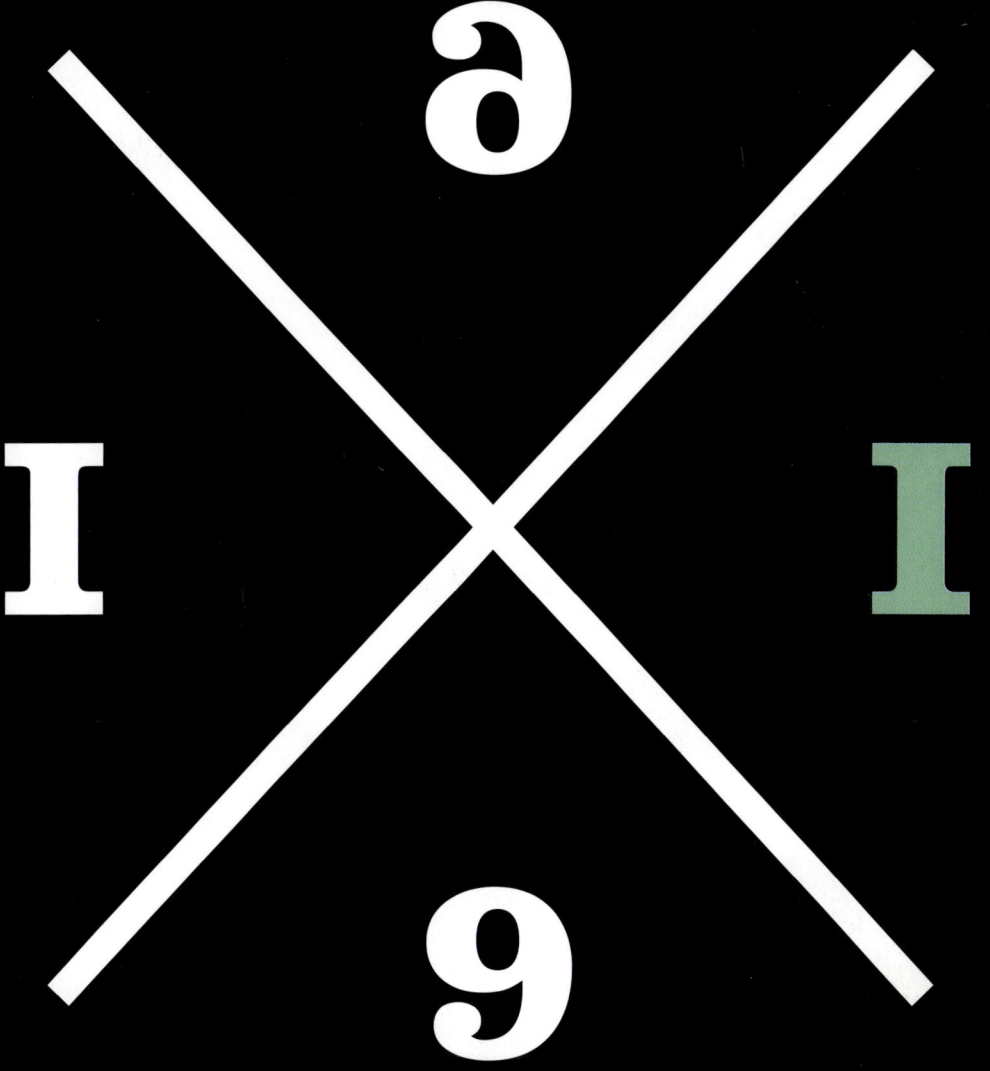

americanillustration o19

NINETEEN

THE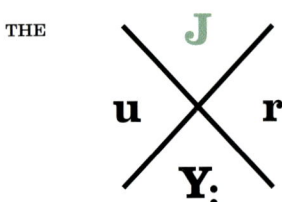

fredwoodward (chairman) ROLLING STONE 01	florianbachleda MAXIMUM GOLF MAGAZINE 02	tombrown TBA+D 03
ruthdiener VIA DESIGN 04	patrickj.b.flynn PJBF DESIGN 05	leanneshapton SATURDAY NIGHT MAGAZINE 06

4

5

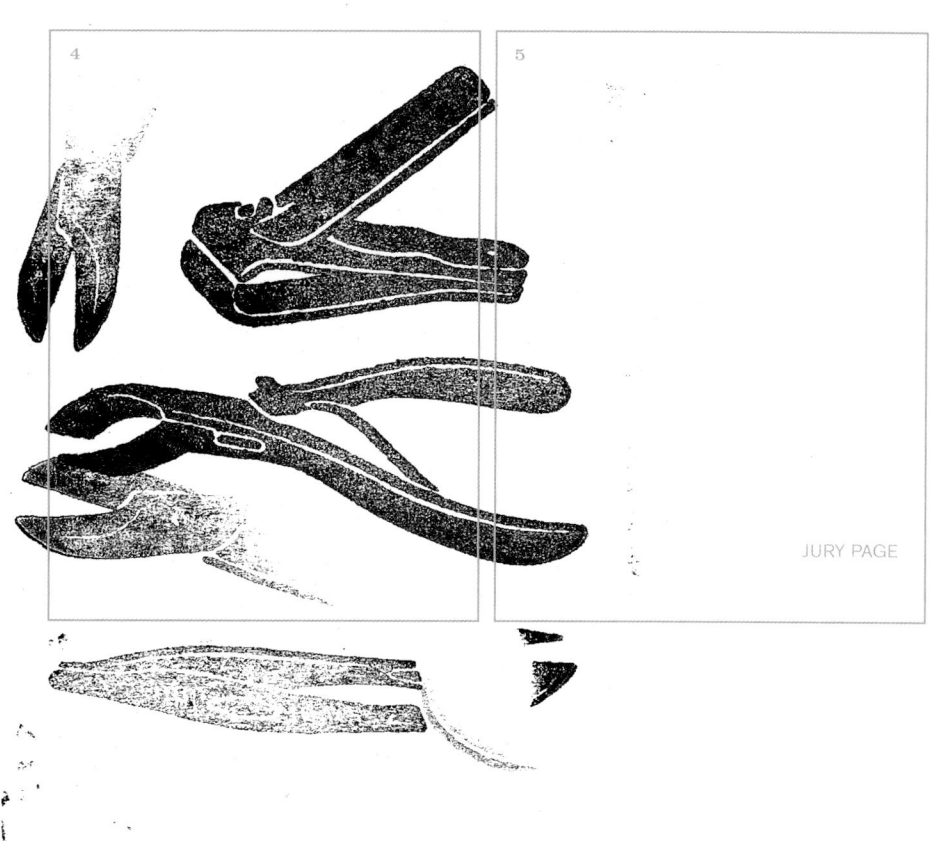

BOOK DESIGN: Tom Brown TBA+D
ASSISTANT DESIGNER: Jenn Roberts
COVER/BOOK ILLUSTRATION: Brian Cronin
CHAIRMAN: Fred Woodward
PUBLISHER: Kenneth Fadner
DIRECTOR: Mark Heflin
CONSULTANT: Peggy Roalf

Special thanks to PARSONS SCHOOL OF DESIGN for providing the space and equipment for the American Illustration 19 judging. The illustrations in this book were originally published in consumer, trade and technical magazines, periodicals, newspapers and their supplements. Others were created for advertisements, promotional design, annual reports, books, cd covers, catalogs, direct mail, self-promotion or were personal works.

Captions and artwork in this book have been supplied by the entrants. While every effort has been made to ensure accuracy, **American Illustration** does not under any circumstances accept any responsibility for errors or omissions. **American Illustration 19** is indexed by illustrator (with address and telephone numbers) and all creative personnel who took part in the creation and utilization of the illustrations in this book.

ISBN:

1886212-14-7

If you are an illustrator, rep., someone who commissions illustration or student and would like to submit work to the next annual competition or if you would like additional copies or back issues, write or call to:

American Illustration
28 West 25th Street, 11th Floor,
New York, NY 10010

TELEPHONE: **(212) 243-5262**   FAX: **(212) 243-5201**
E-MAIL: aiap@idt.net
or go to our web site at **www.ai-ap.com**

••
Distributor to the United States and Canada:
D.A.P./DISTRIBUTED ART PUBLISHERS
155 Sixth Avenue, 2nd Floor
New York, NY 10013-1507
TELEPHONE: (212) 627-1999
FAX: (212) 627-9484

••
Distributor to the Rest of the World:
HARPERCOLLINS INTERNATIONAL
10 East 53rd Street
New York, NY 10022-5299
TELEPHONE: (212) 207-7000
FAX: (212) 207-6927

PRINTER: Dai Nippon, Hong Kong

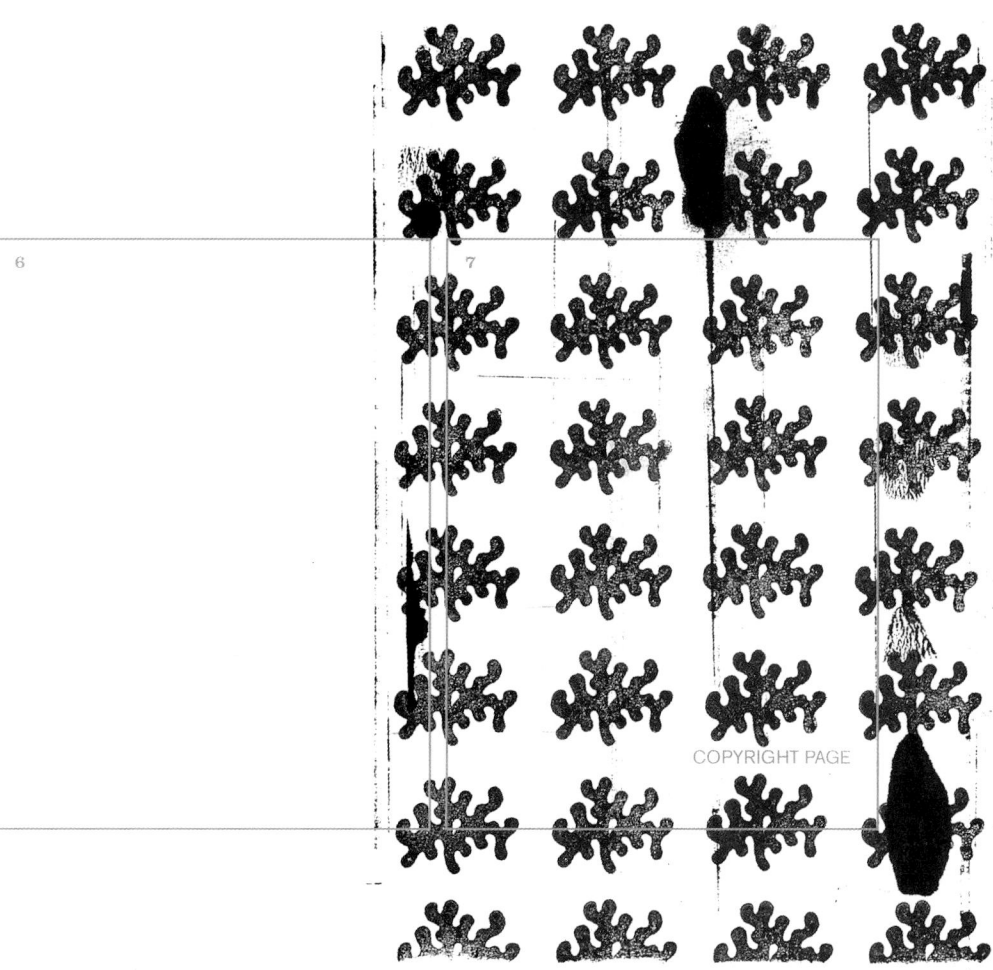

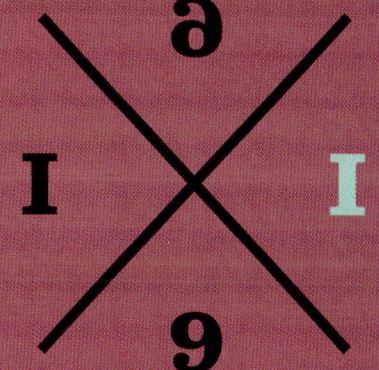

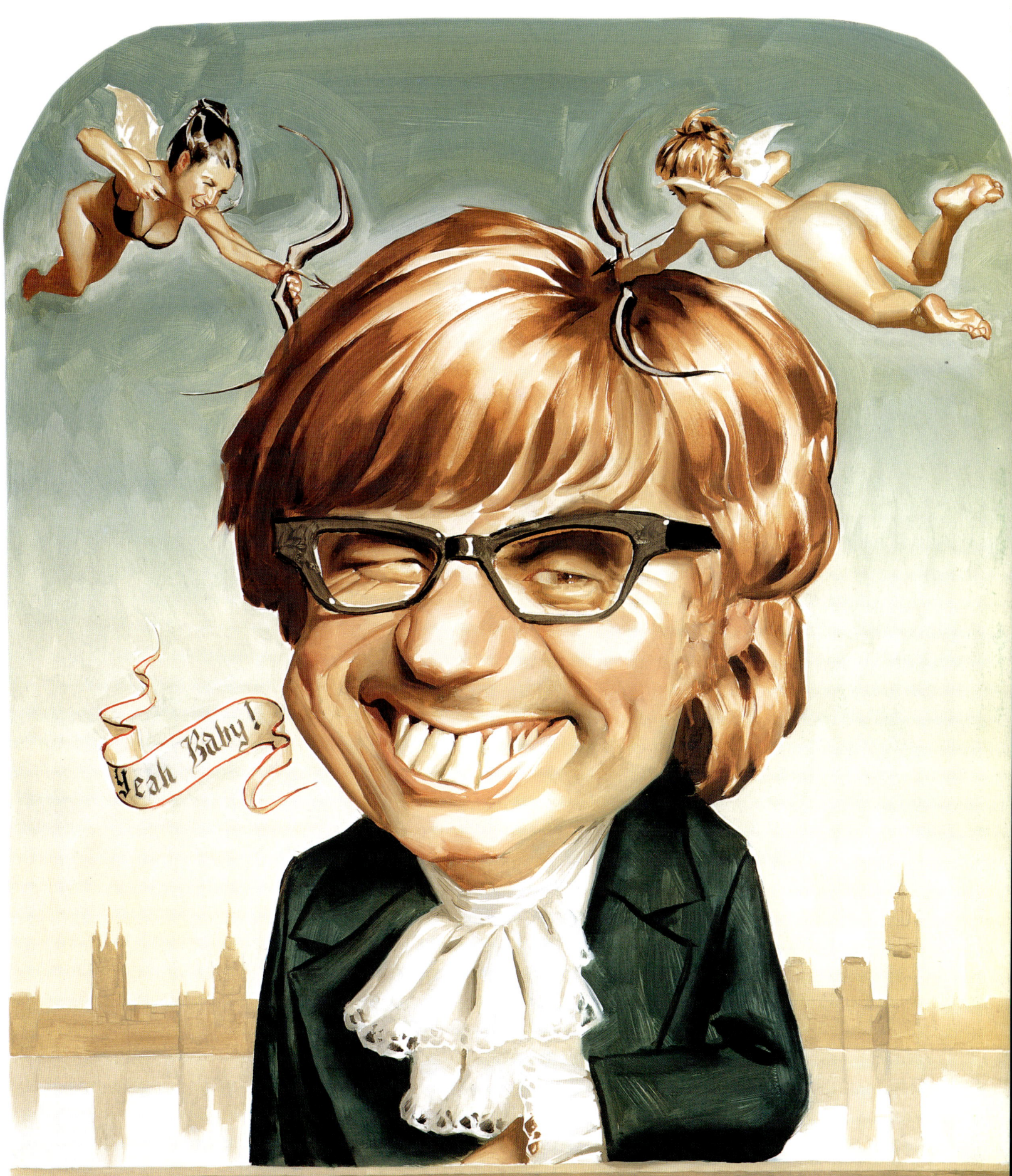

AUSTIN DANGER POWERS

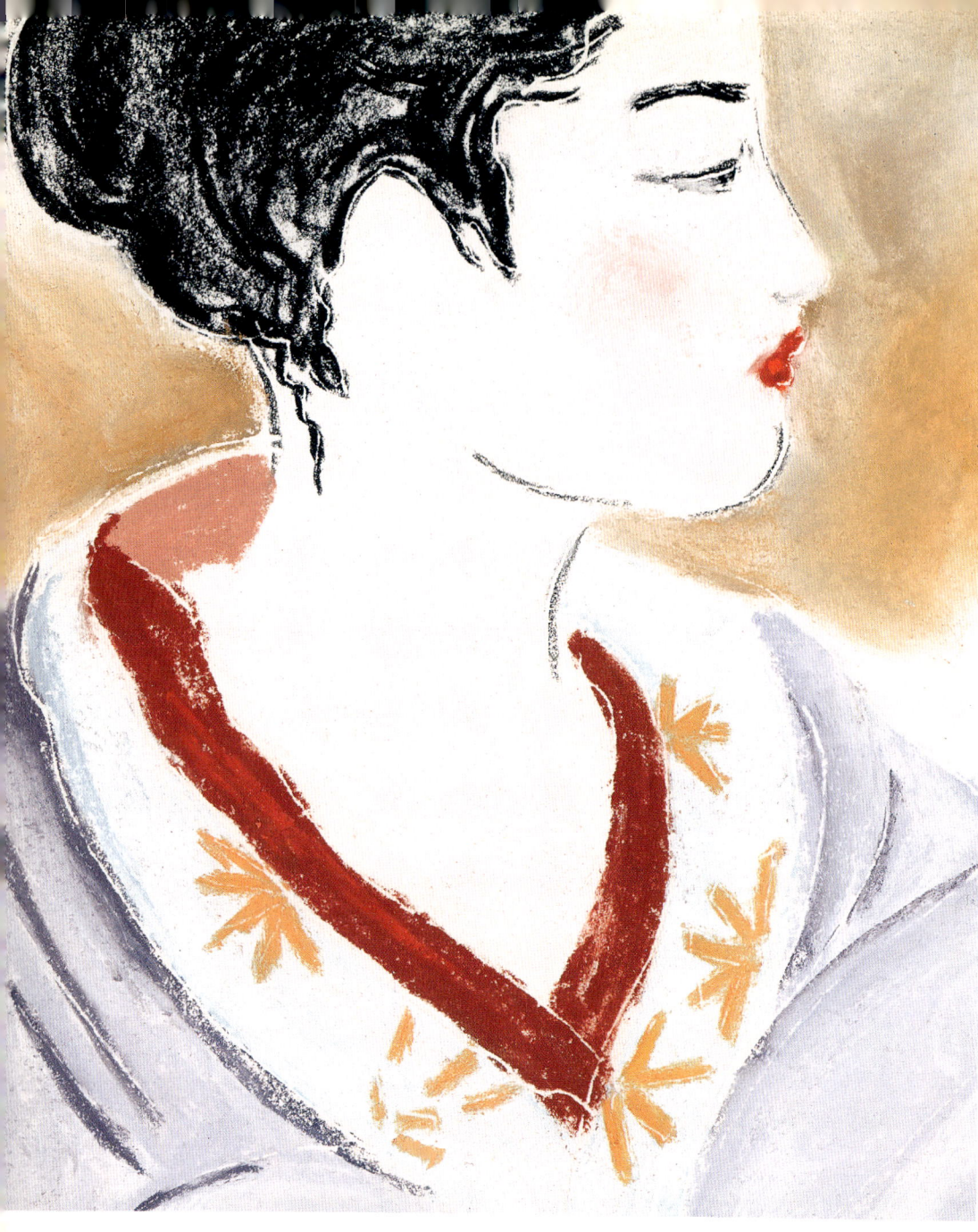

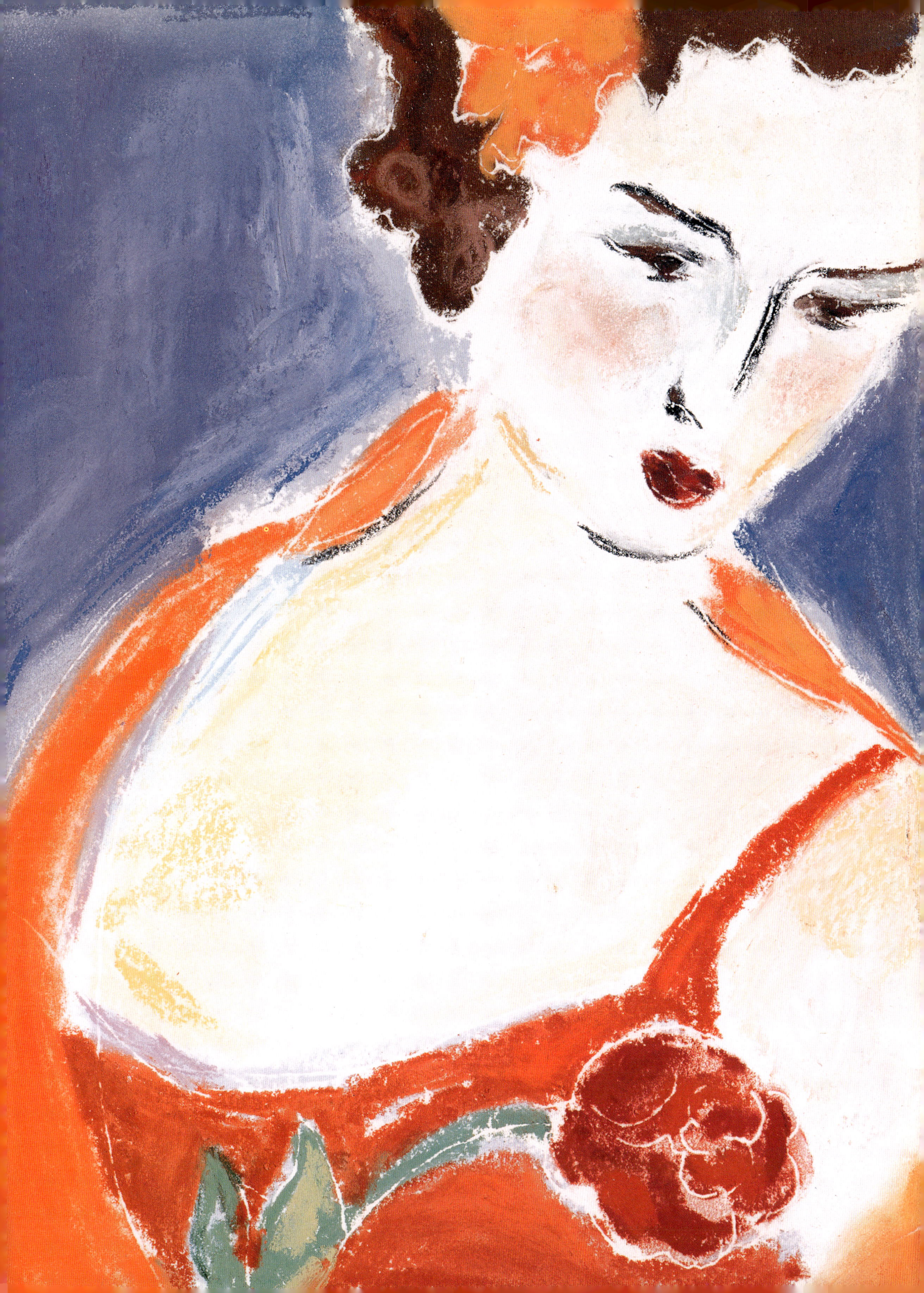

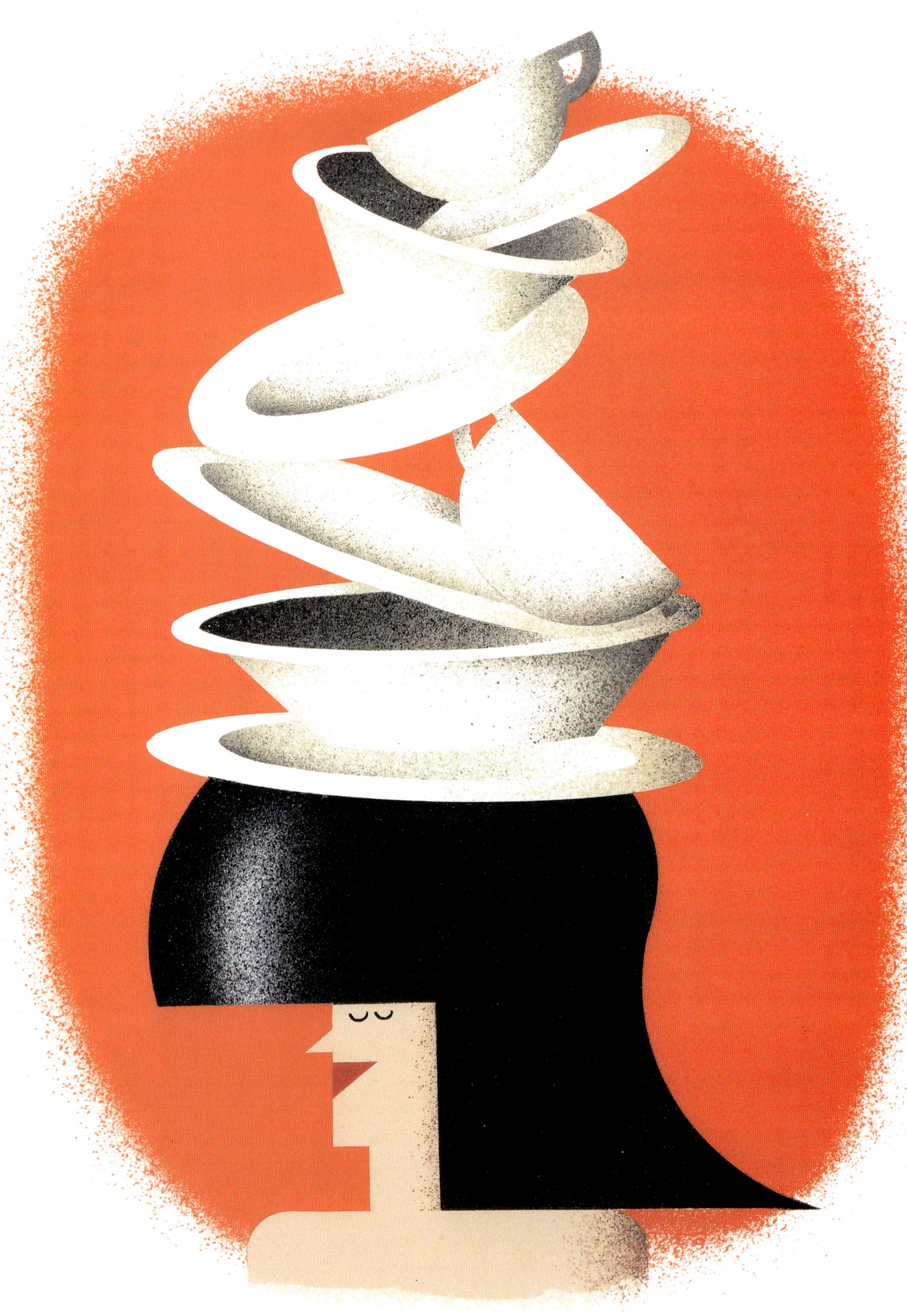

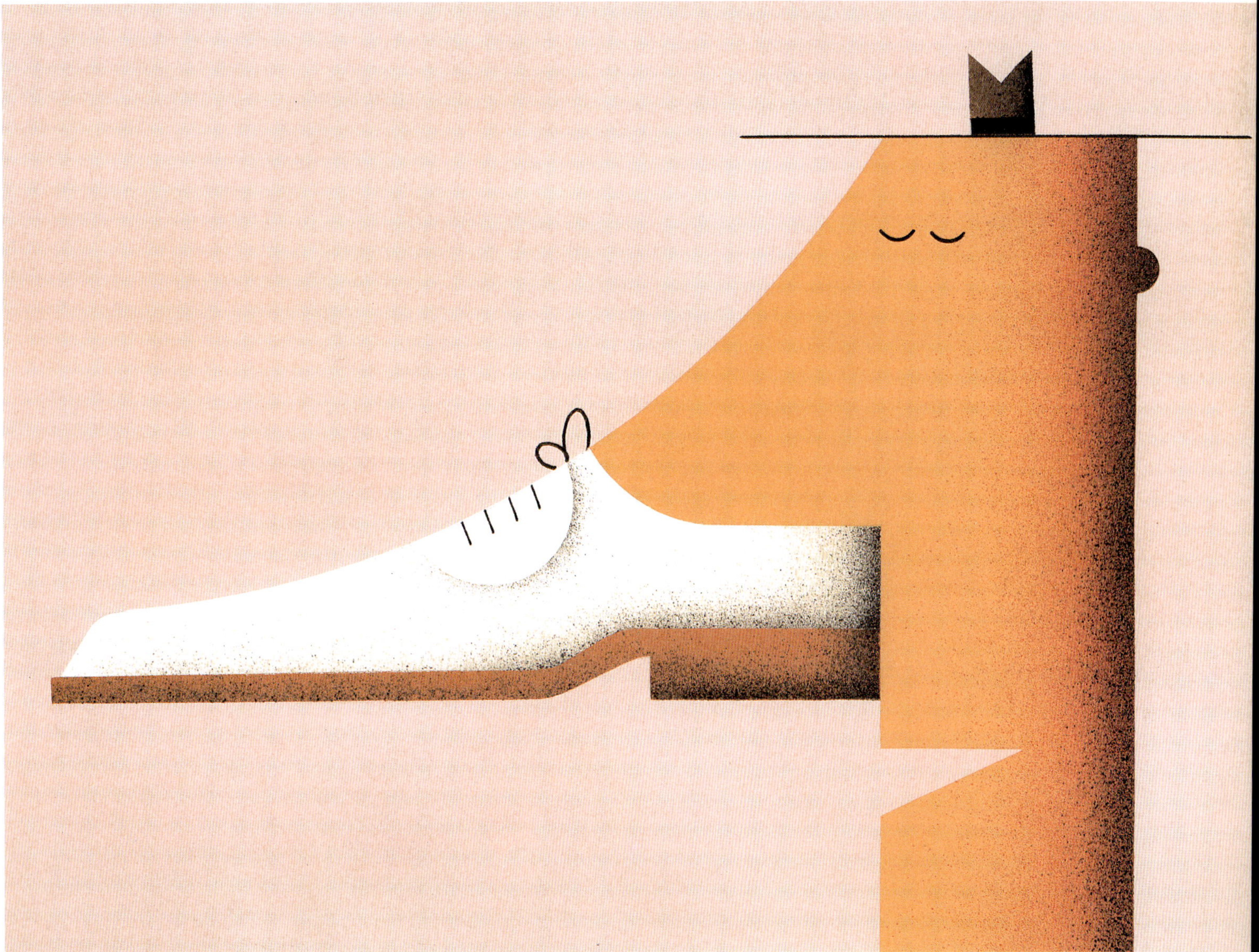

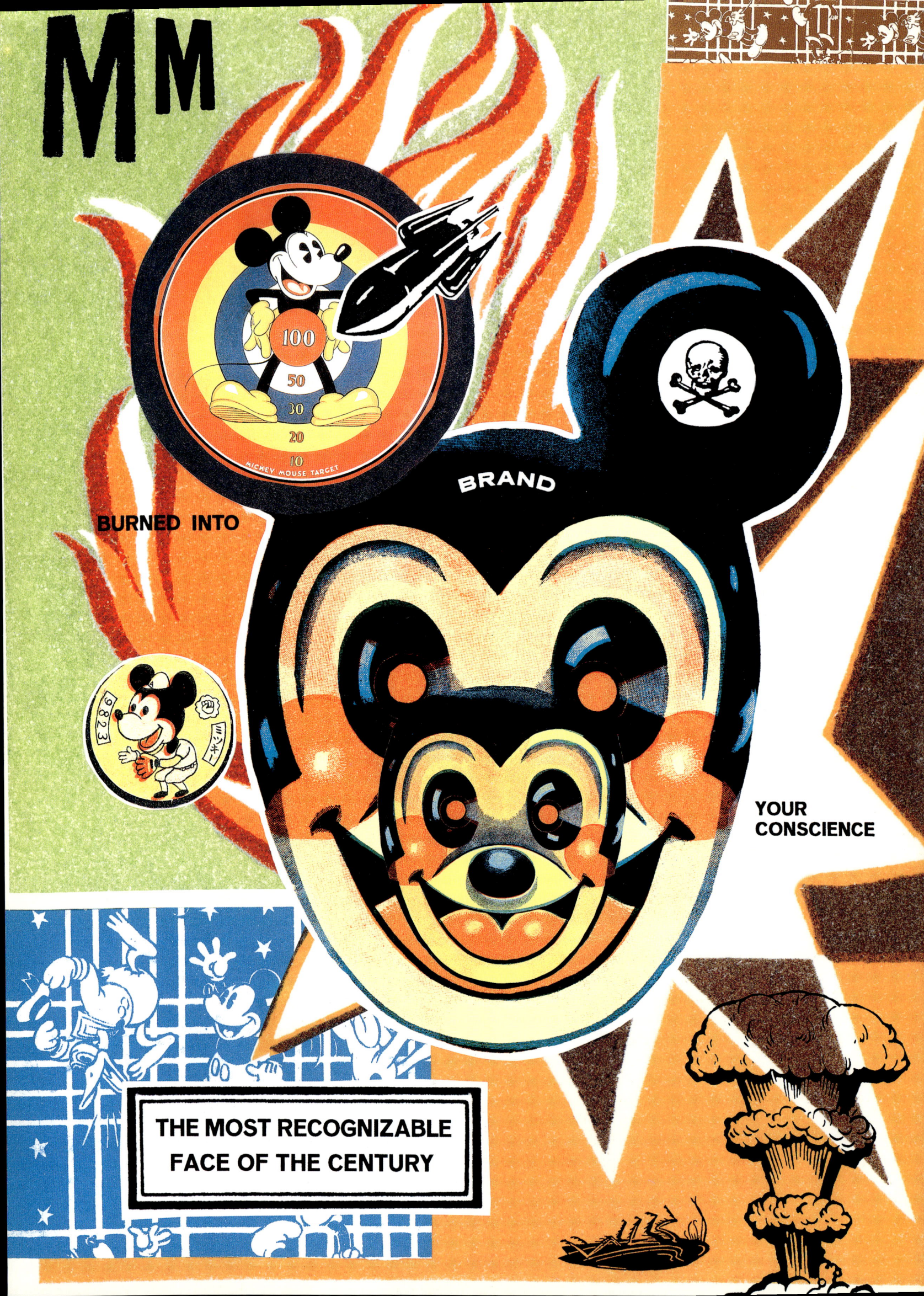

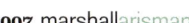

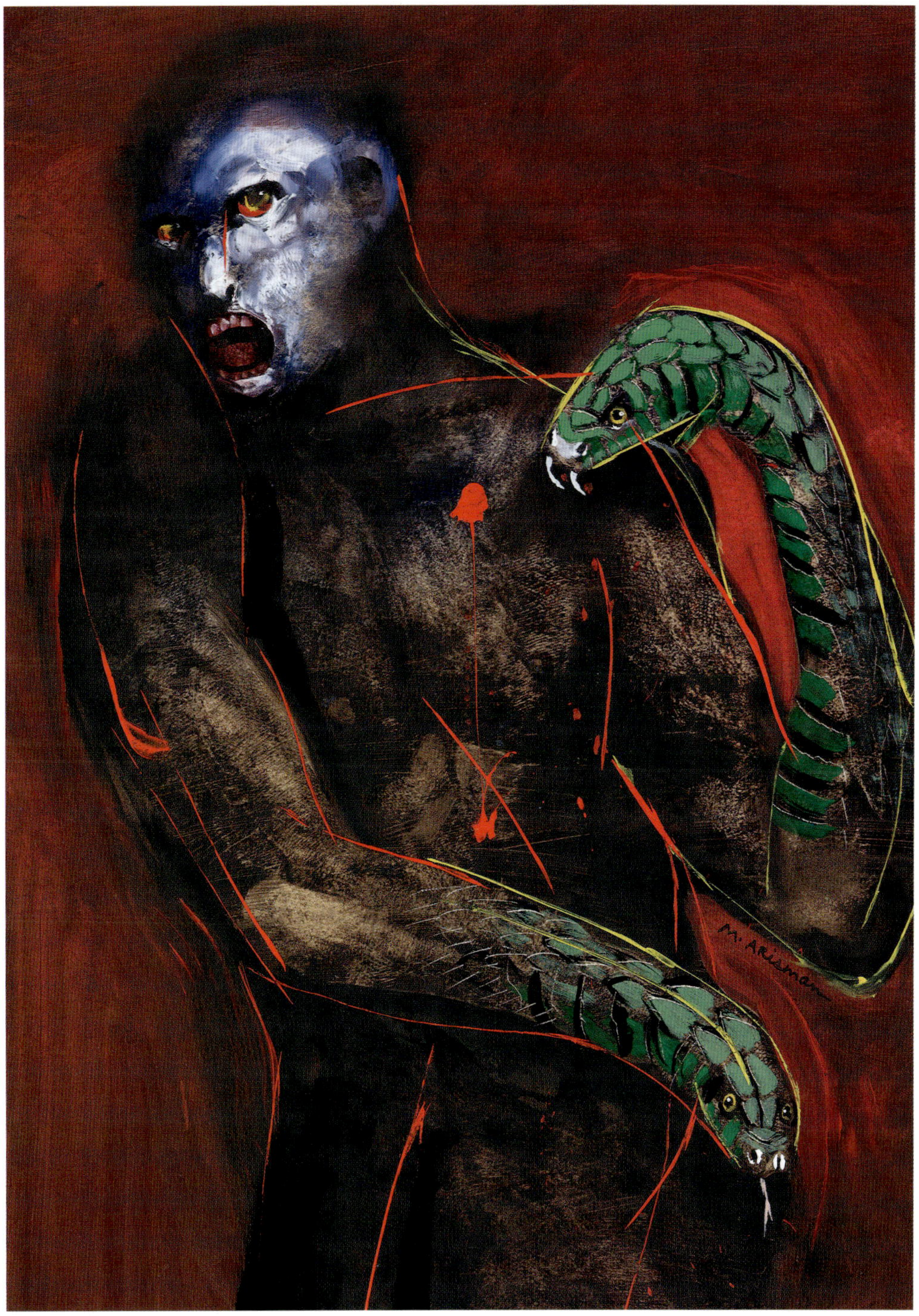

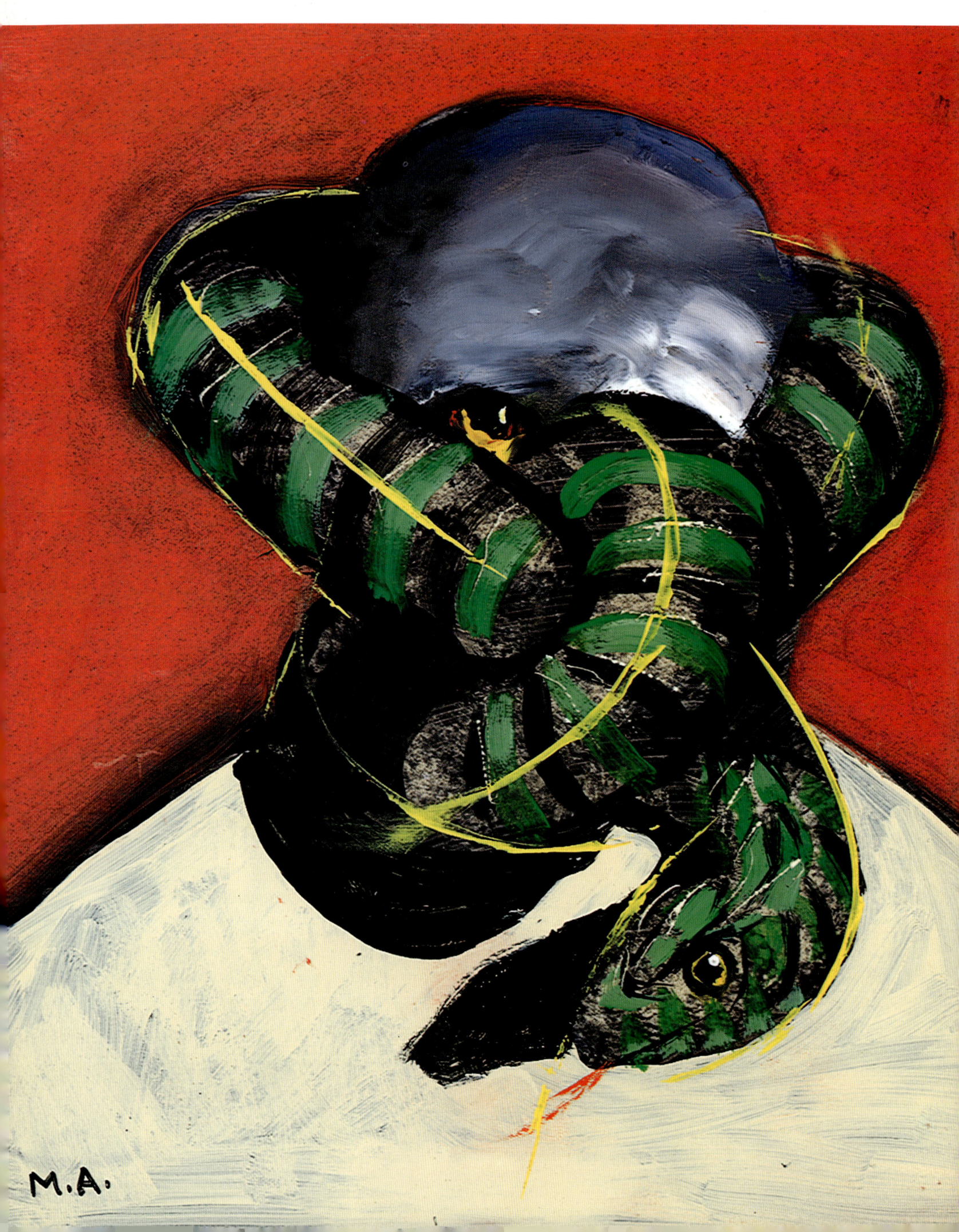

M.A.

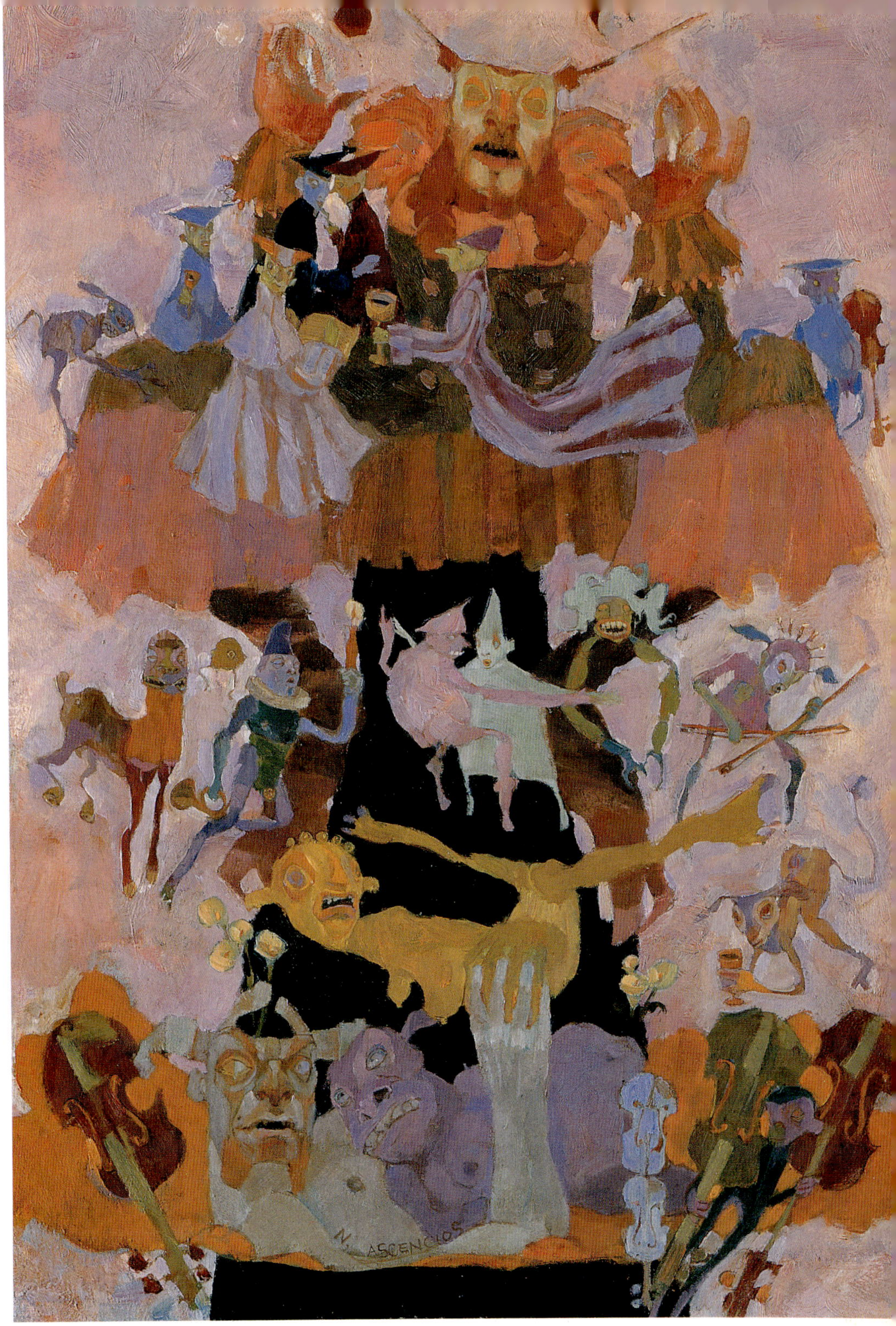

009 n.ascencios

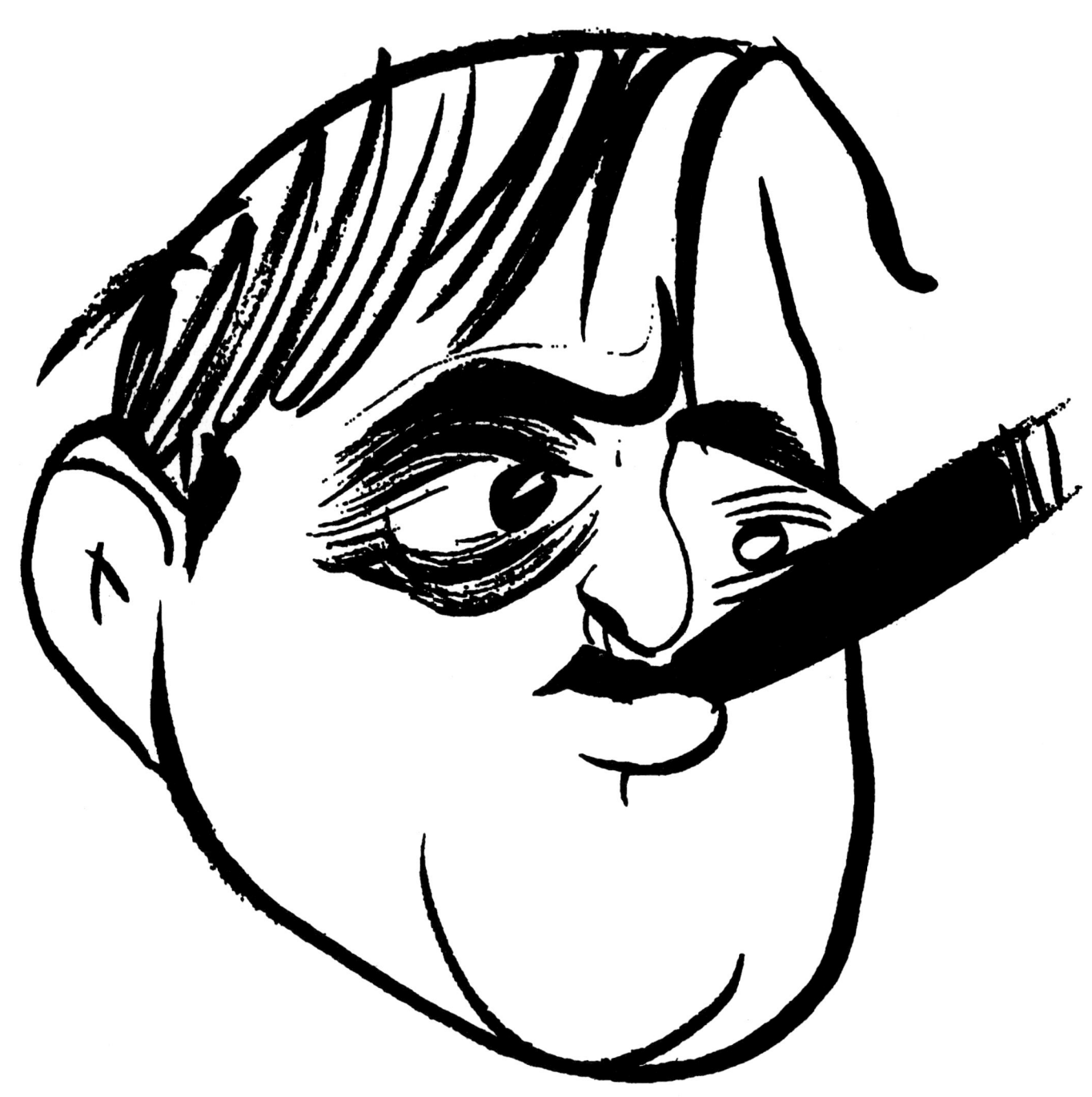

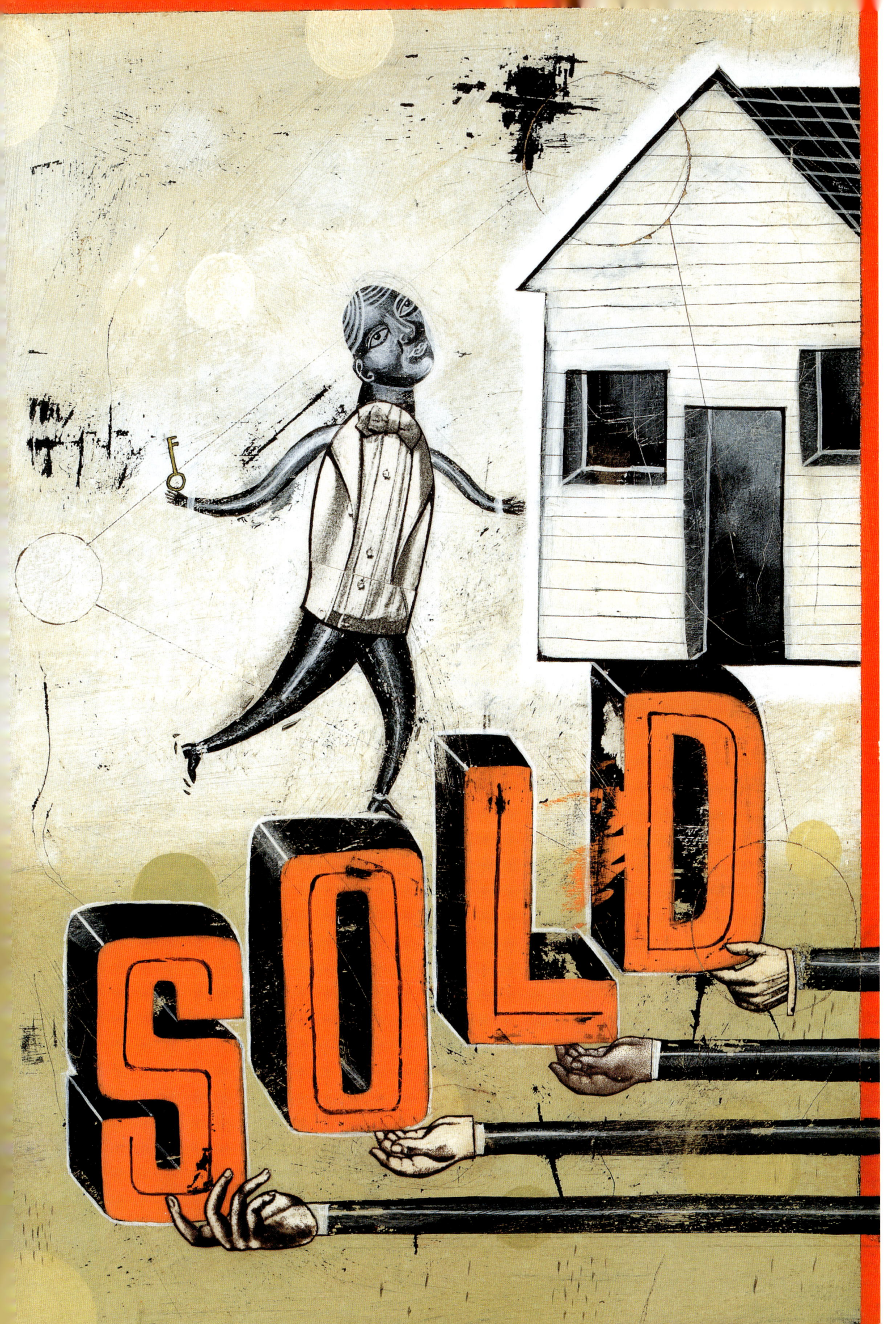

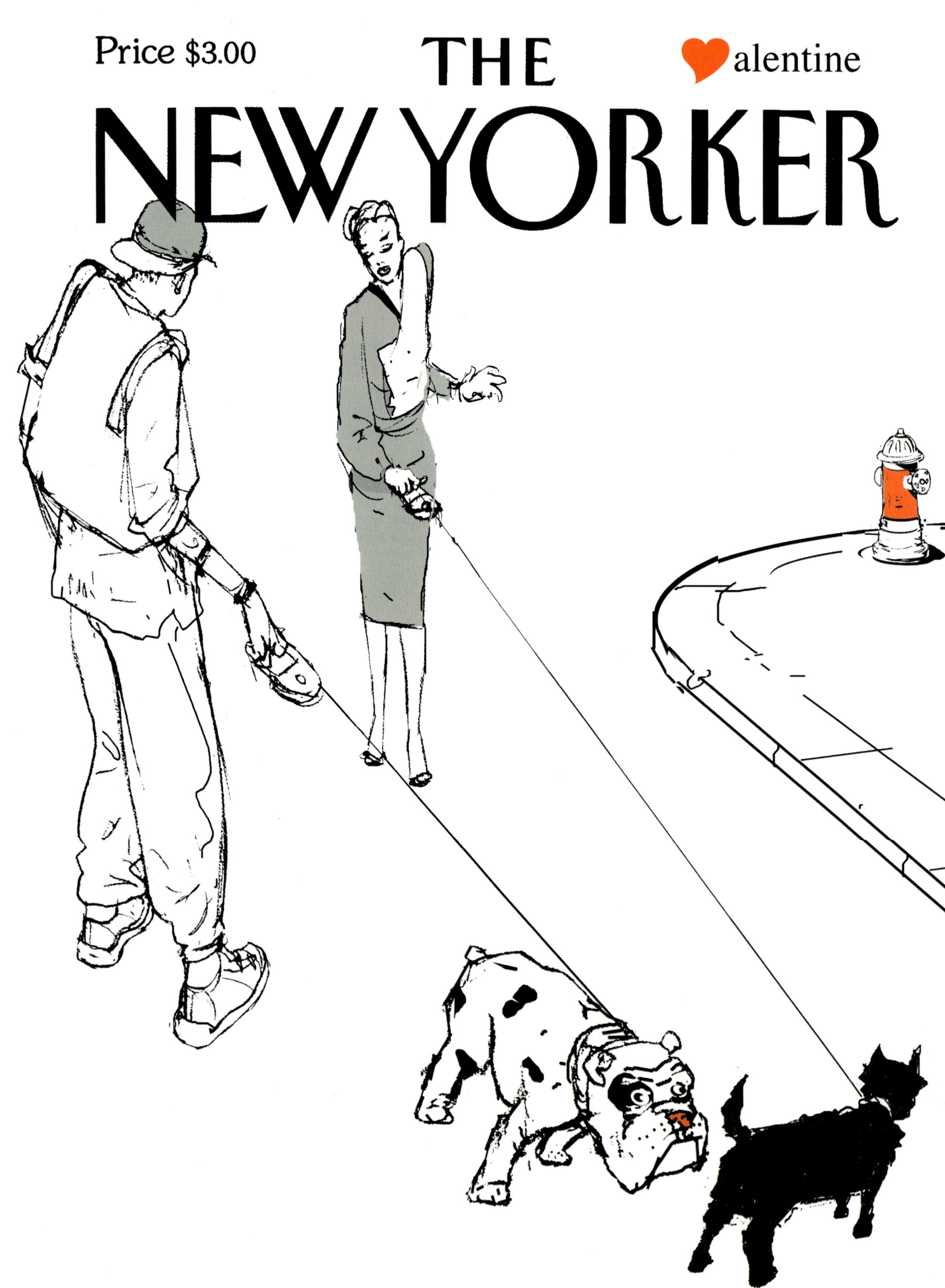

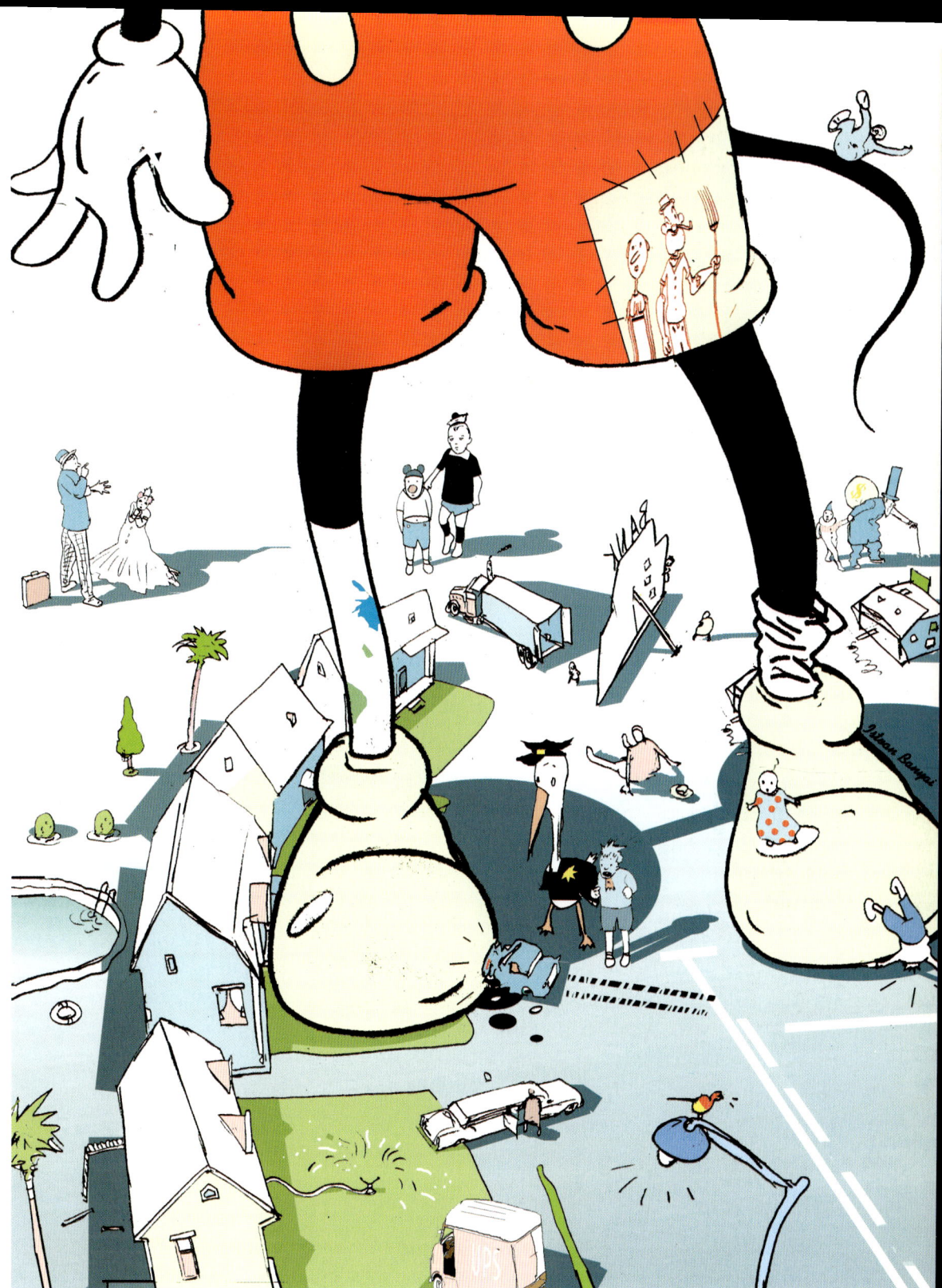

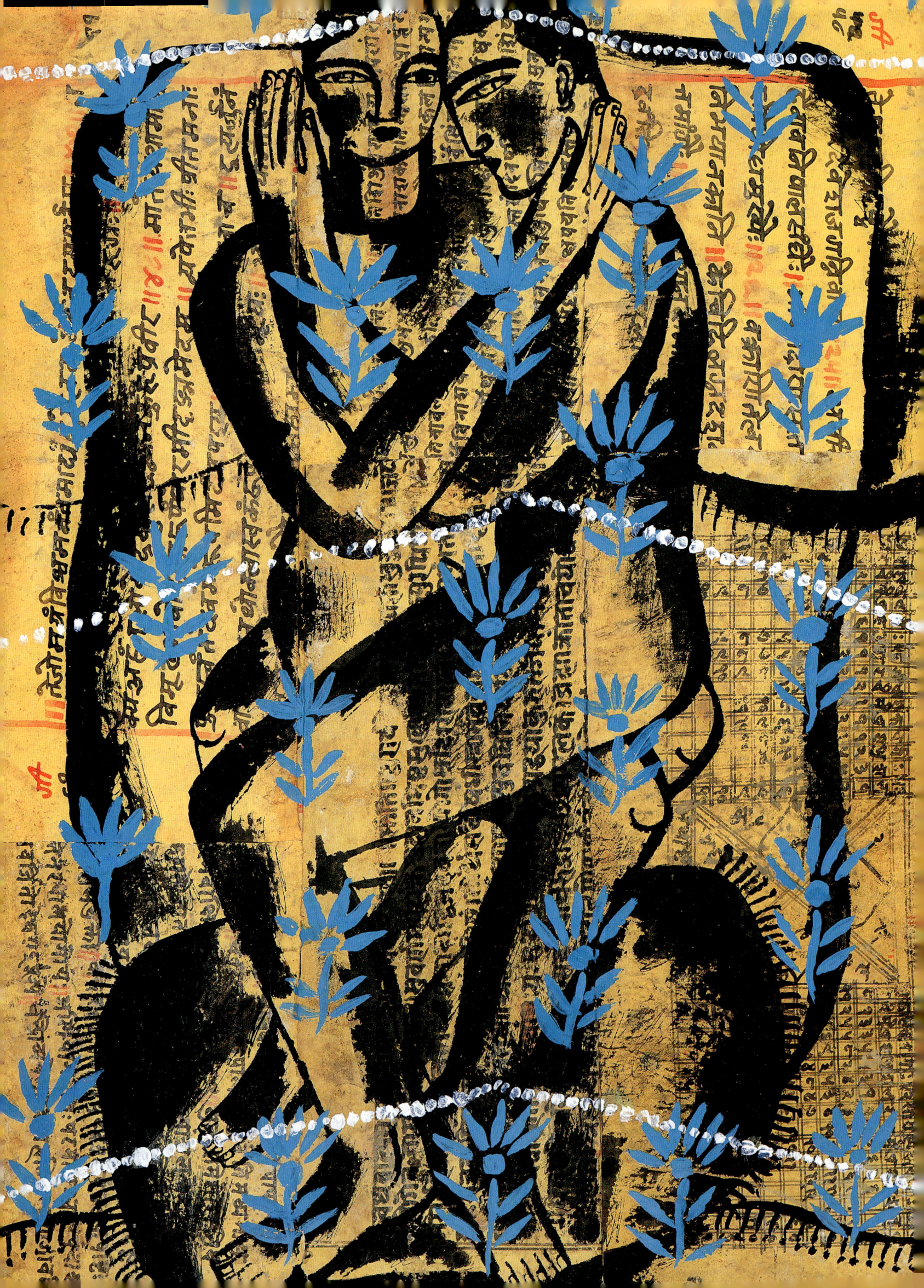

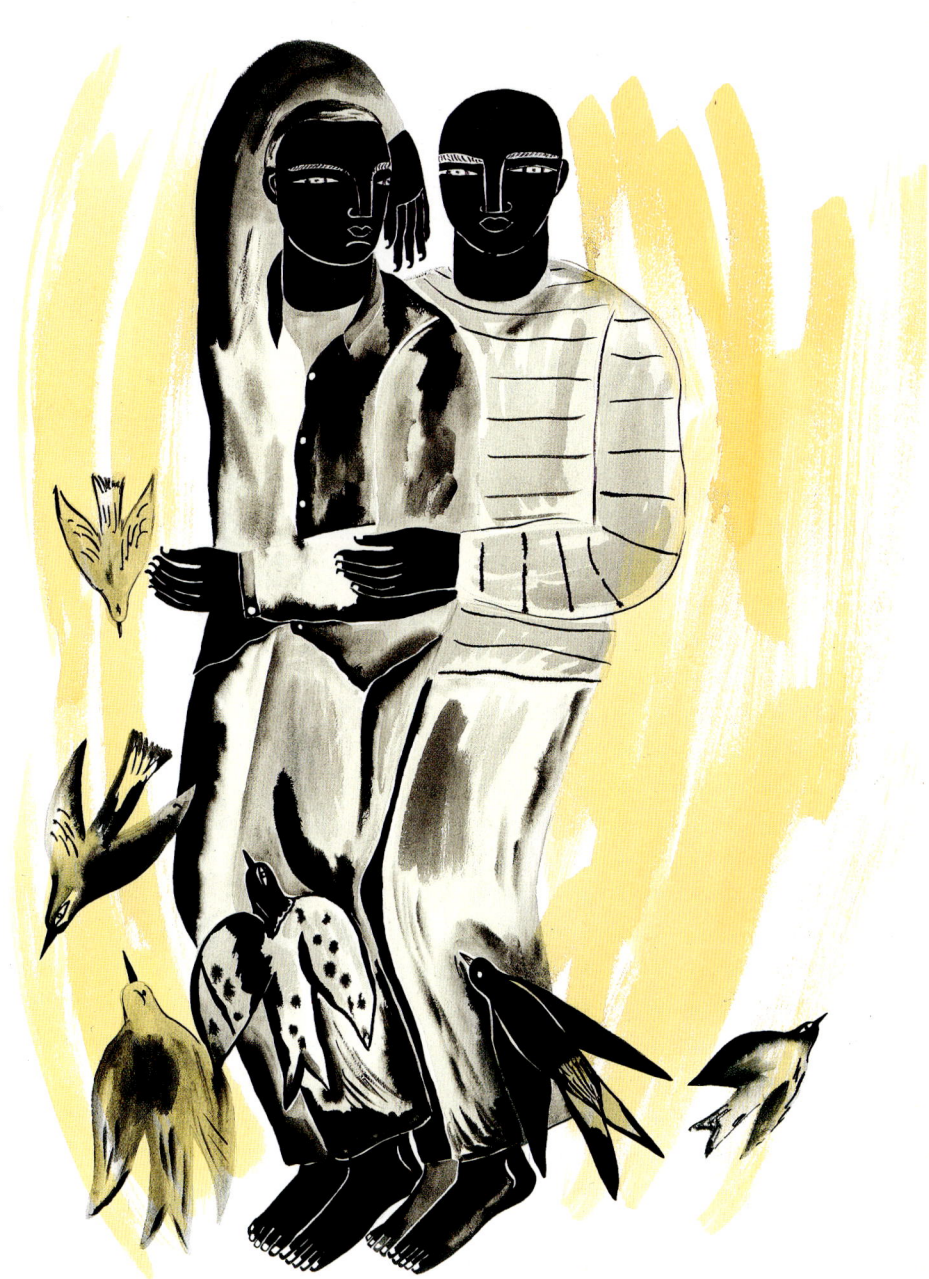

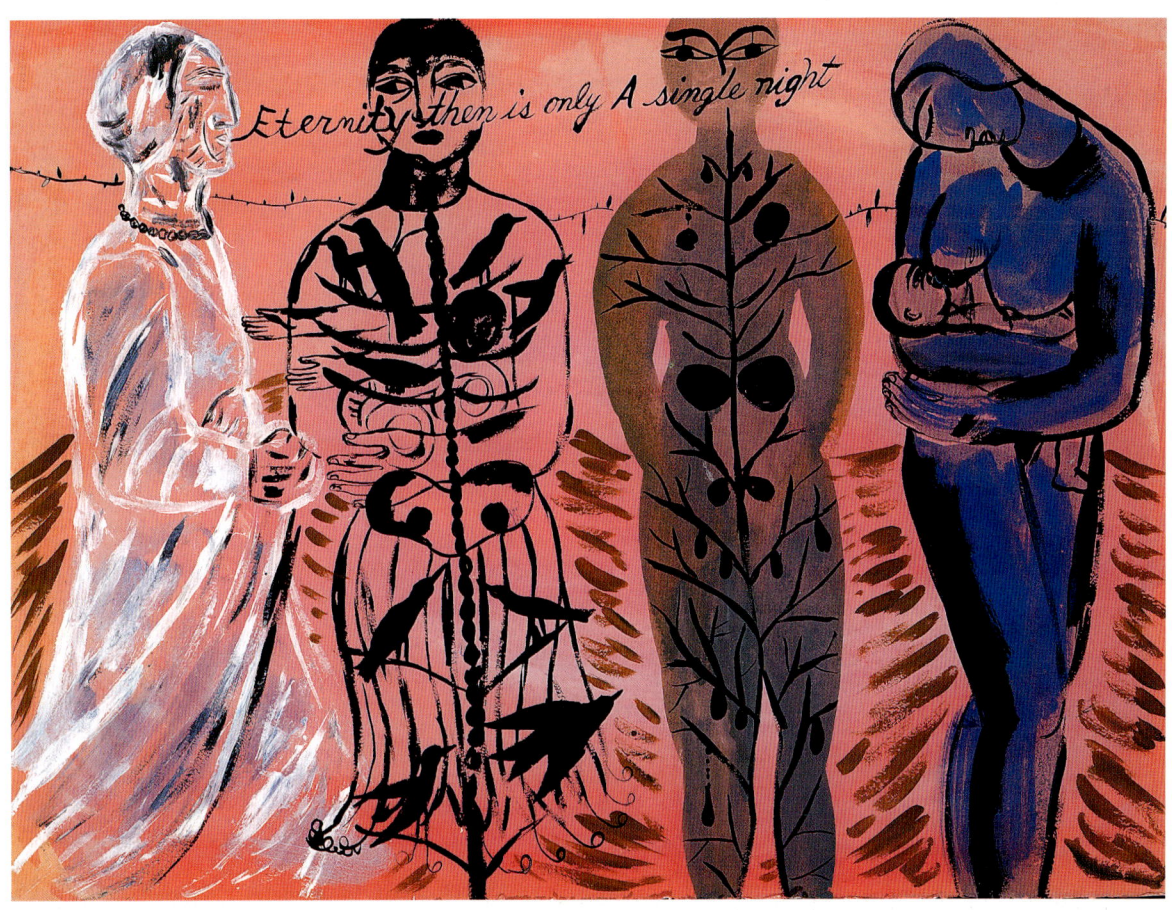

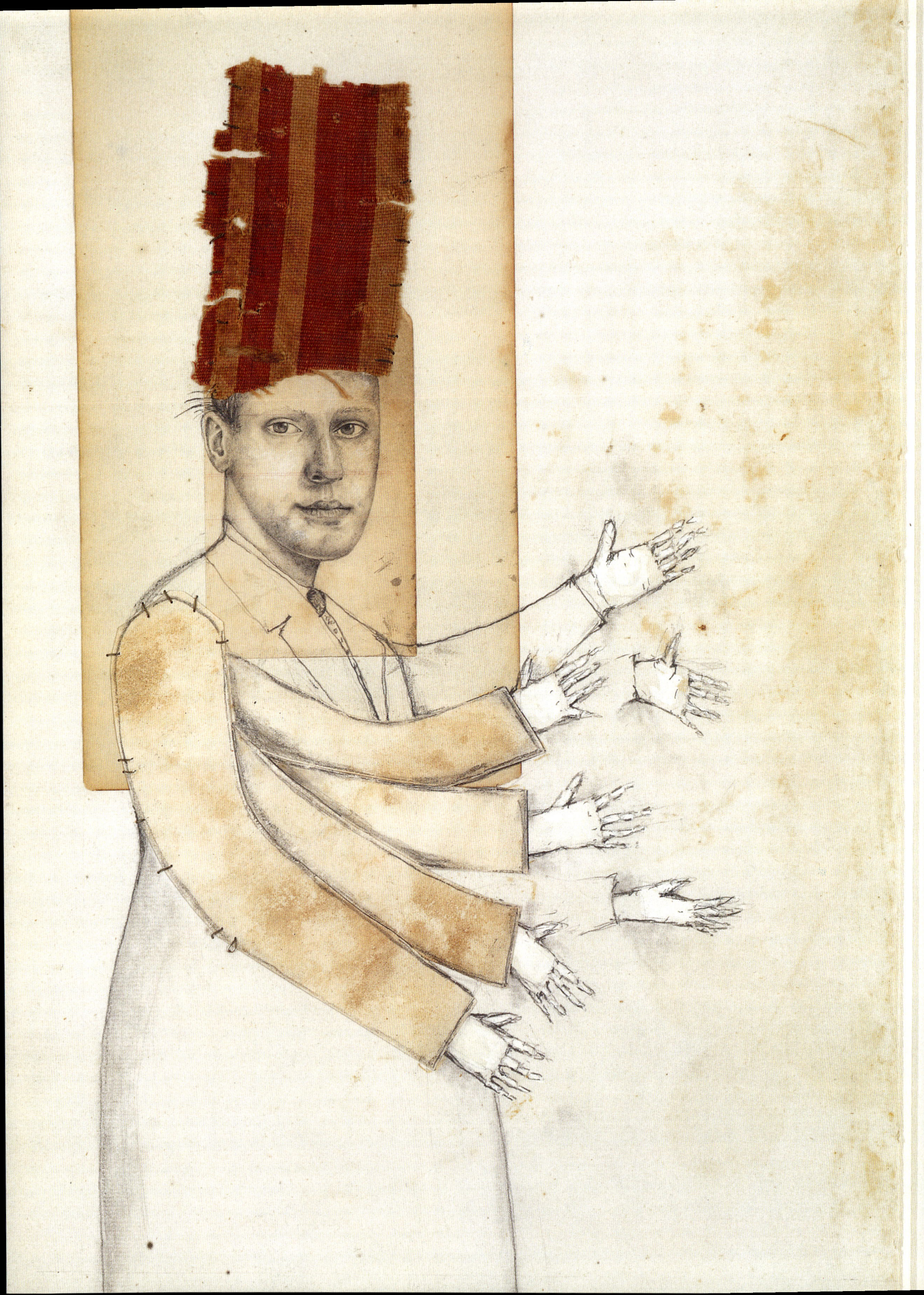

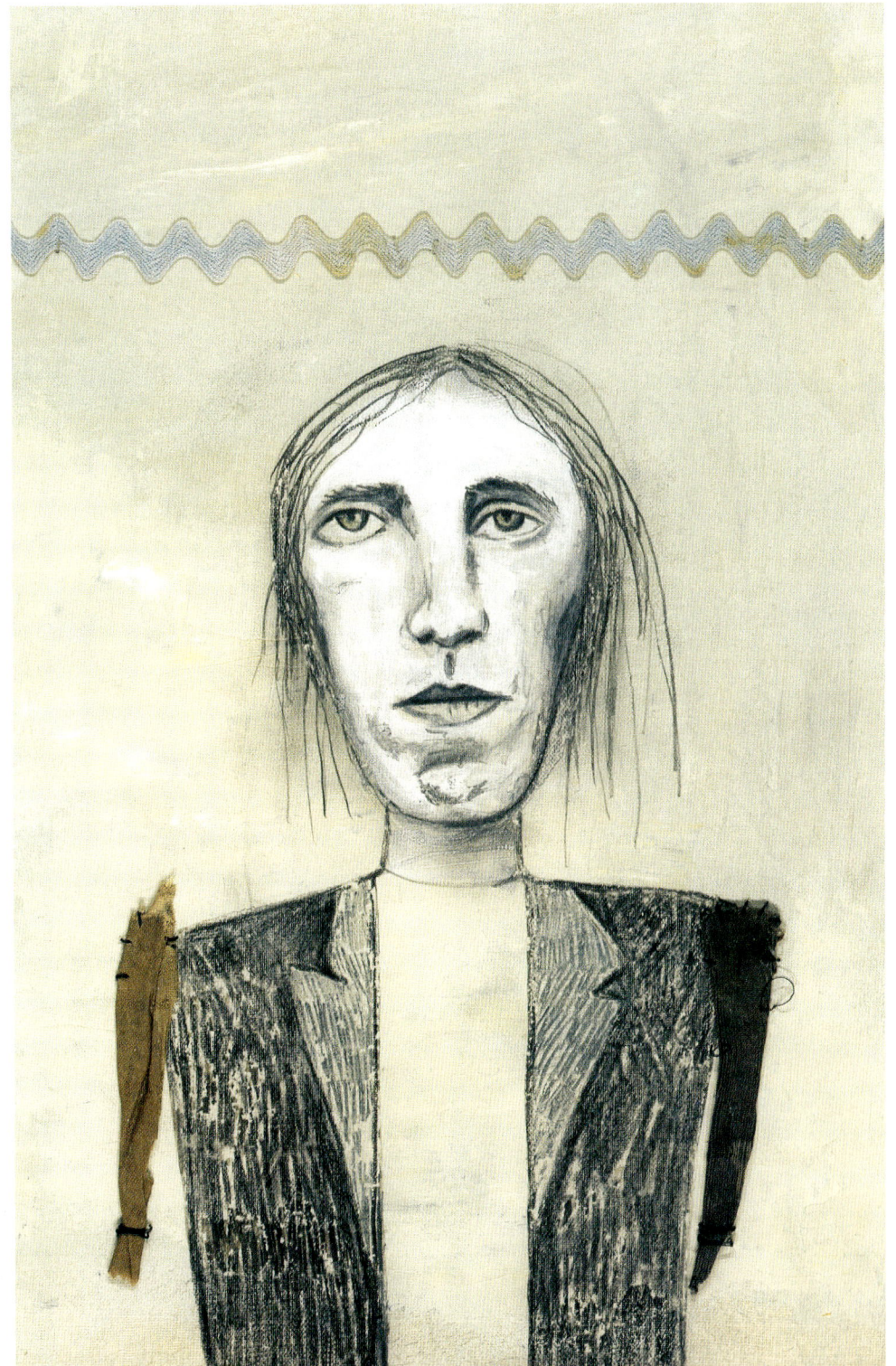

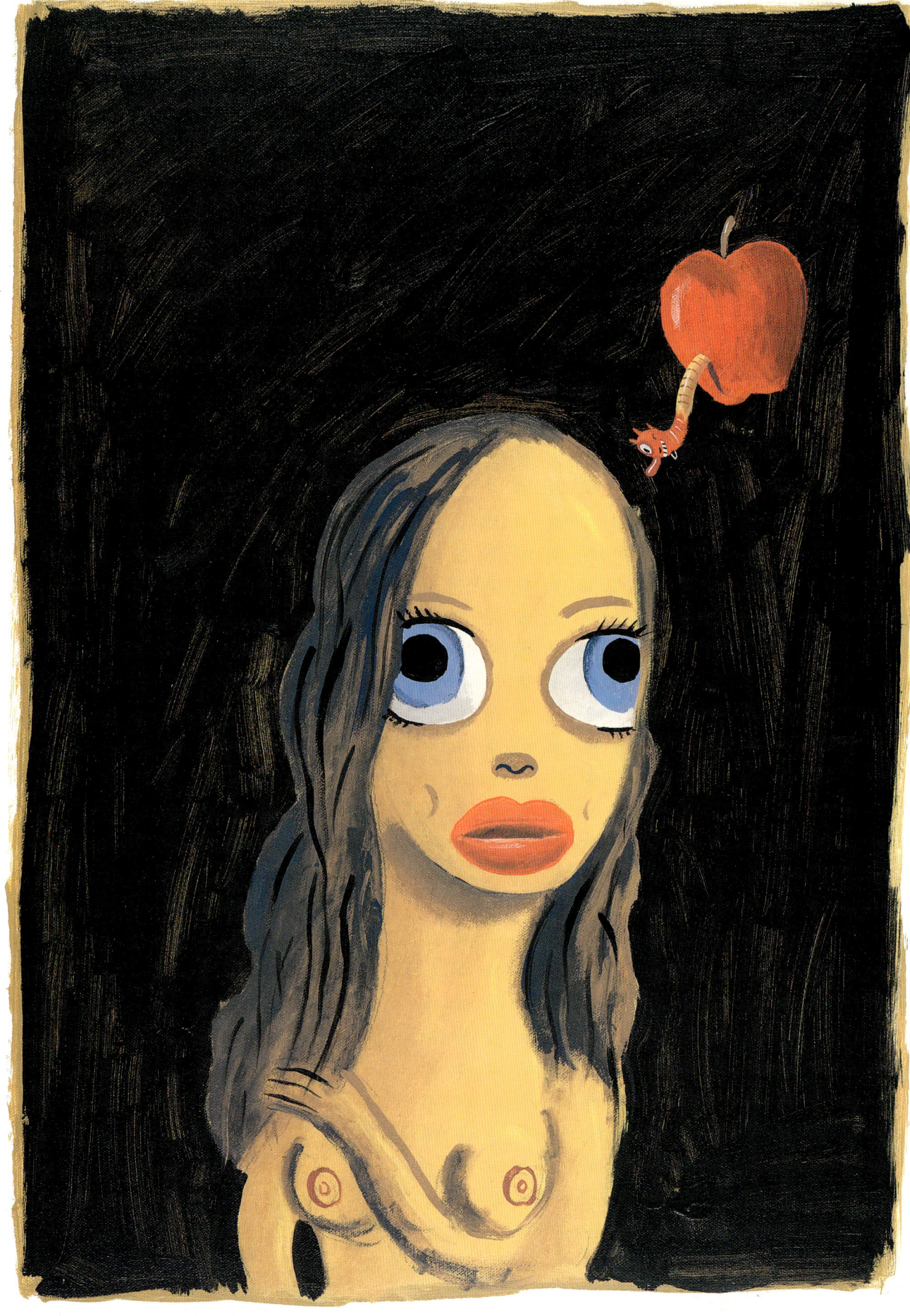

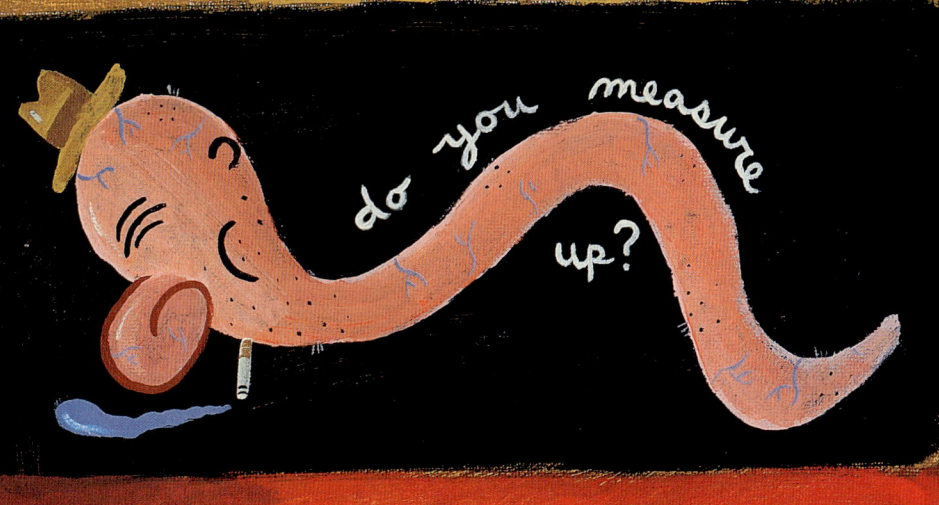

do you measure up?

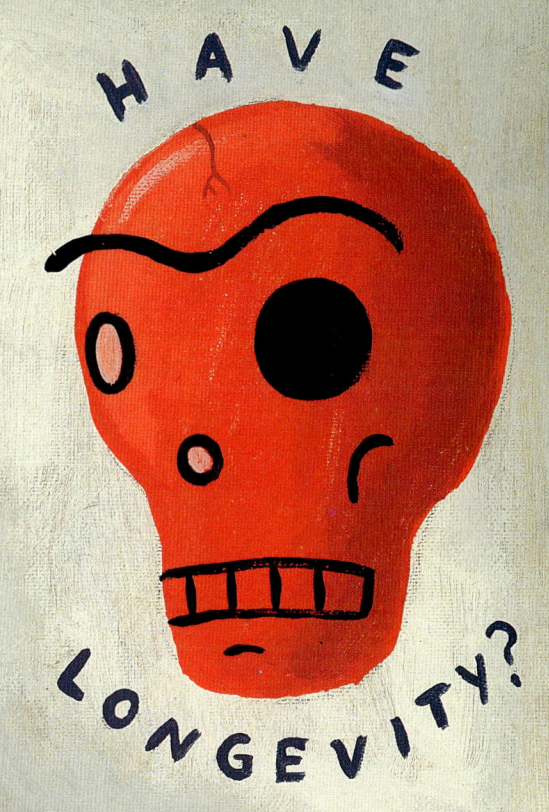

HAVE LONGEVITY?

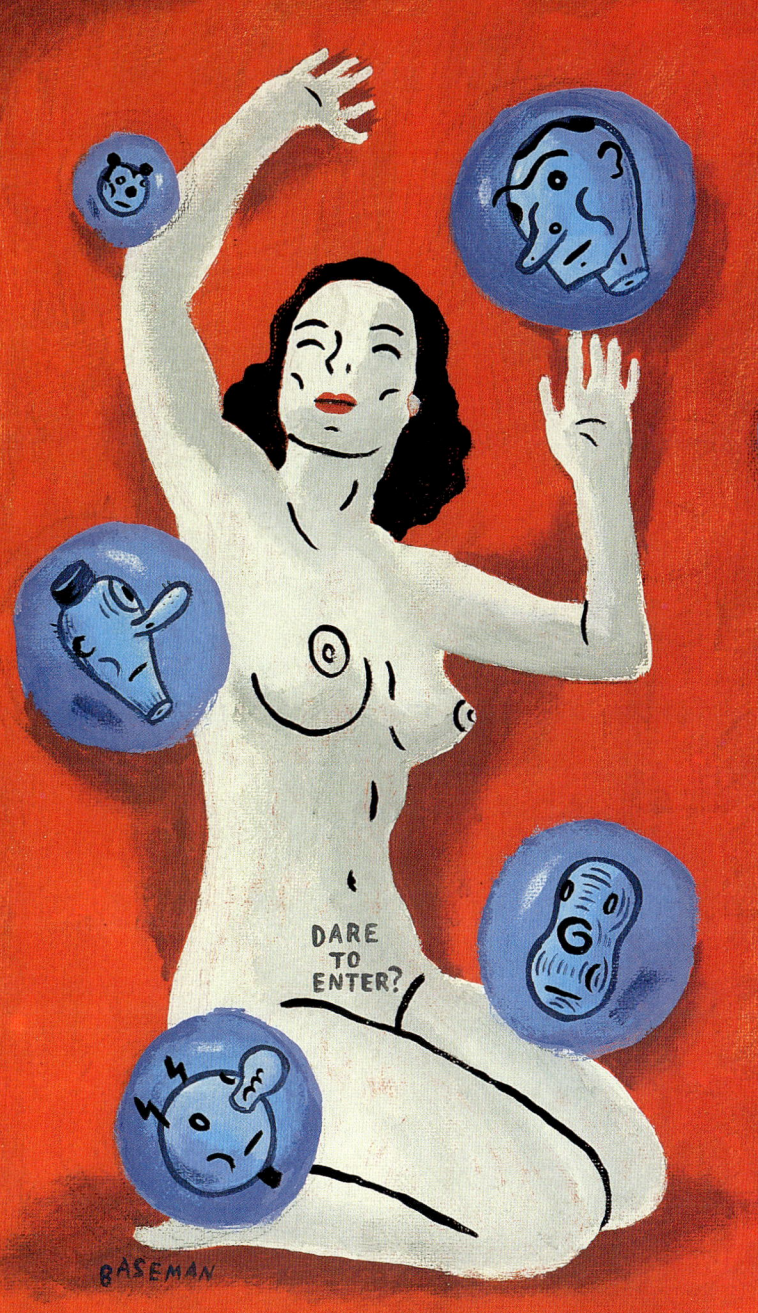

DARE TO ENTER?

BASEMAN

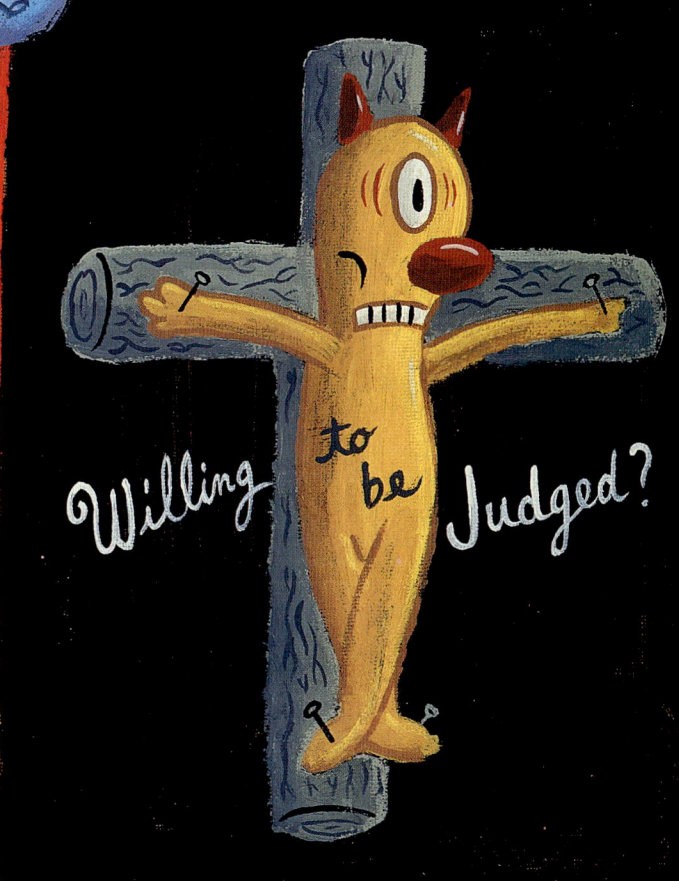

Willing to be Judged?

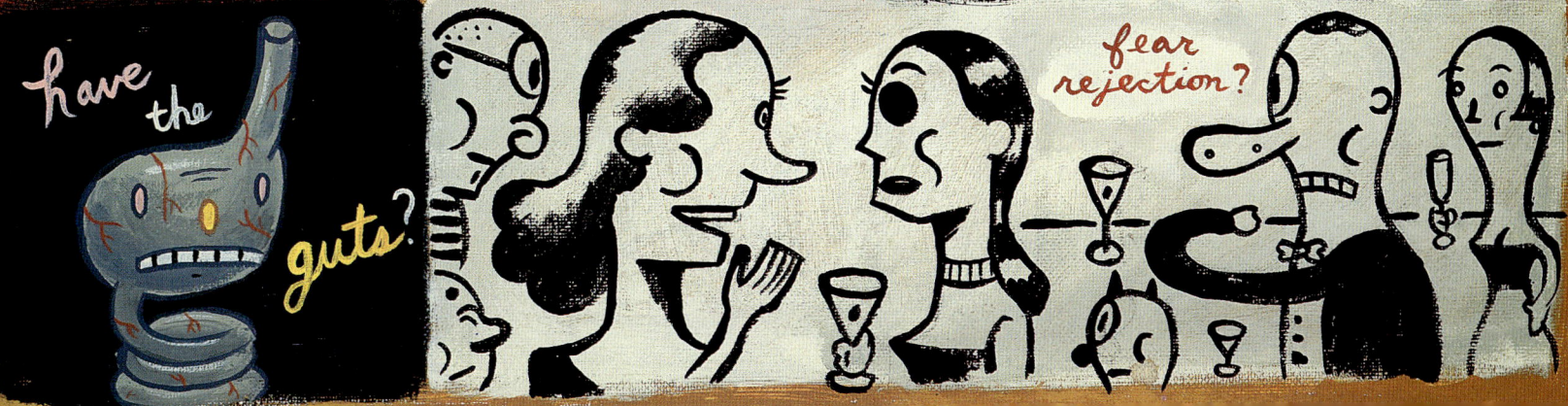

have the guts?

fear rejection?

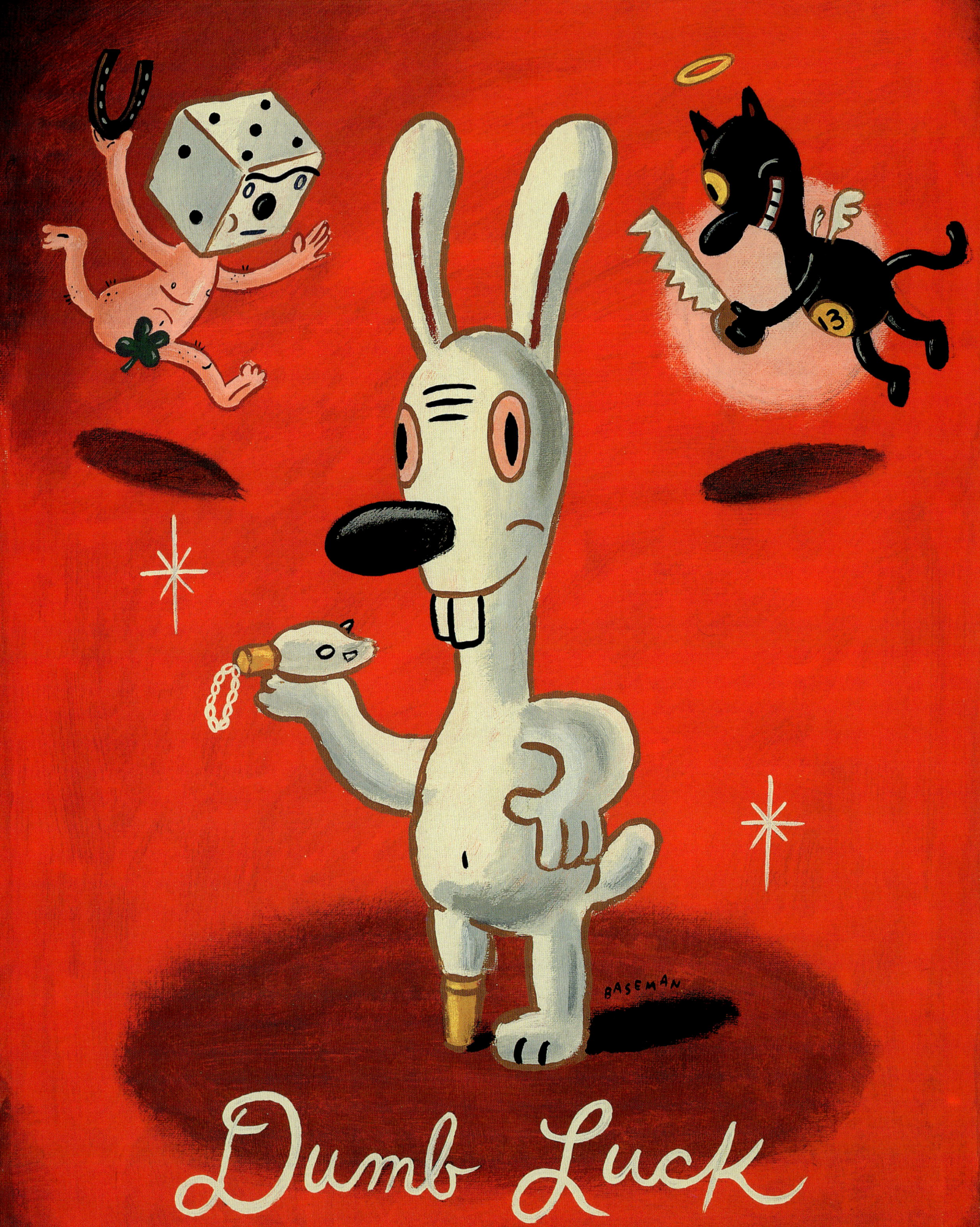

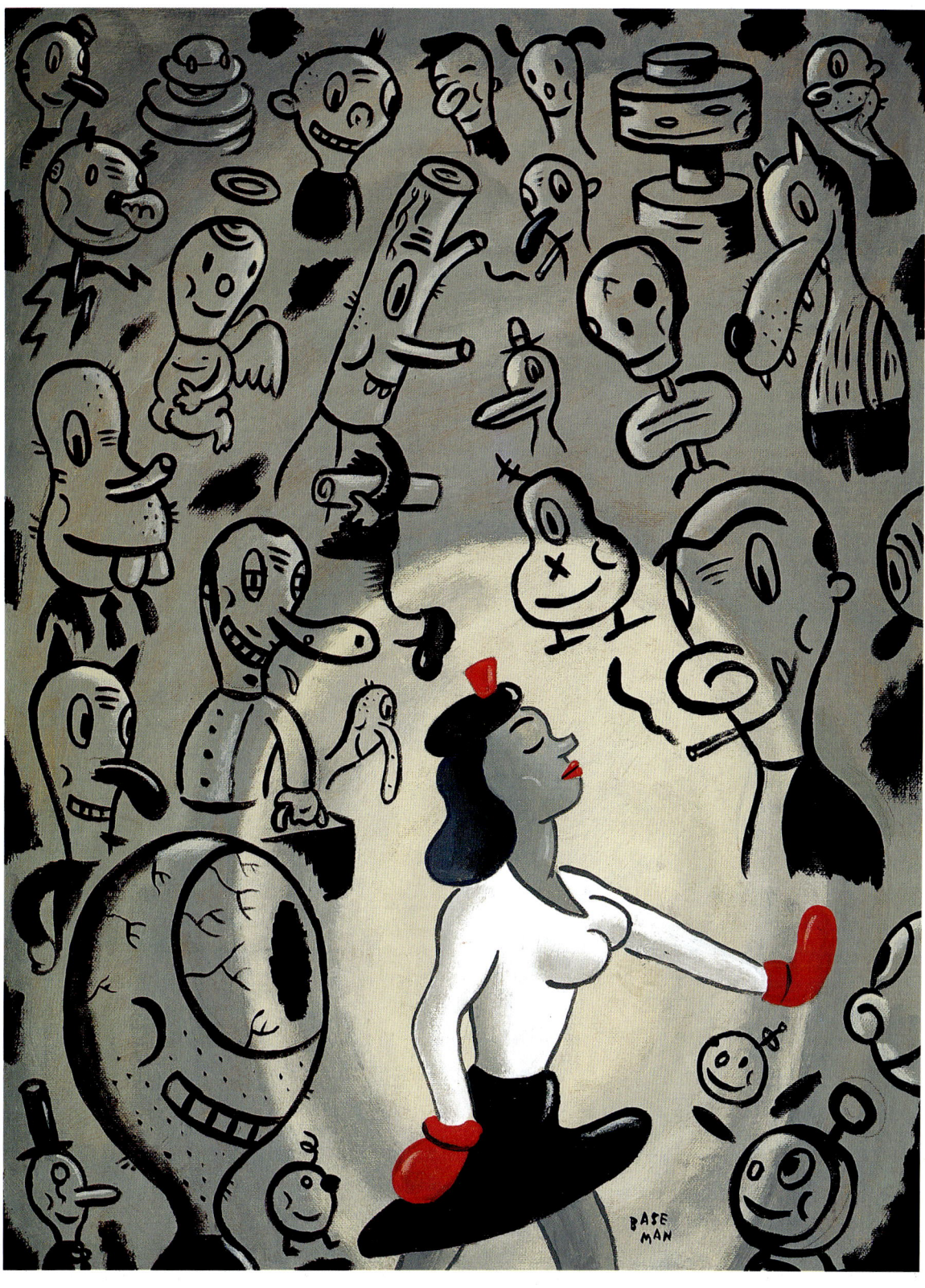

023 melinda beck

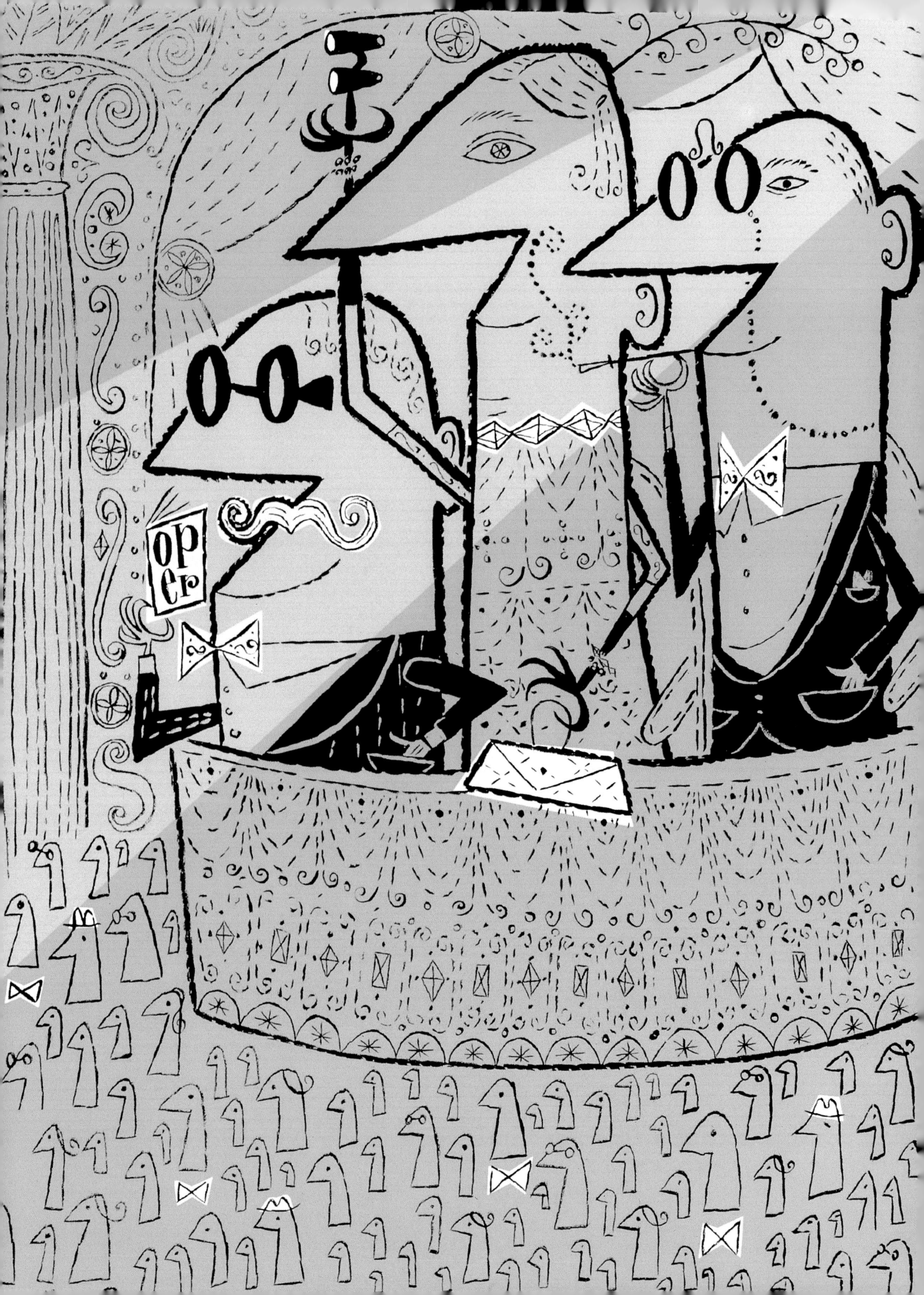

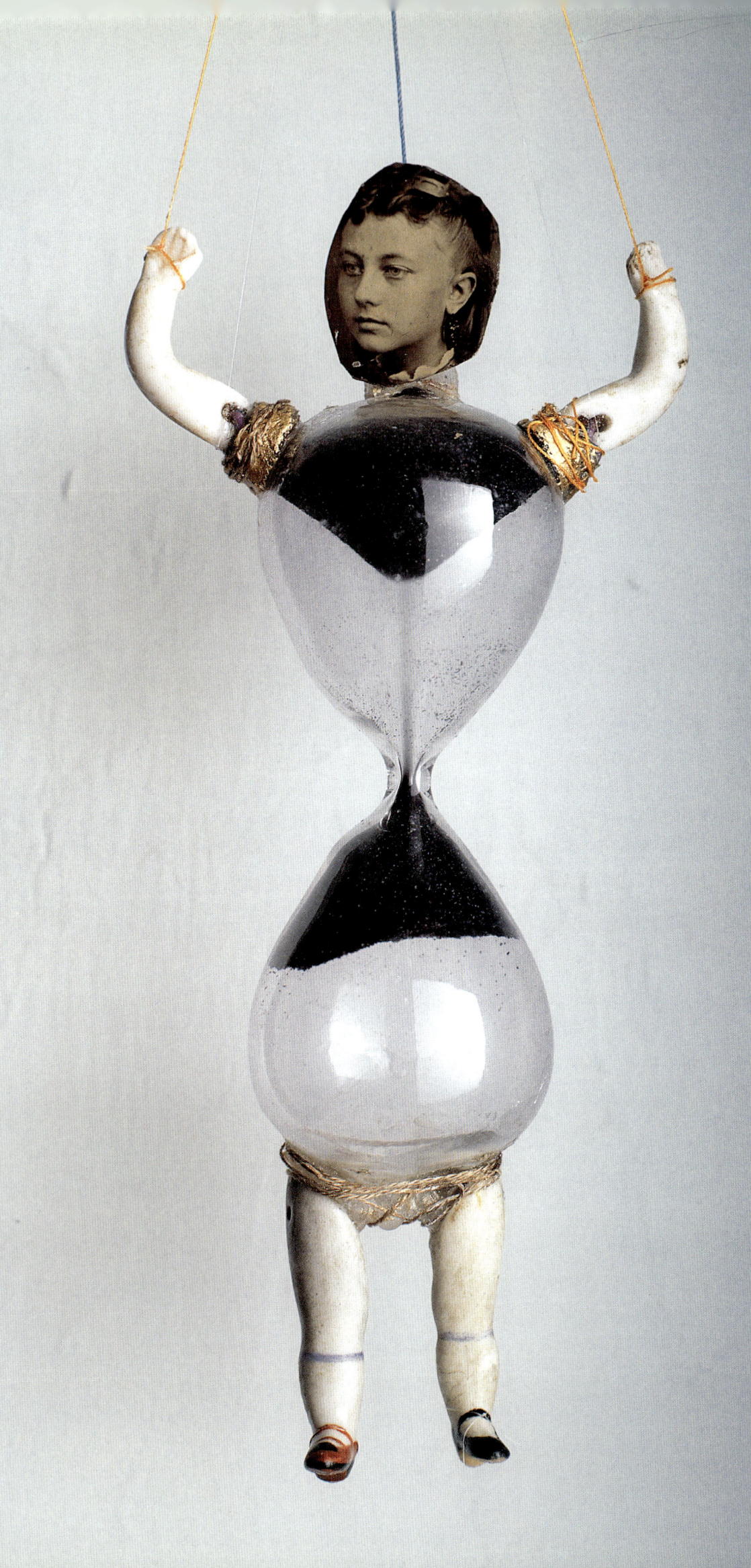

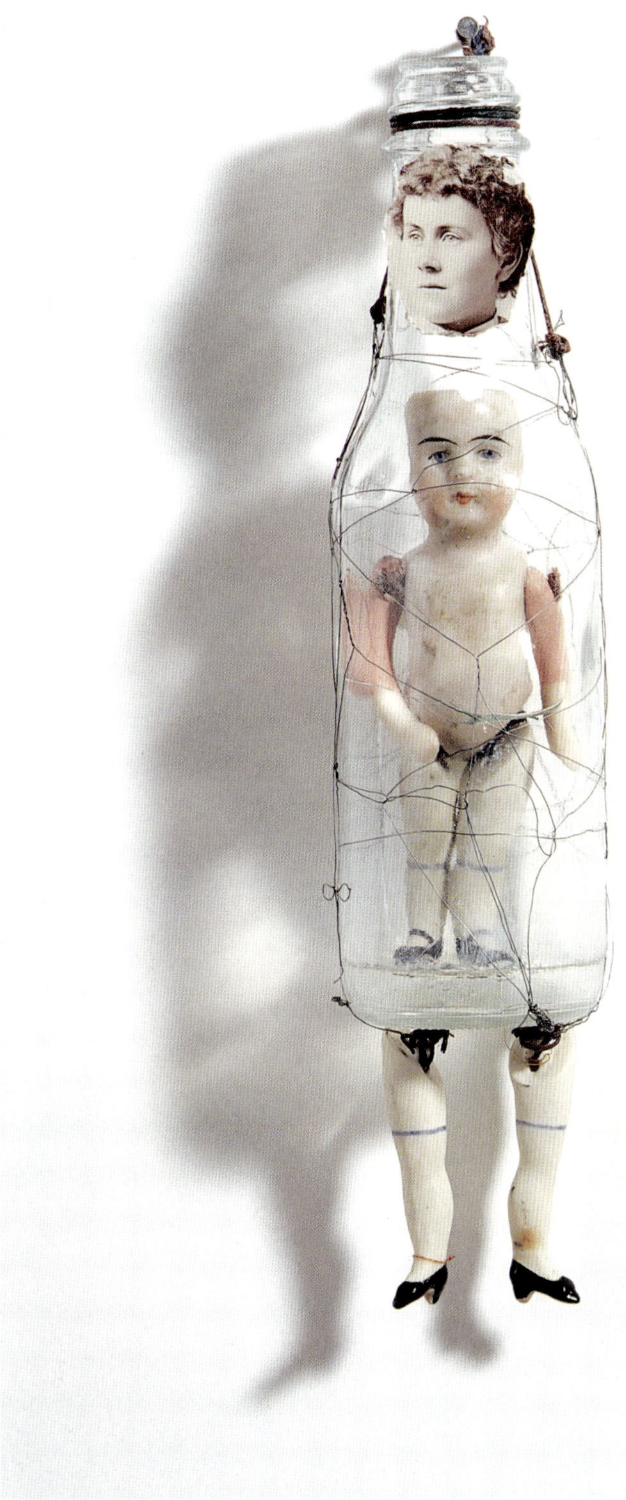

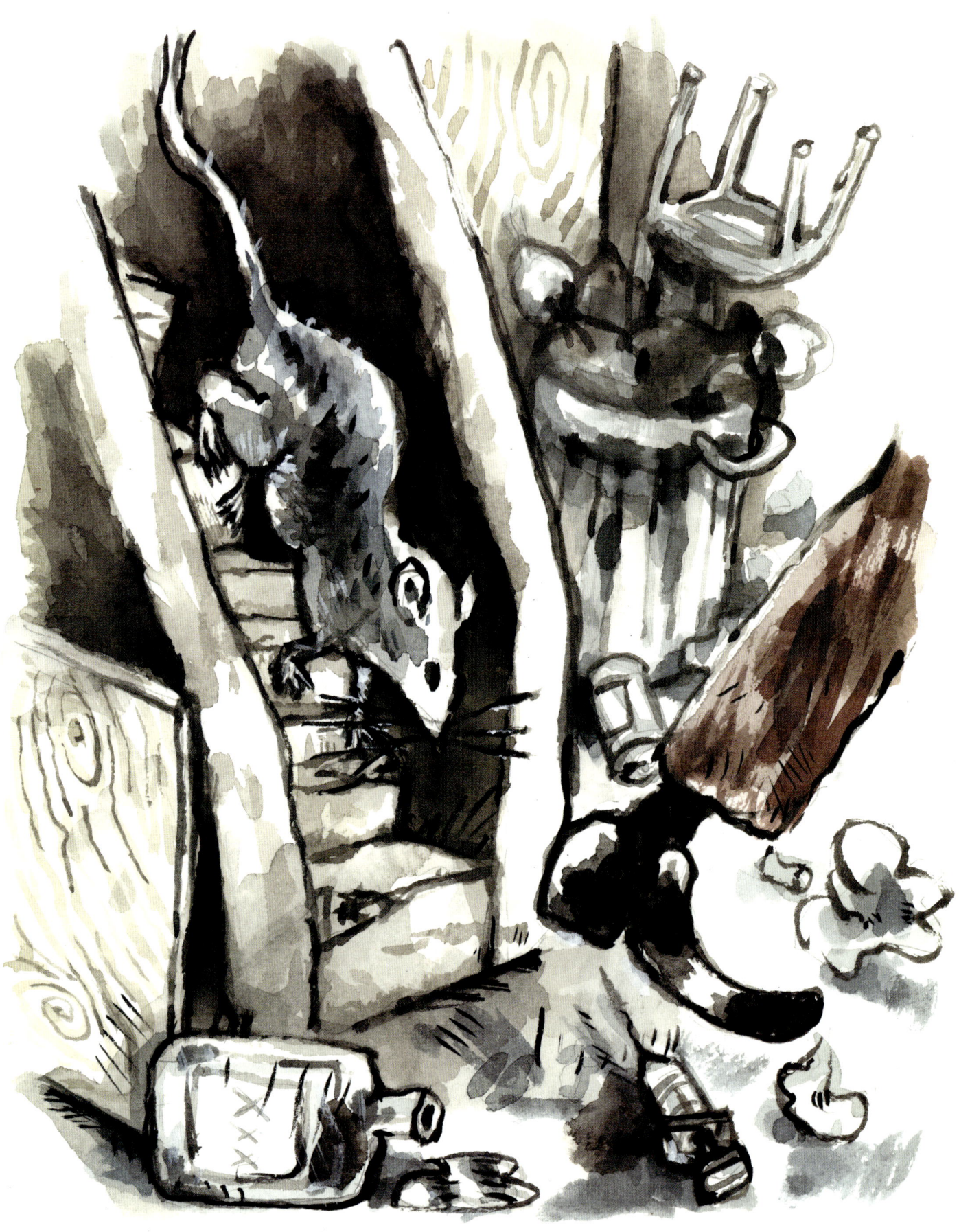

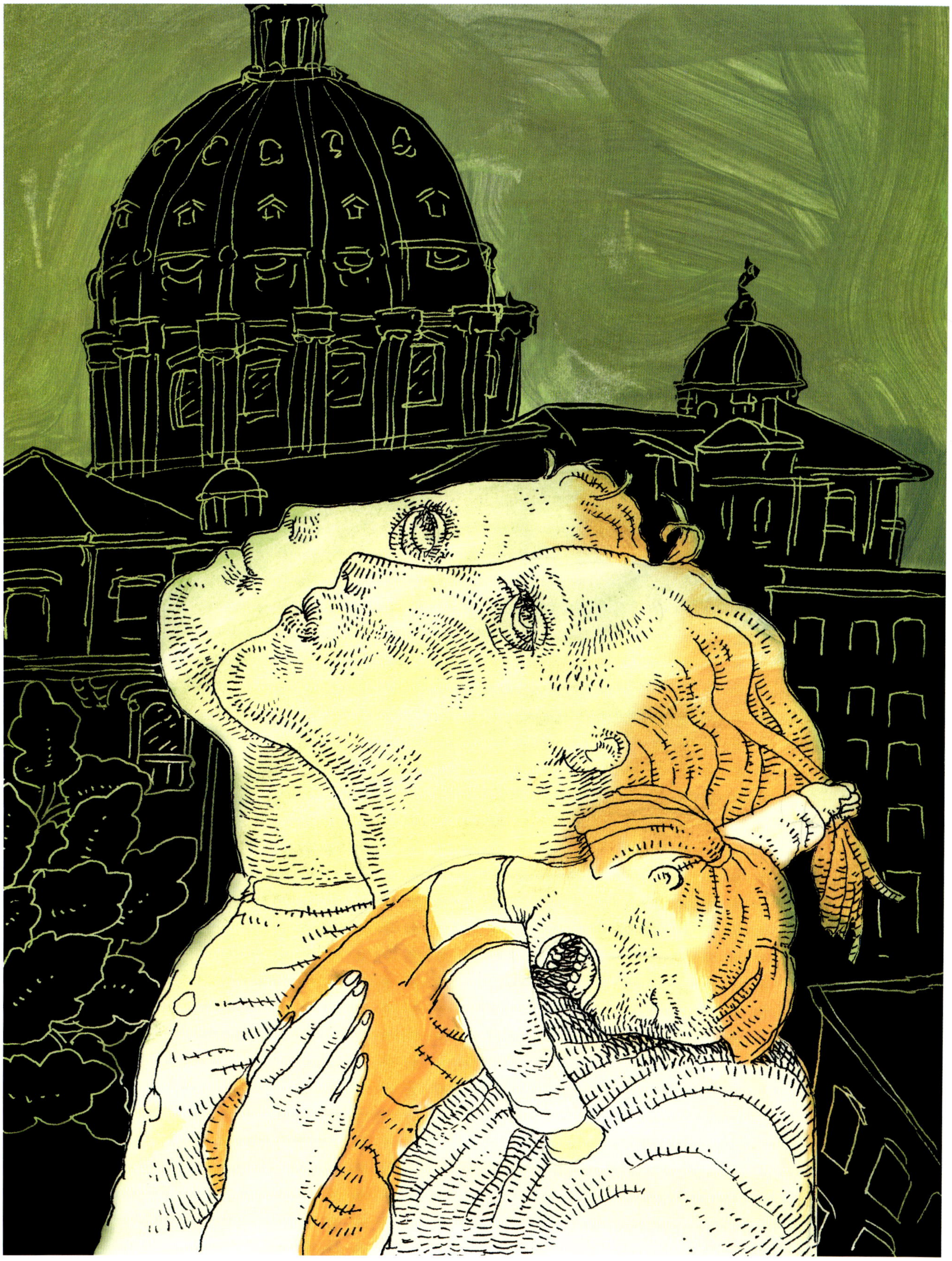

027 wesleybedrosian

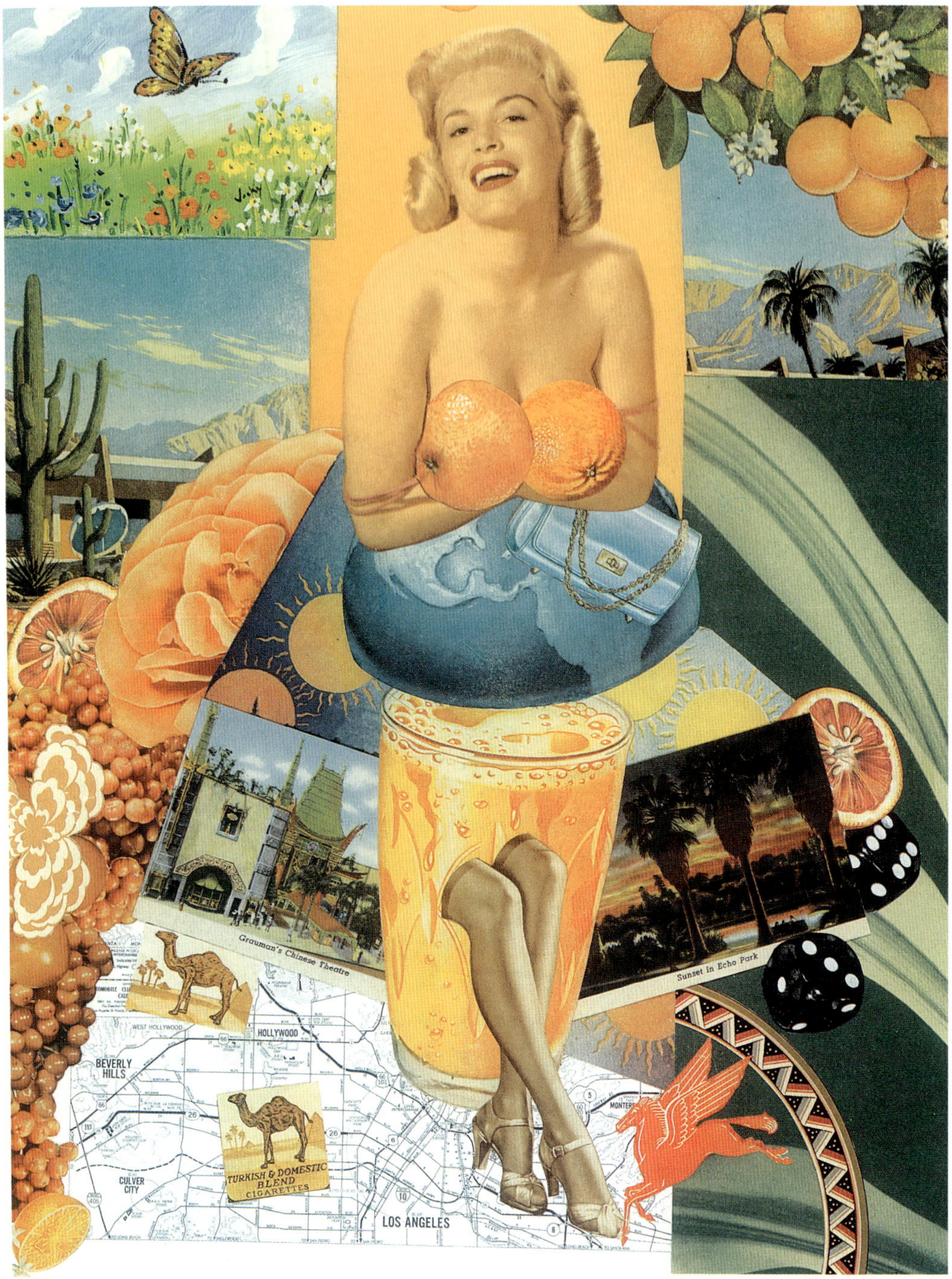

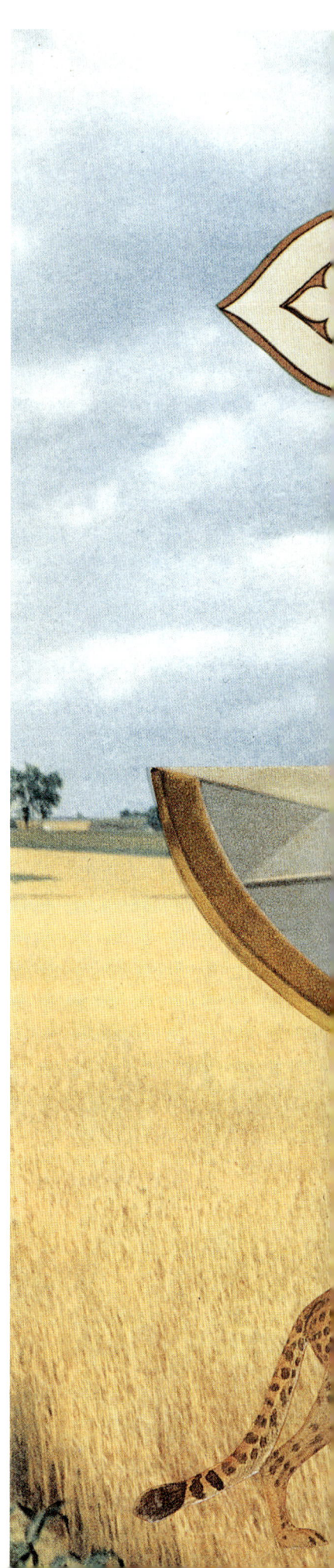

028|029 lynnbennett

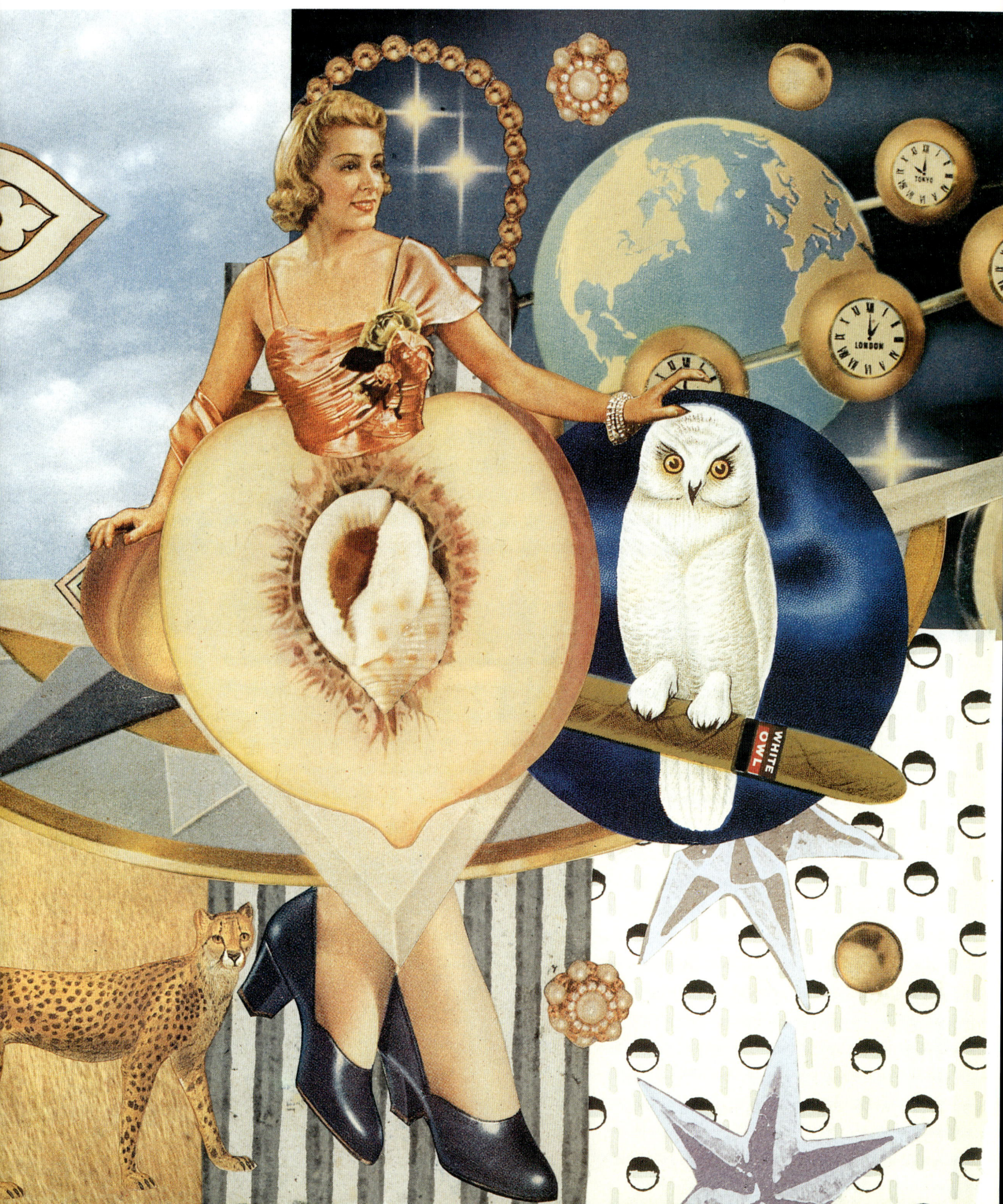

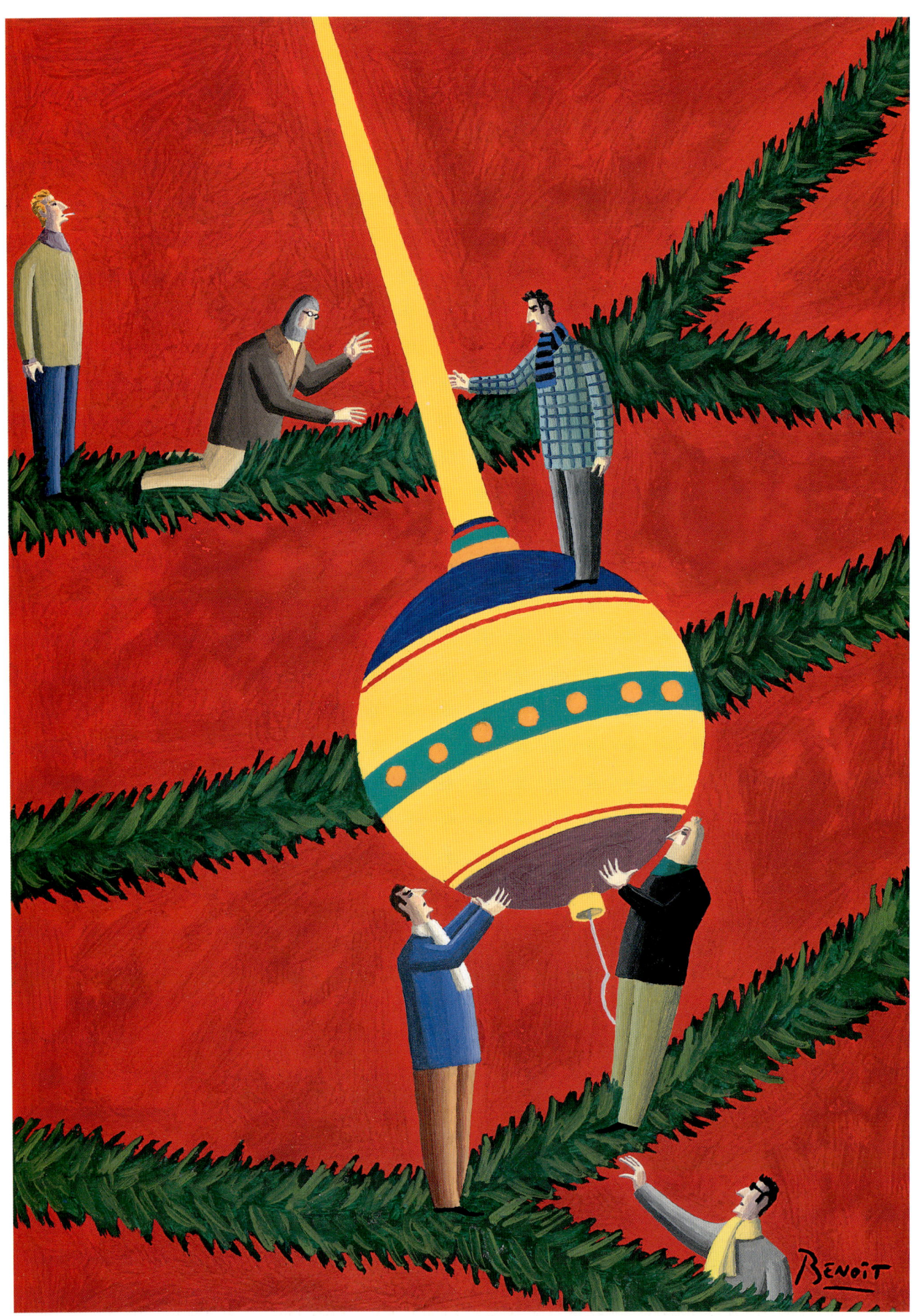

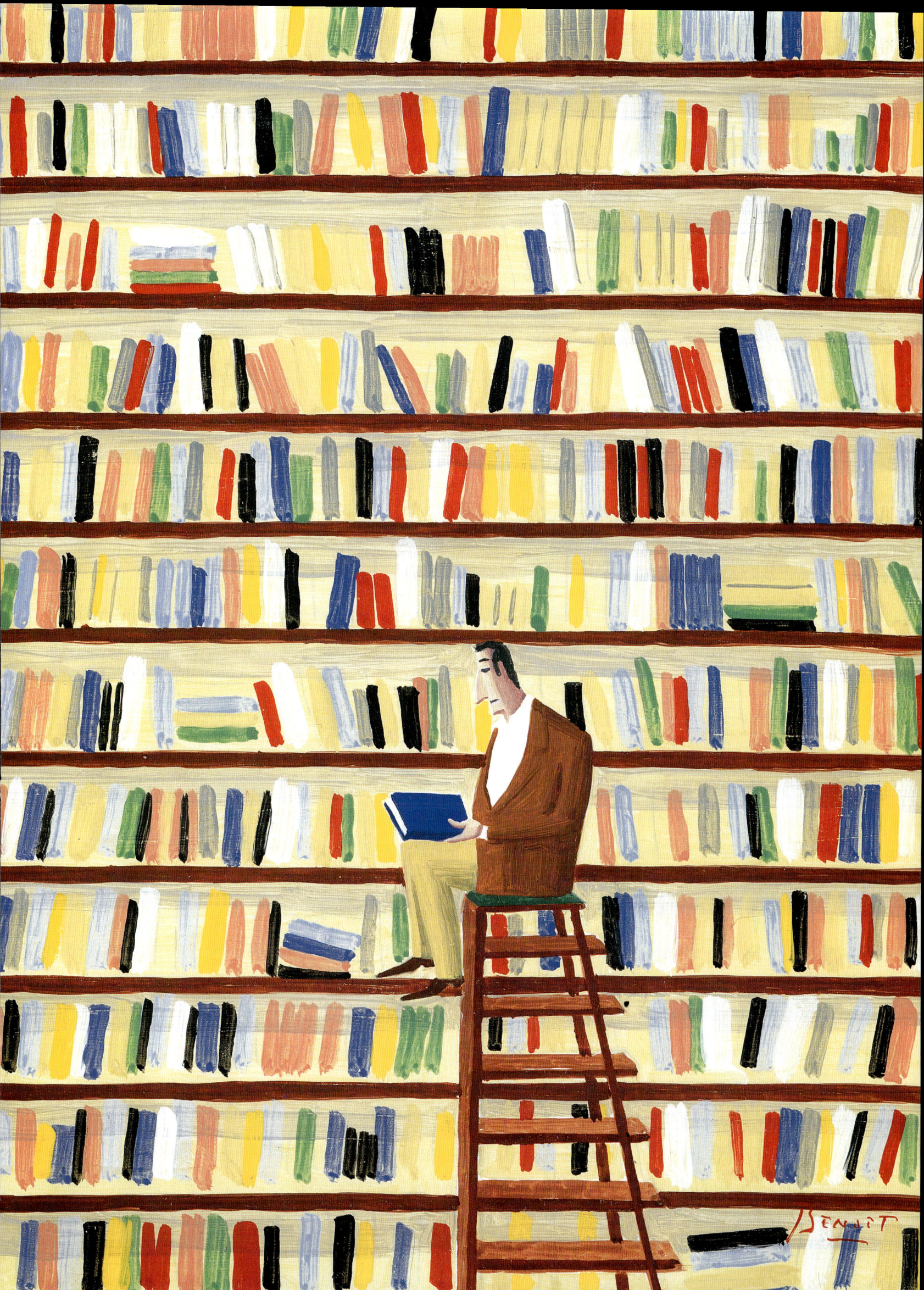

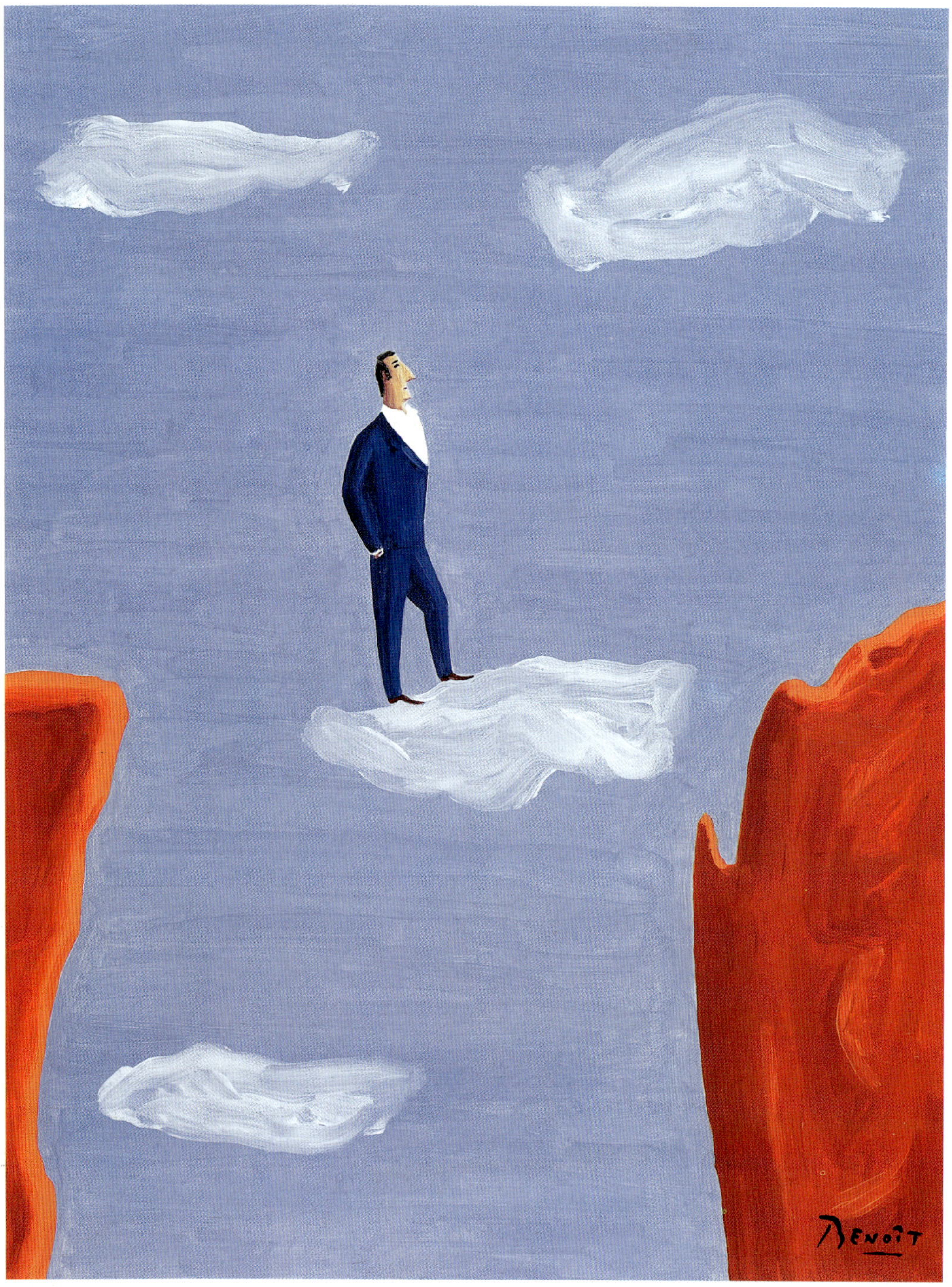

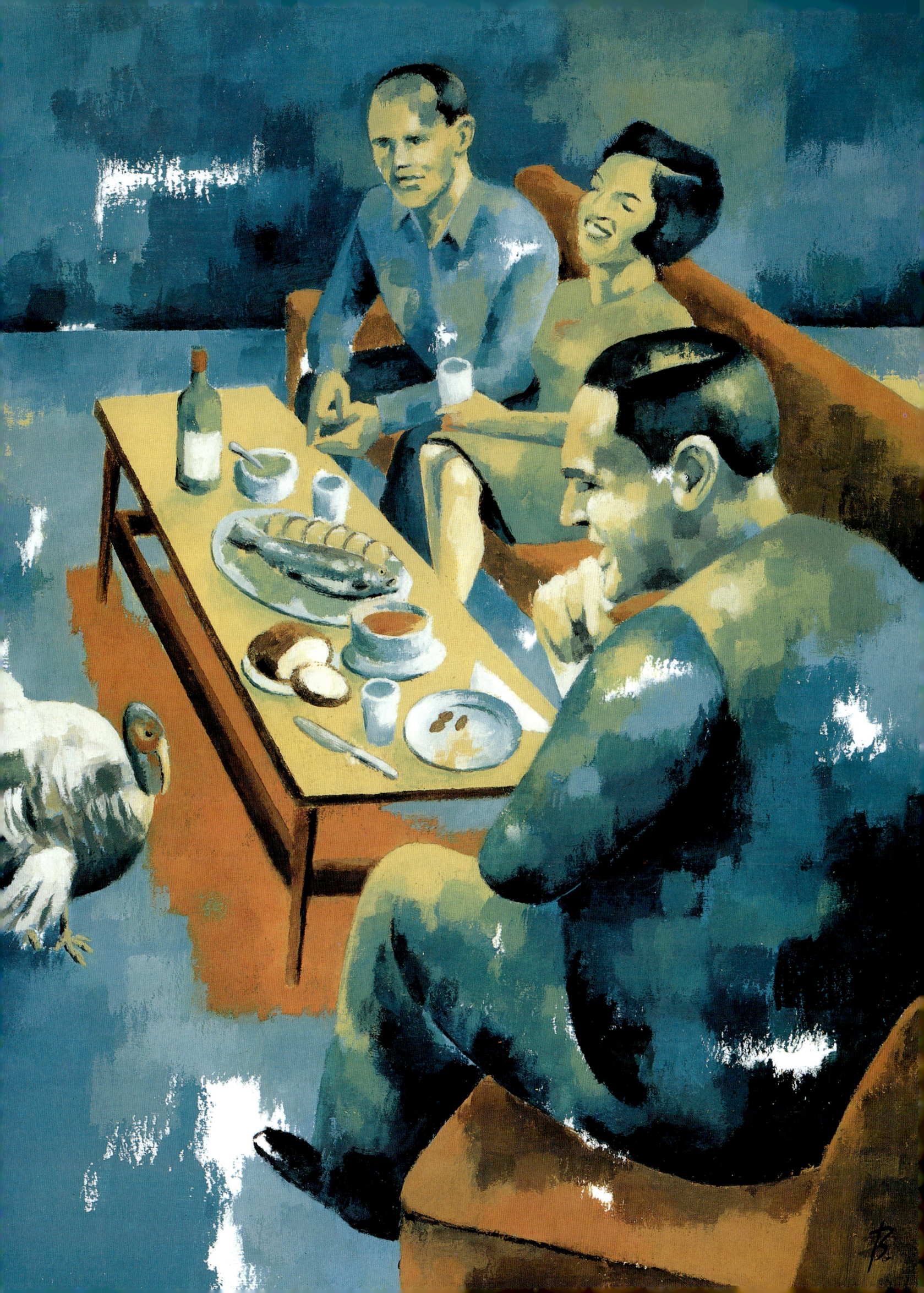

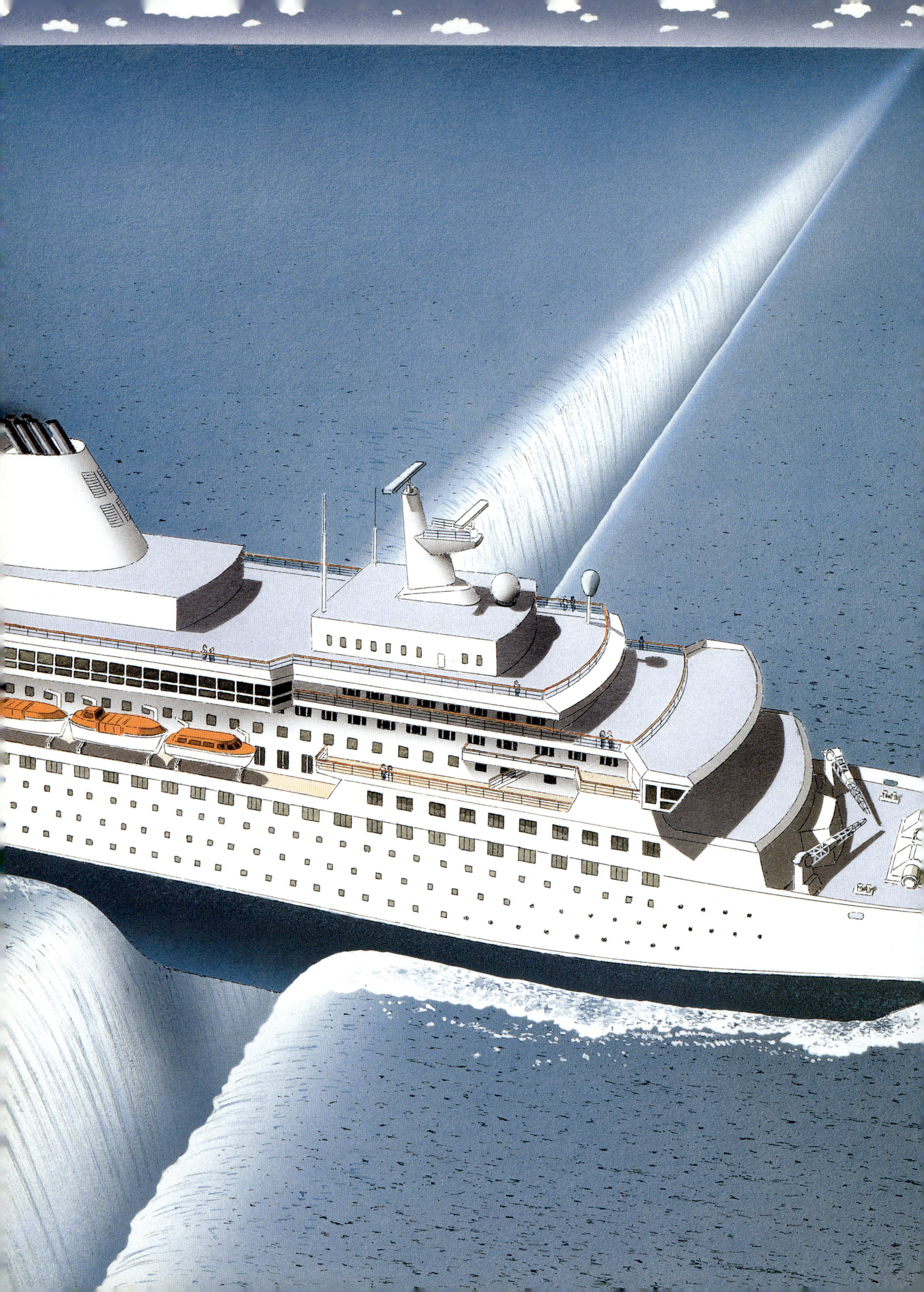

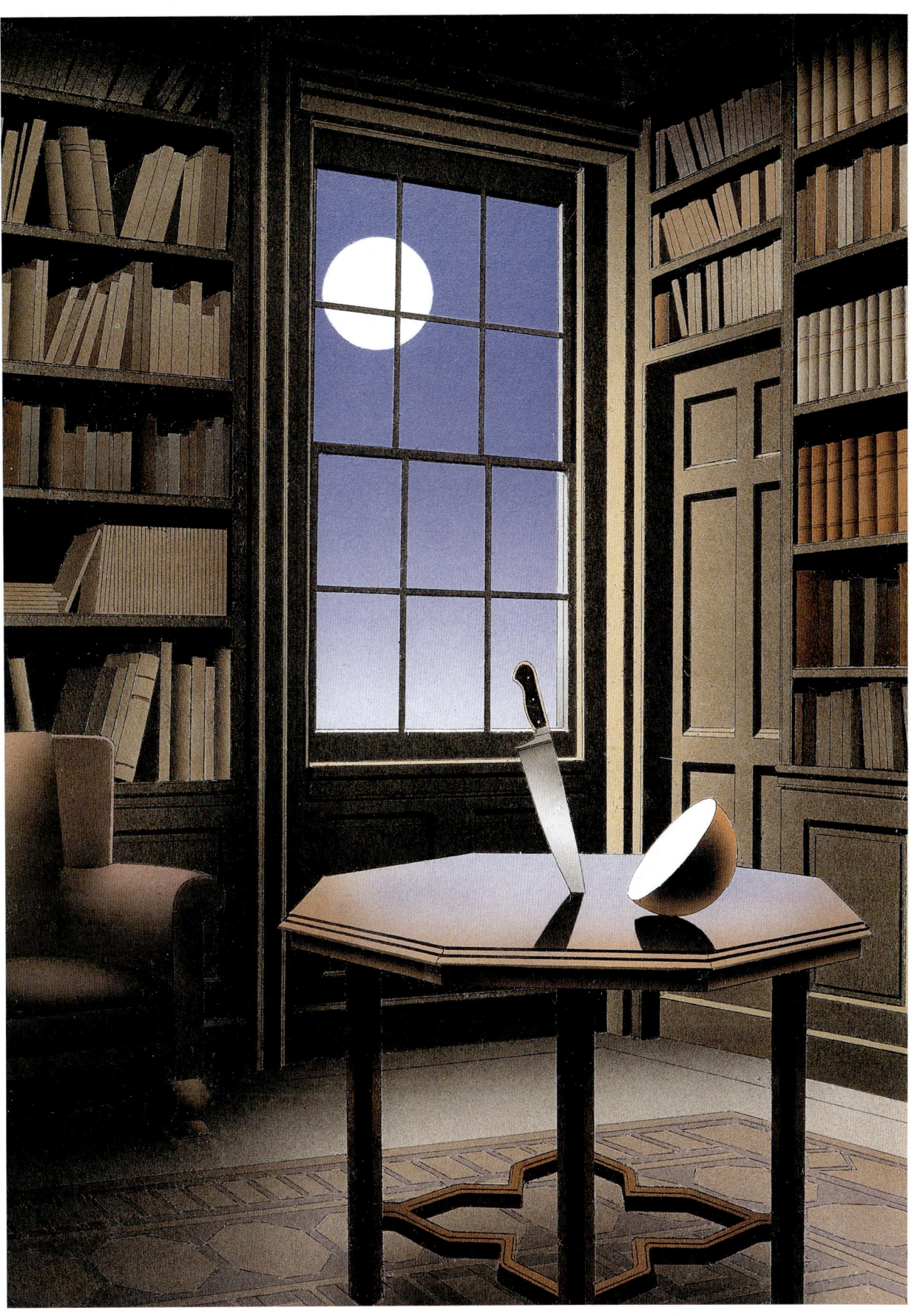

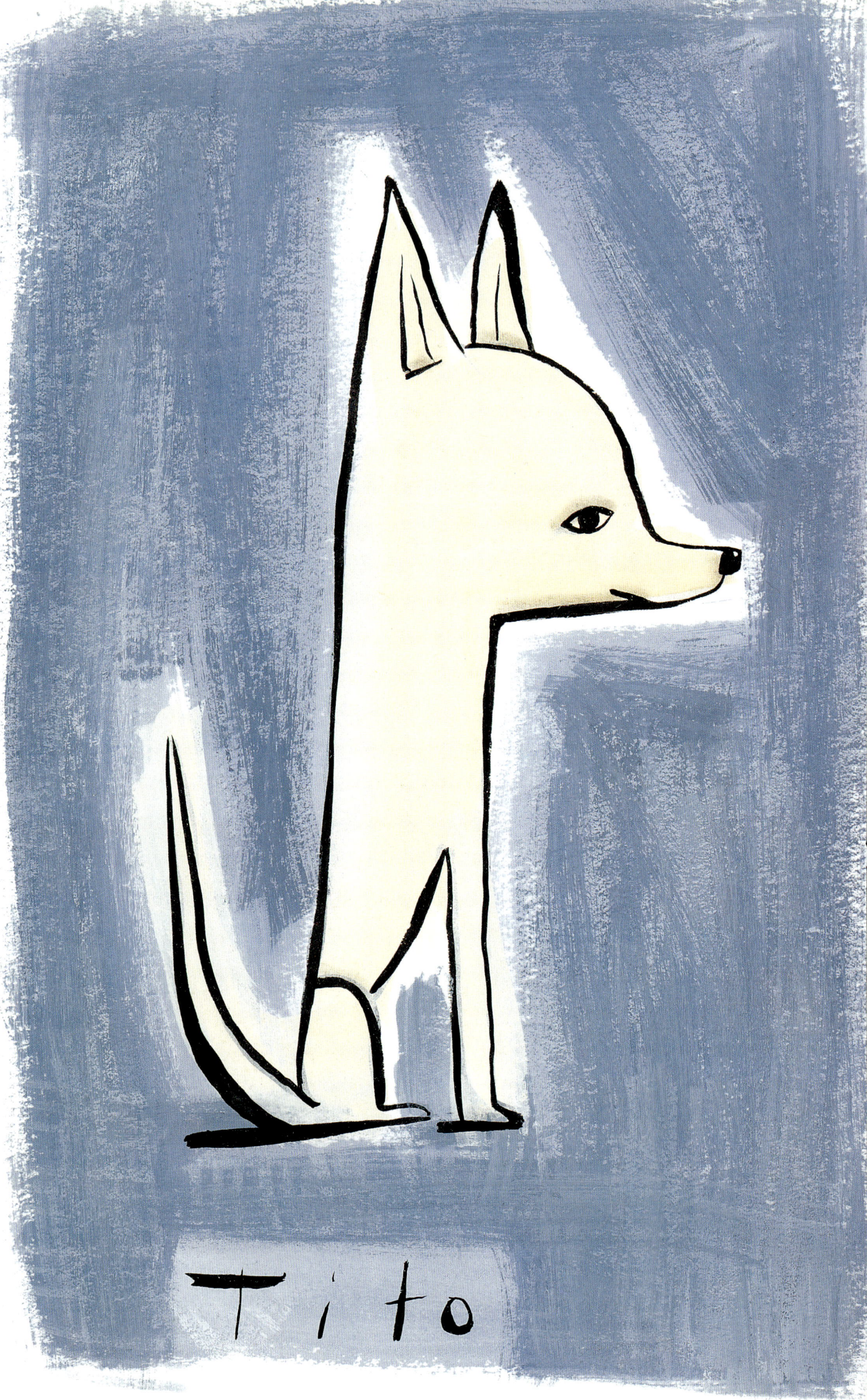

Tito

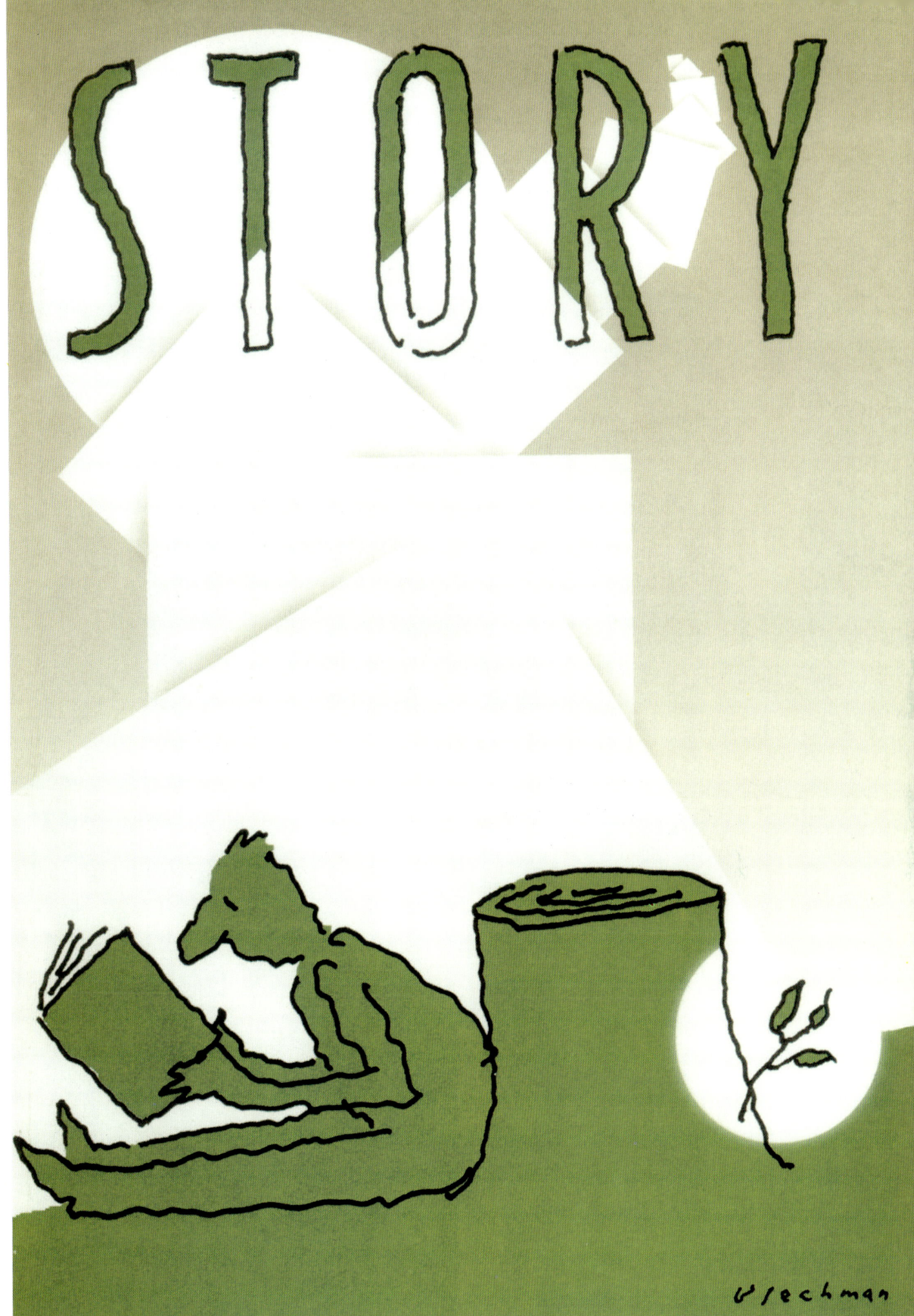

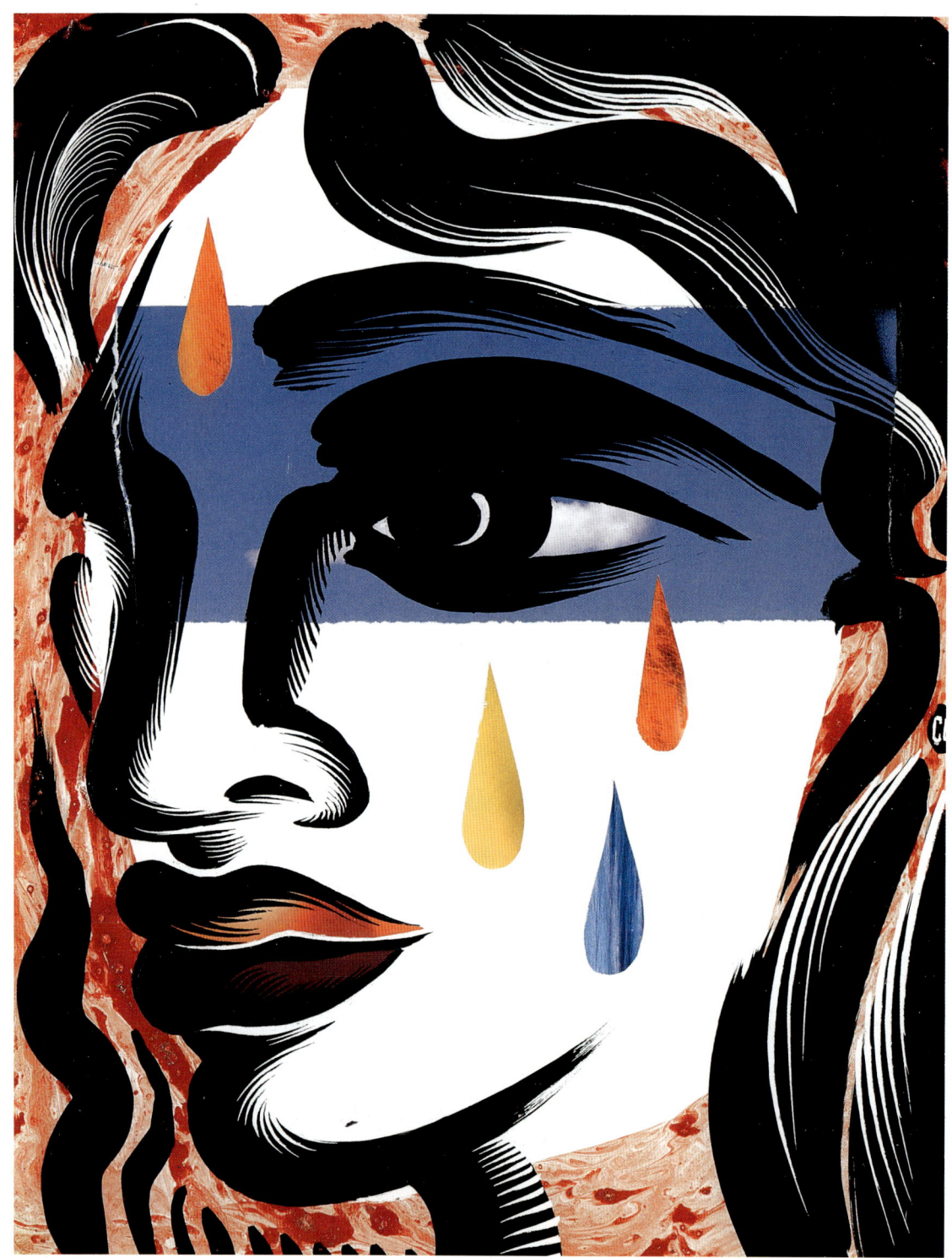

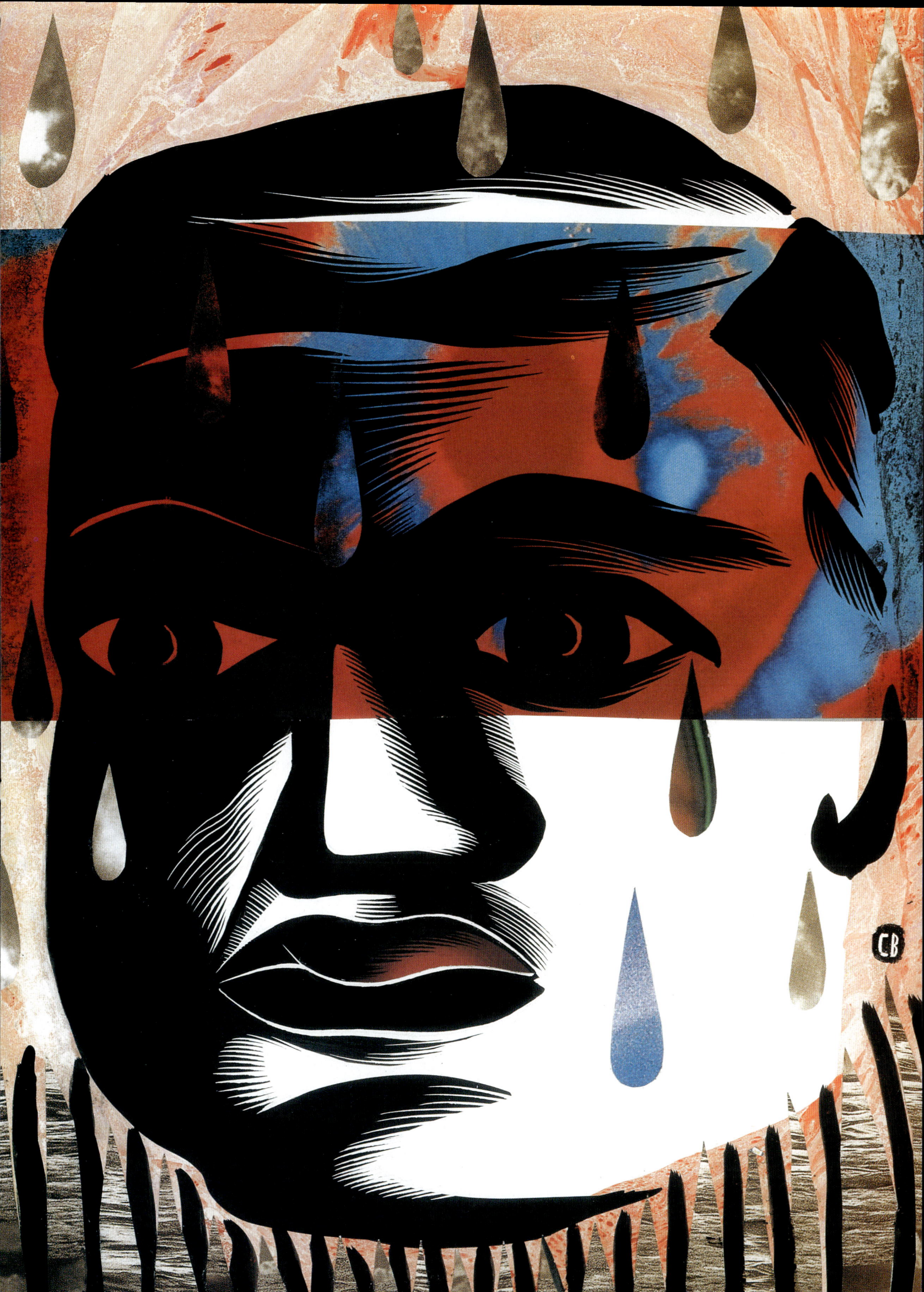

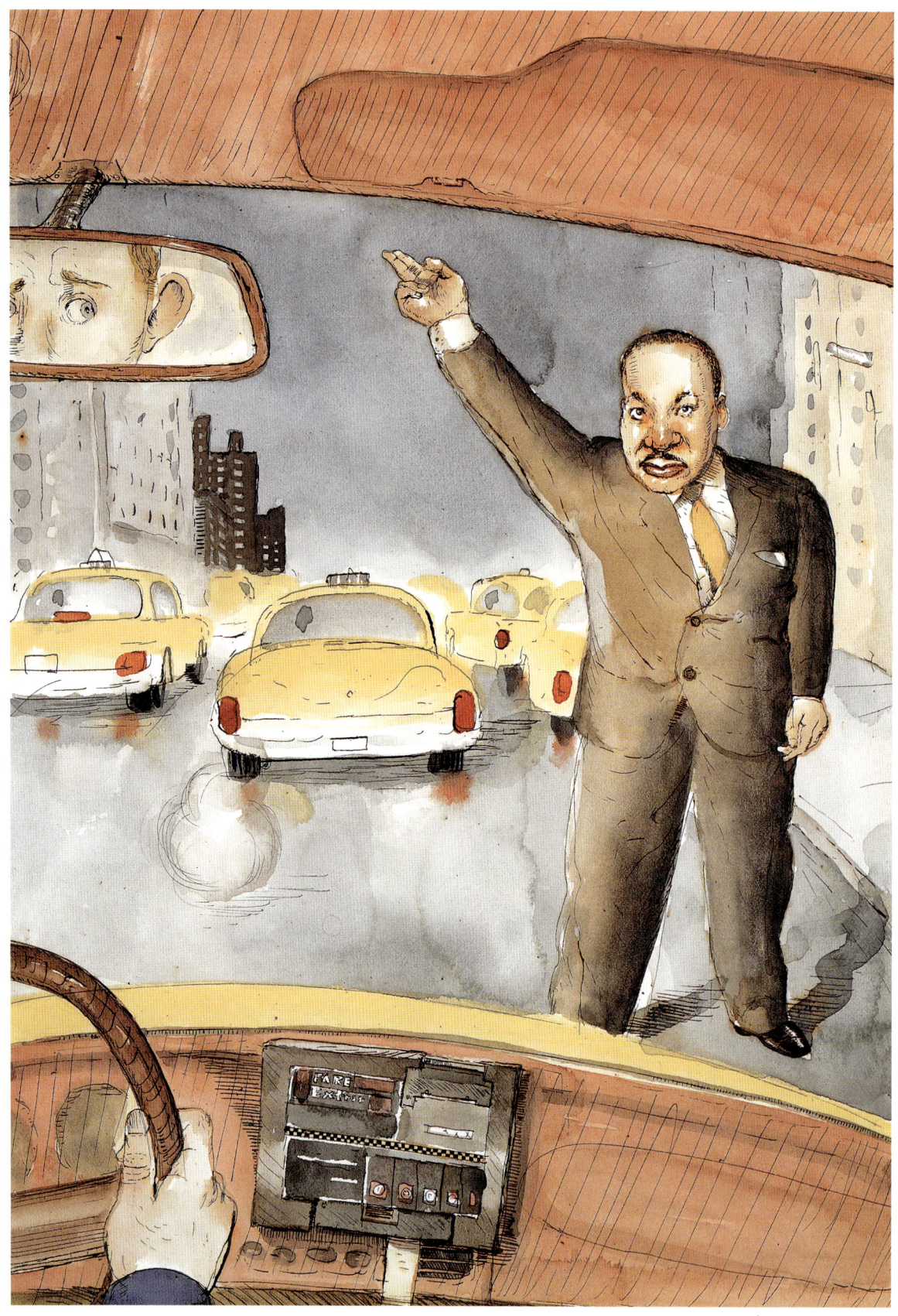

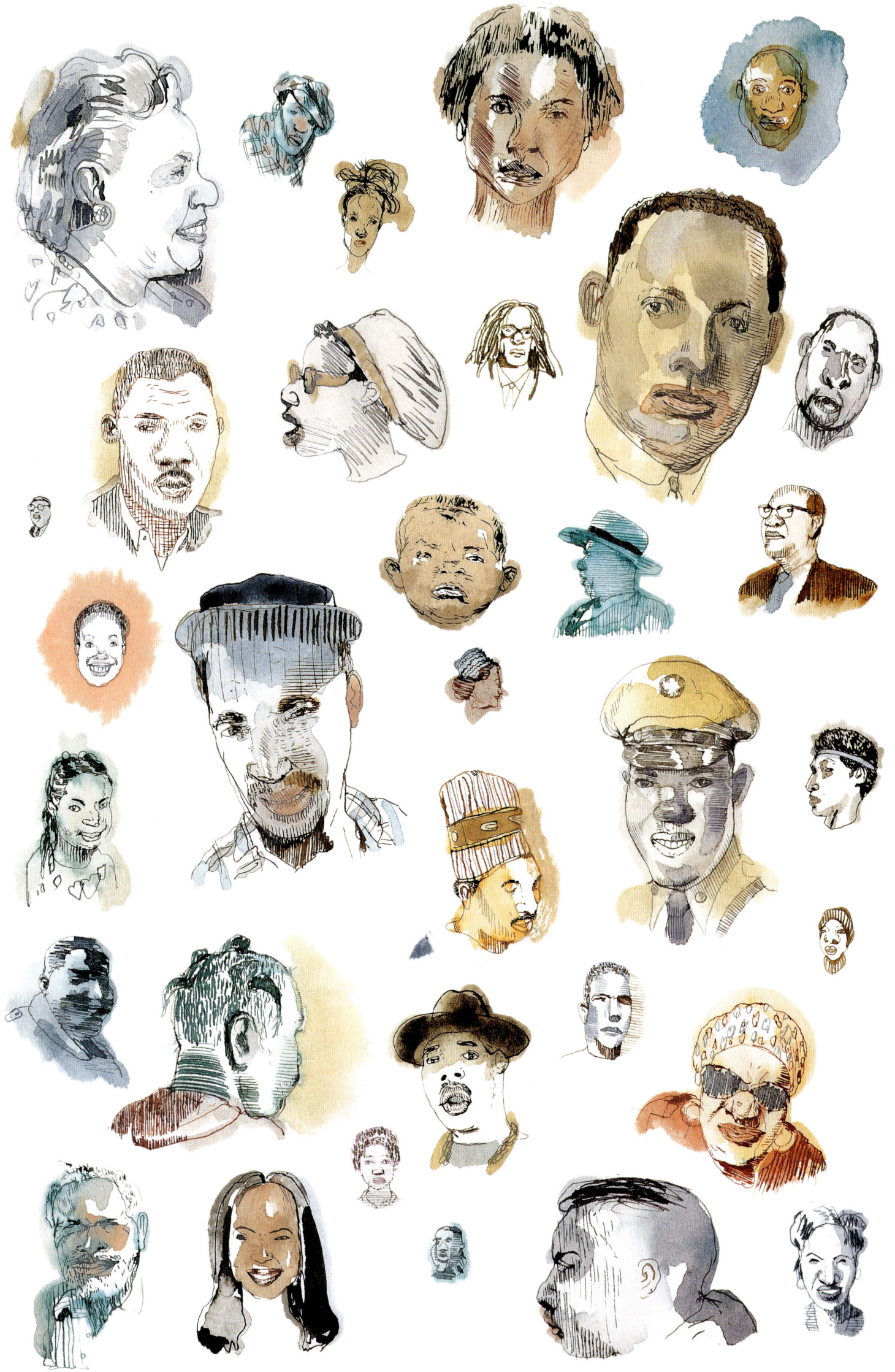

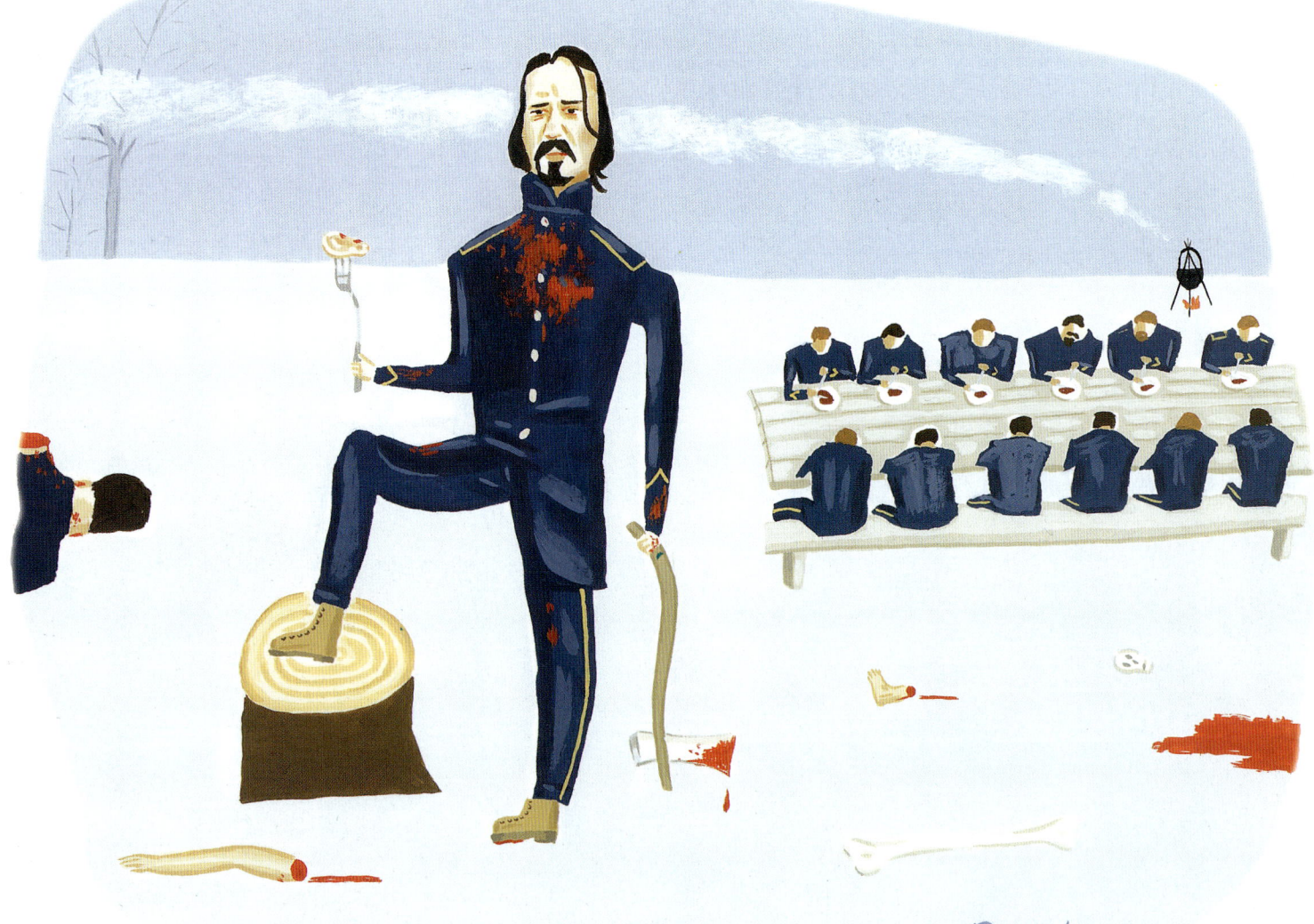

BoRda

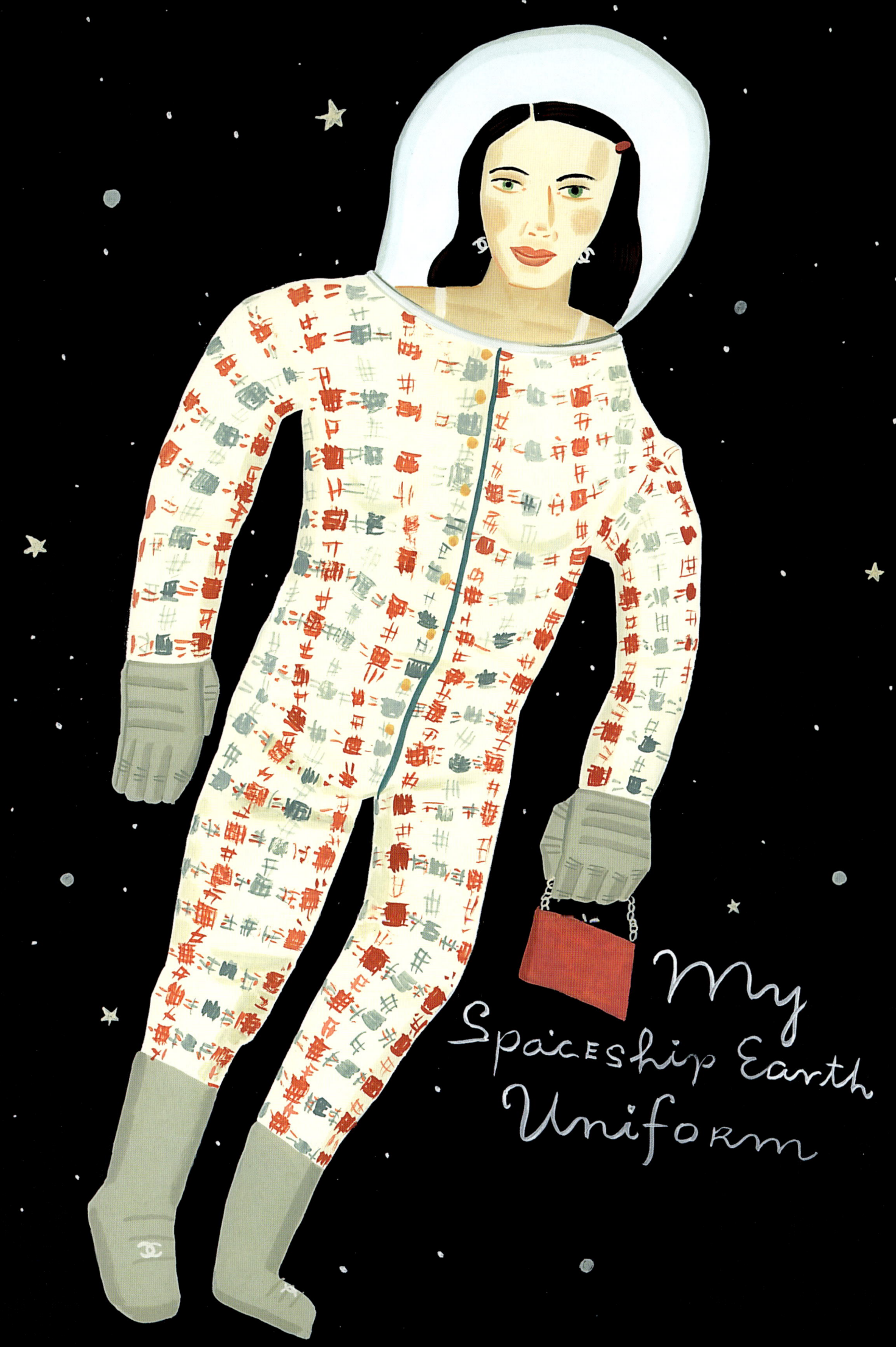

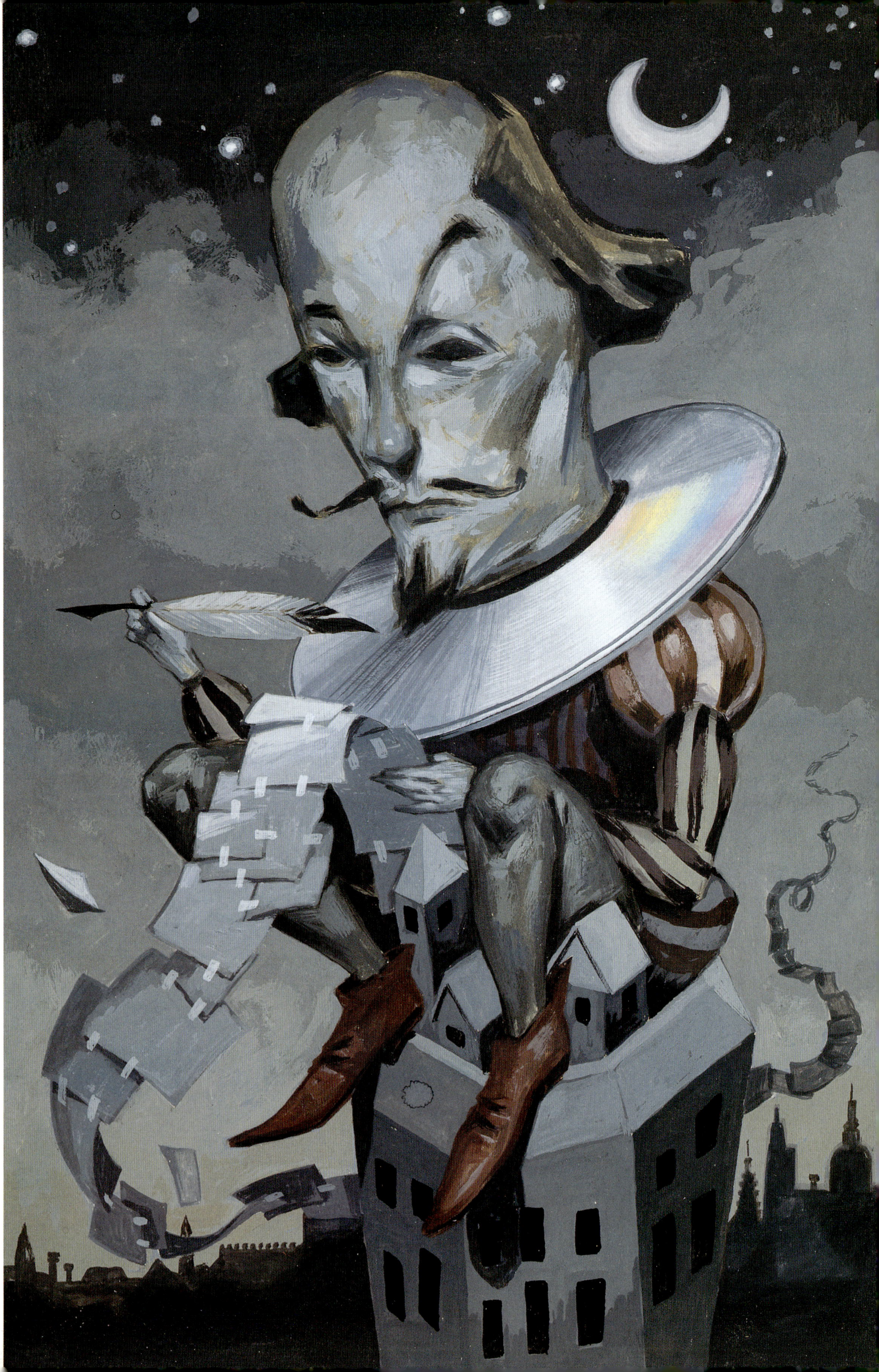

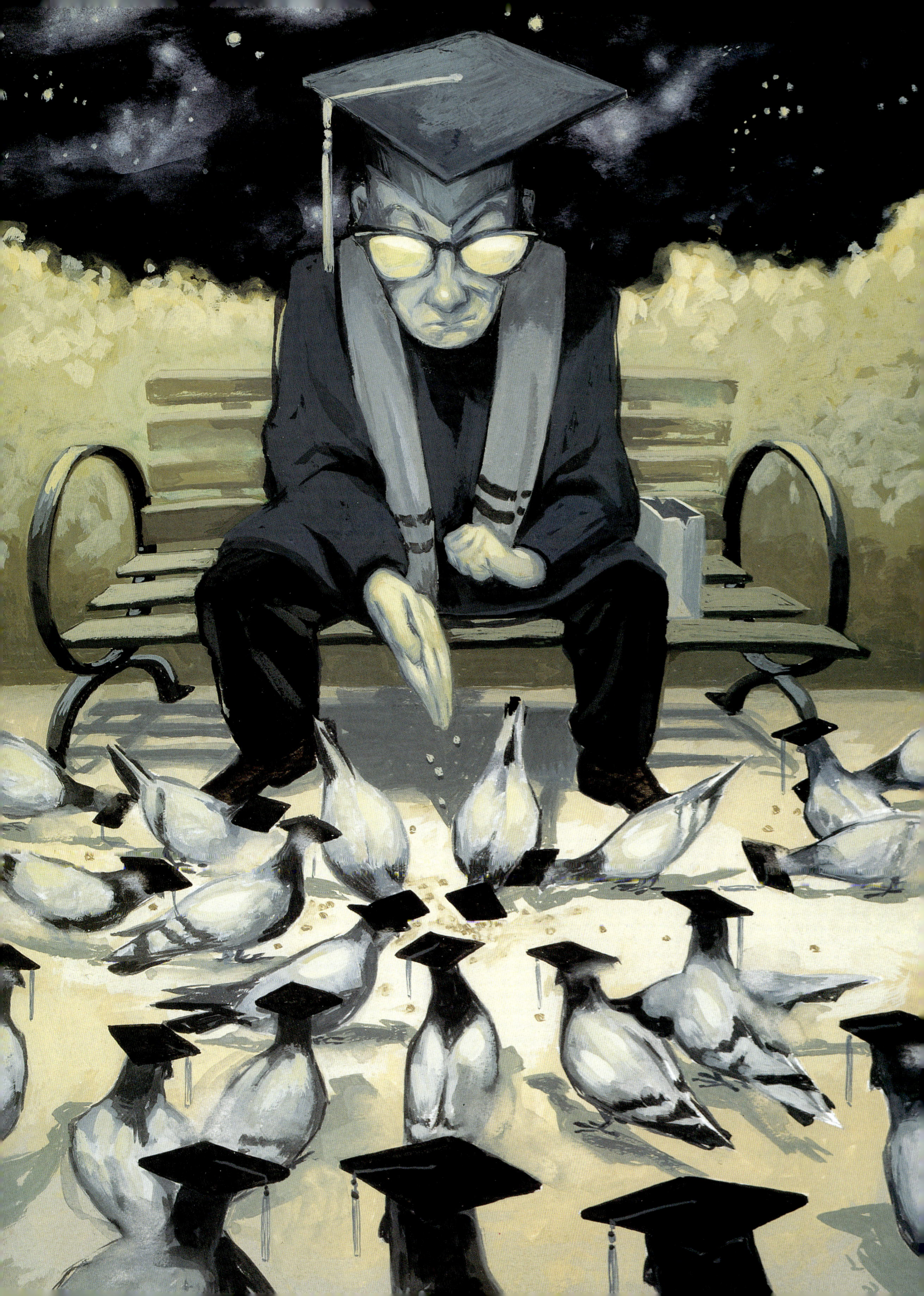

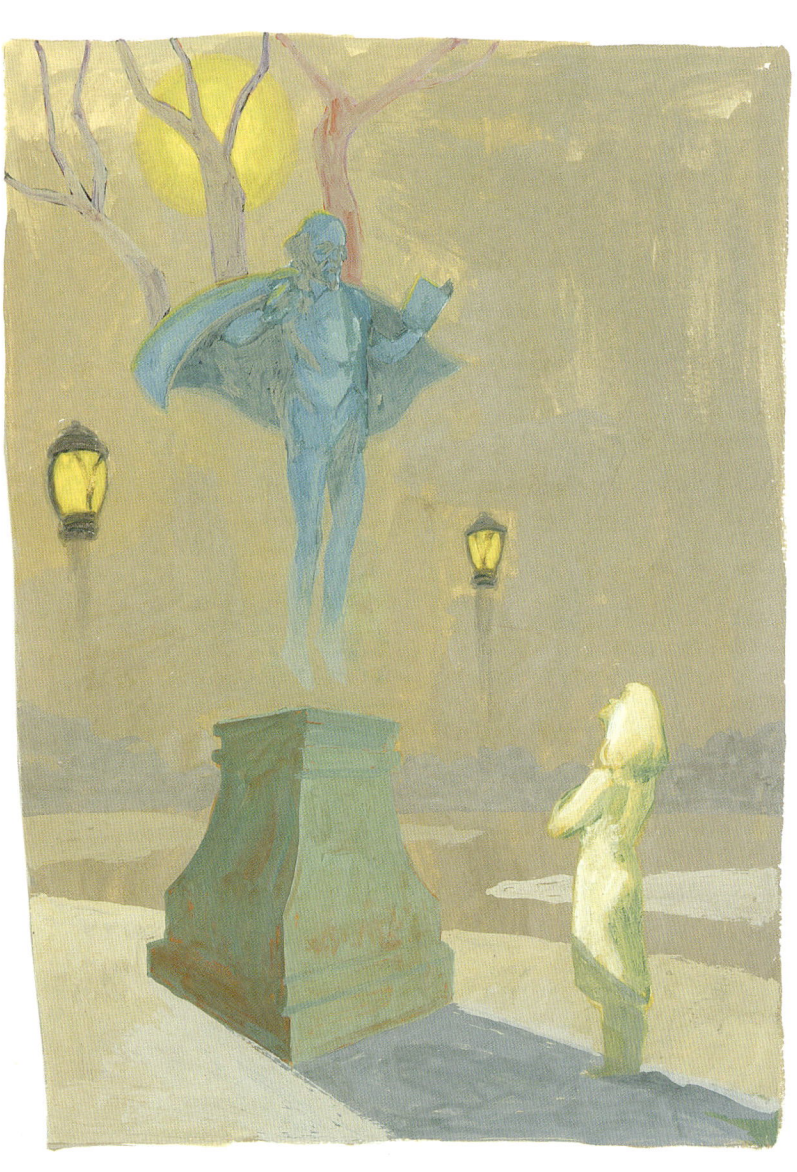

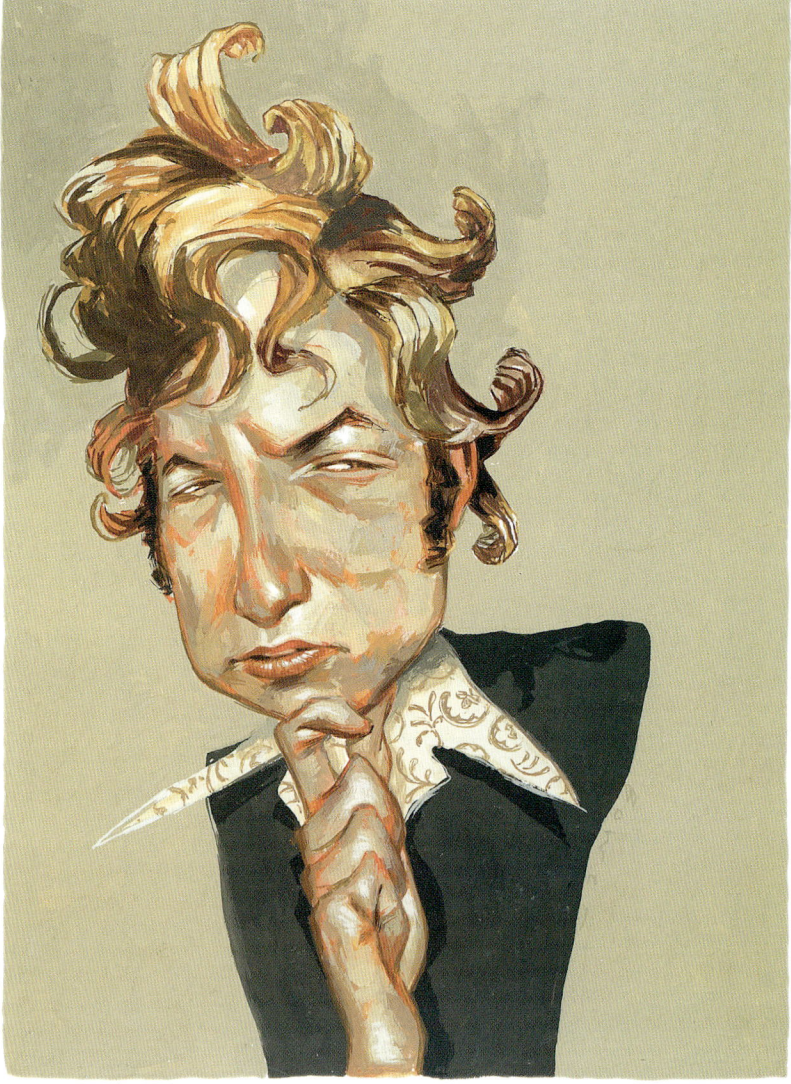

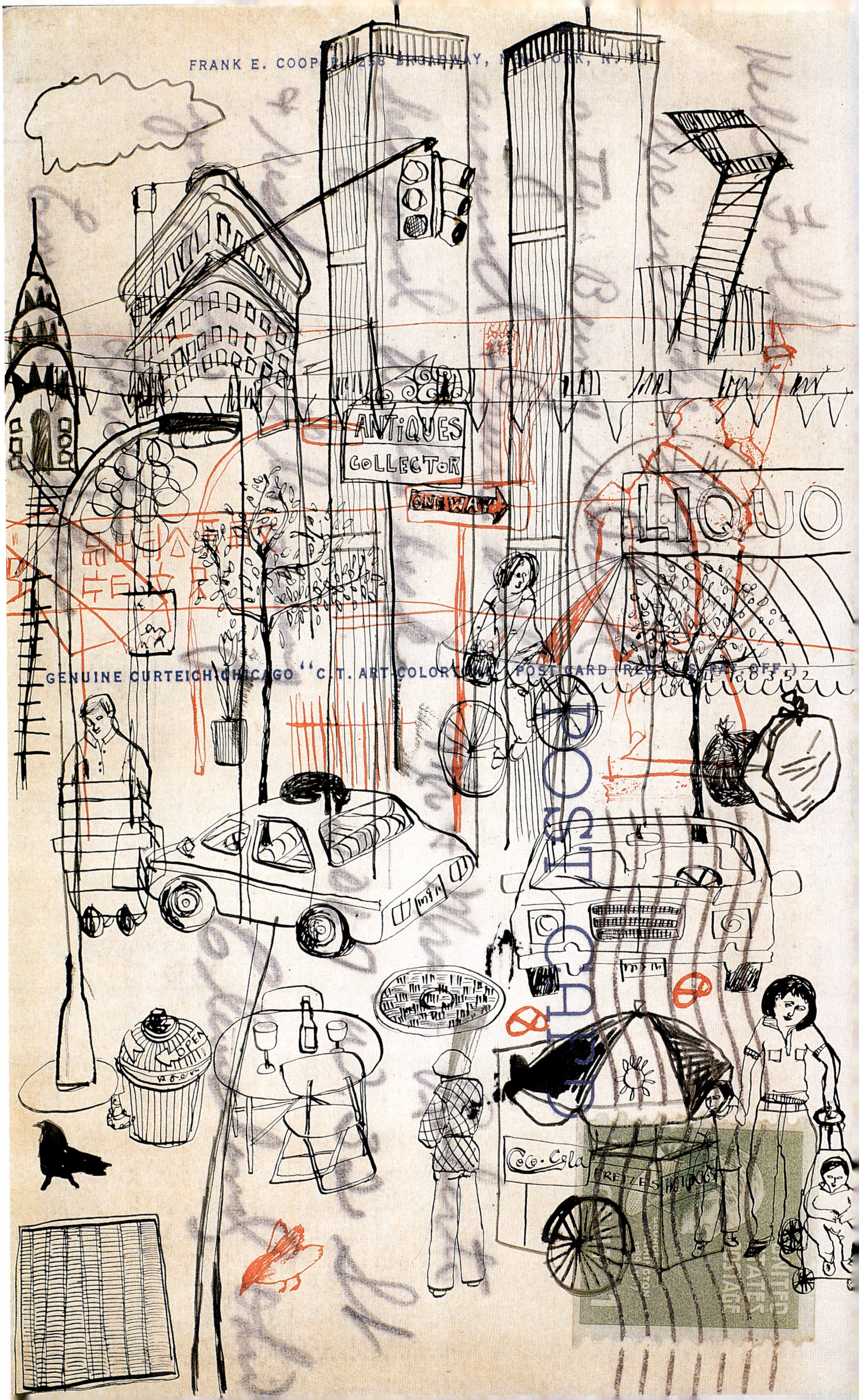

FRANK E. COOPER, 258 BROADWAY, NEW YORK, N.Y.

ANTIQUES
COLLECTOR

ONE WAY

LIQUO

GENUINE CURTEICH CHICAGO "C.T. ART COLORTONE" POST CARD (REG. U.S. PAT. OFF.)

POST CARD

Coca-Cola

PRETZELS

UNITED STATES POSTAGE

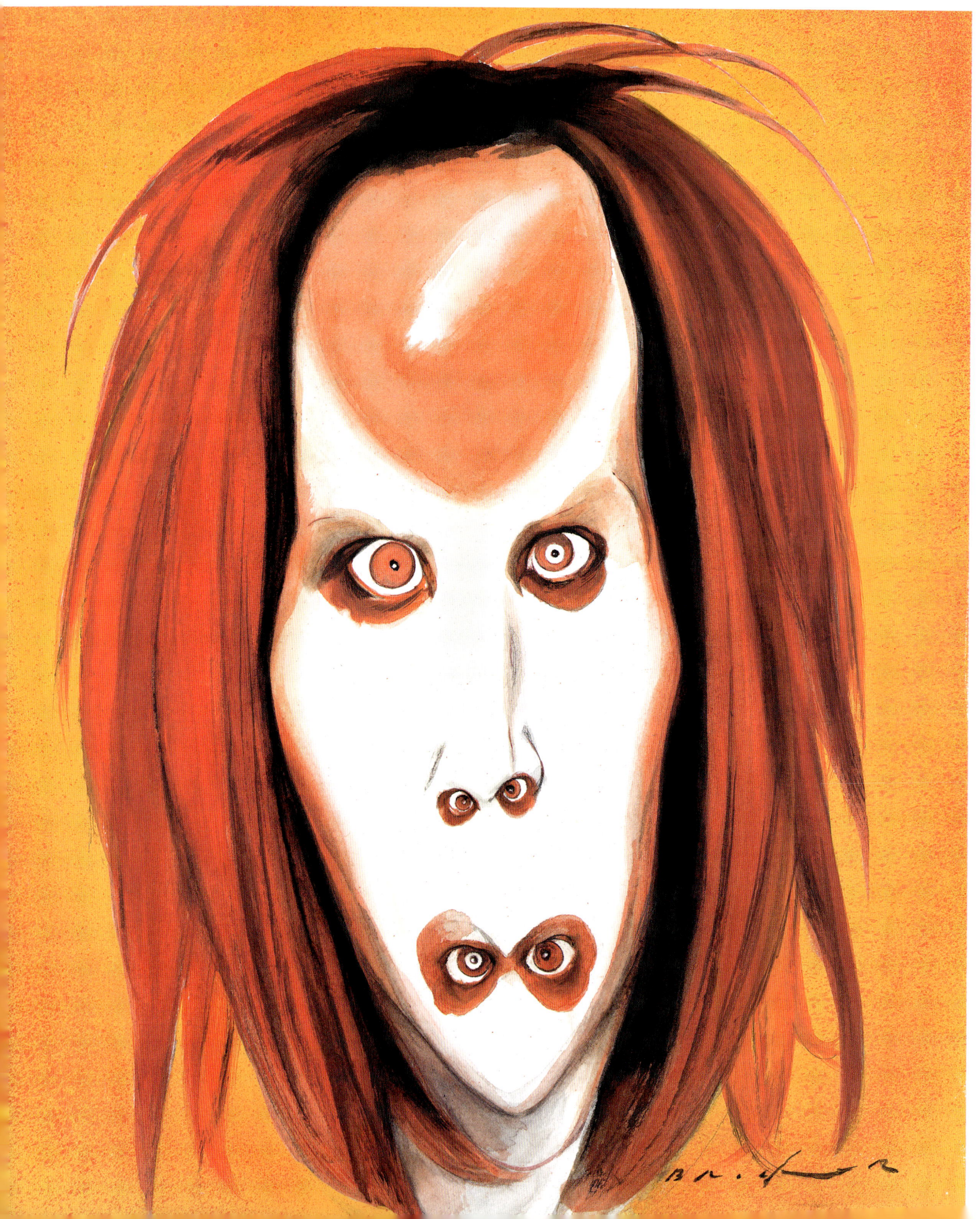

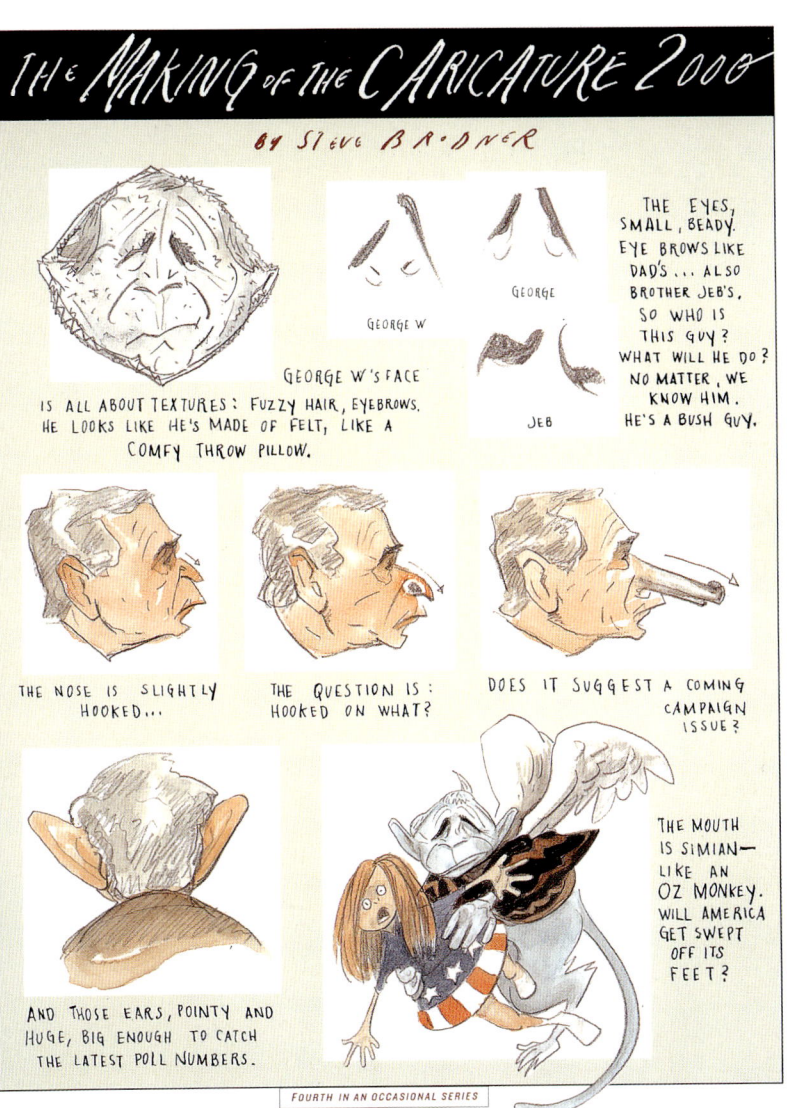

THE MAKING OF THE CARICATURE 2000
BY STEVE BRODNER

GEORGE W'S FACE IS ALL ABOUT TEXTURES: FUZZY HAIR, EYEBROWS. HE LOOKS LIKE HE'S MADE OF FELT, LIKE A COMFY THROW PILLOW.

GEORGE W

GEORGE

JEB

THE EYES, SMALL, BEADY. EYE BROWS LIKE DAD'S... ALSO BROTHER JEB'S, SO WHO IS THIS GUY? WHAT WILL HE DO? NO MATTER, WE KNOW HIM. HE'S A BUSH GUY.

THE NOSE IS SLIGHTLY HOOKED...

THE QUESTION IS: HOOKED ON WHAT?

DOES IT SUGGEST A COMING CAMPAIGN ISSUE?

AND THOSE EARS, POINTY AND HUGE, BIG ENOUGH TO CATCH THE LATEST POLL NUMBERS.

THE MOUTH IS SIMIAN— LIKE AN OZ MONKEY. WILL AMERICA GET SWEPT OFF ITS FEET?

FOURTH IN AN OCCASIONAL SERIES

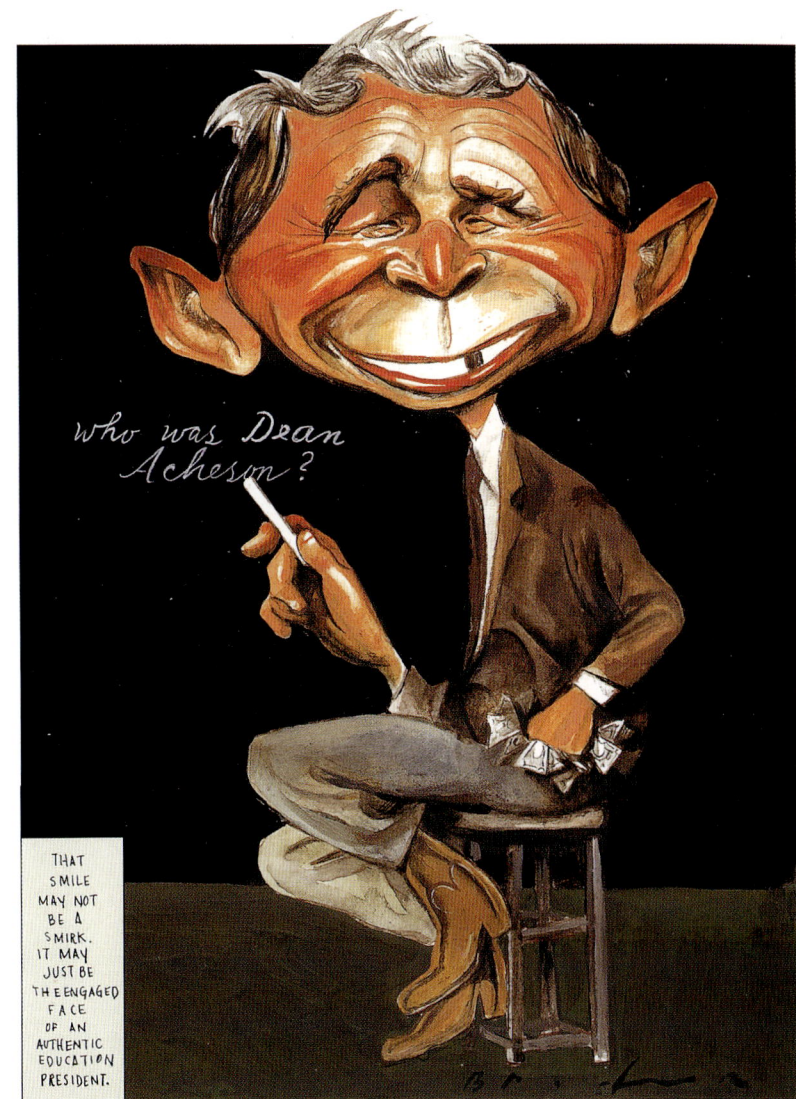

who was Dean Acheson?

THAT SMILE MAY NOT BE A SMIRK. IT MAY JUST BE THE ENGAGED FACE OF AN AUTHENTIC EDUCATION PRESIDENT.

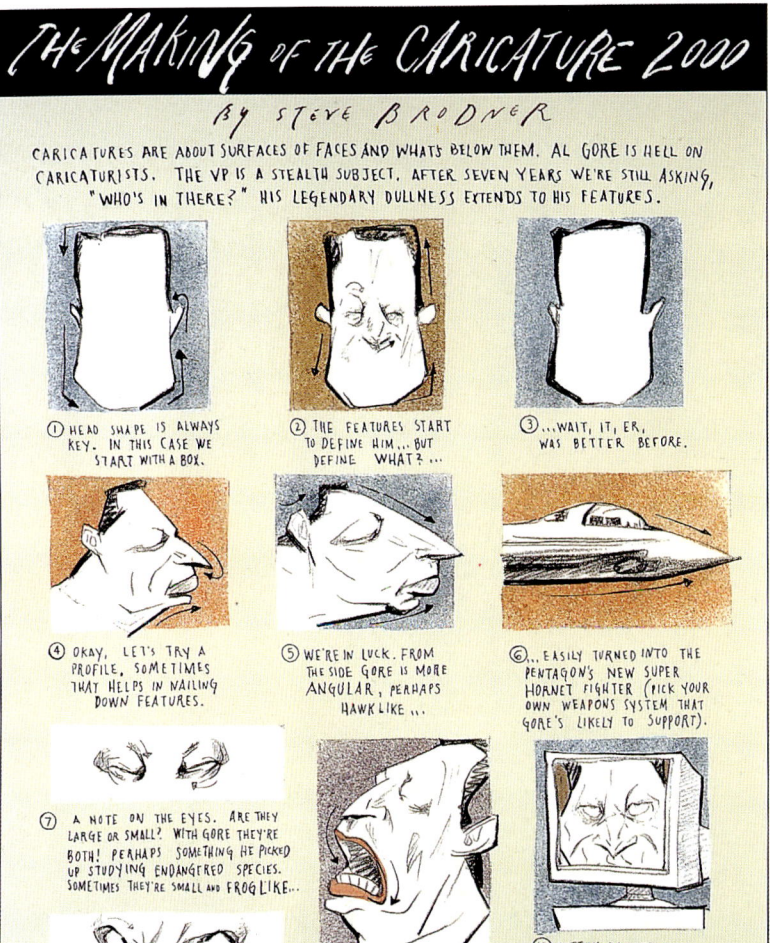

THE MAKING OF THE CARICATURE 2000
BY STEVE BRODNER

CARICATURES ARE ABOUT SURFACES OF FACES AND WHAT'S BELOW THEM. AL GORE IS HELL ON CARICATURISTS. THE VP IS A STEALTH SUBJECT. AFTER SEVEN YEARS WE'RE STILL ASKING, "WHO'S IN THERE?" HIS LEGENDARY DULLNESS EXTENDS TO HIS FEATURES.

① HEAD SHAPE IS ALWAYS KEY. IN THIS CASE WE START WITH A BOX.

② THE FEATURES START TO DEFINE HIM... BUT DEFINE WHAT?...

③ ...WAIT, IT, ER, WAS BETTER BEFORE.

④ OKAY, LET'S TRY A PROFILE, SOMETIMES THAT HELPS IN NAILING DOWN FEATURES.

⑤ WE'RE IN LUCK. FROM THE SIDE GORE IS MORE ANGULAR, PERHAPS HAWK LIKE...

⑥ ...EASILY TURNED INTO THE PENTAGON'S NEW SUPER HORNET FIGHTER (PICK YOUR OWN WEAPONS SYSTEM THAT GORE'S LIKELY TO SUPPORT).

⑦ A NOTE ON THE EYES. ARE THEY LARGE OR SMALL? WITH GORE THEY'RE BOTH! PERHAPS SOMETHING HE PICKED UP STUDYING ENDANGERED SPECIES. SOMETIMES THEY'RE SMALL AND FROG LIKE...

⑧ ...OTHER TIMES THEY'RE LIKE LARGE SPOTTED OWL'S EYES.

⑨ LIP ALERT: GORE, IT MUST BE NOTED, HAS JULIA ROBERTS' LIPS. THEY RUN ALL OVER HIS LOWER FACE.

⑩ GETTING BACK TO THE SQUARE SHAPE. ISN'T IT AN APPROPRIATE ONE FOR THE INVENTOR OF THE INTERNET? SO, FINALLY, IS AL GORE A HYPERLINK TO A GOOD SITE...

FIRST IN AN OCCASIONAL SERIES

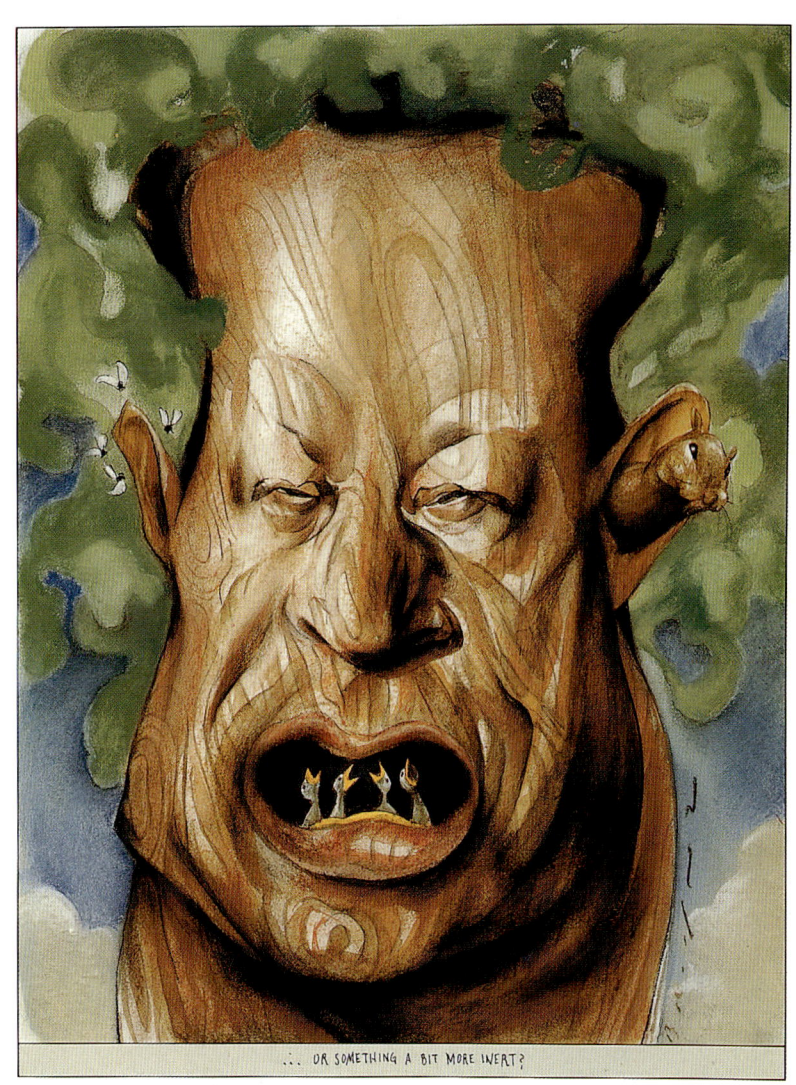

... OR SOMETHING A BIT MORE INERT?

THE MAKING OF THE CARICATURE 2000

BY STEVE BRODNER

A RHODES SCHOLAR, BILL BRADLEY IS PERHAPS THE BRAINIEST CANDIDATE OF THE BUNCH. HIS HEAD IS A GOOD CLUE... A KIND OF LIGHT BULB — LIKE OLD REDDY KILOWATT. THE FOLDS IN THE LOWER FACE SEEM LIKE A PUDDLE OF MOLASSES THAT THE BULB IS STUCK IN.

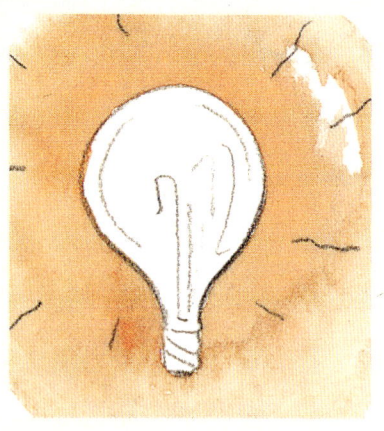 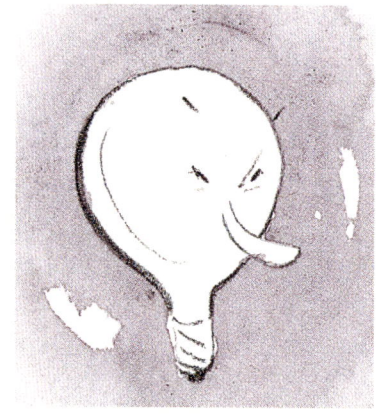 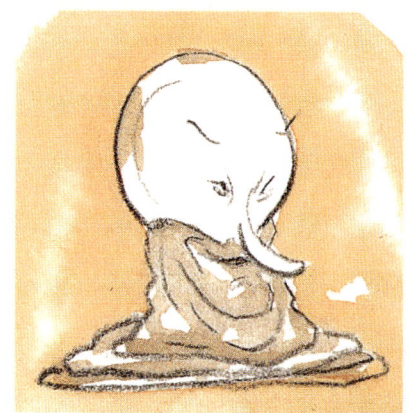

PEOPLE HAVE COMMENTED ON HIS "JACK NICHOLSON" EYES.

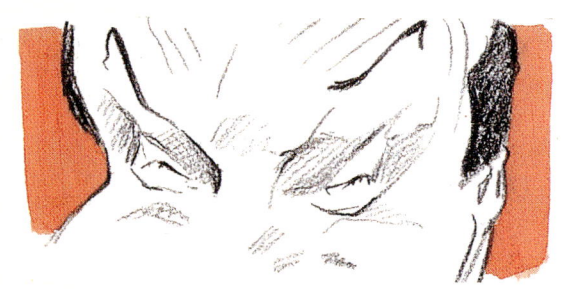 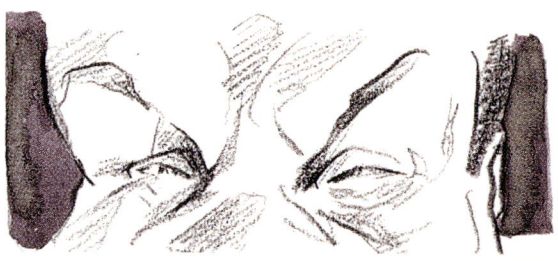

THEY'RE ACTUALLY MORE IN THE STYLE OF CAMPAIGN CONTRIBUTOR MICHAEL EISNER.

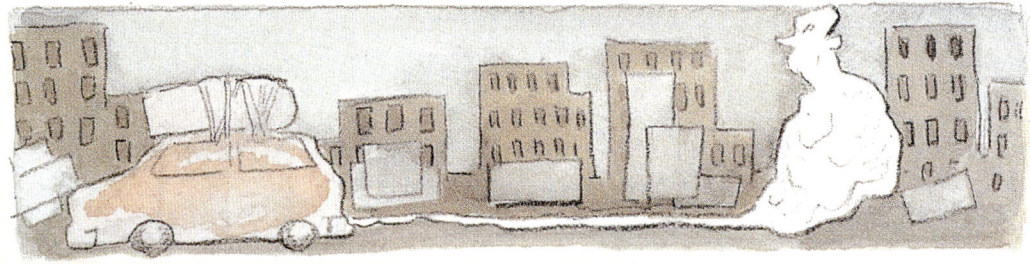 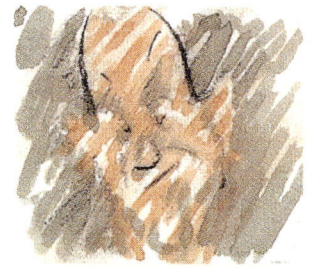

FORMER SEN. PAUL SIMON DESCRIBED BRADLEY AS BEING ON HIS OWN CLOUD. HOW ABOUT DUST CLOUDS GATHERING IN A NAFTA-DEVASTATED TOWN?

WARM AND FUZZY HE MAY NOT BE — AT LEAST NOT WARM.

PAUL WELLSTONE SAID THAT "THERE'S A HUGE VOID BRADLEY CAN FILL". THAT HAS ALREADY HAPPENED. THERE'S THE VOID IN CLINTON'S RHETORIC...

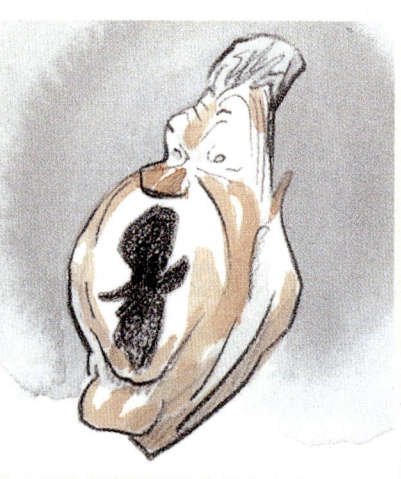 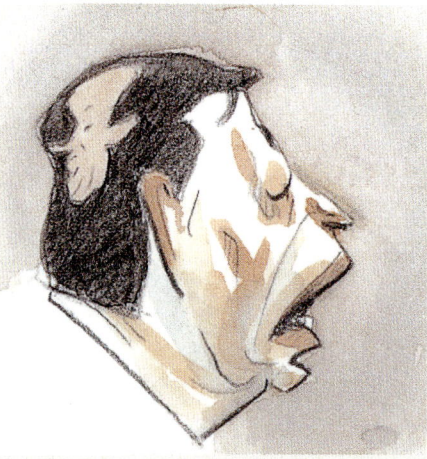

... AND THE VOID IN GORE'S HAIRLINE.

THIRD IN AN OCCASIONAL SERIES

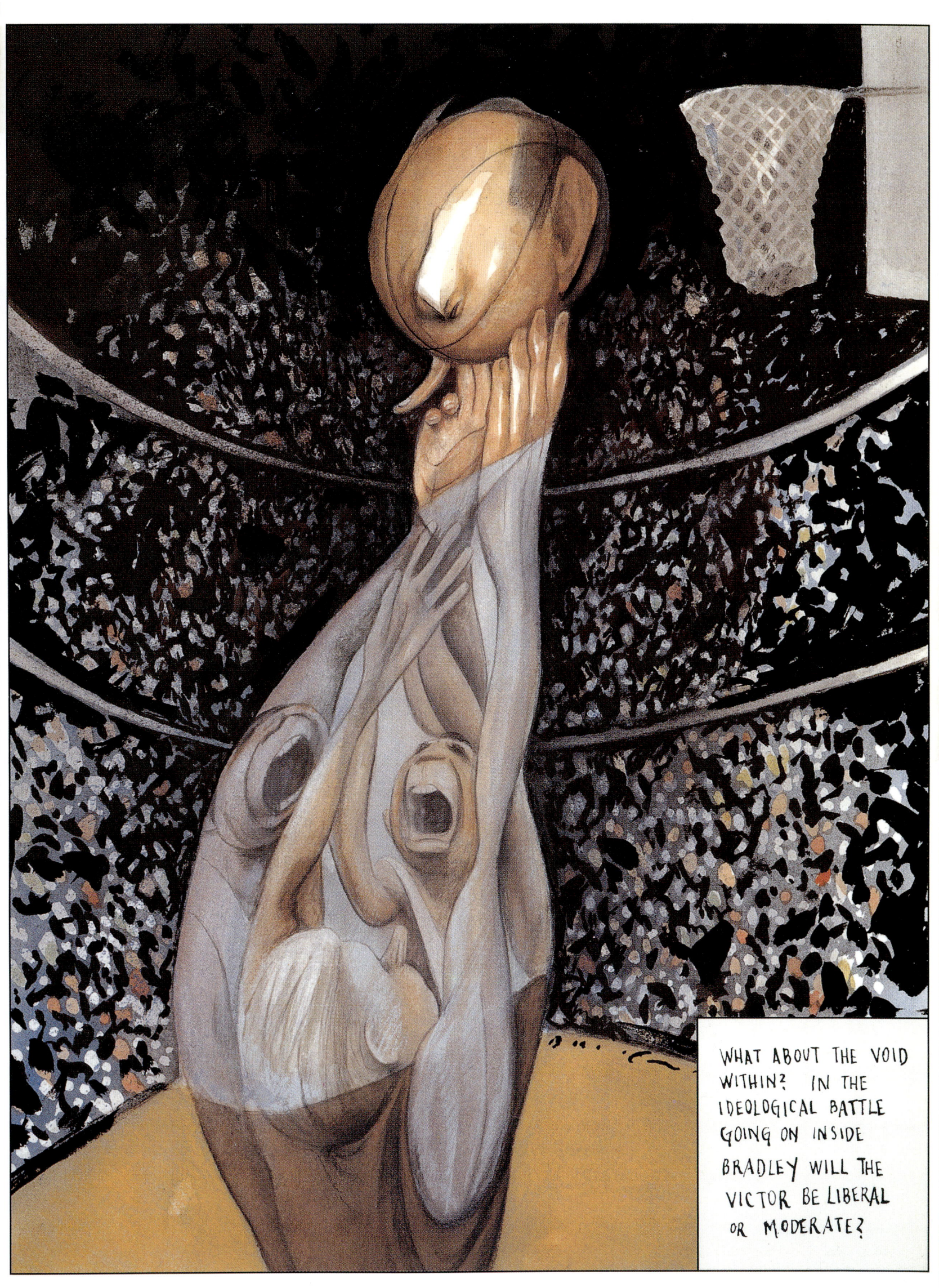

WHAT ABOUT THE VOID WITHIN? IN THE IDEOLOGICAL BATTLE GOING ON INSIDE BRADLEY WILL THE VICTOR BE LIBERAL OR MODERATE?

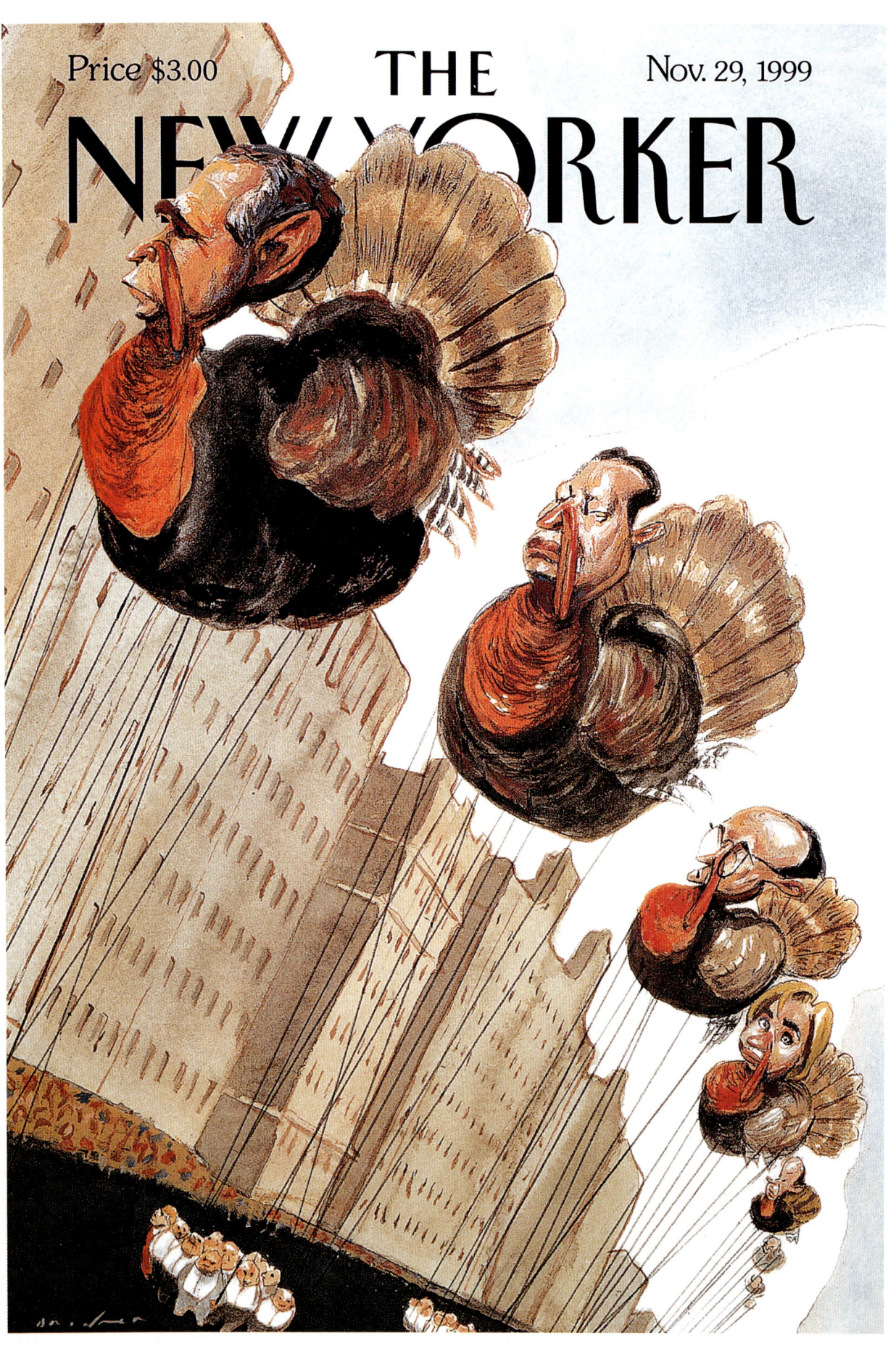

Price $3.00   THE   Nov. 29, 1999

NEW YORKER

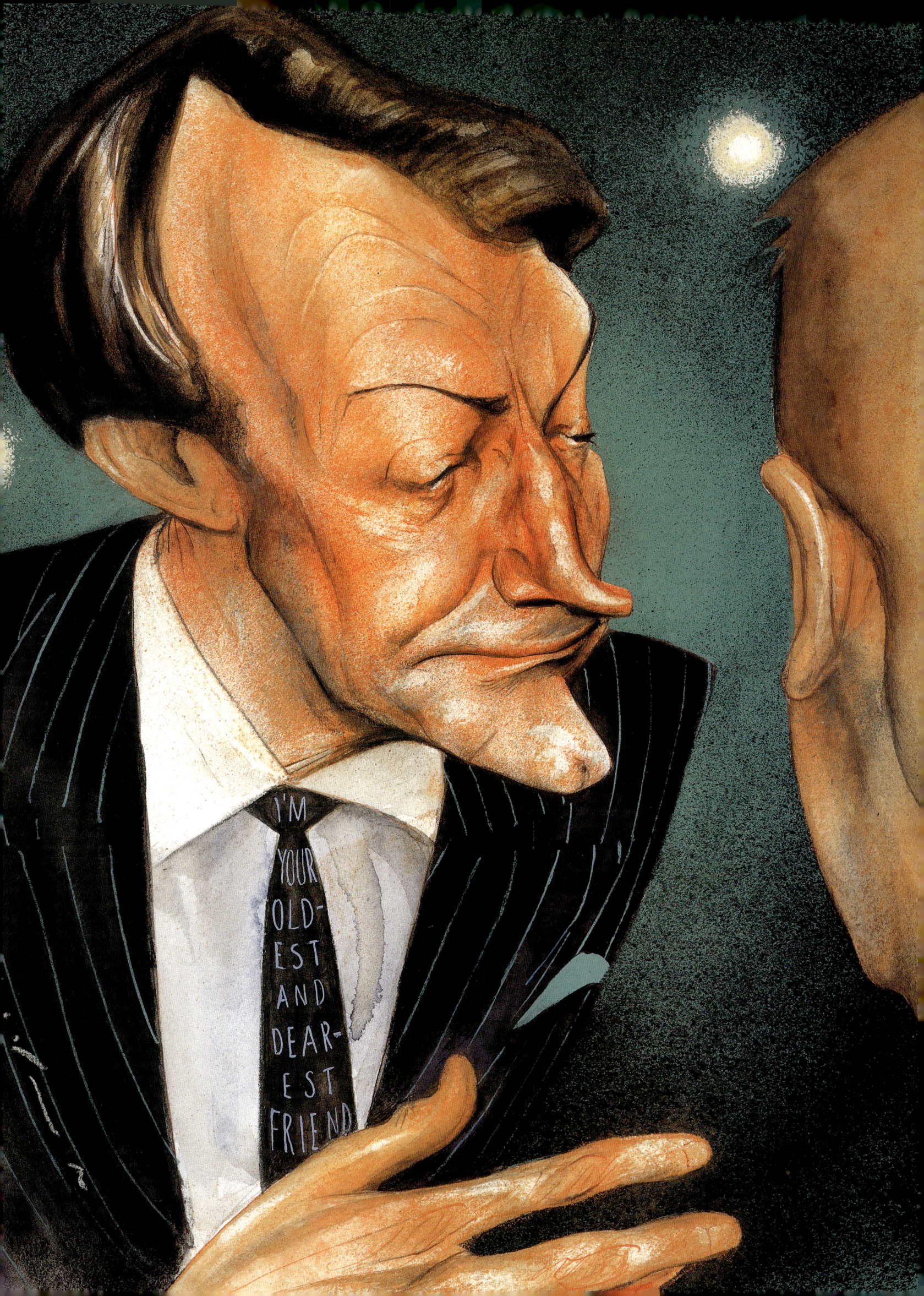

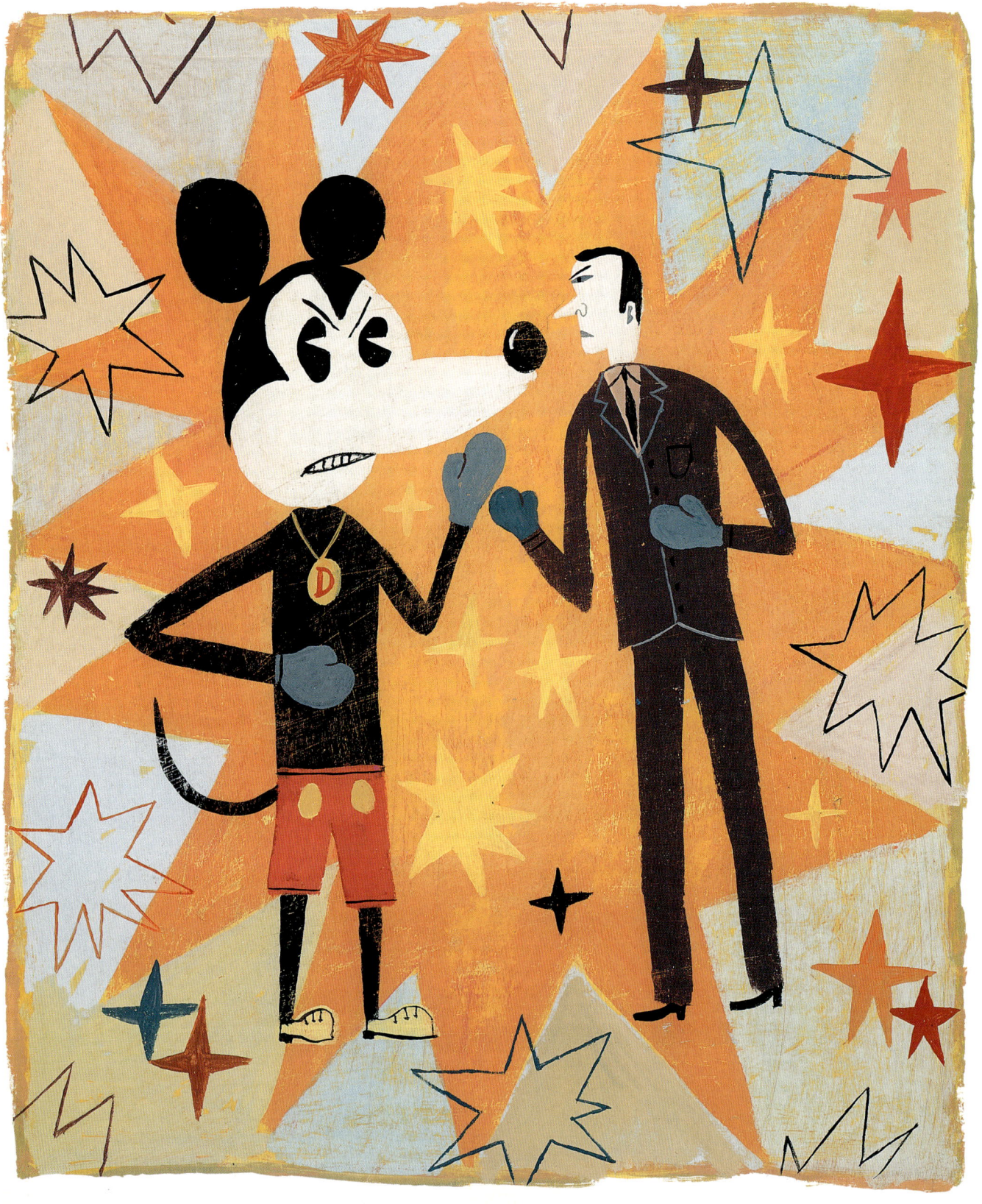

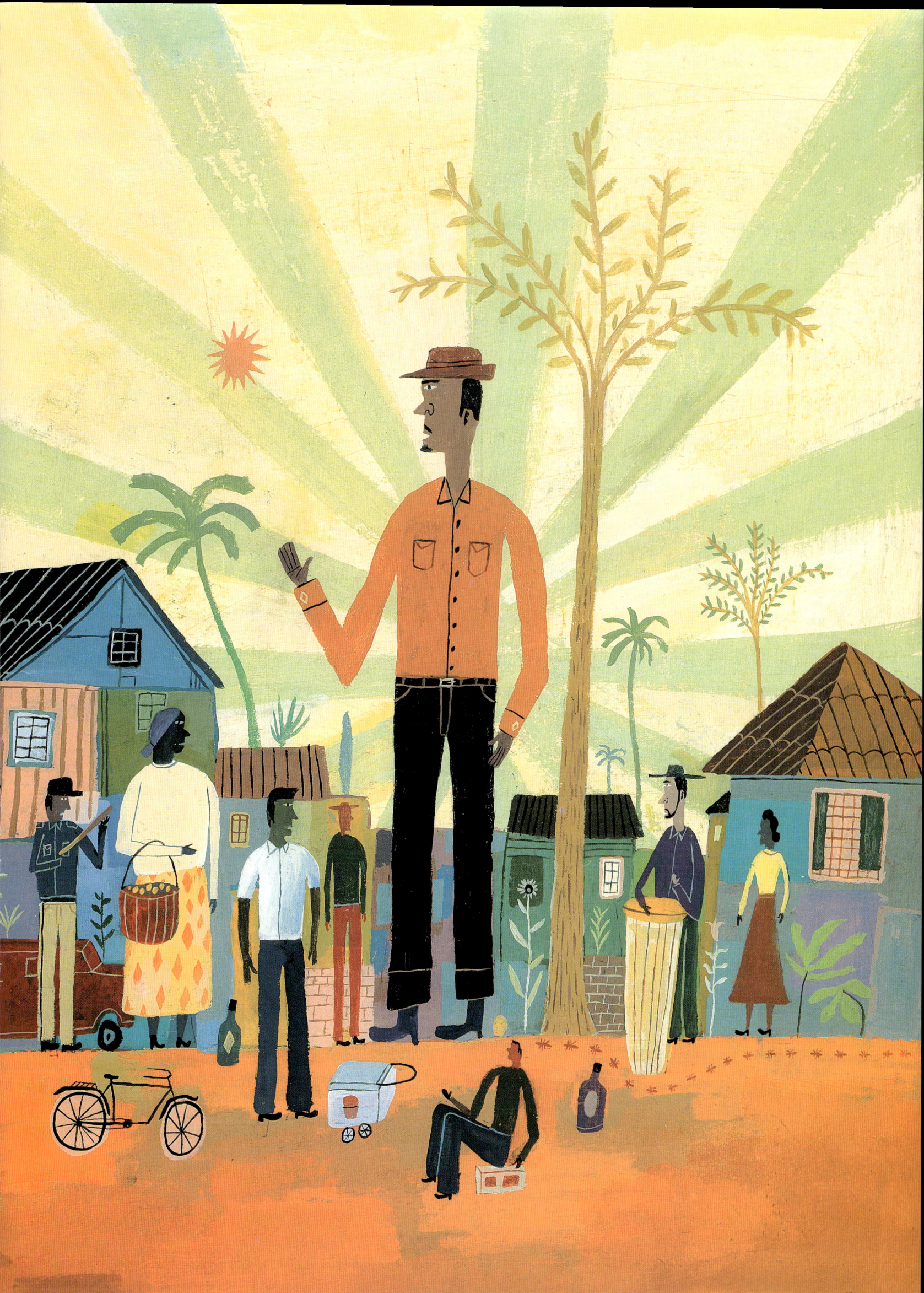

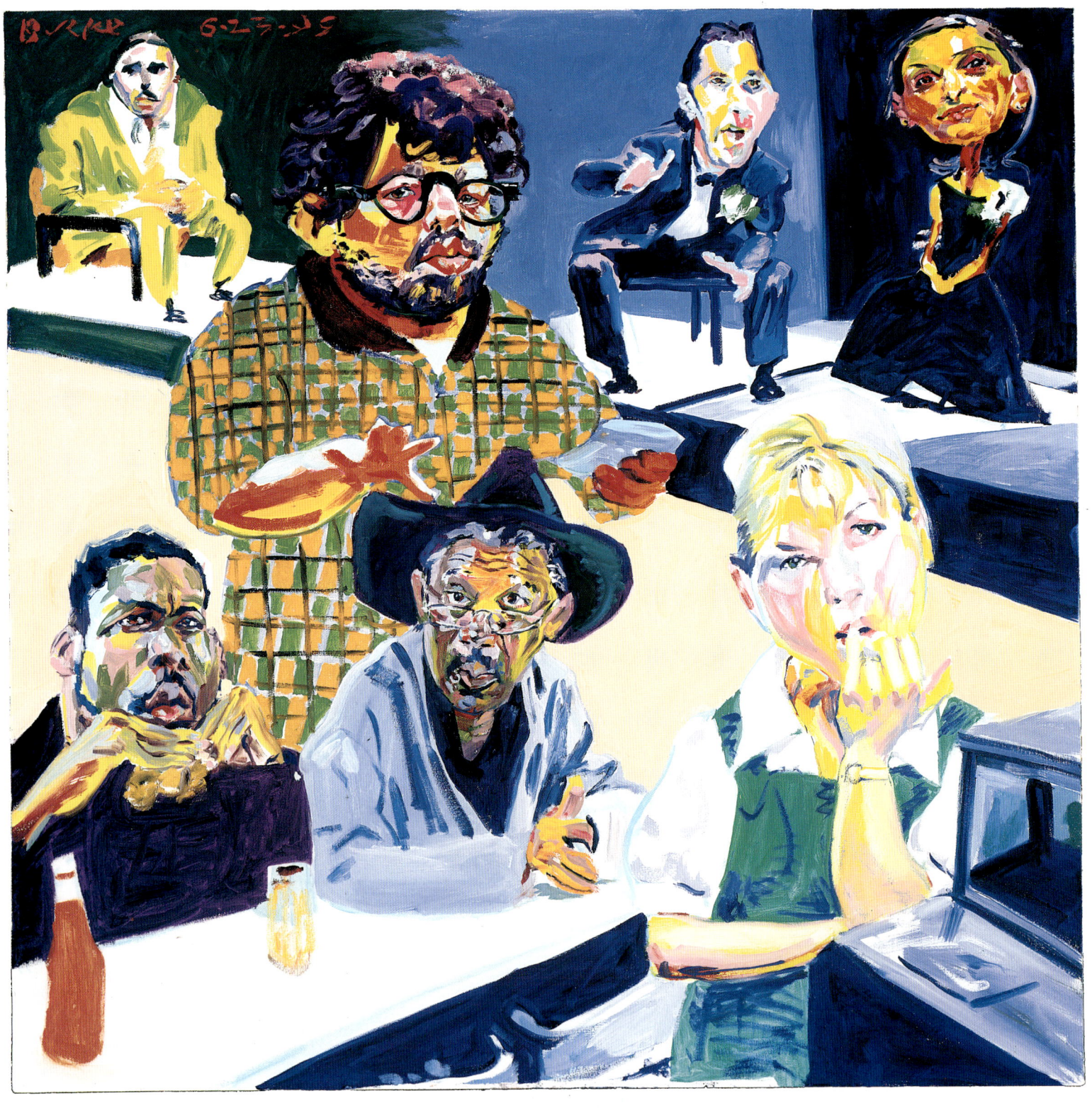

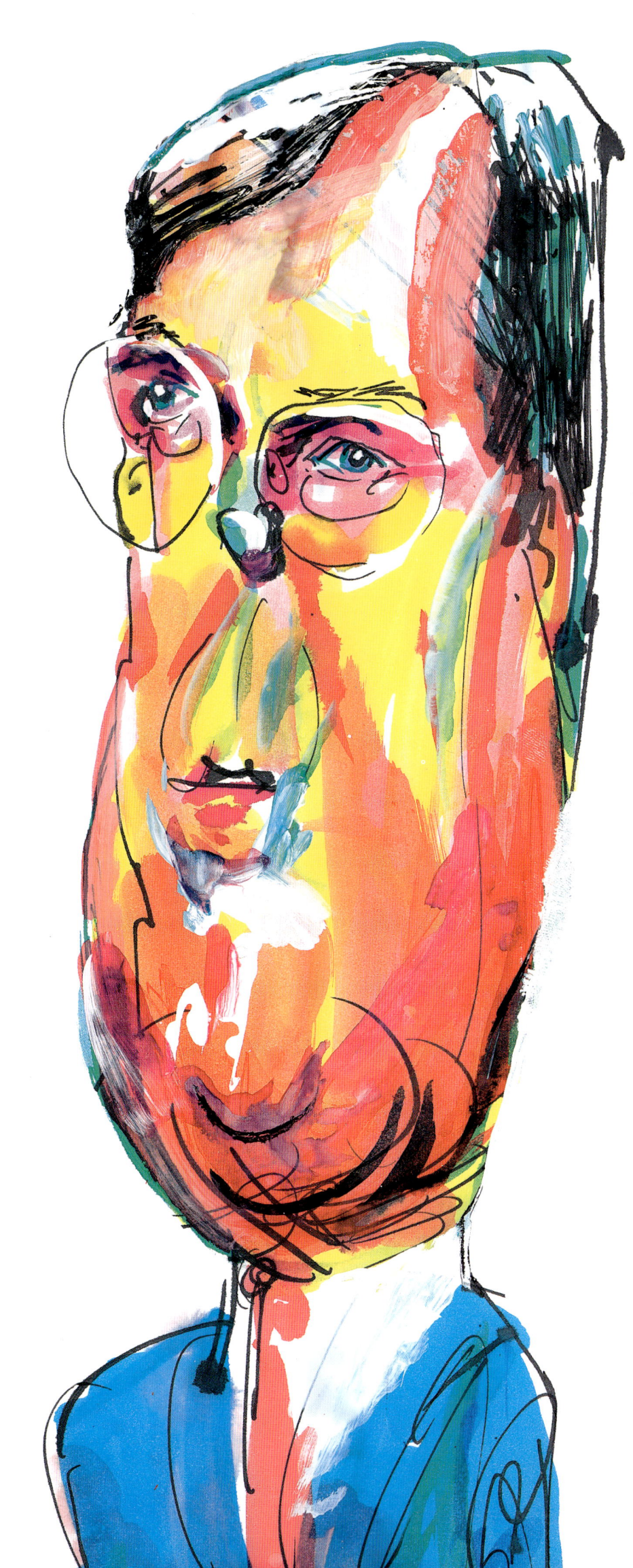

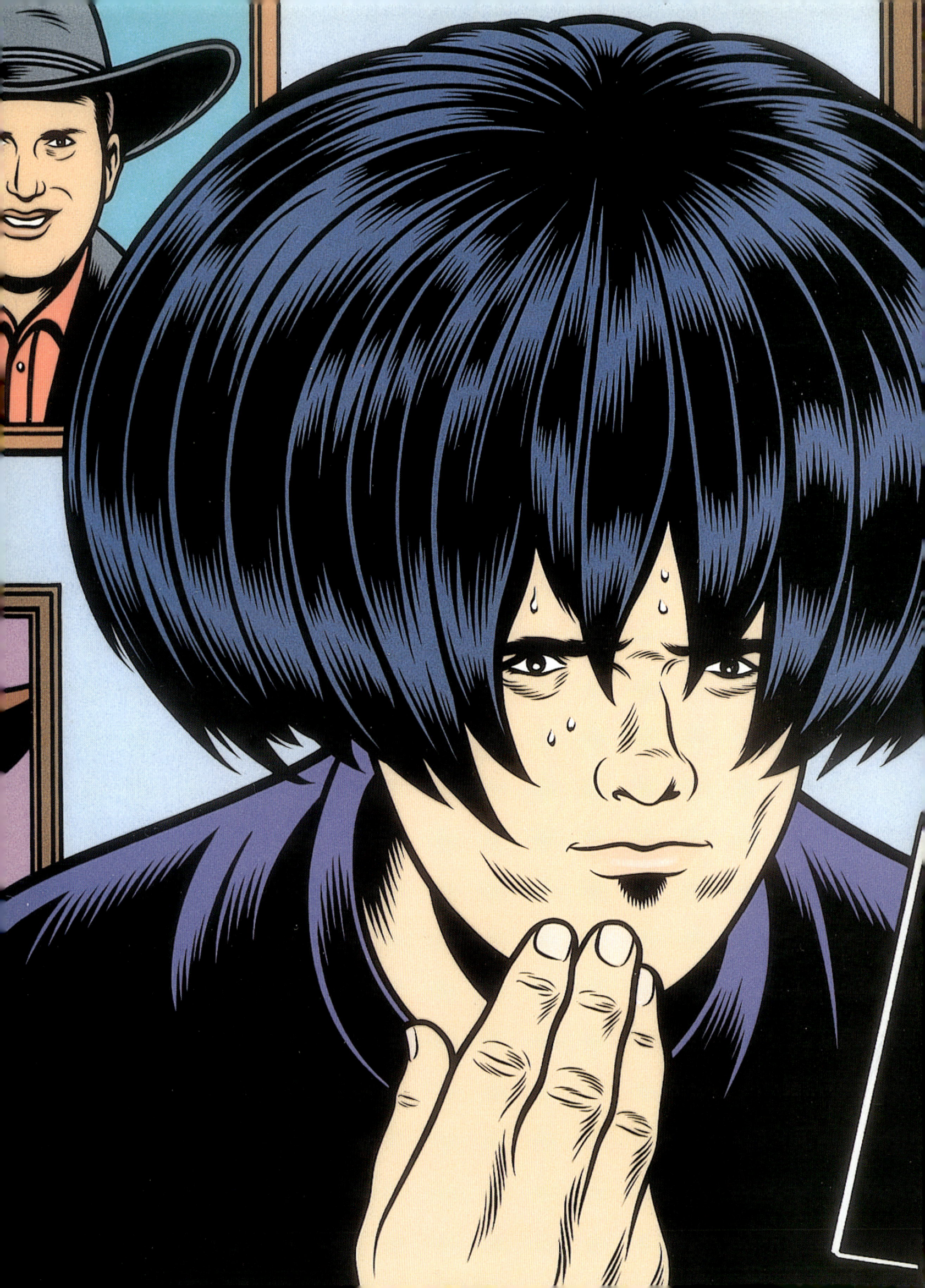

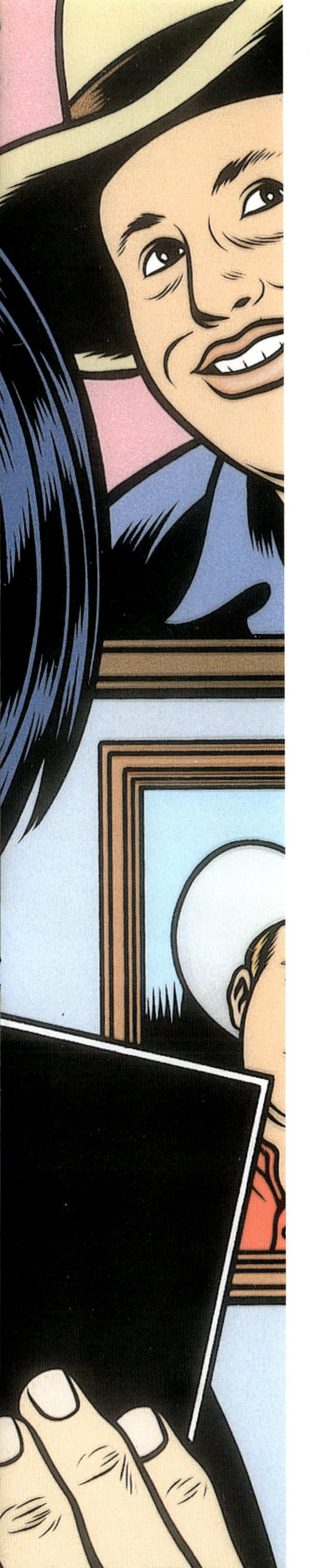

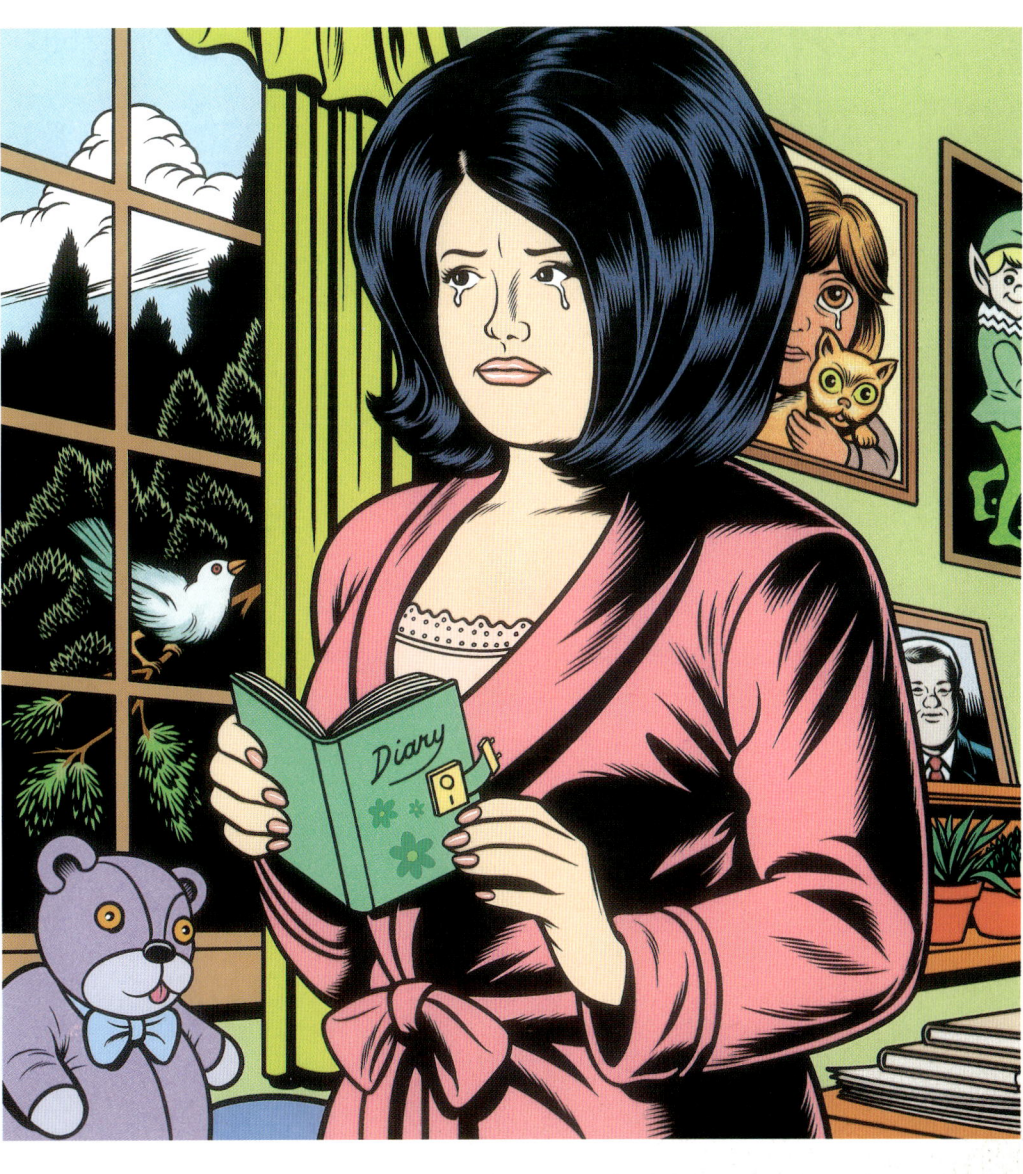

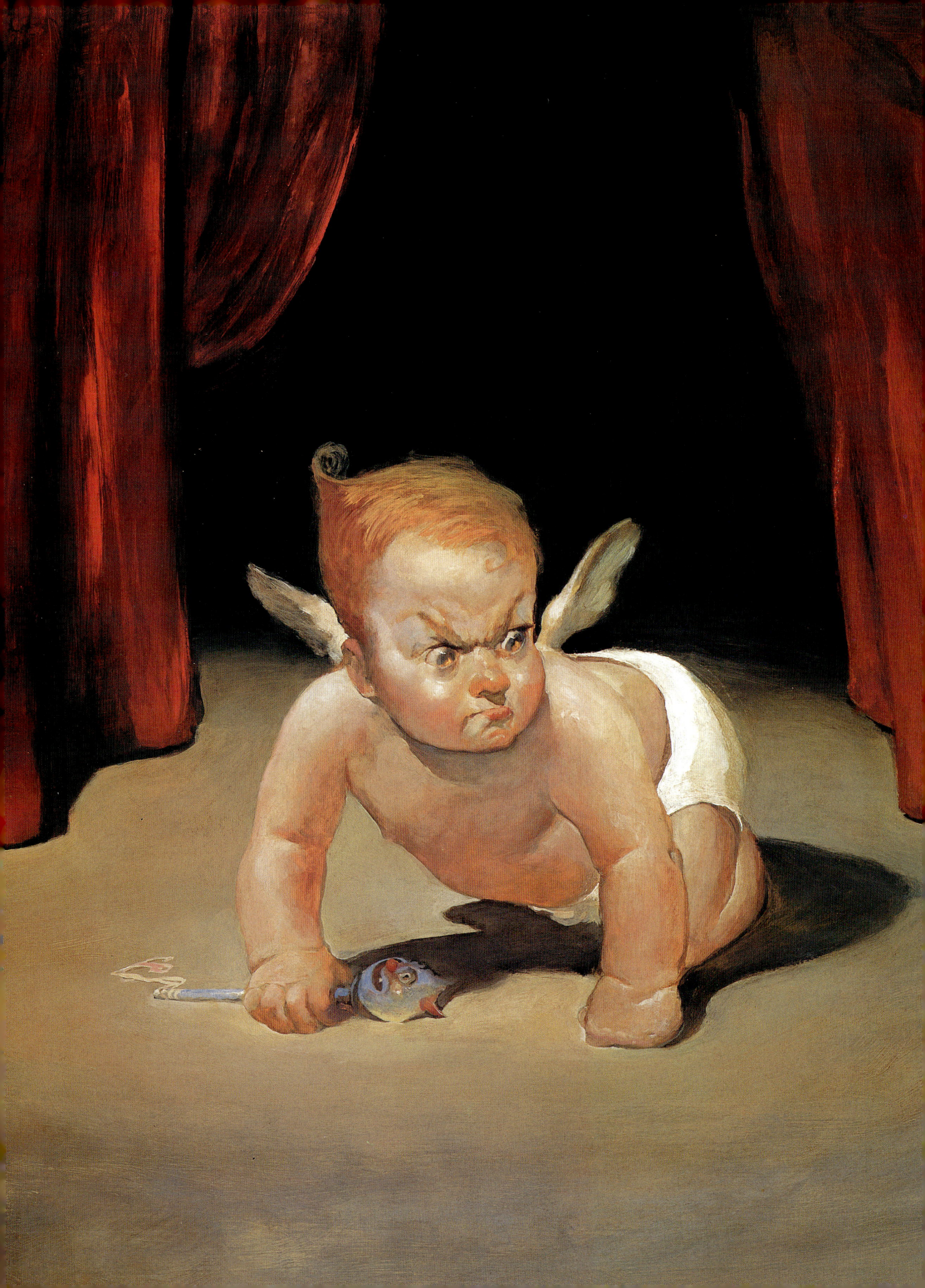

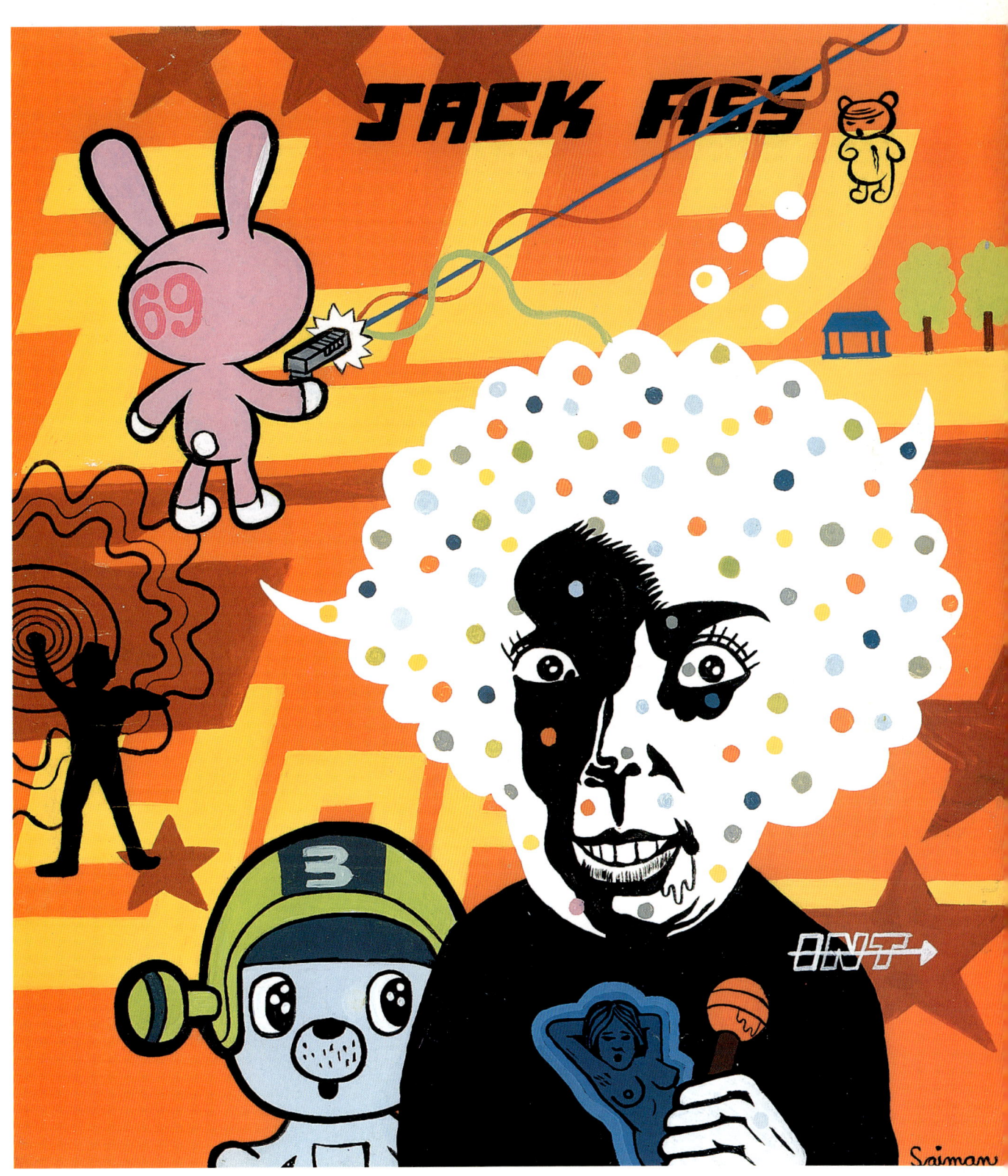

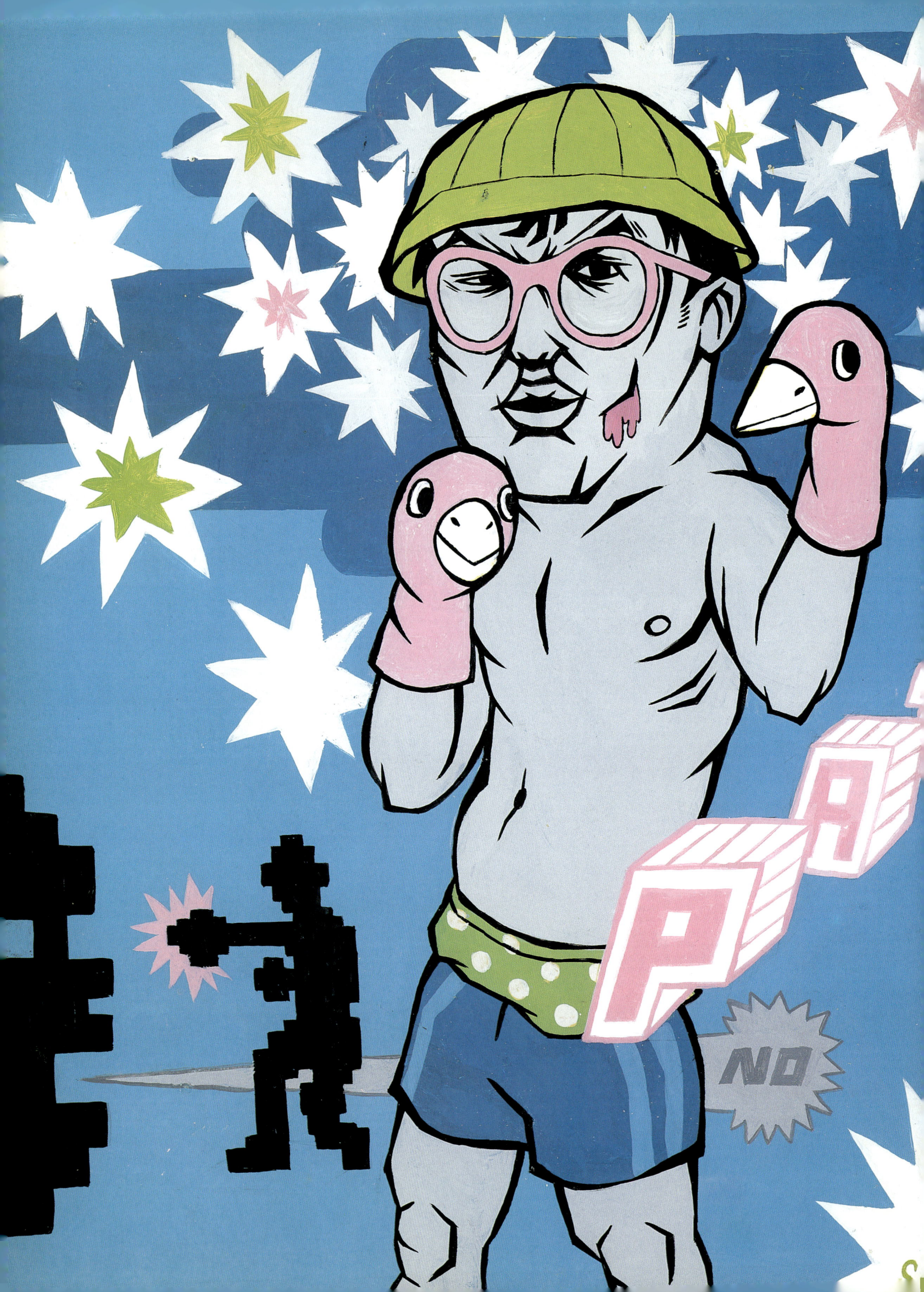

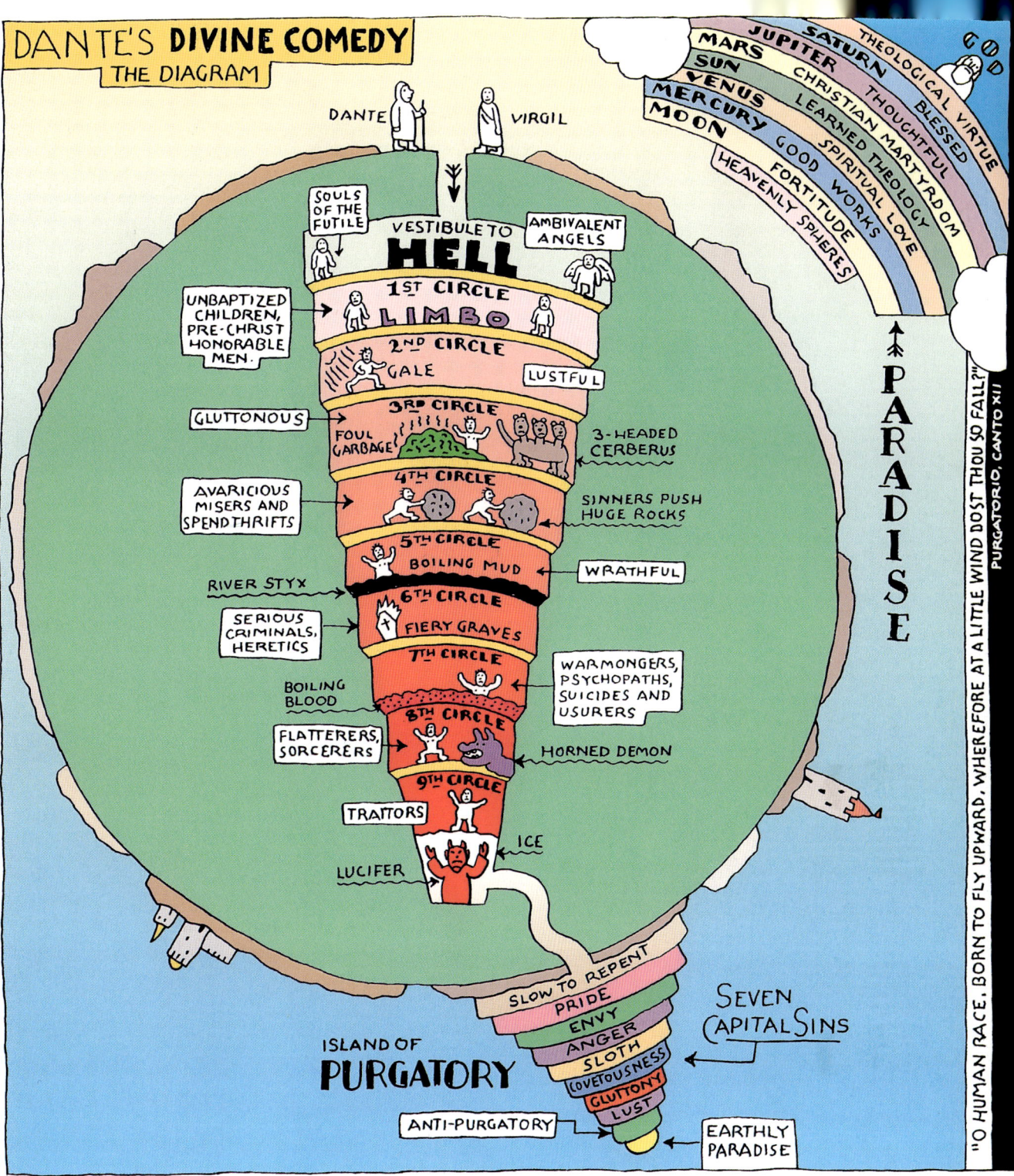

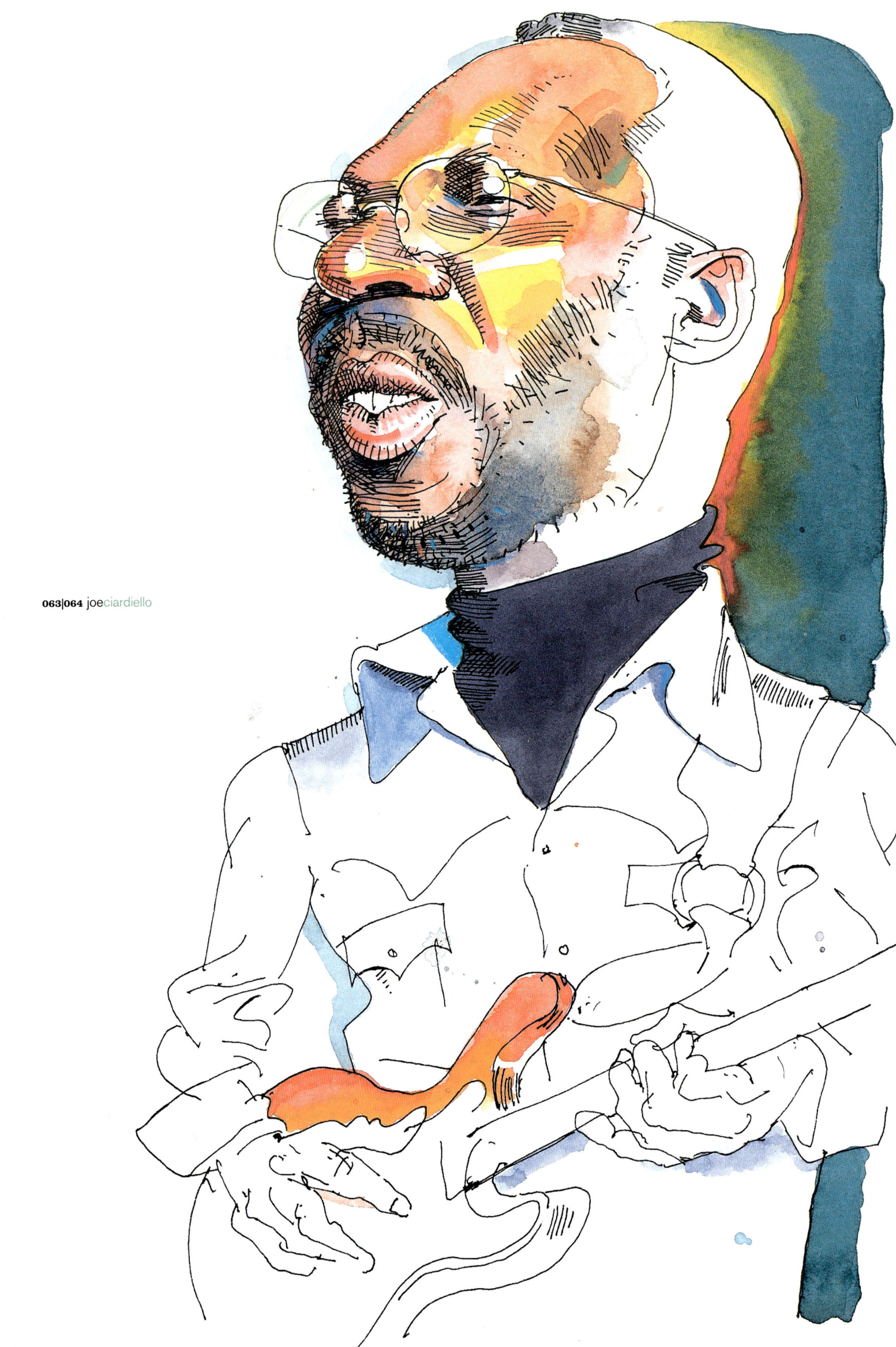

..Samuel.Beckett..

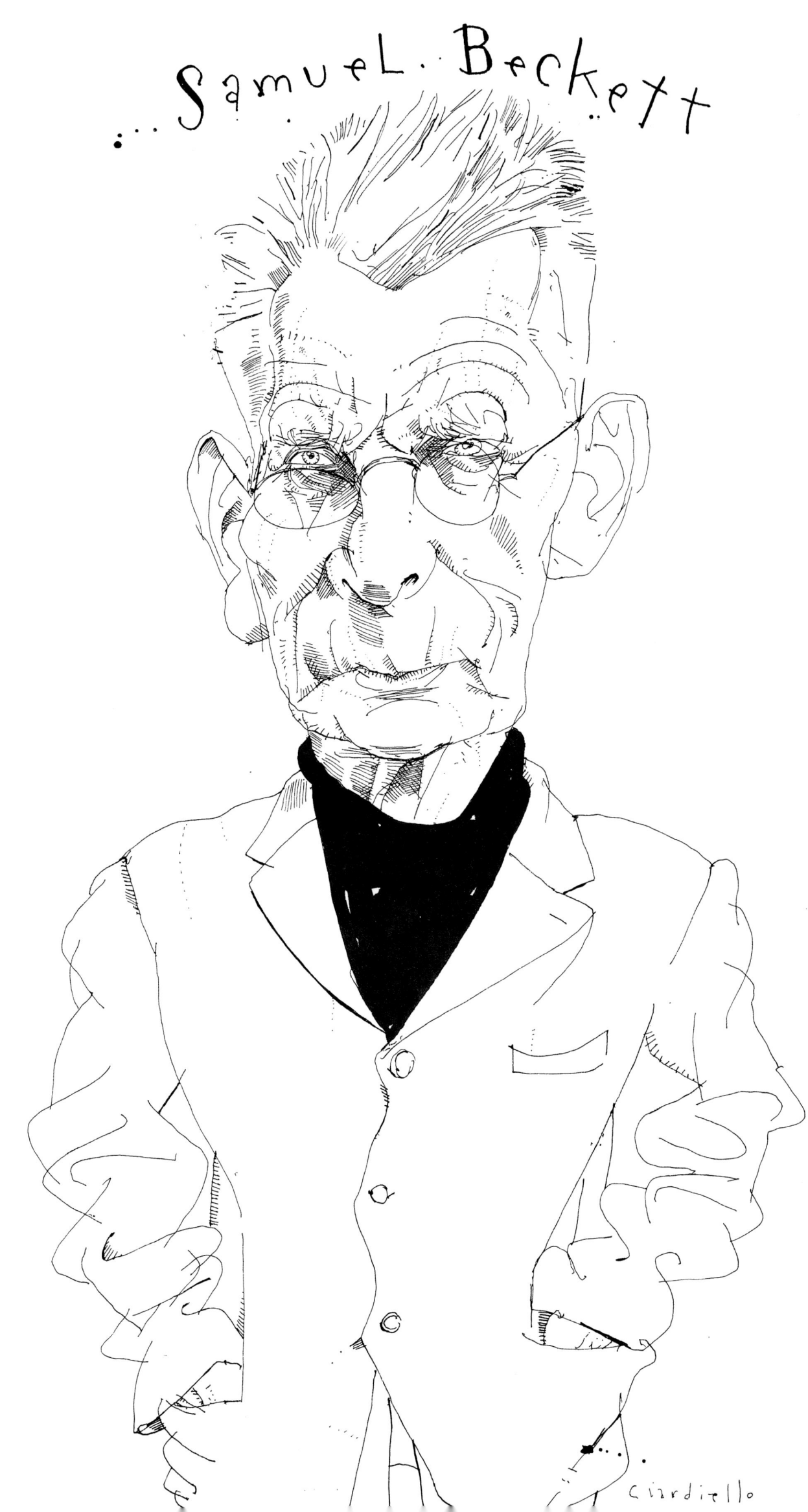

Ciardiello

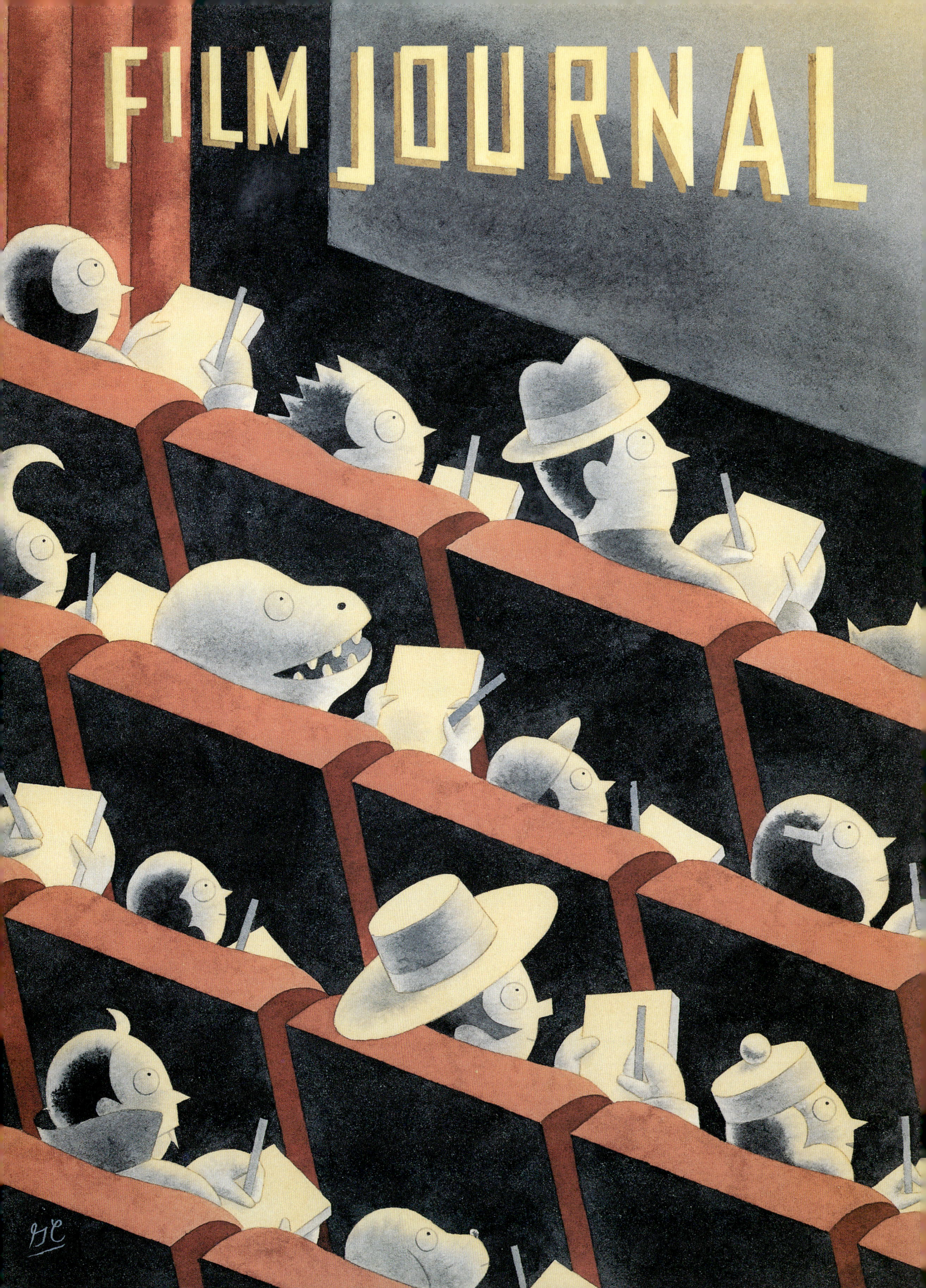

065|066 gregclarke

DOGGY STYLES *of the* 21ST CENTURY

Fur-de-Lis	Flea-Bag Chic	Neo-Pilgrimism
Dogma Chic	Douglas Fur	Hamptons Hip
Cossack Cool	Post(man)-Punk	Bald Beagle

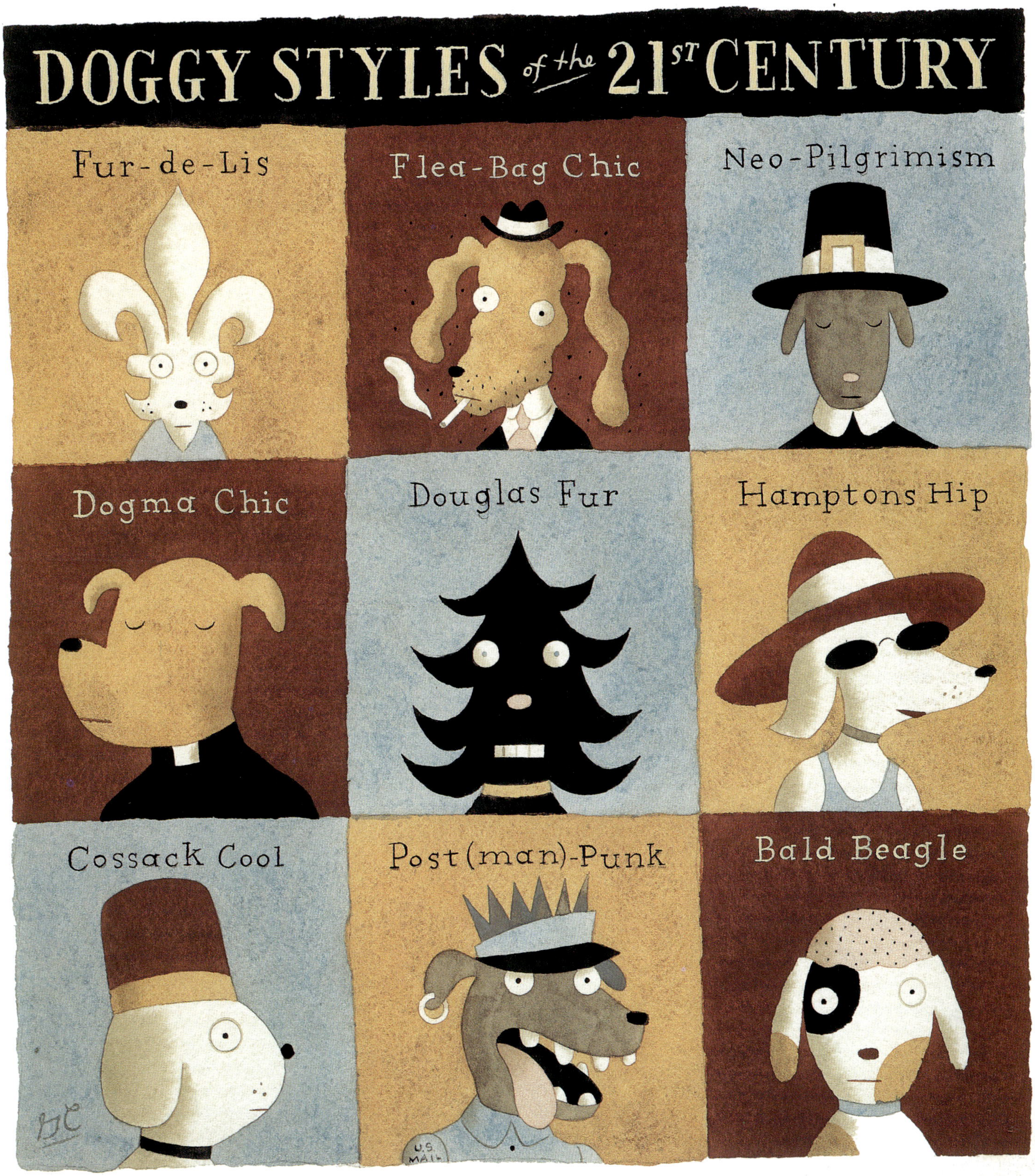

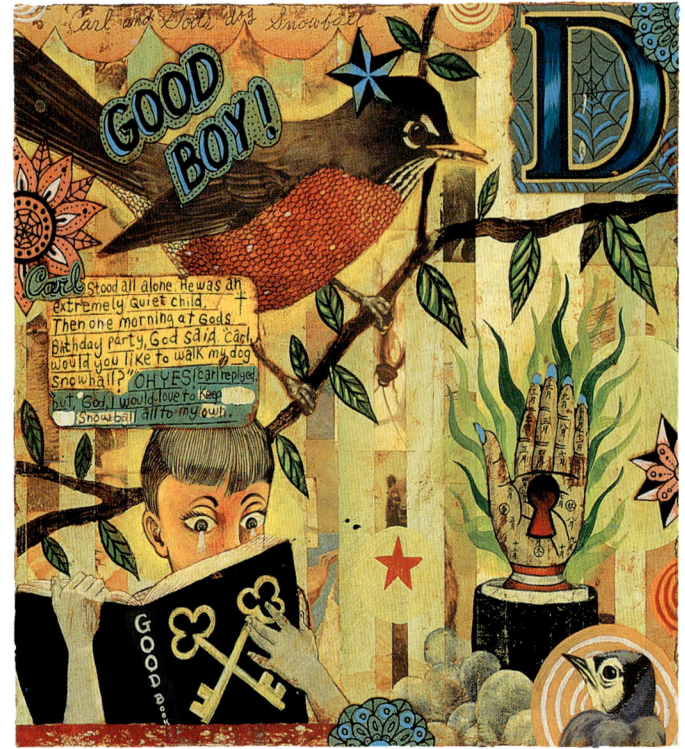

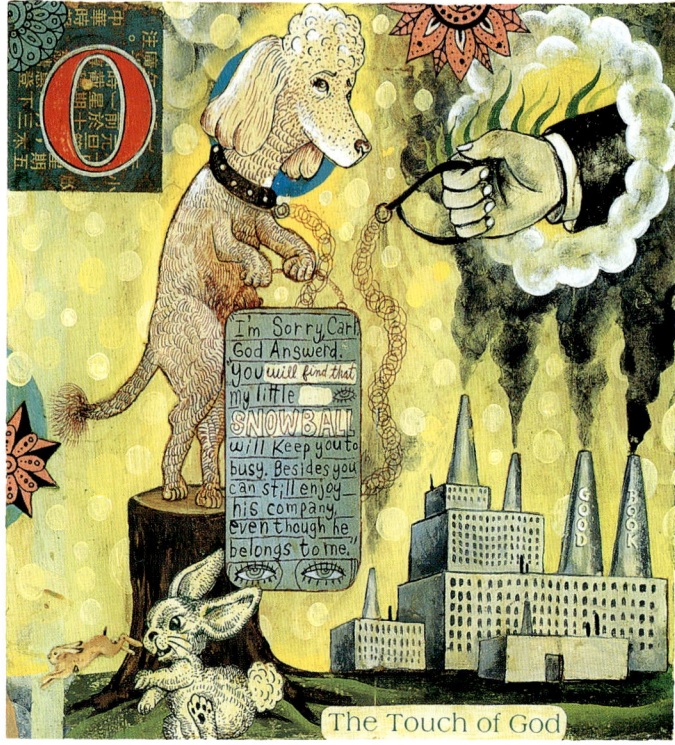

The Touch of God

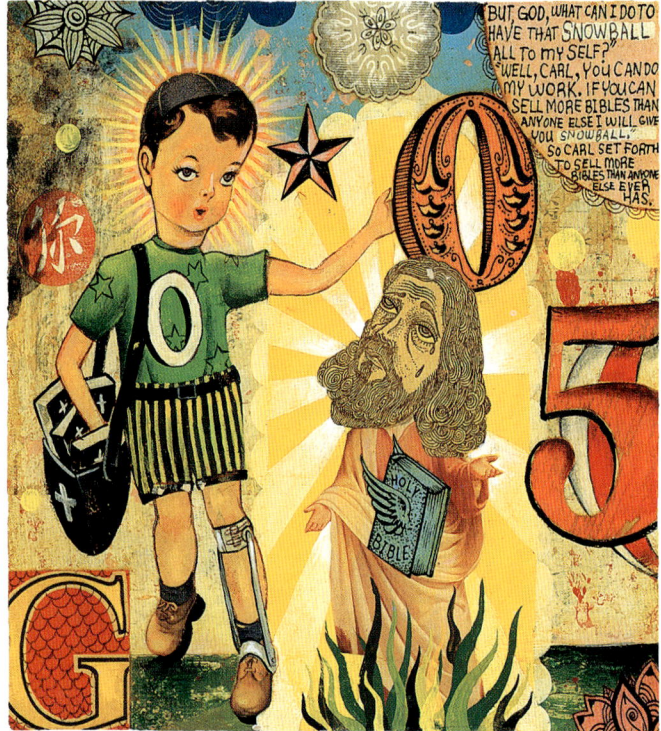

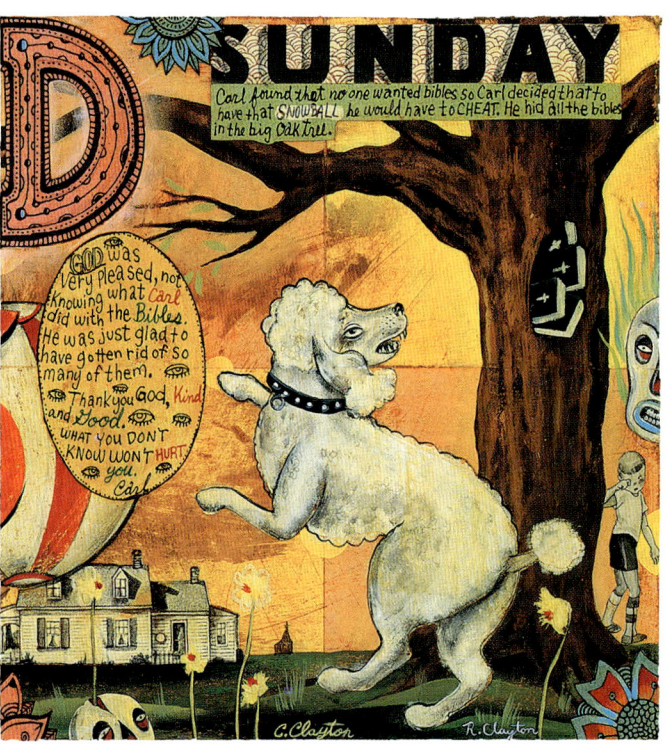

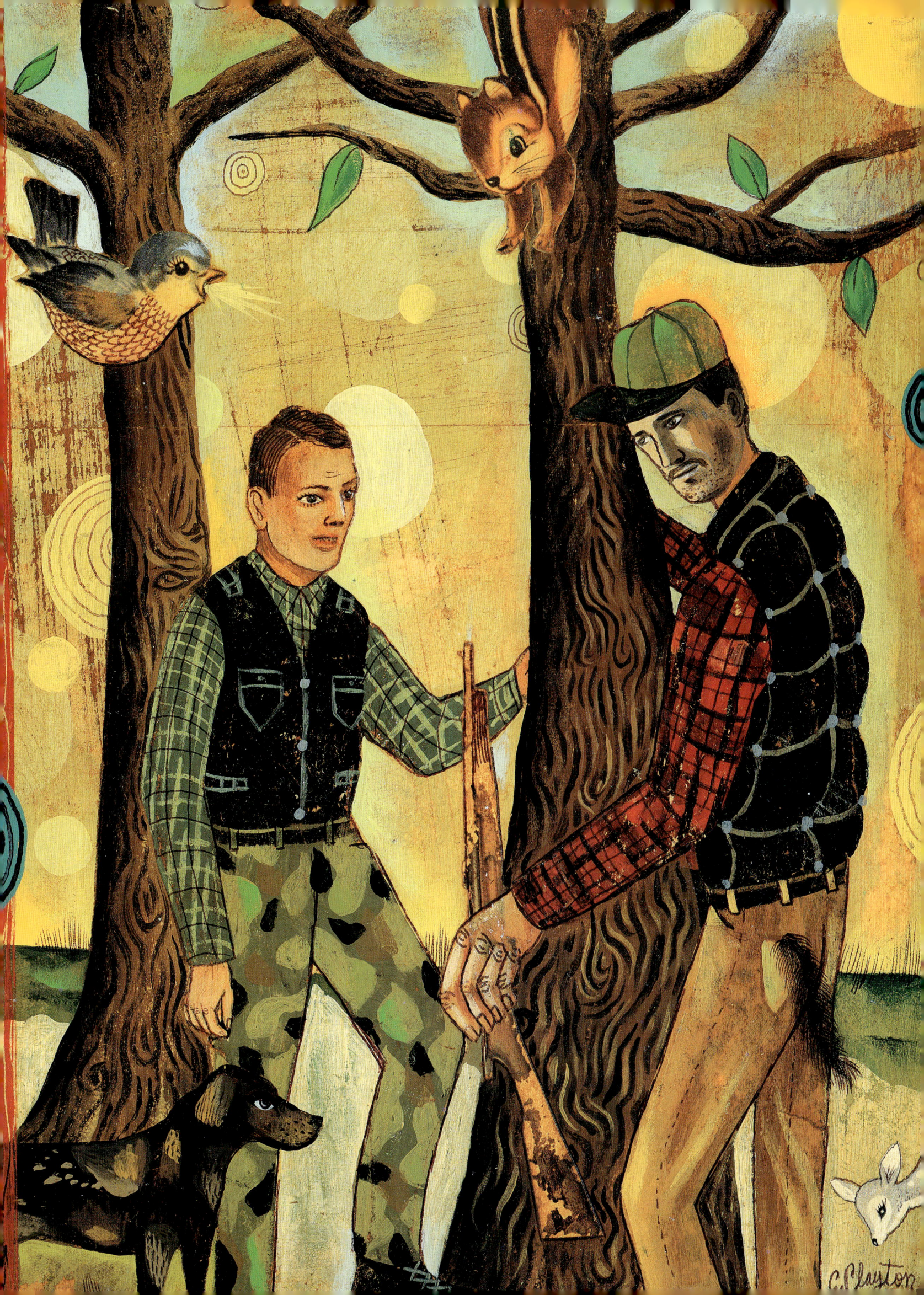

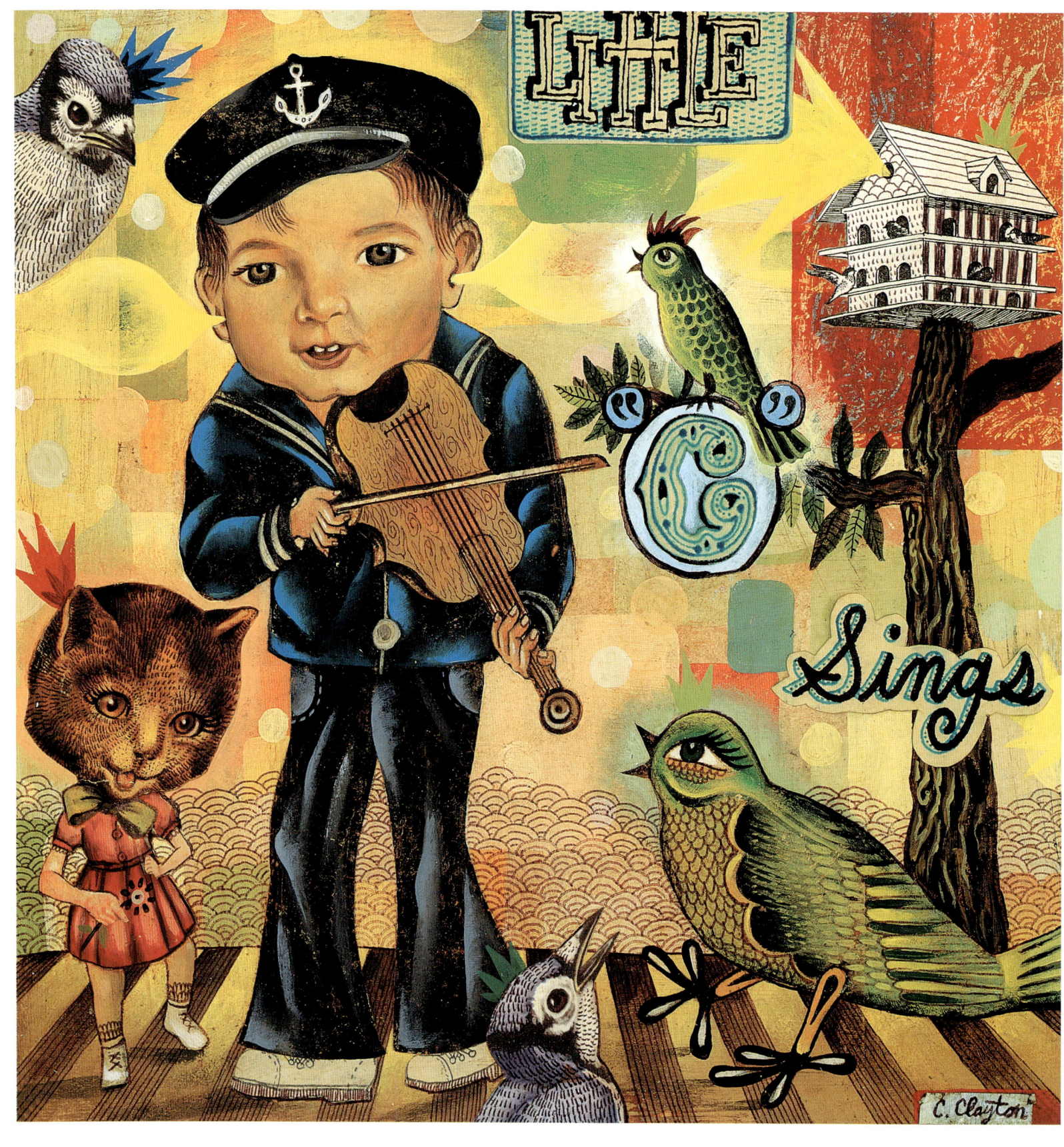

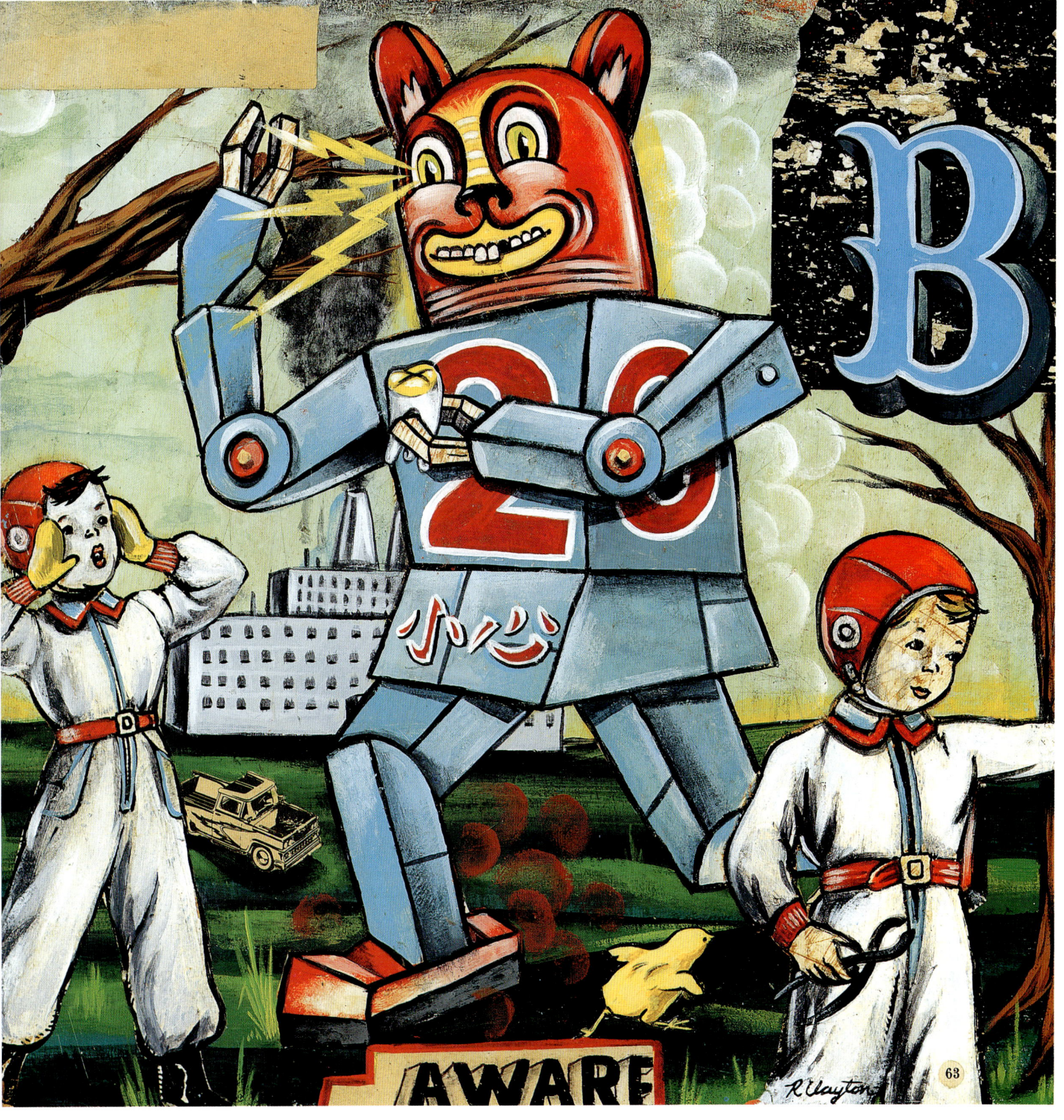

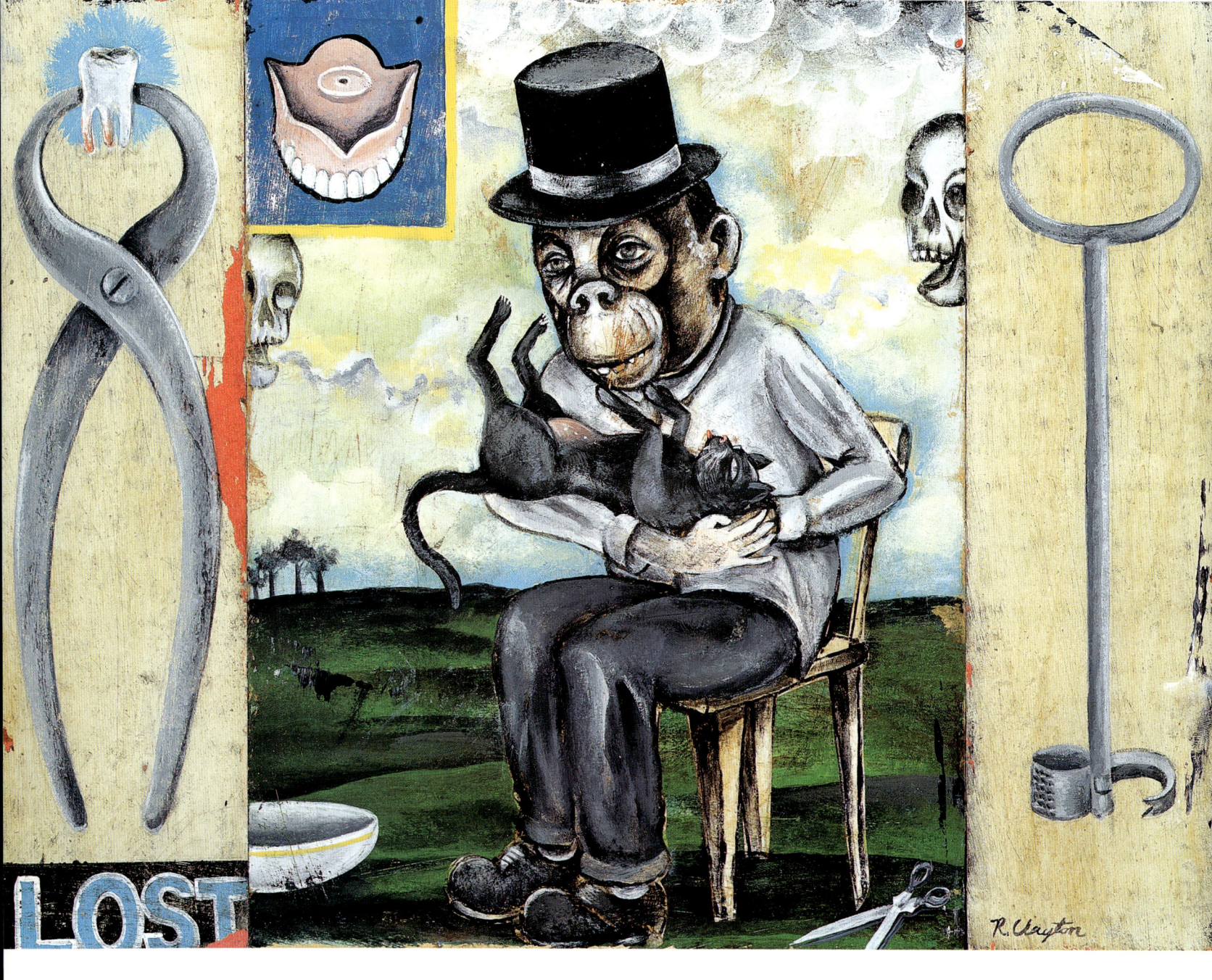

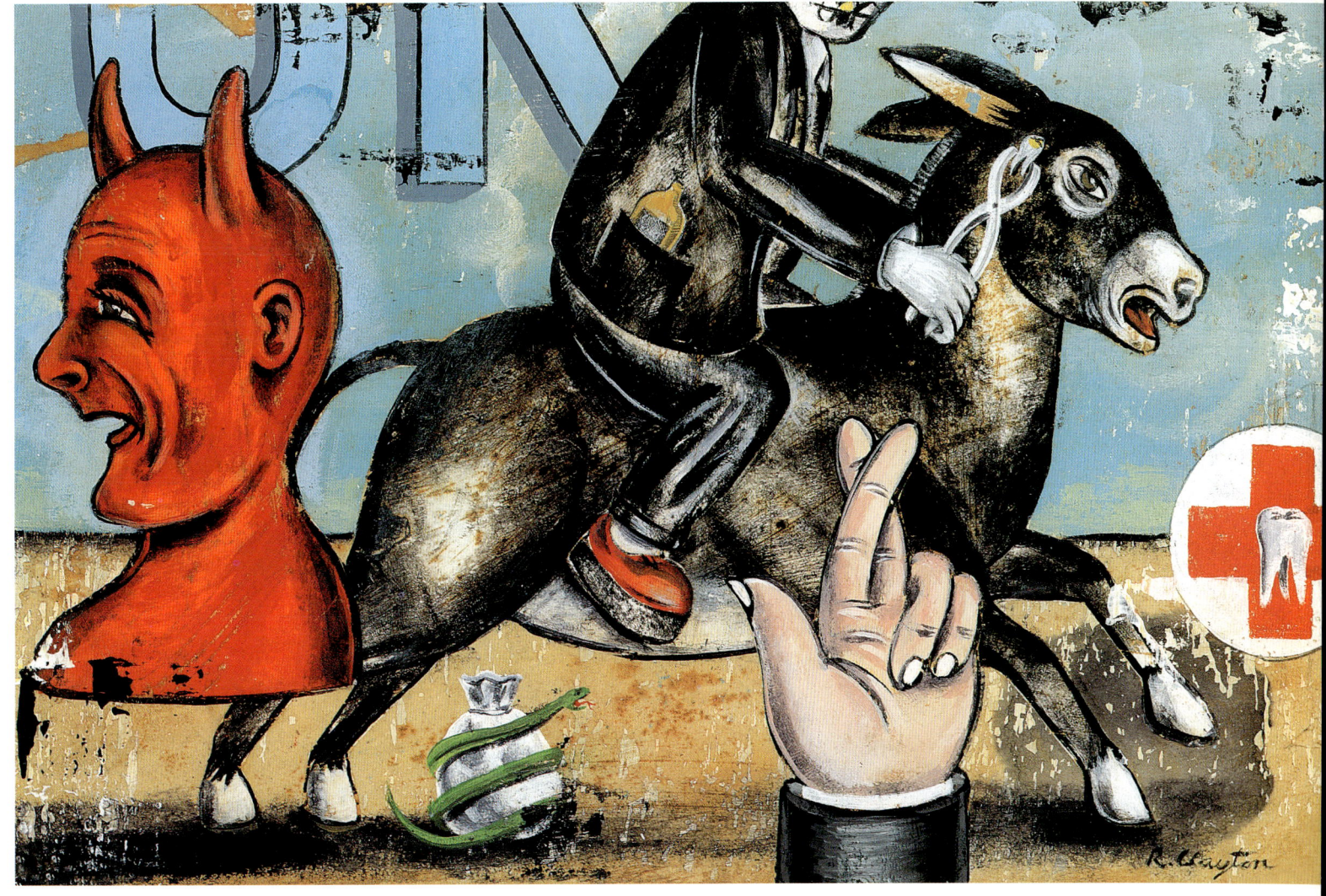

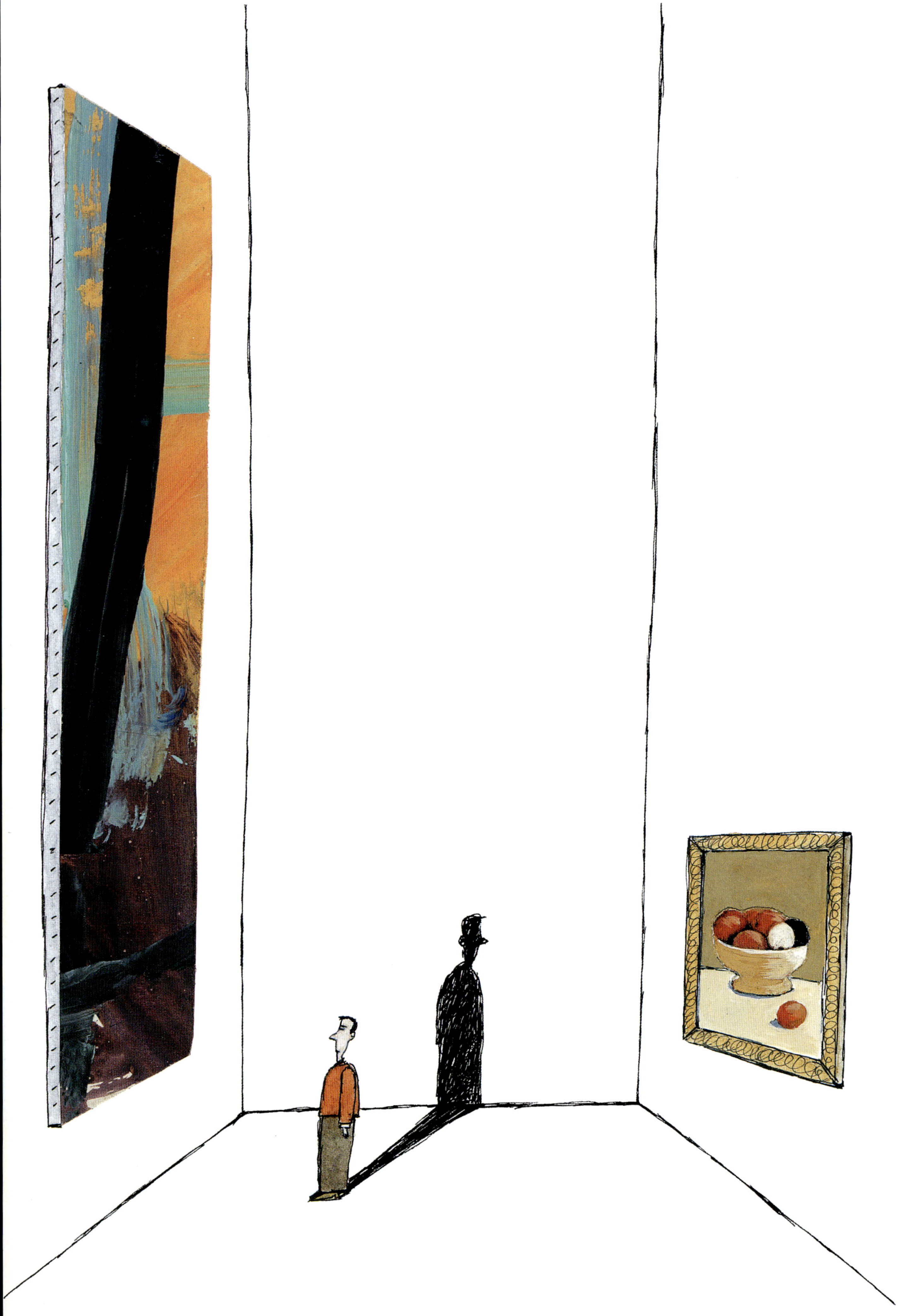

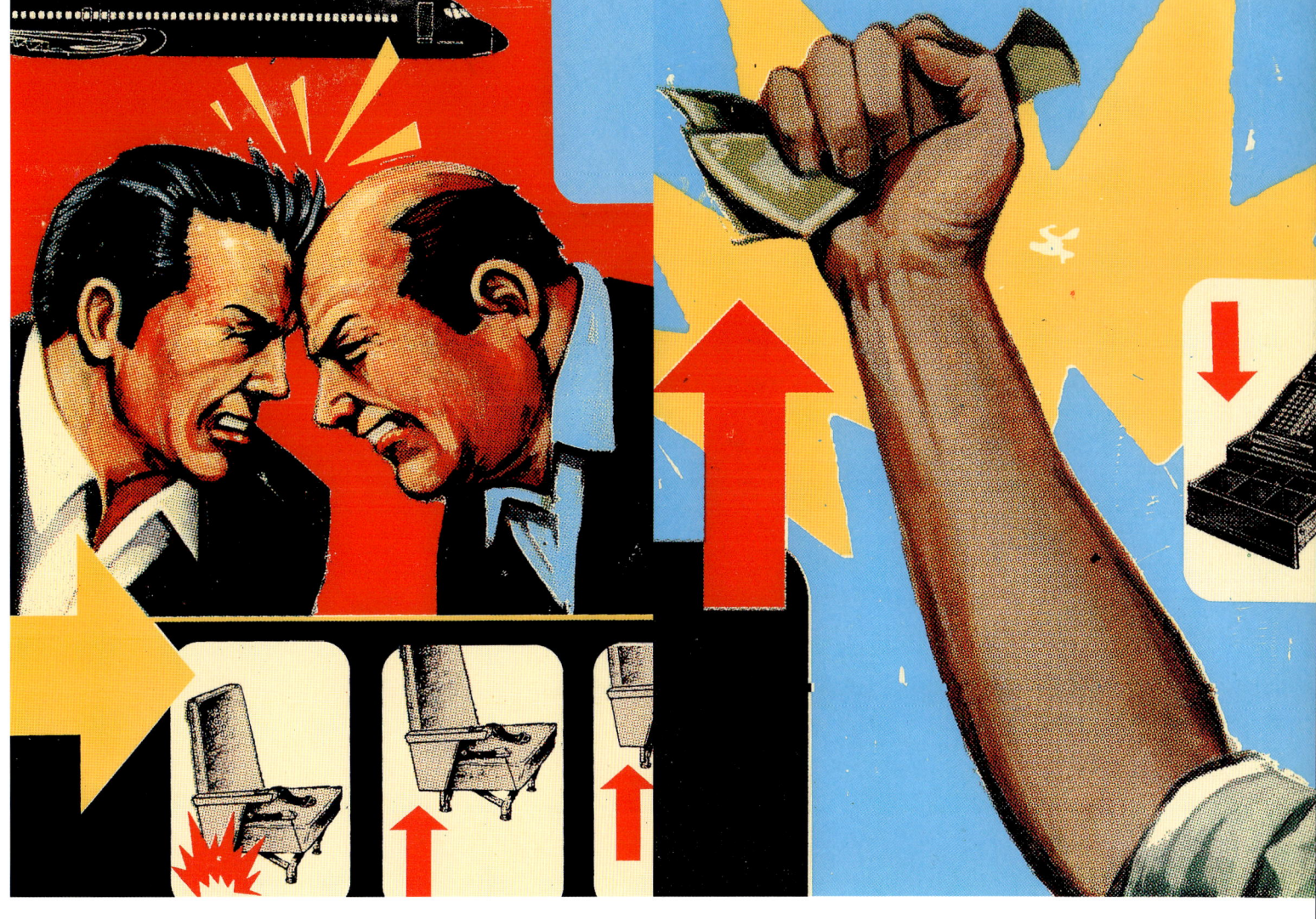

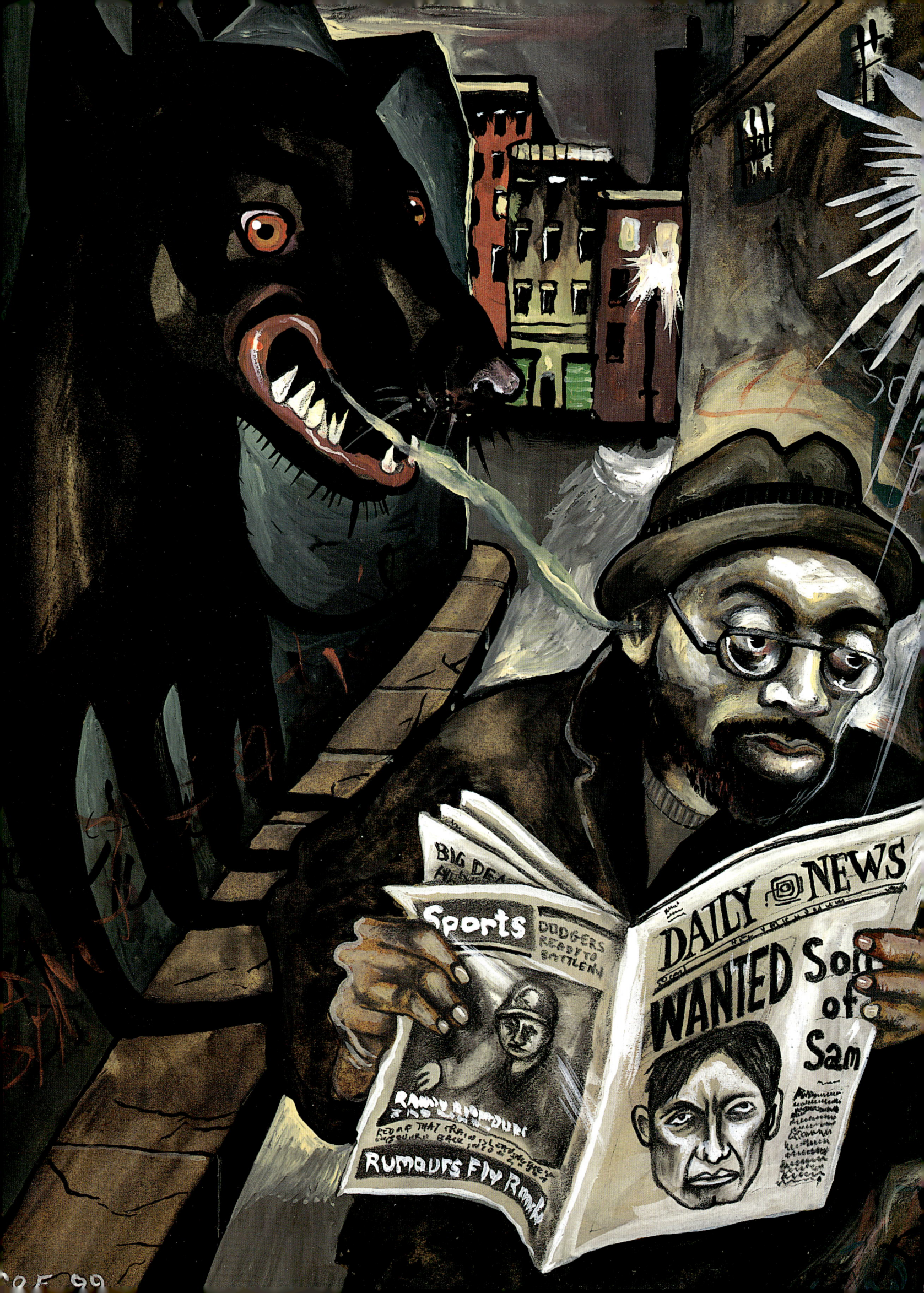

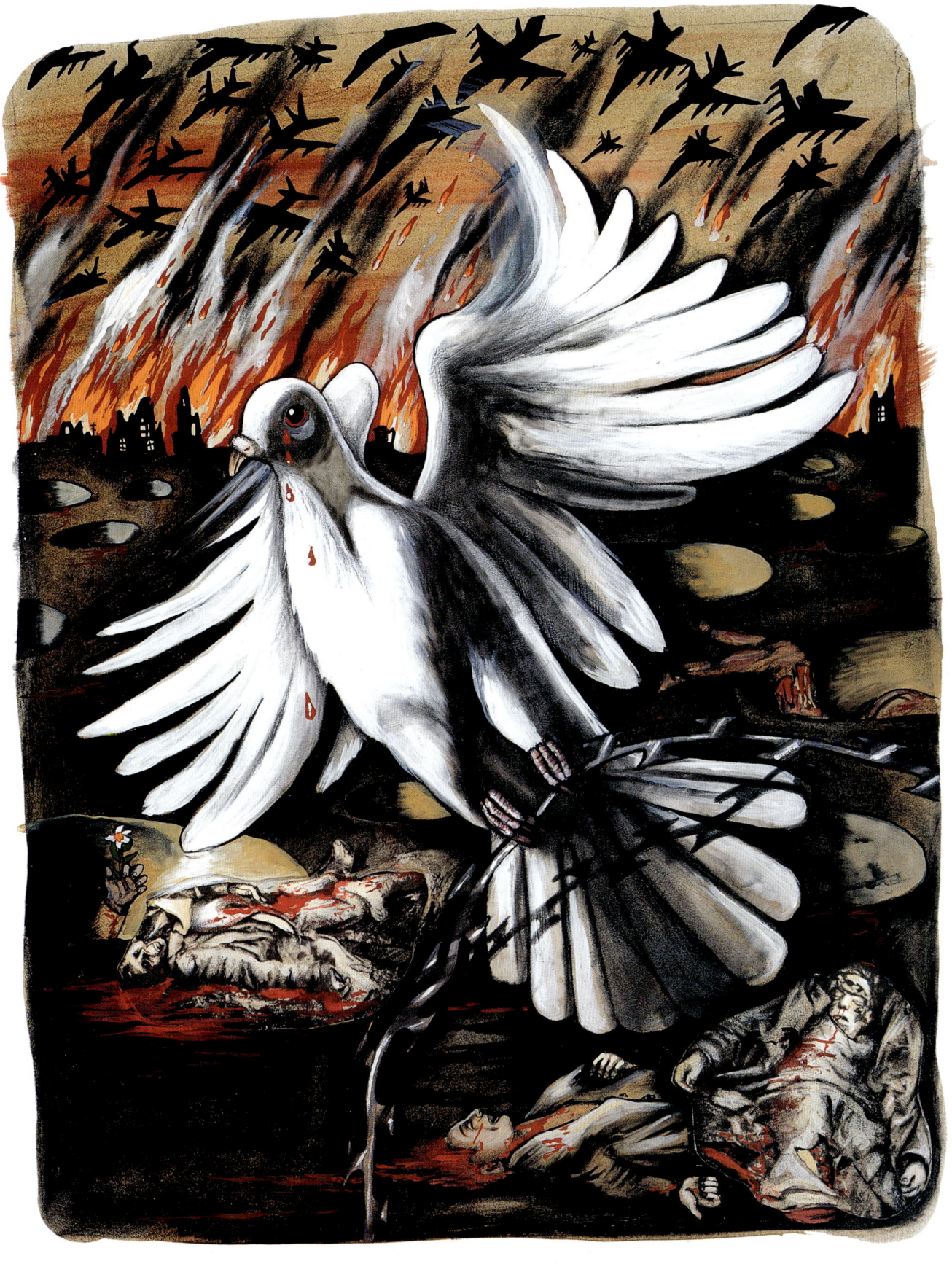

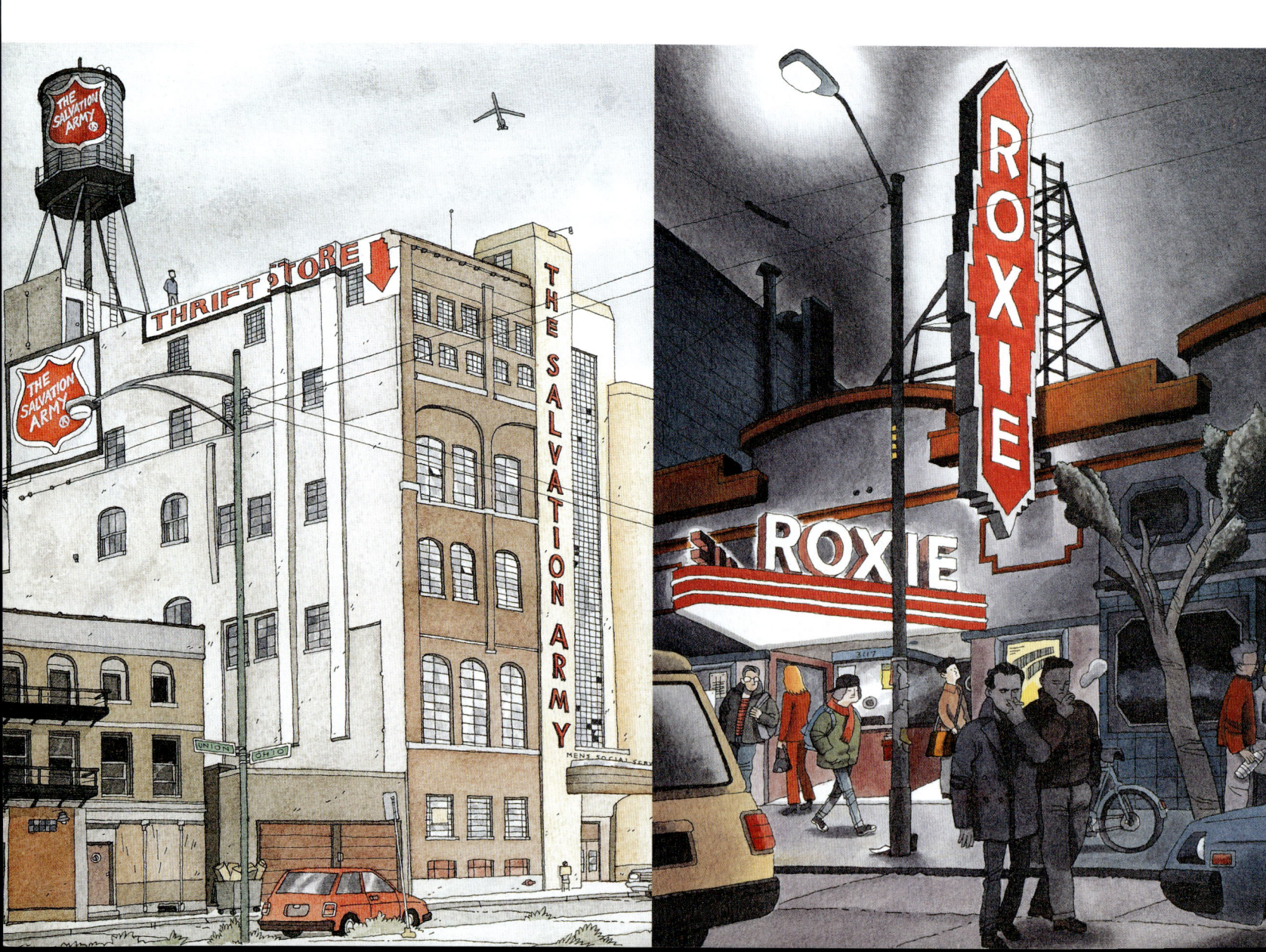

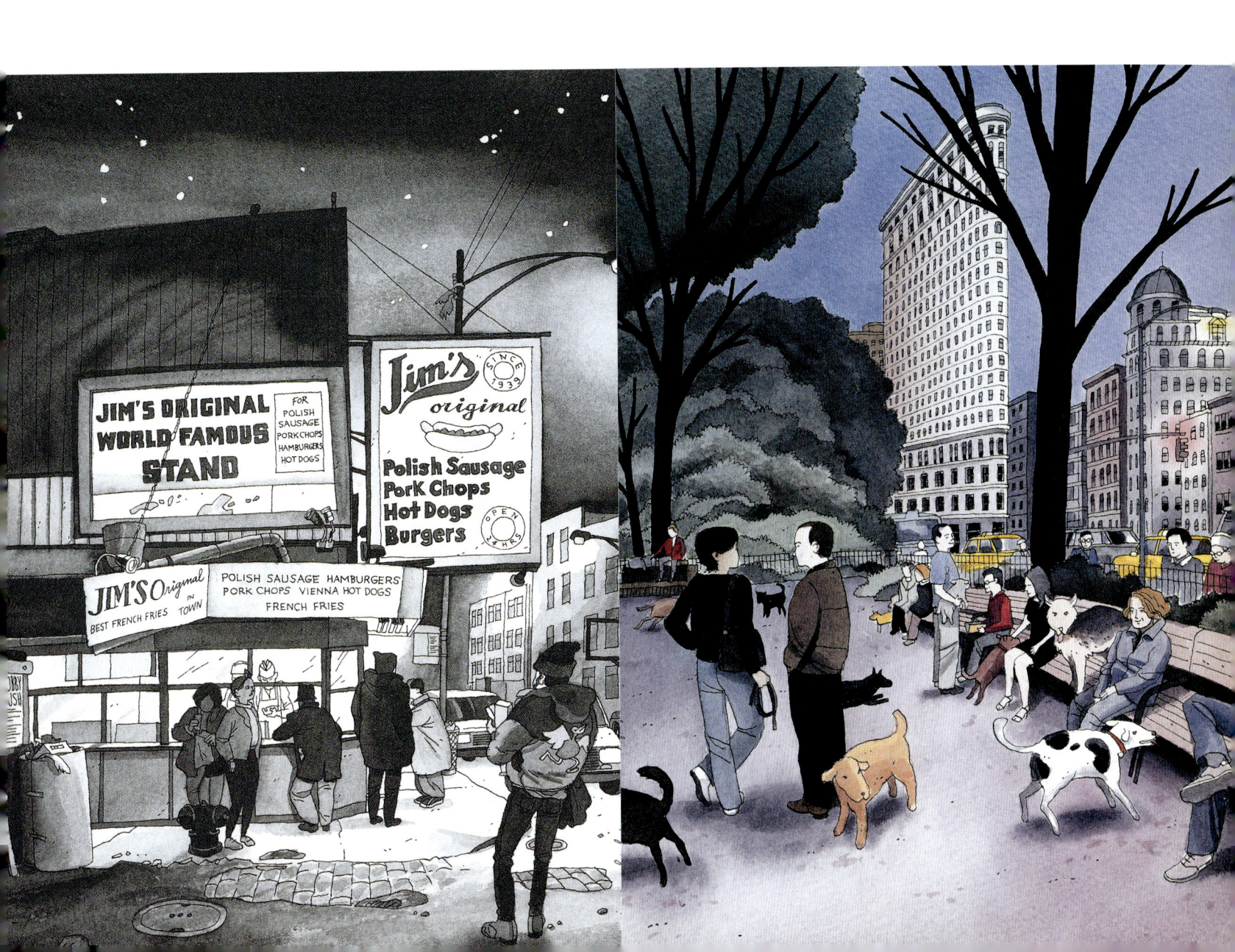

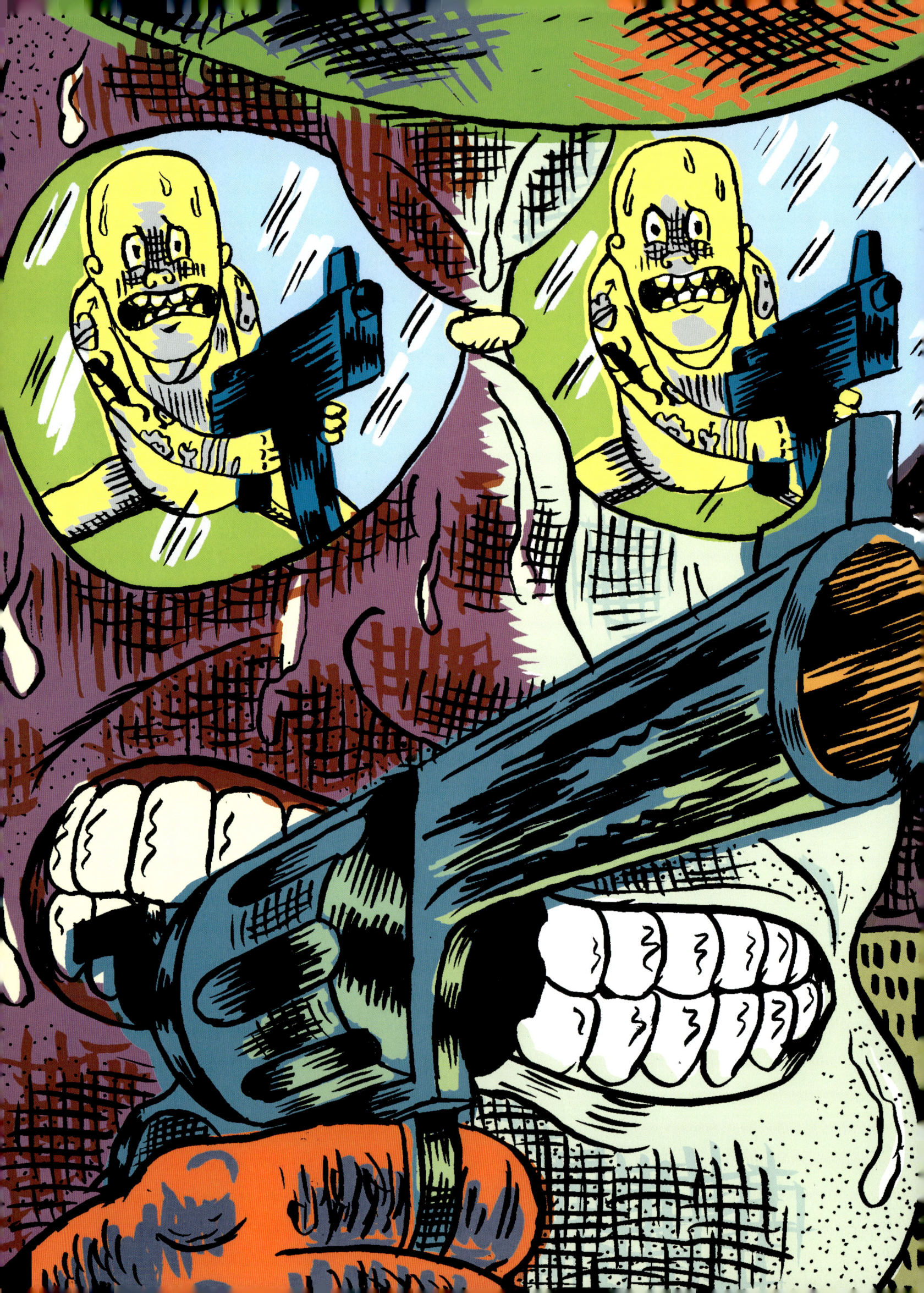

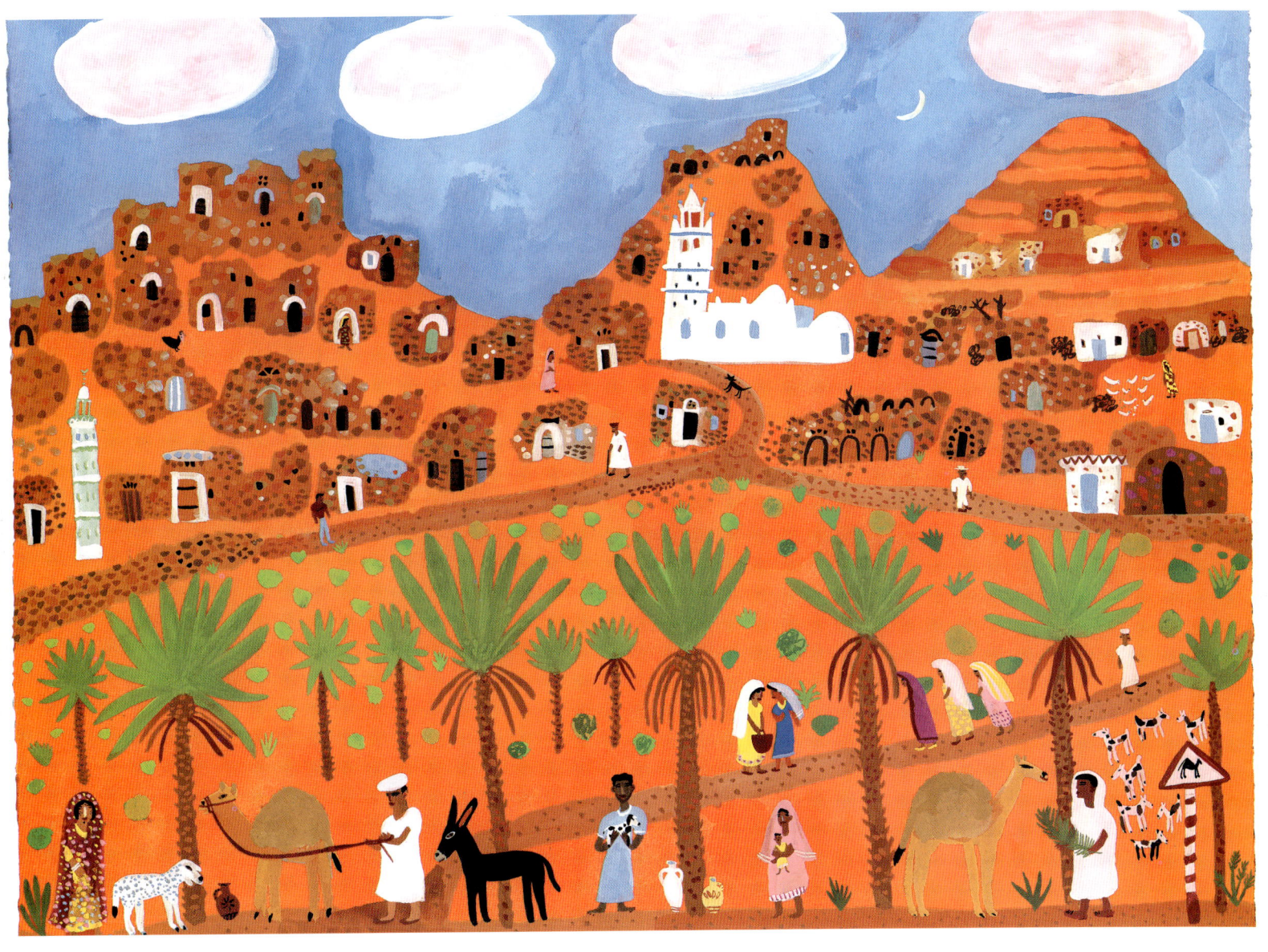

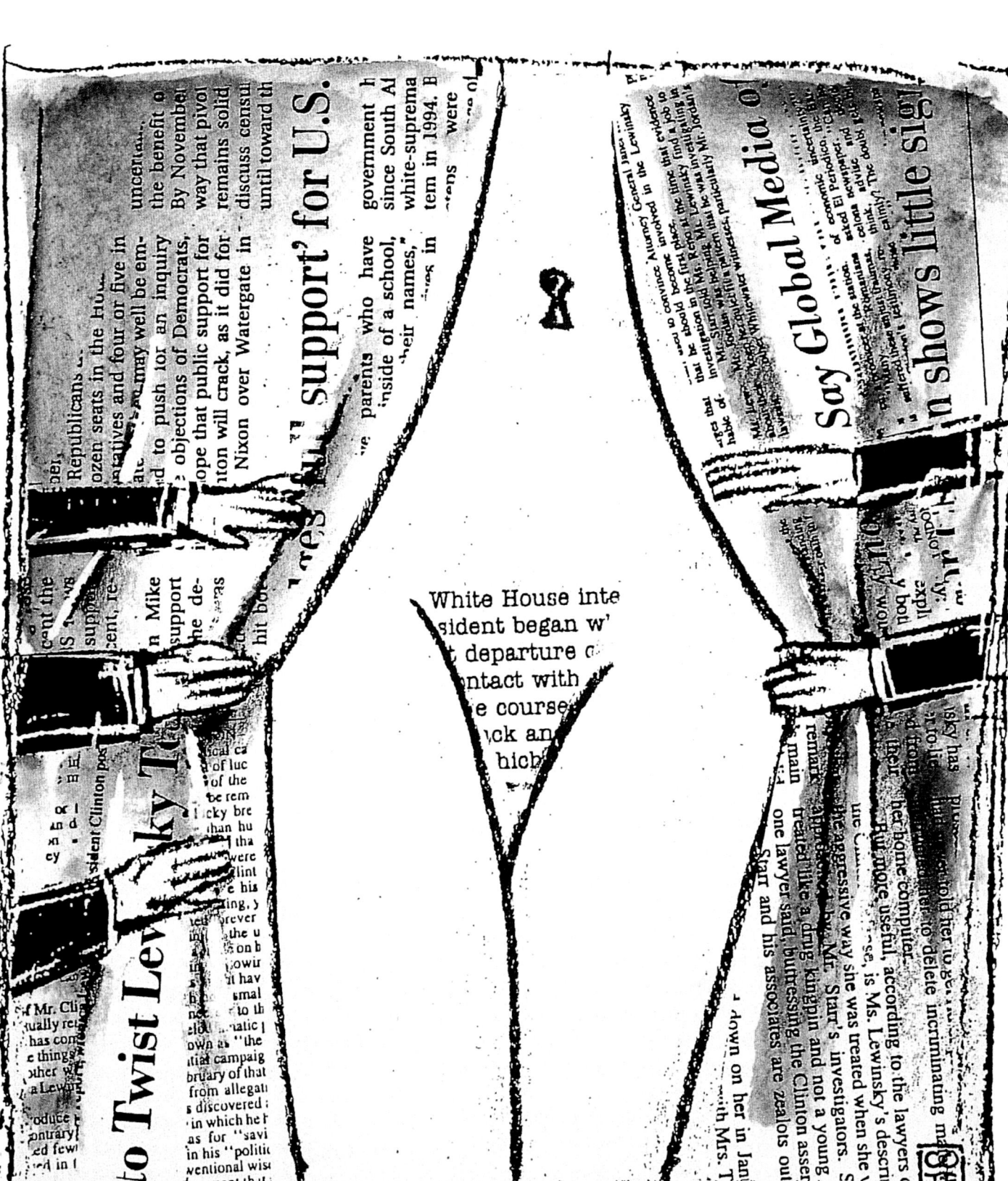

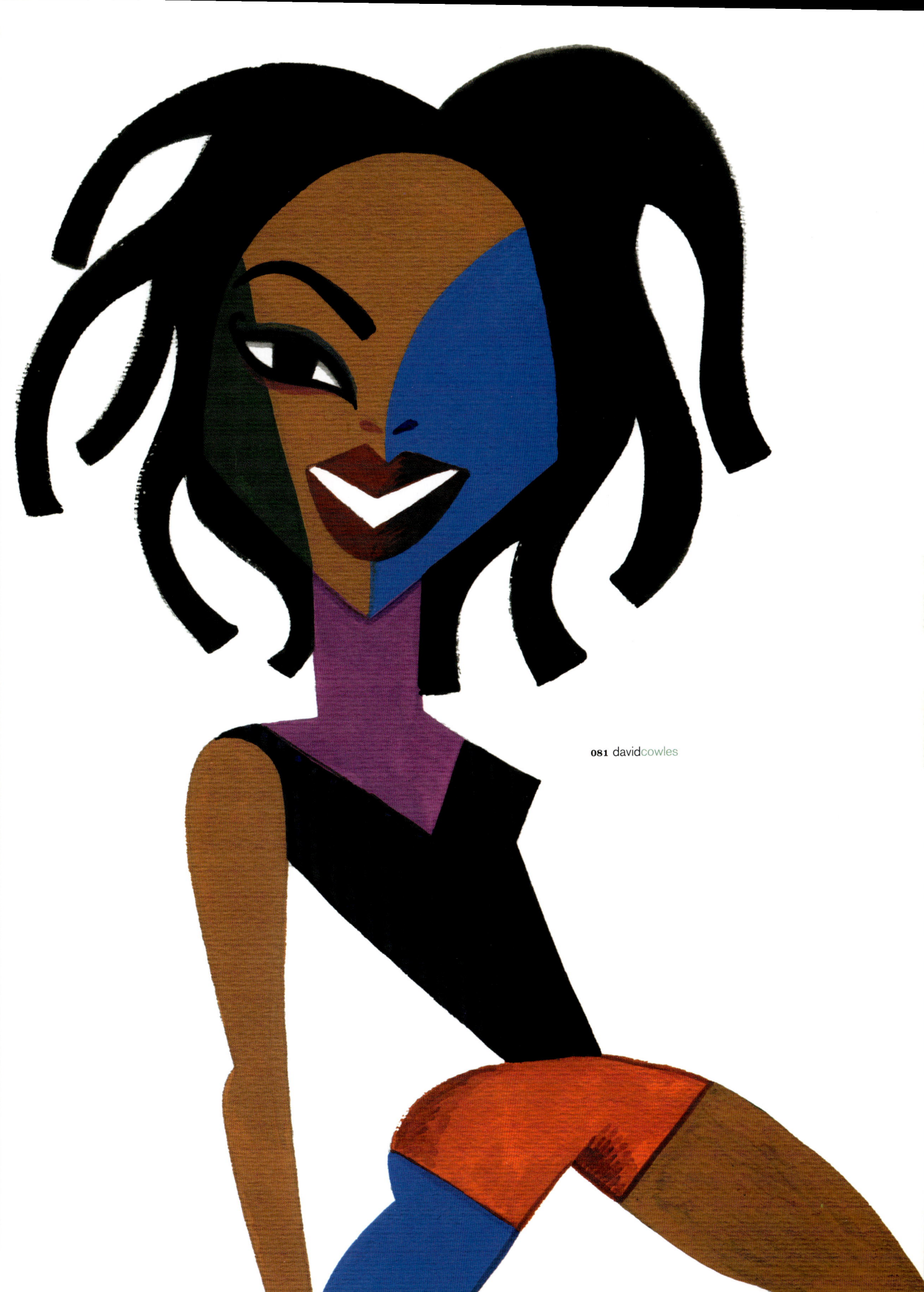

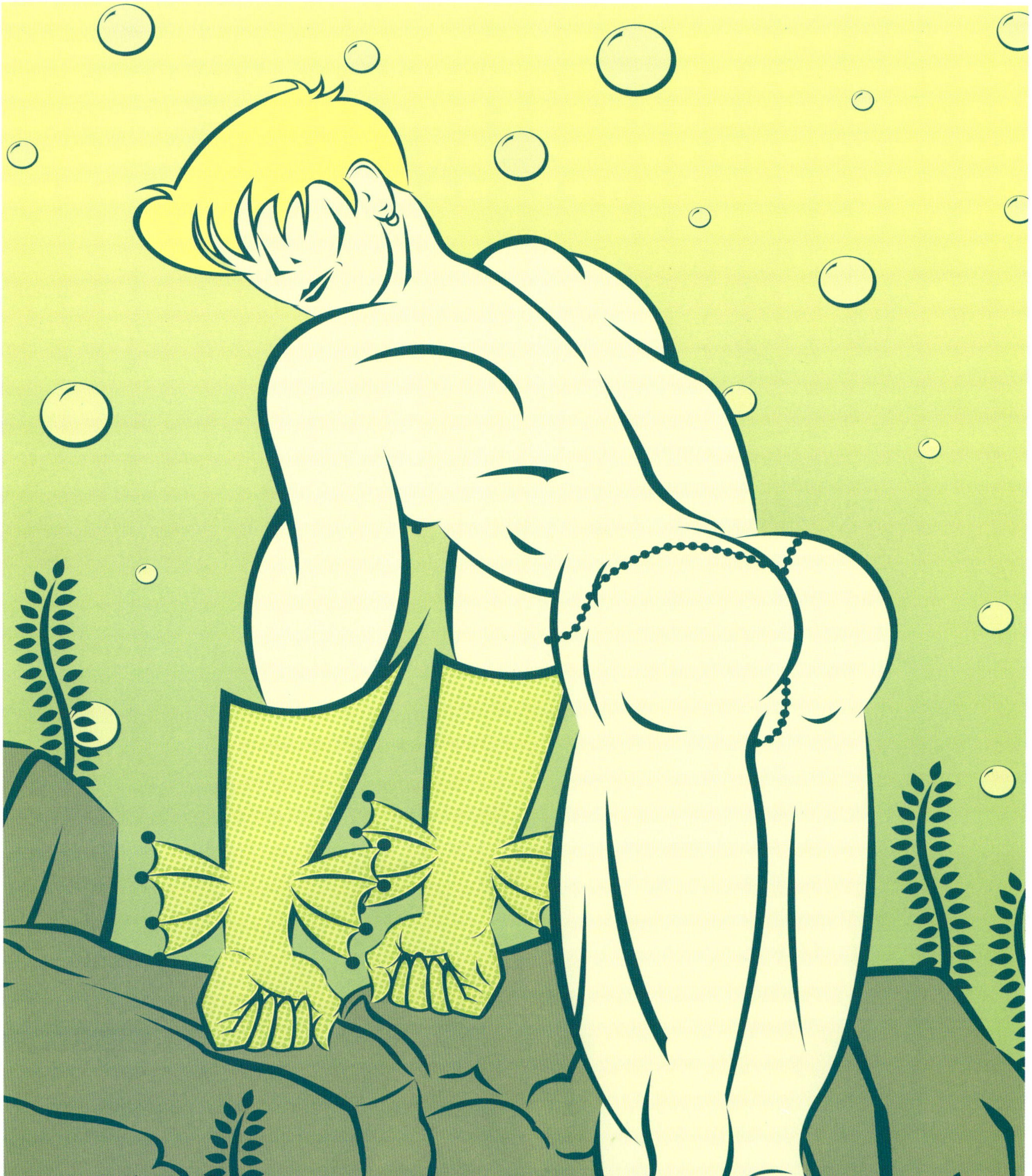

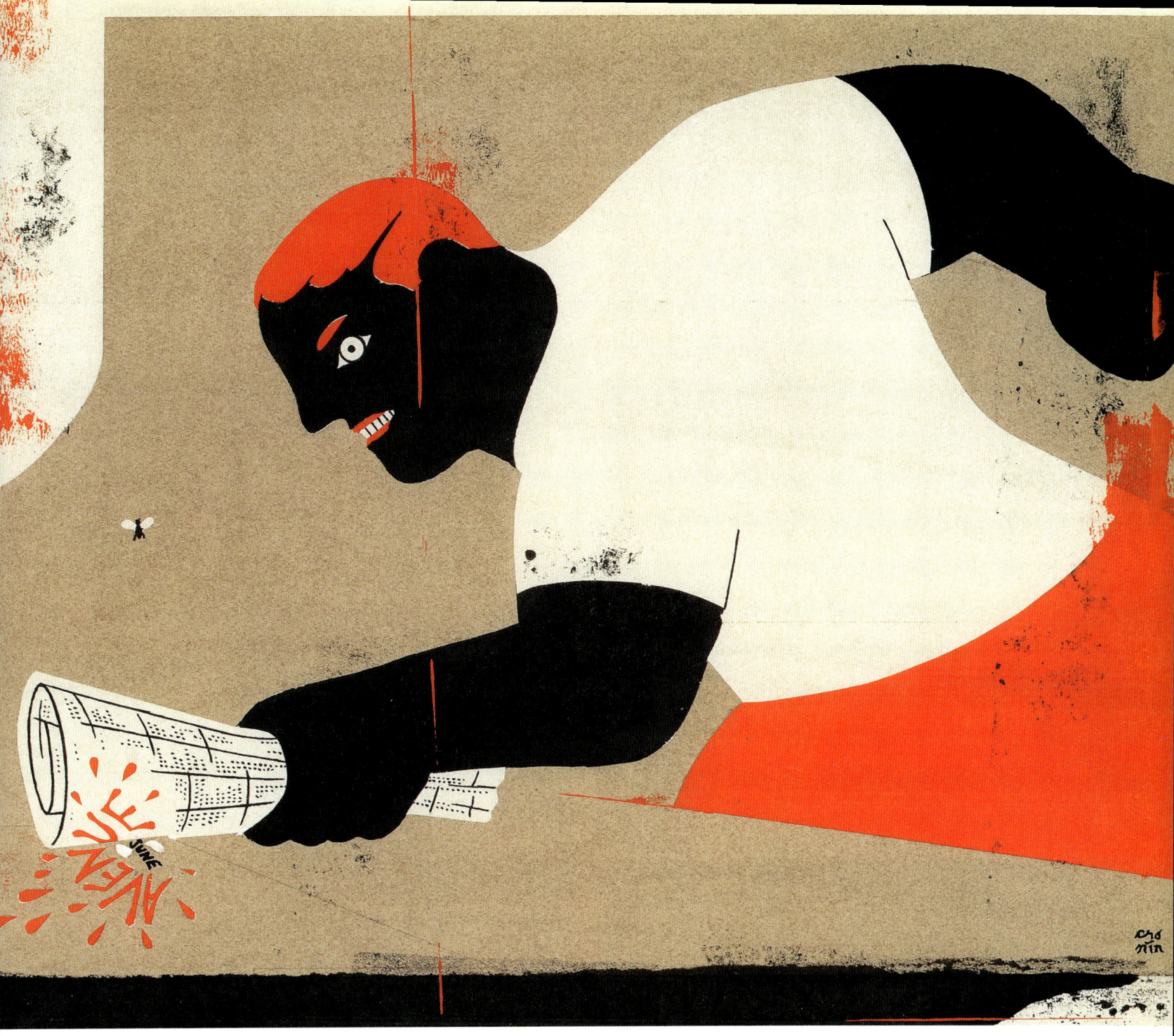

cronin

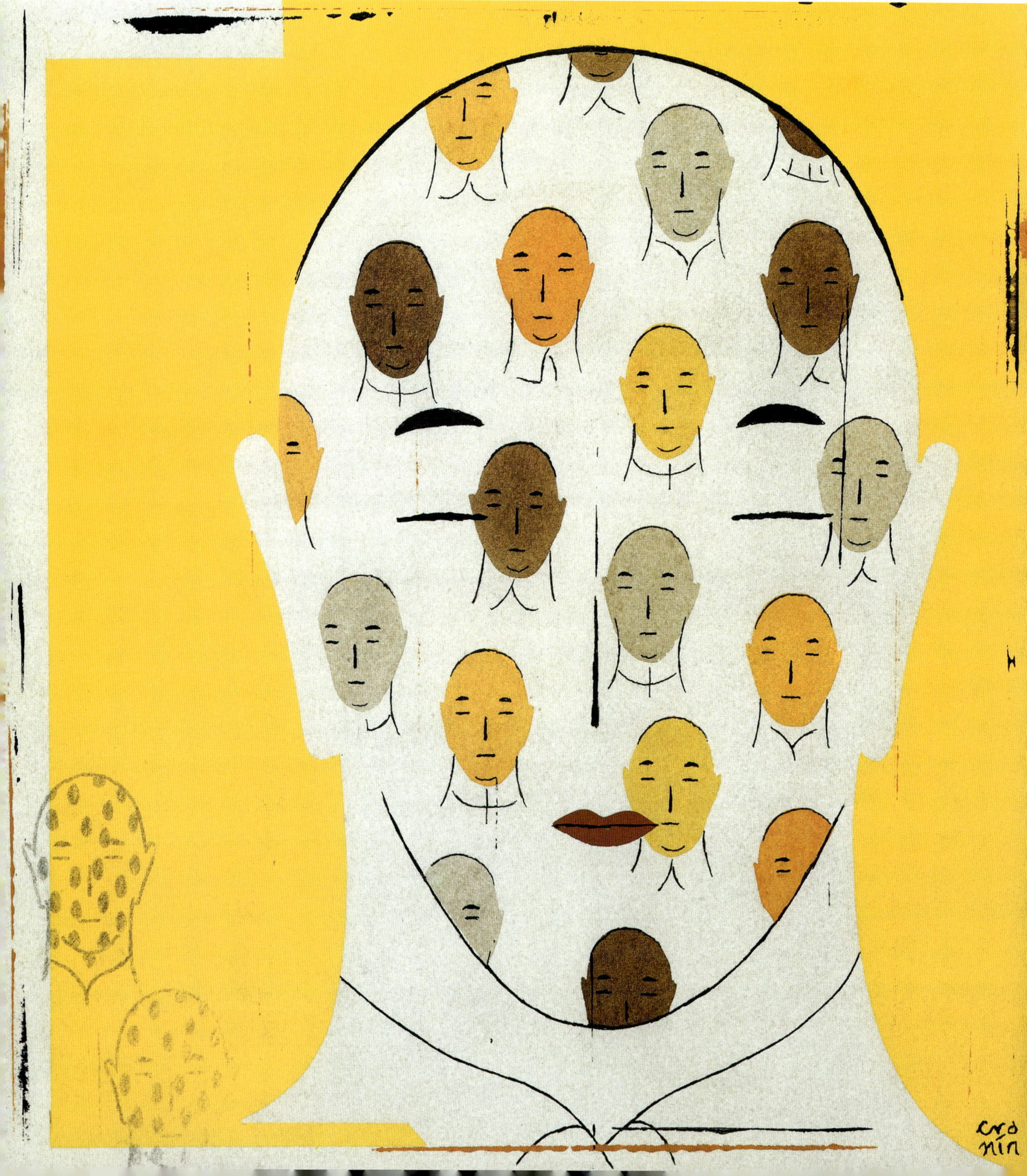

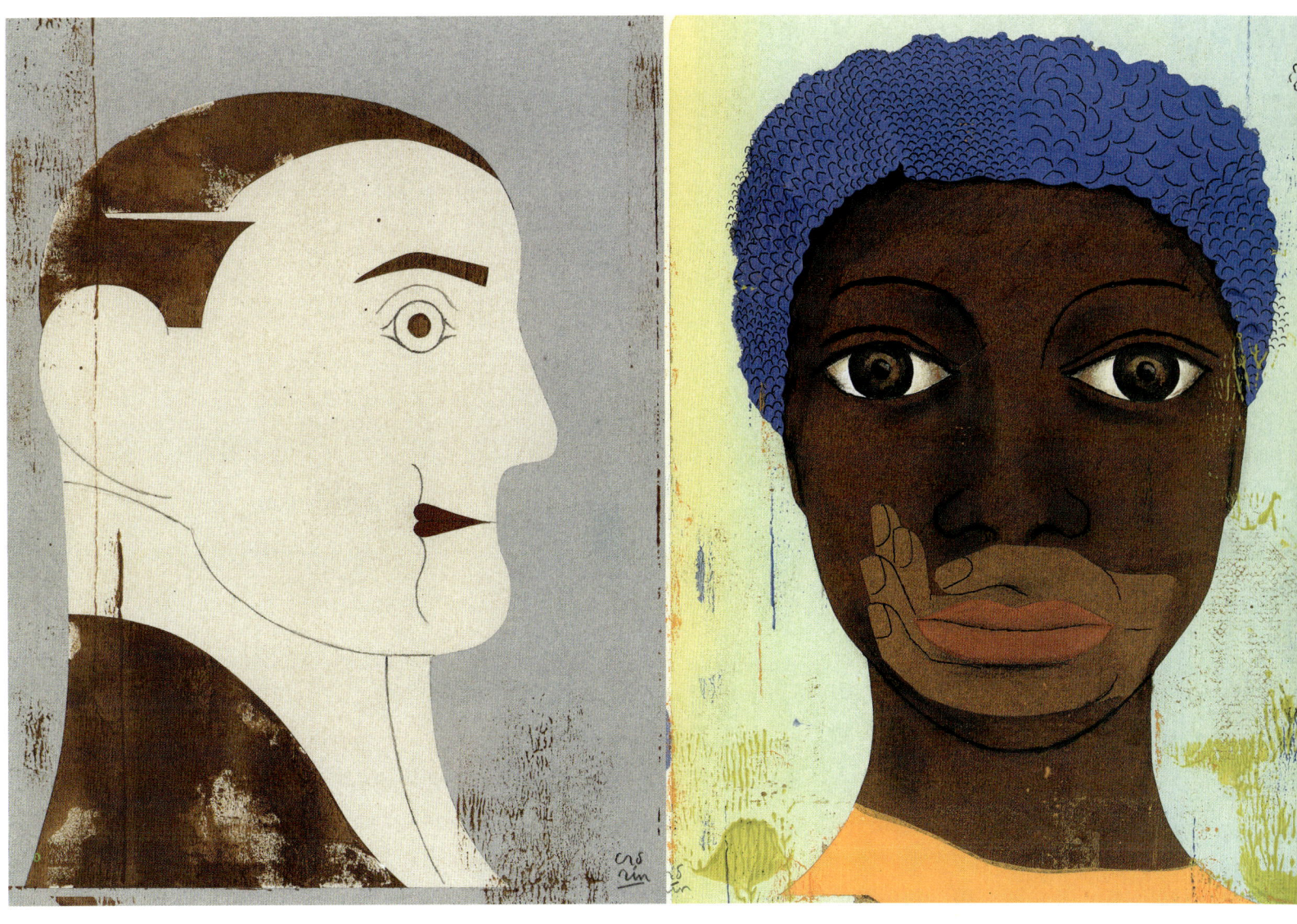

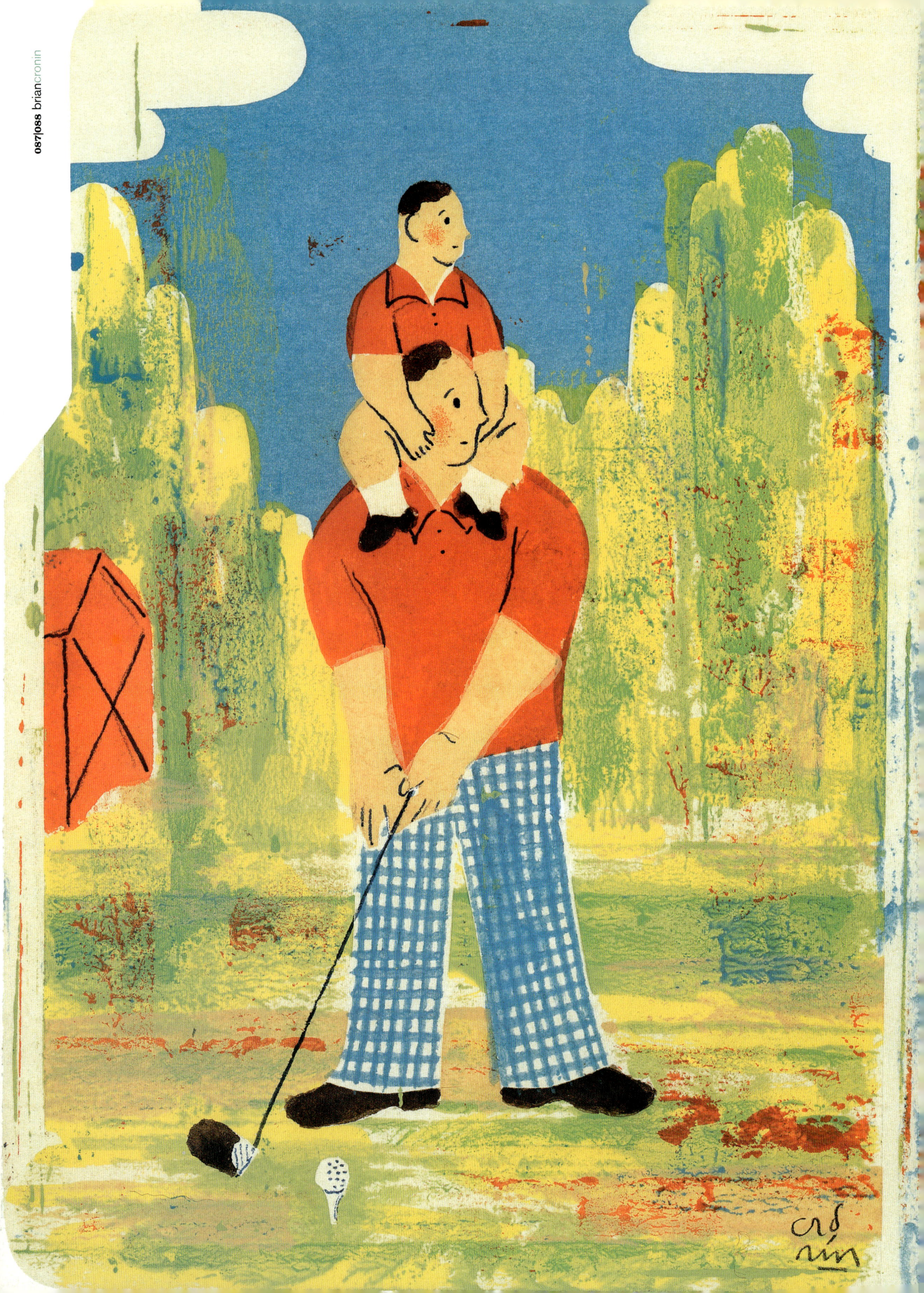

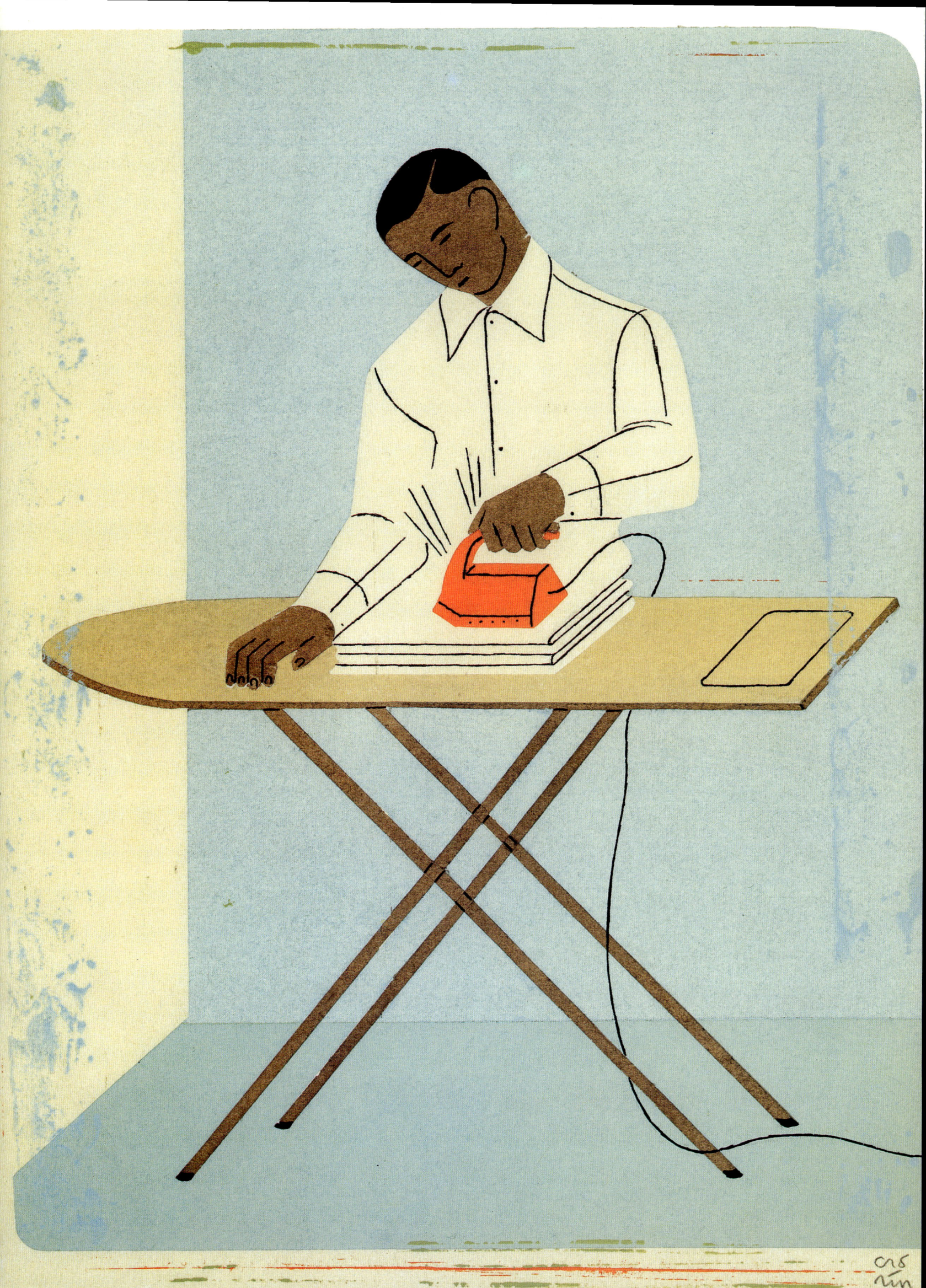

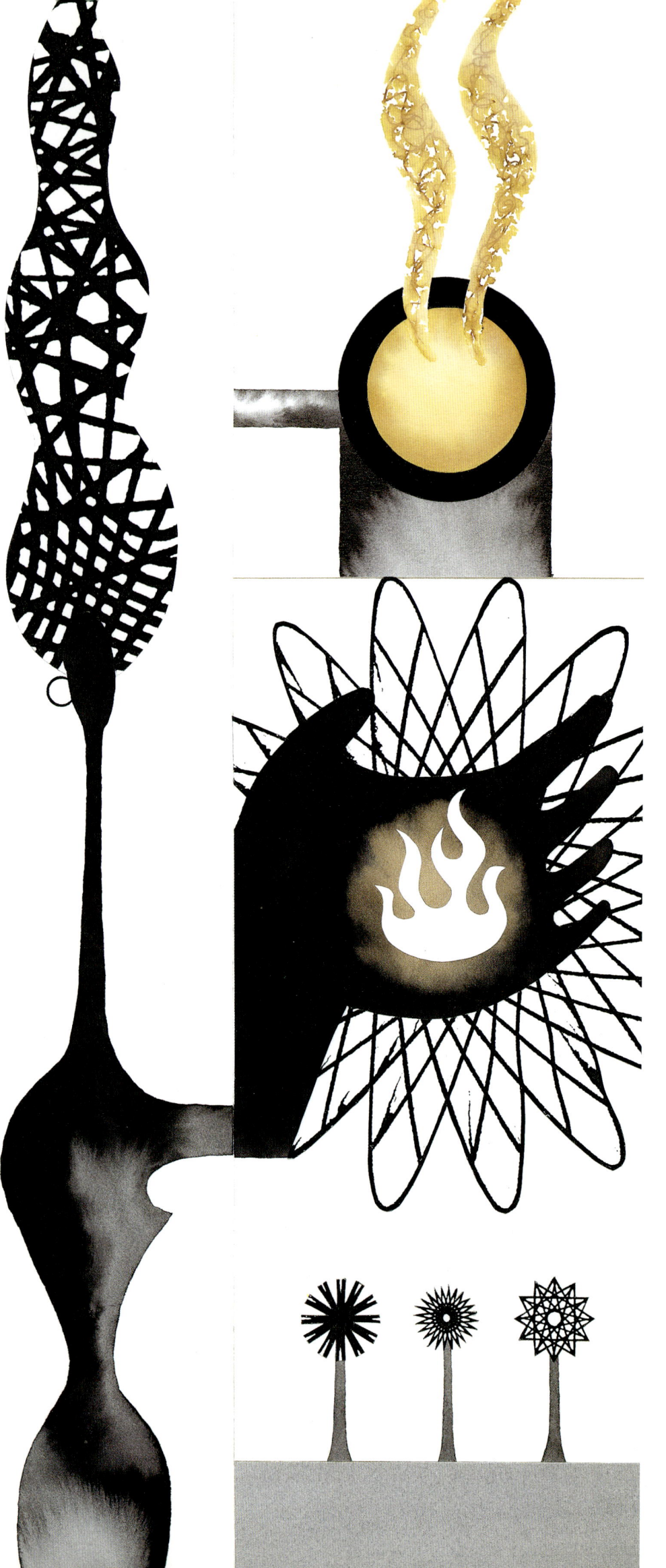

089 pauldallas

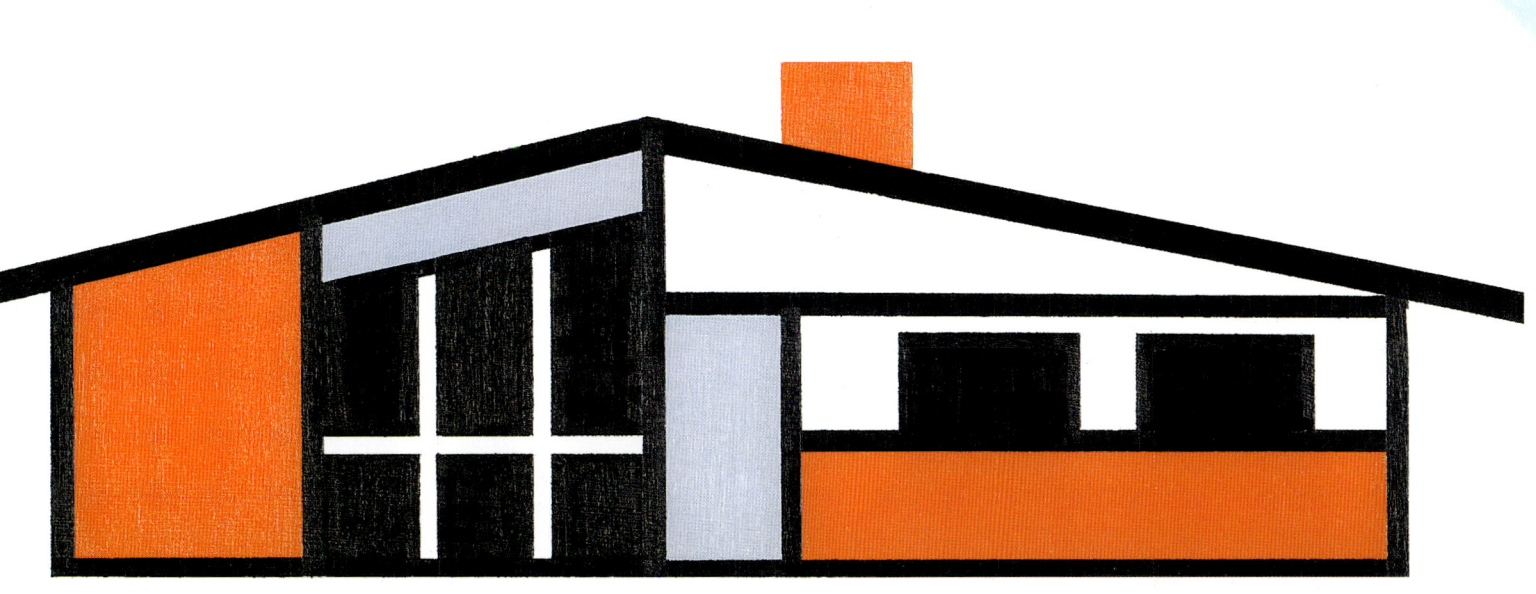

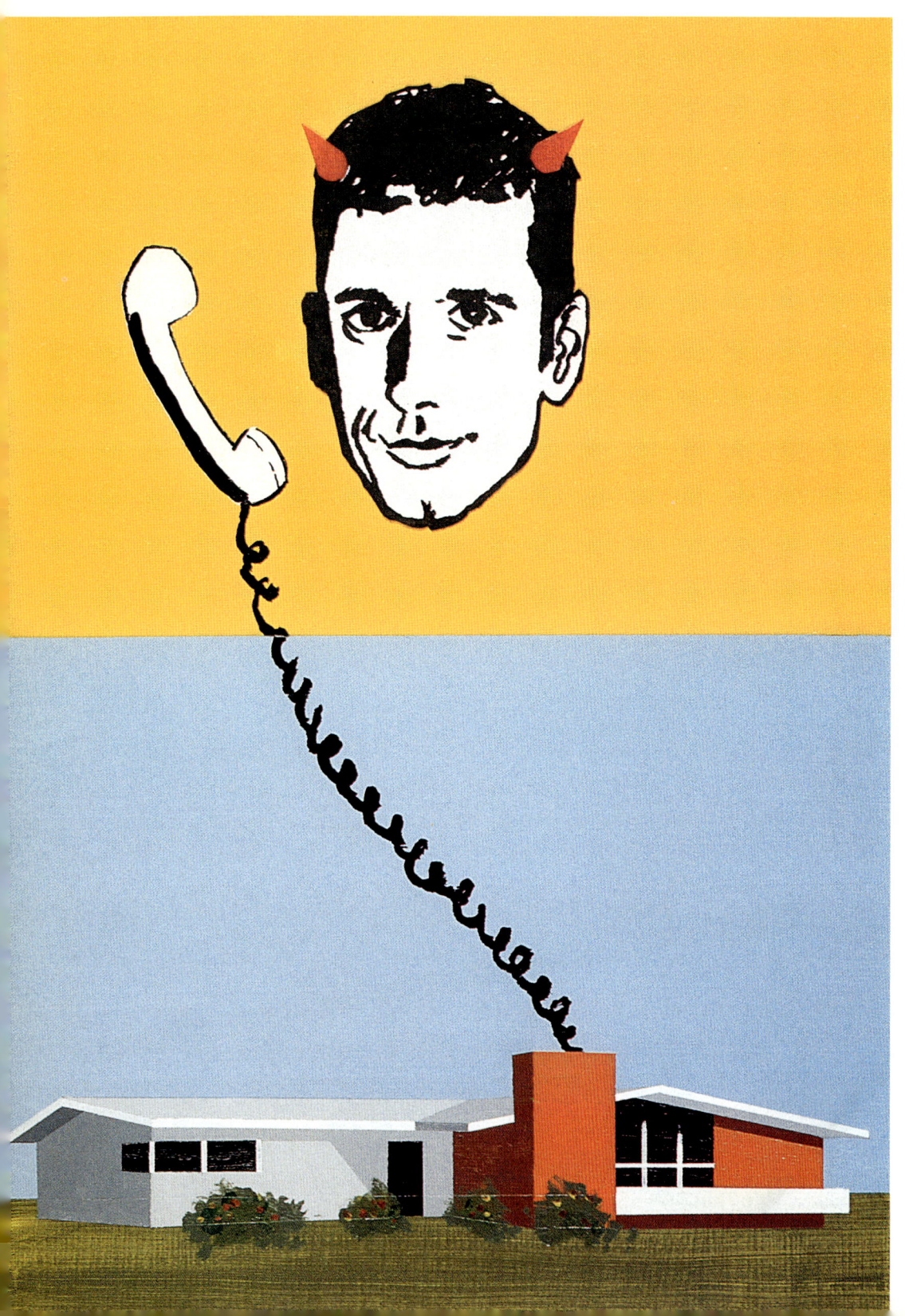

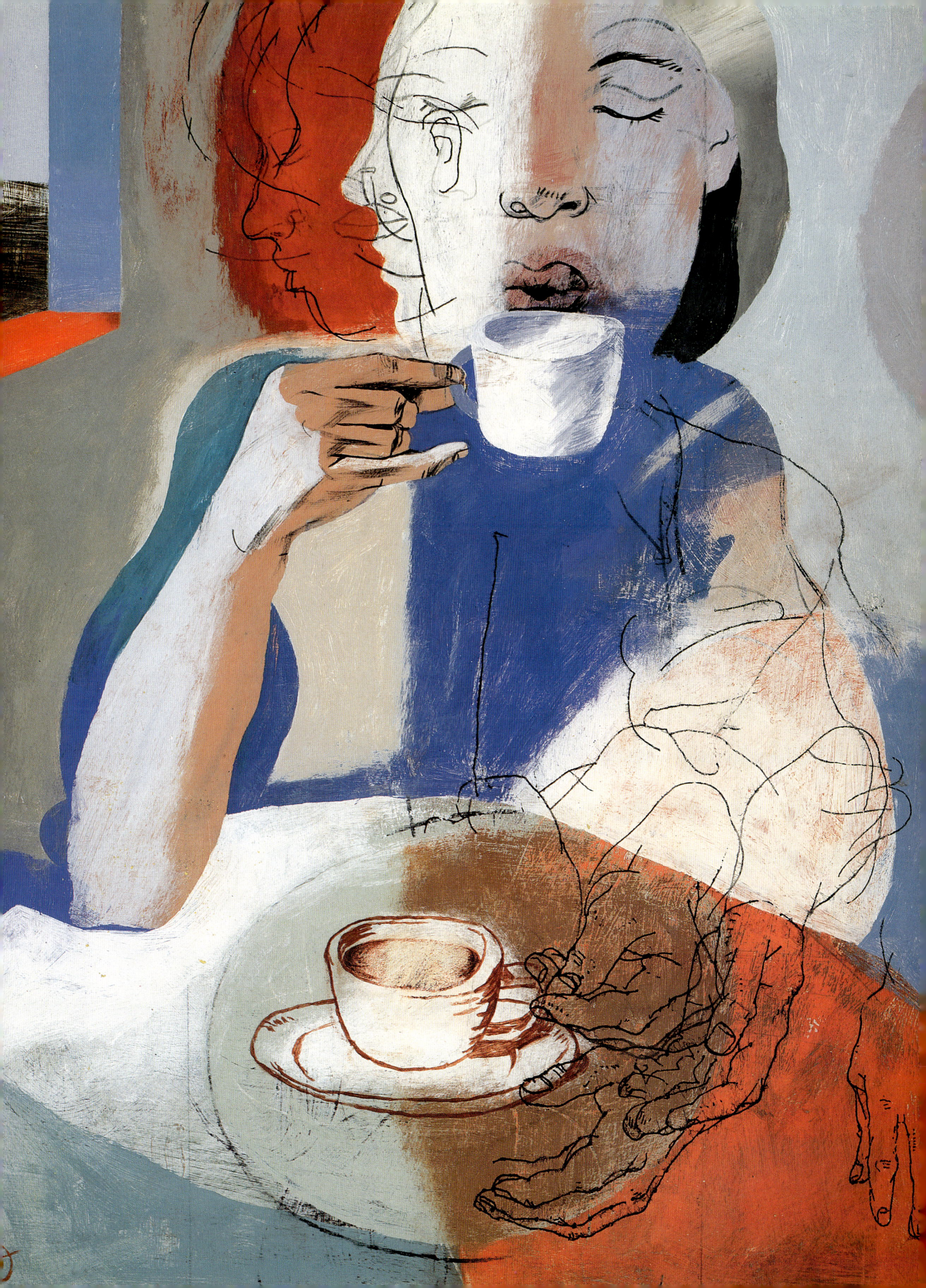

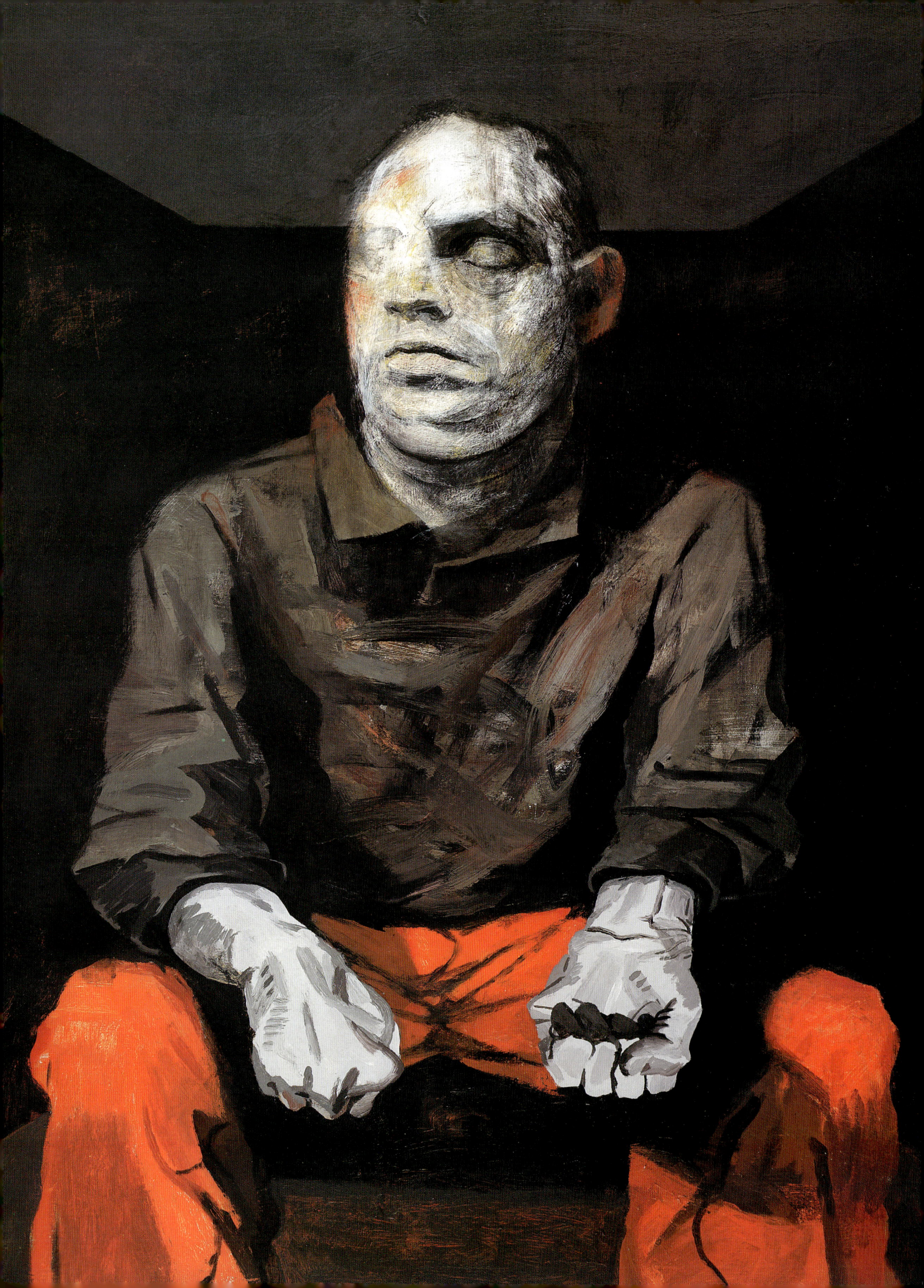

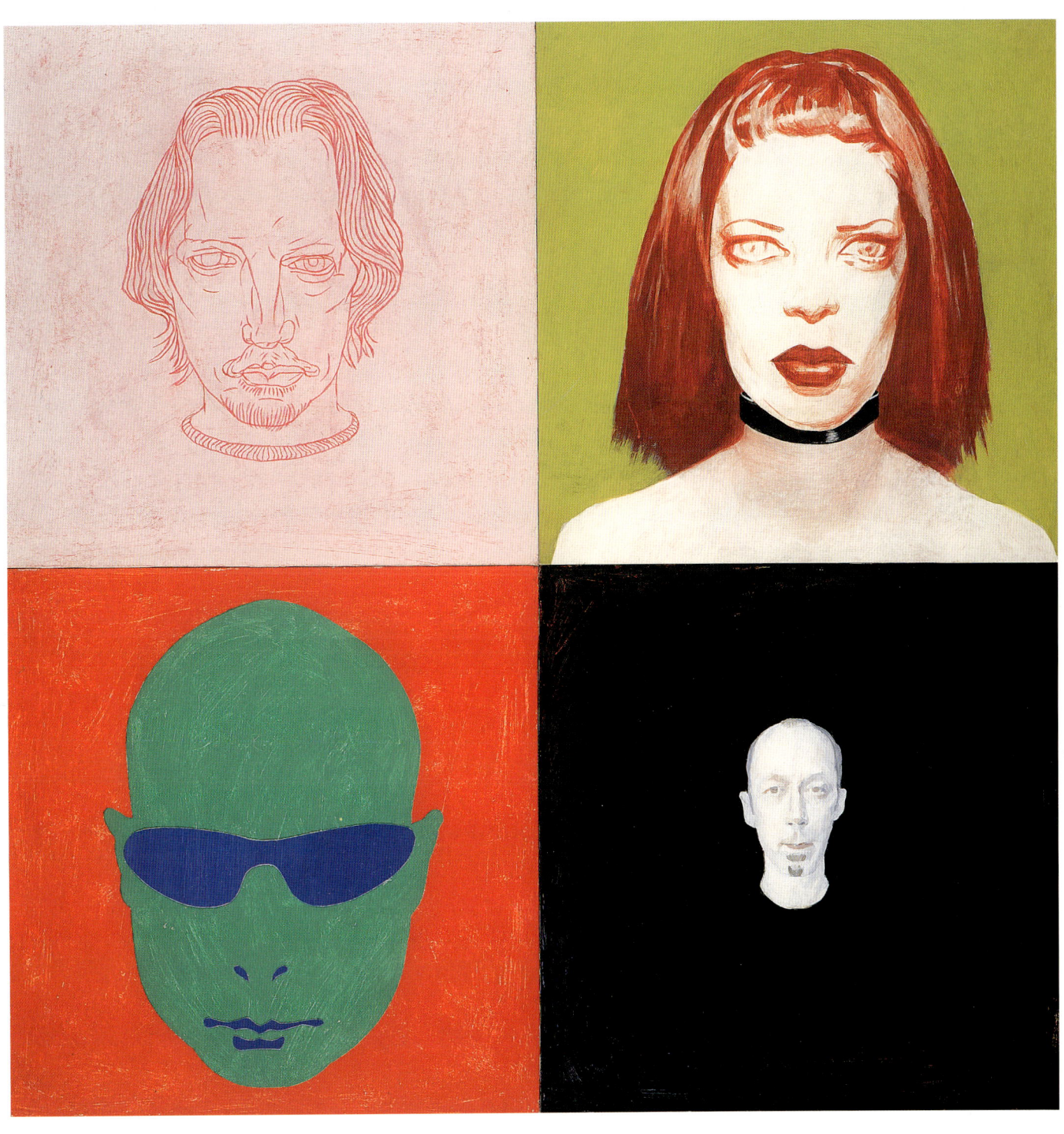

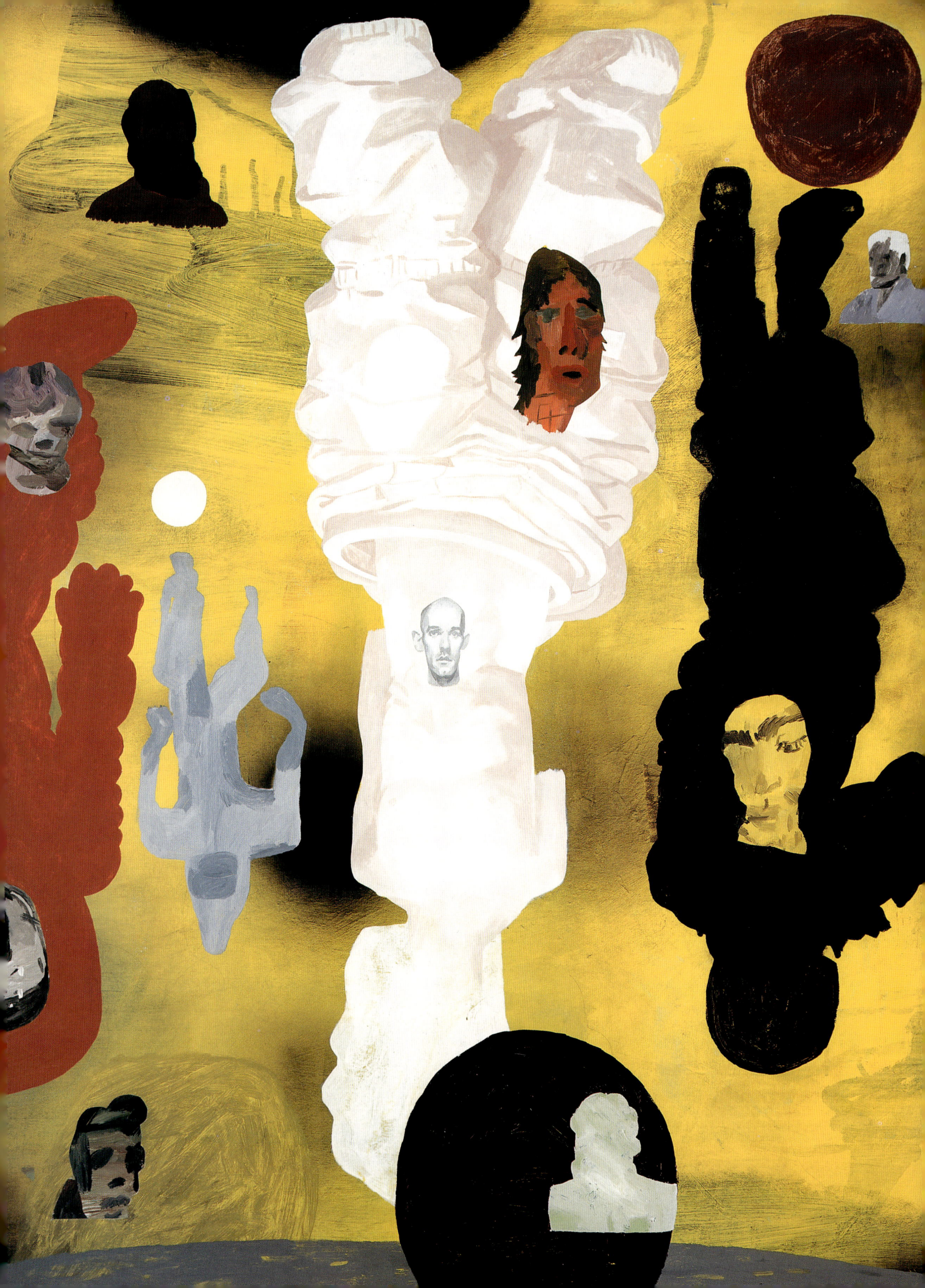

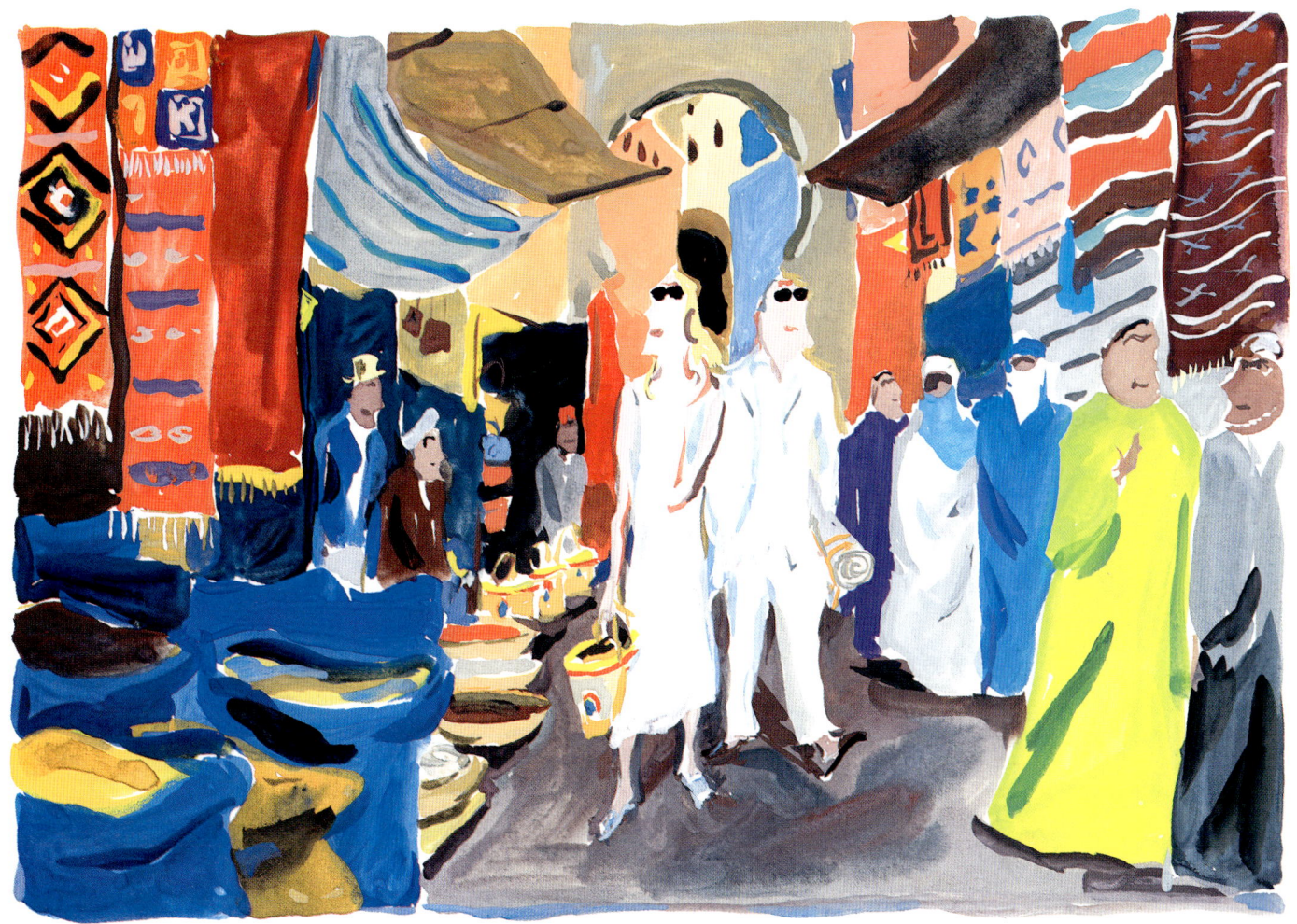

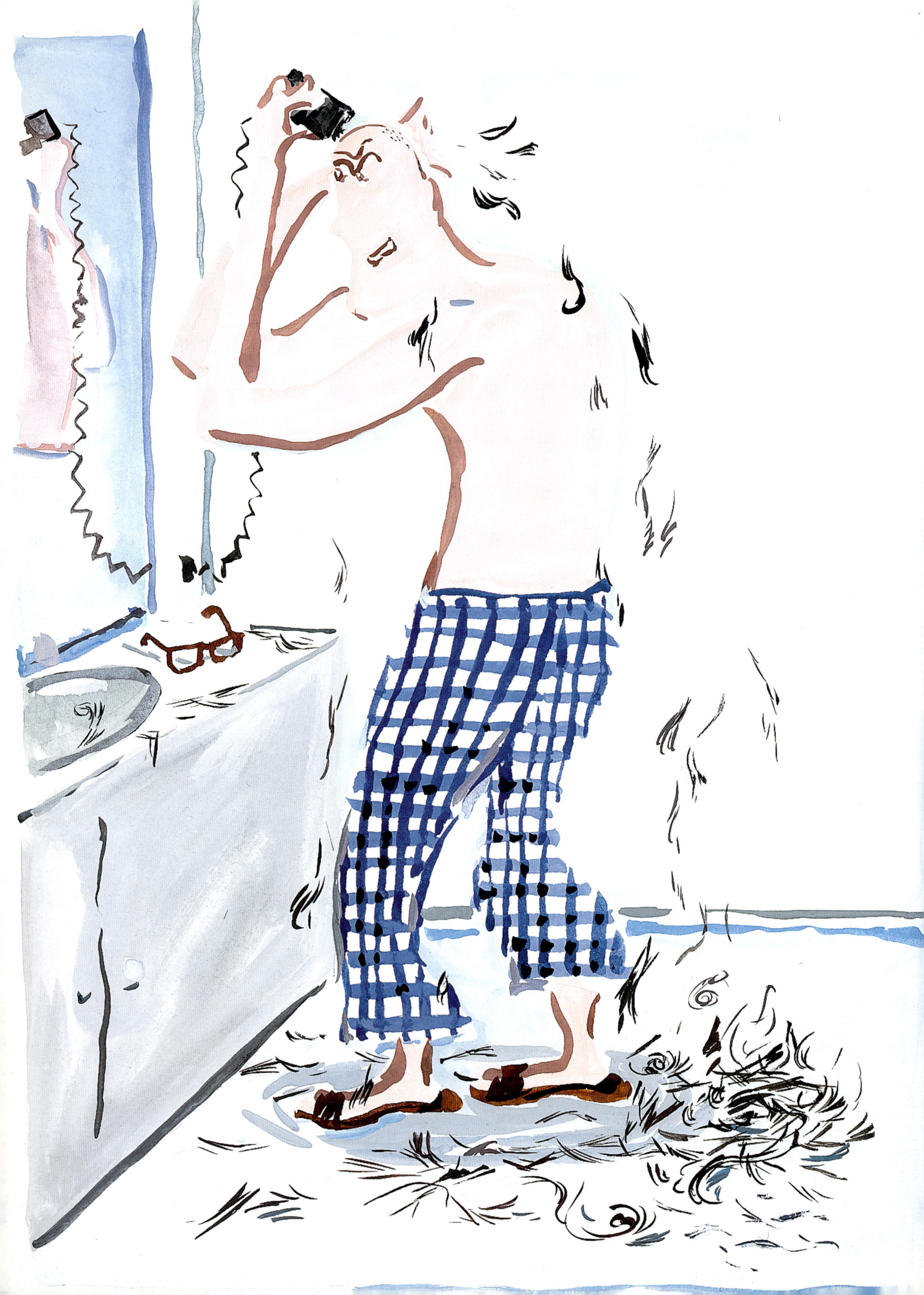

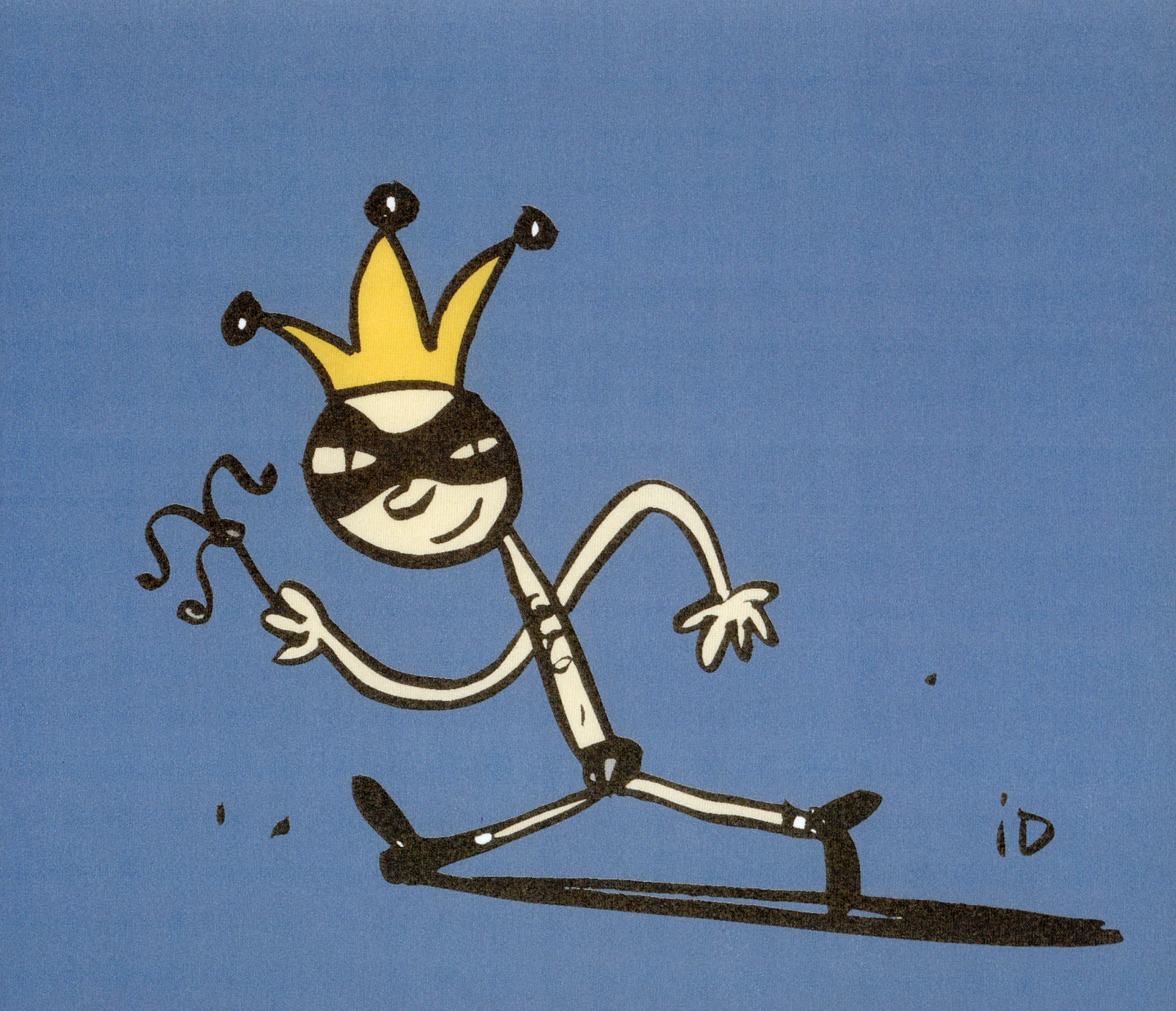

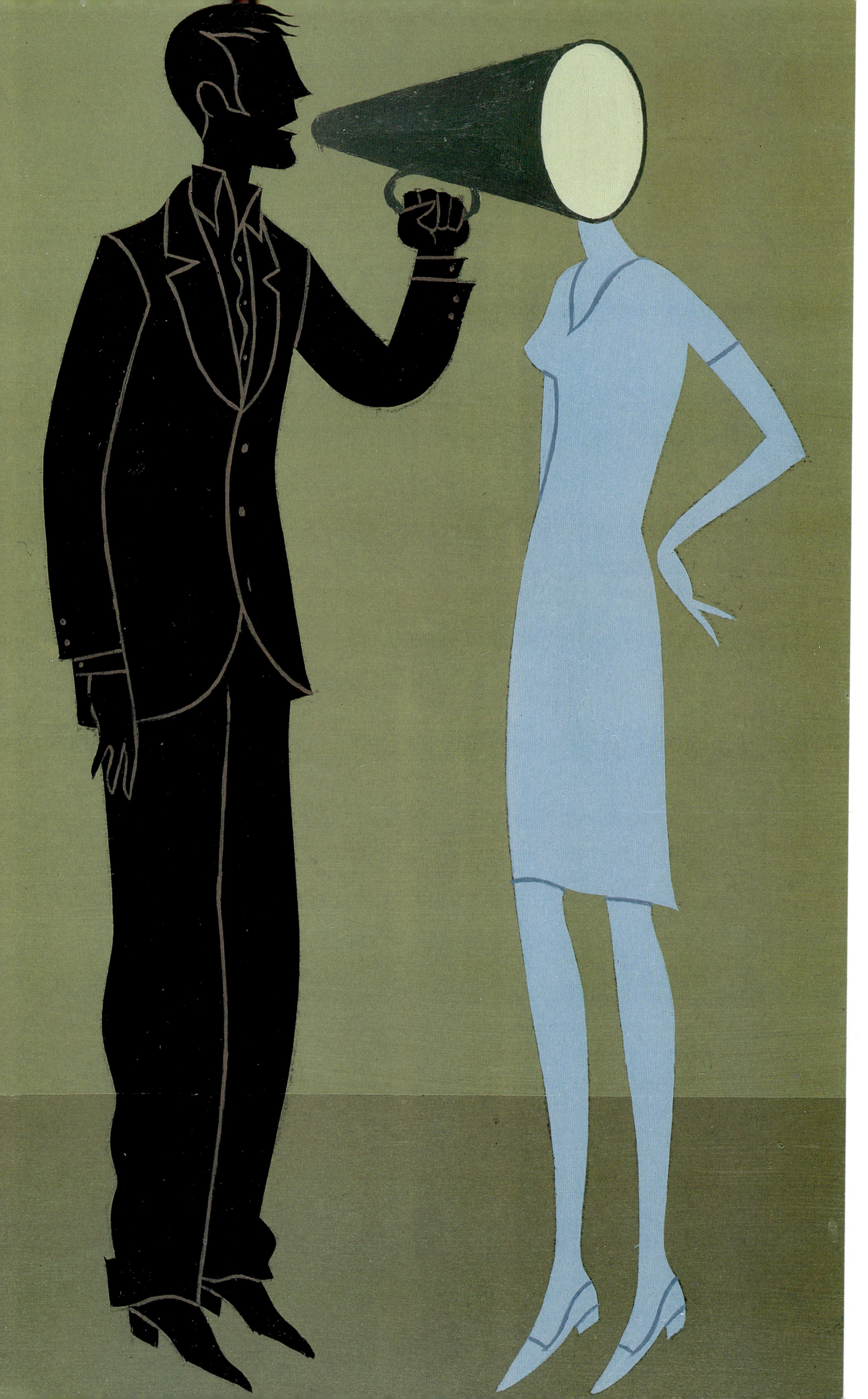

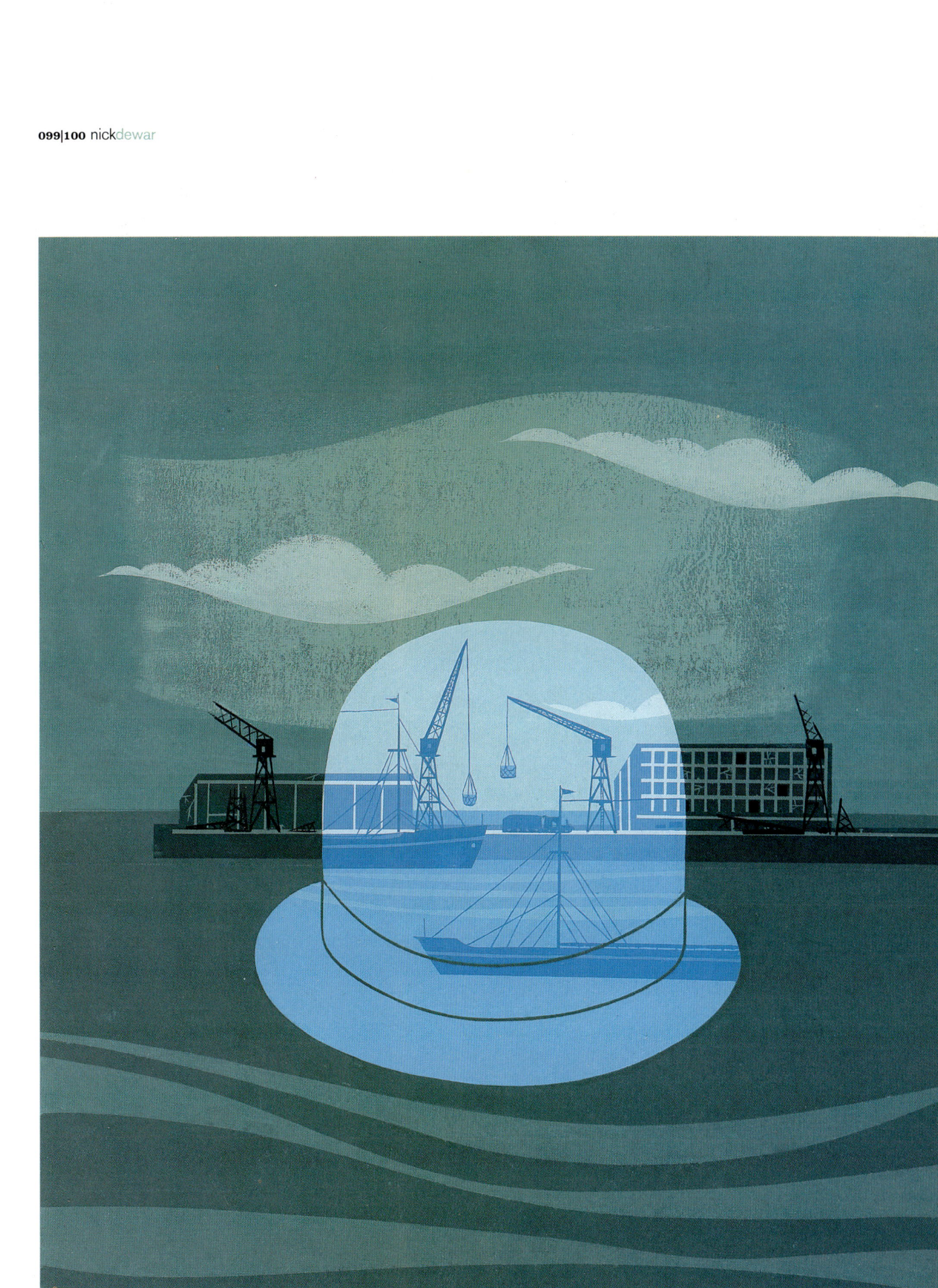

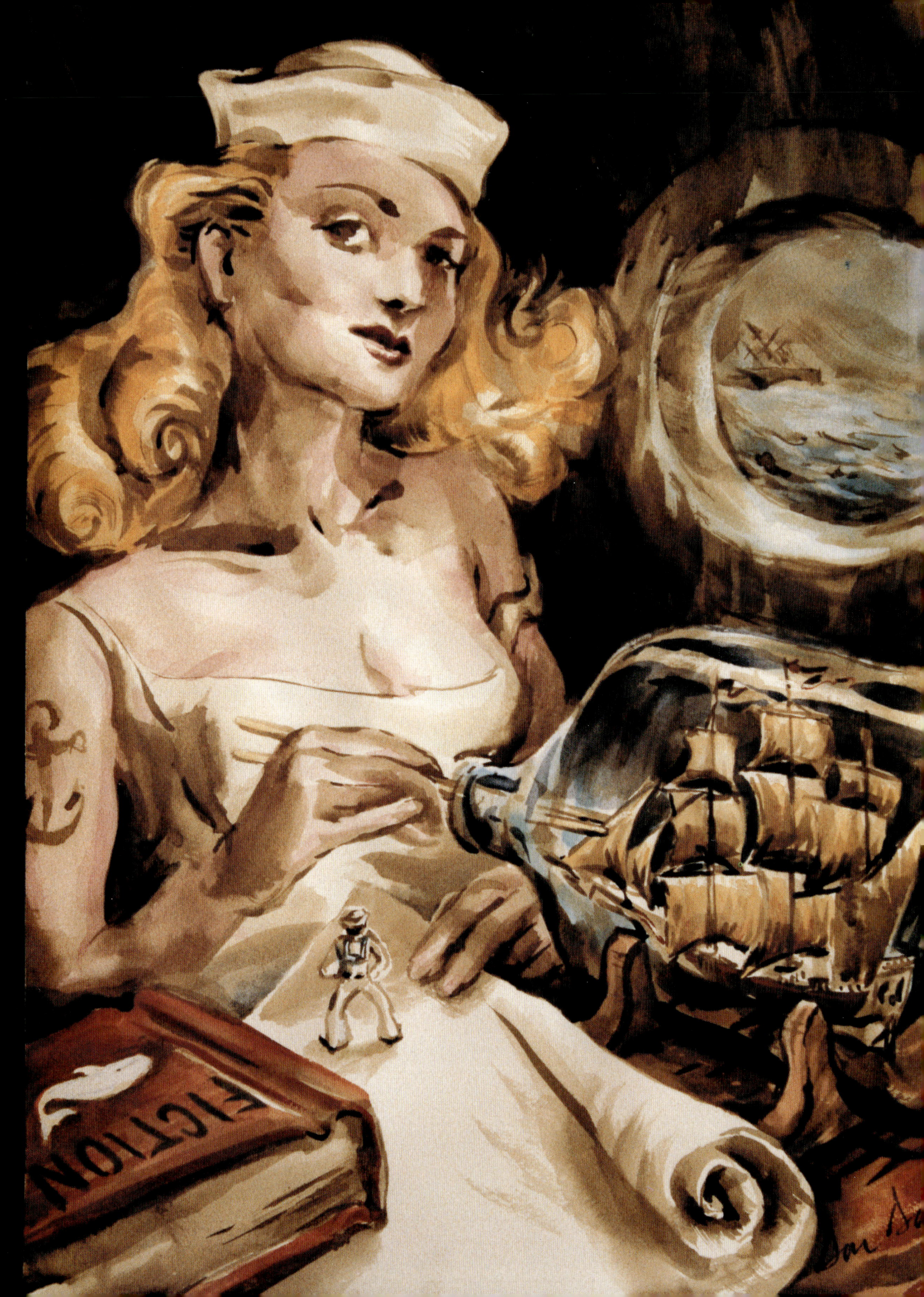

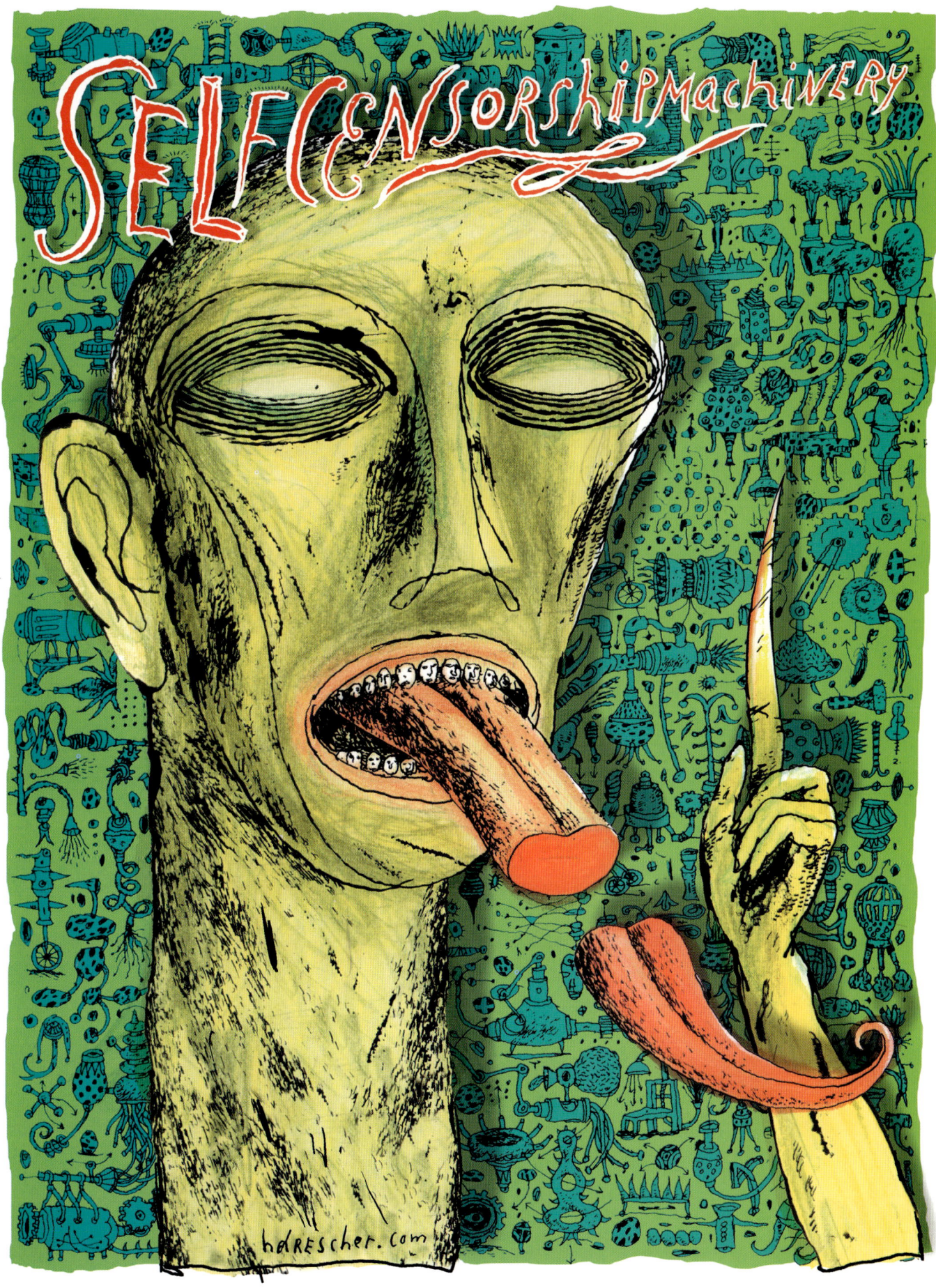

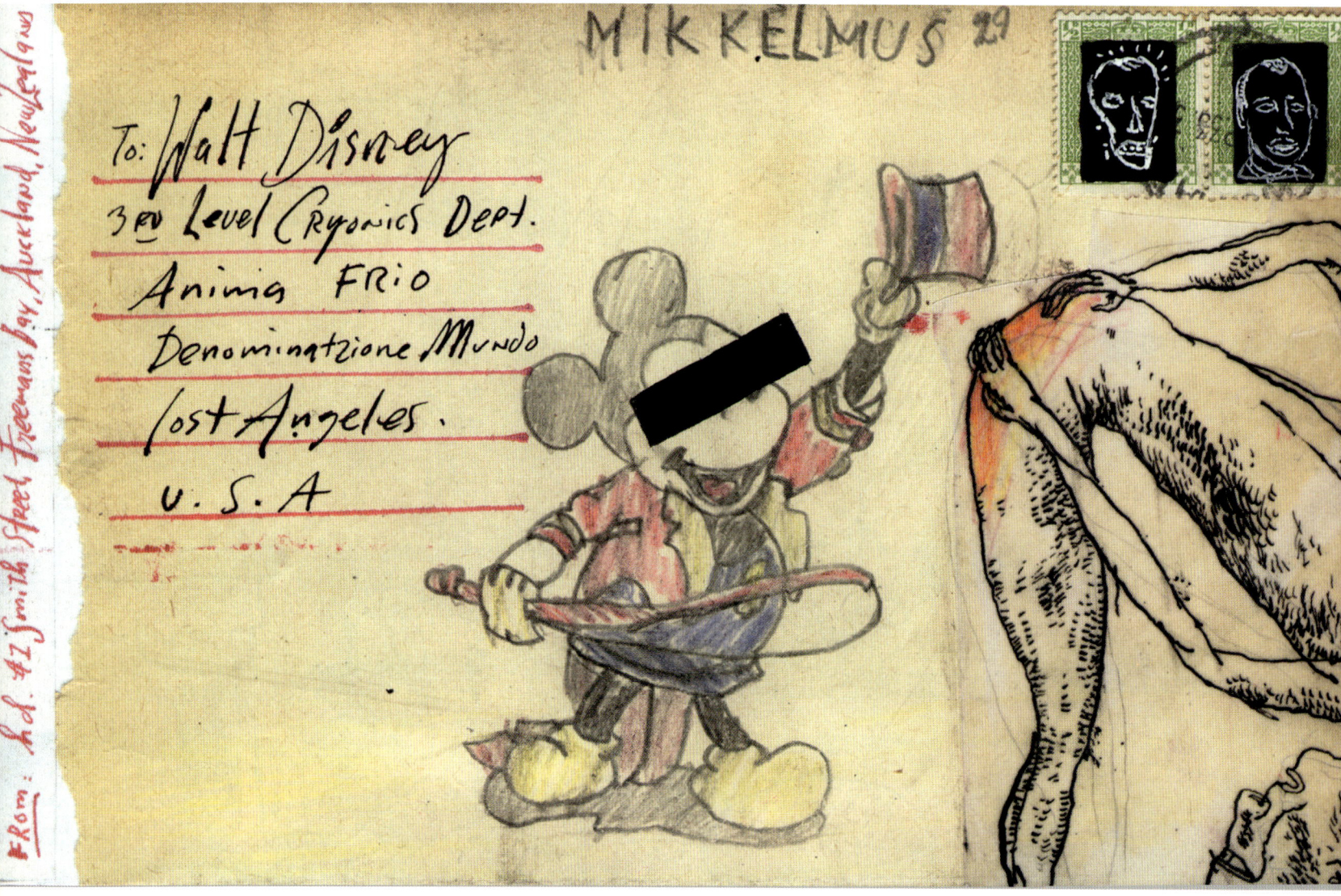

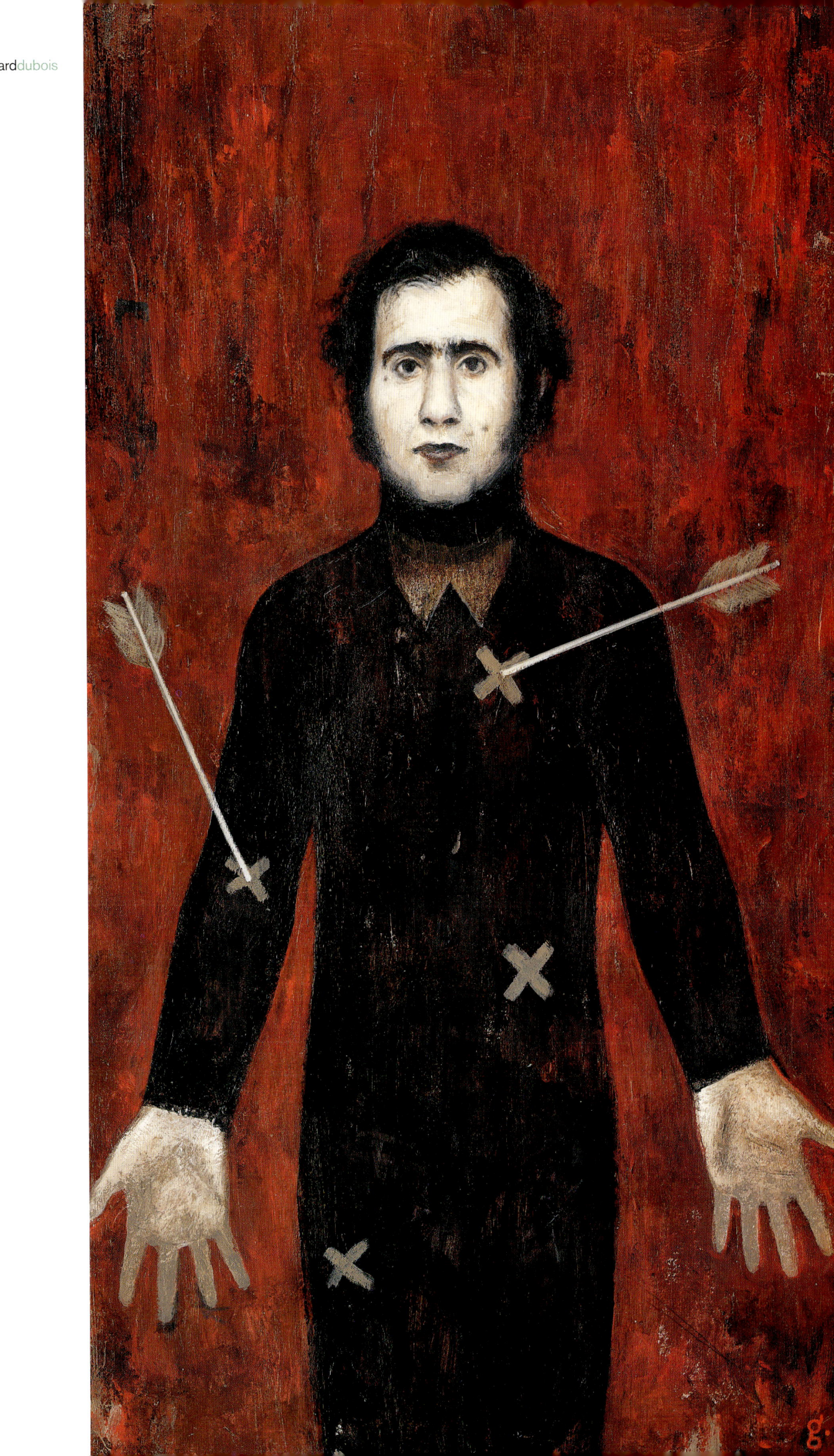

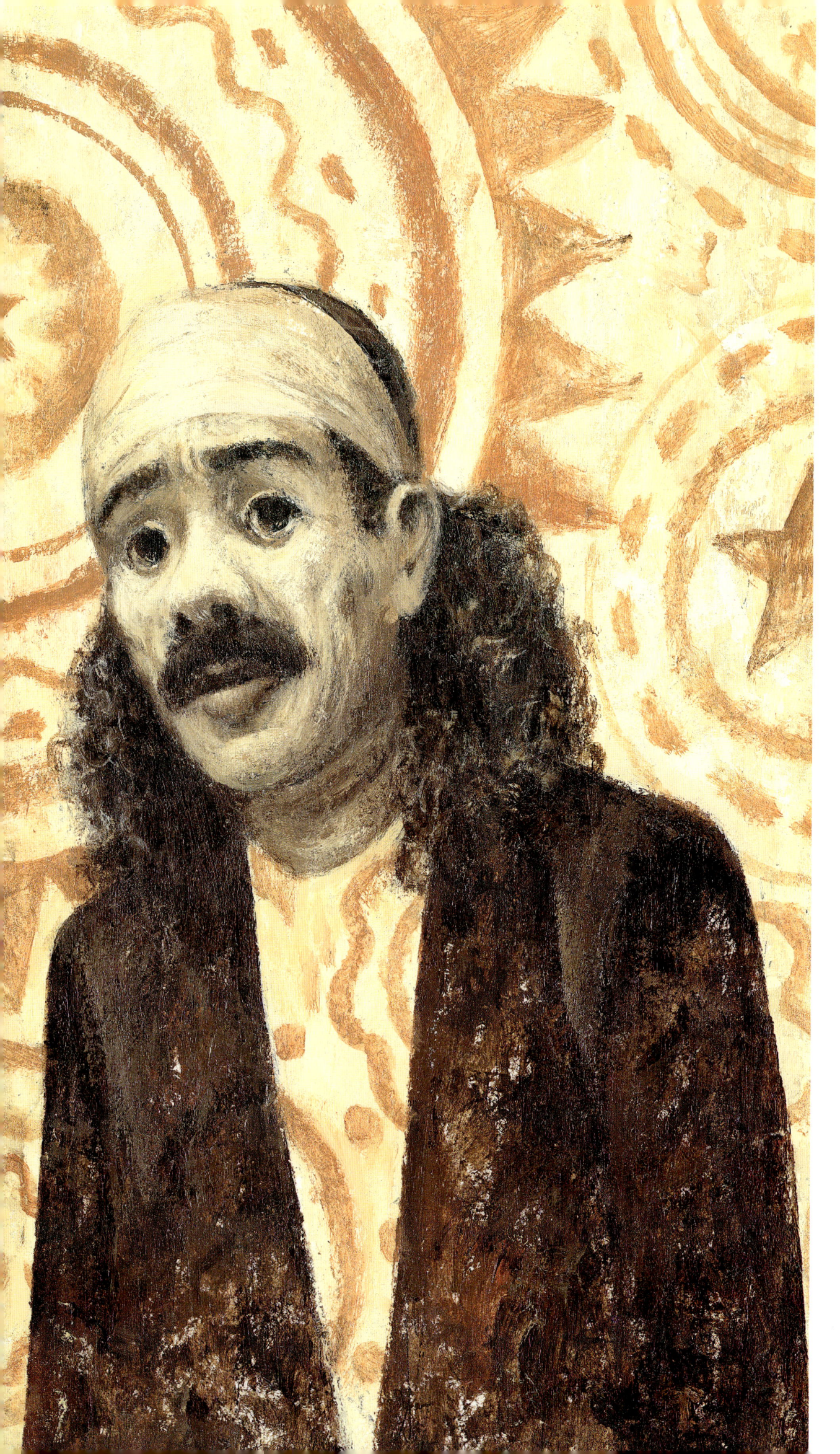

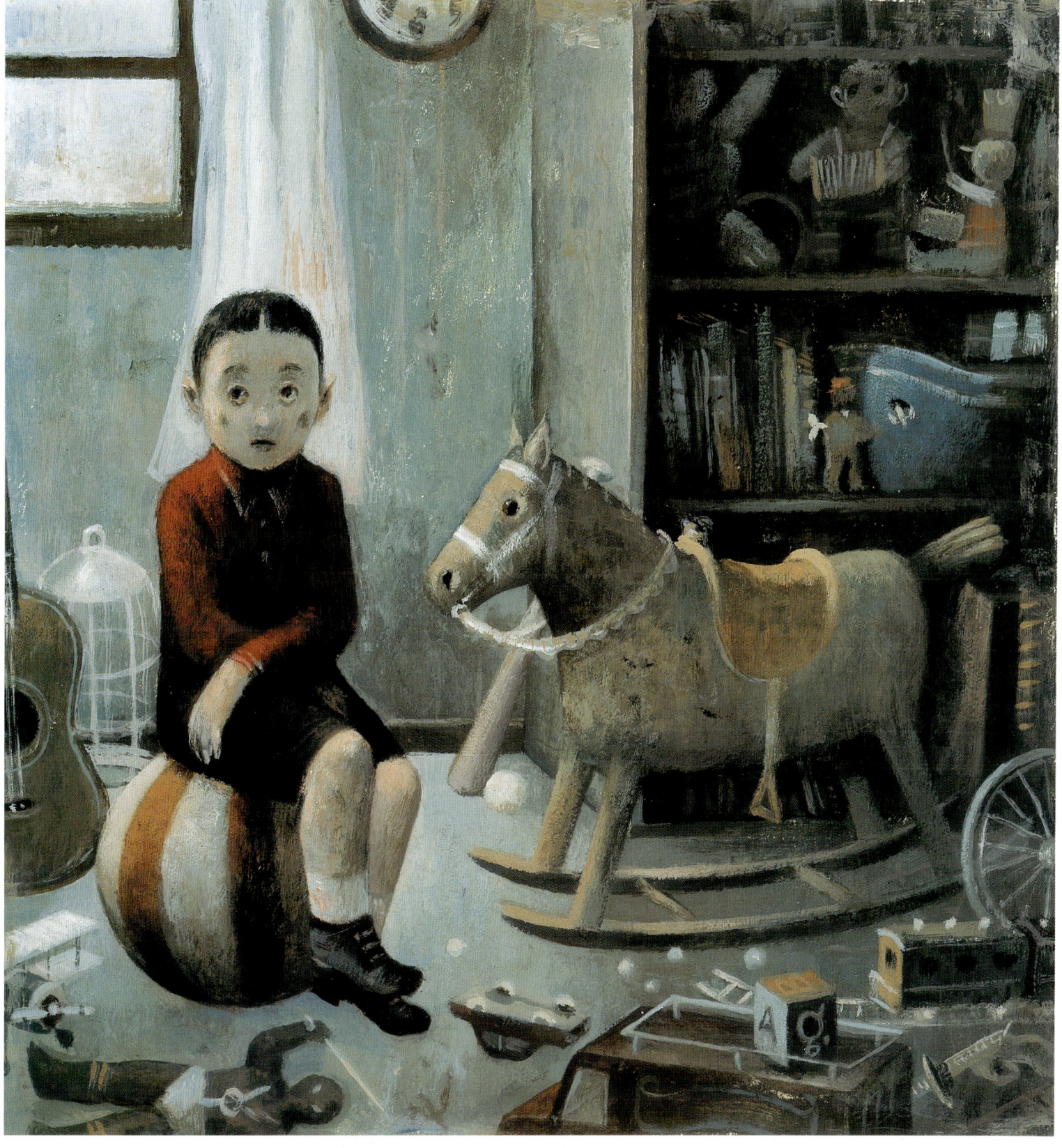

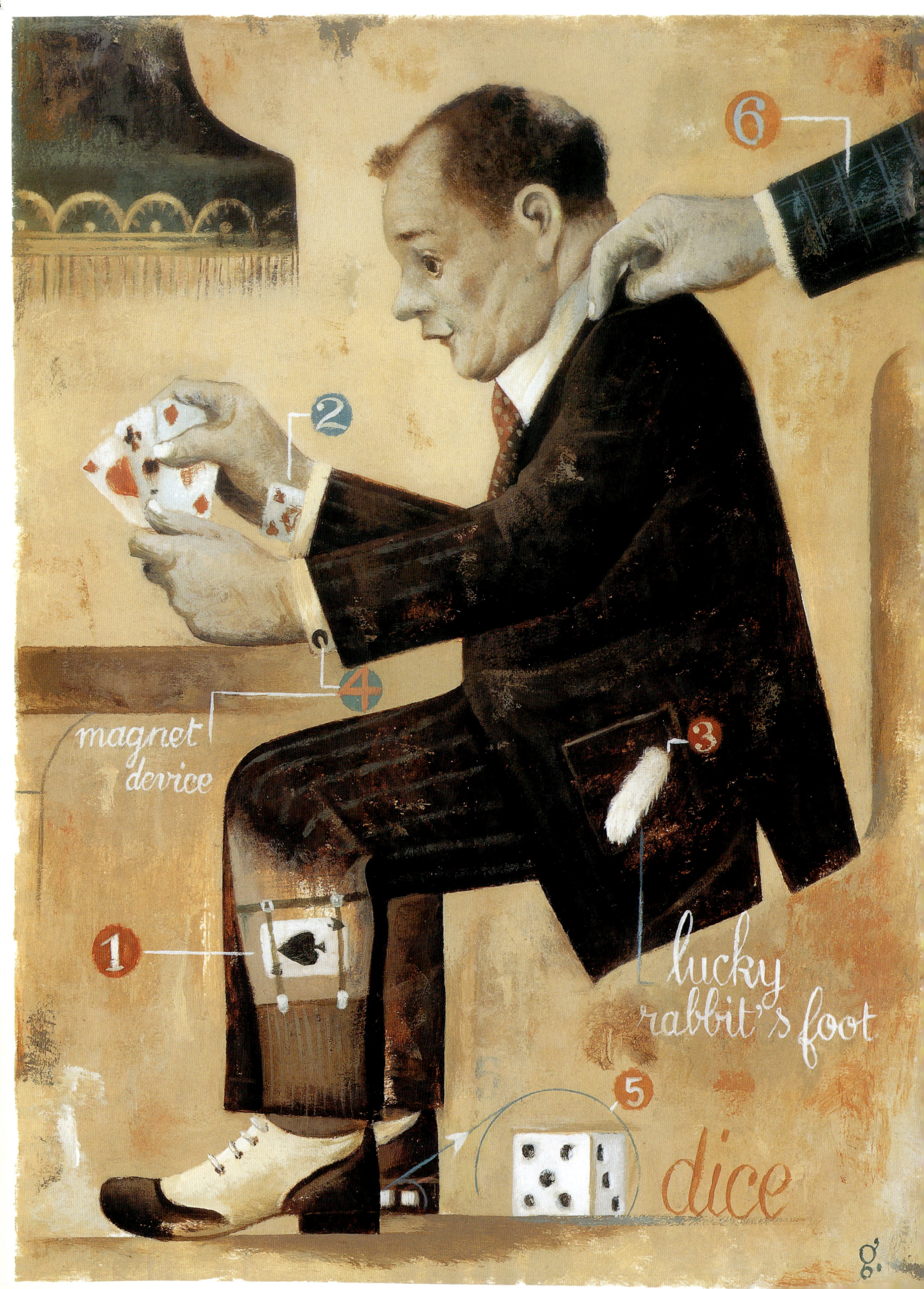

6

2

magnet
device

4

3

1

lucky
rabbit's foot

5

dice

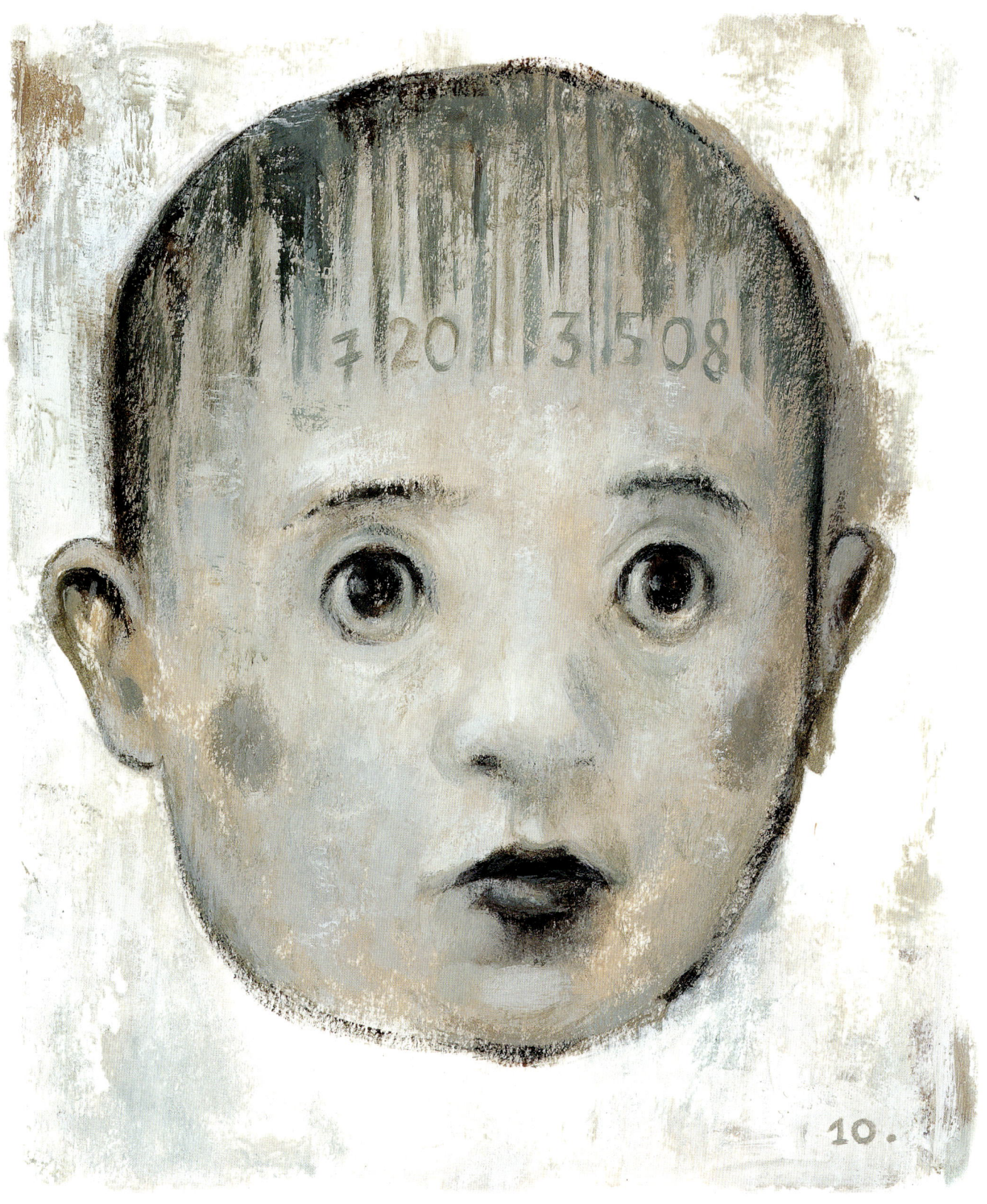

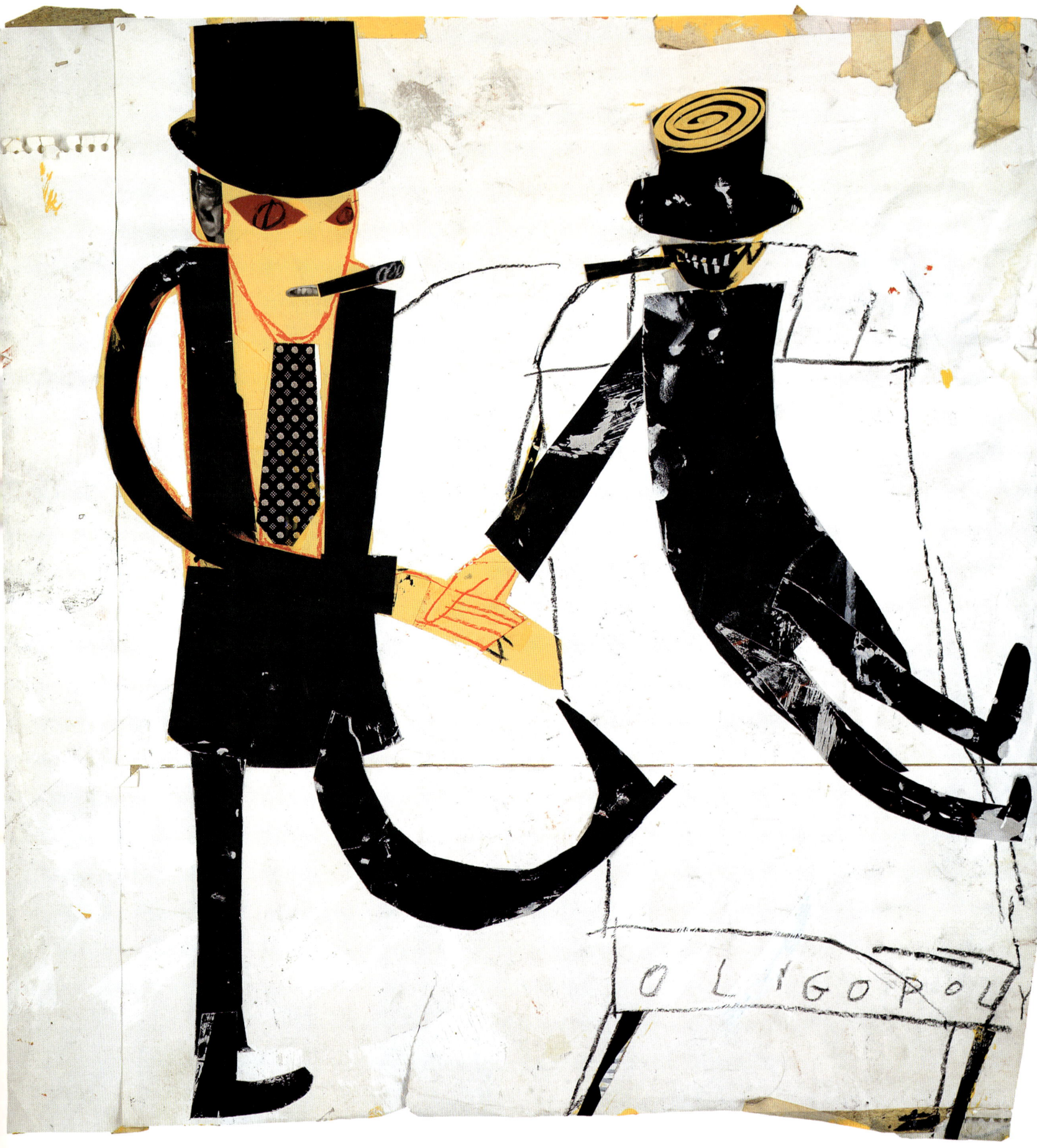

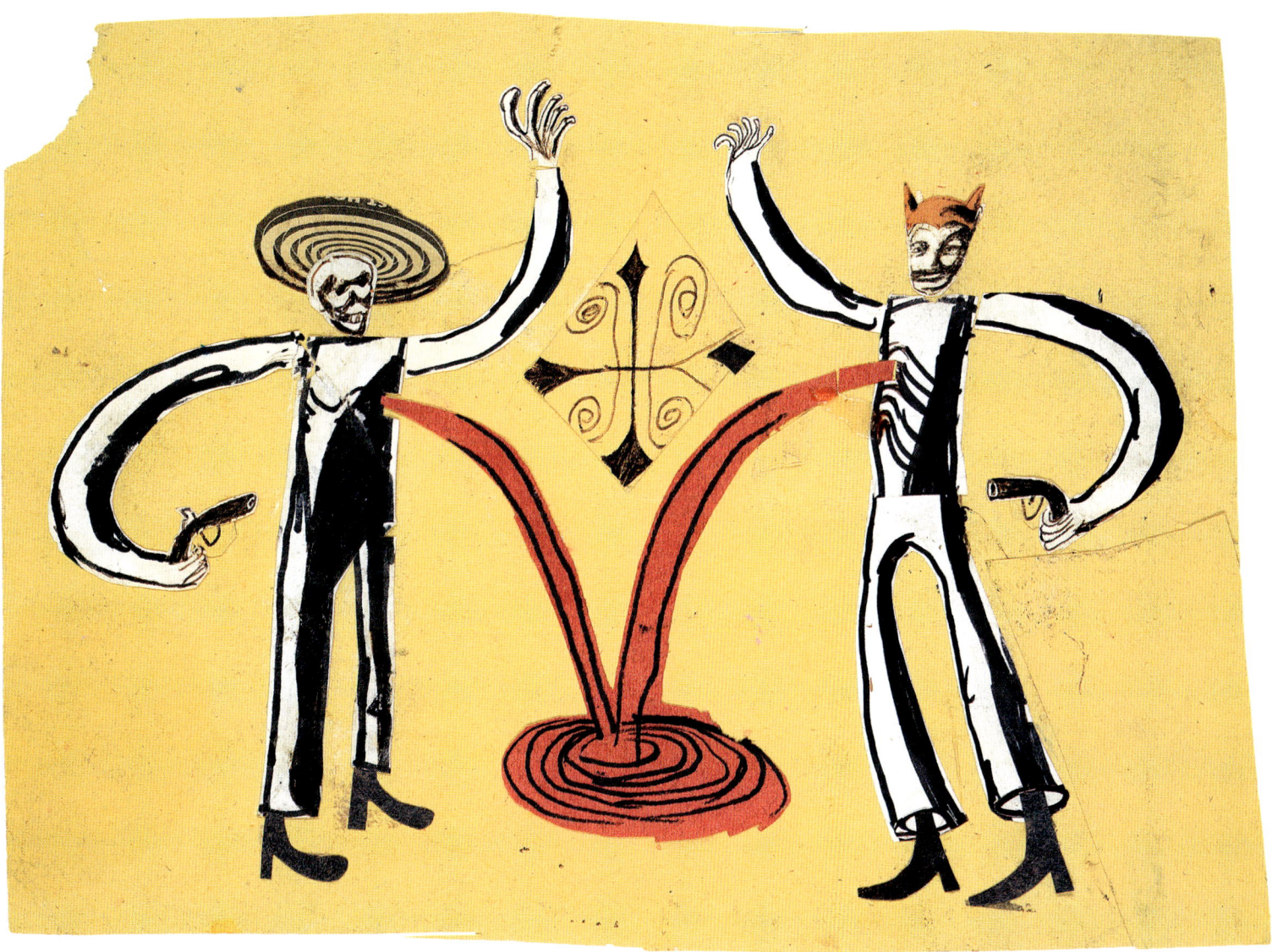

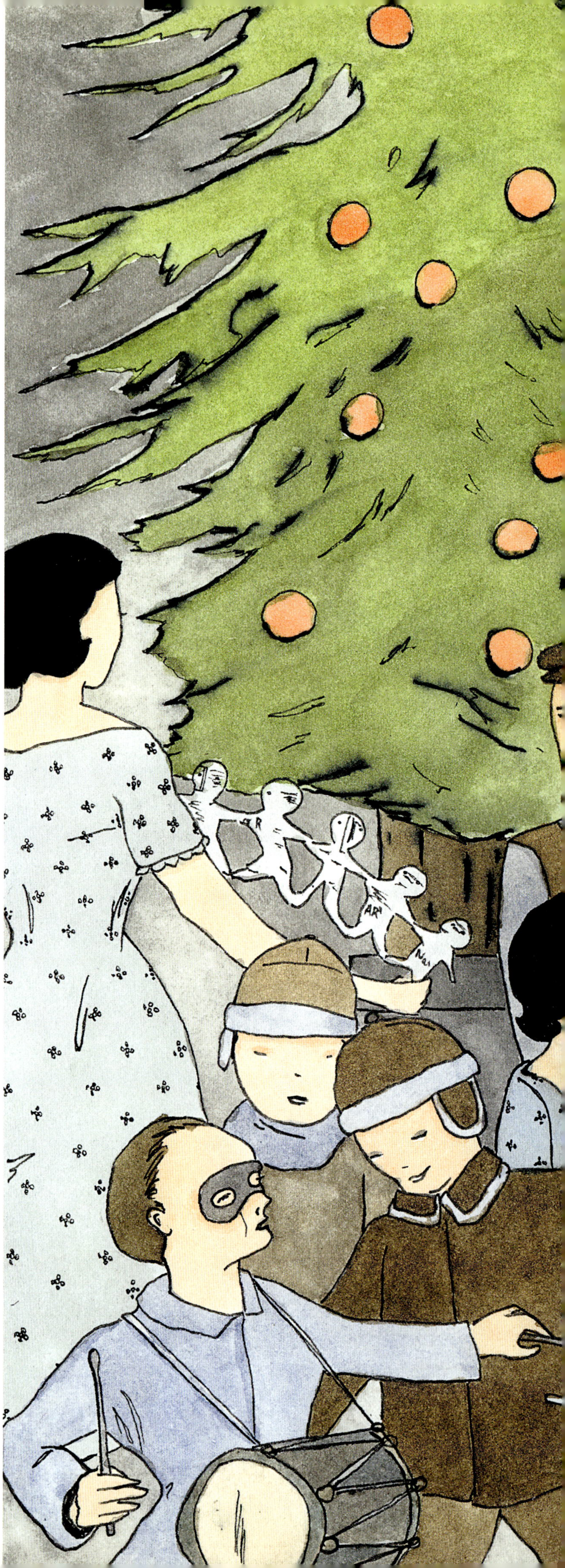

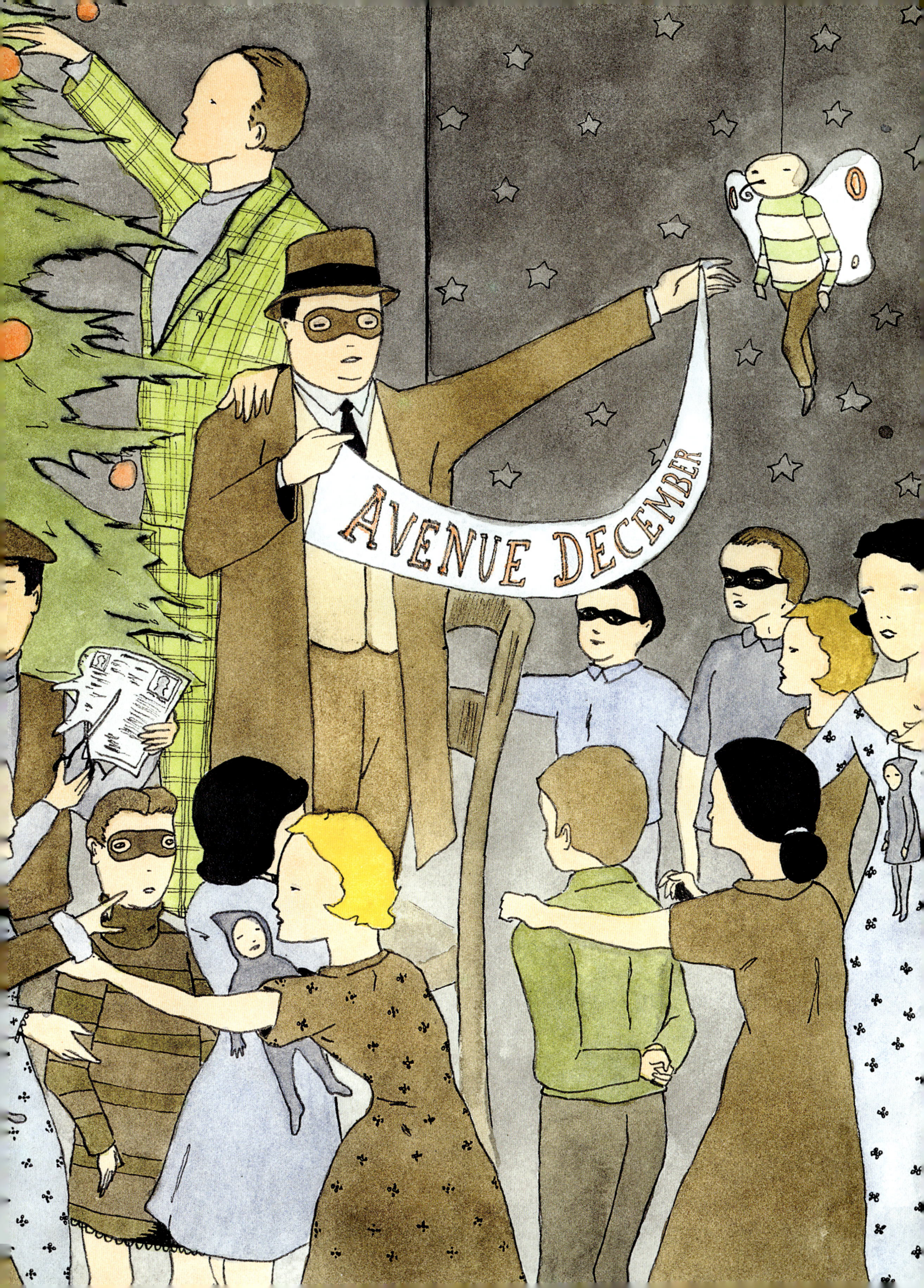

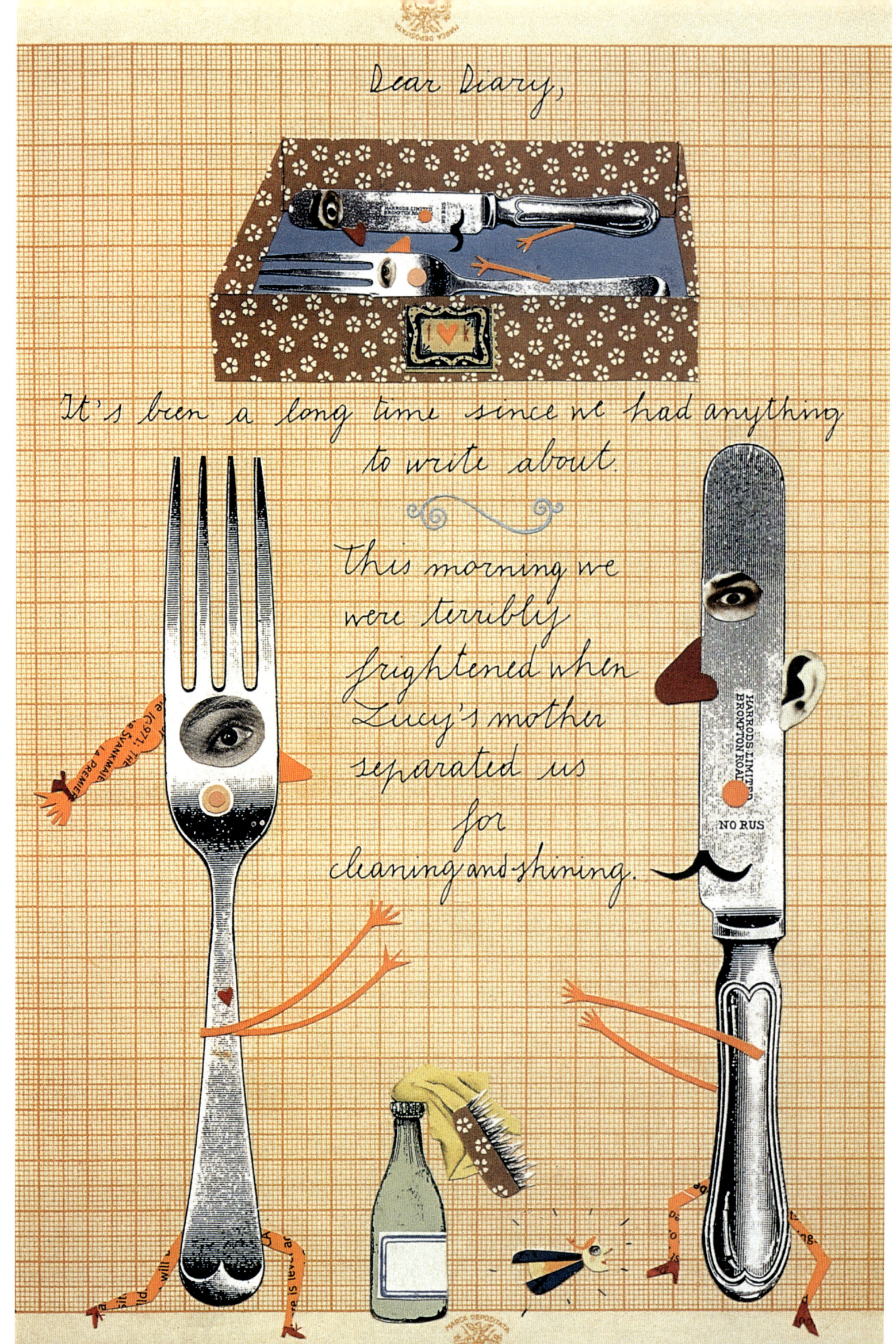

Dear Diary,

It's been a long time since we had anything to write about.

This morning we were terribly frightened when Lucy's mother separated us for cleaning and shining.

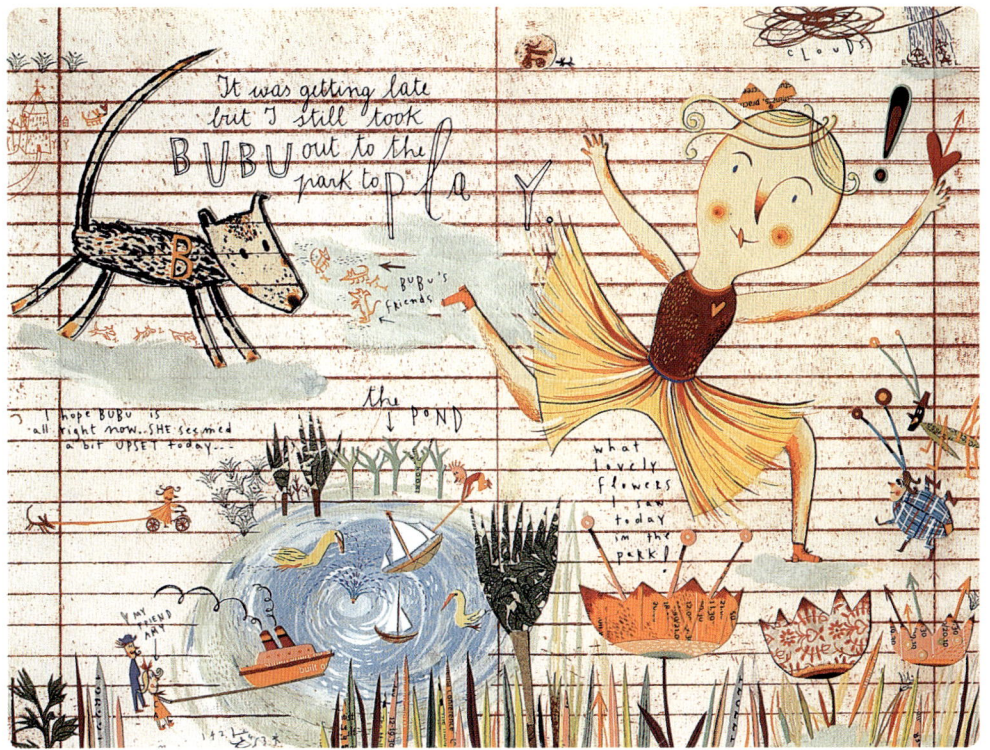

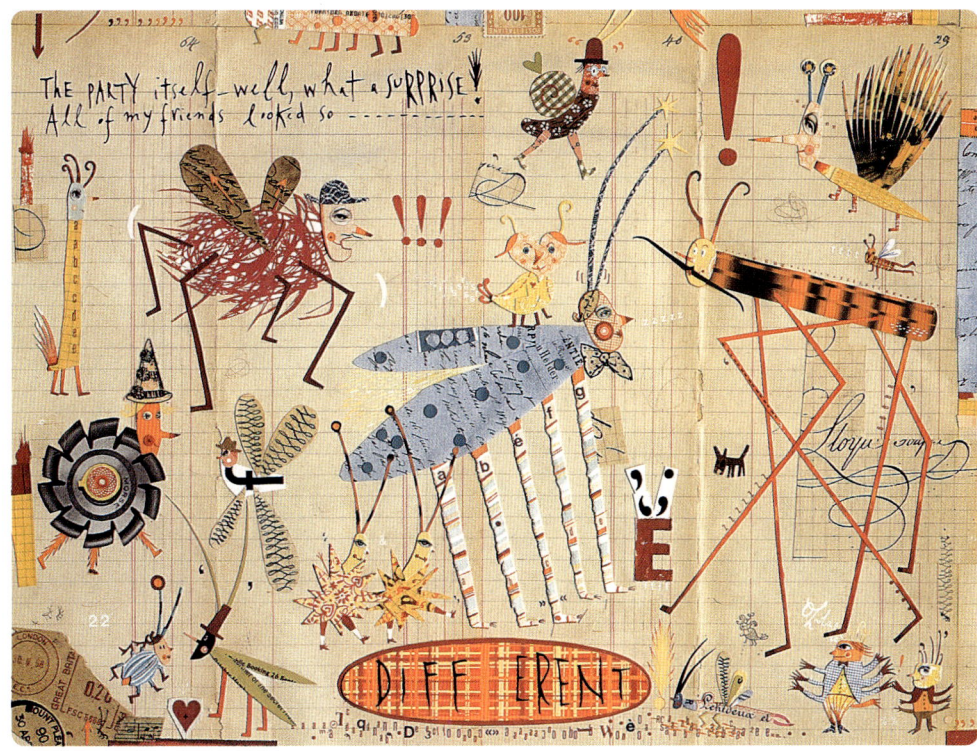

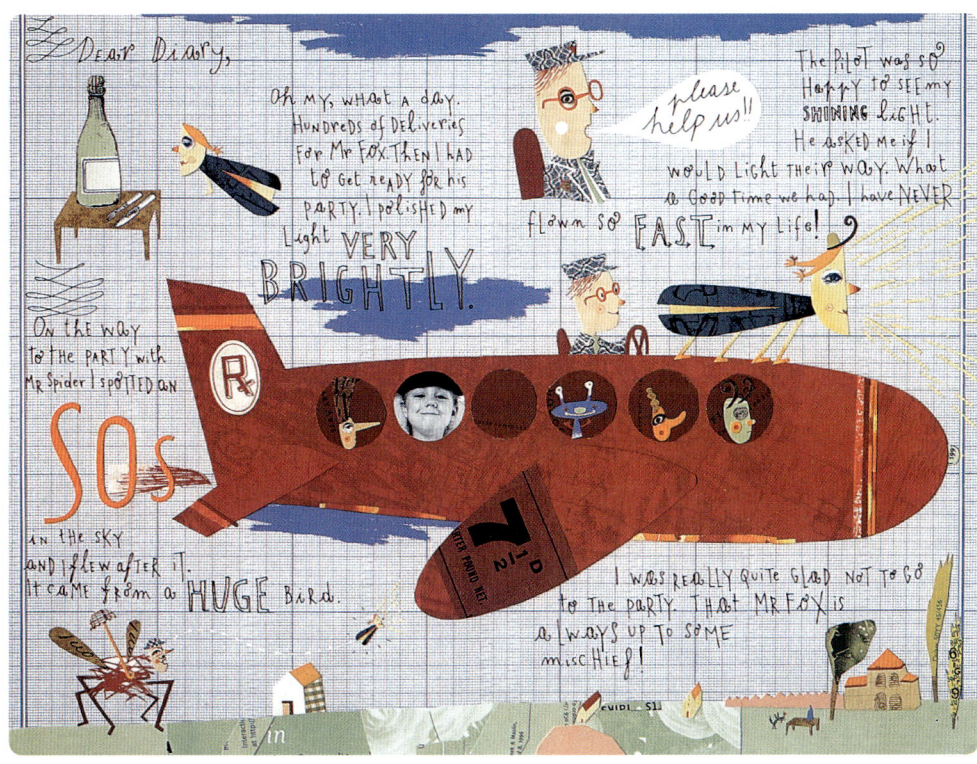

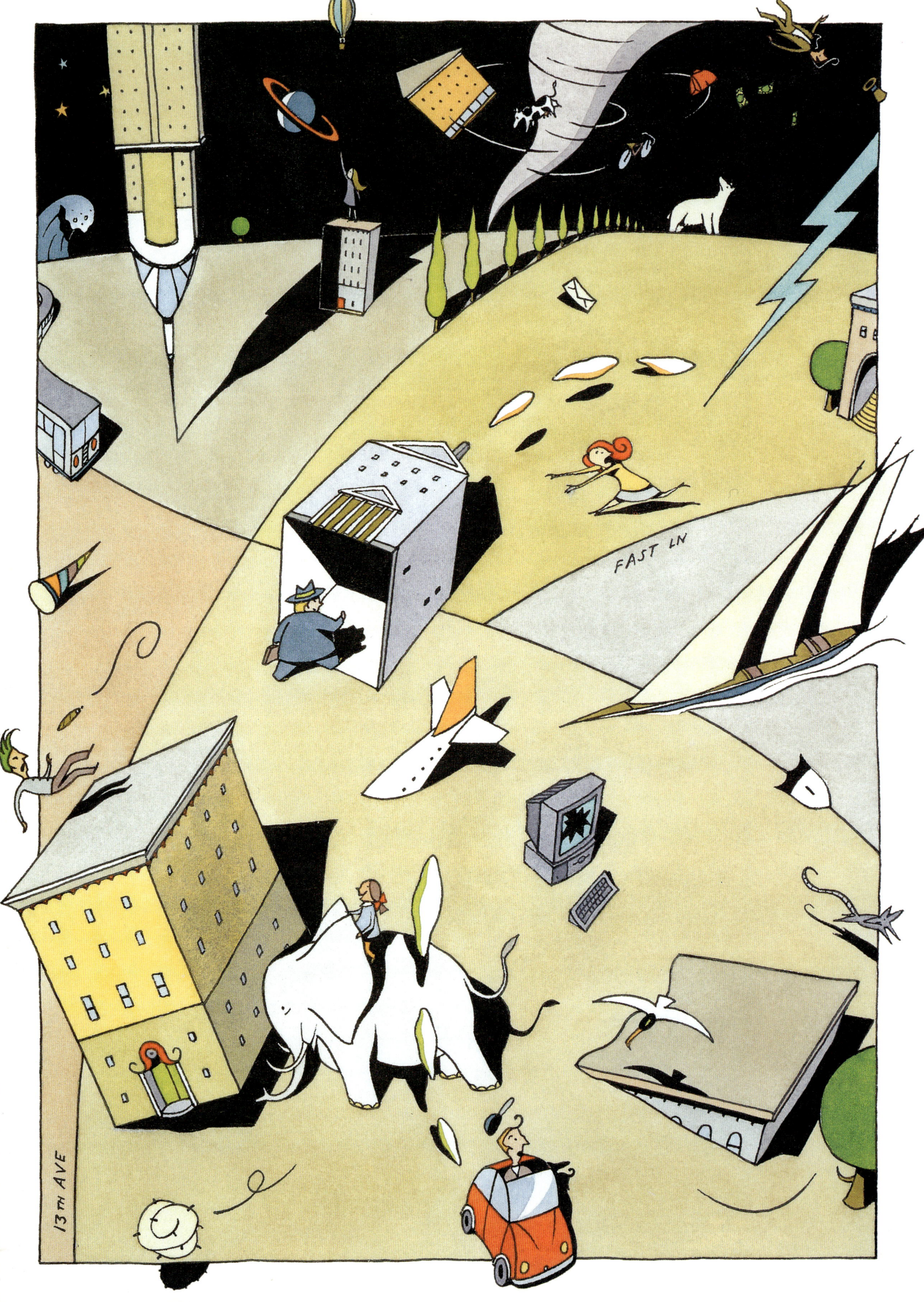

FAST LN

13th AVE

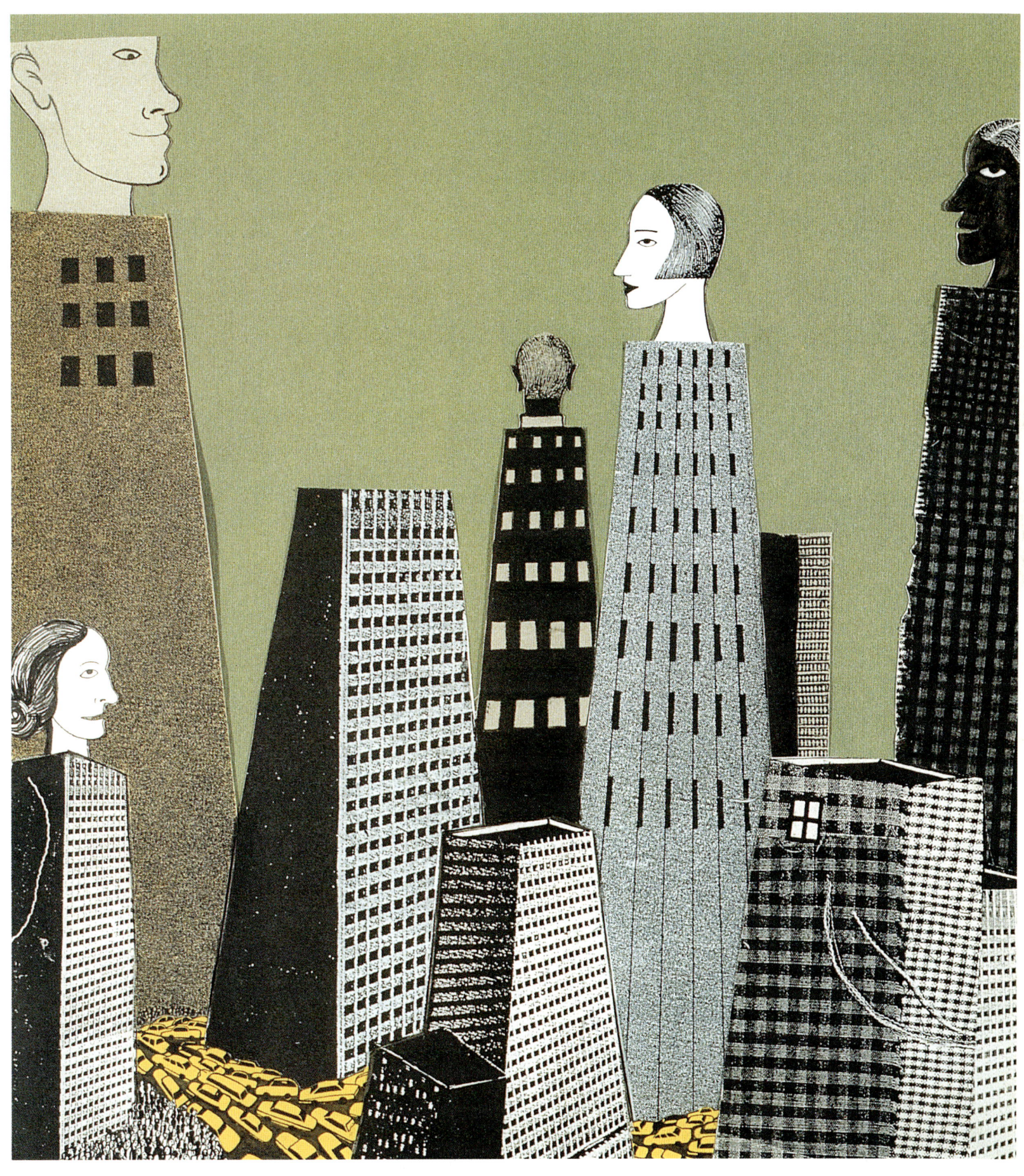

A B-
RUSH
WITH
INK

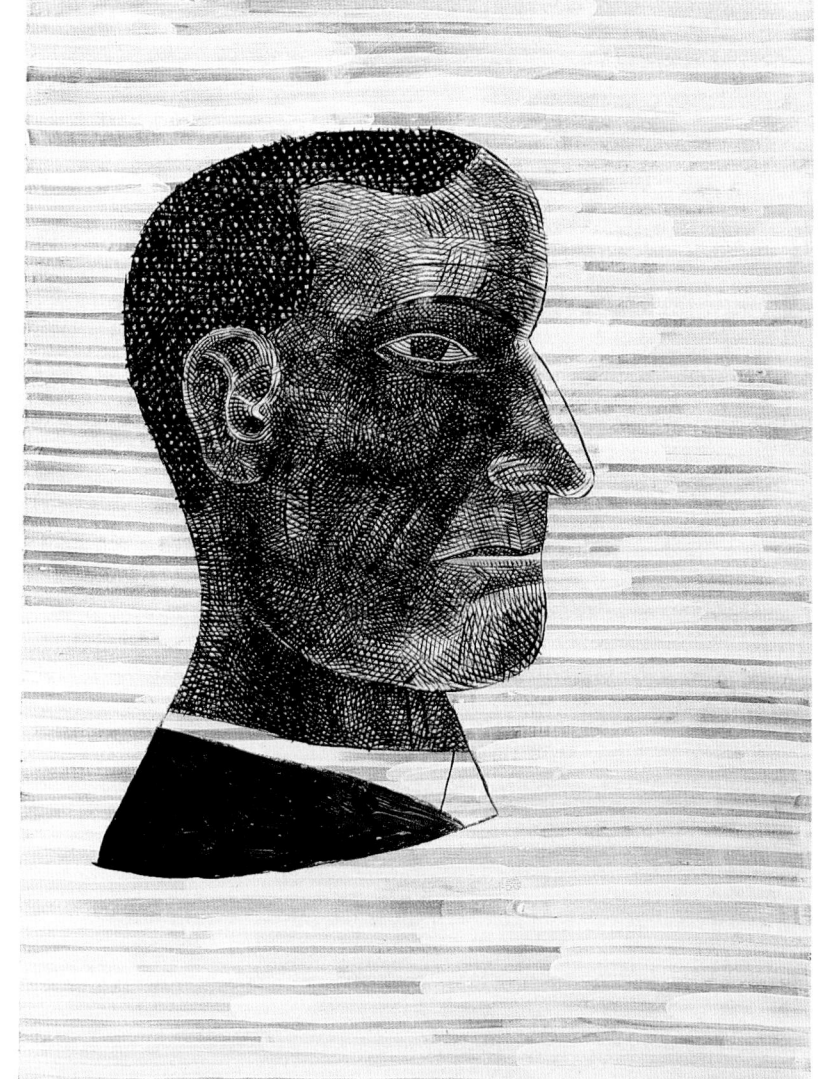

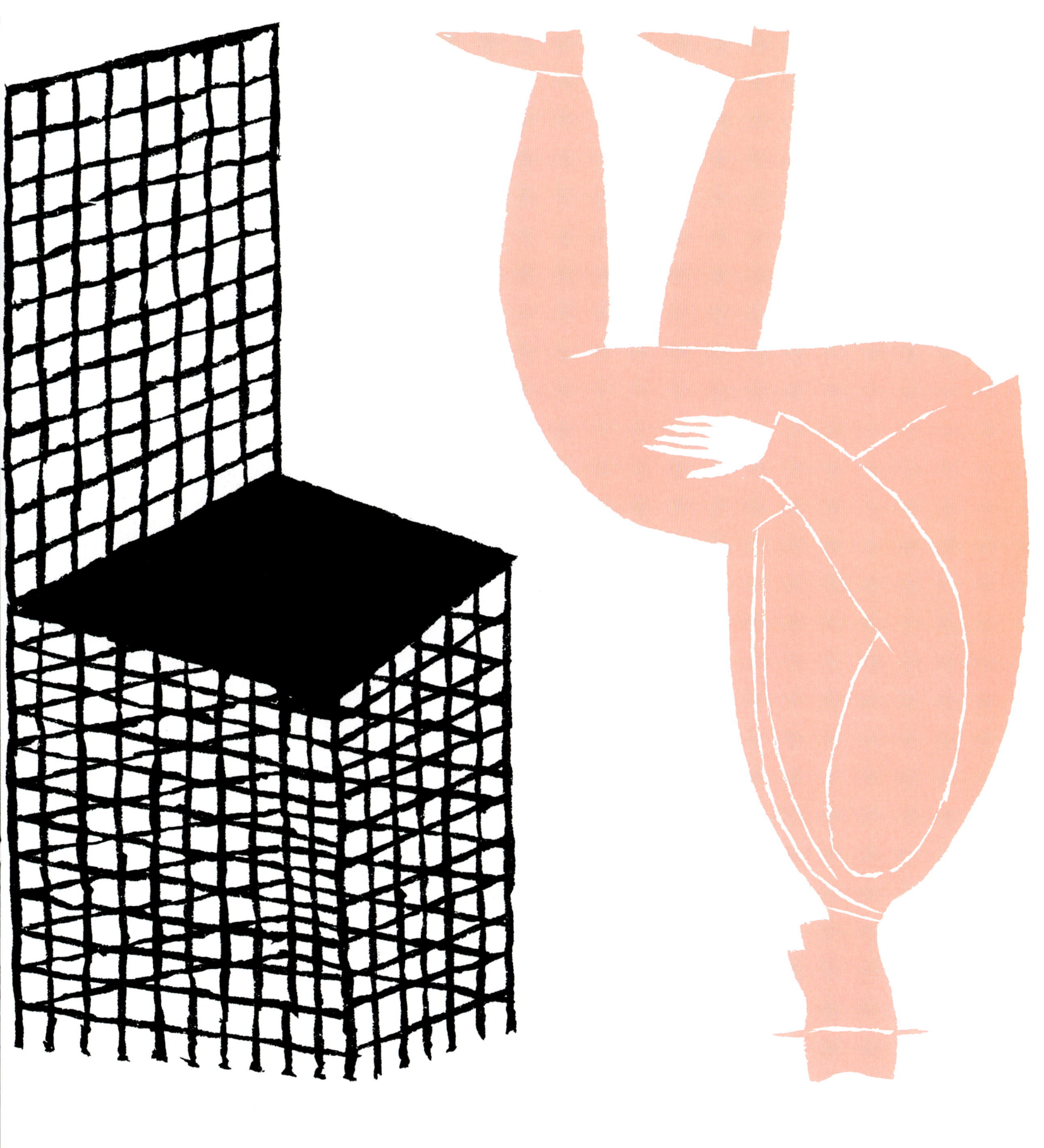

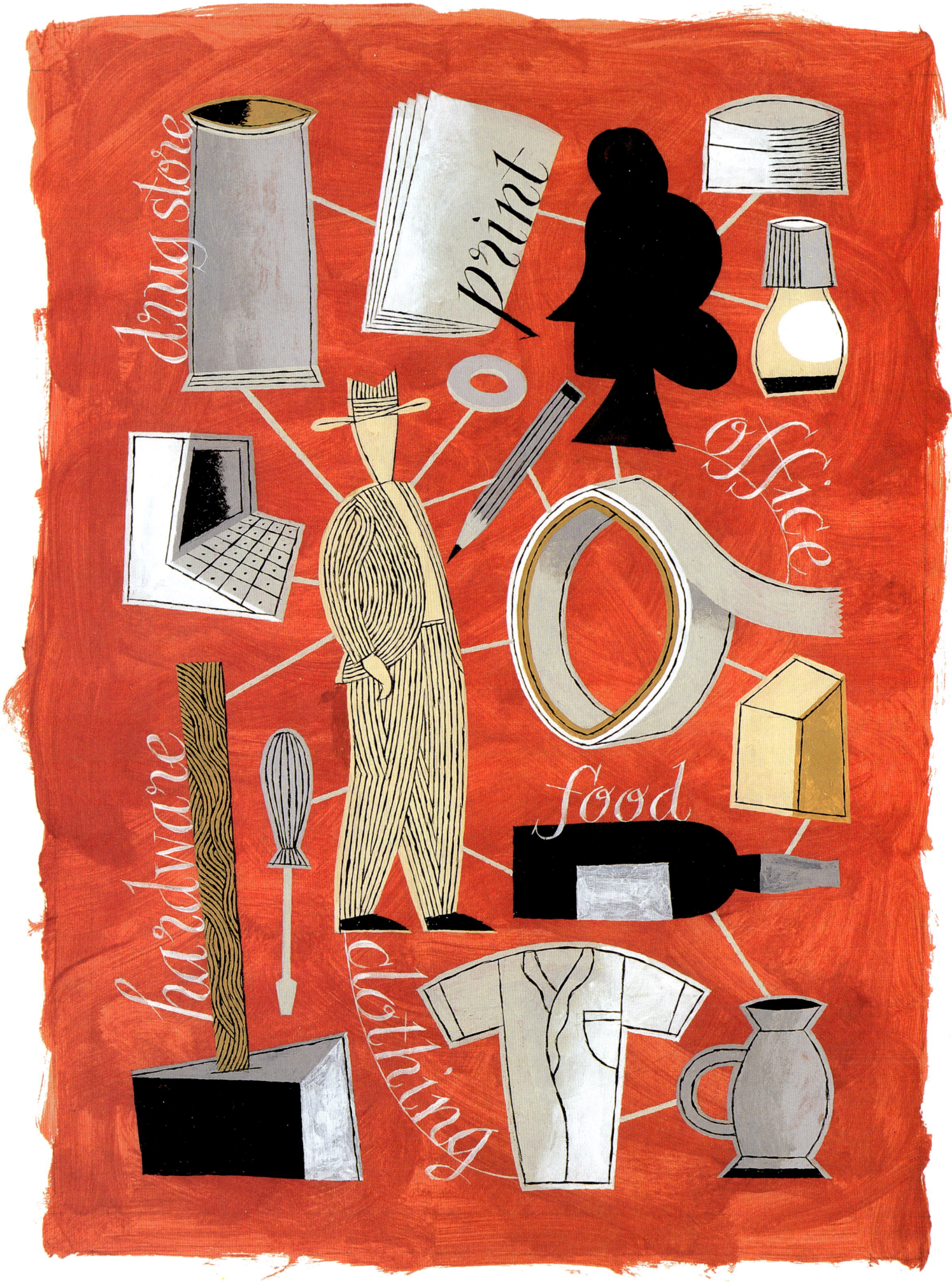

drug store

print

office

food

hardware

clothing

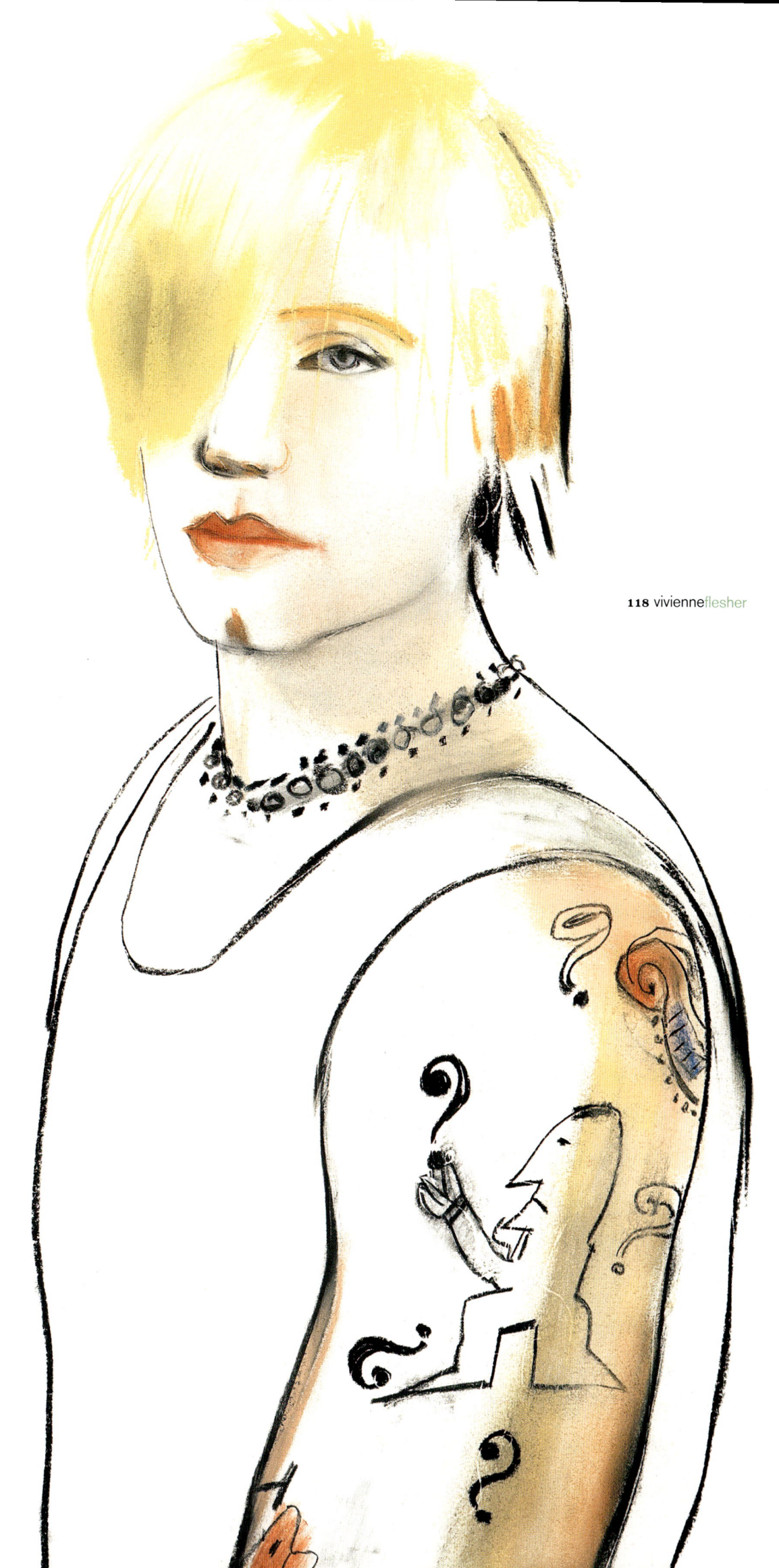

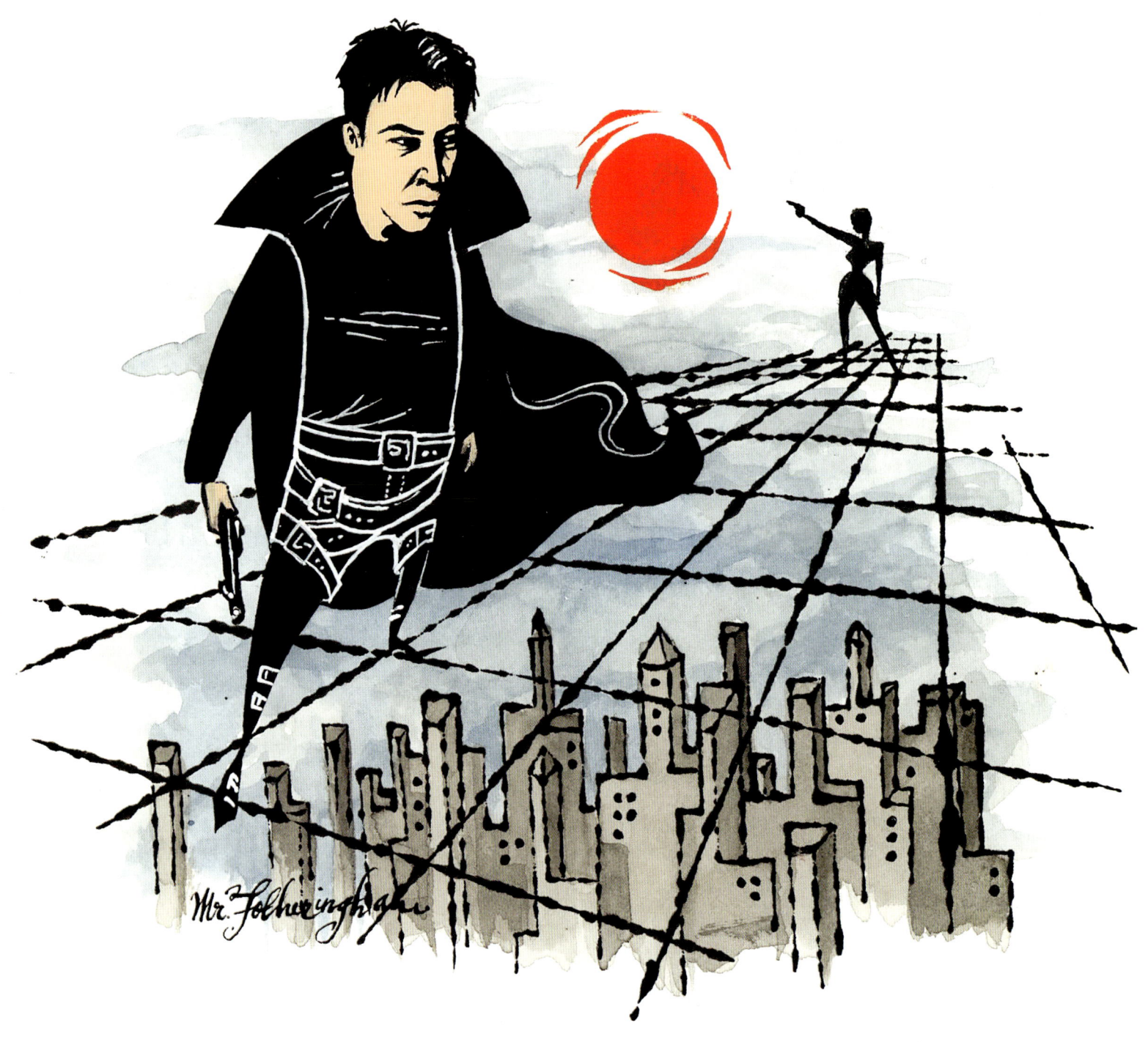

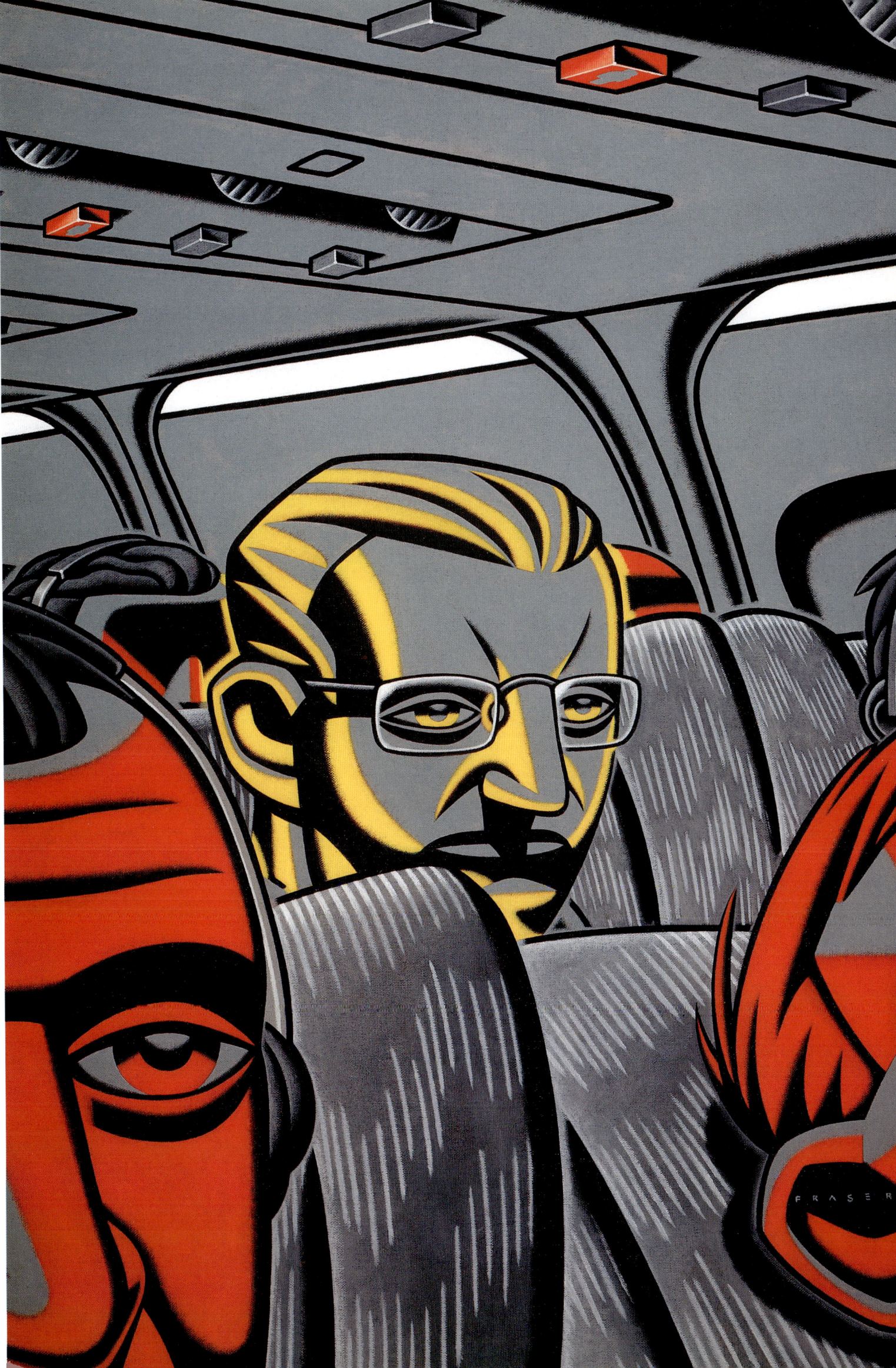

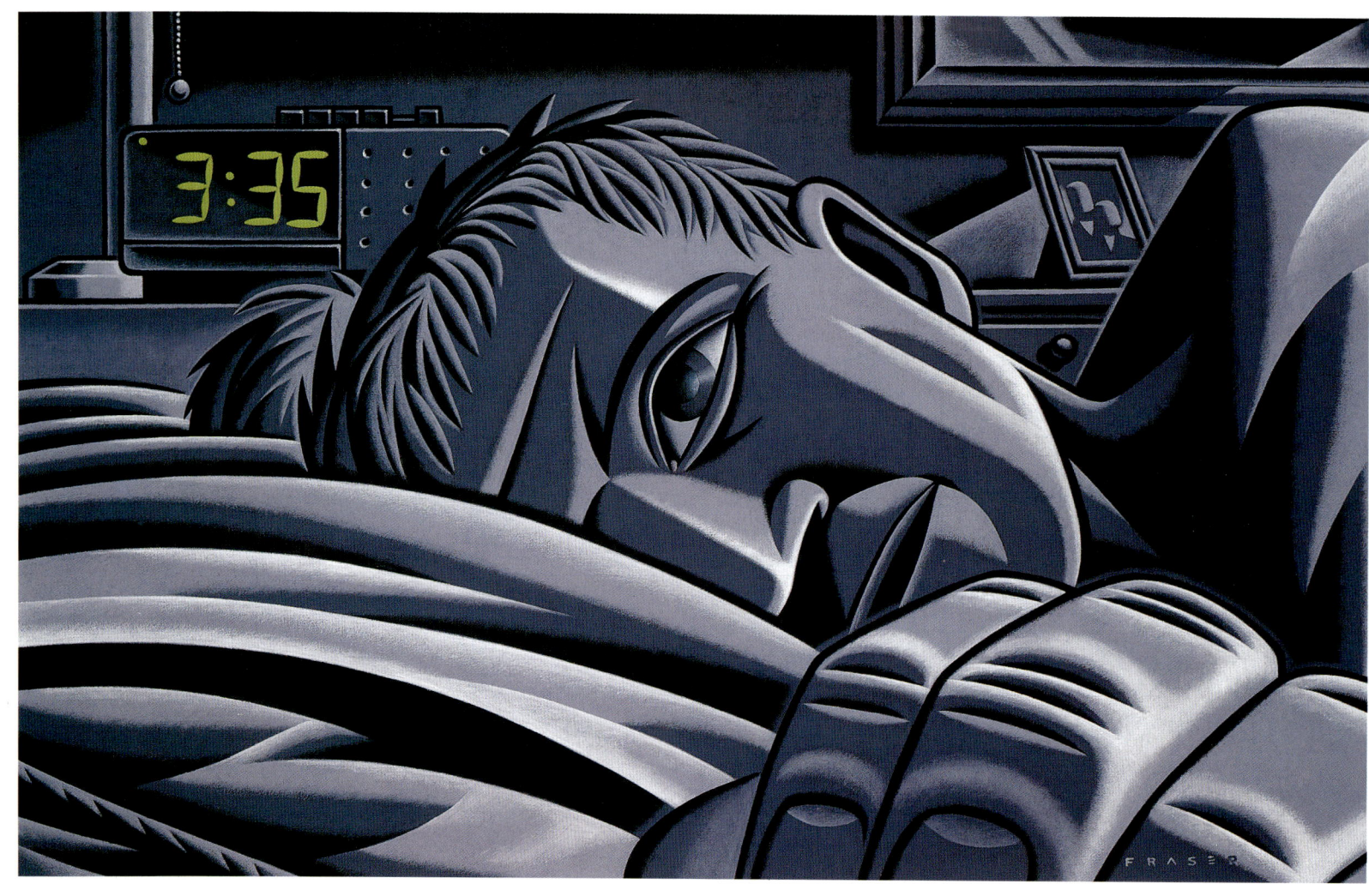

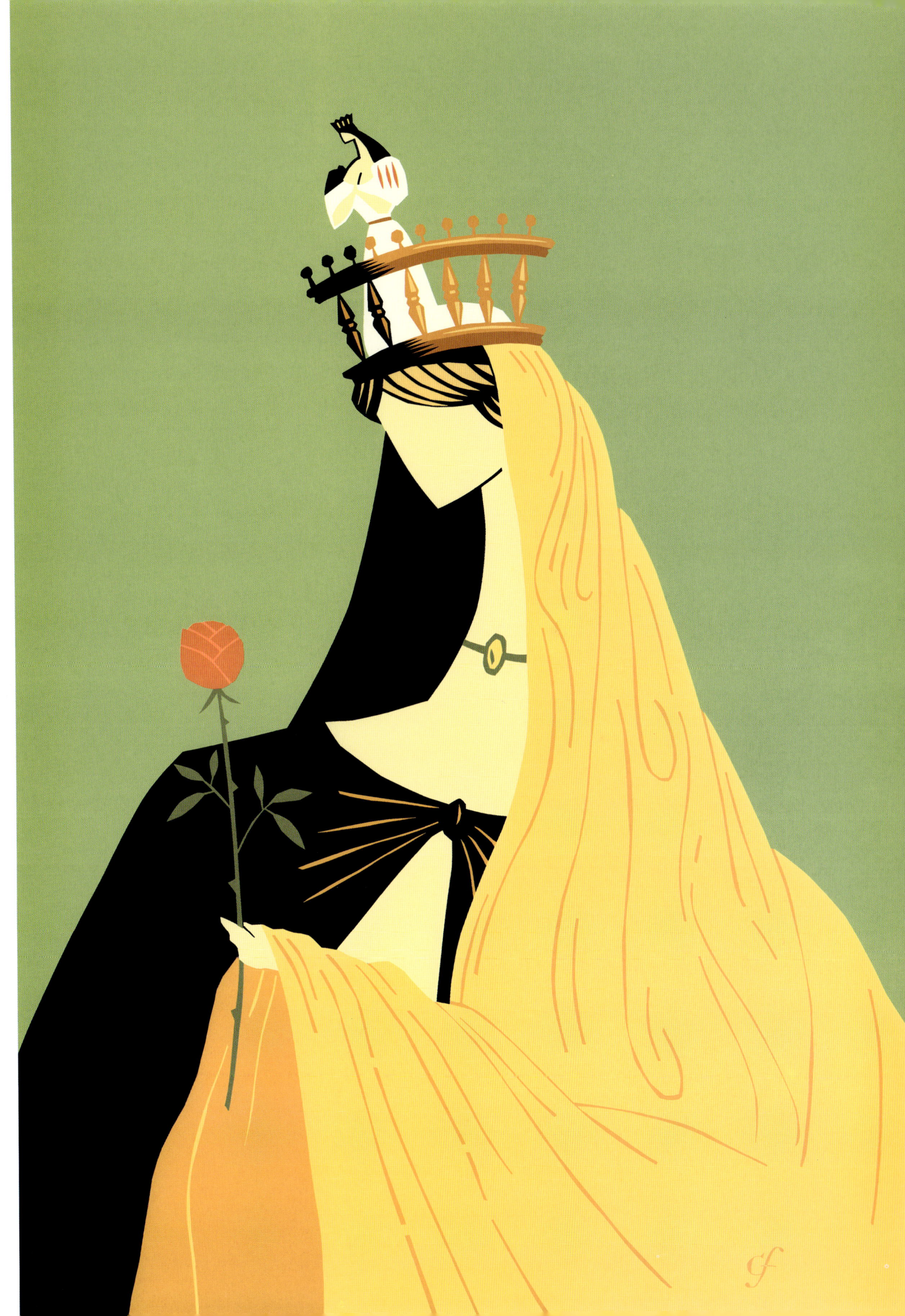

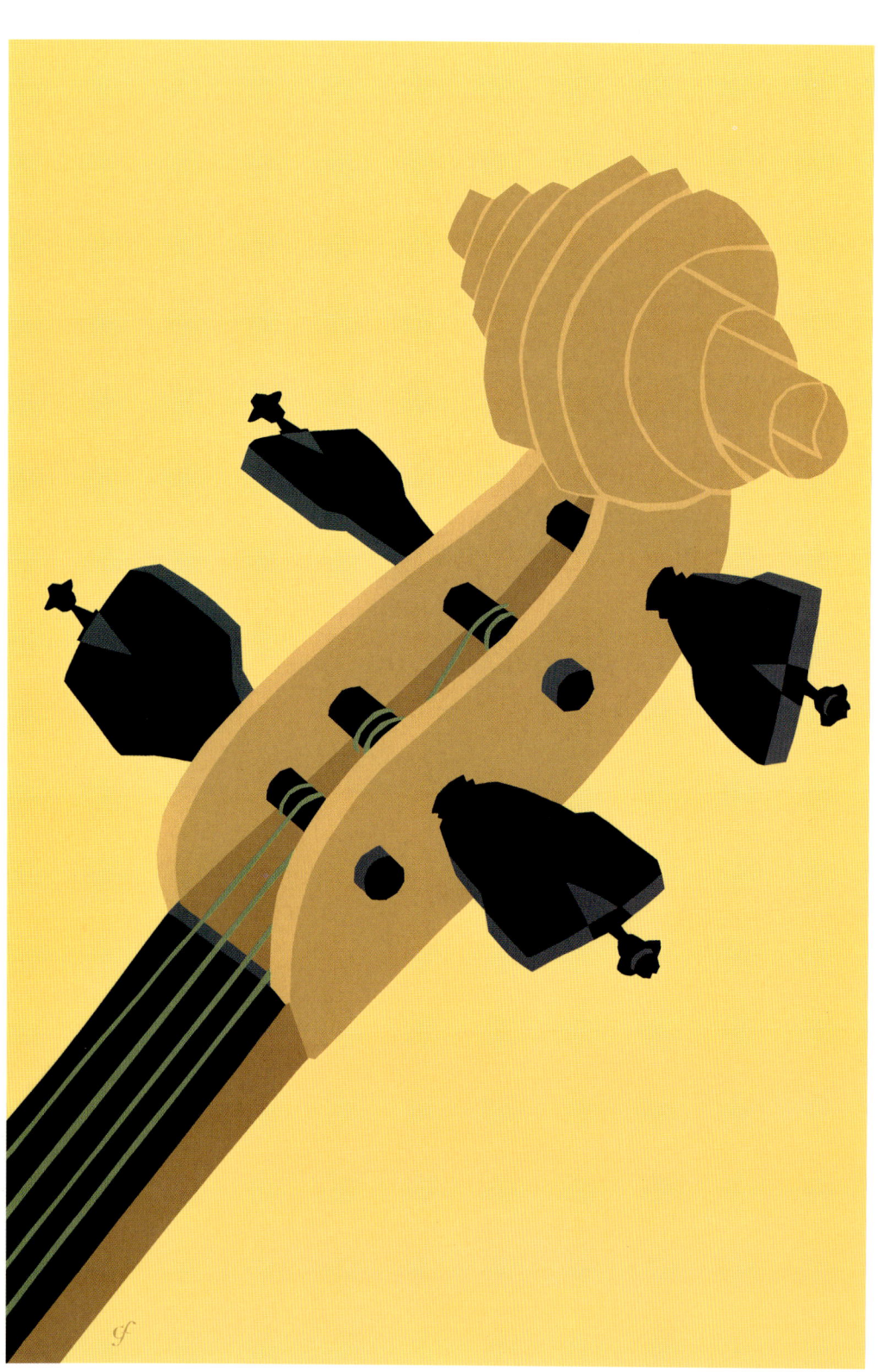

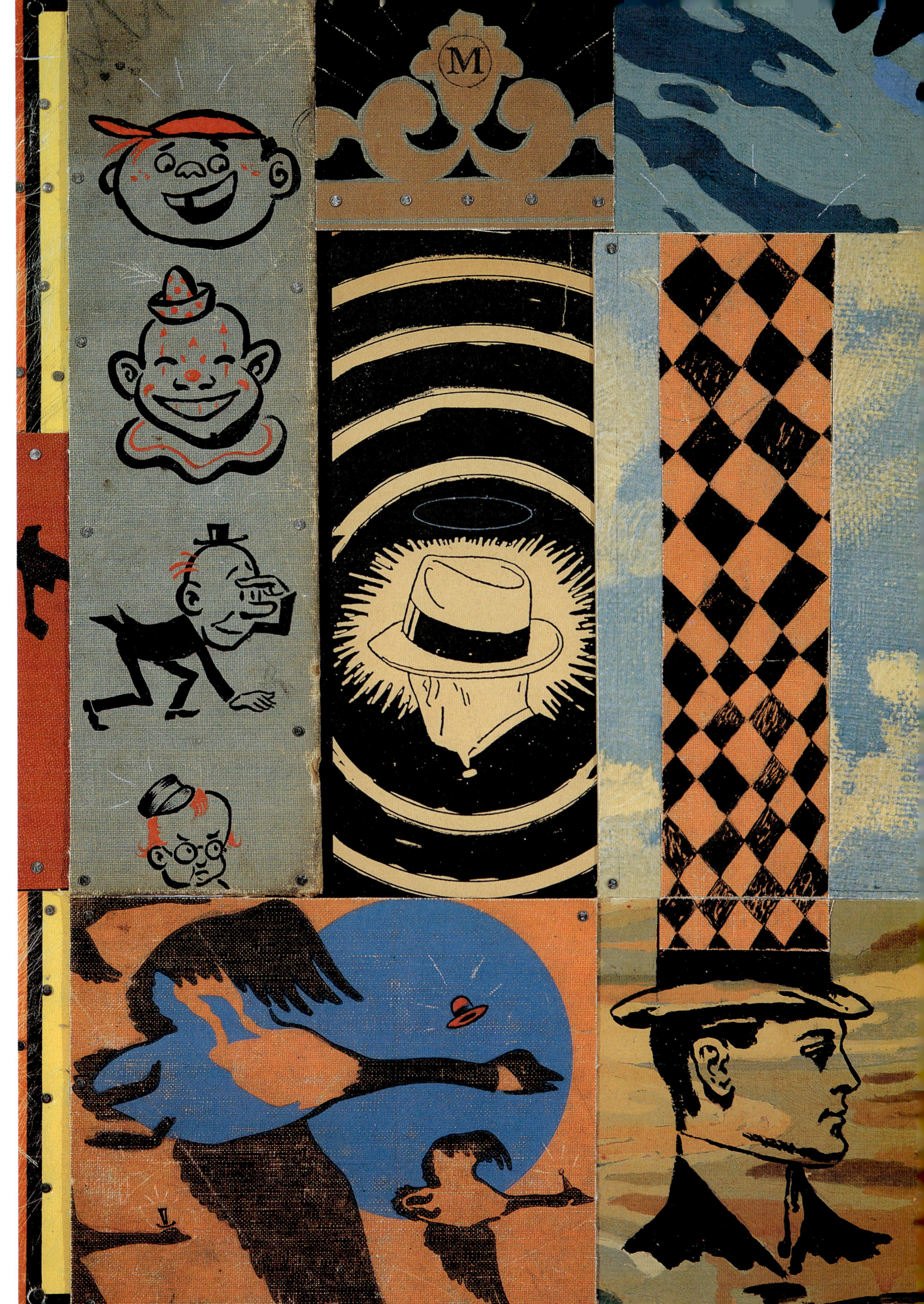

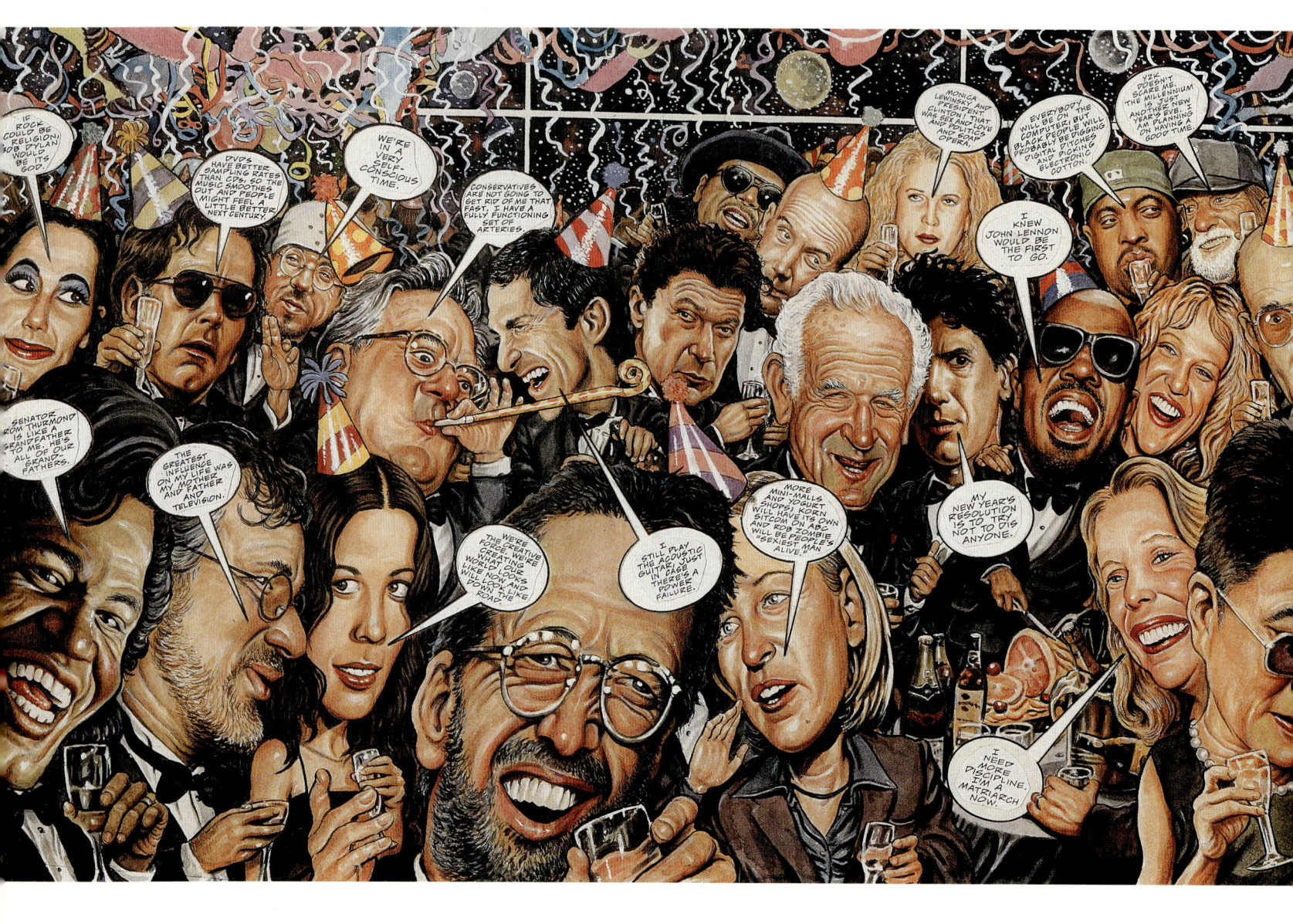

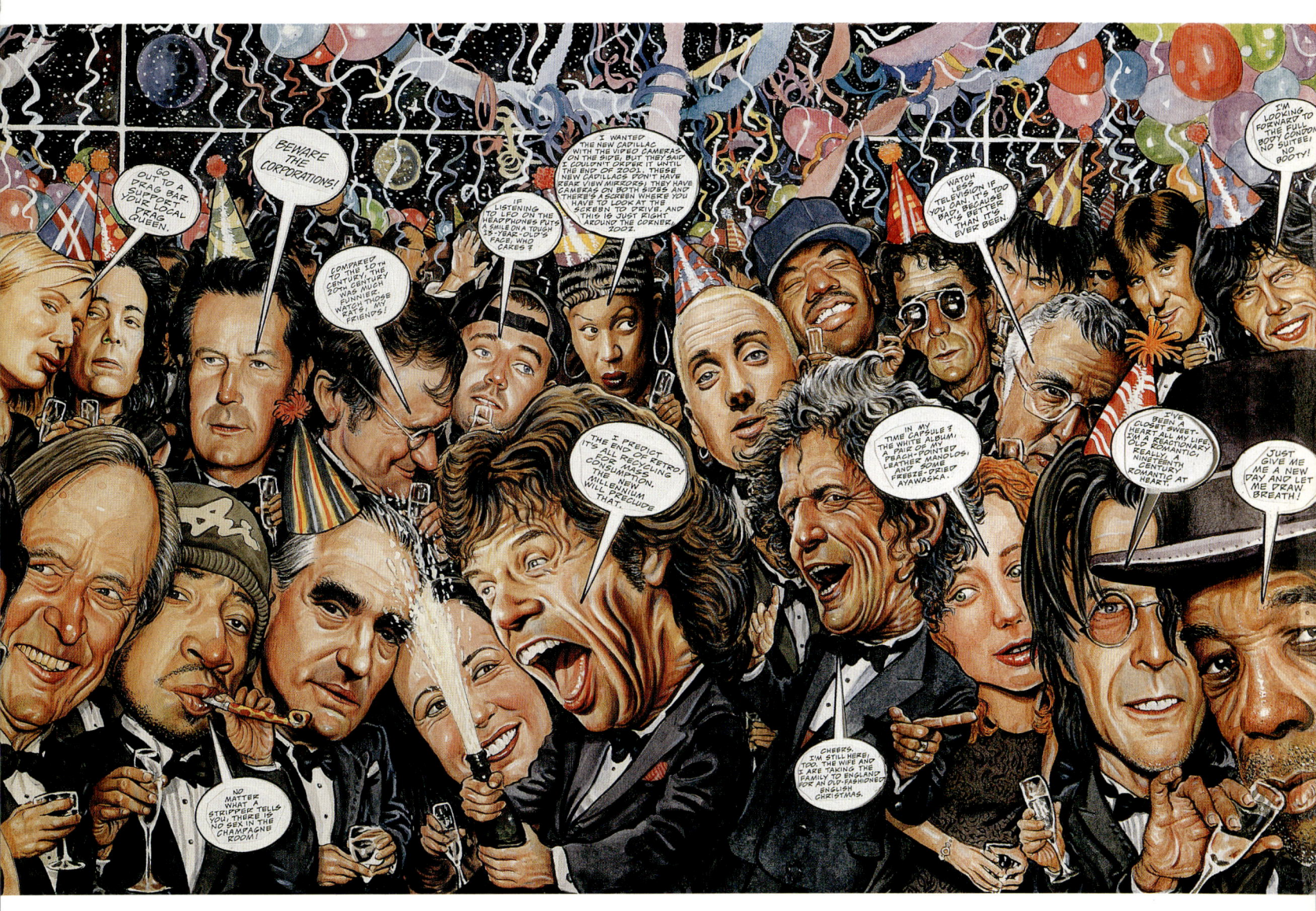

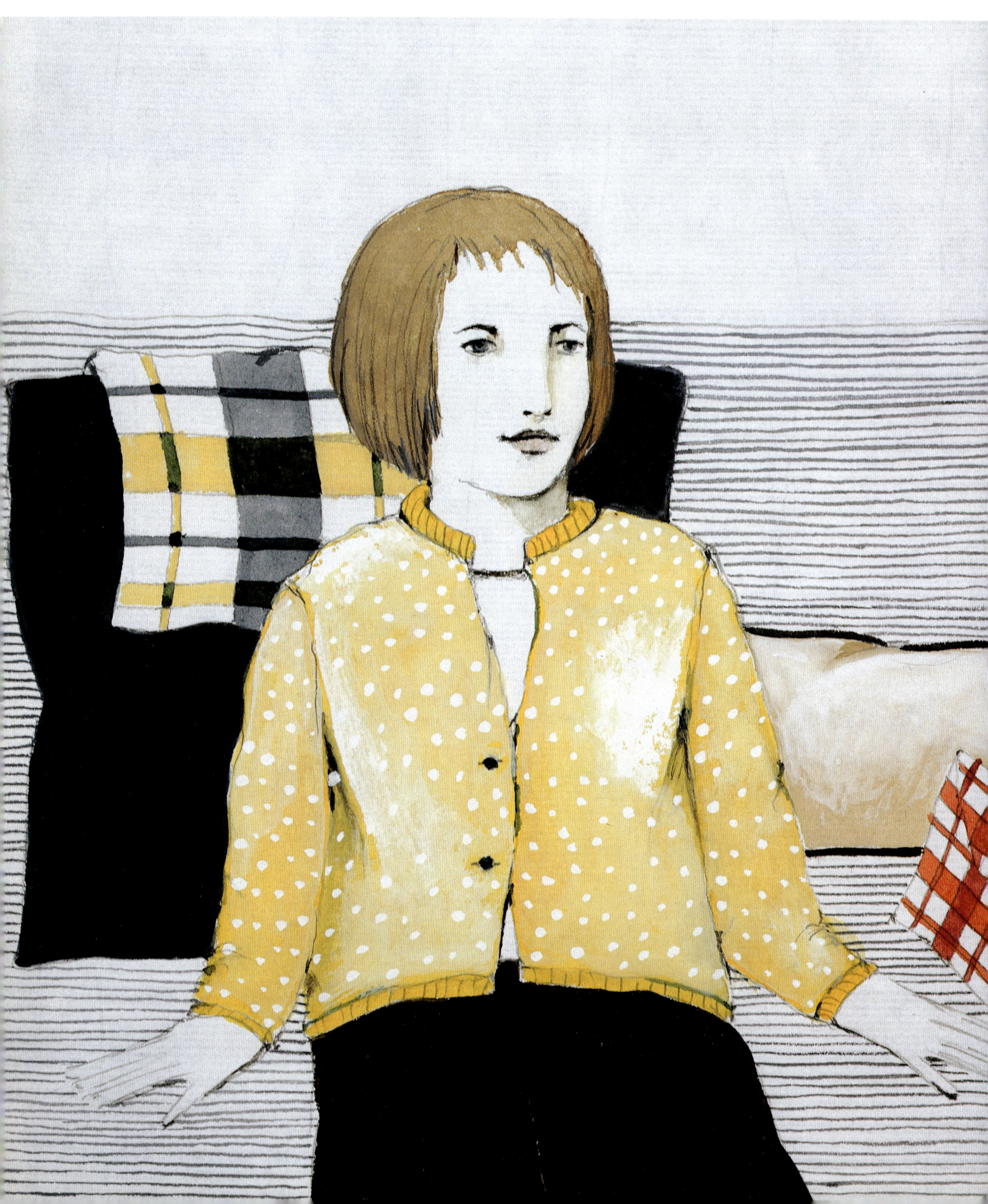

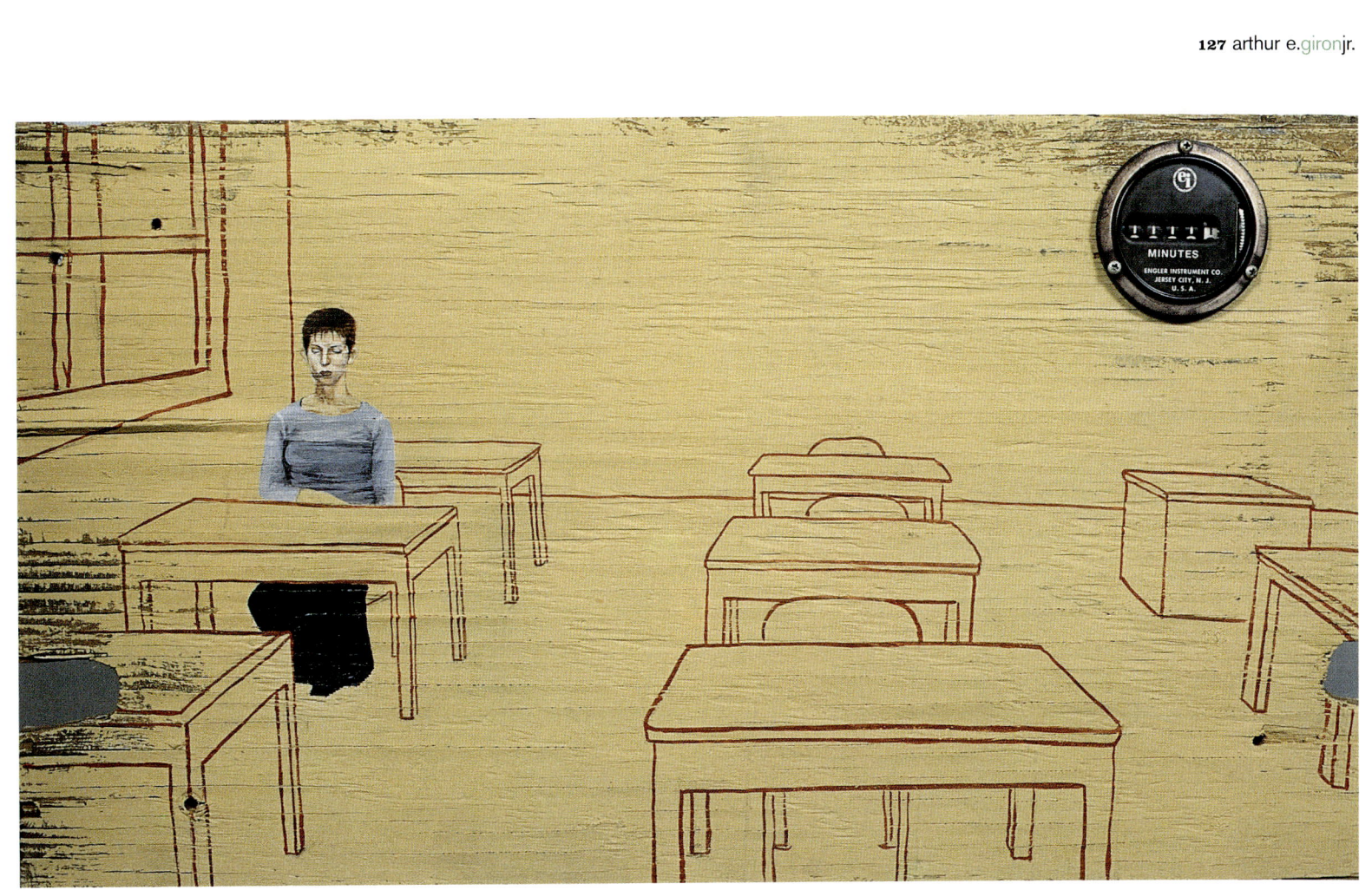

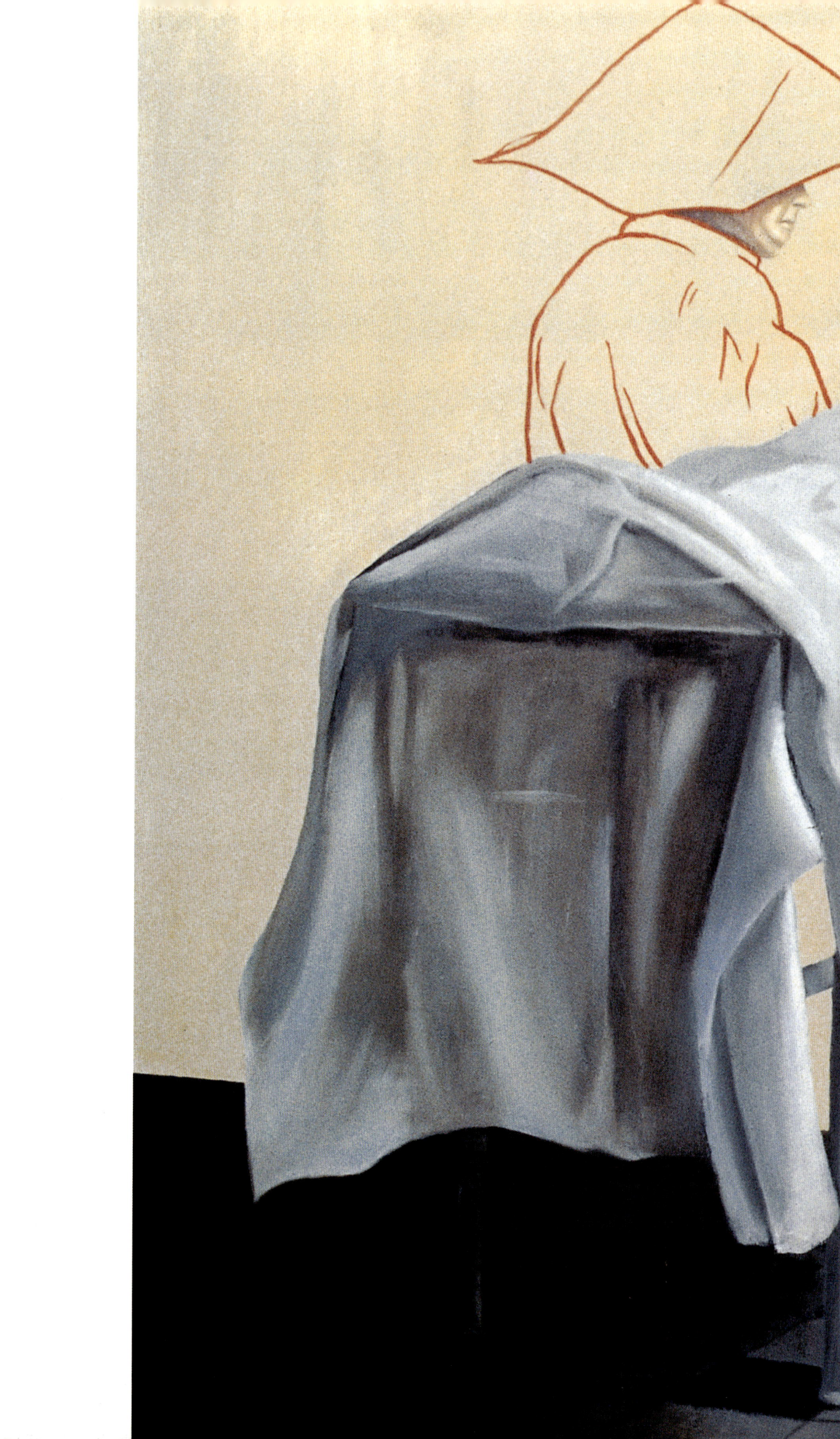

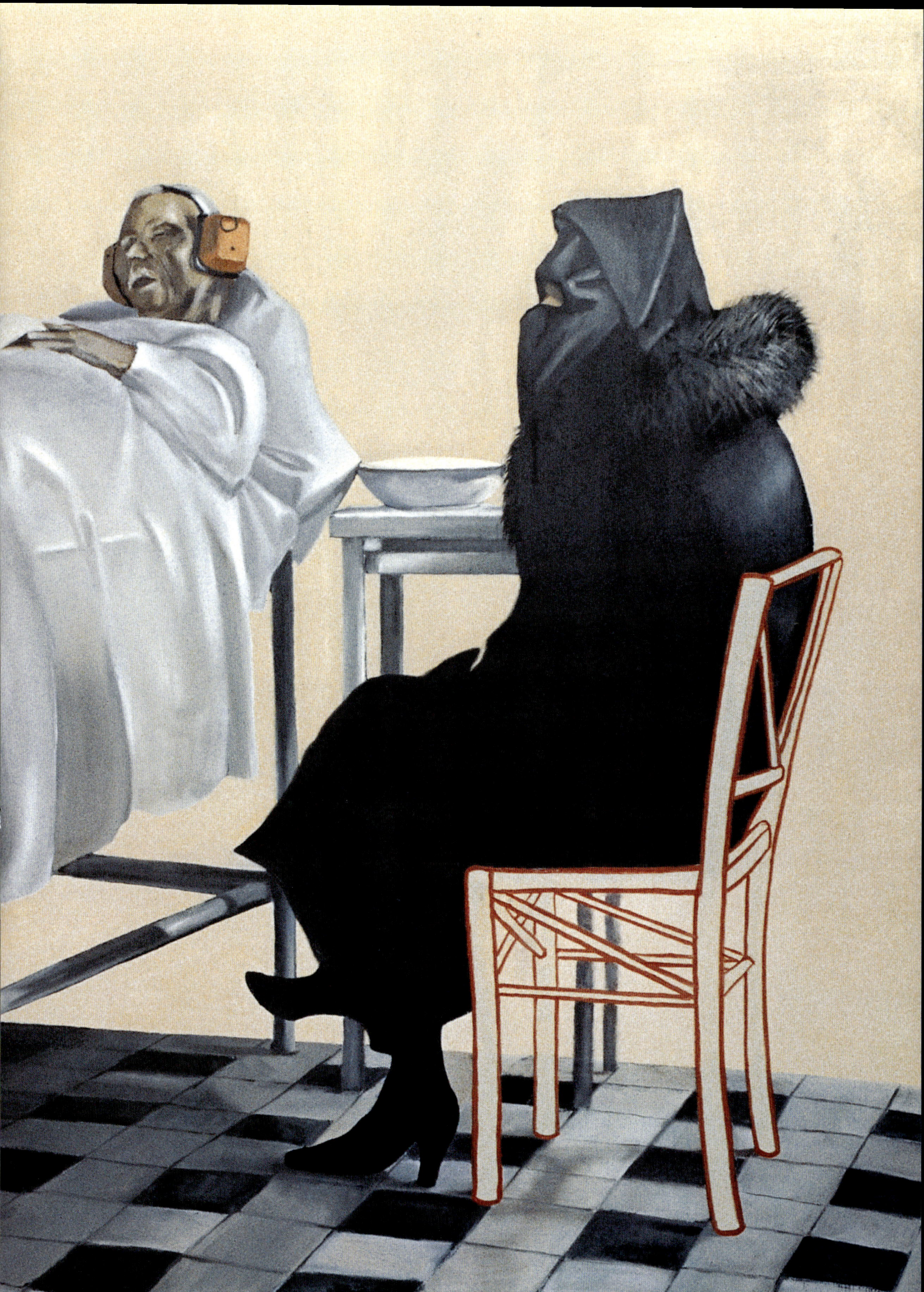

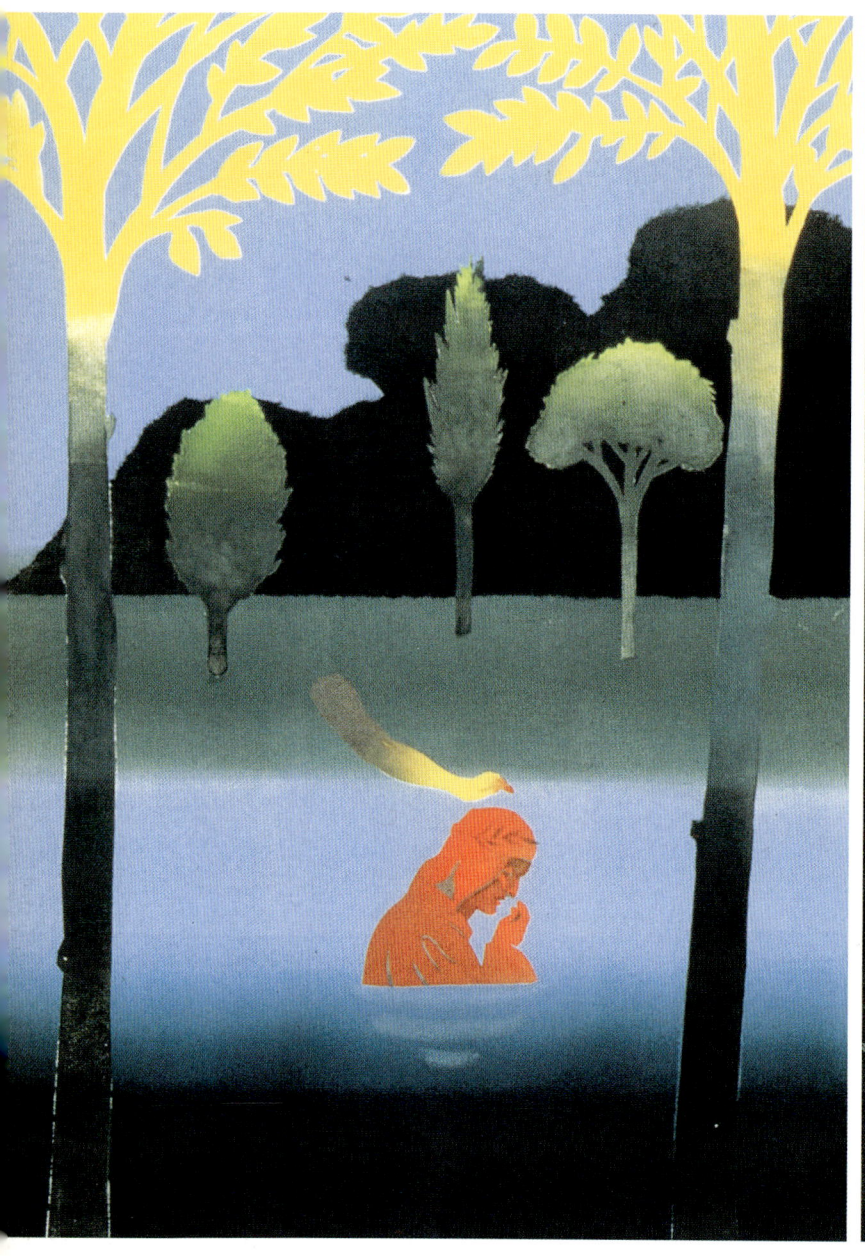

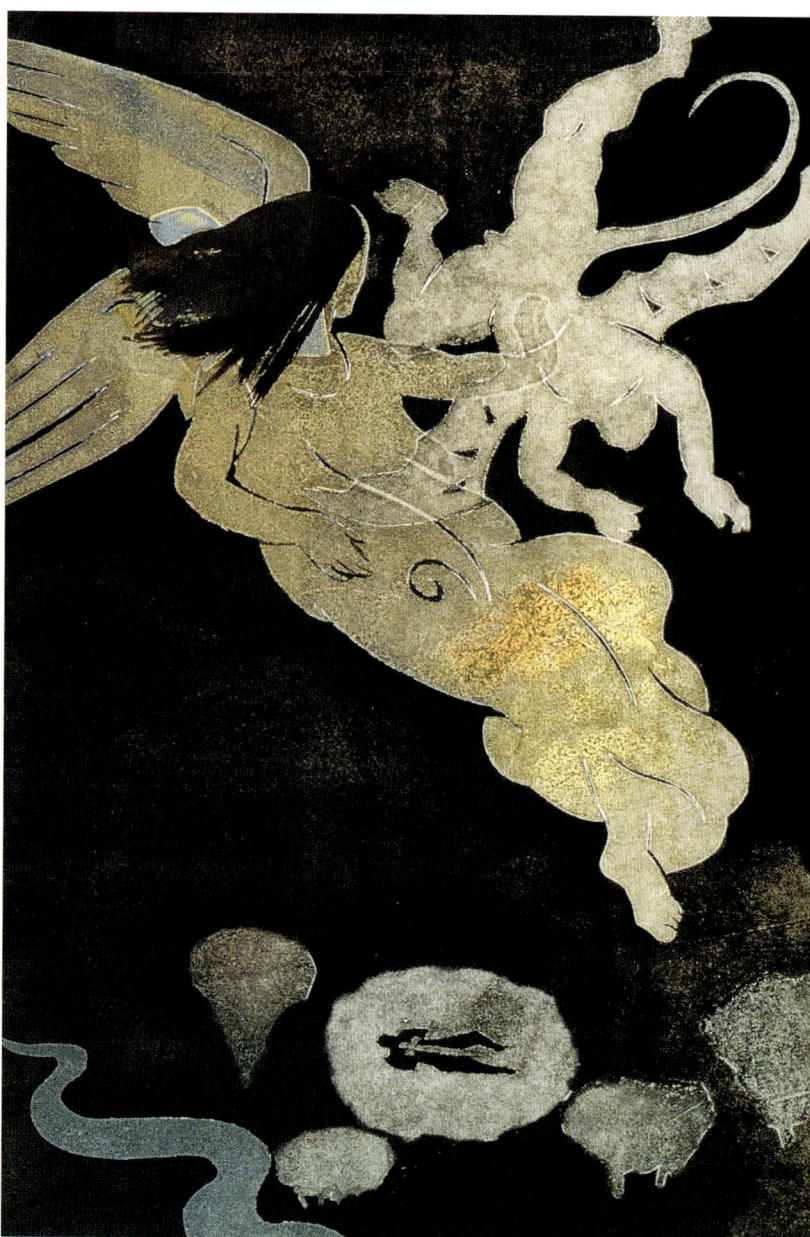

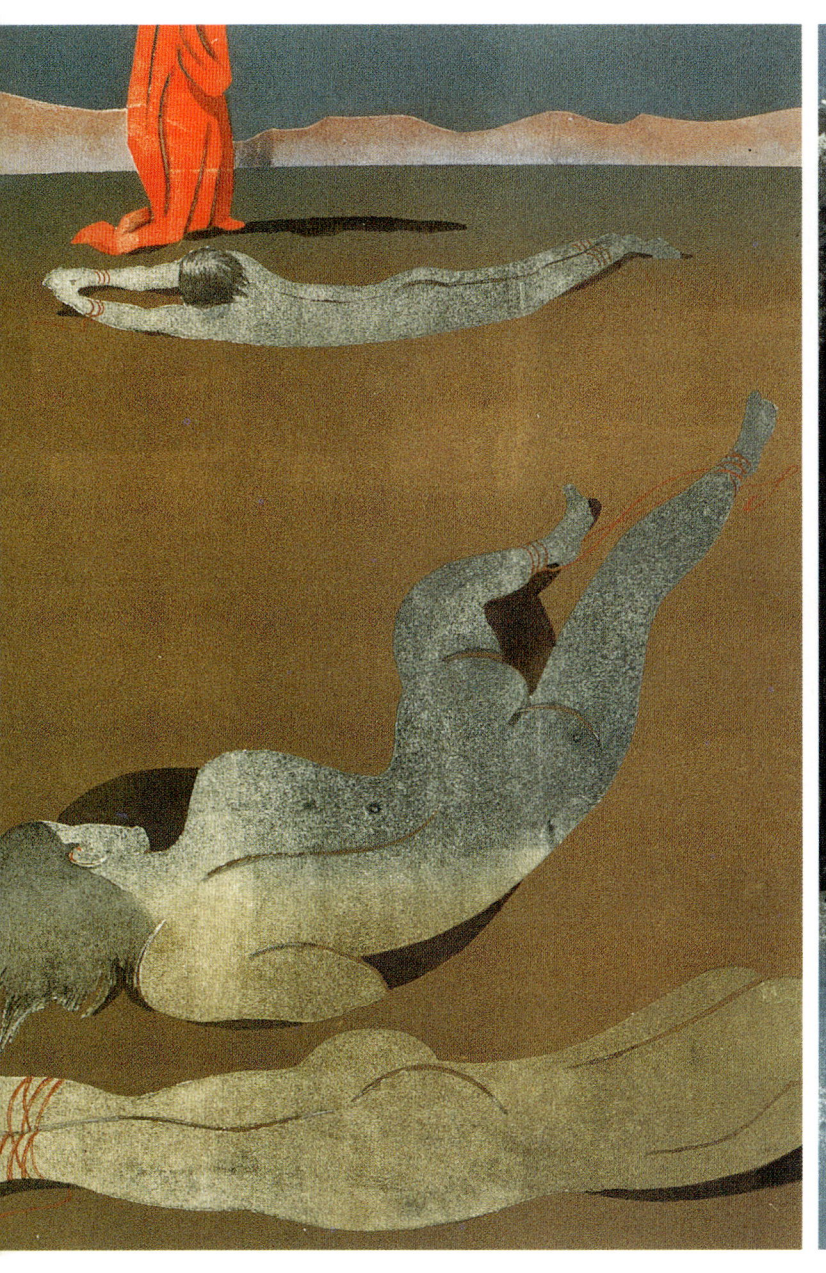
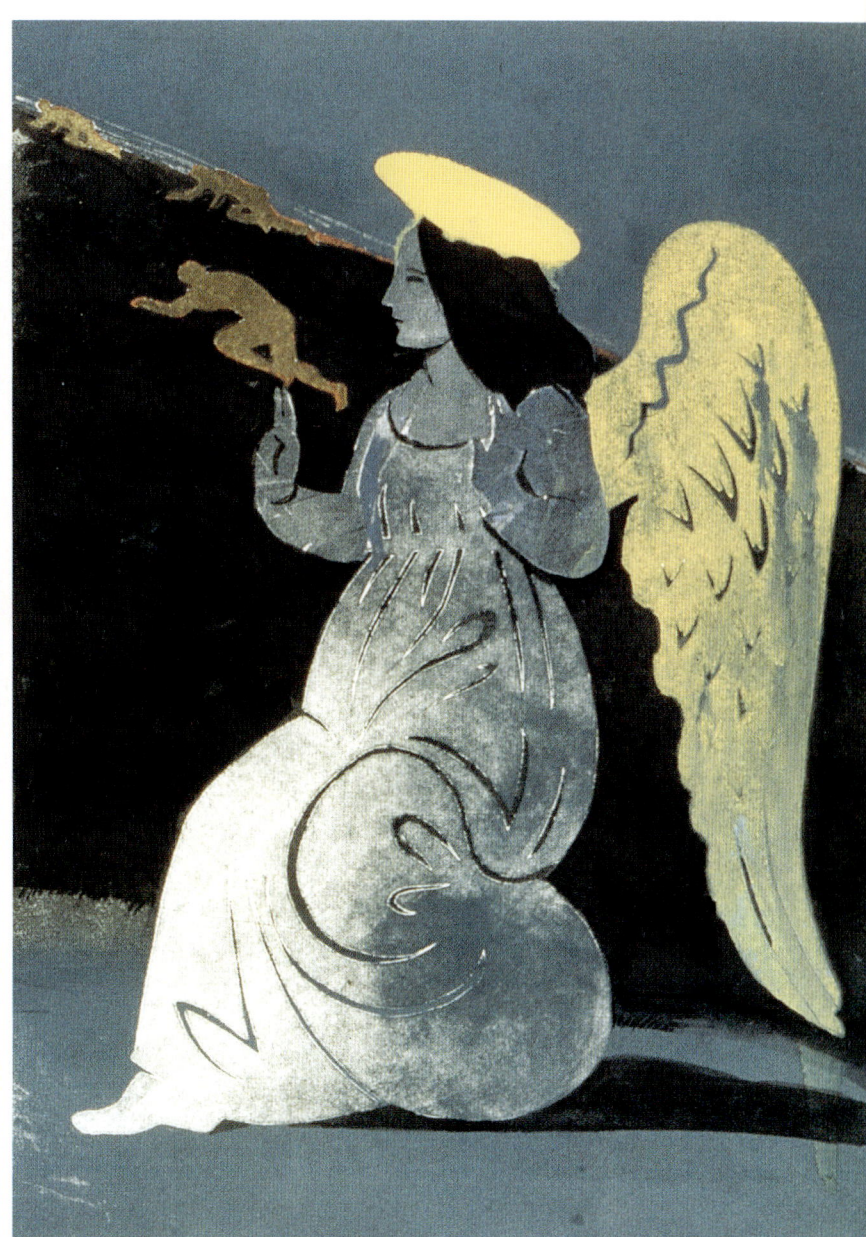

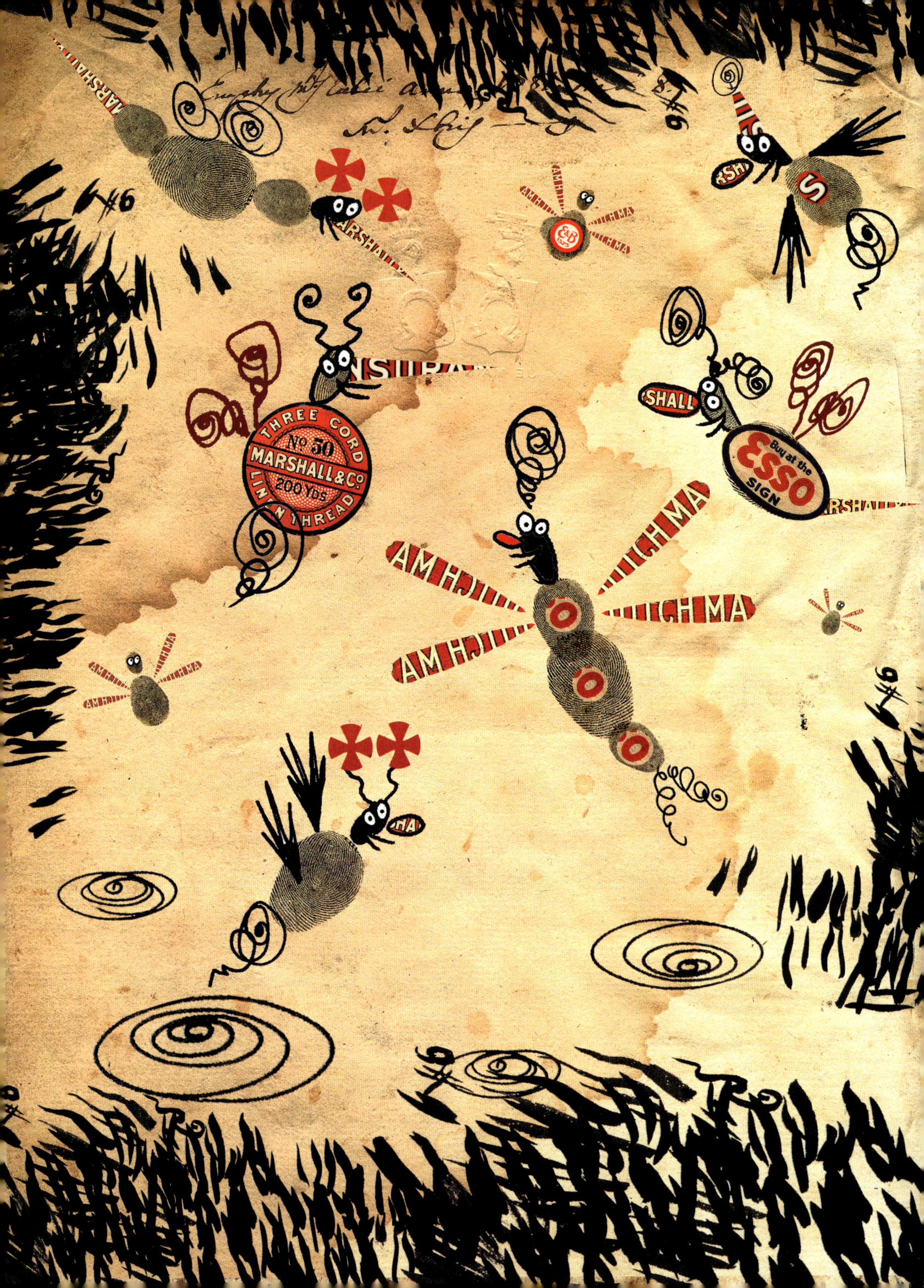

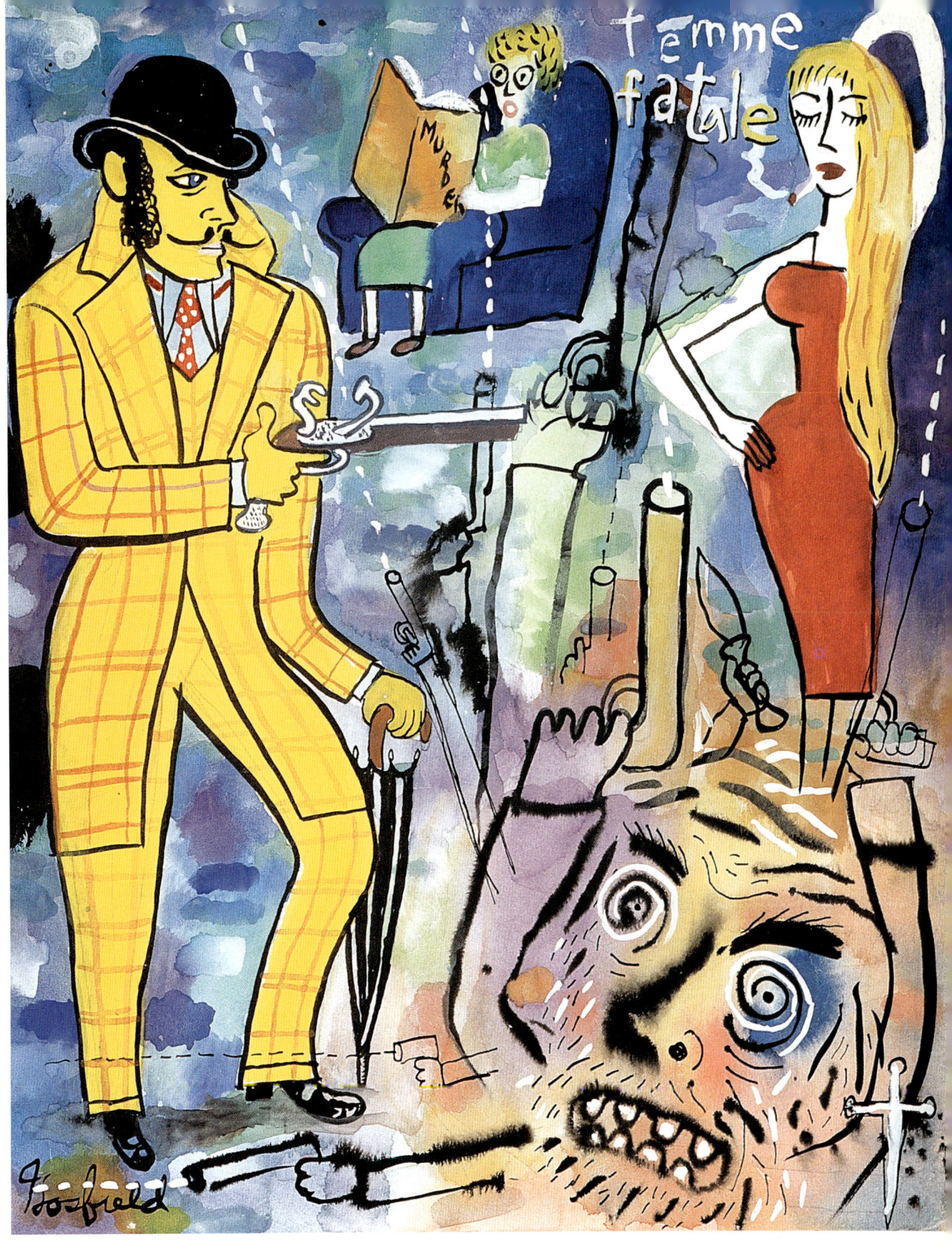

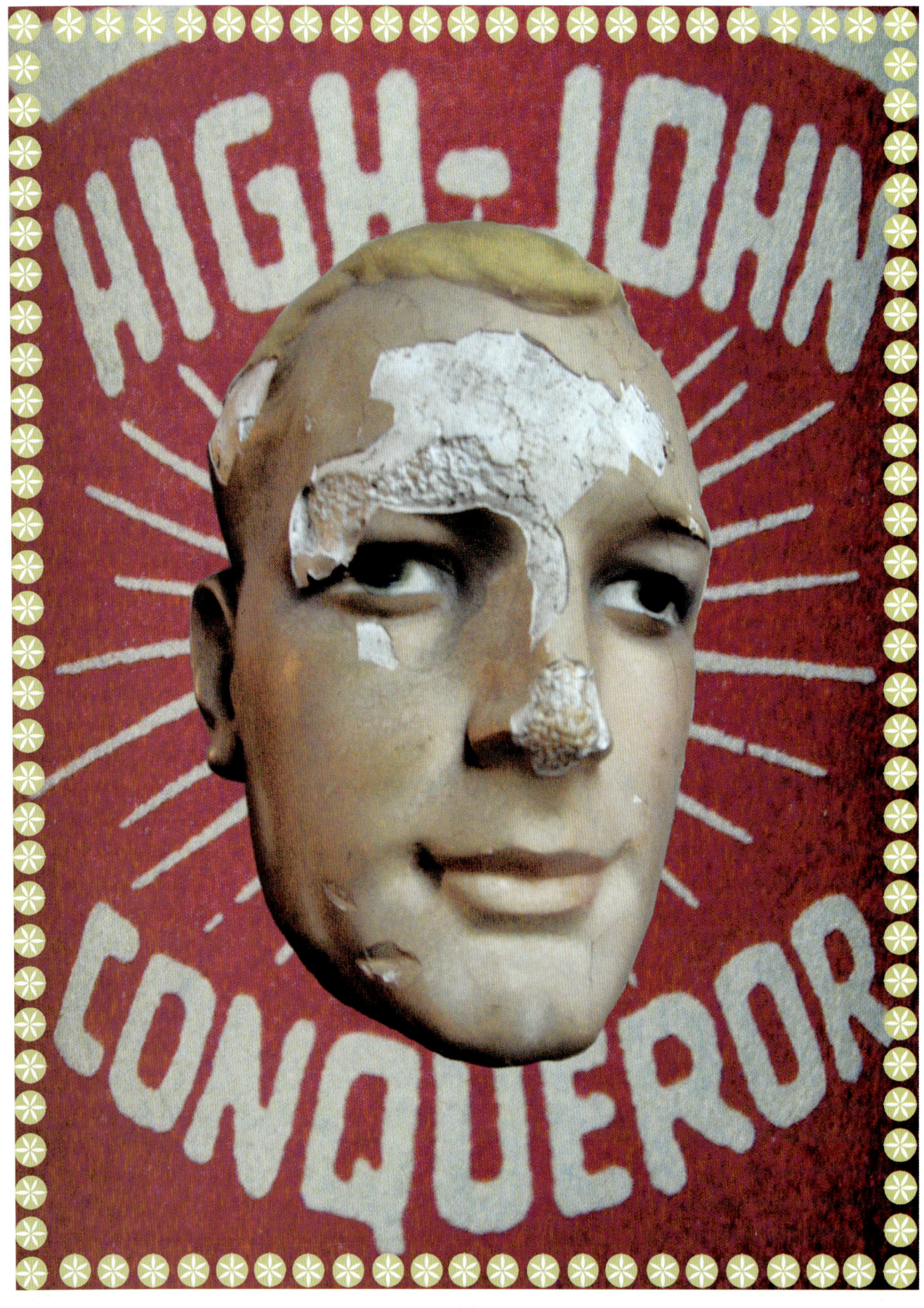

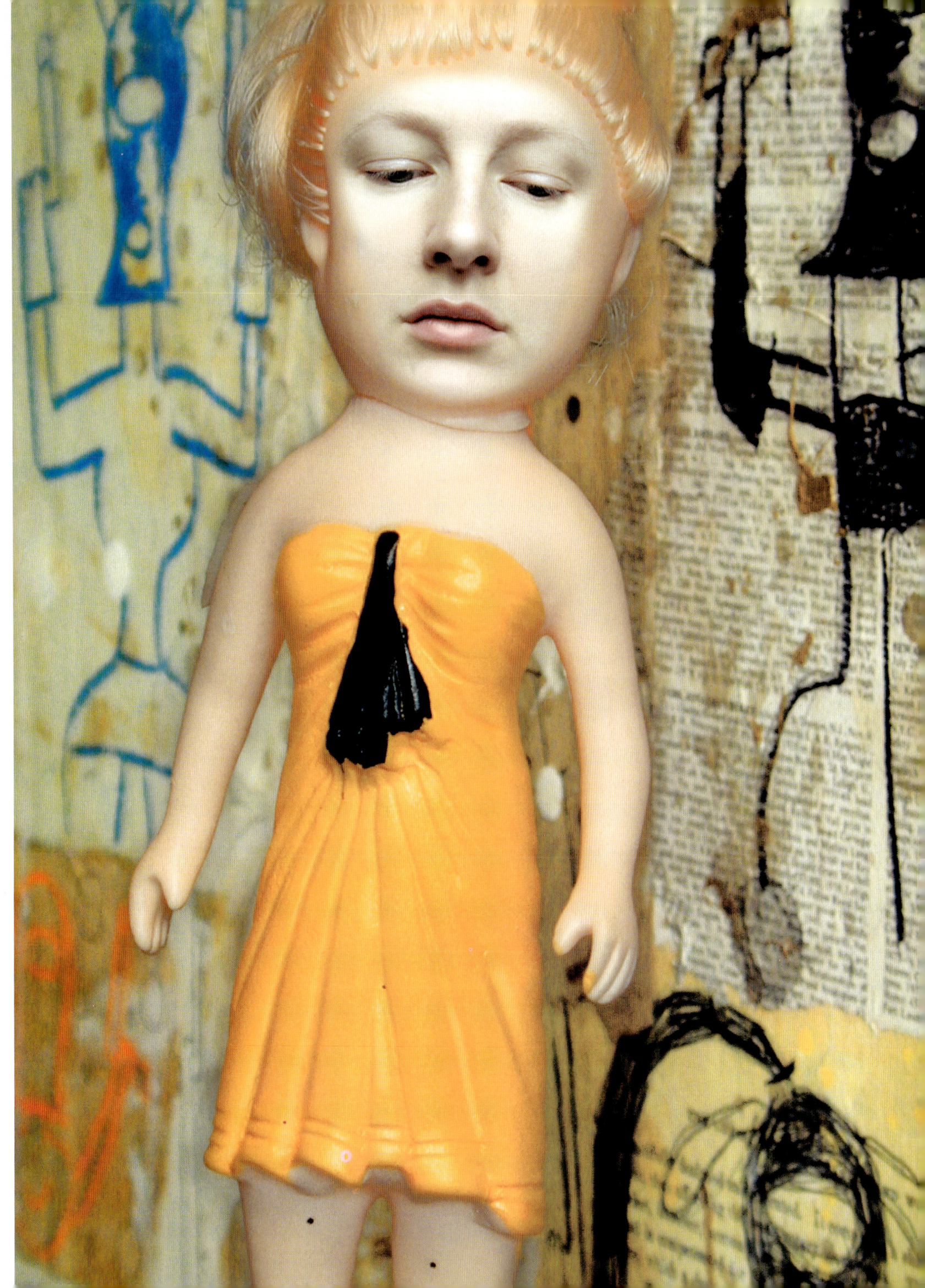

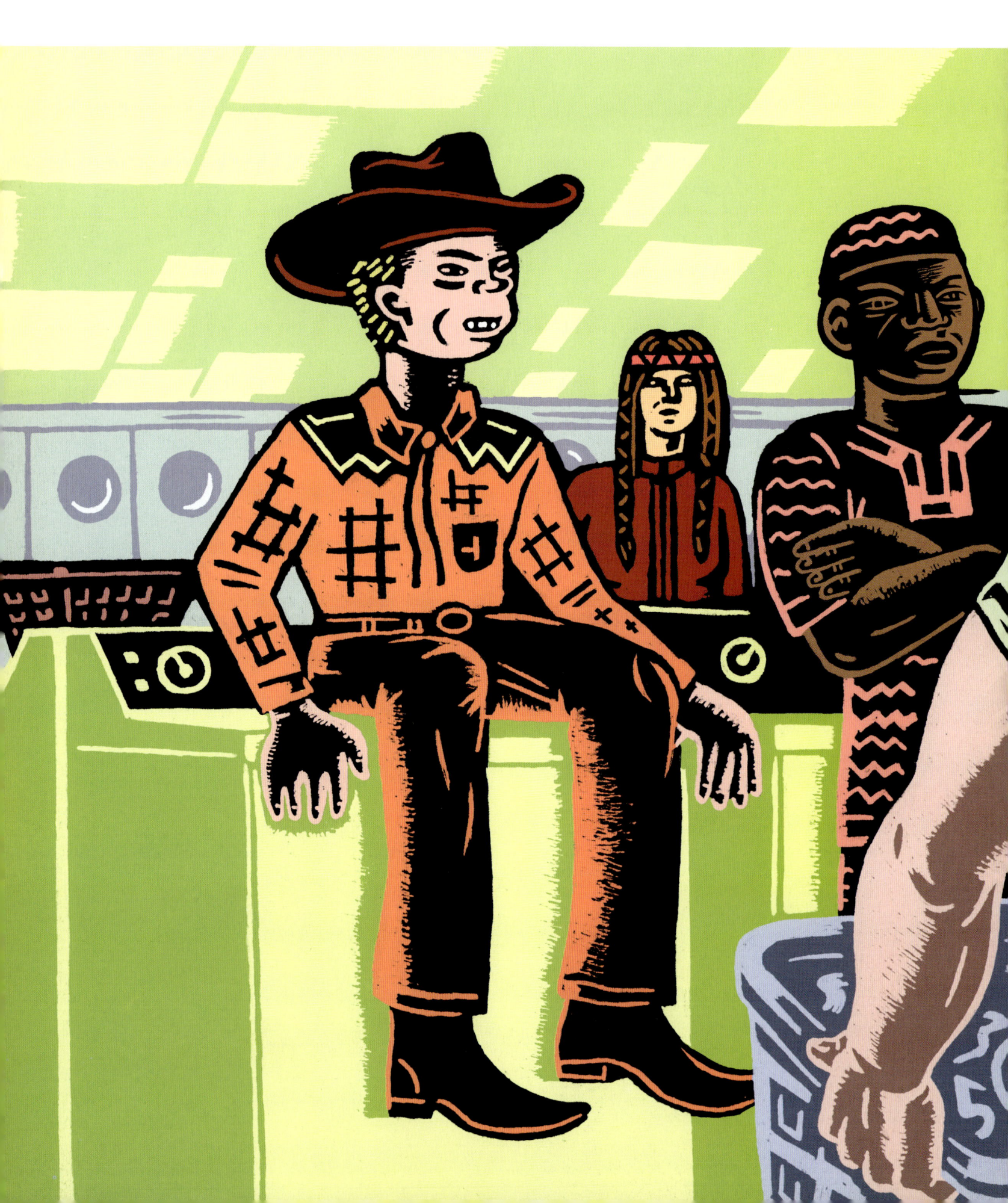

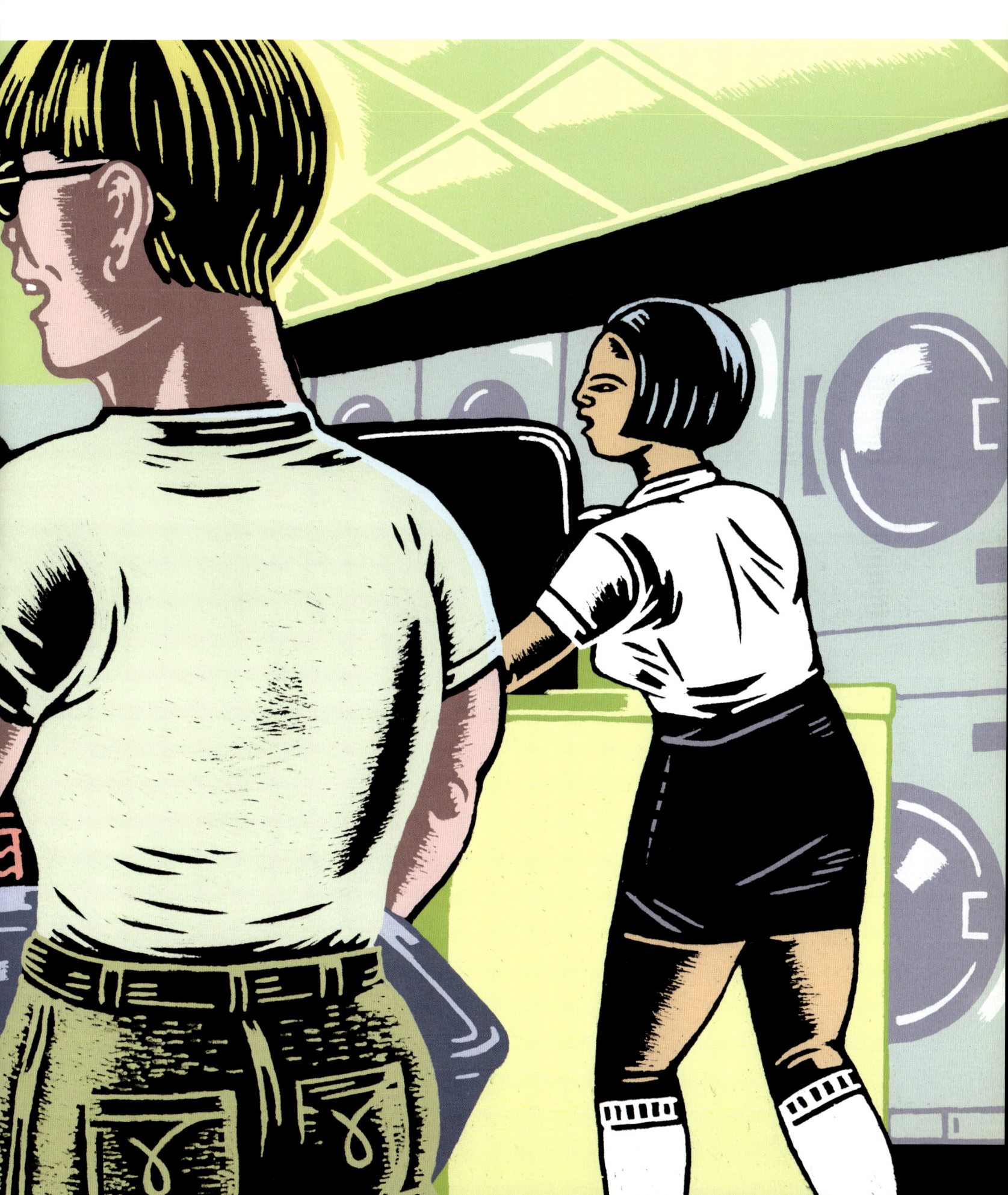

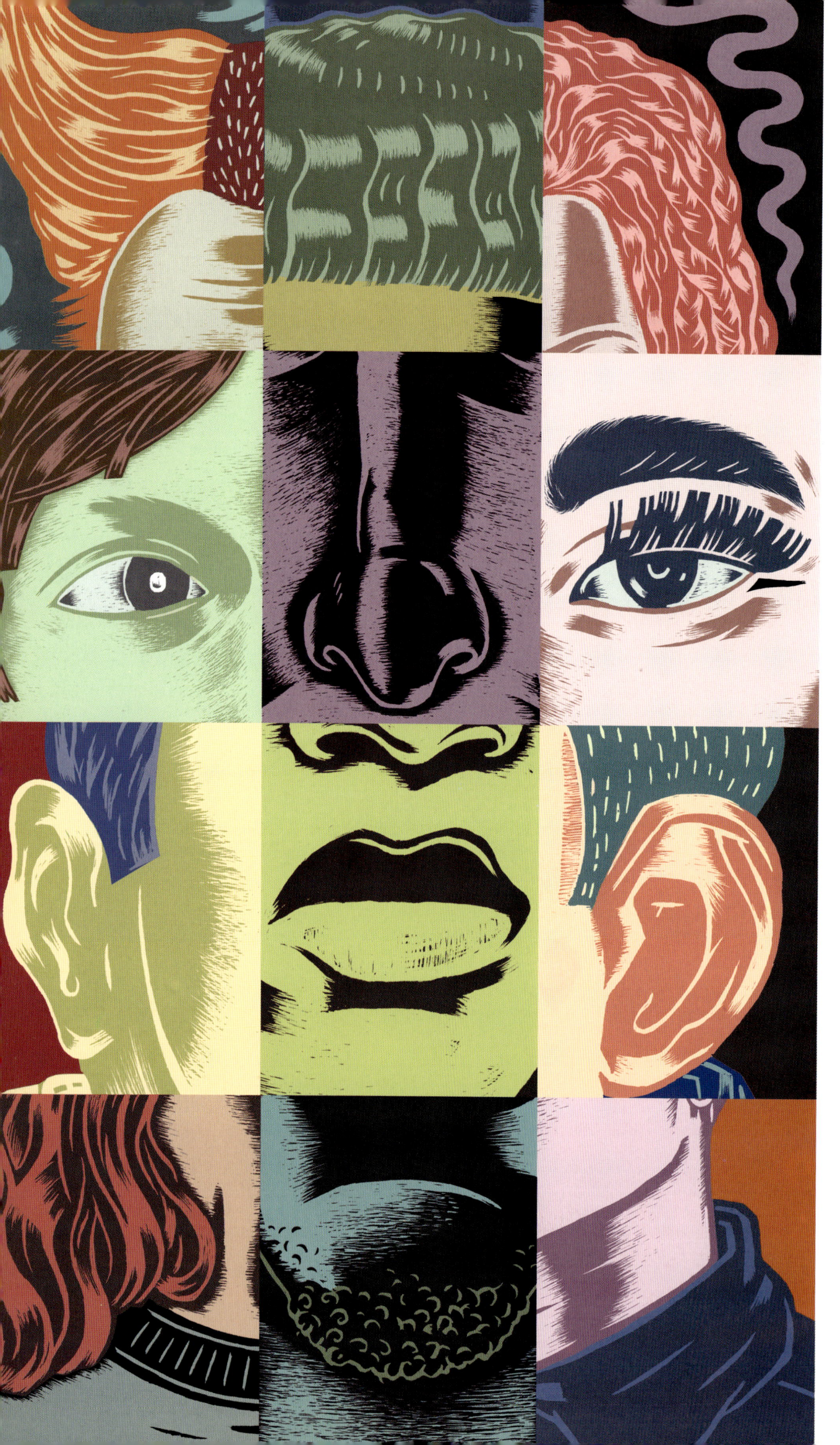

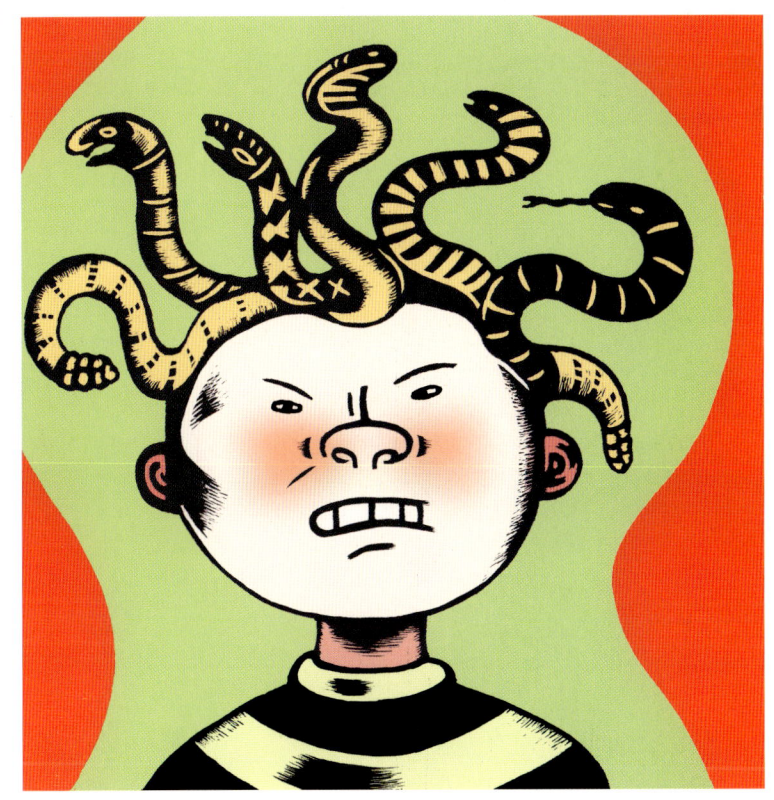
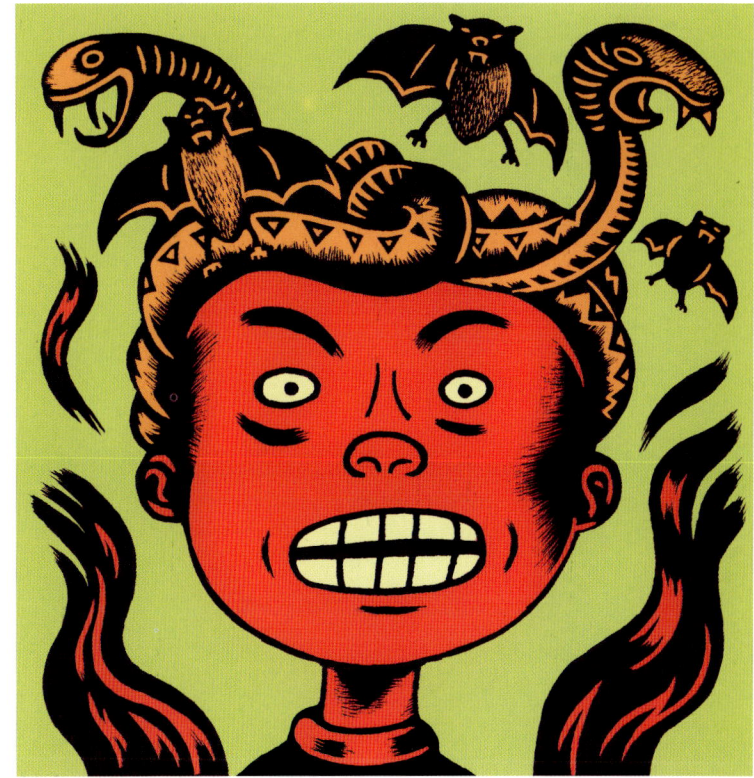
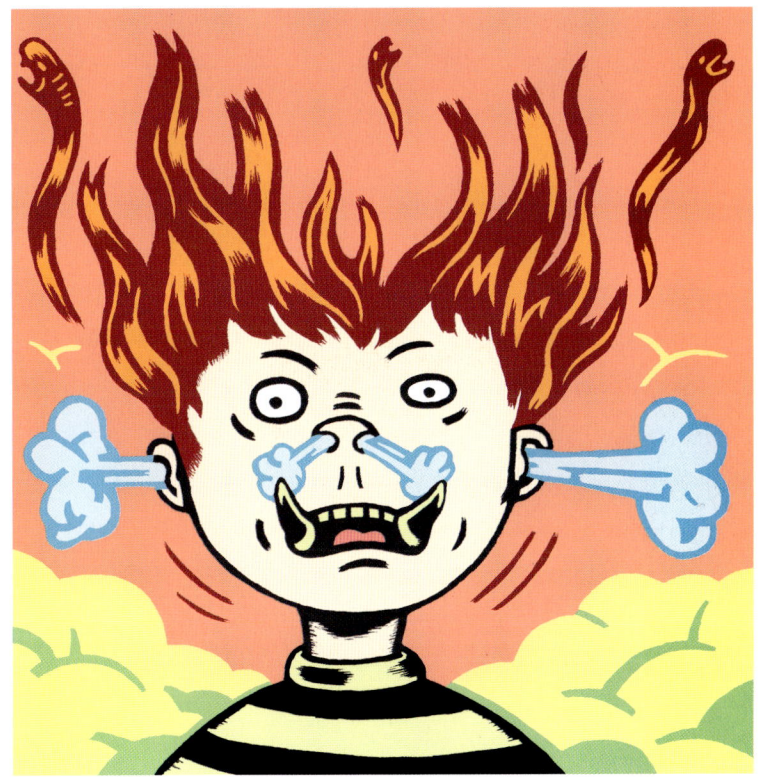
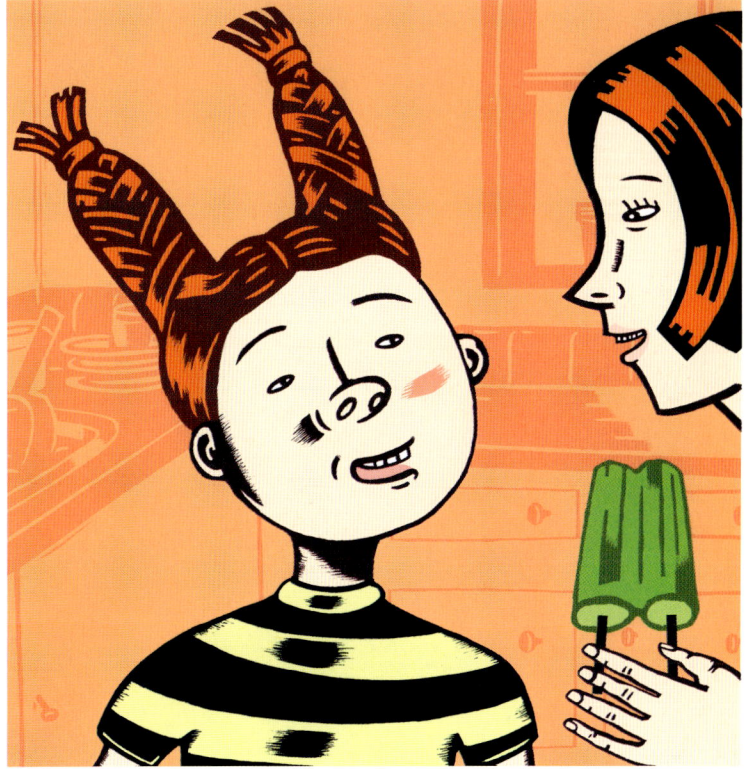

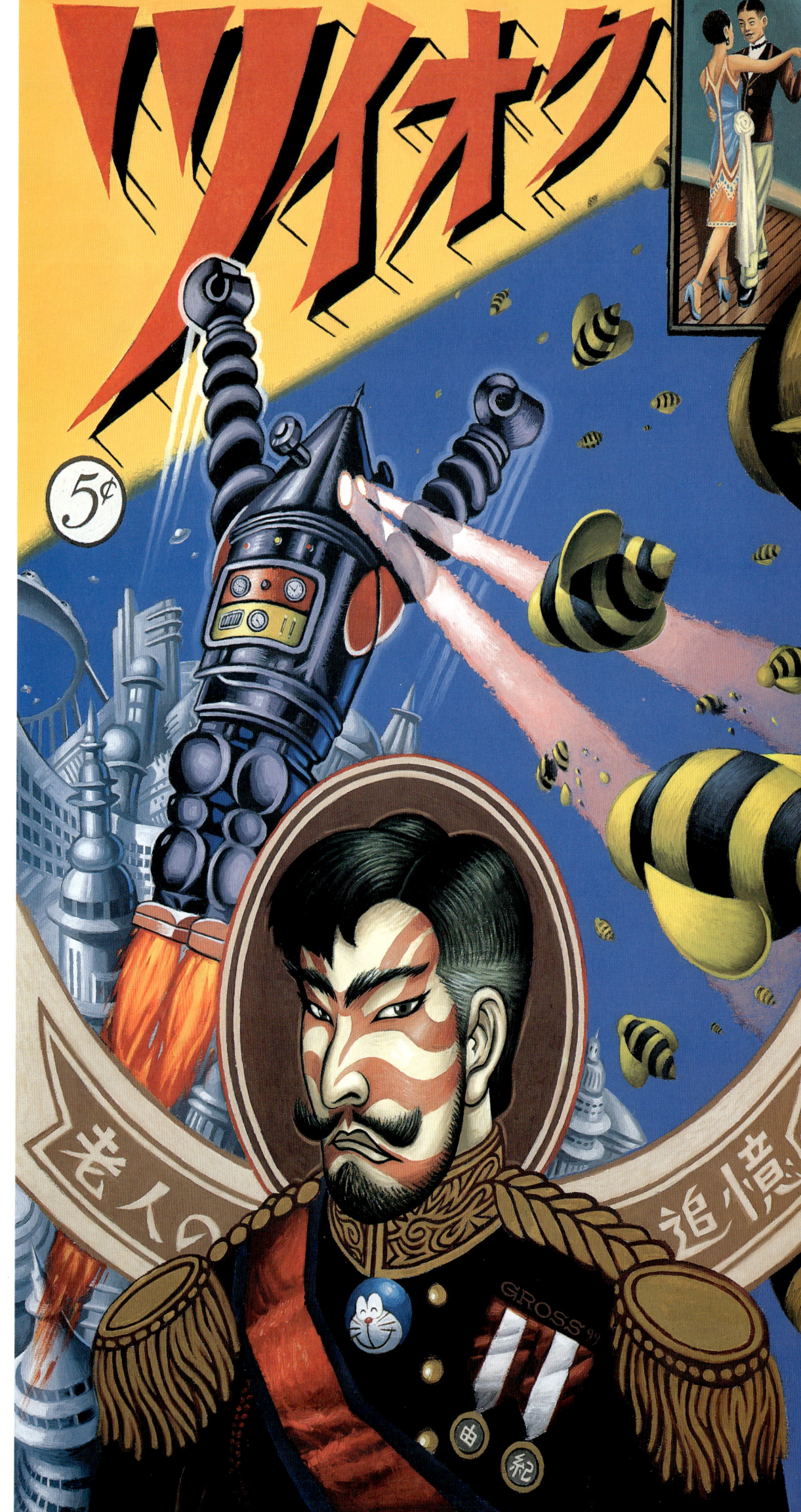

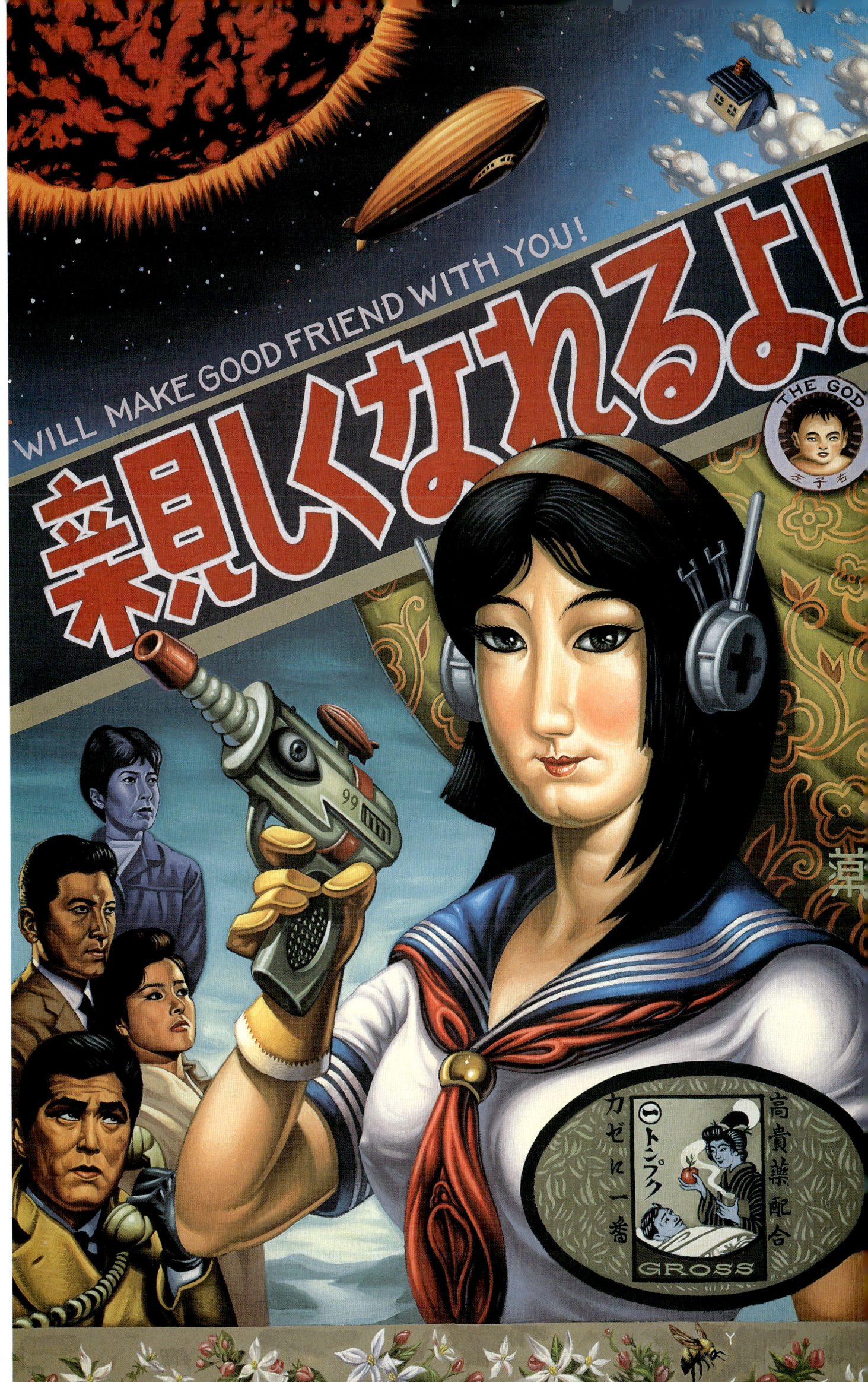

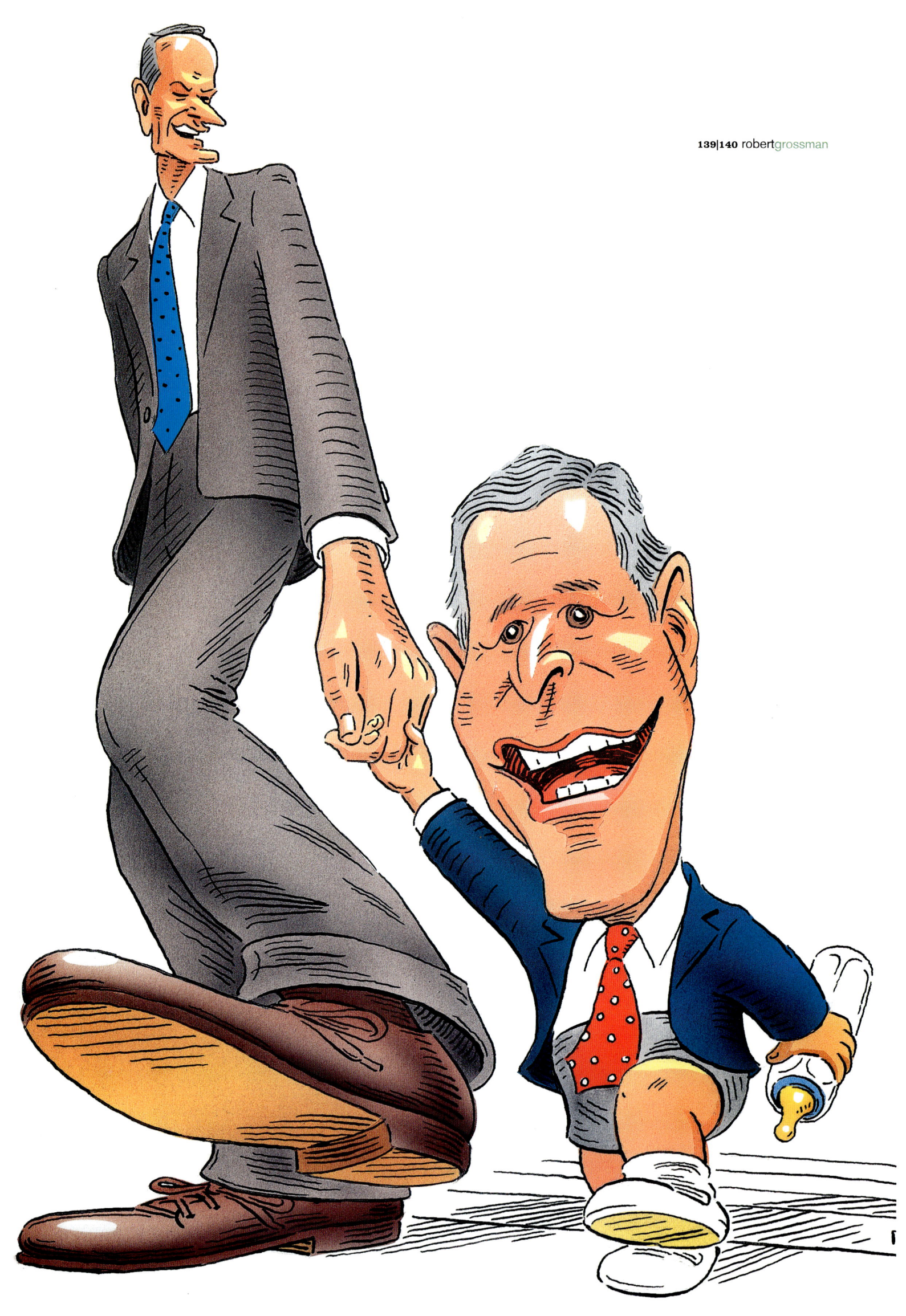

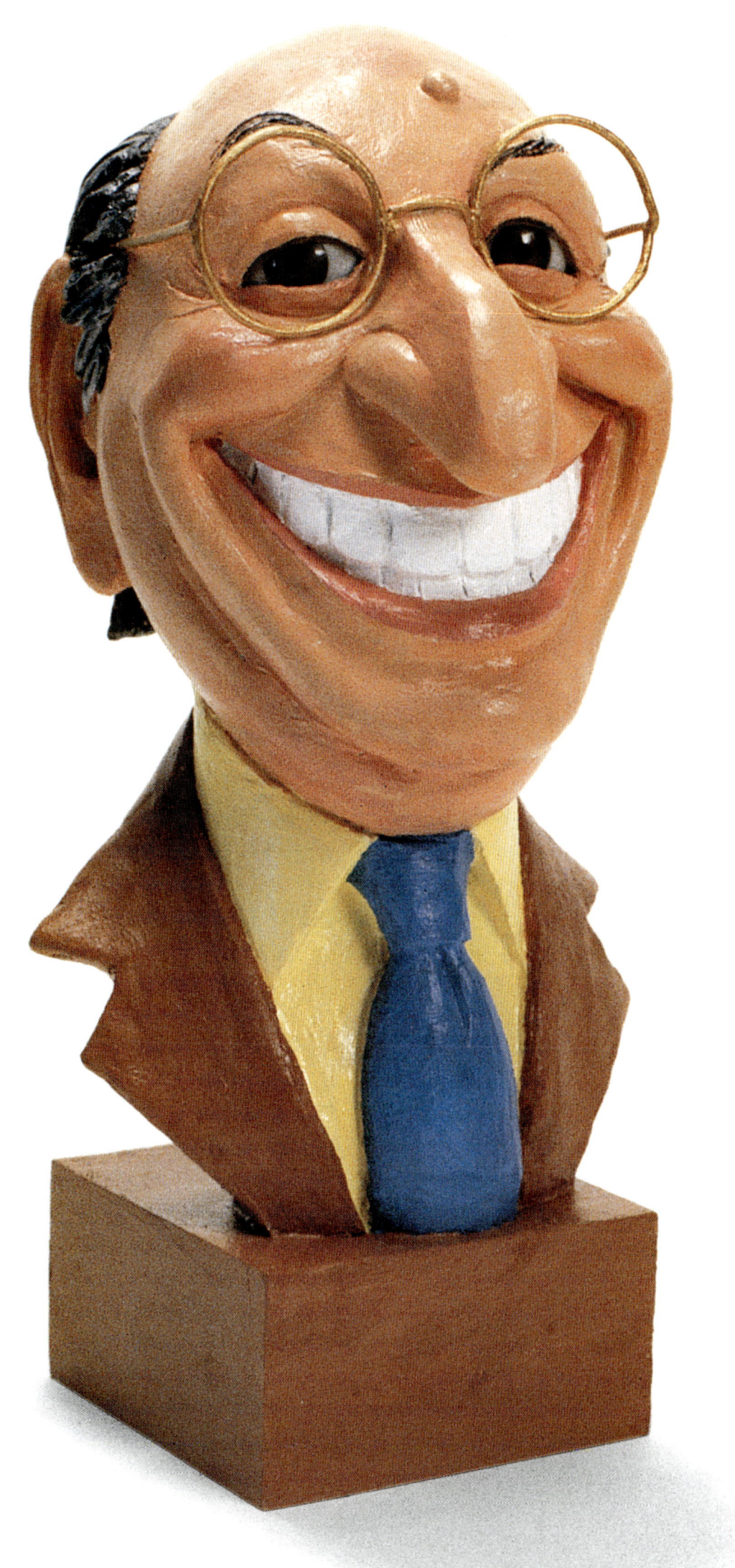

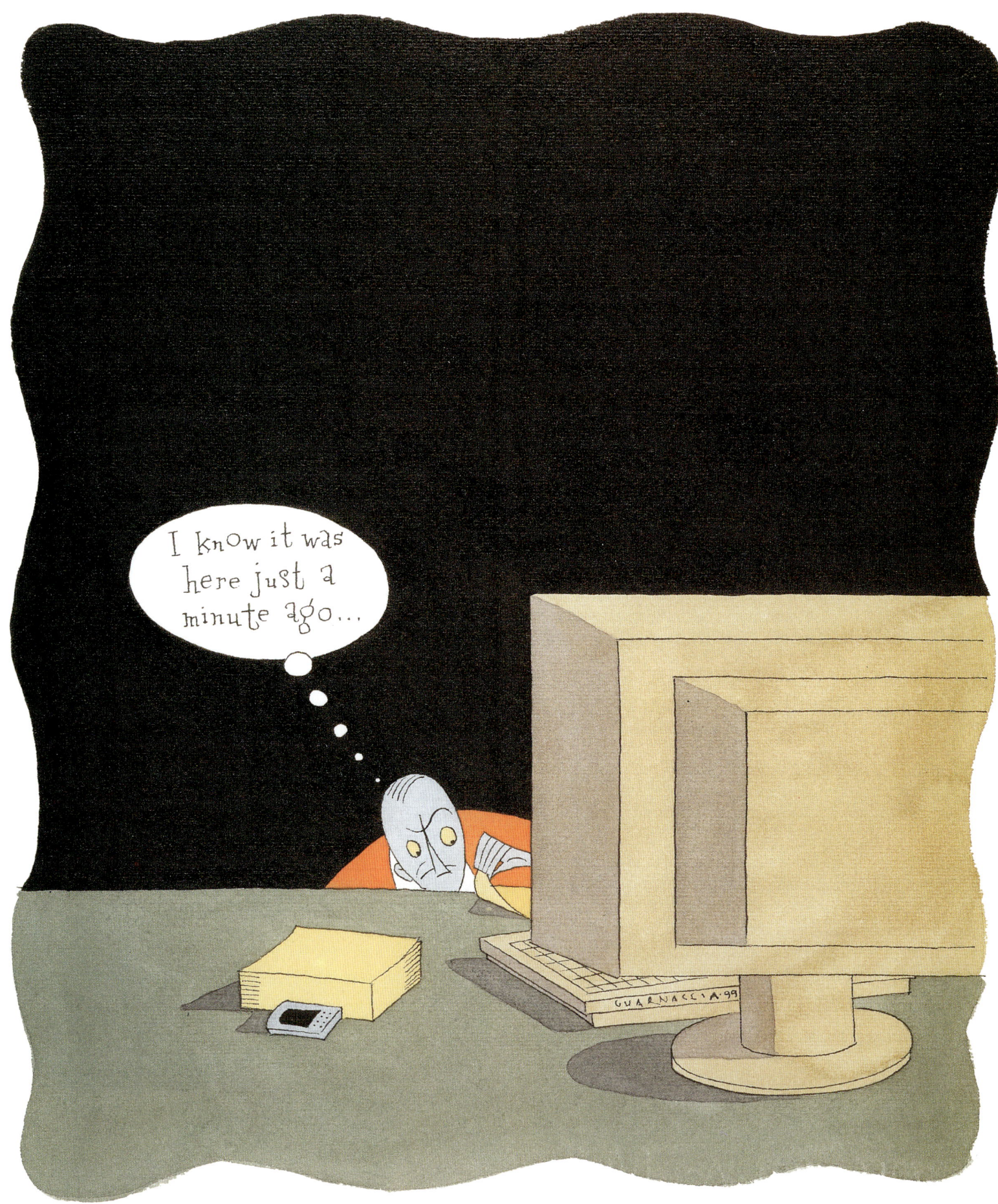

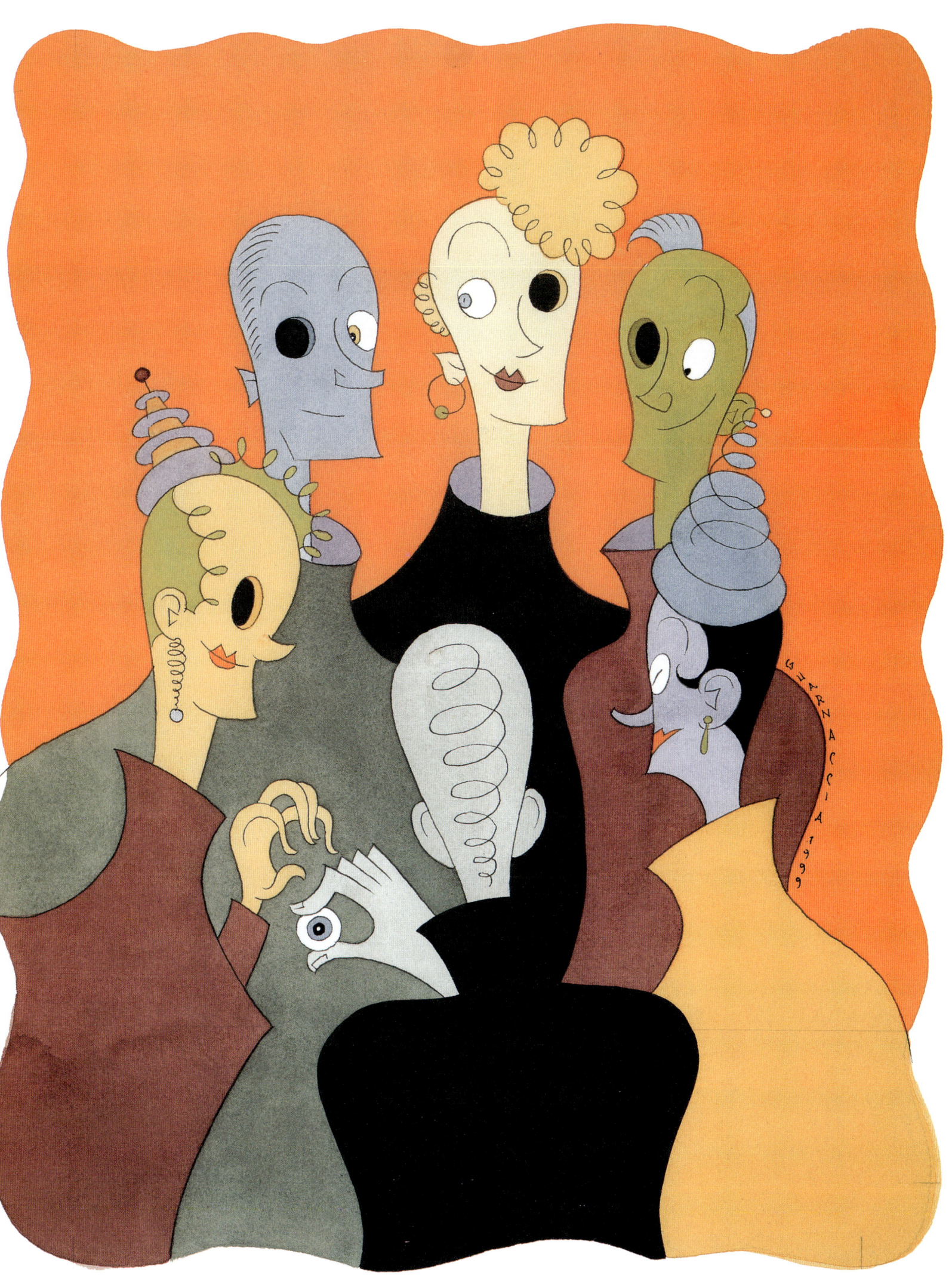

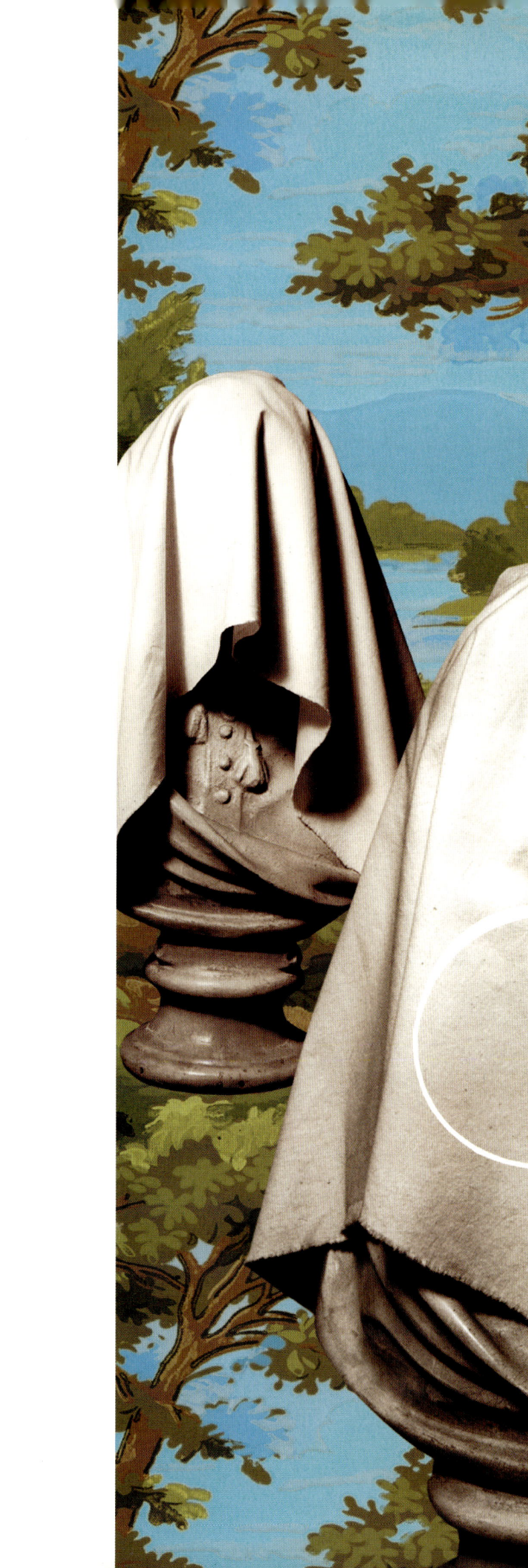

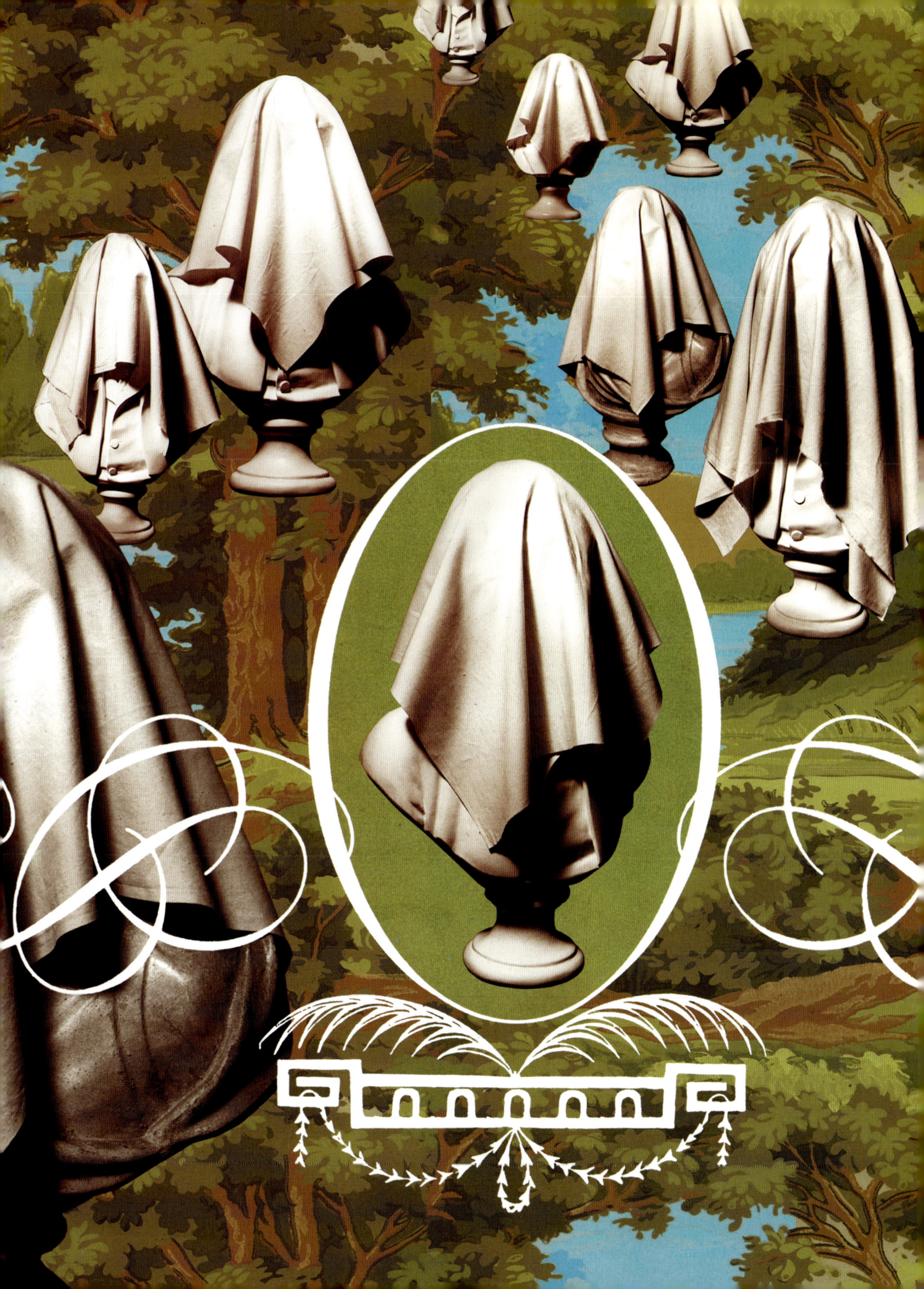

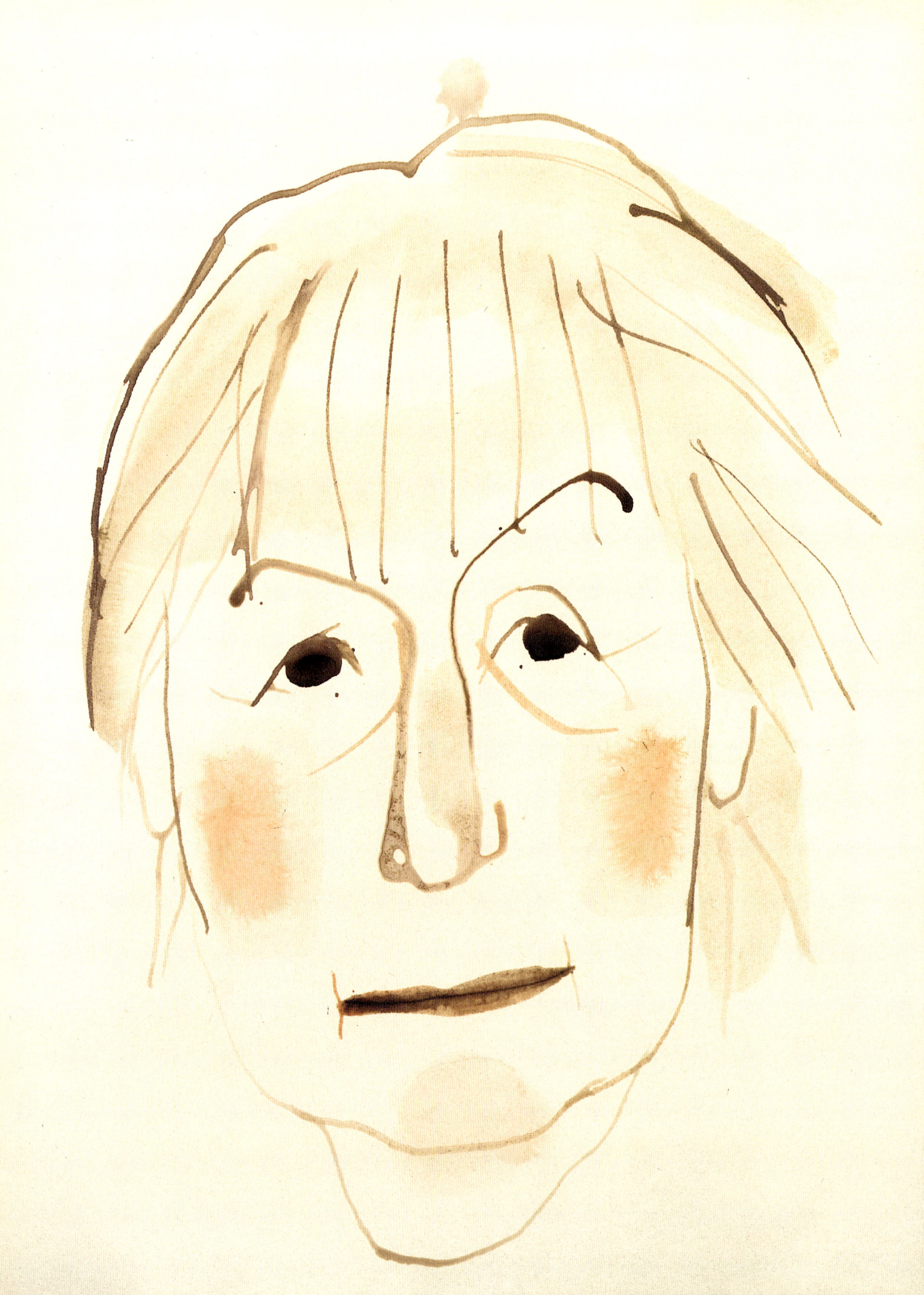

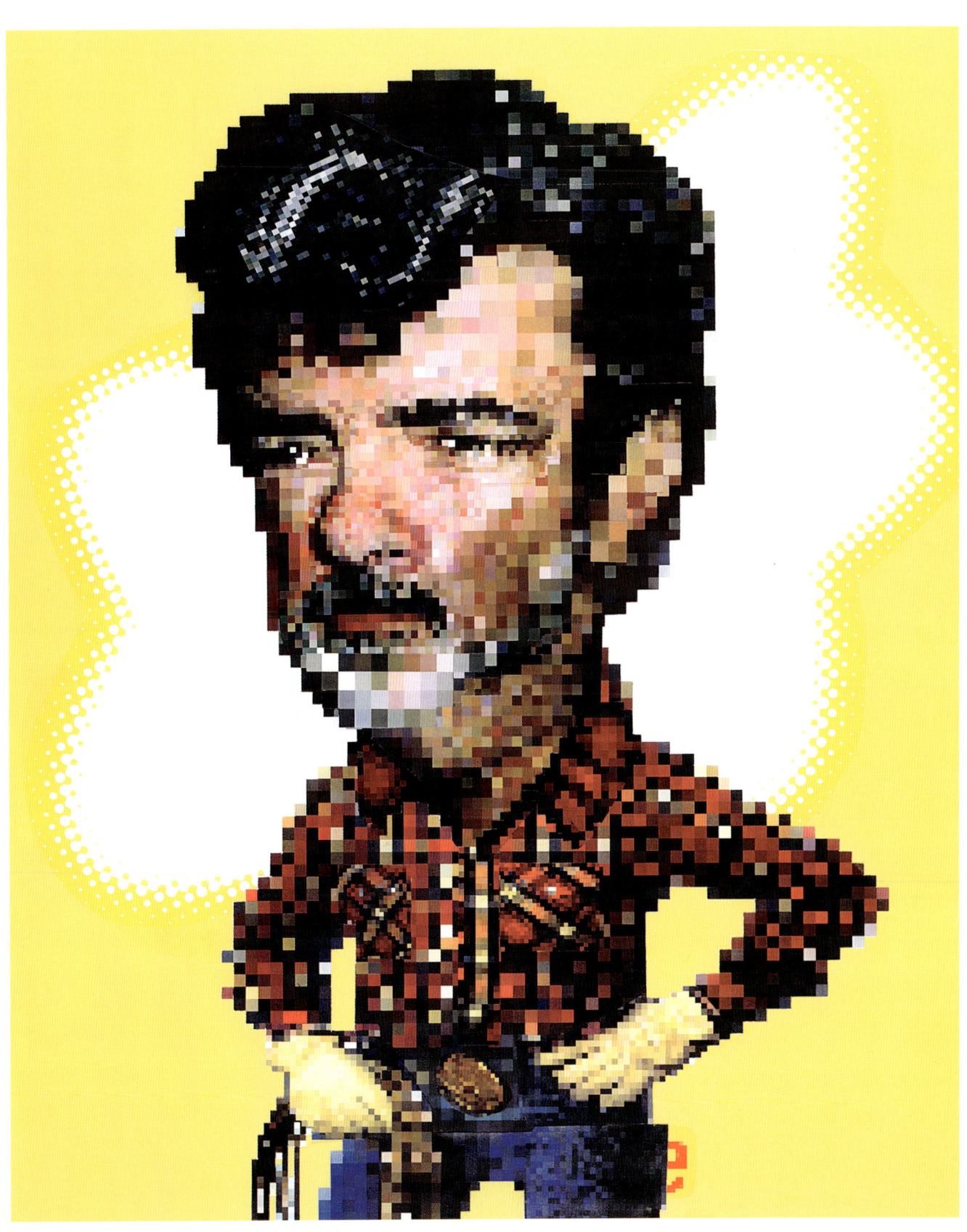

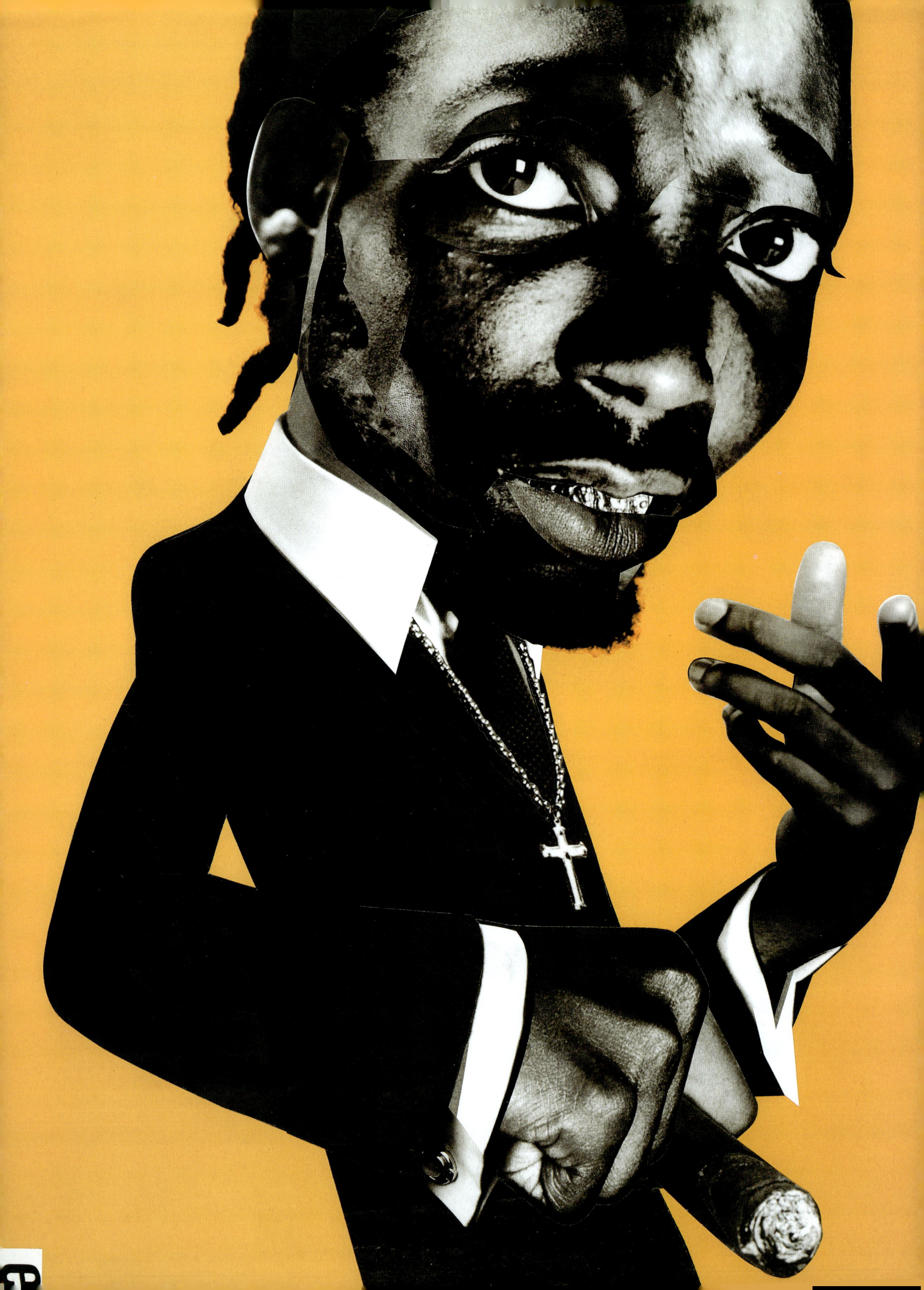

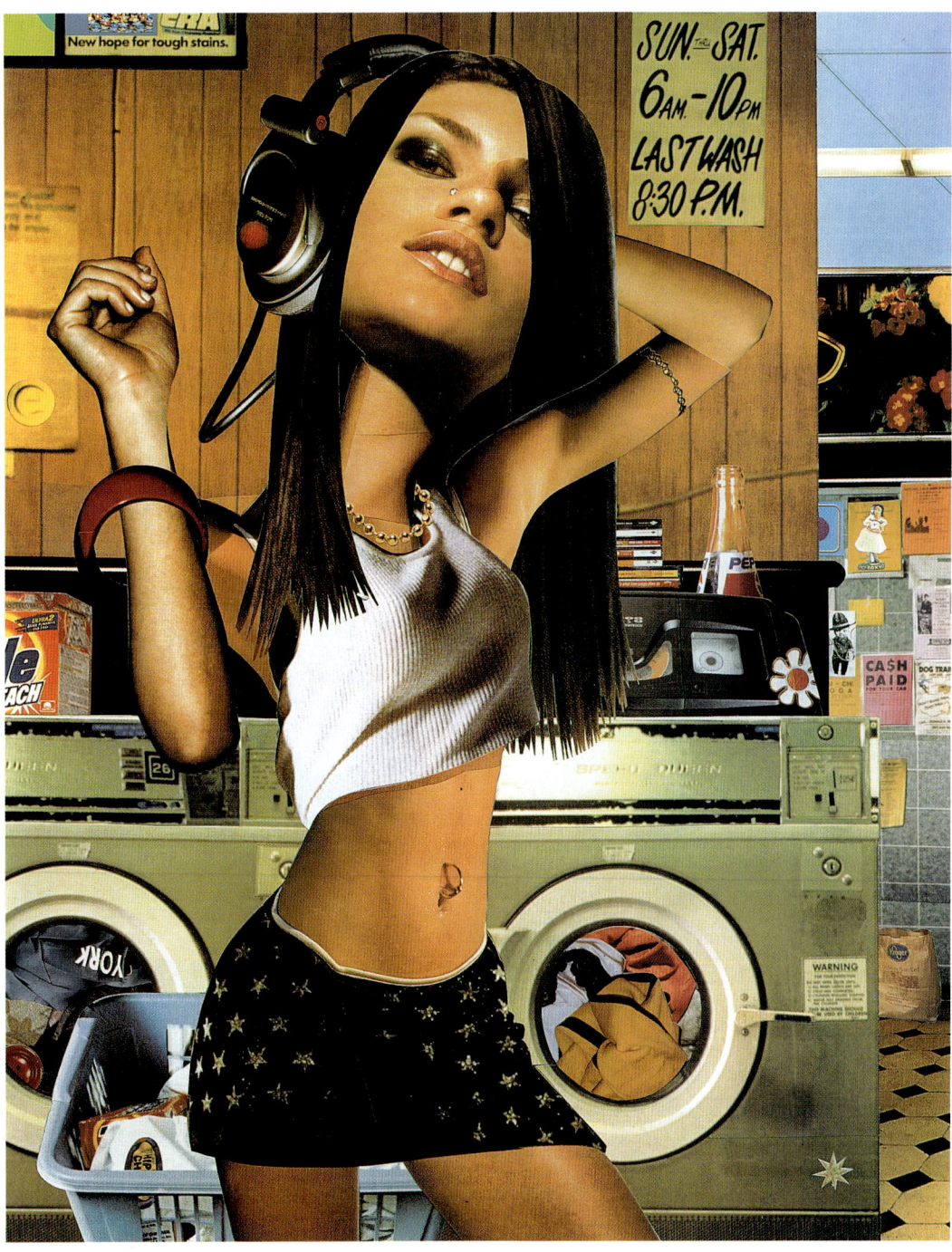

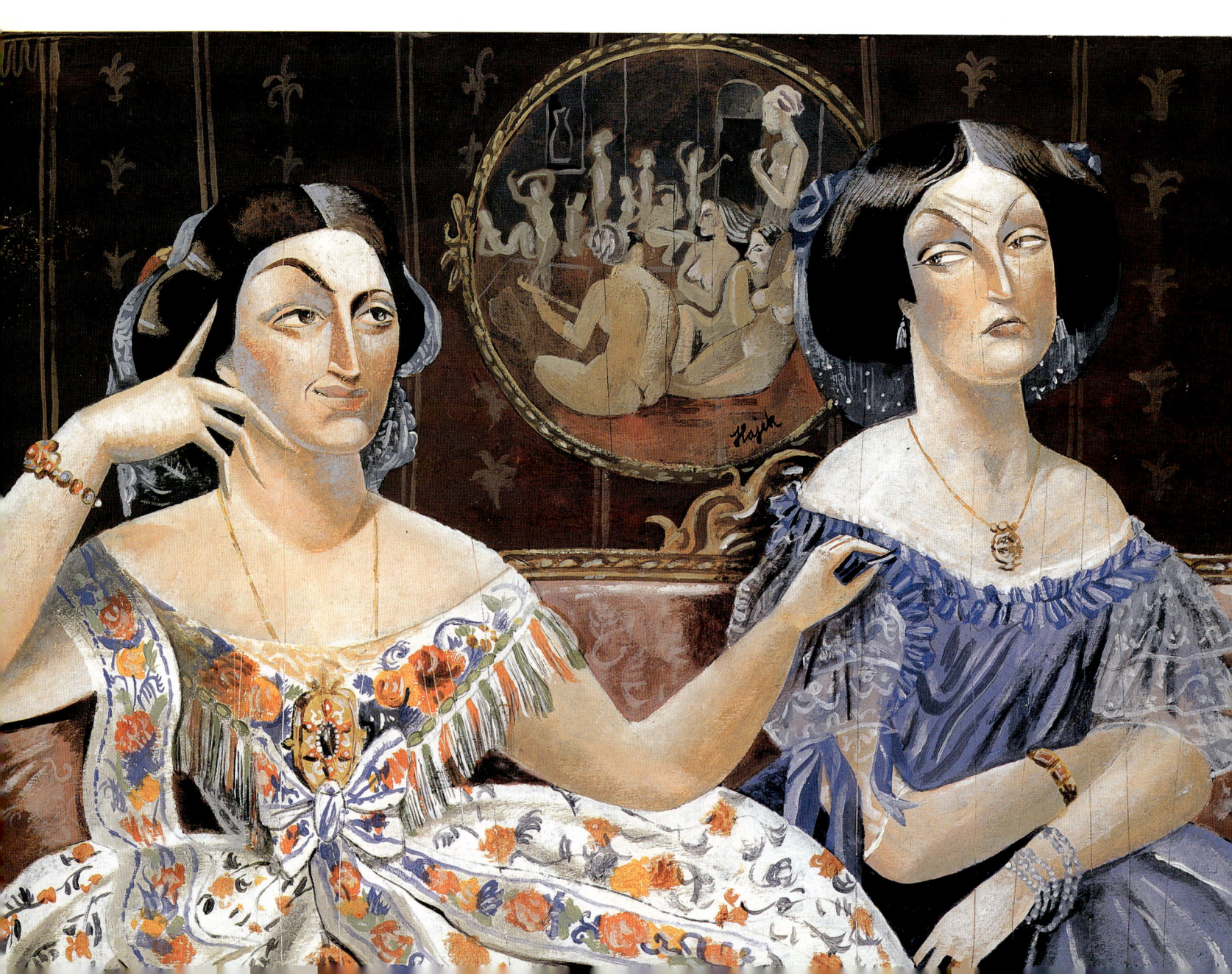

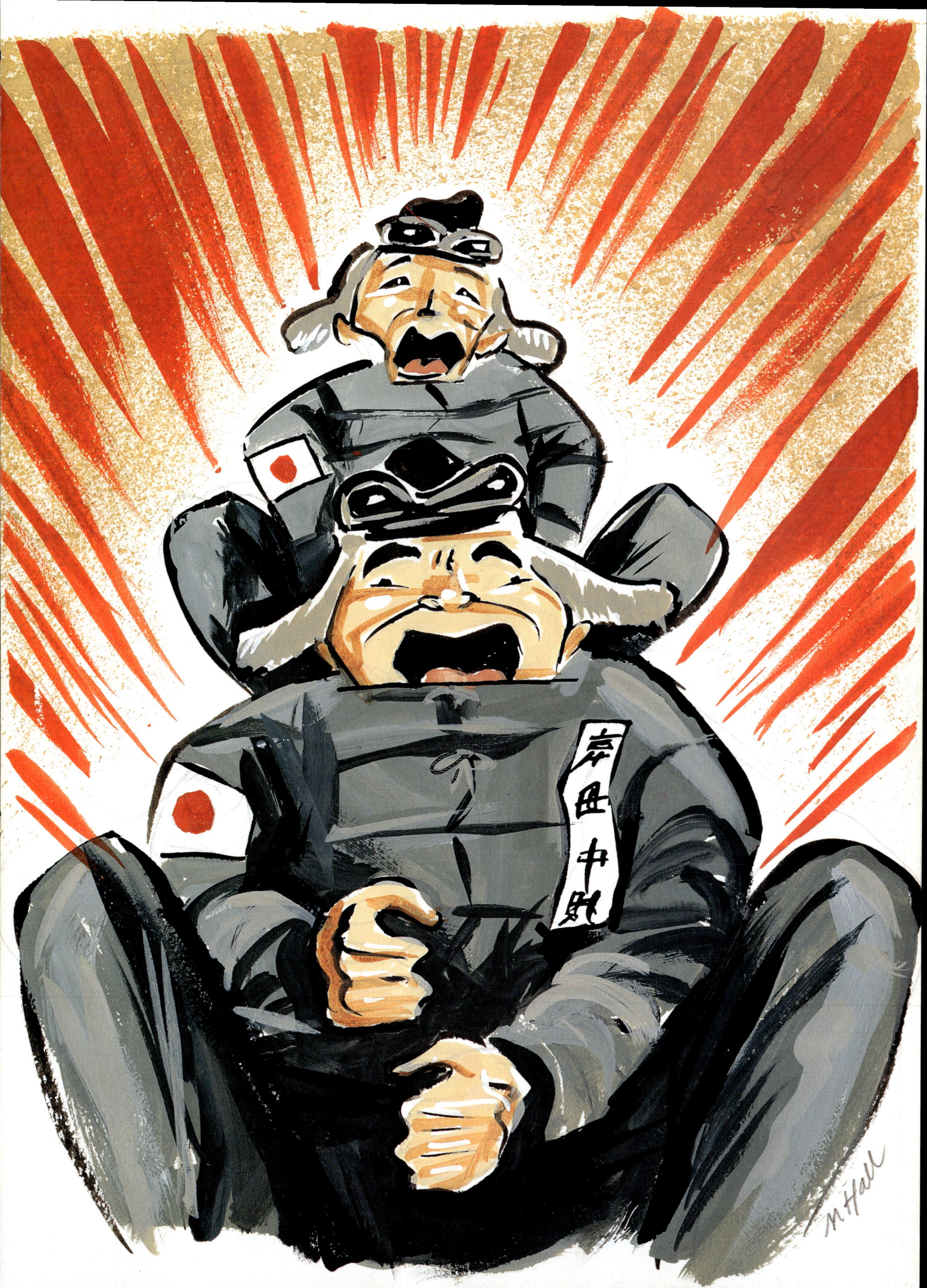

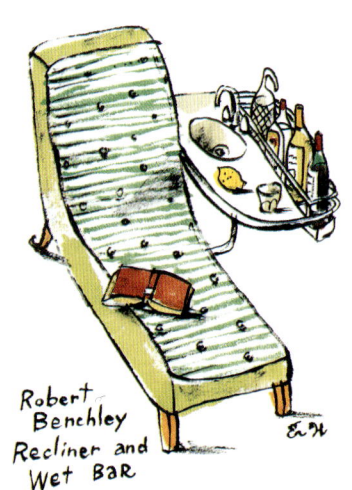

Robert
Benchley
Recliner and
Wet Bar

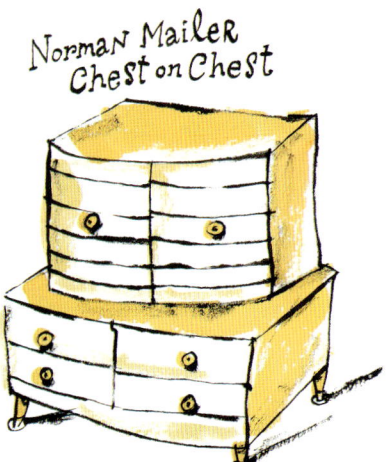

Norman Mailer
Chest on Chest

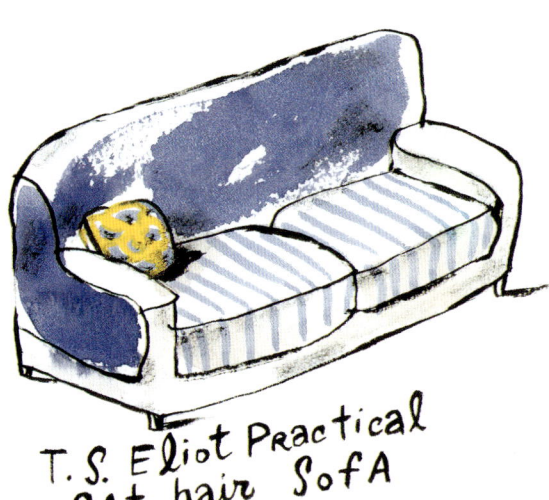

T.S. Eliot Practical
Cat hair Sofa

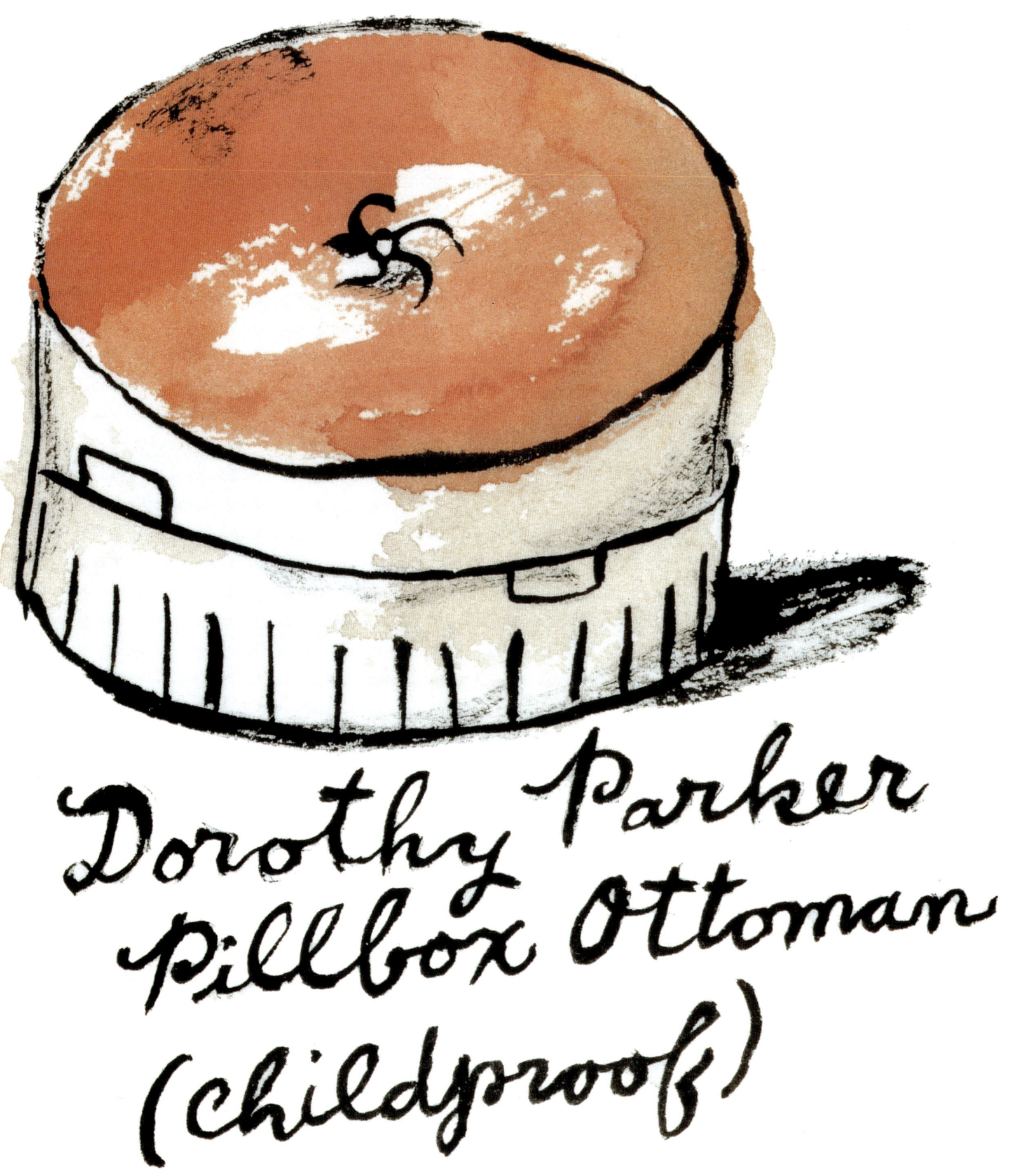

Dorothy Parker
Pillbox Ottoman
(childproof)

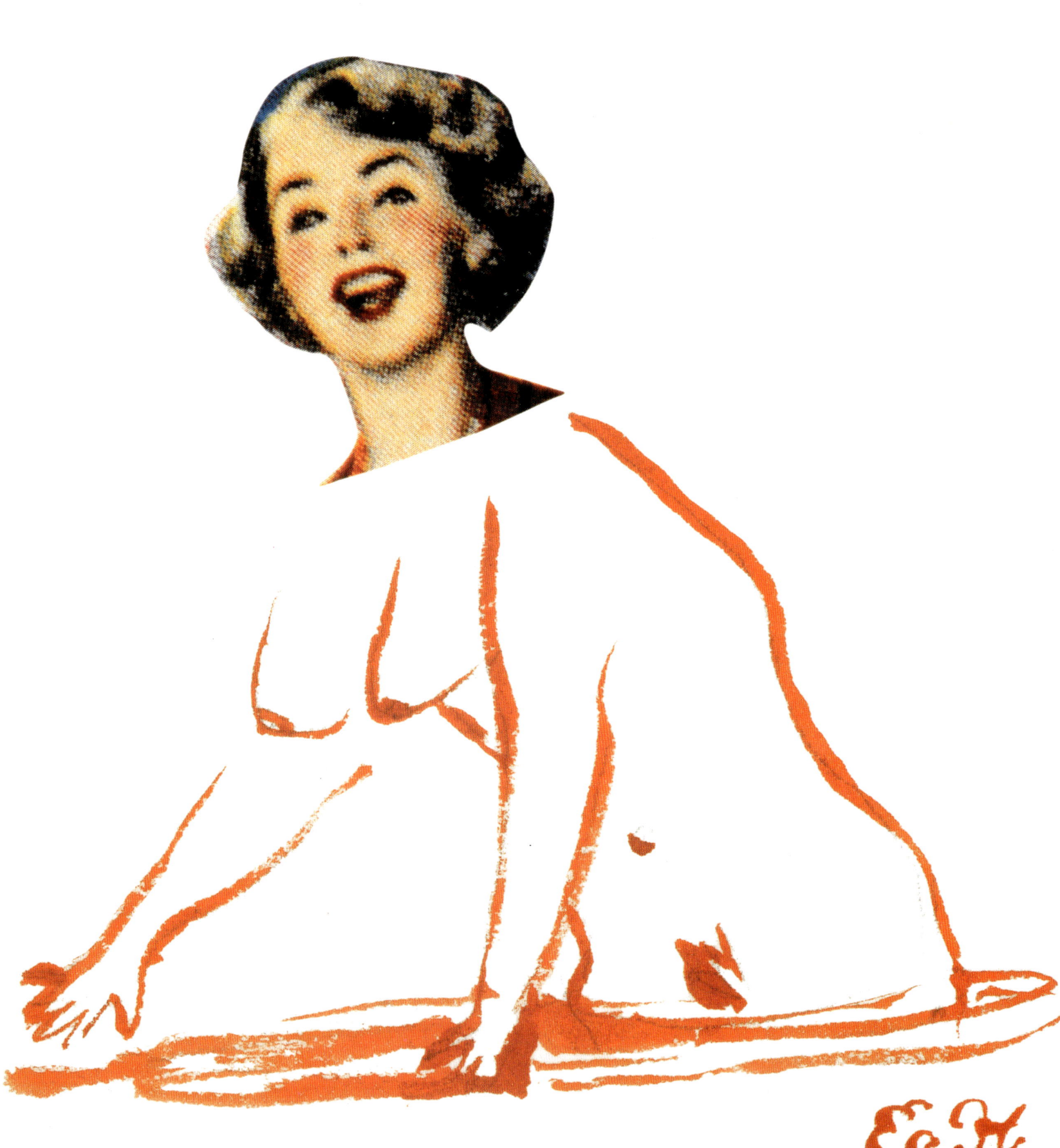

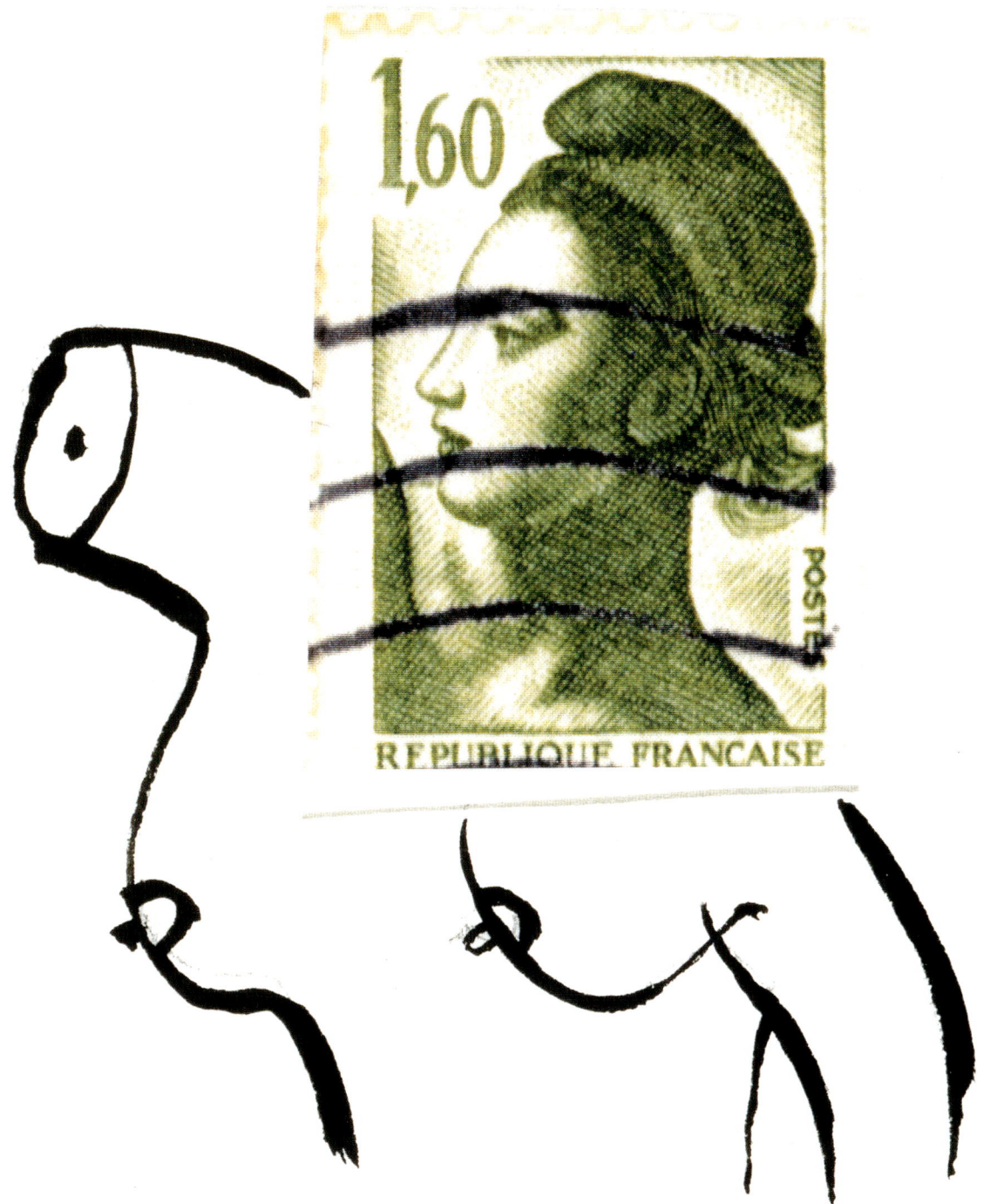

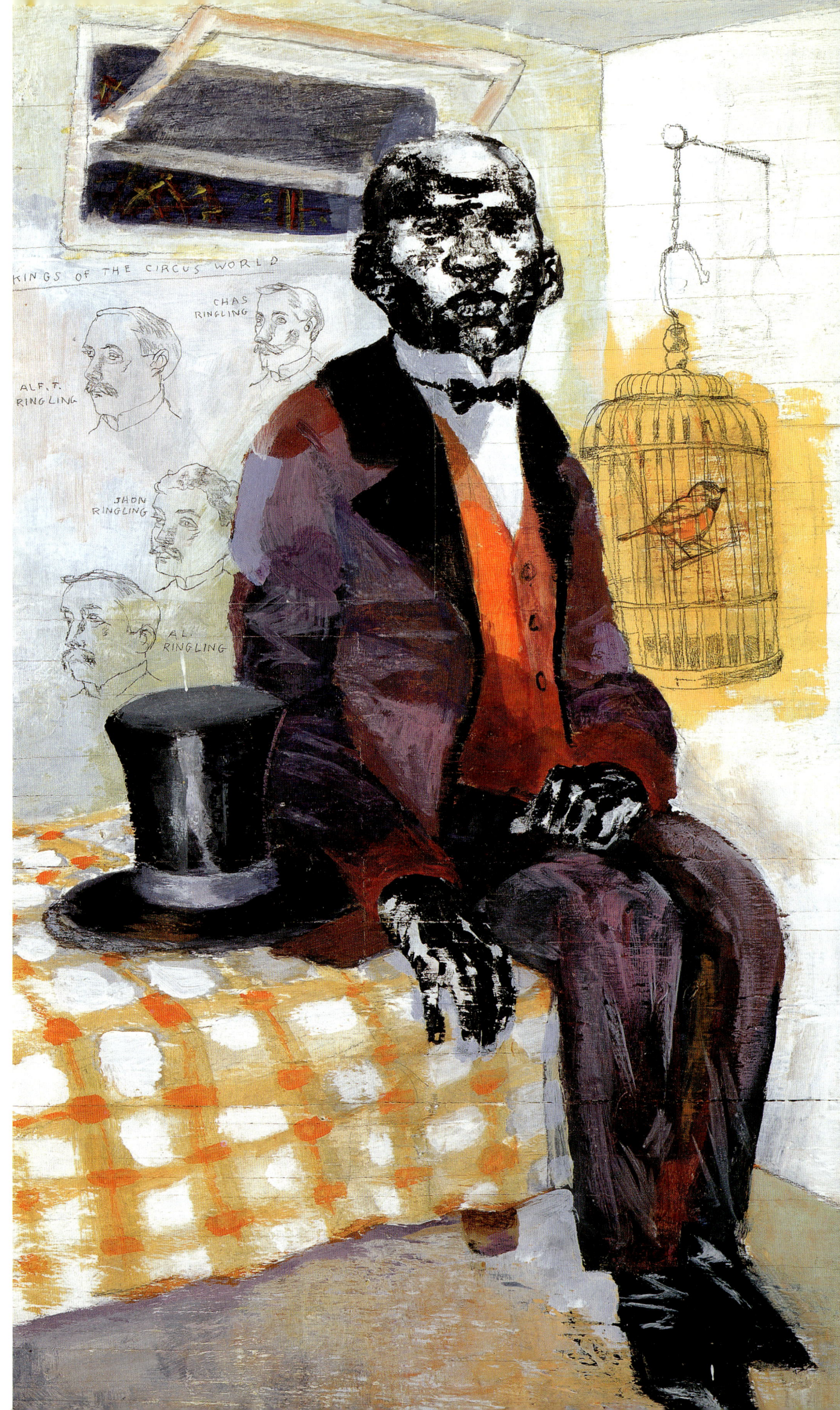

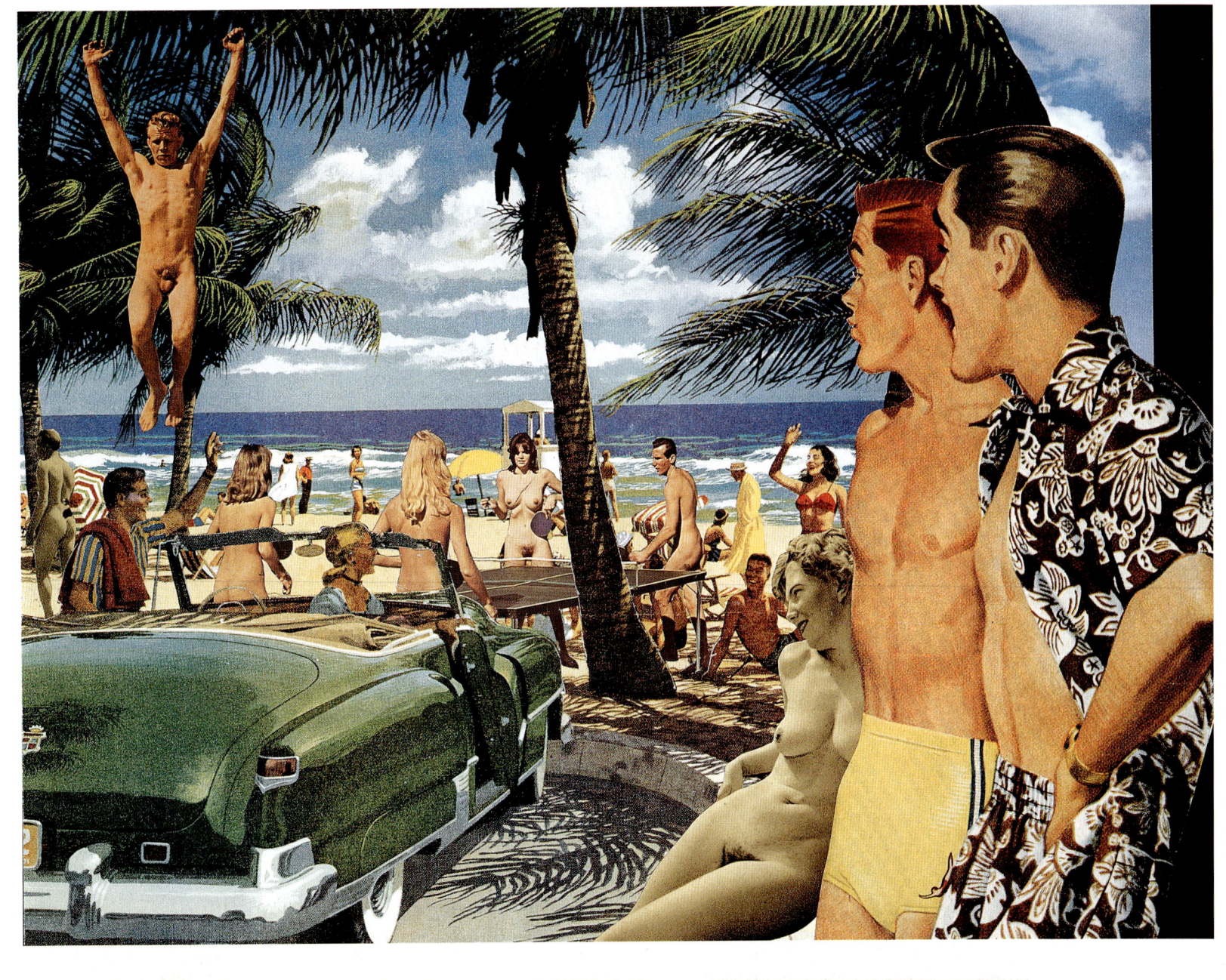

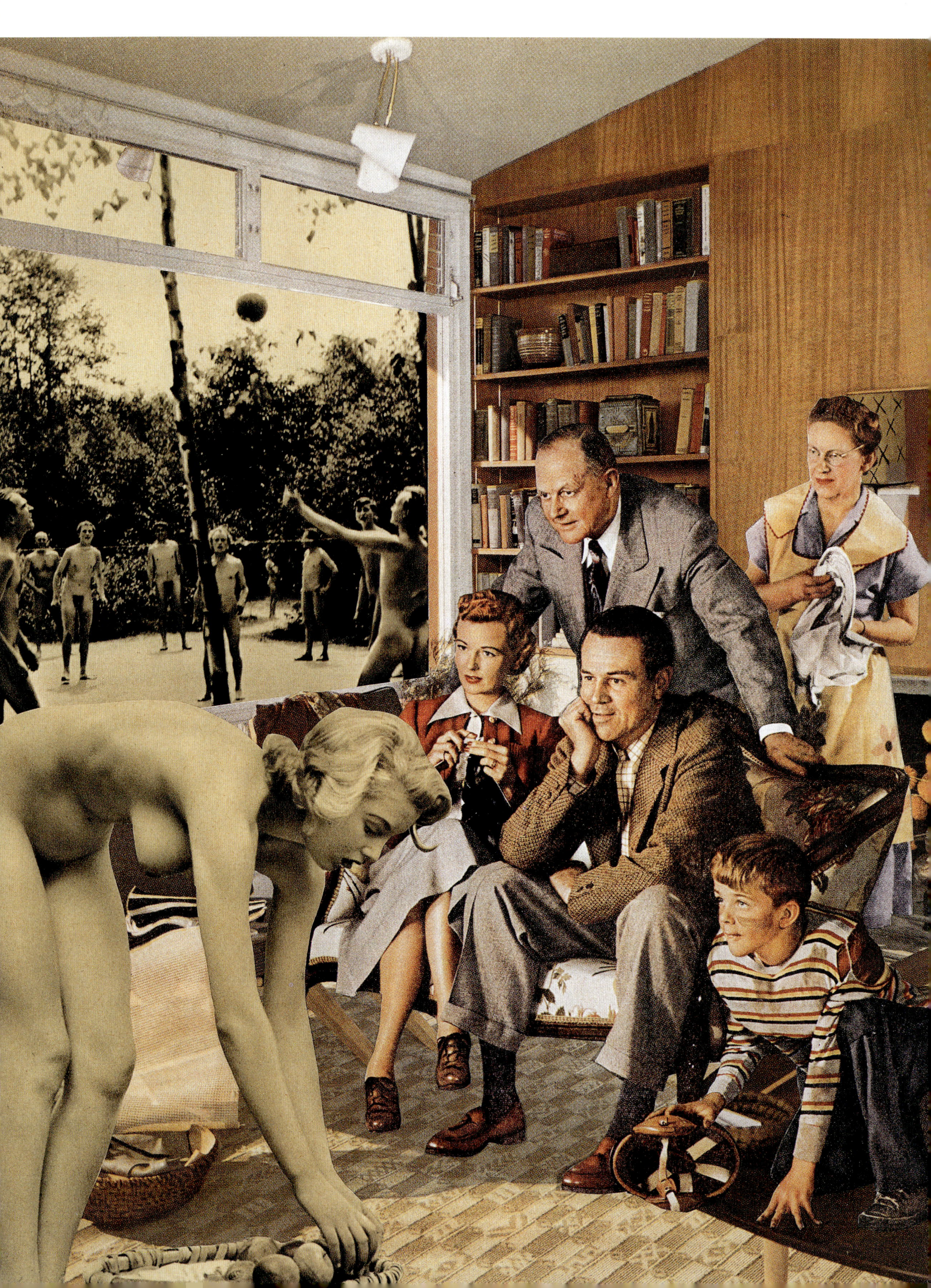

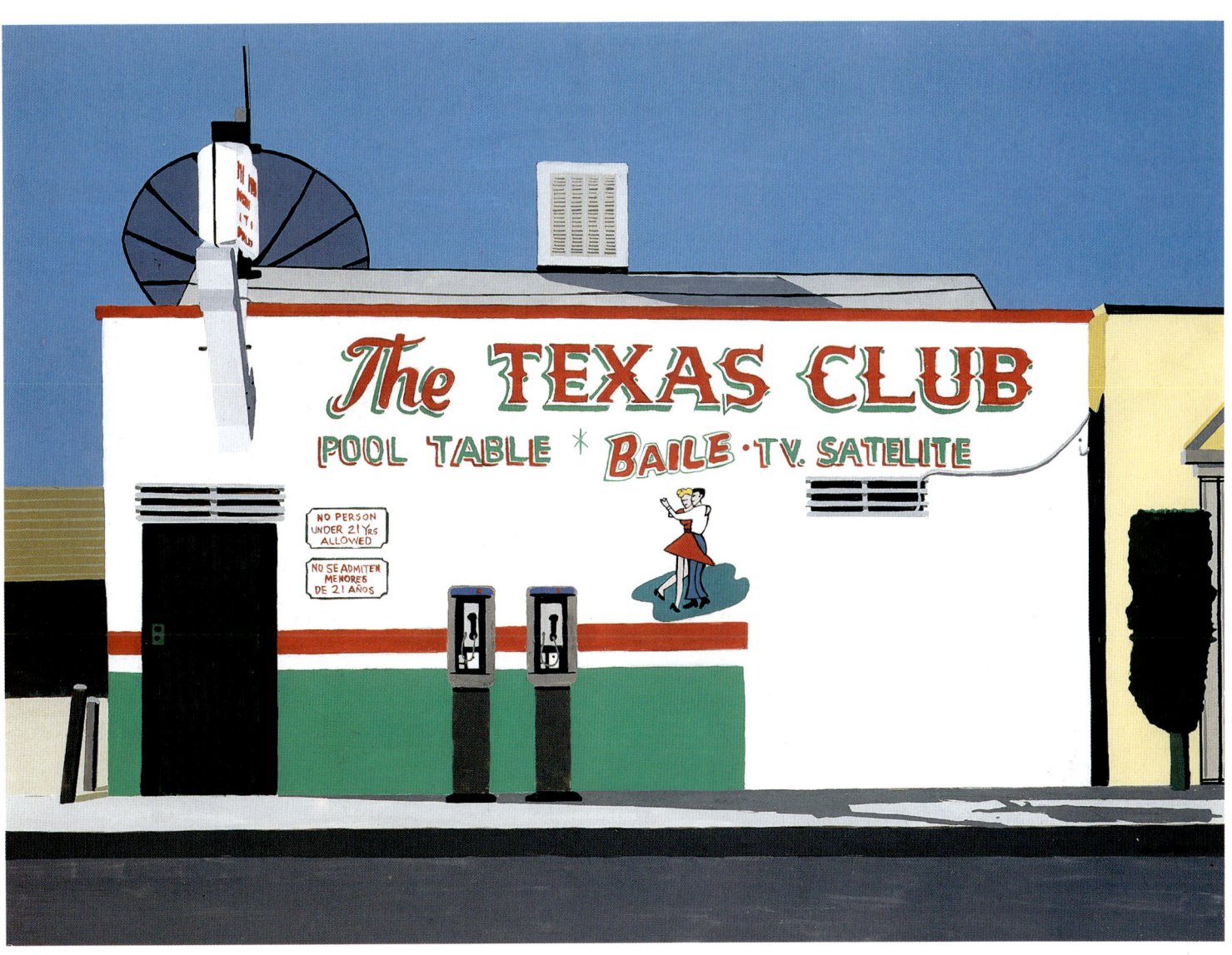

155|156 jimheimann

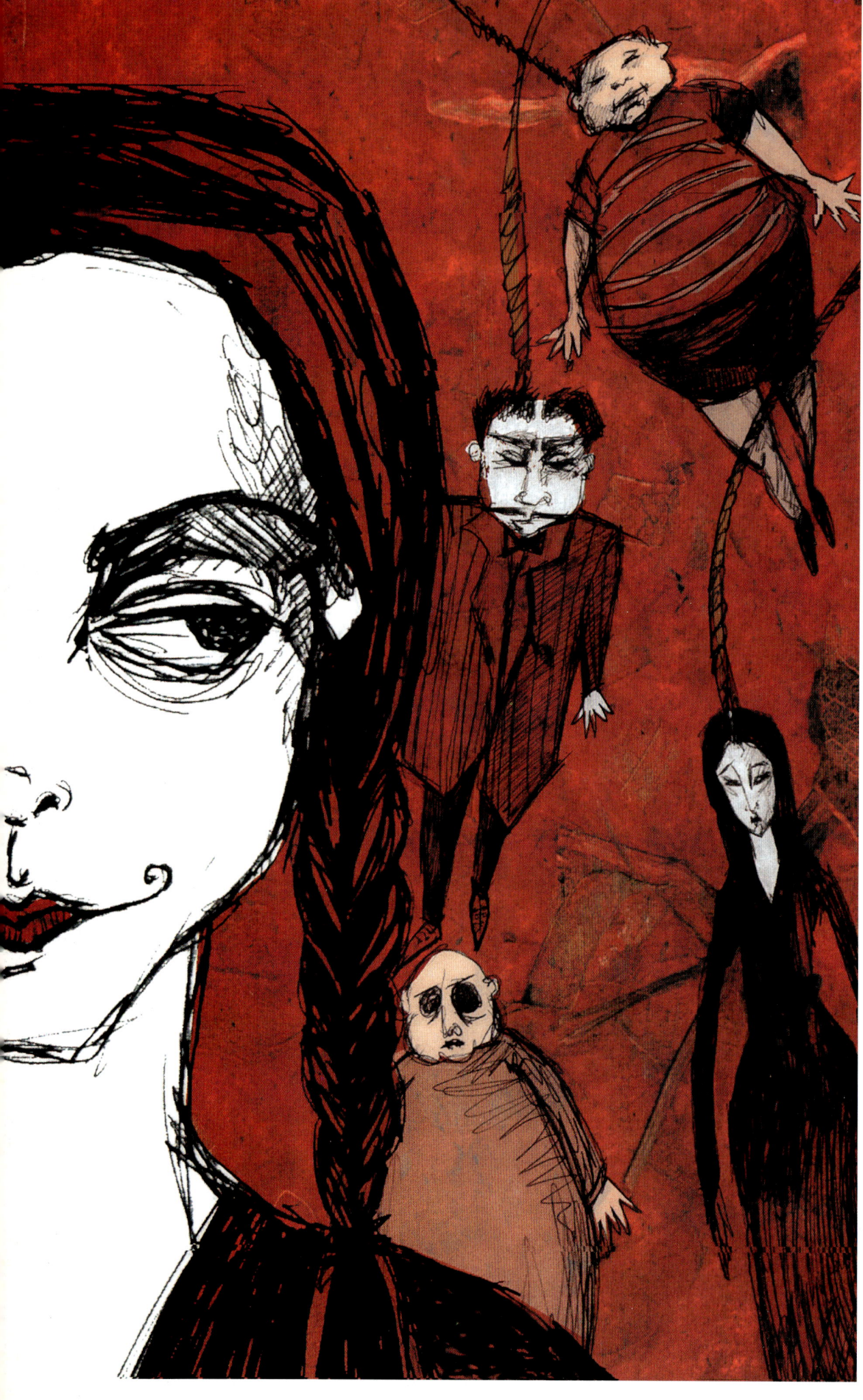

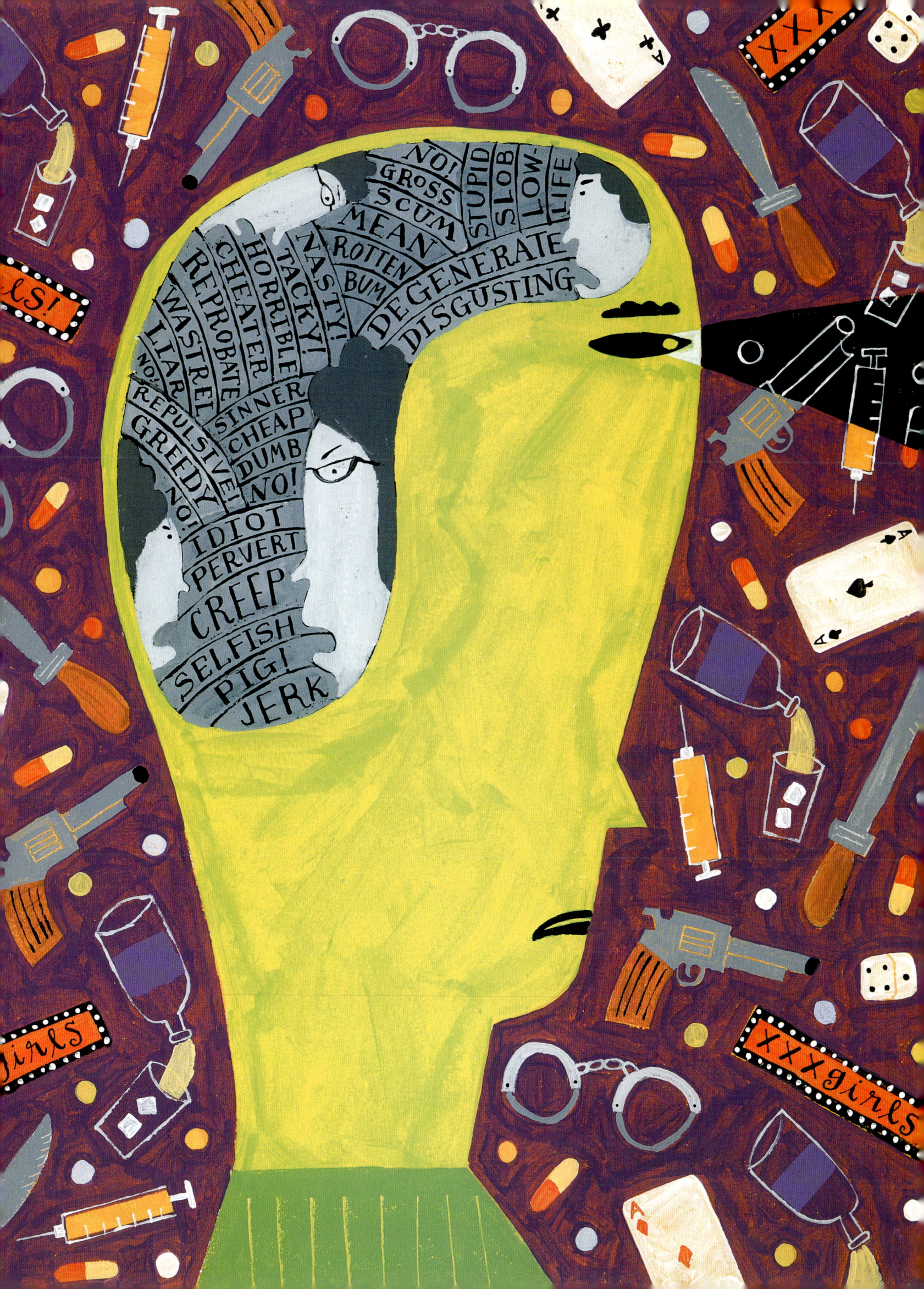

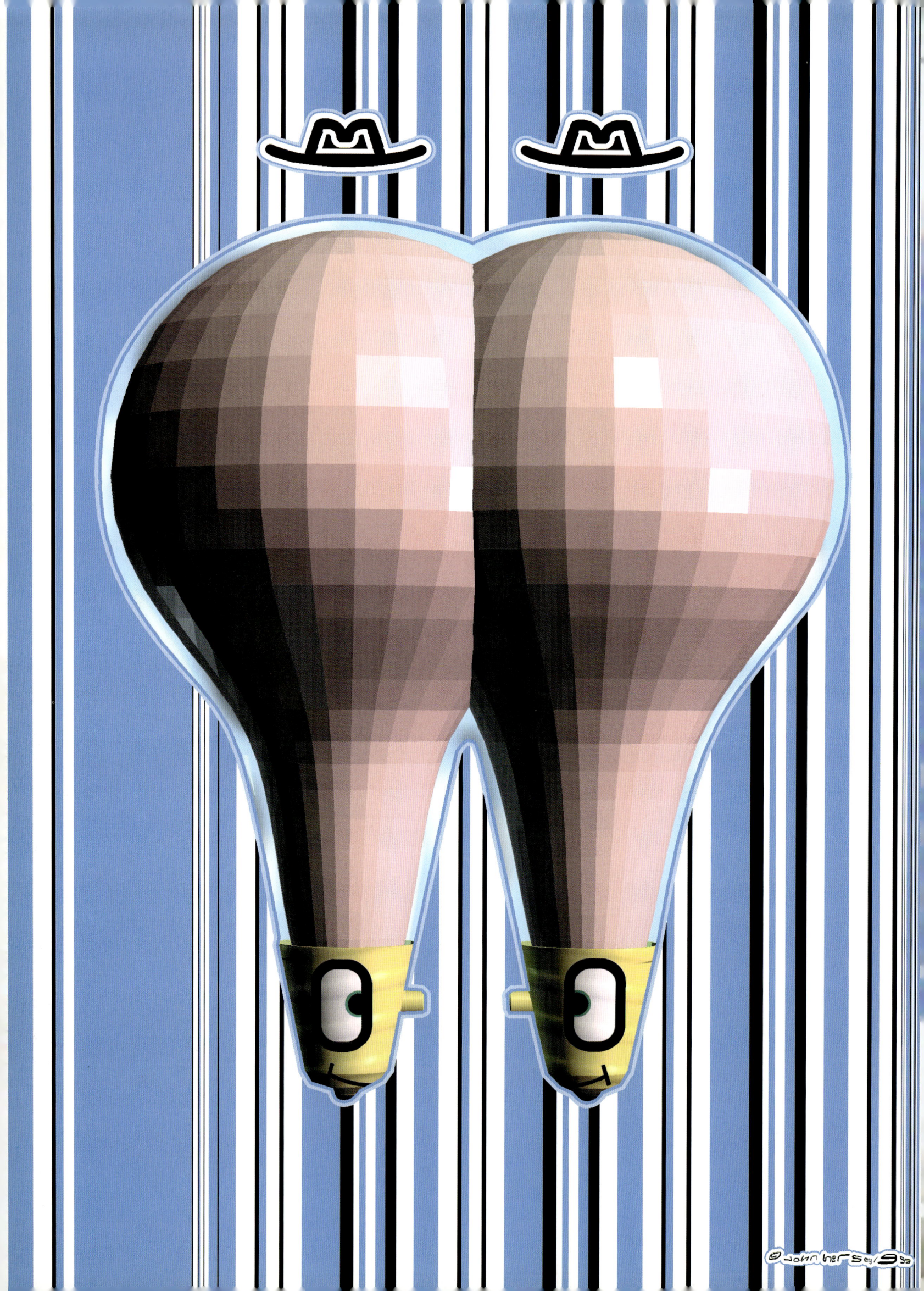

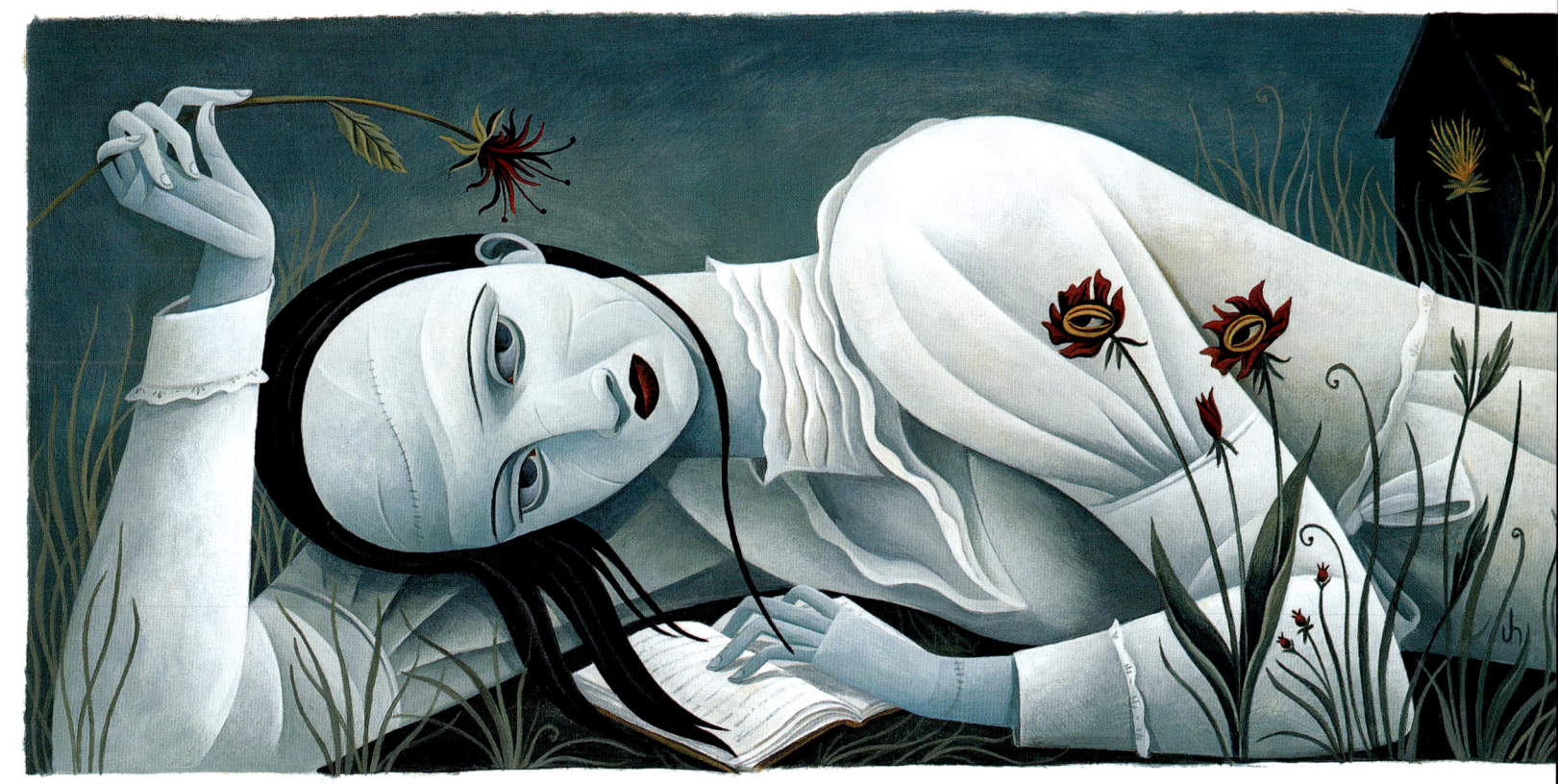

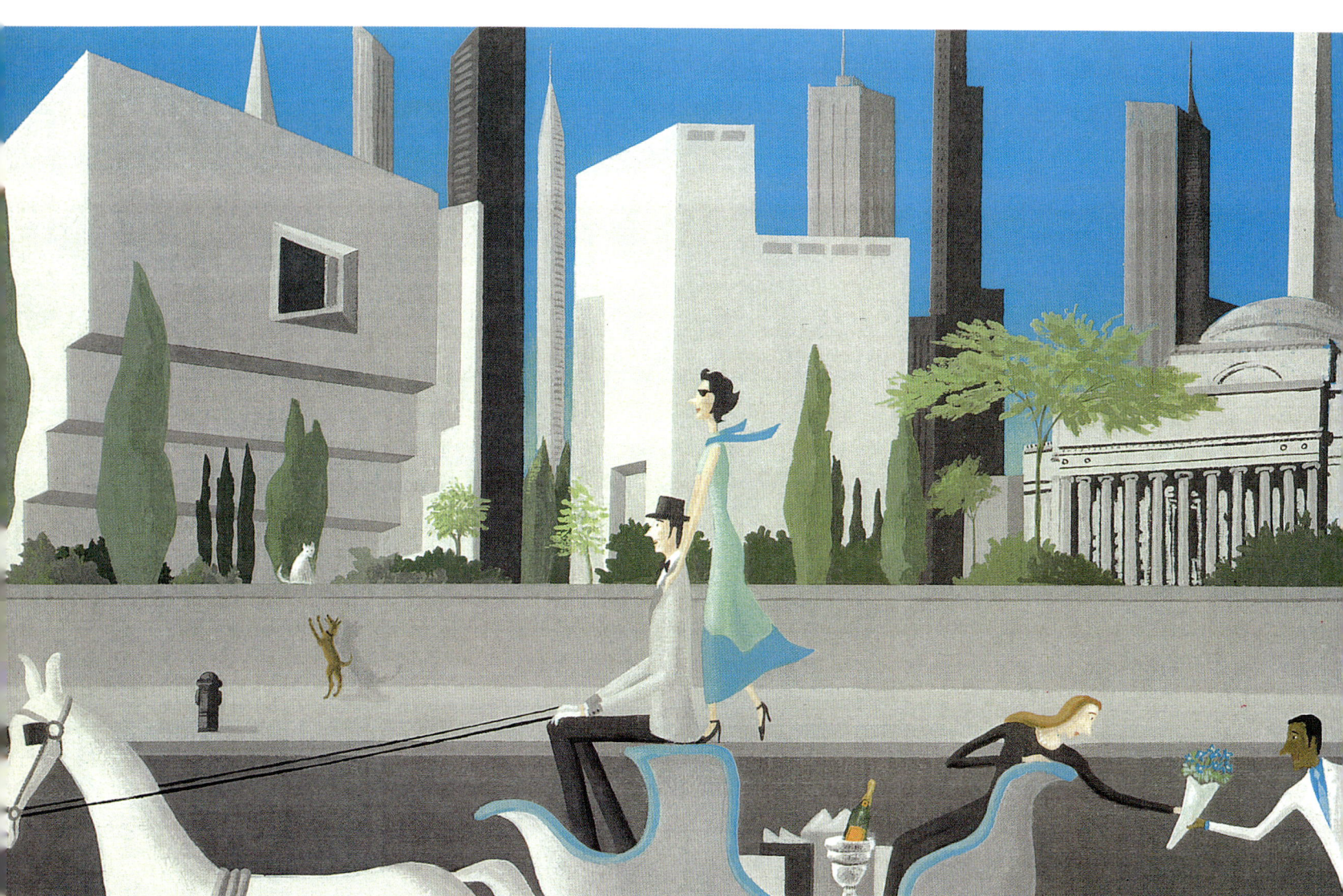

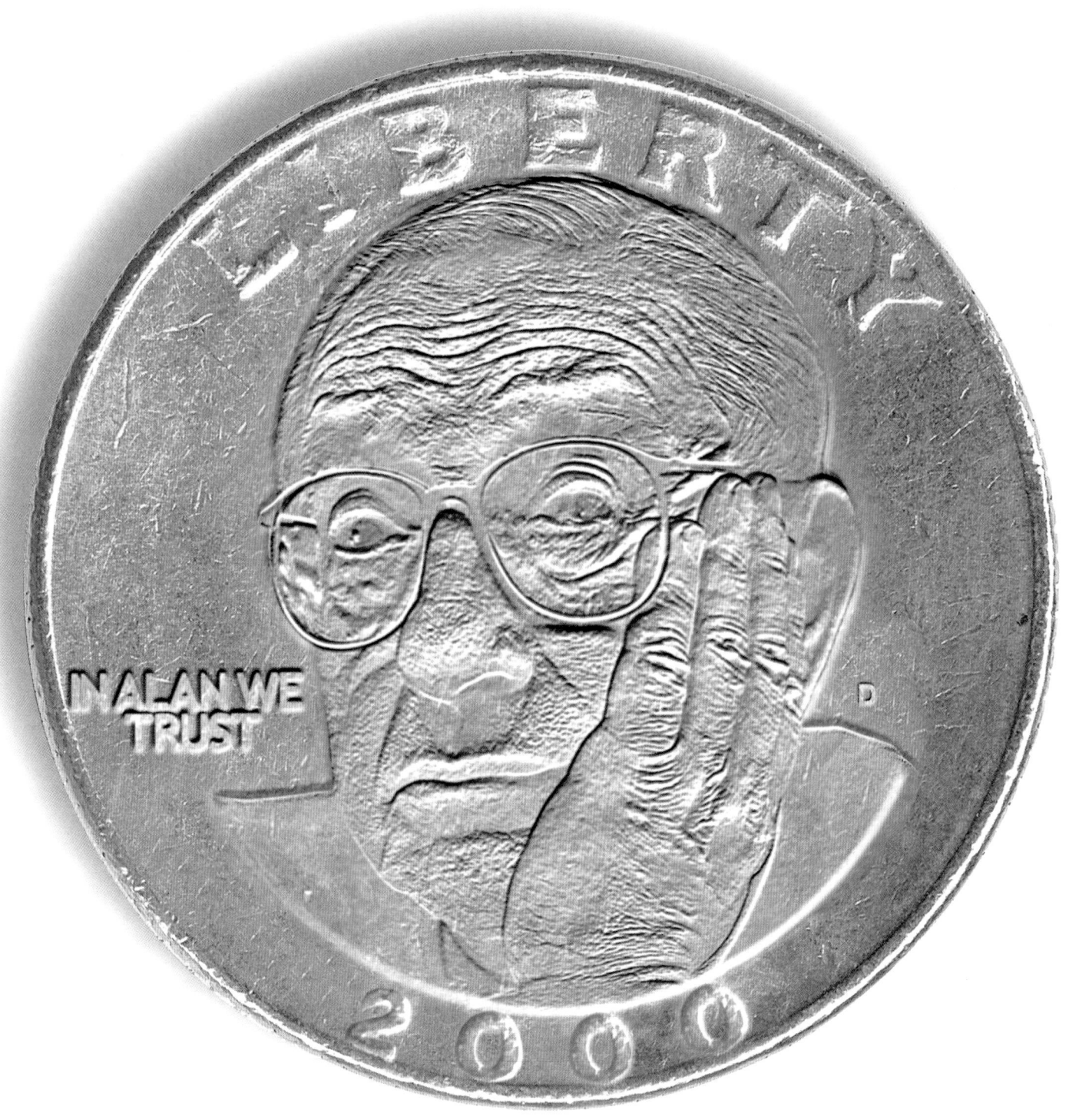

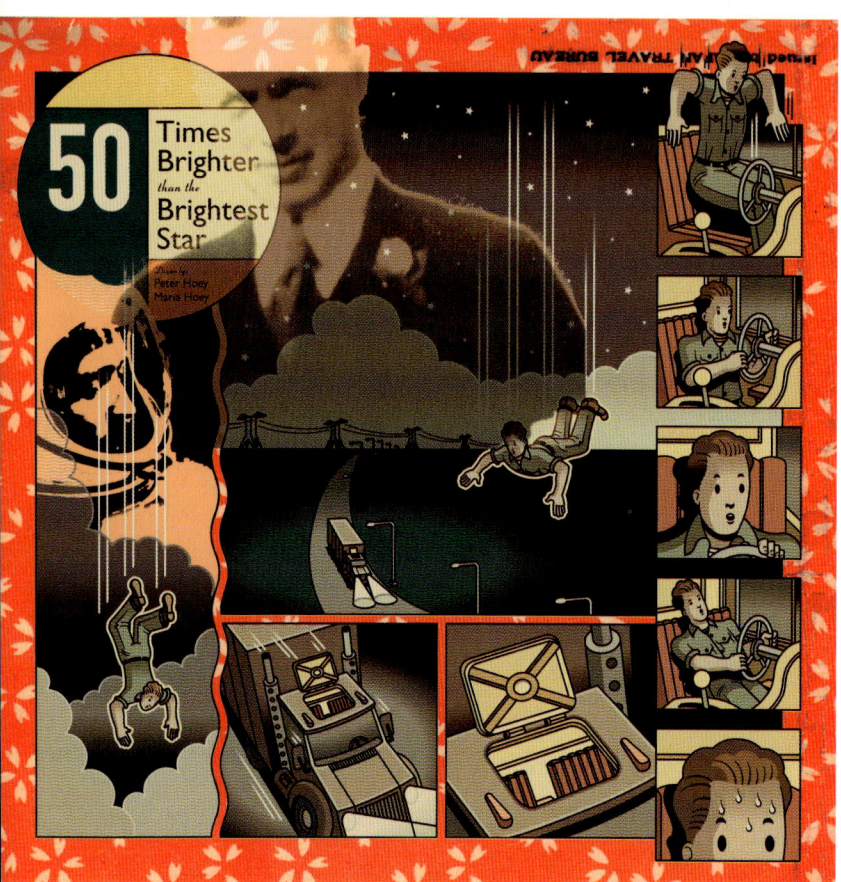
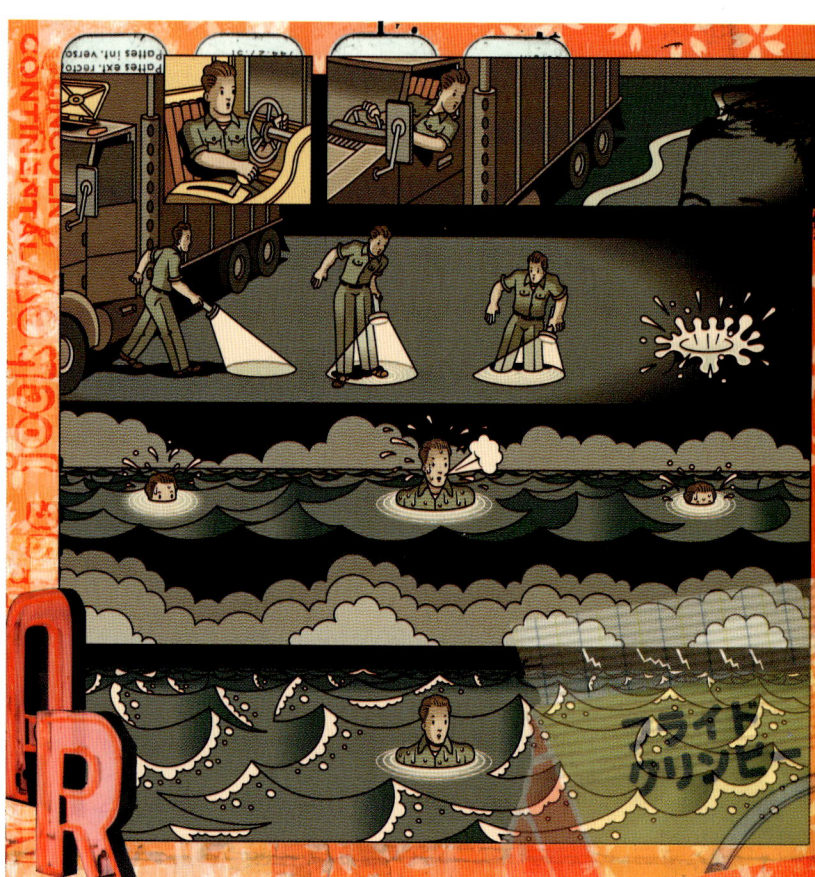

163 peter&mariahoey

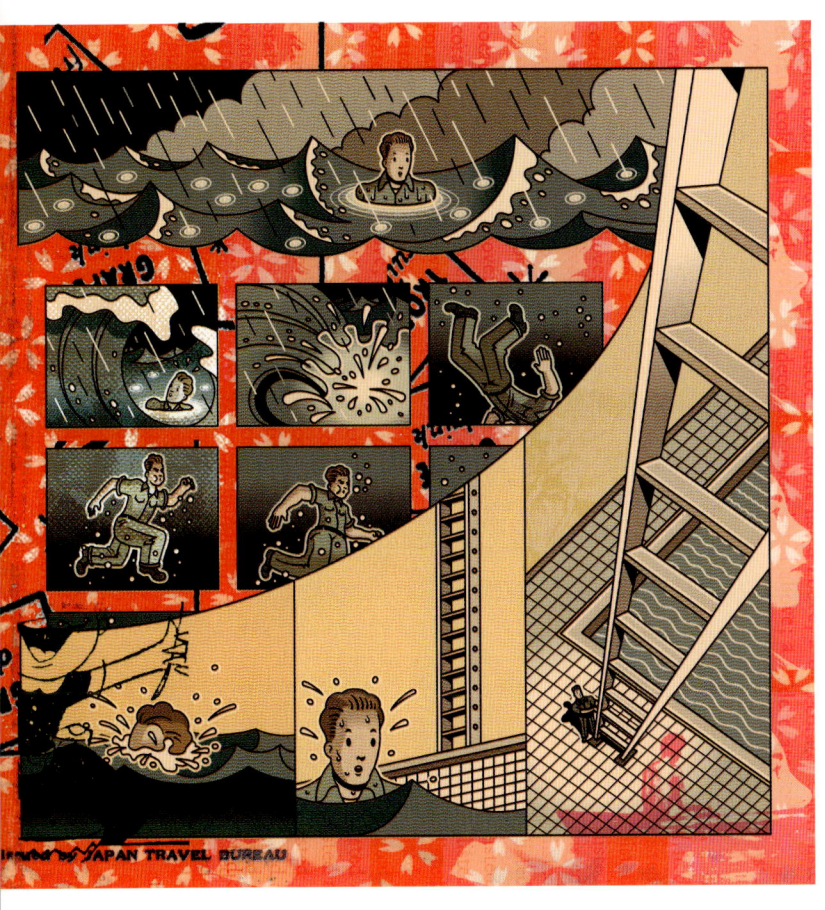

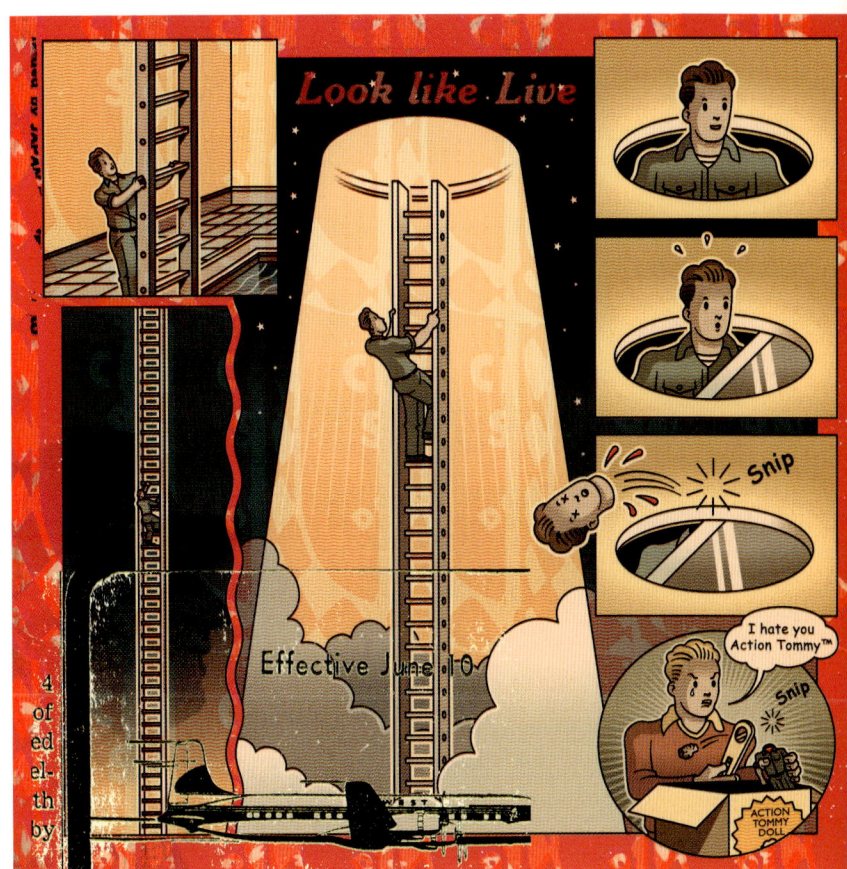

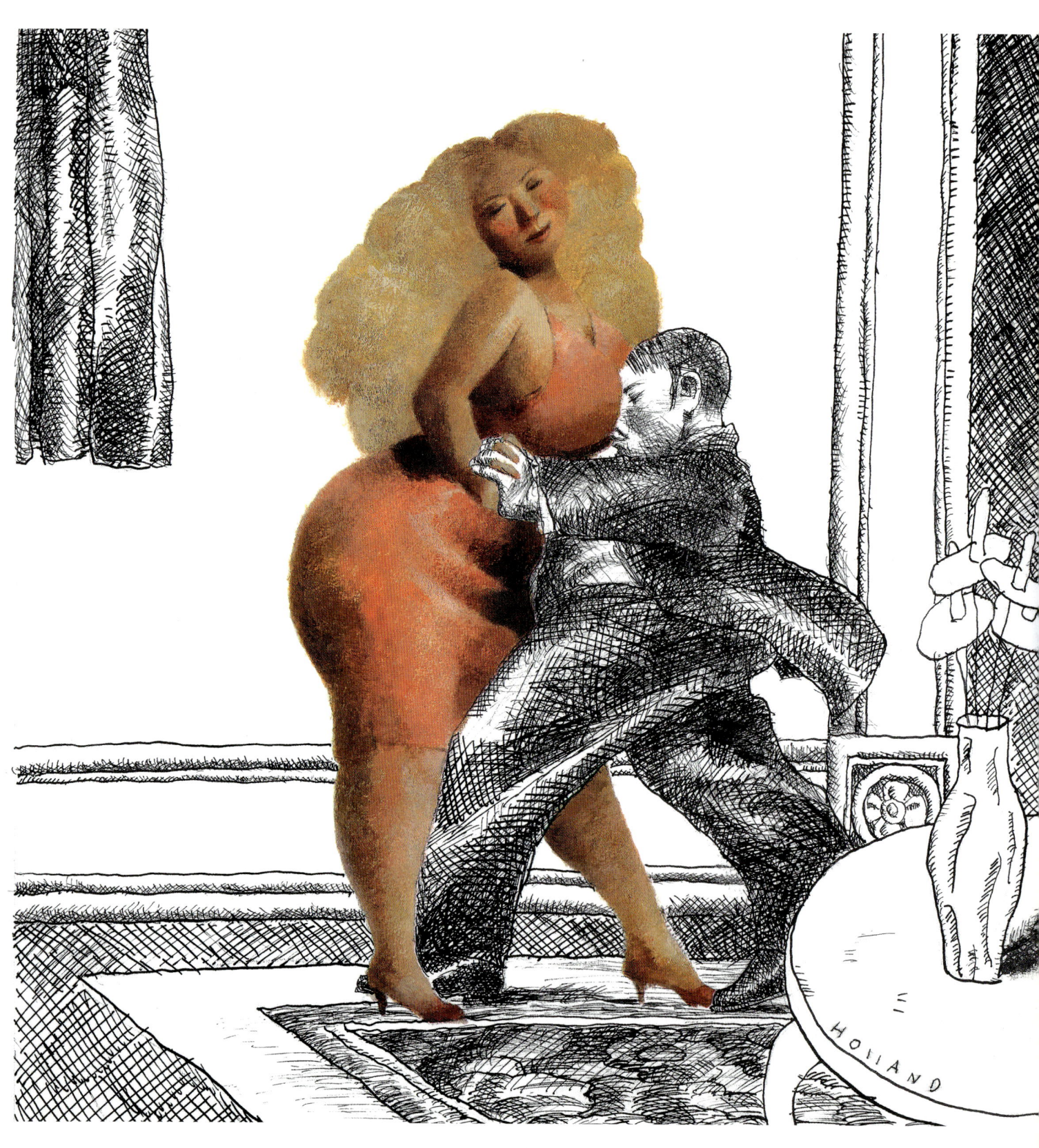

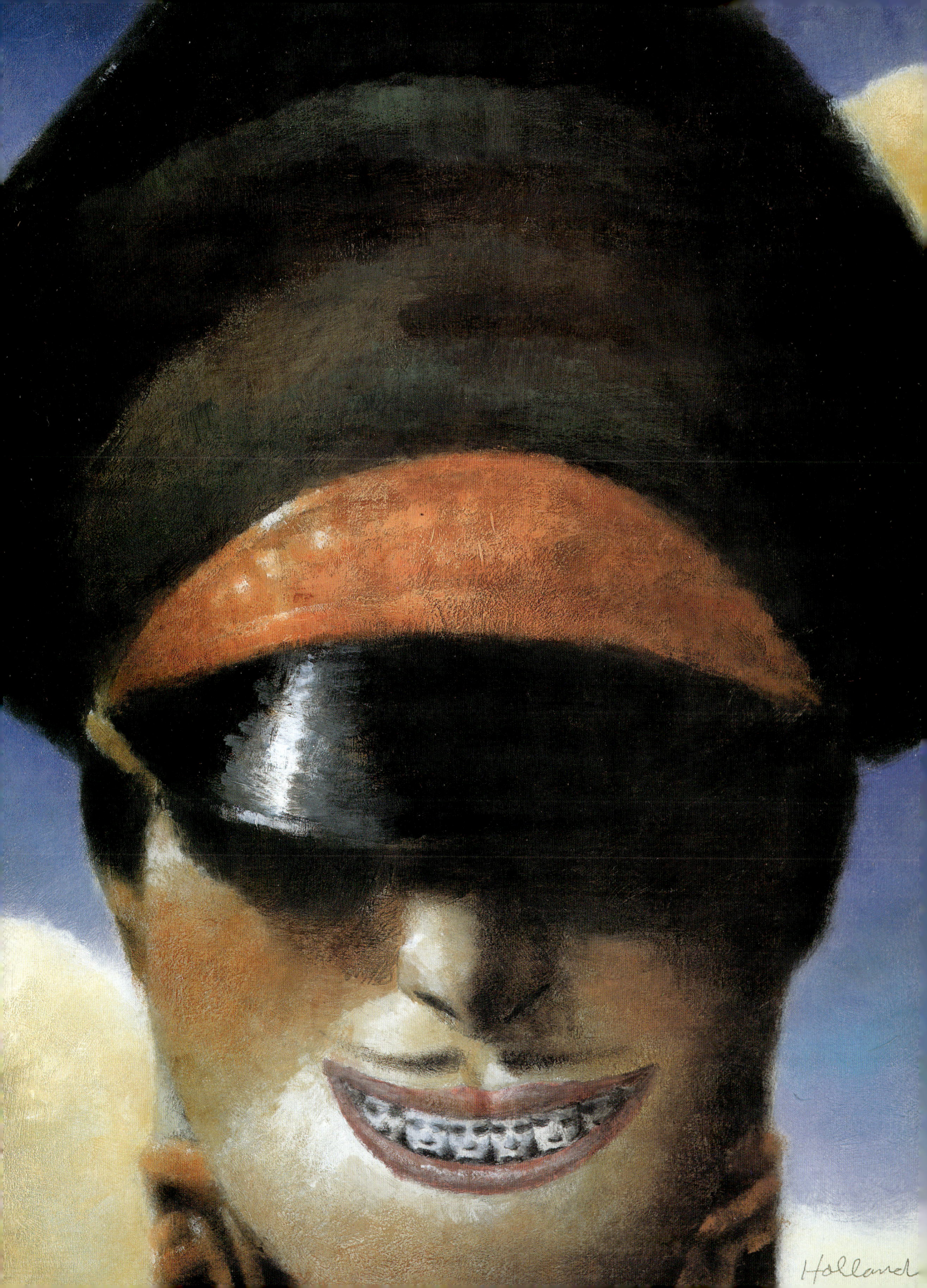

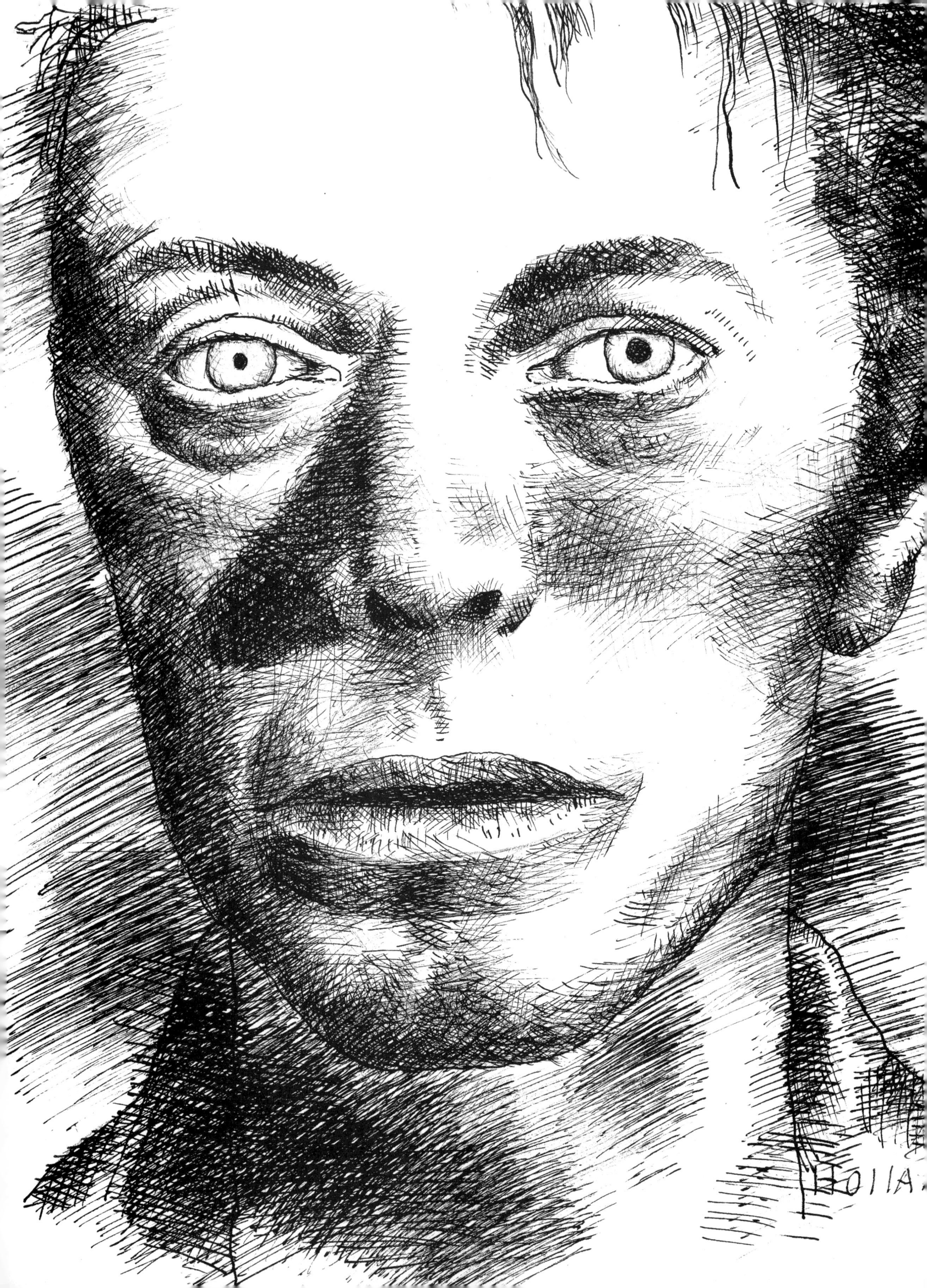

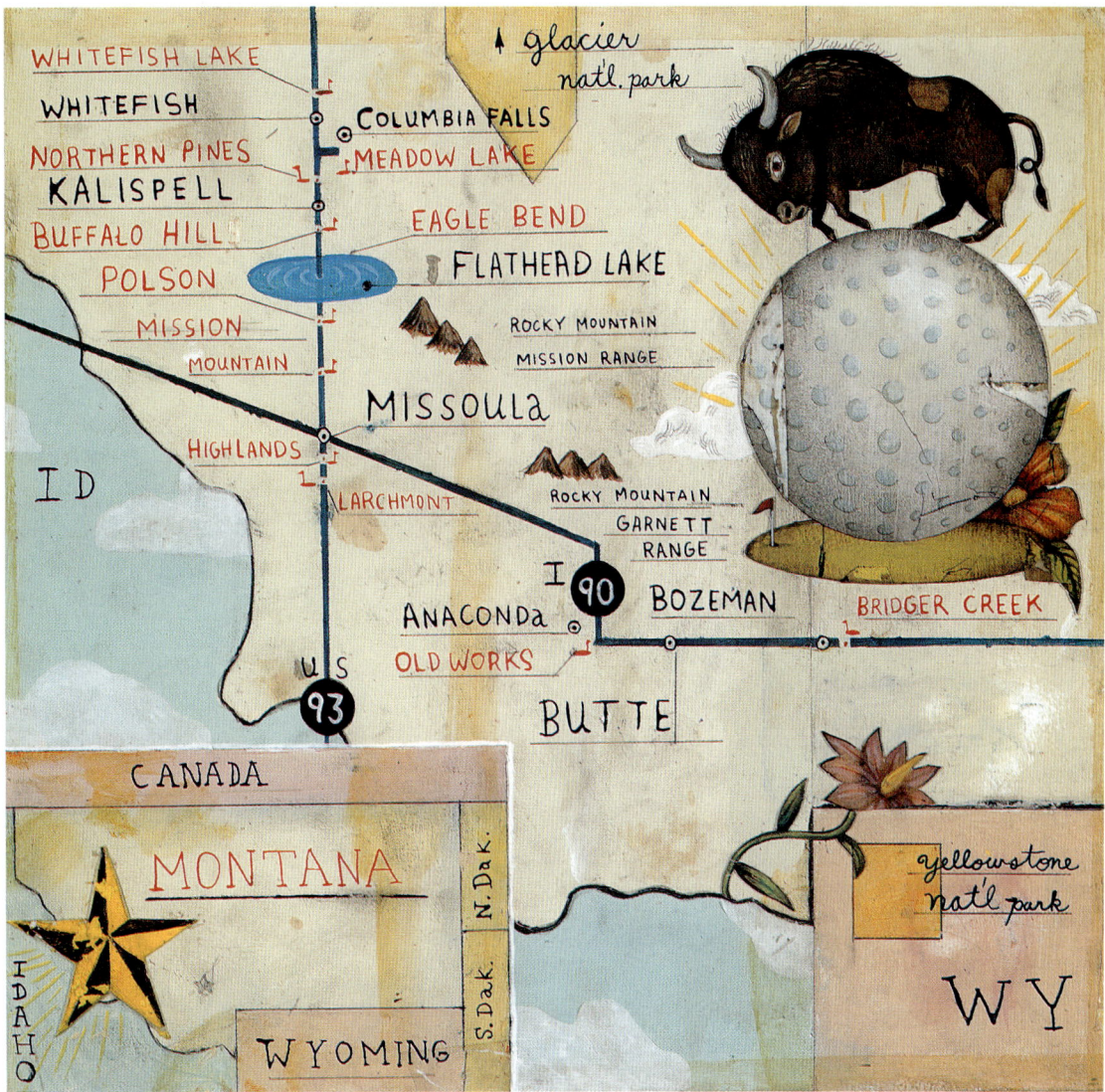

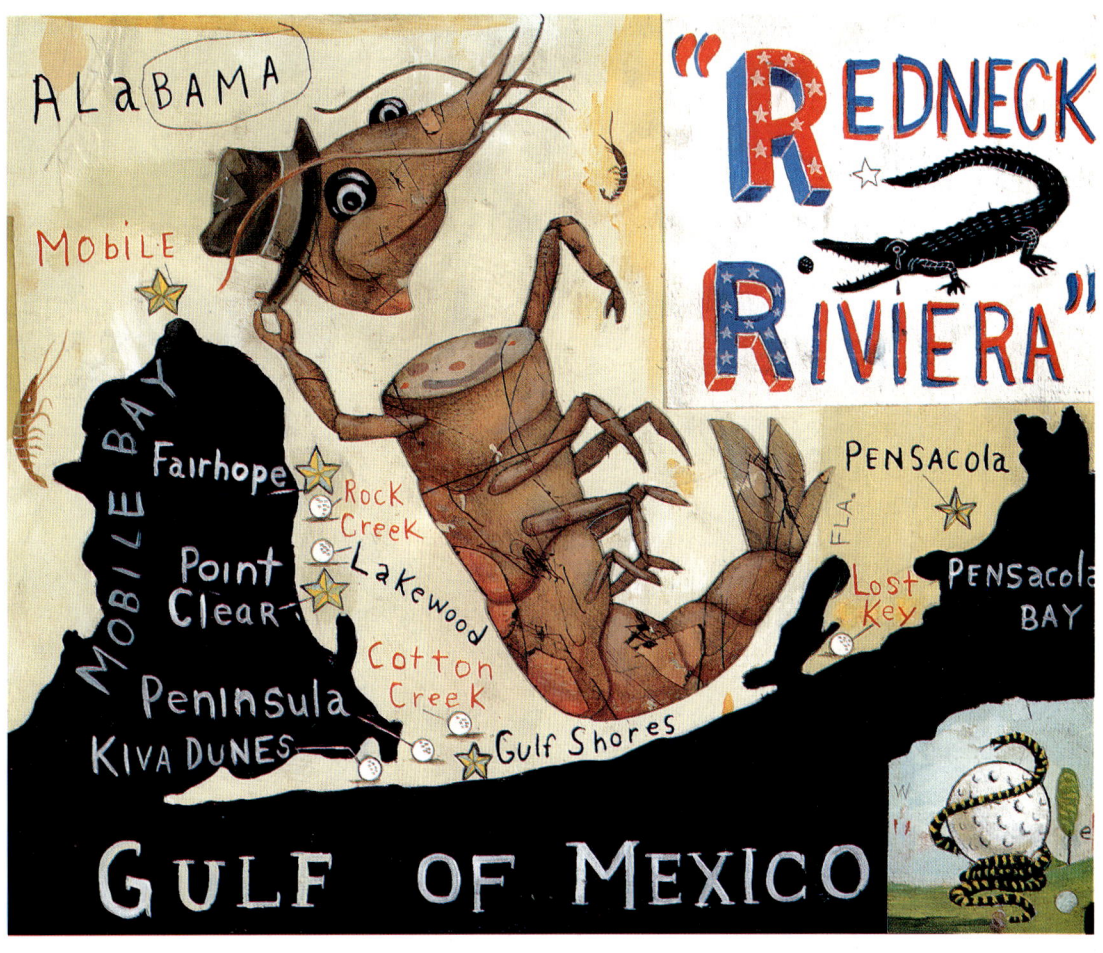

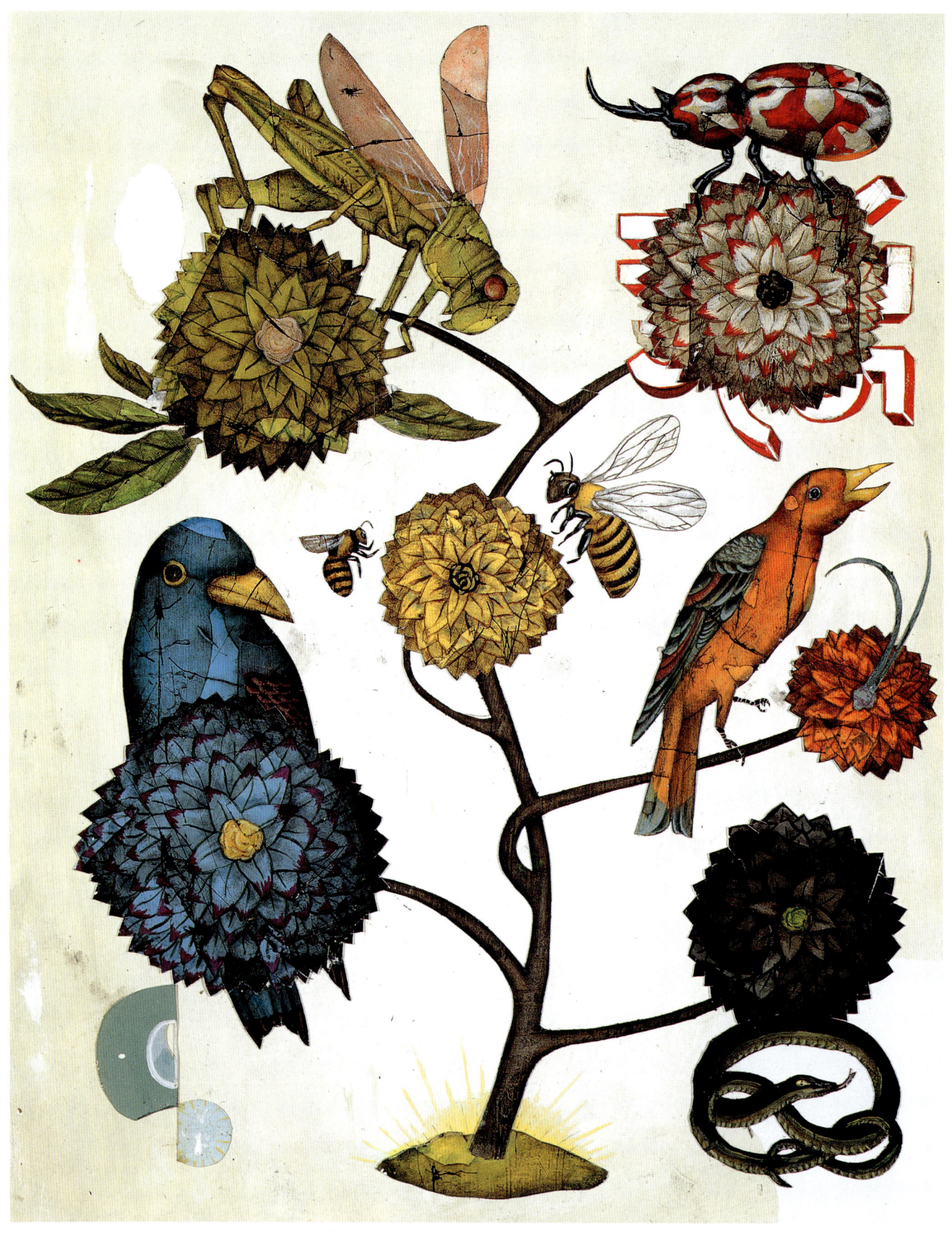

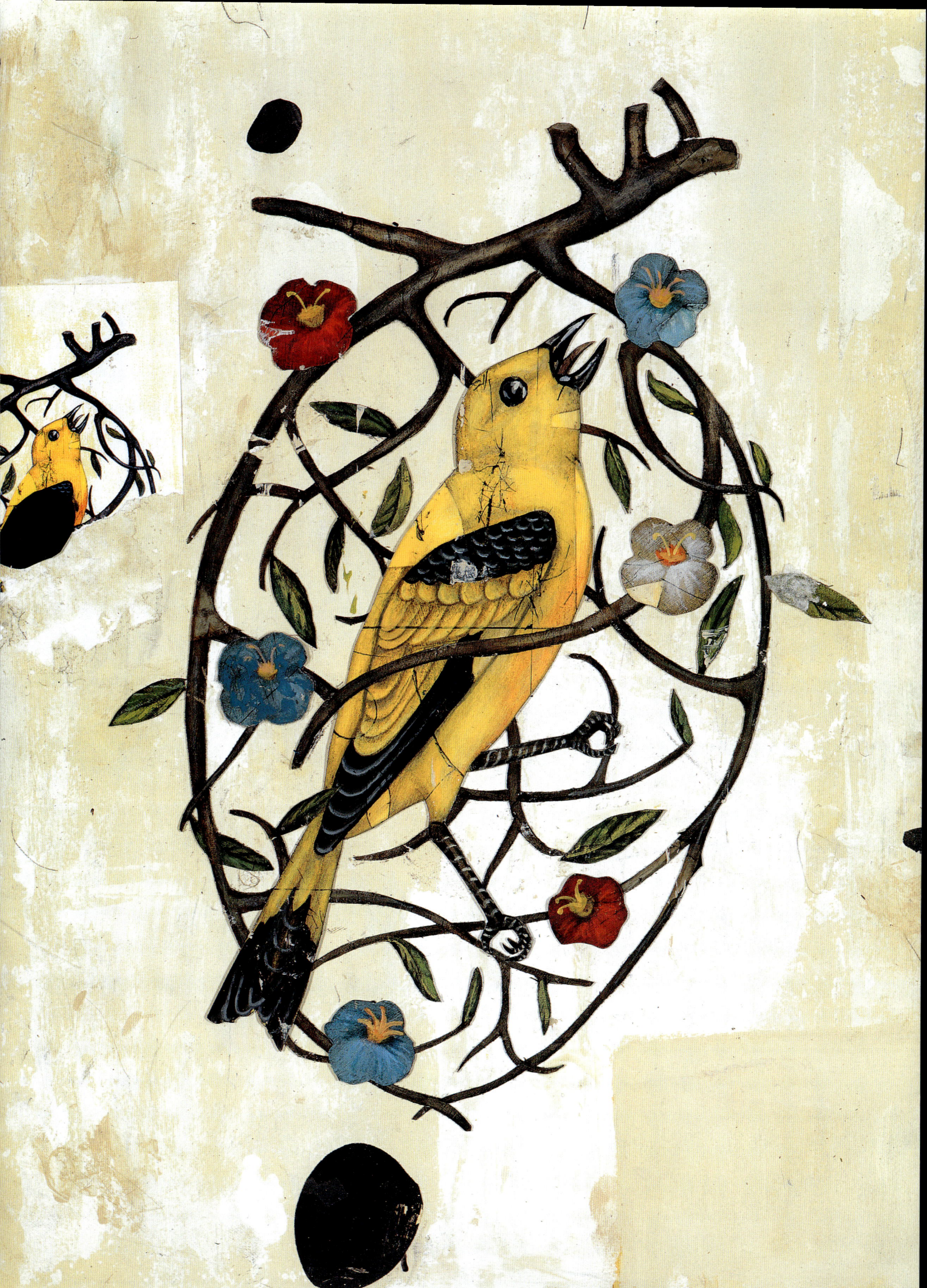

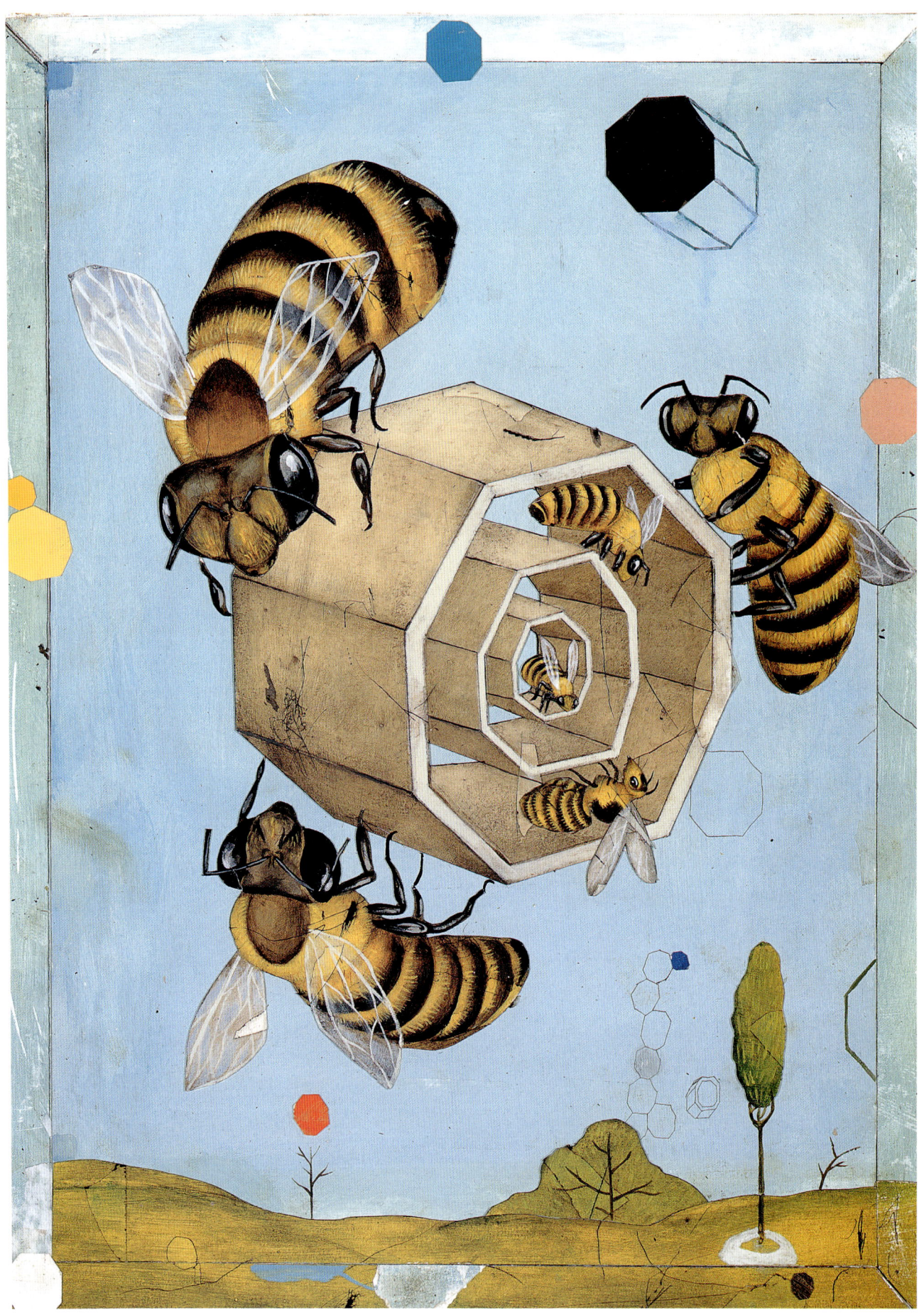

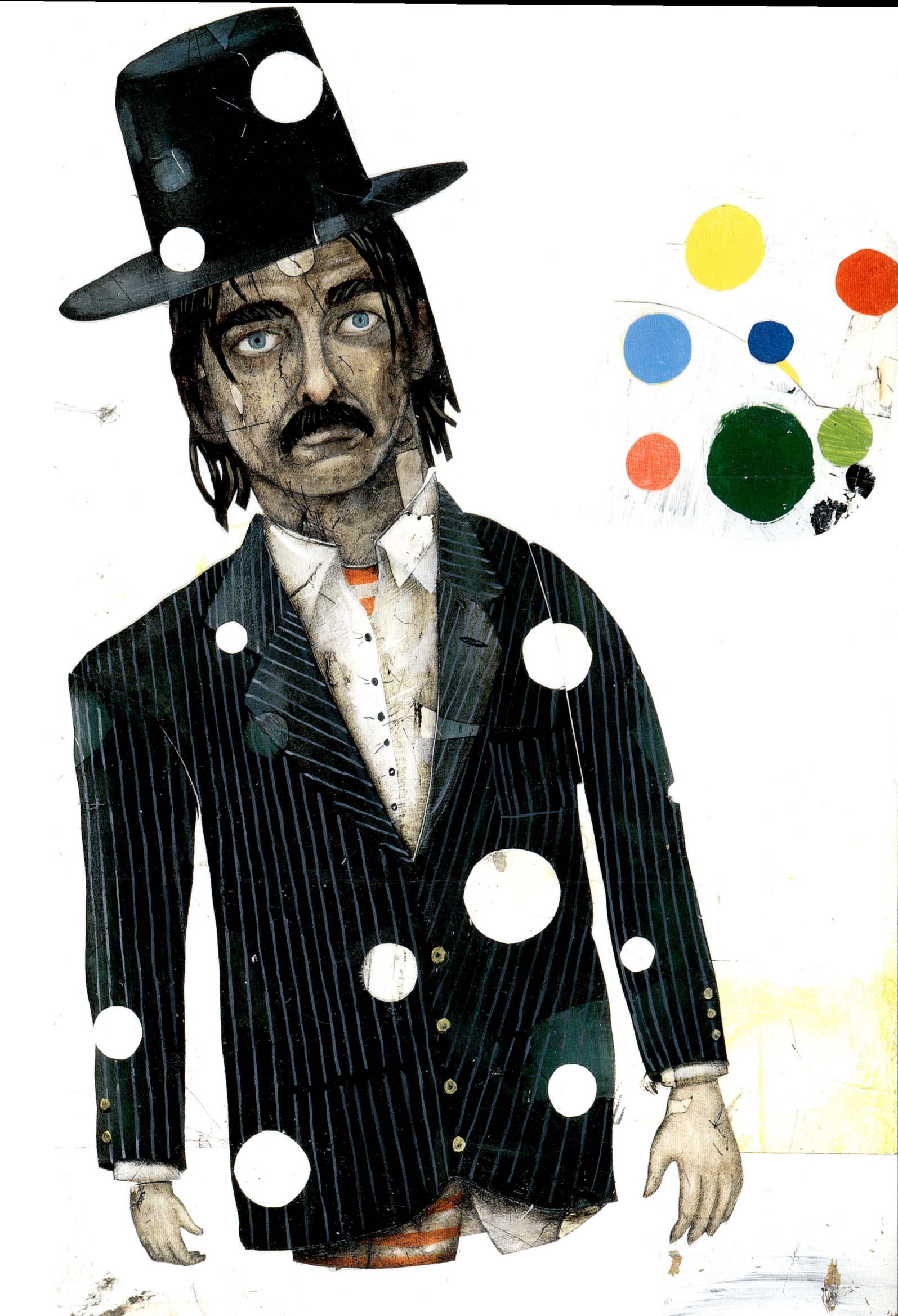

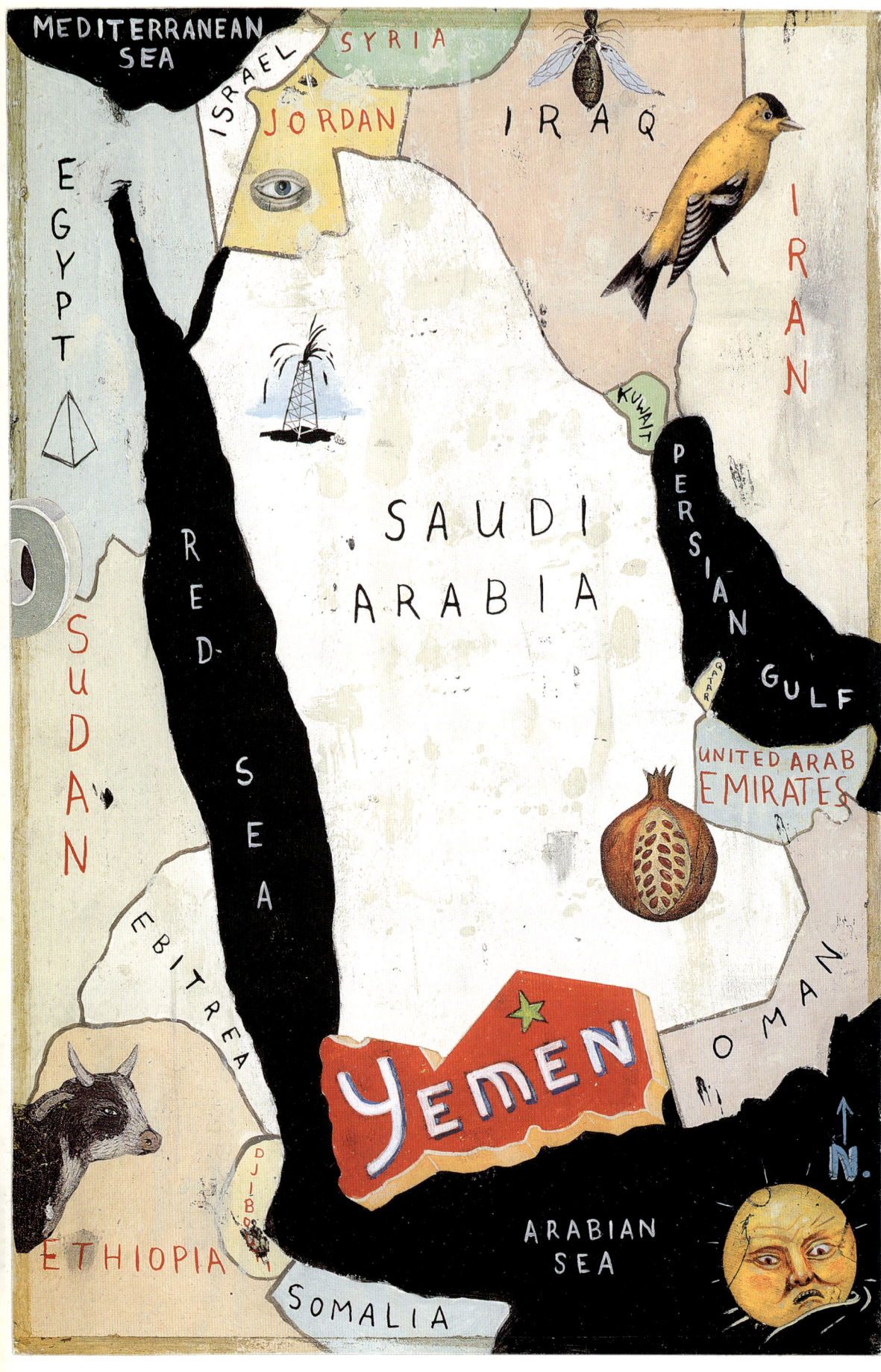

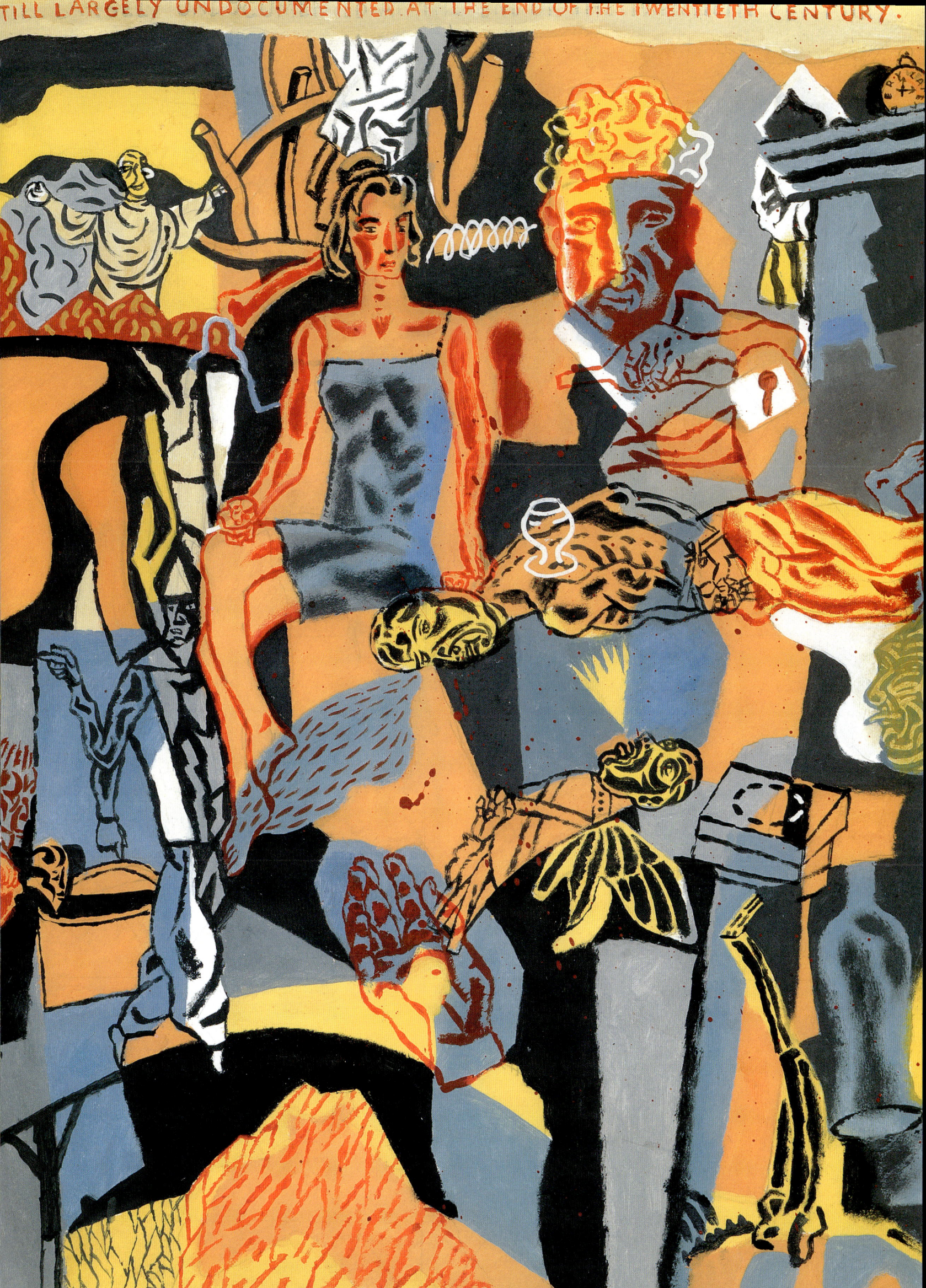

...TILL LARGELY UNDOCUMENTED AT THE END OF THE TWENTIETH CENTURY.

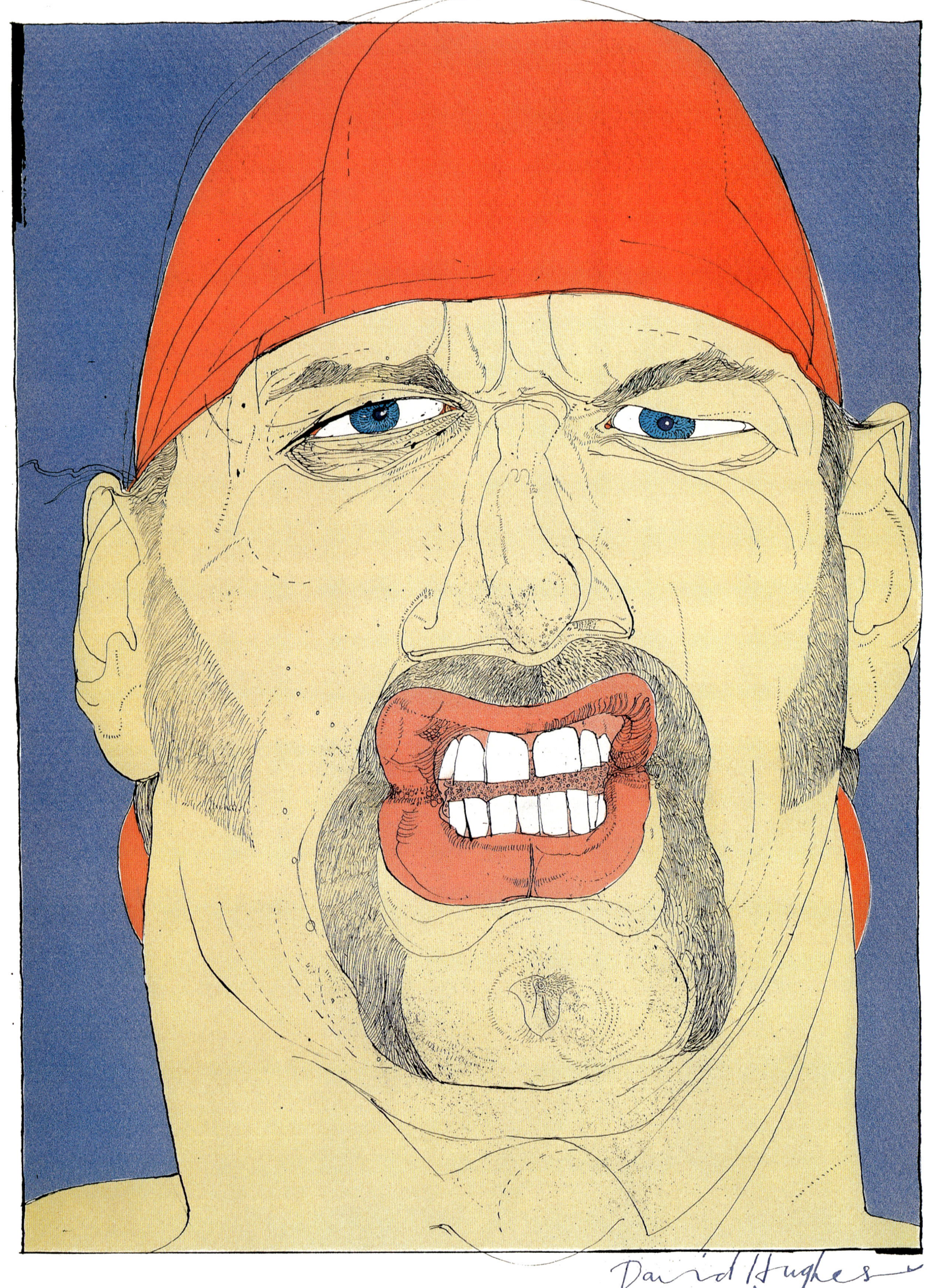

David Hughes

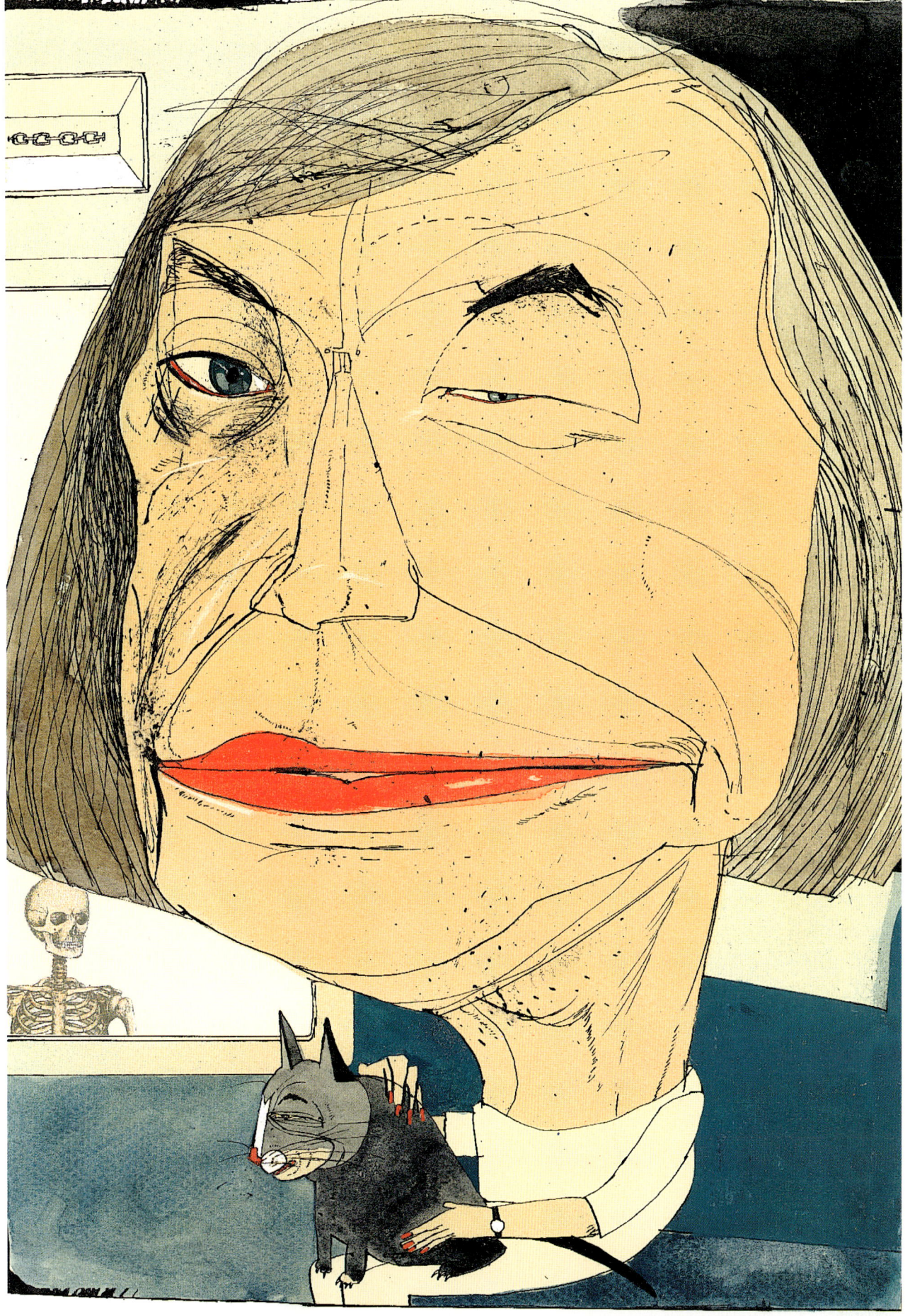

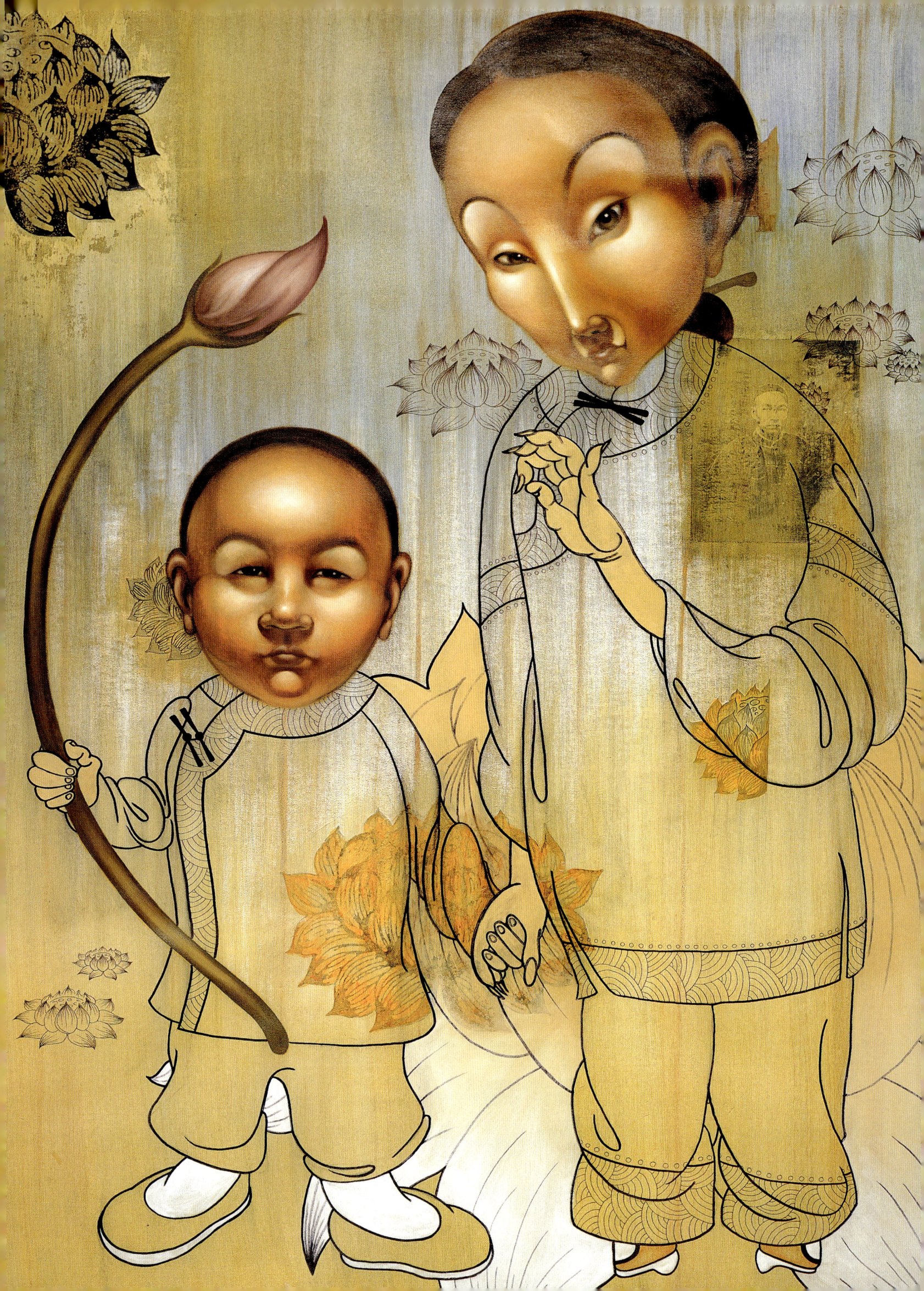

178 mirkoilić

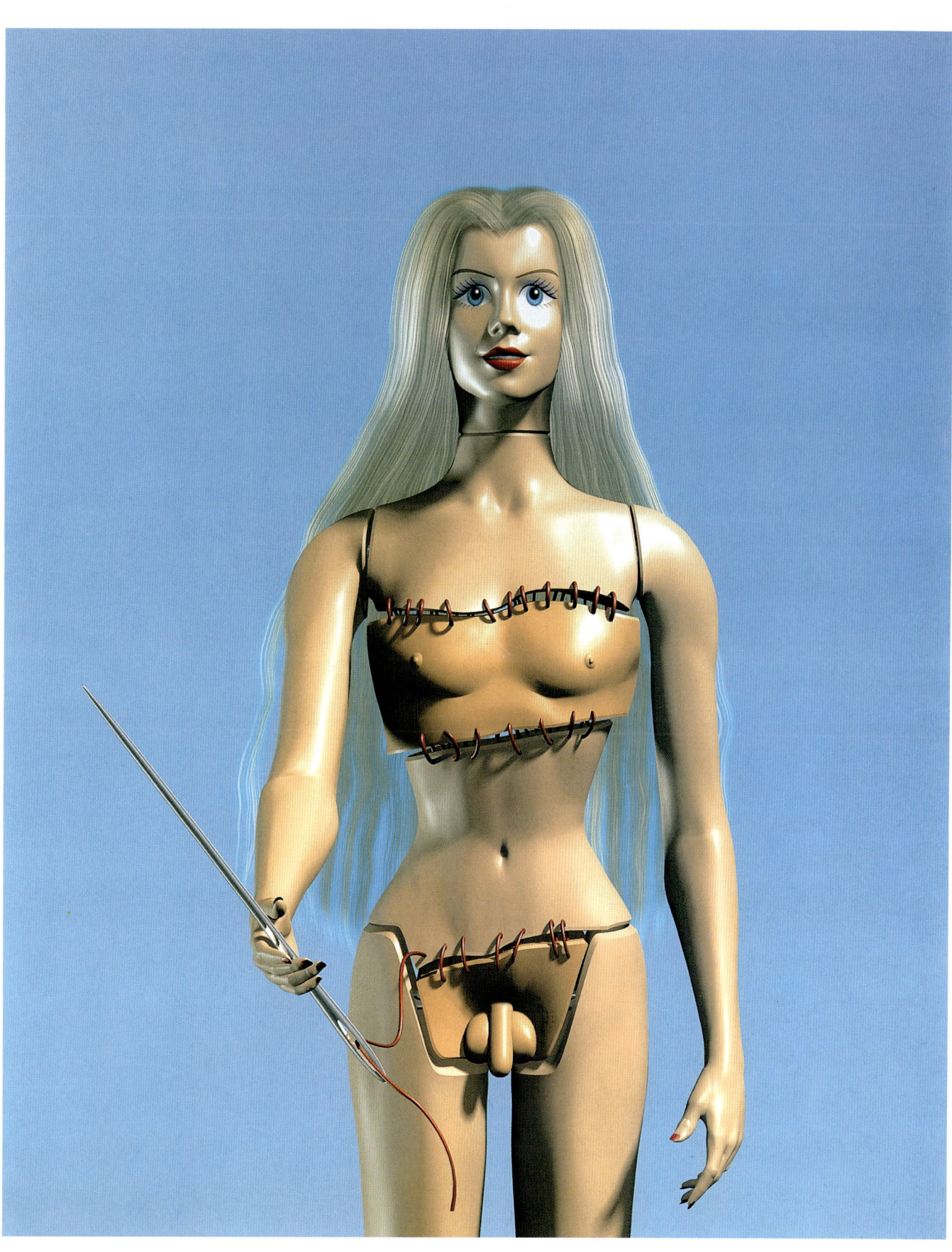

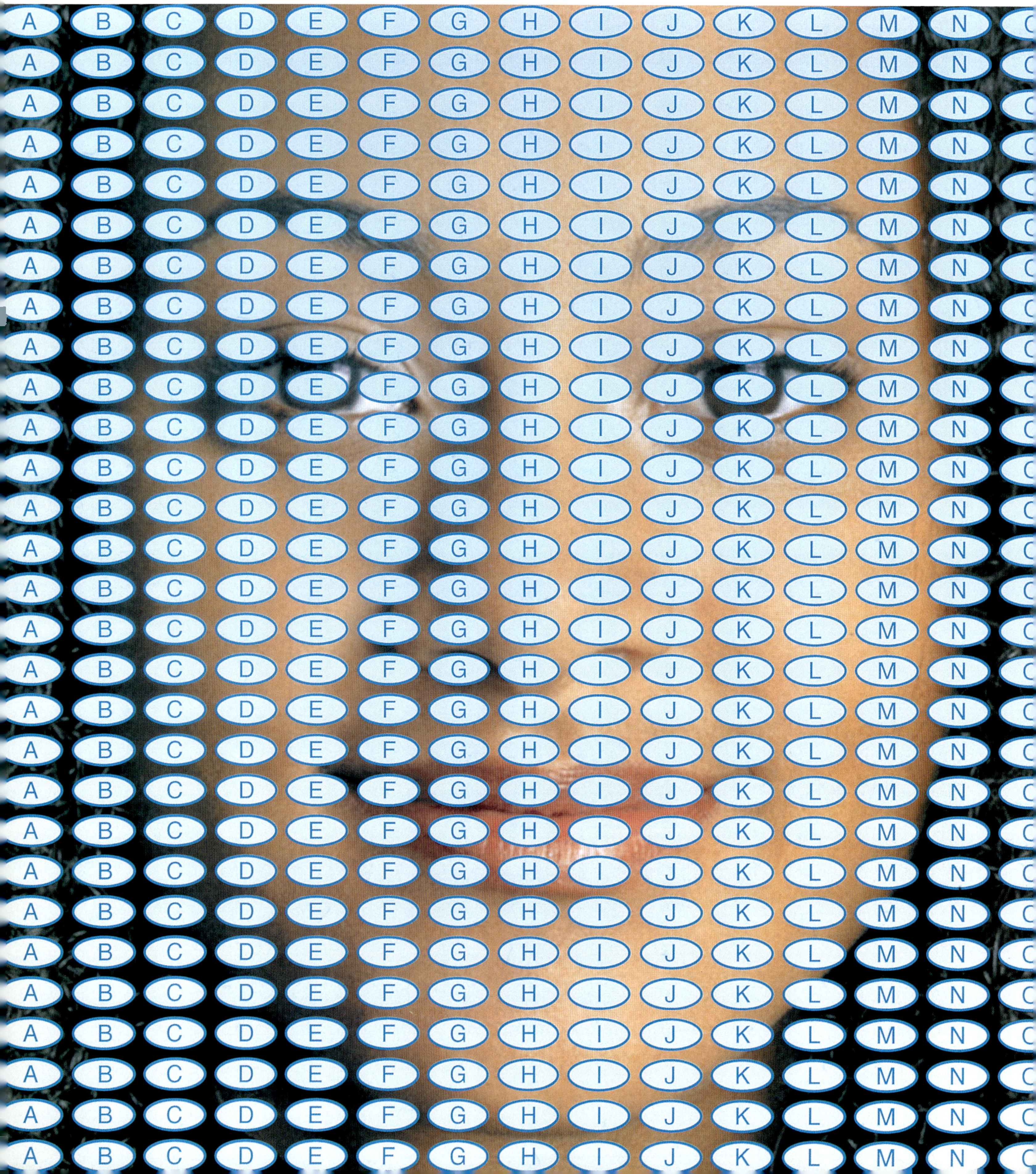

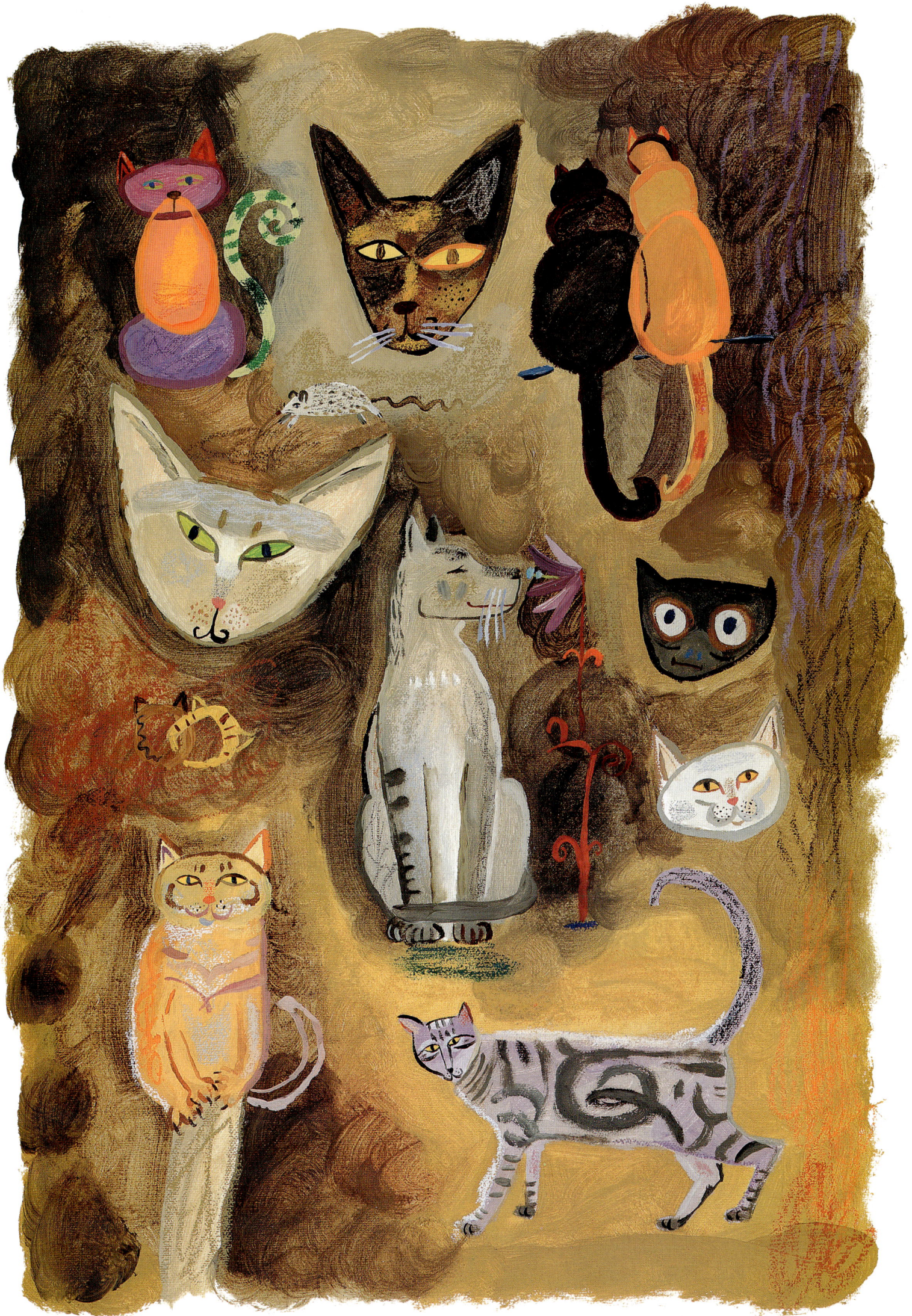

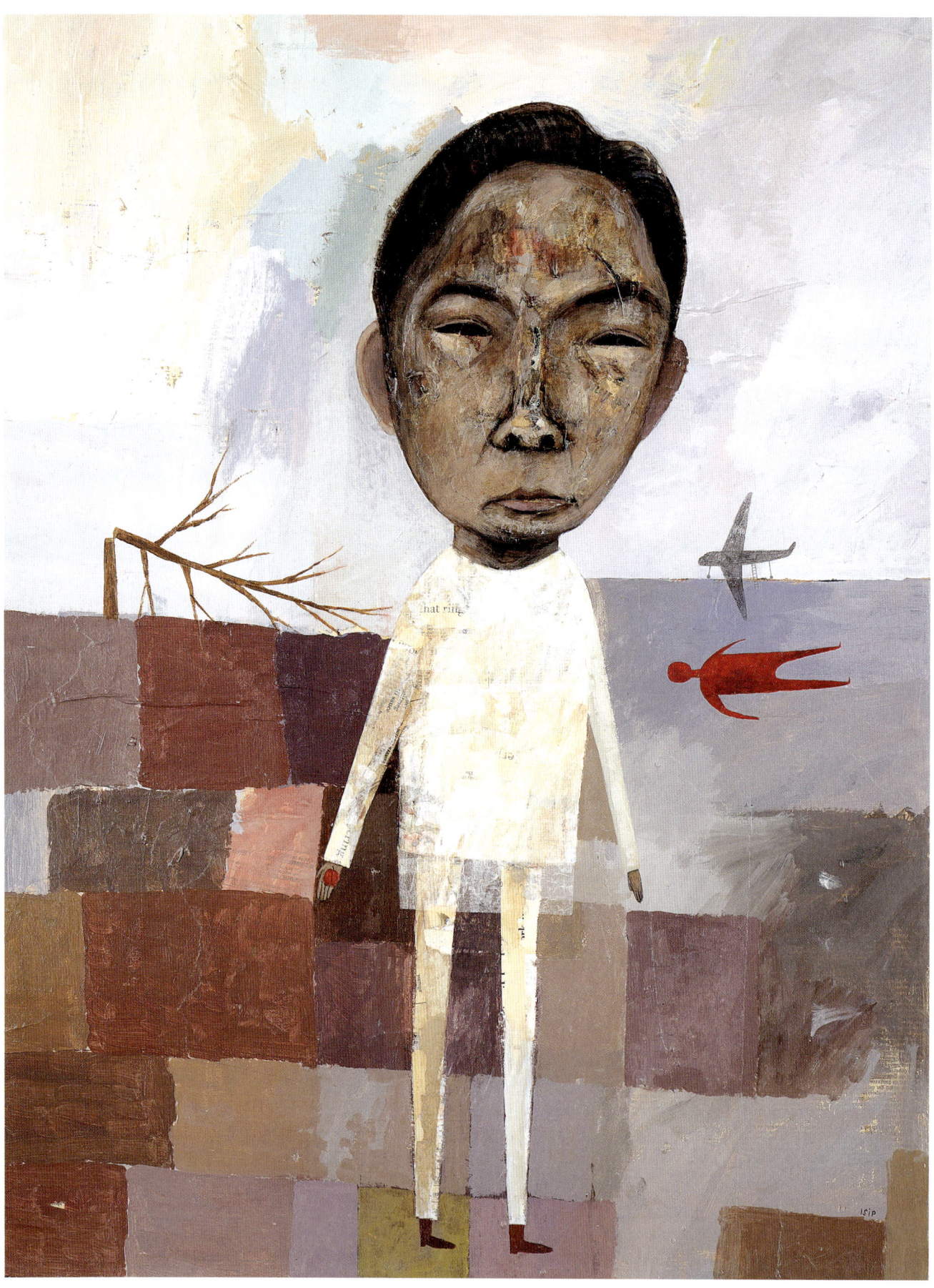

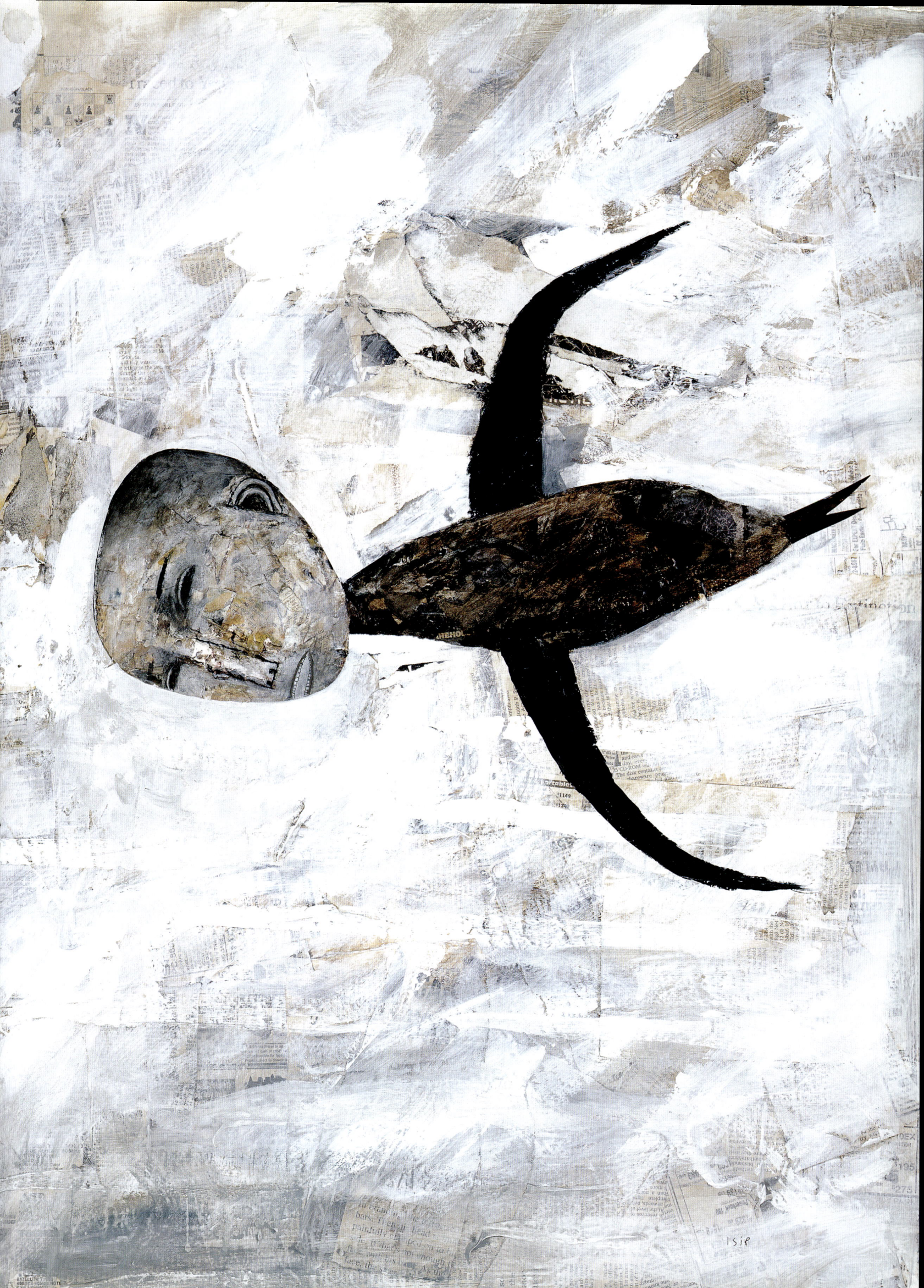

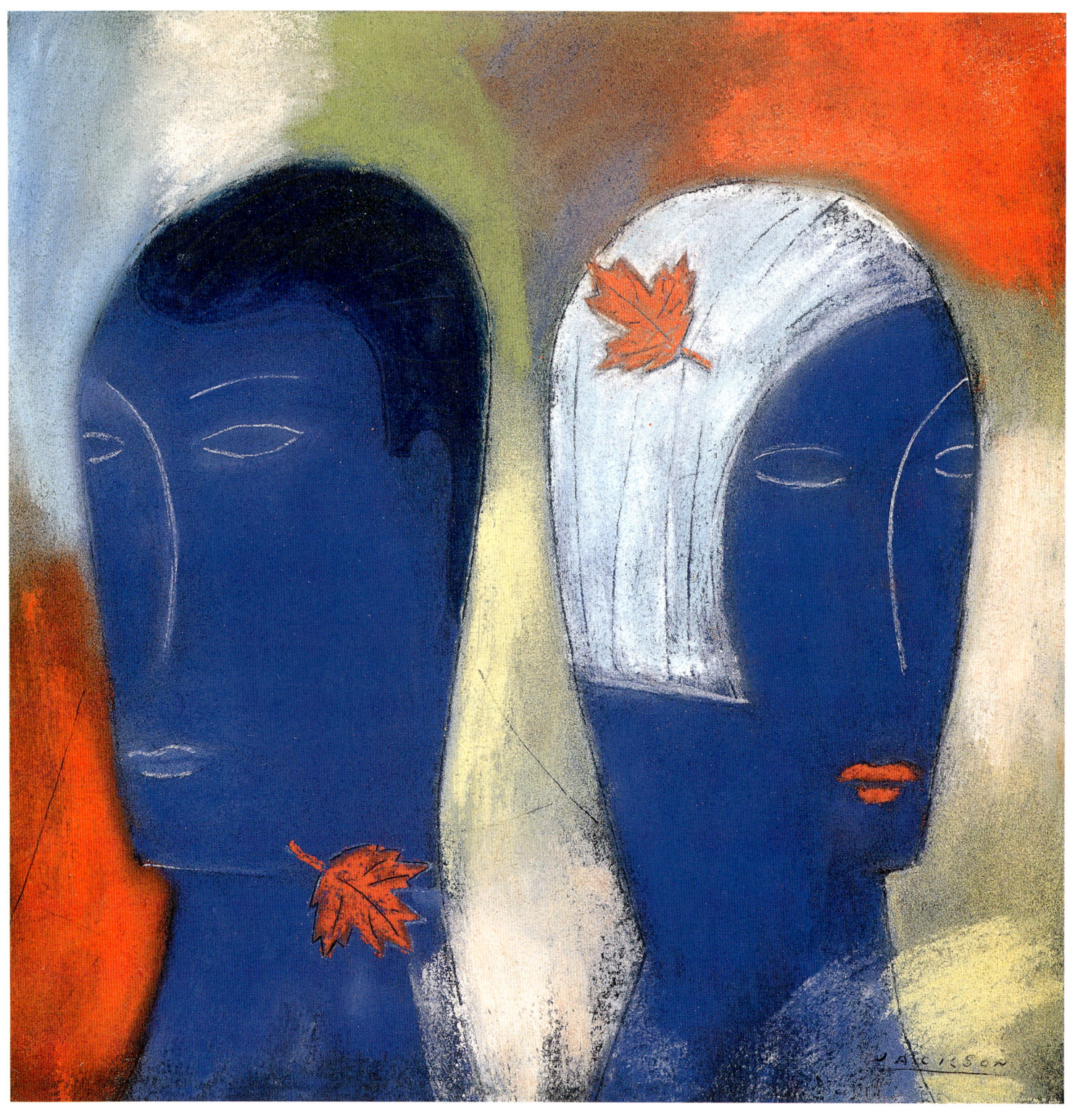

183|184 jeff jackson

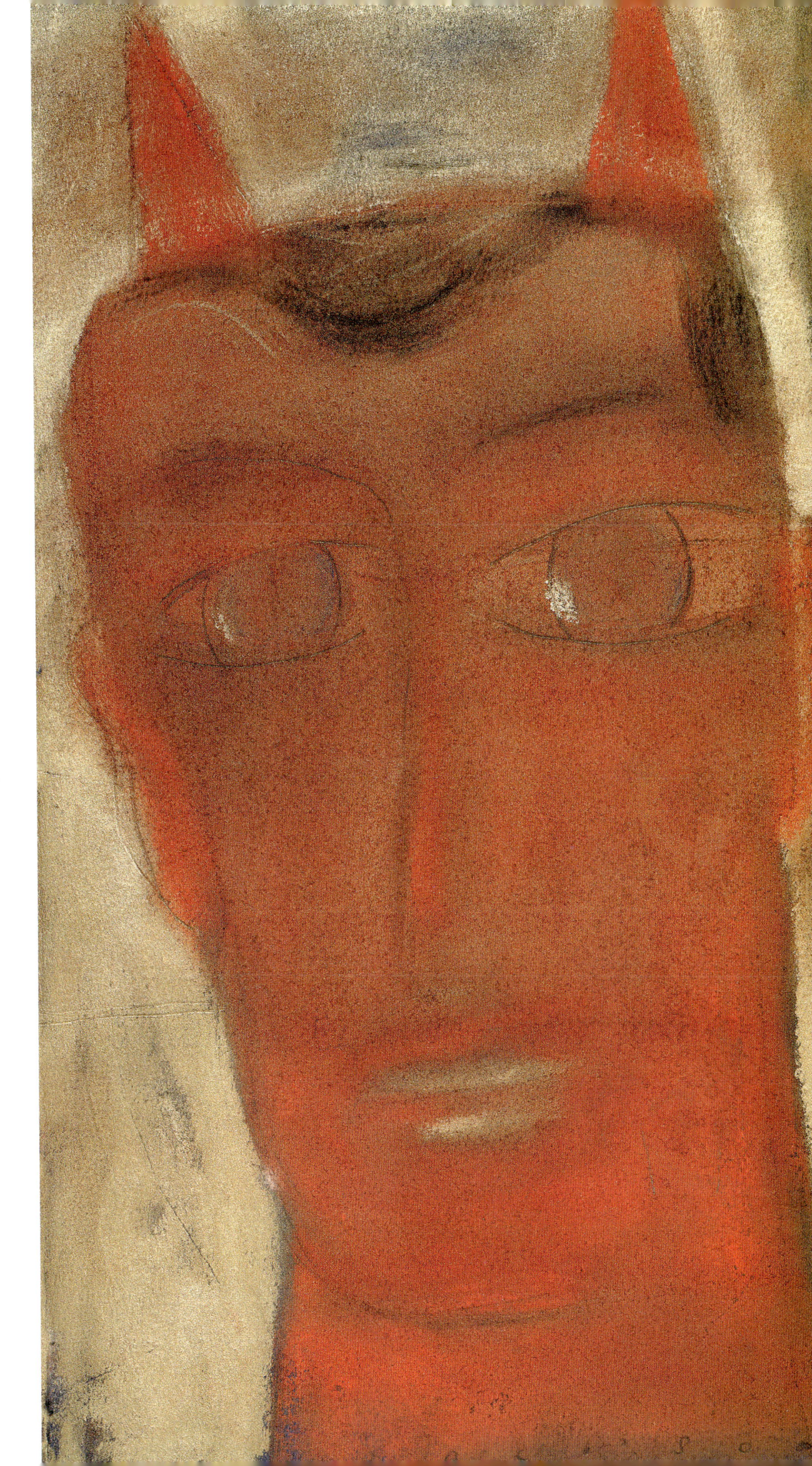

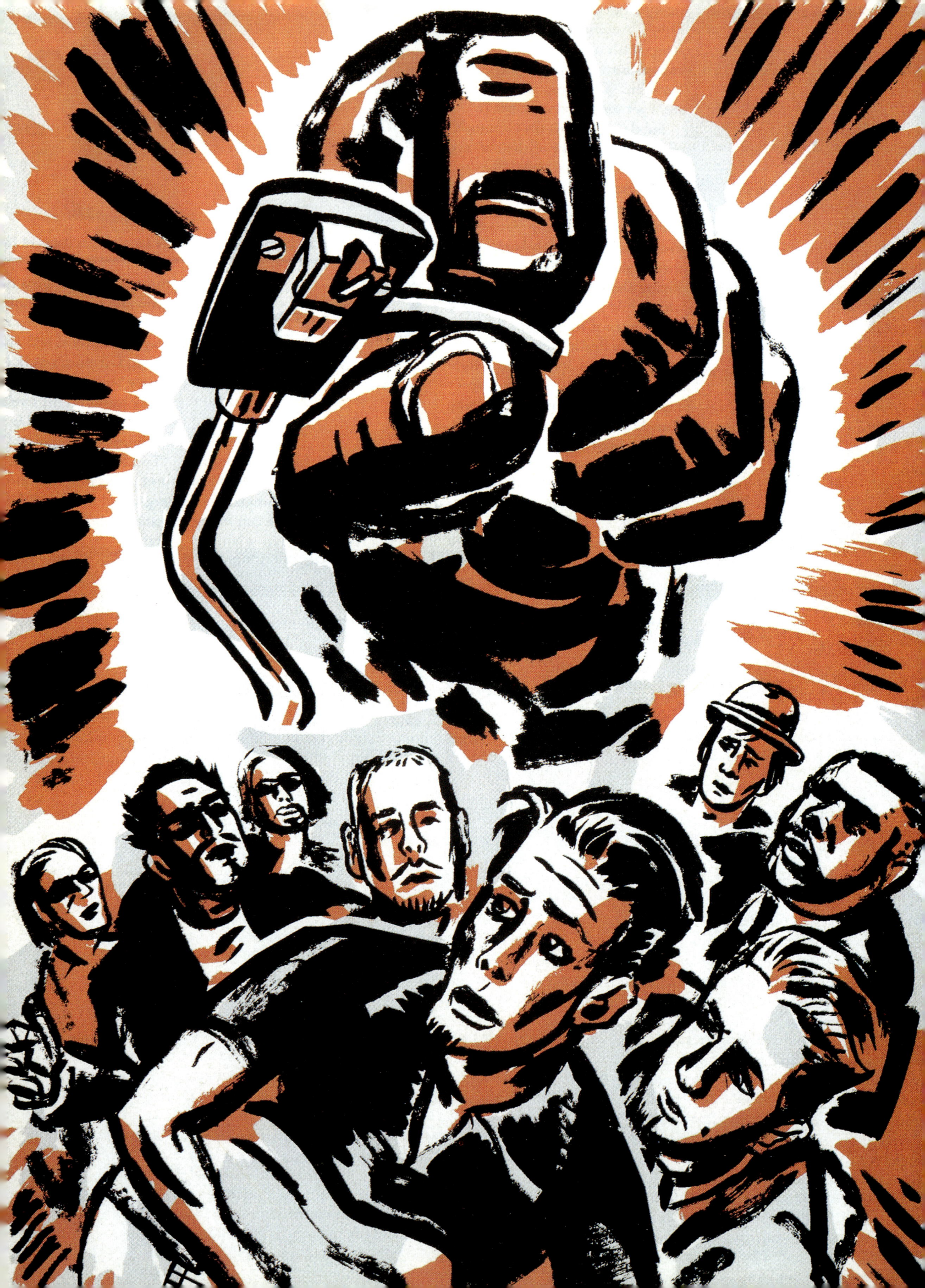

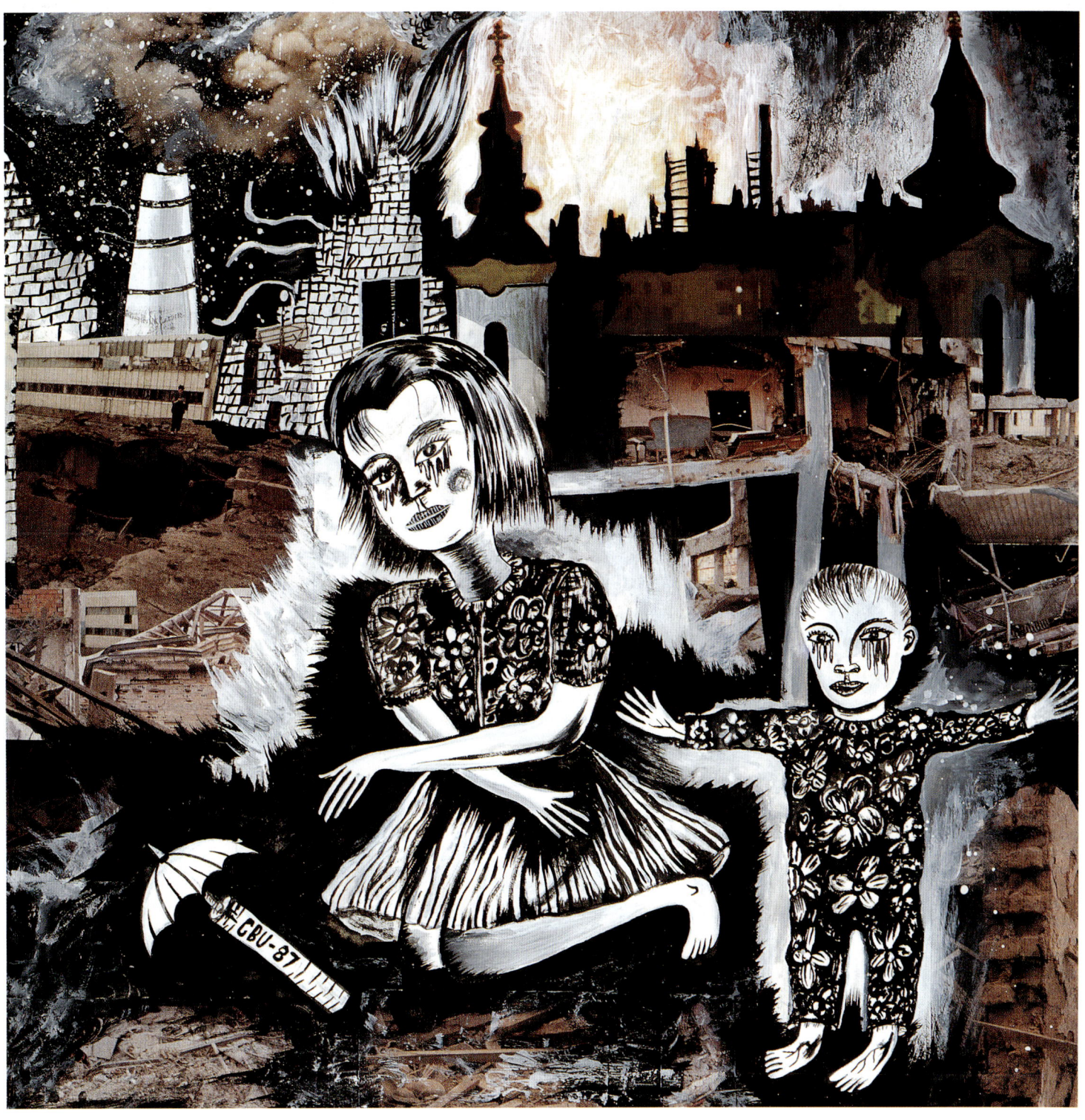

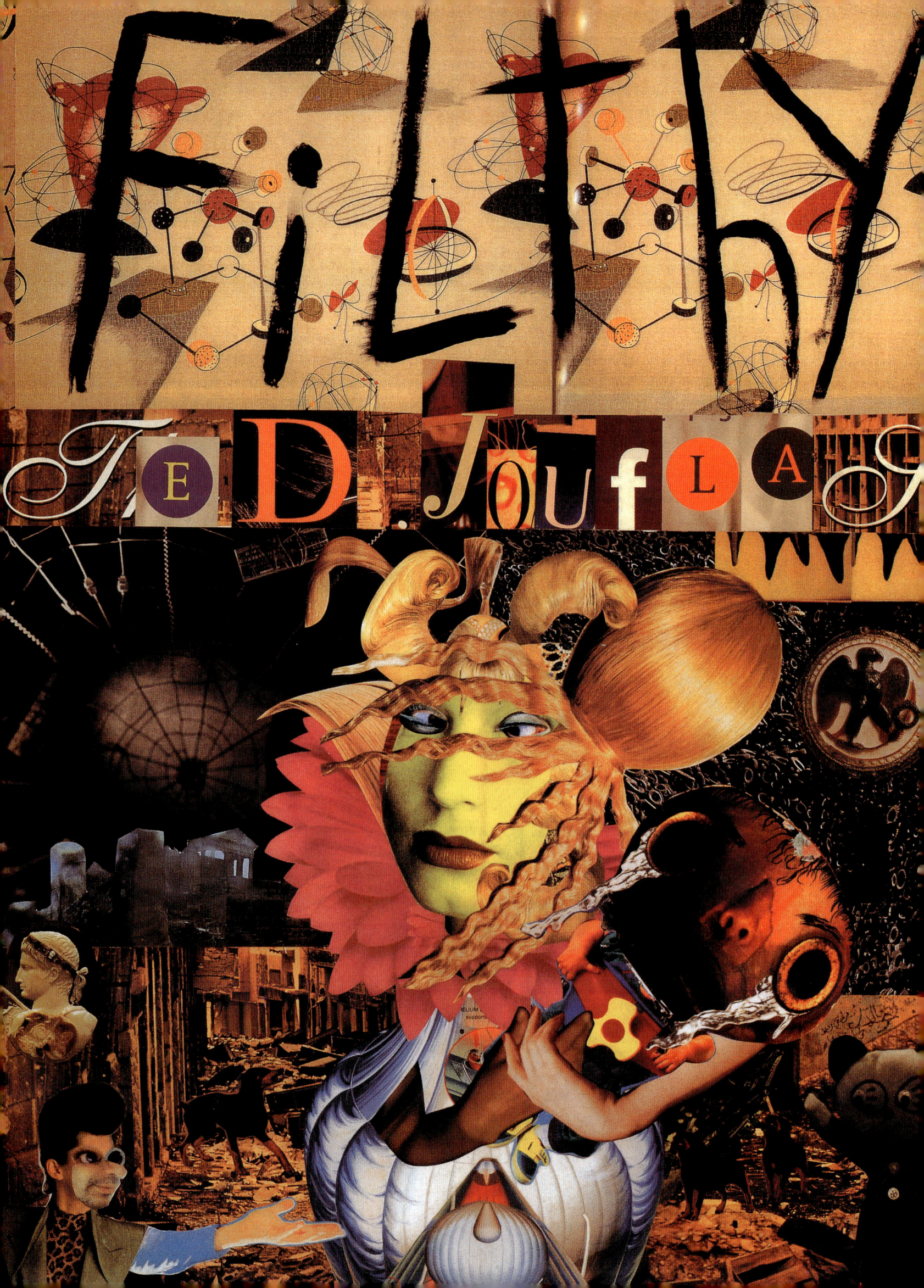

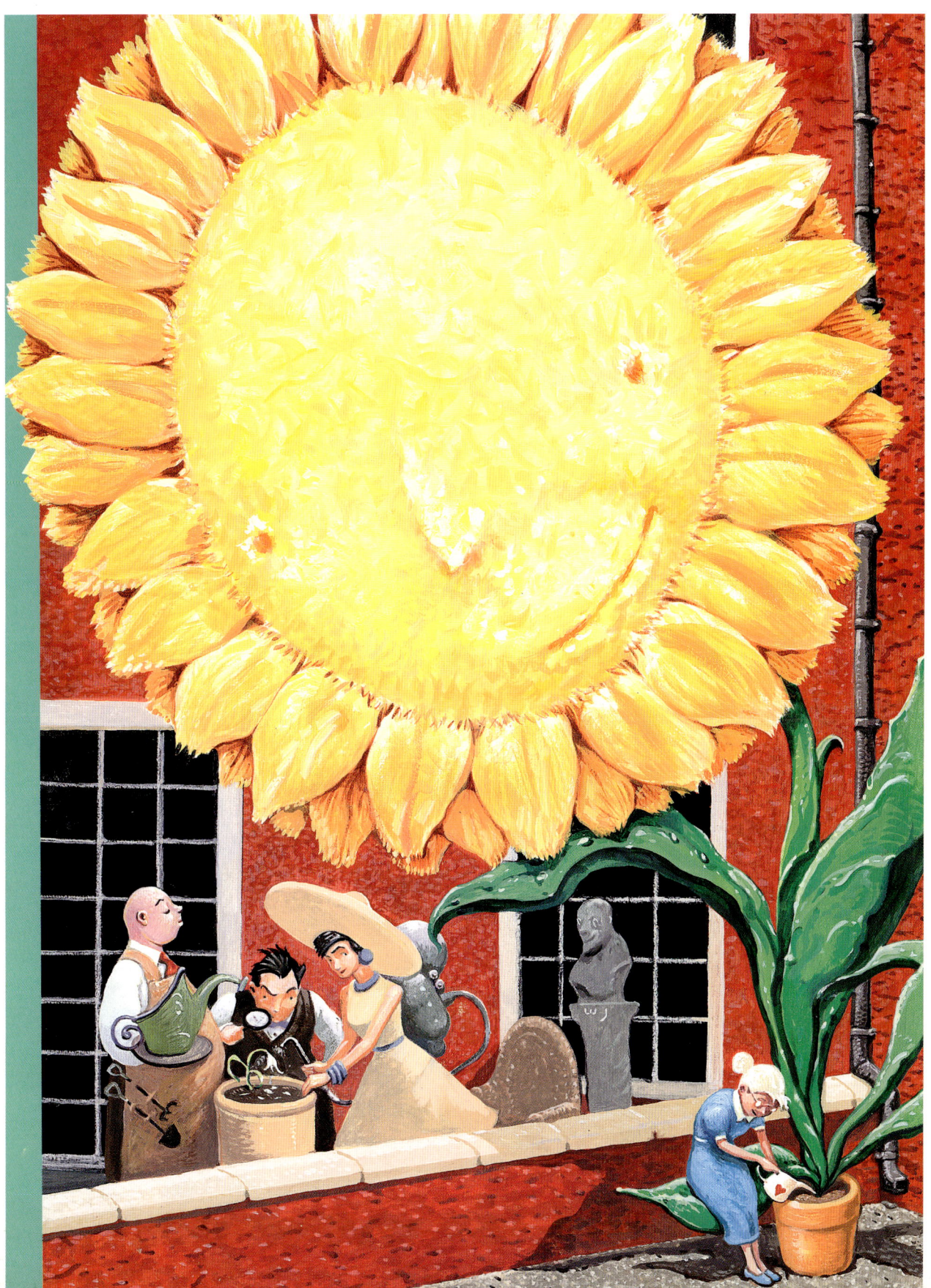

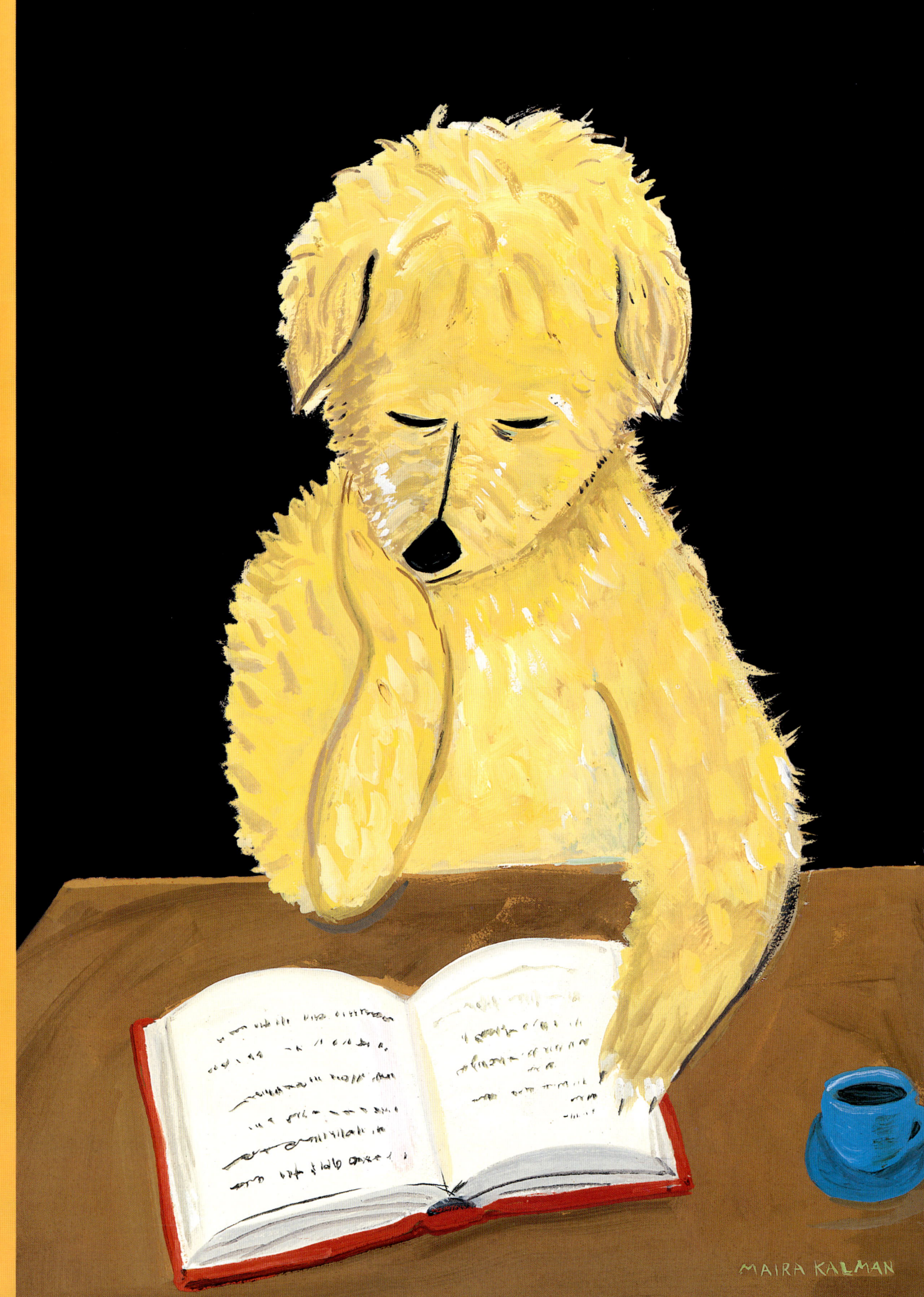

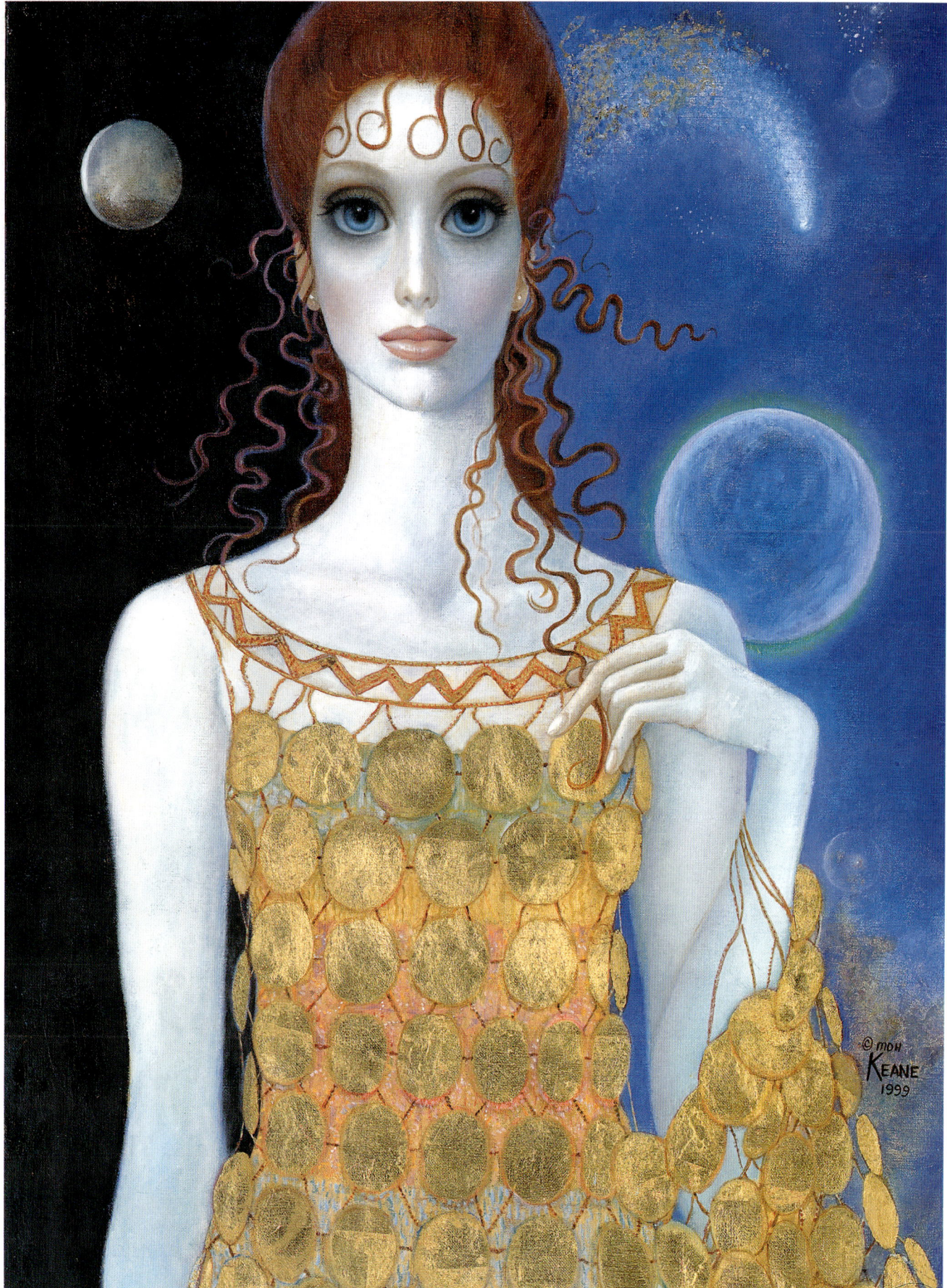

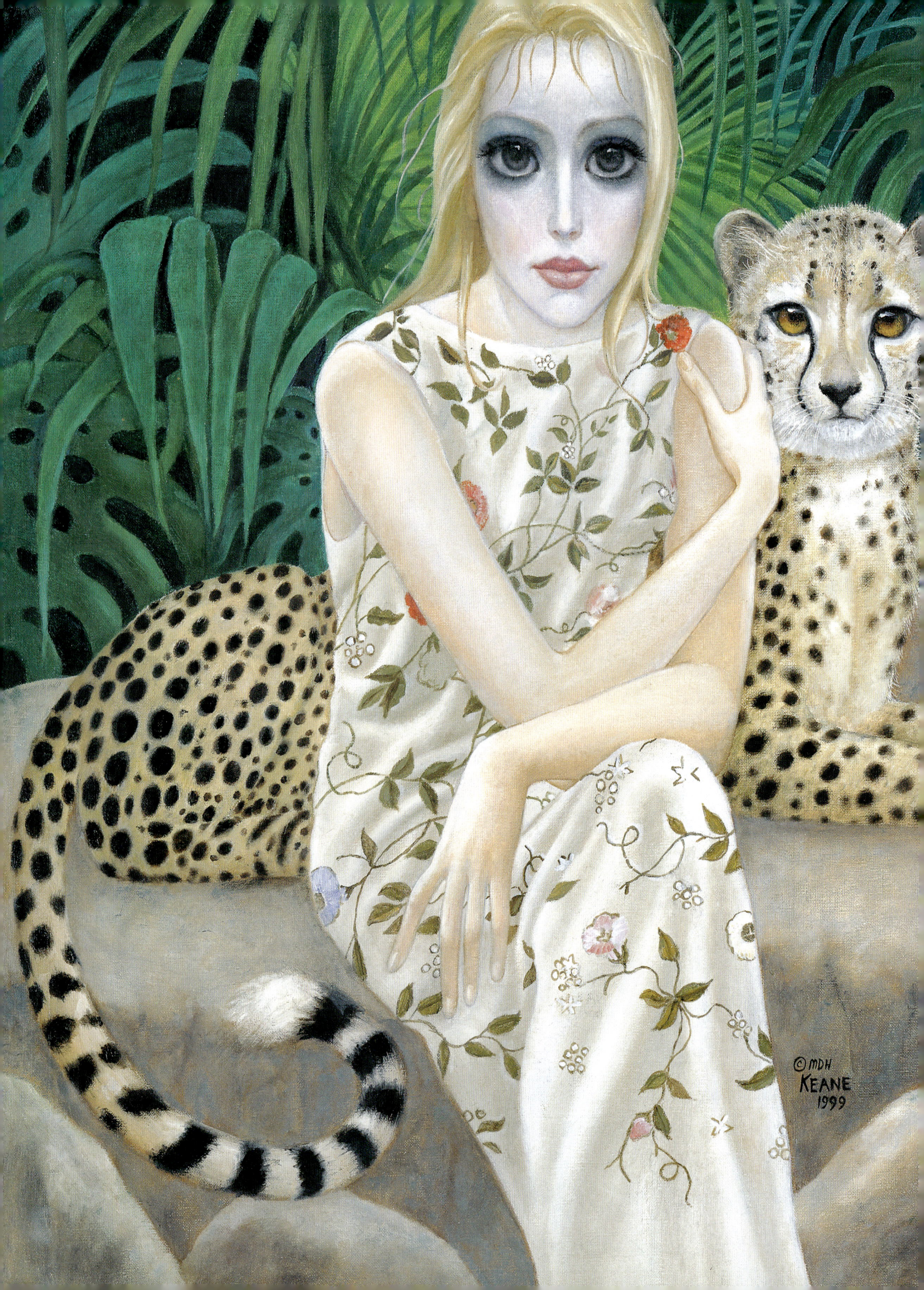

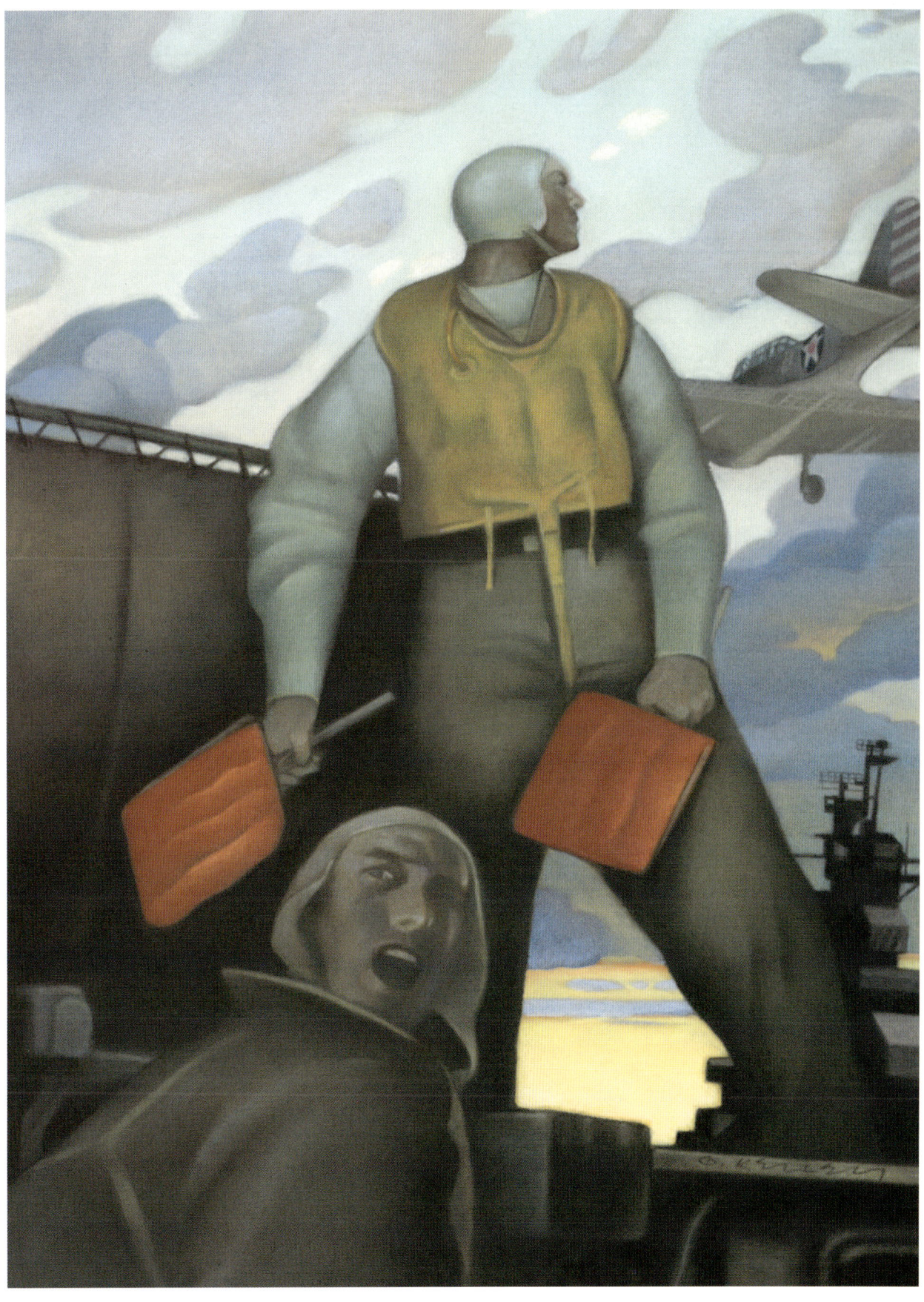

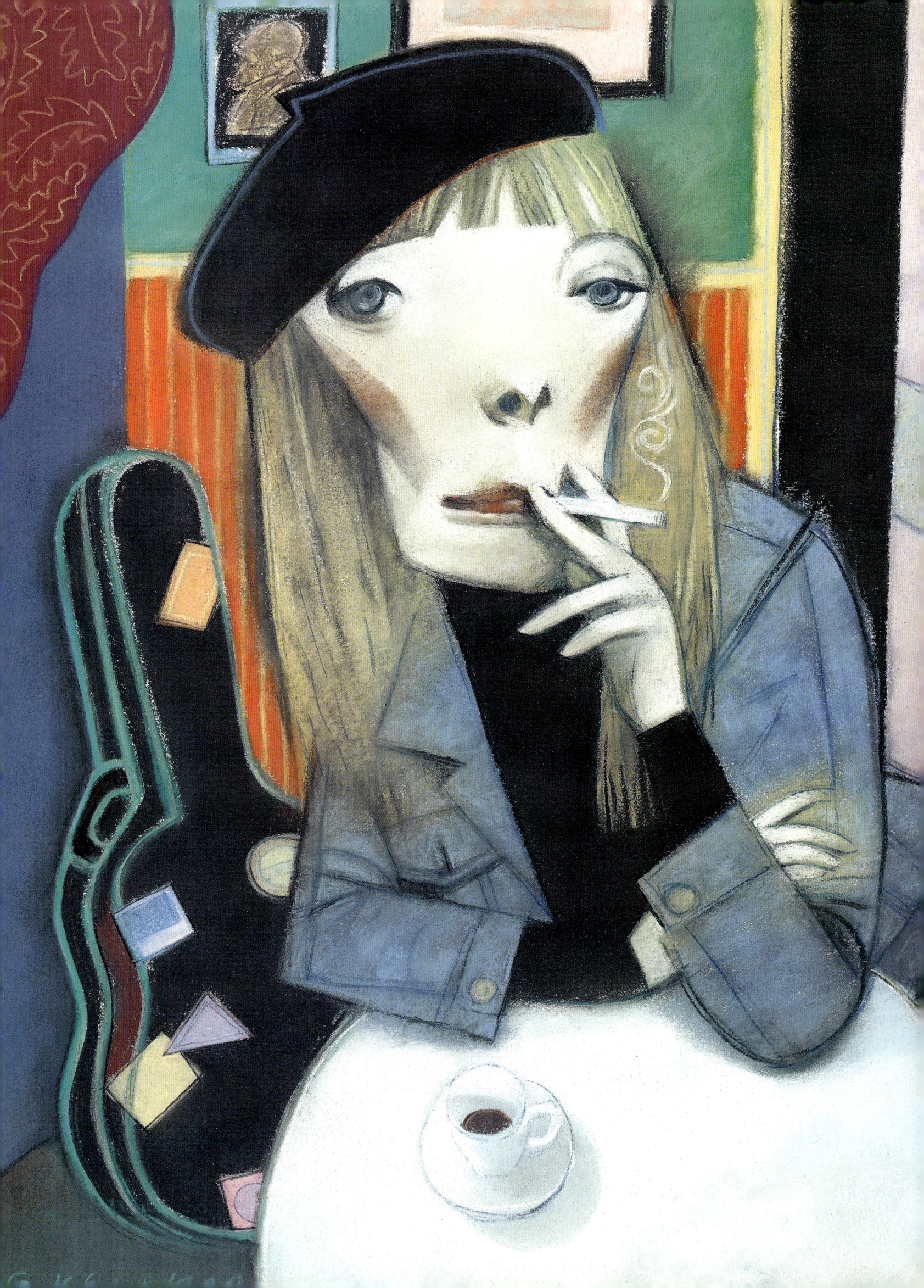

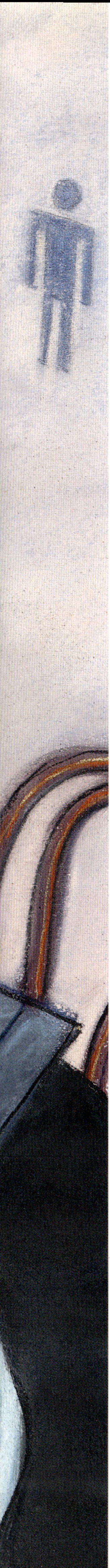

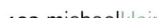

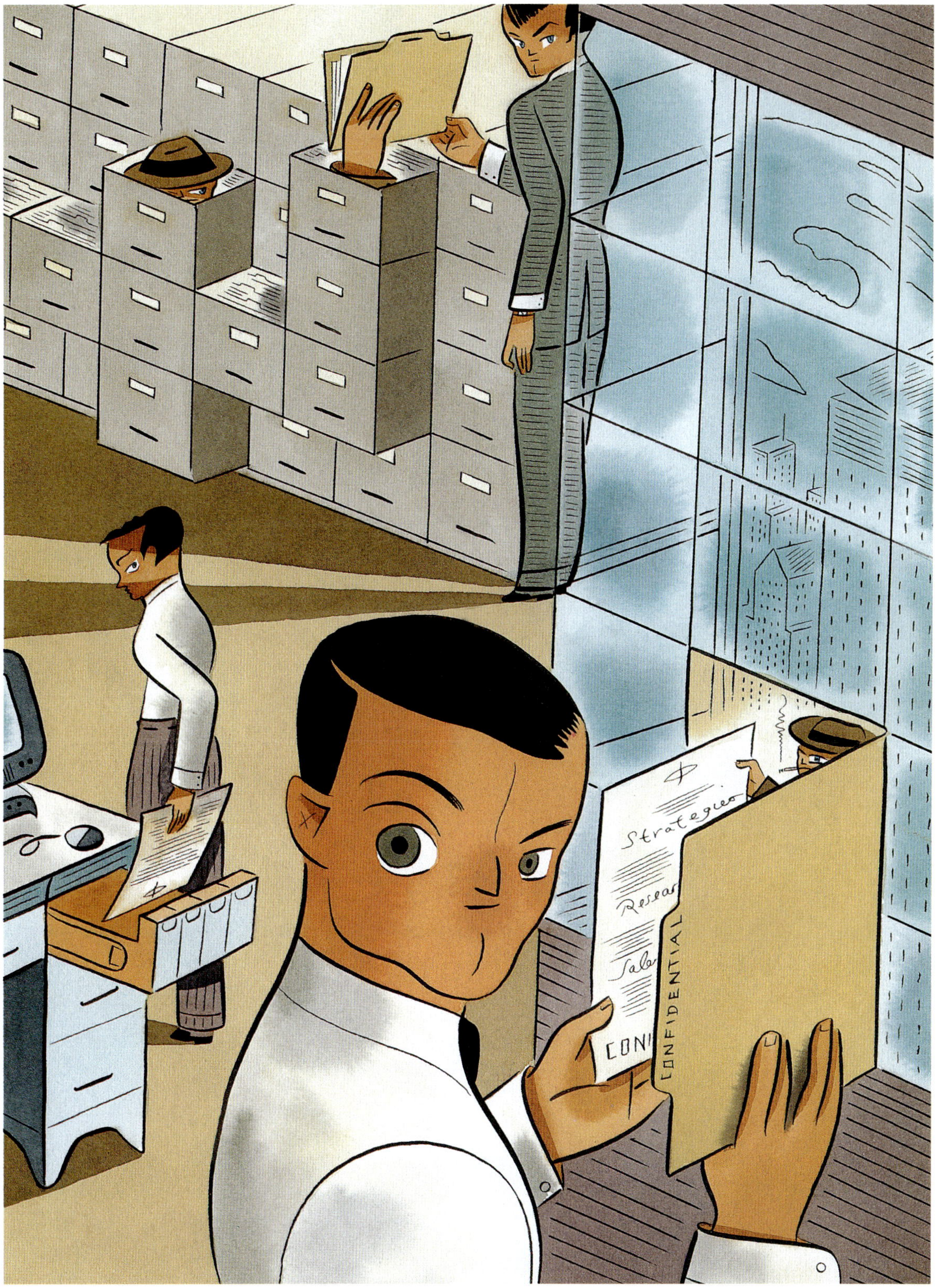

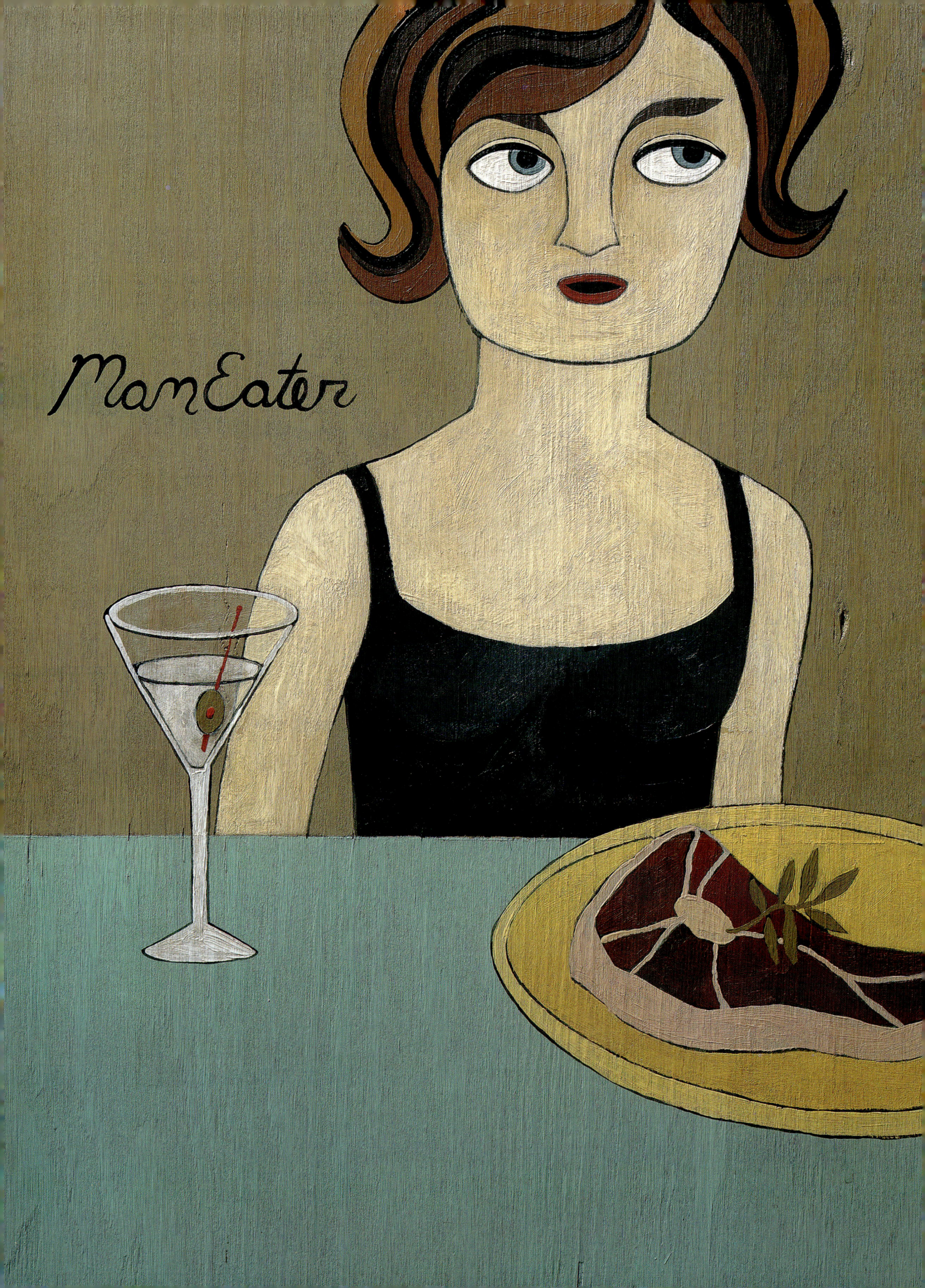

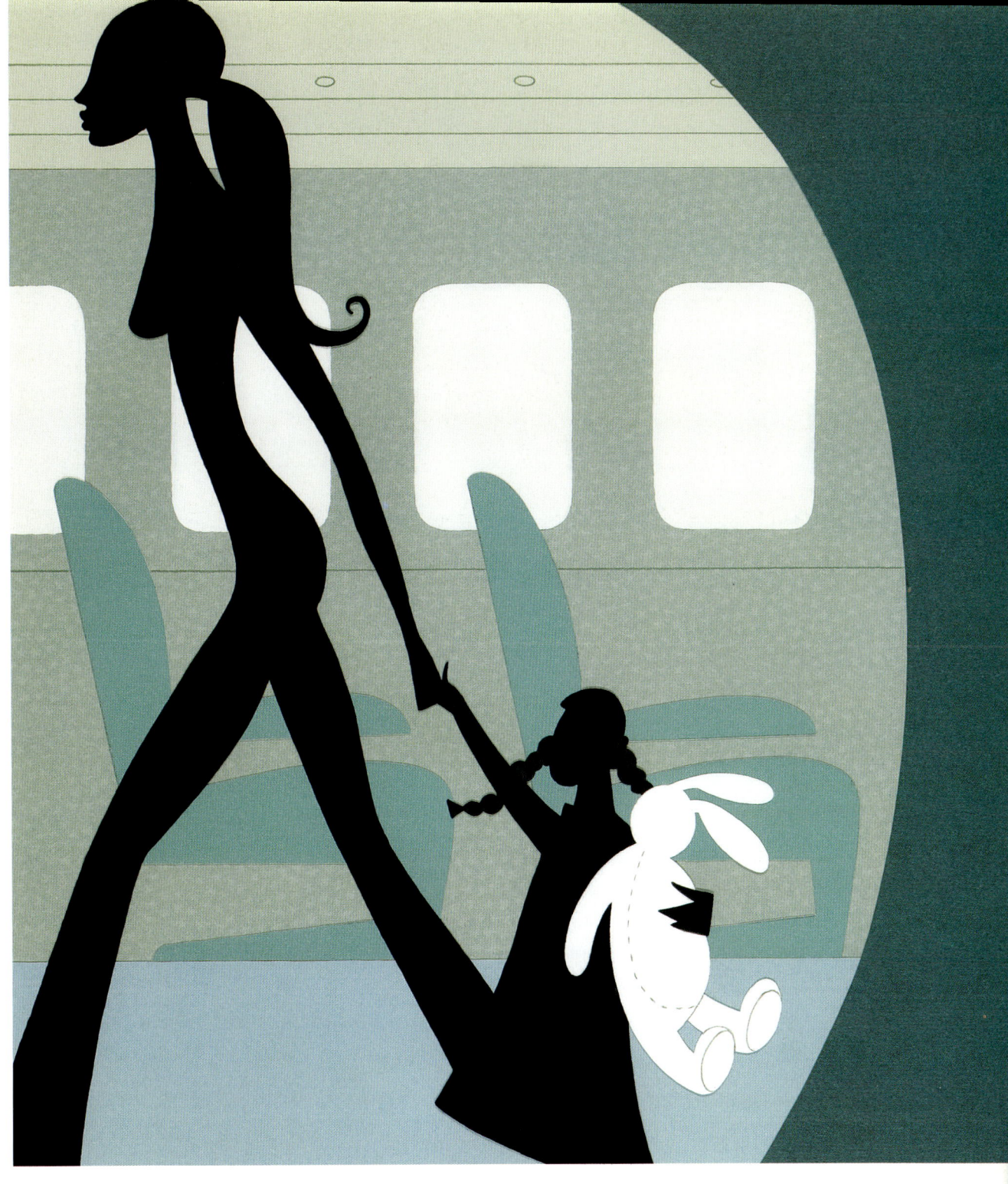

195 anjakroencke

194 trishakrauss

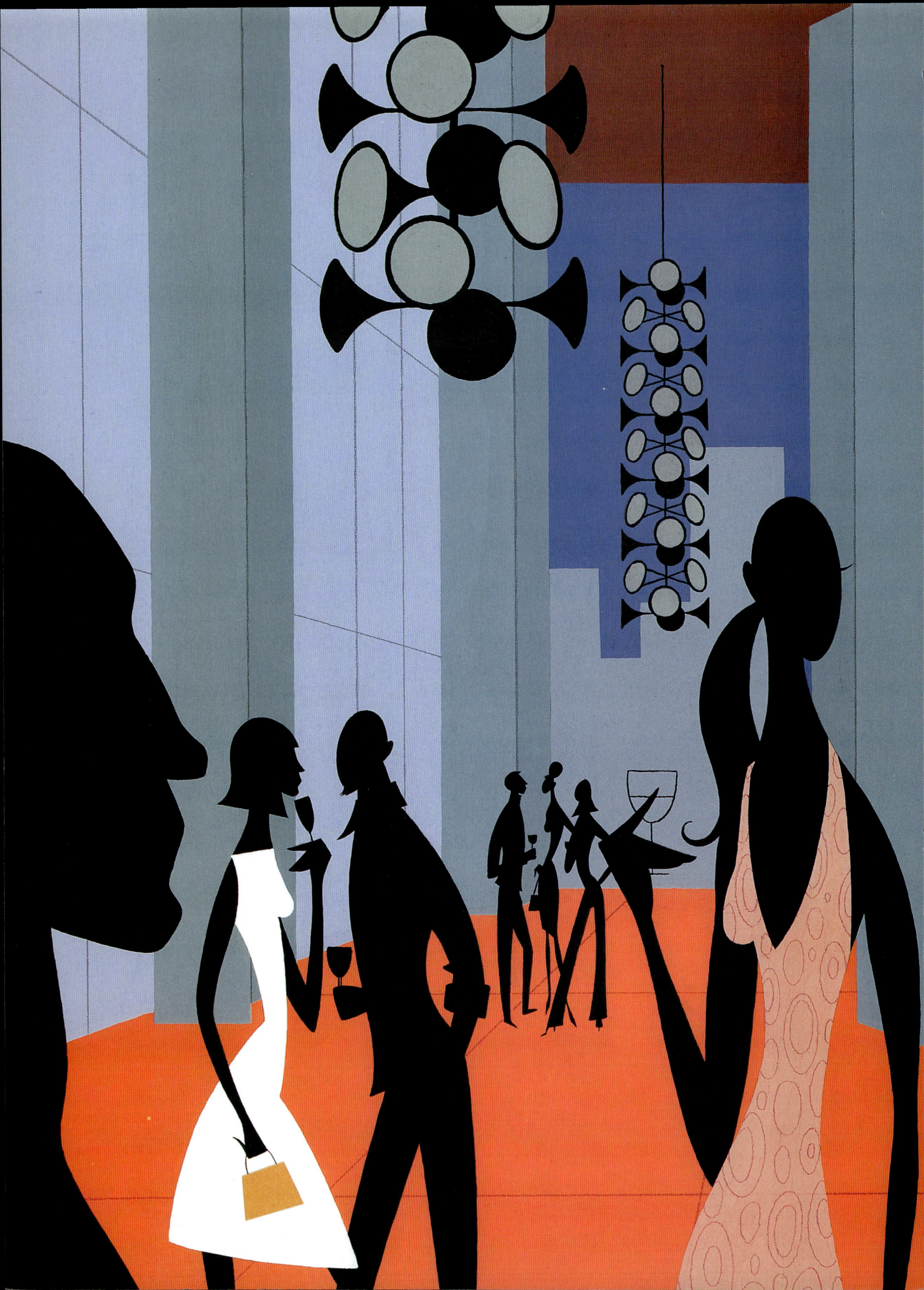

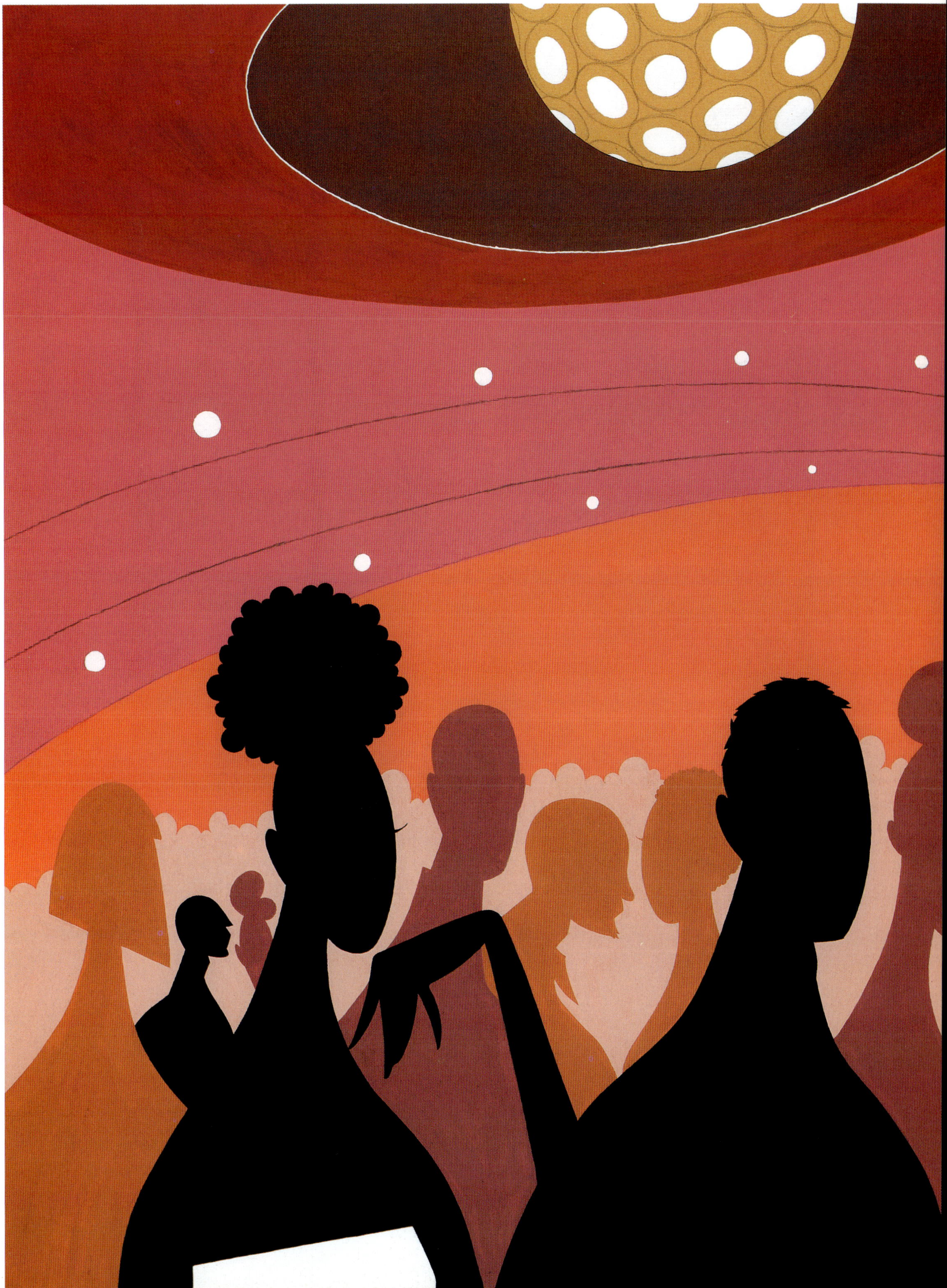

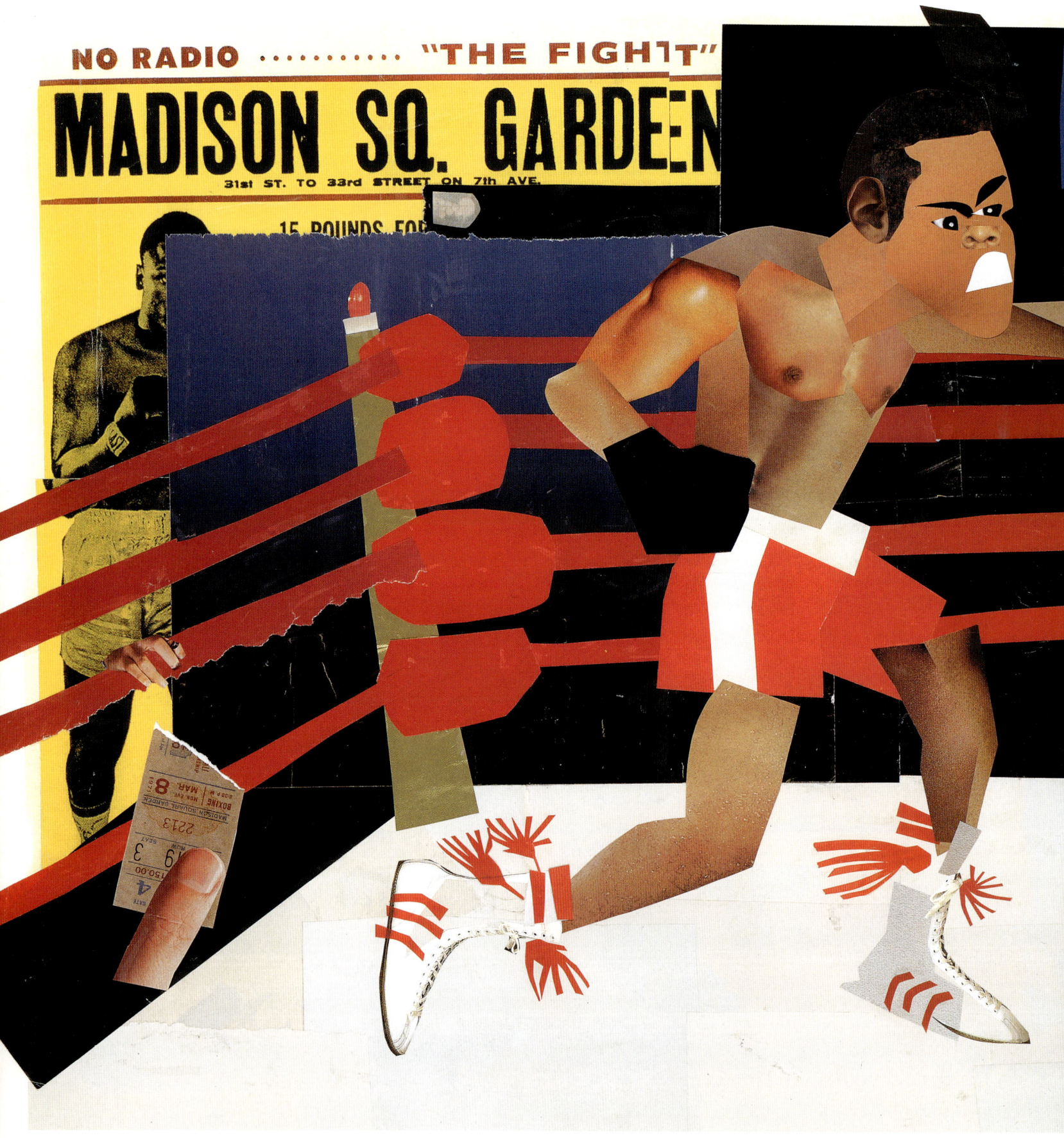

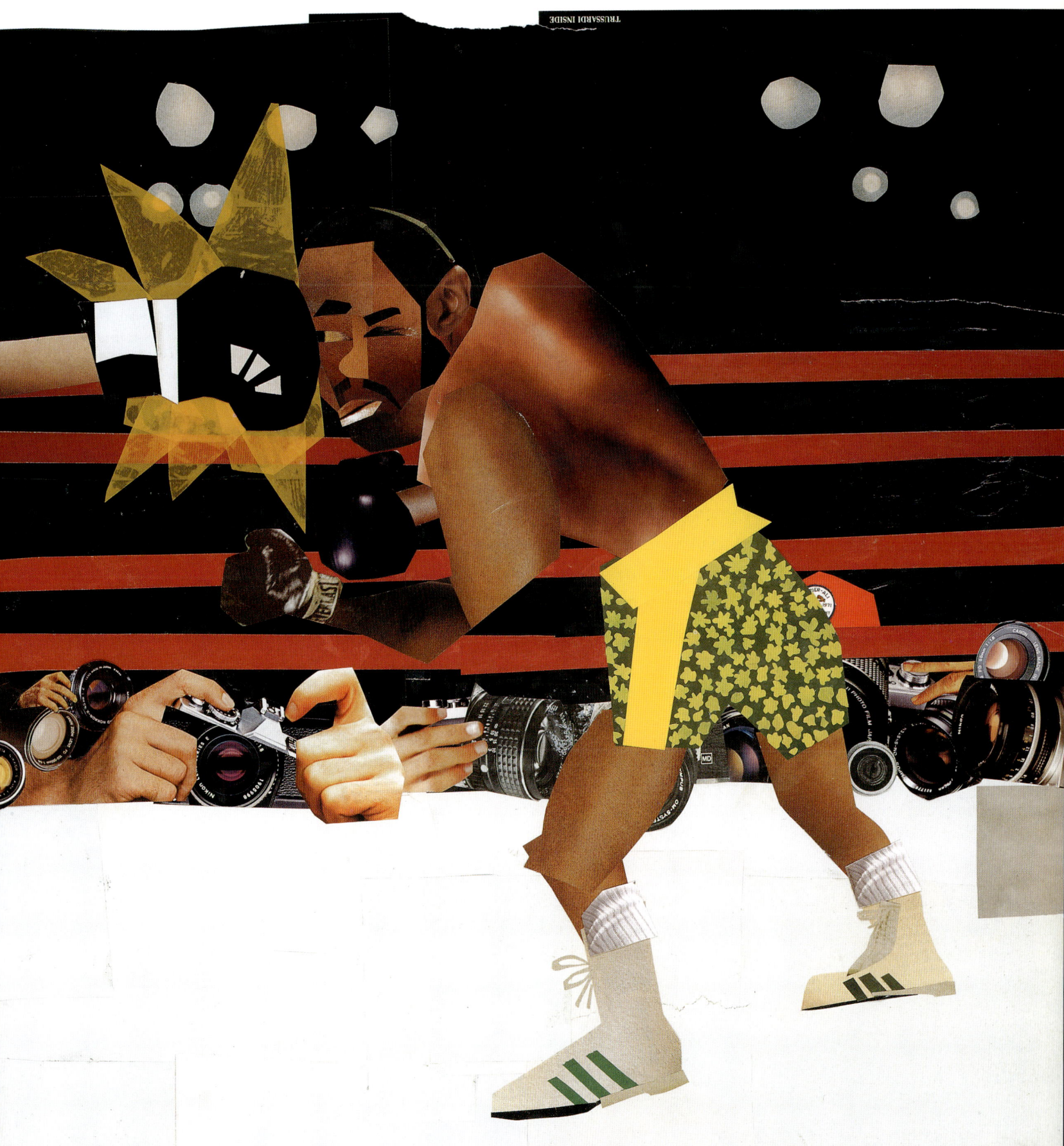

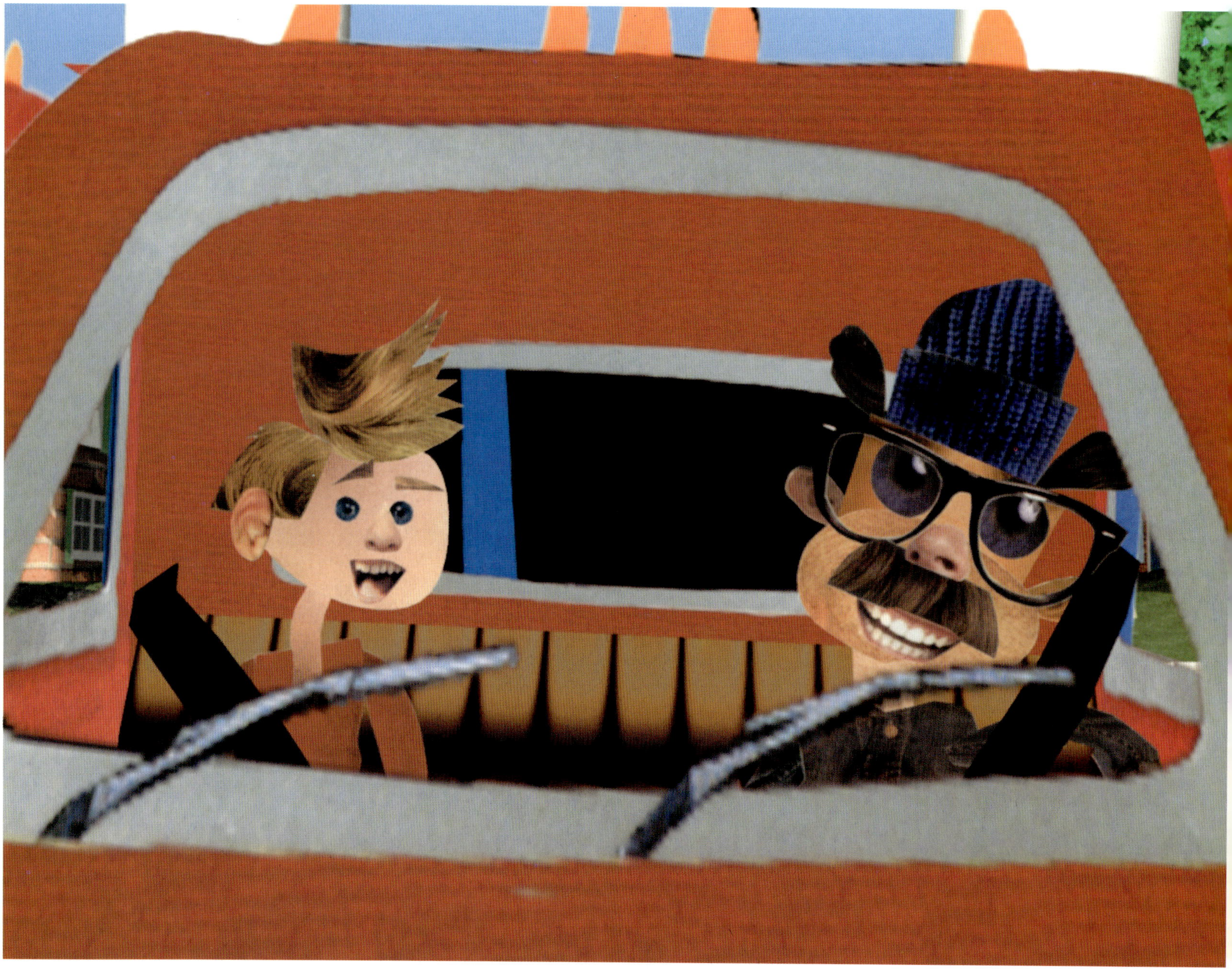

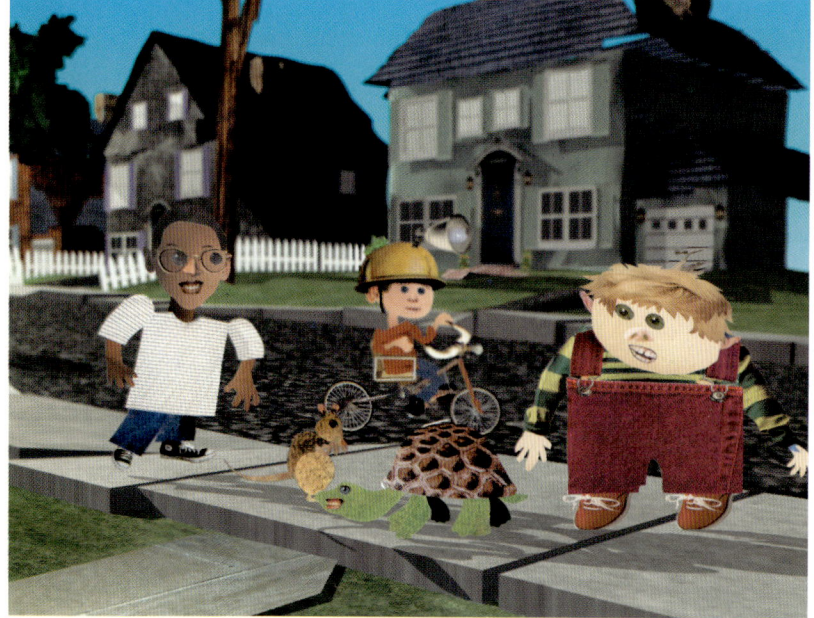
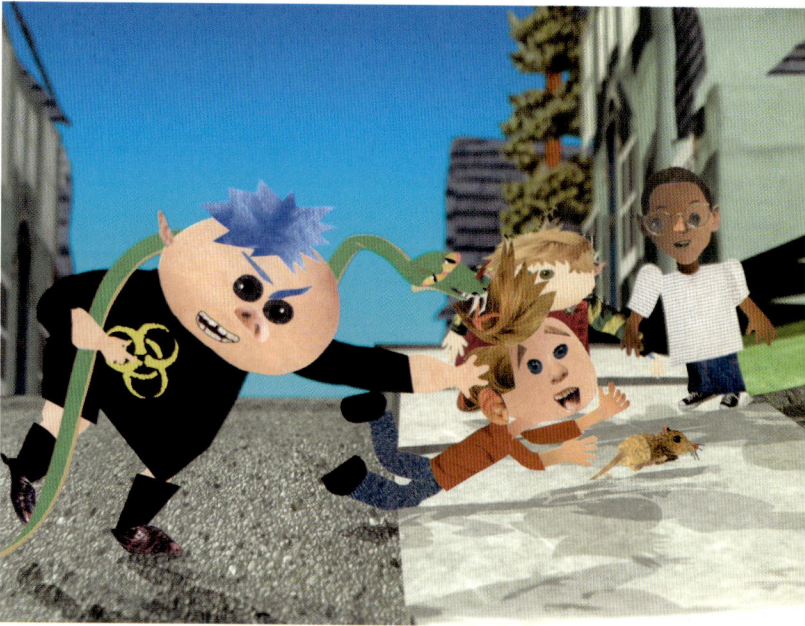

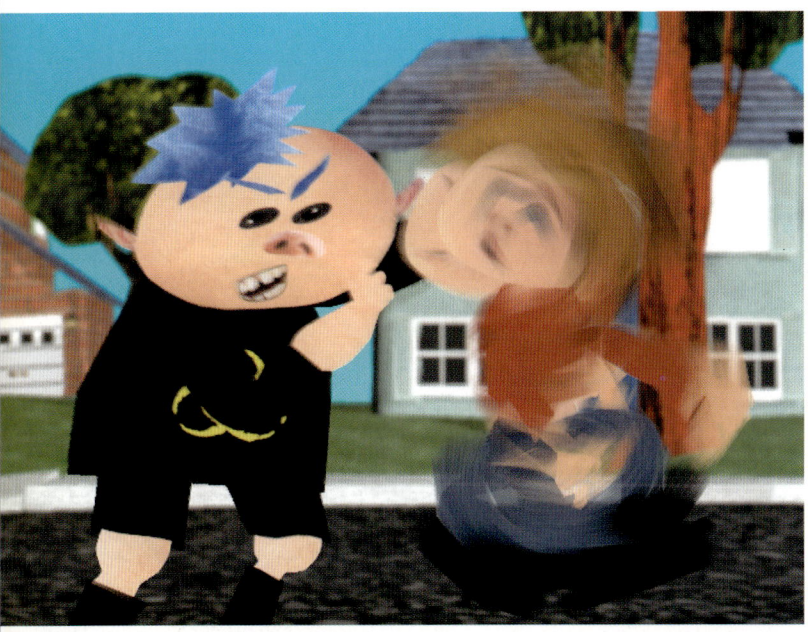
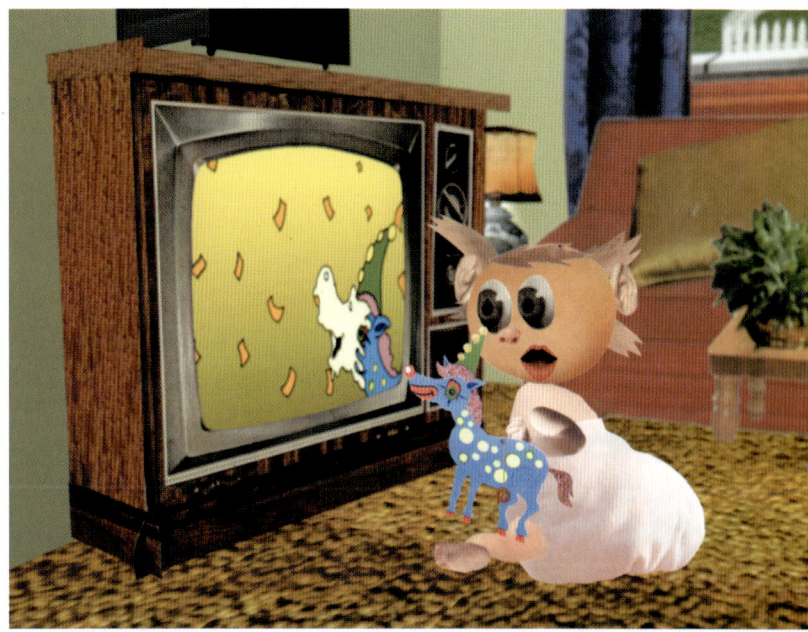
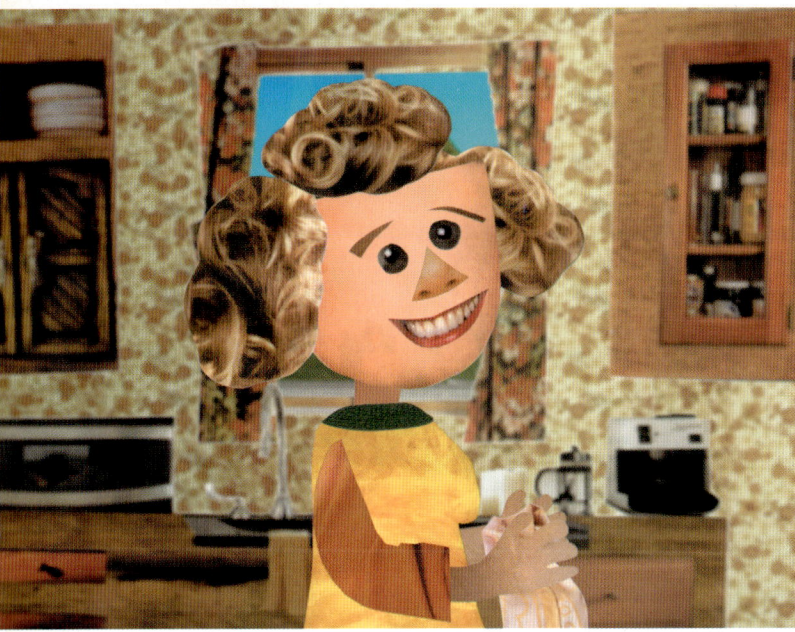
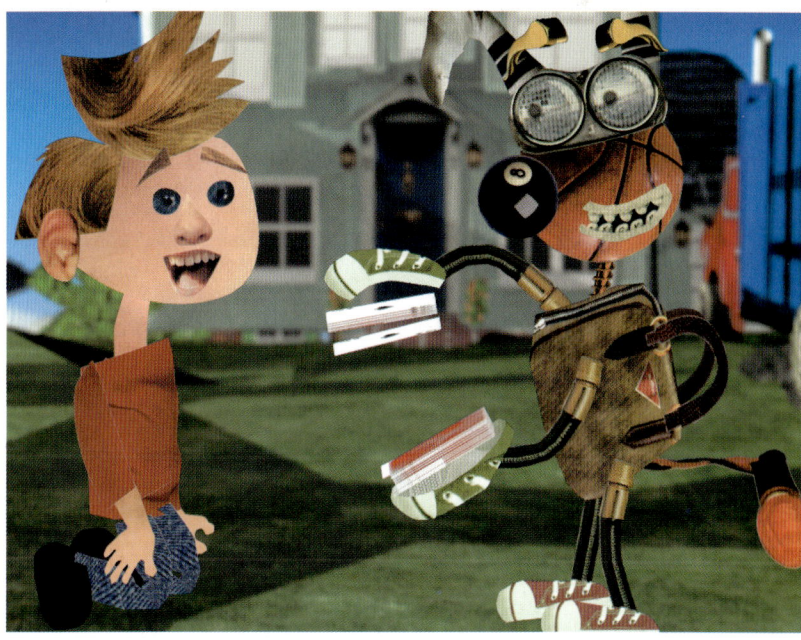
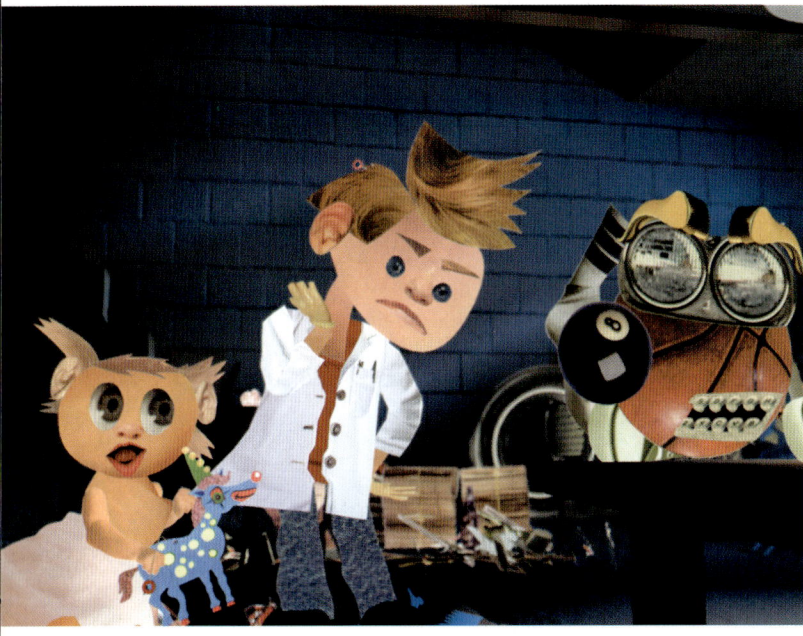
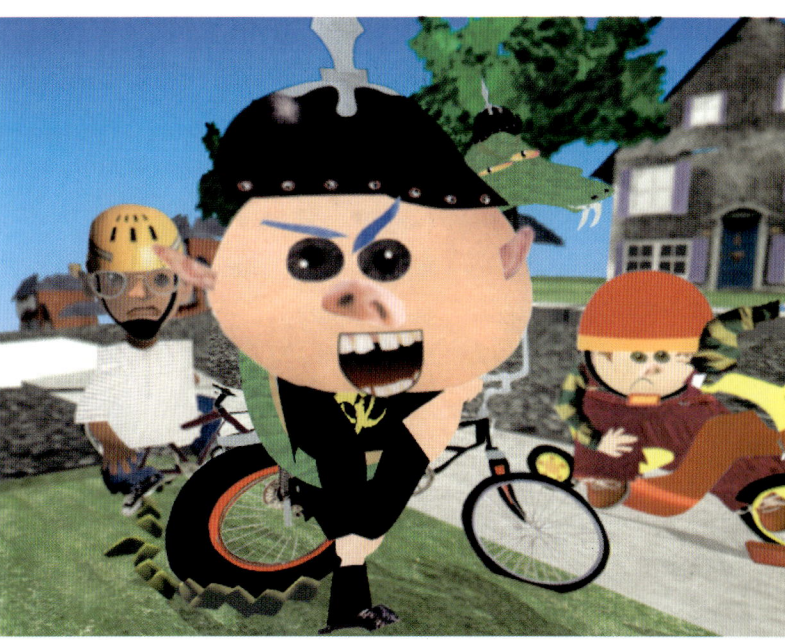

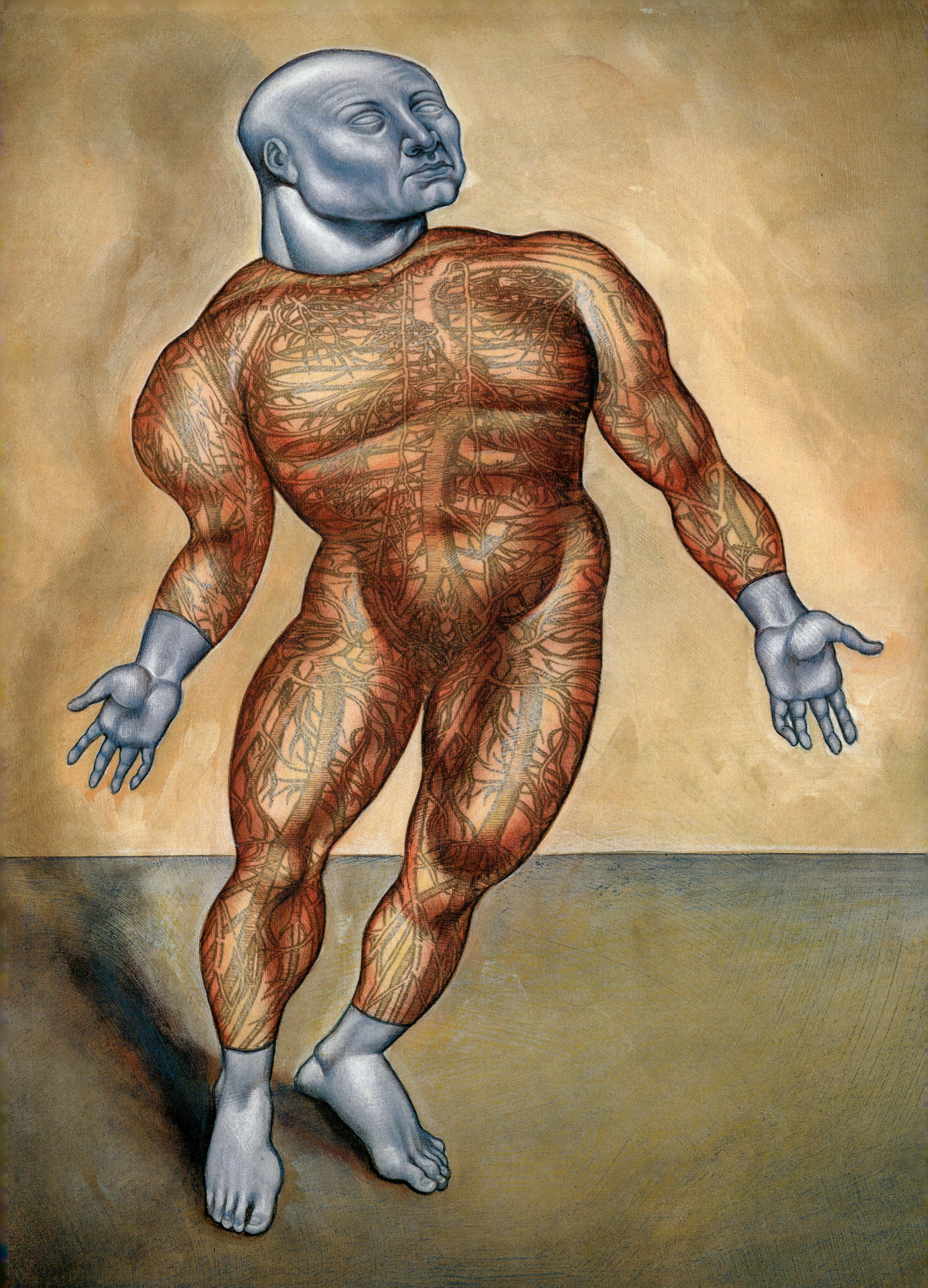

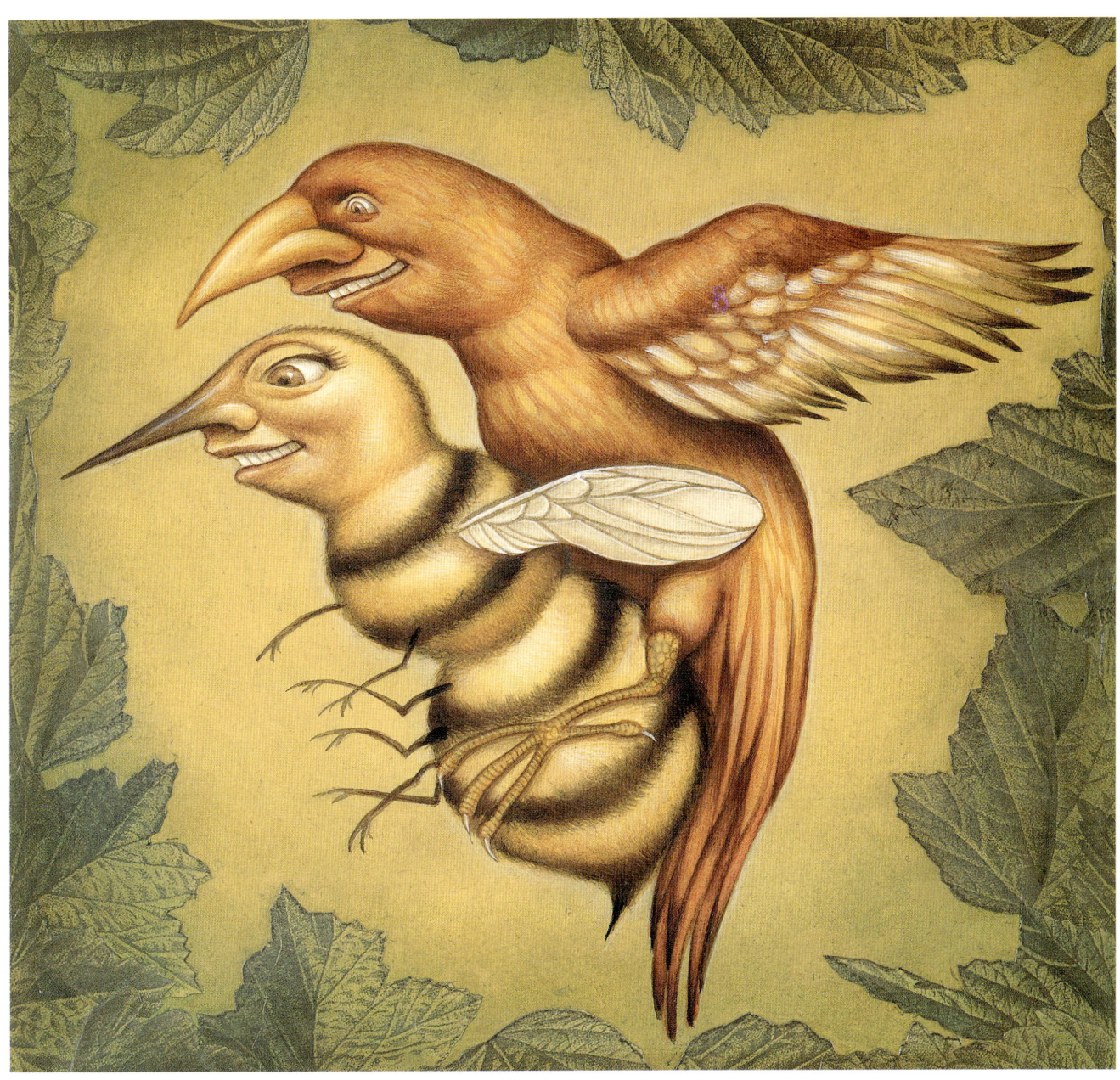

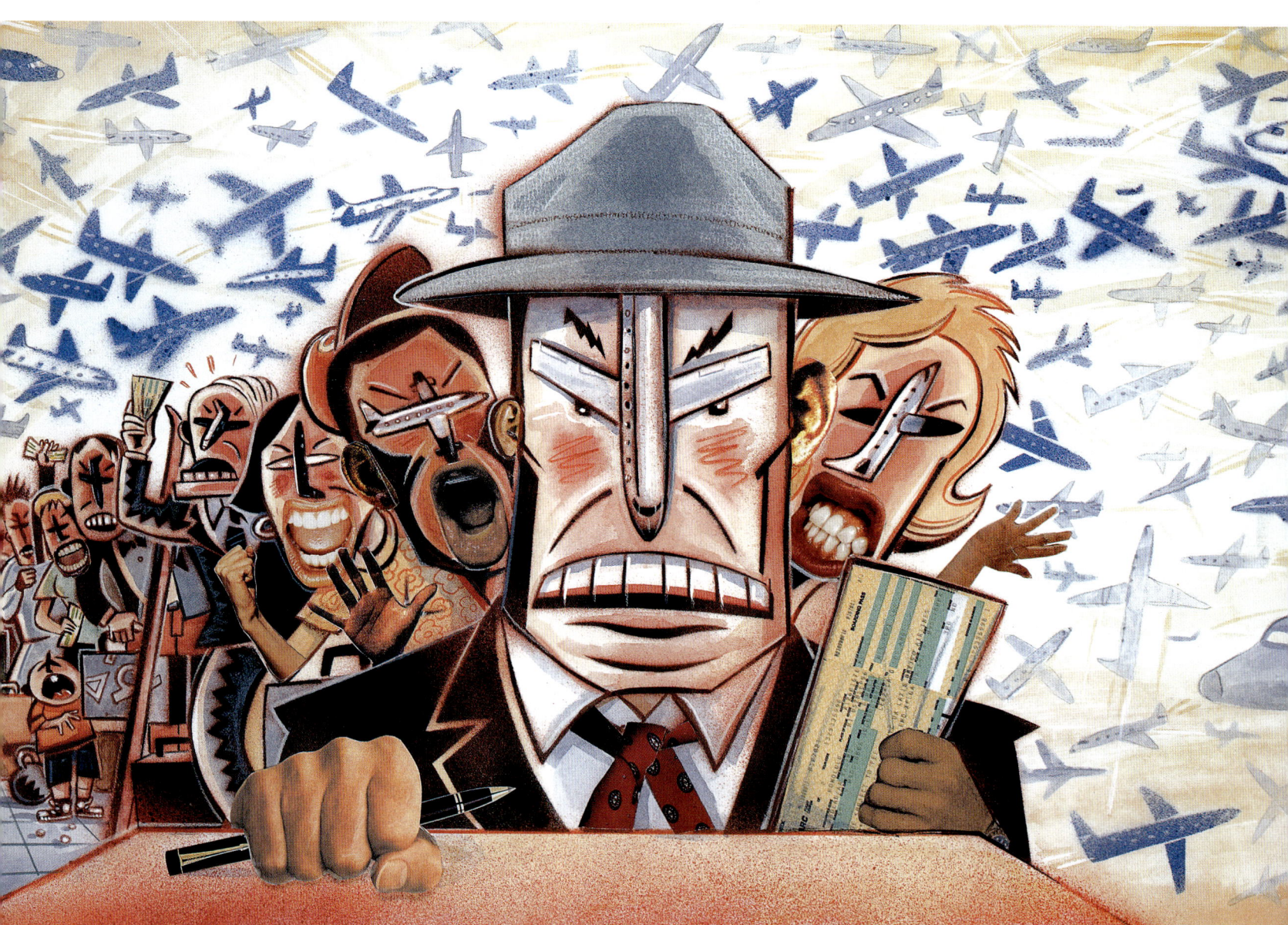

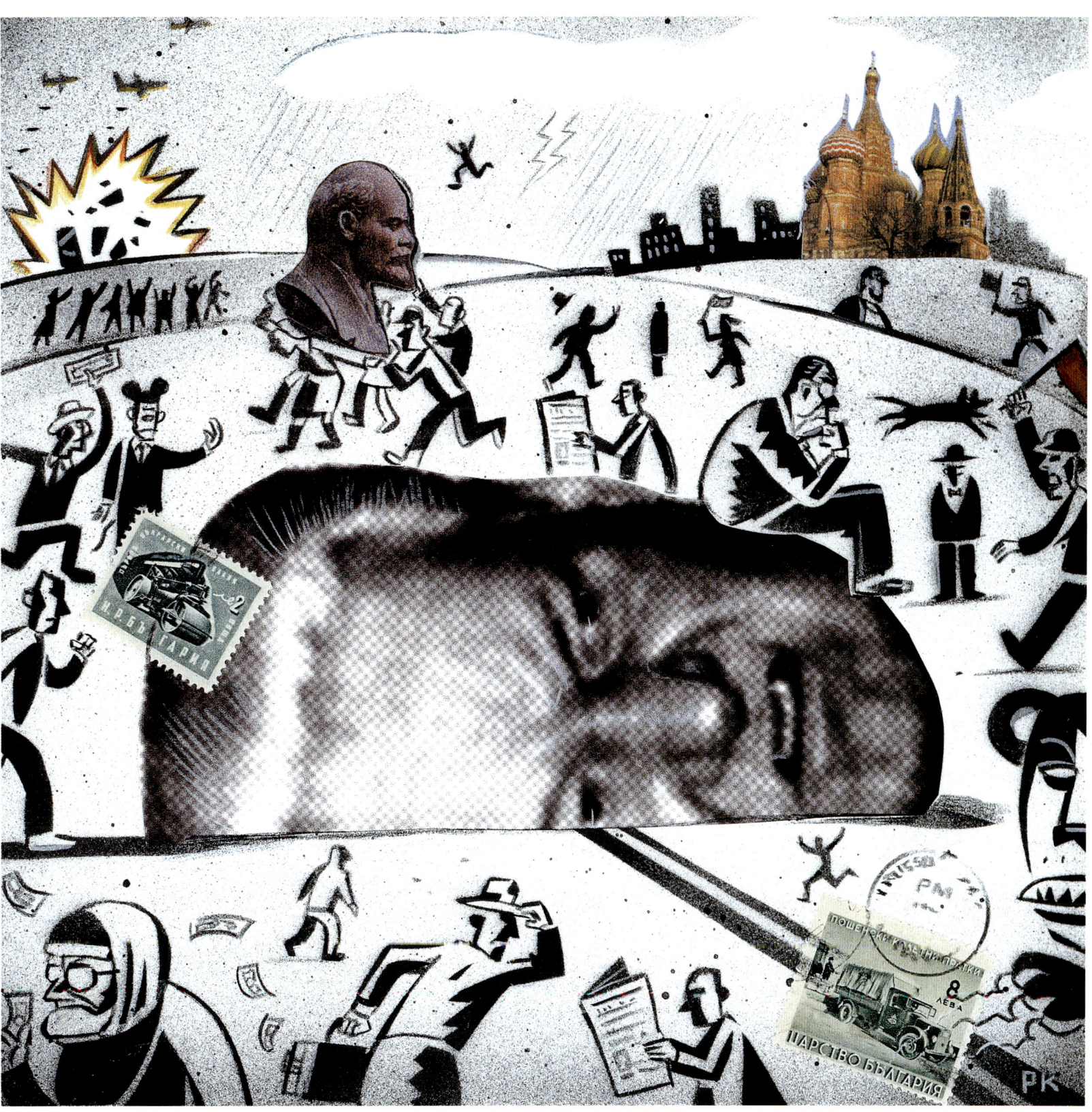

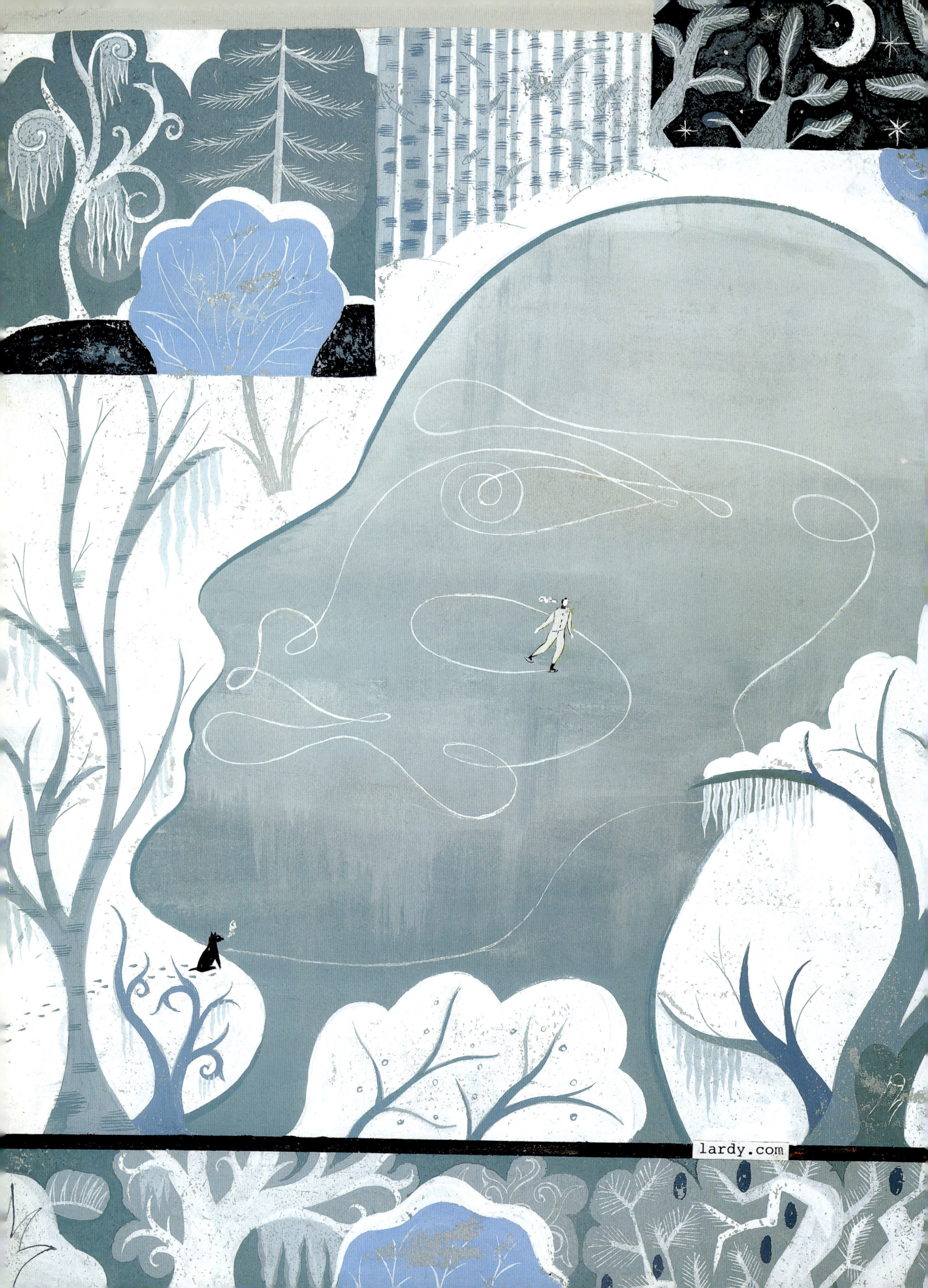

lardy.com

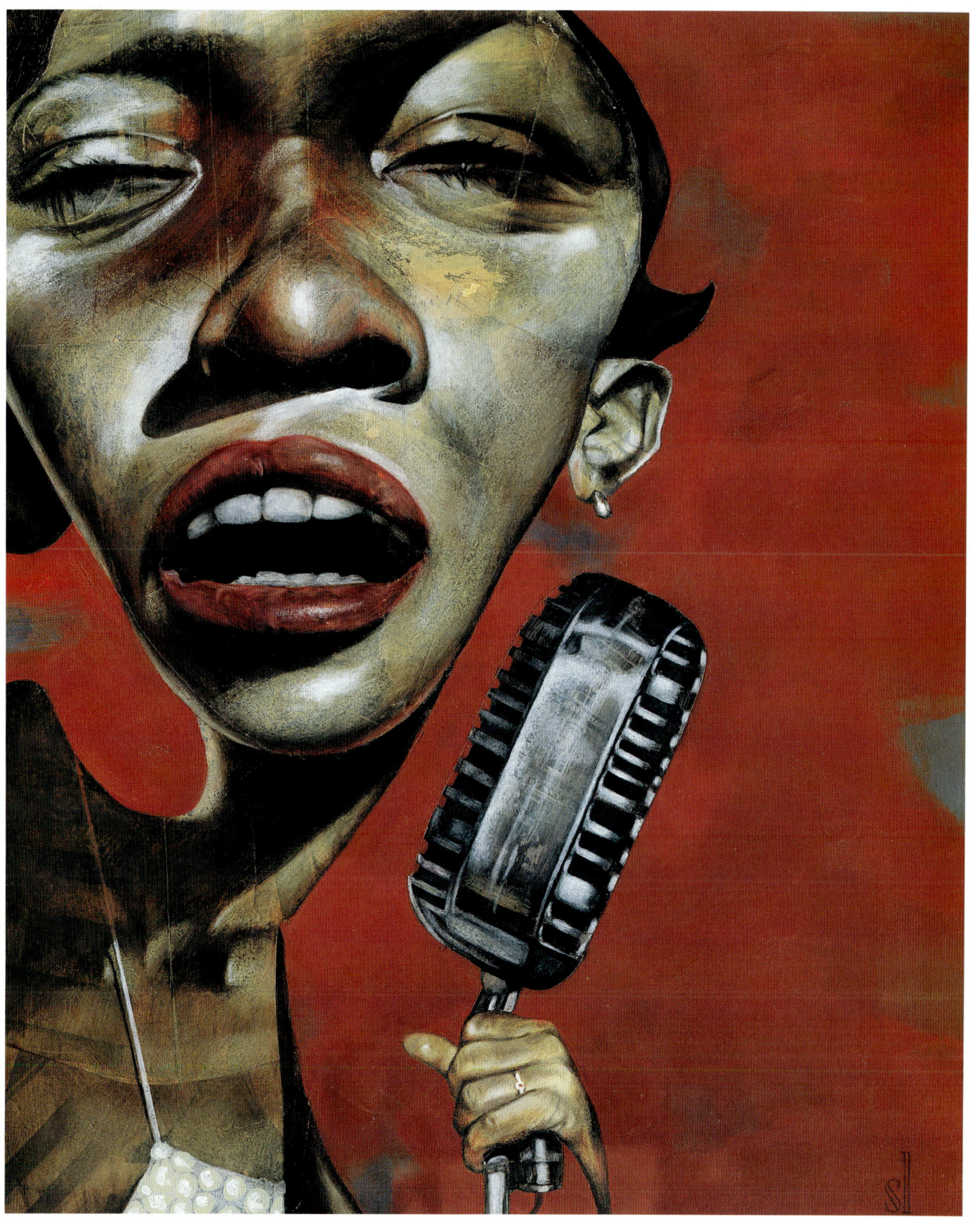

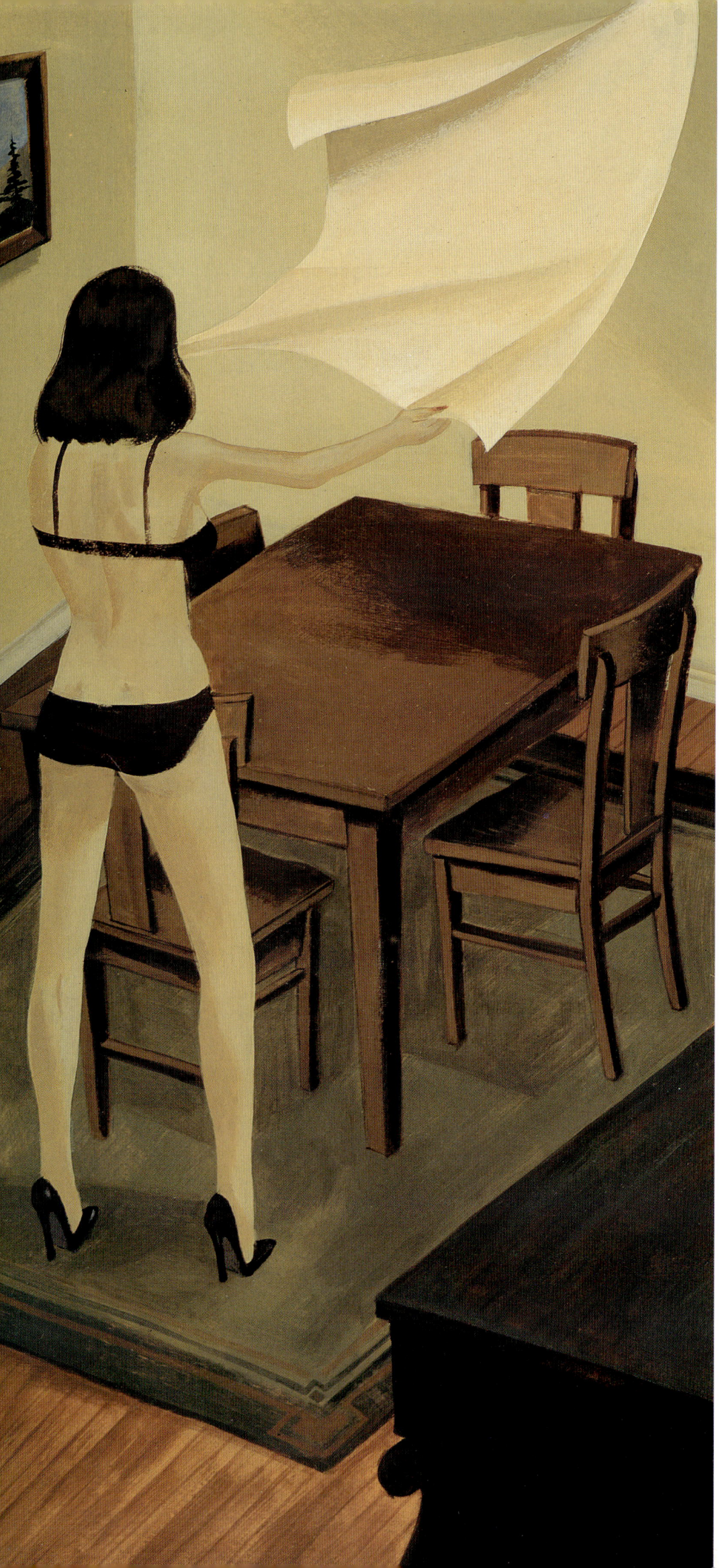

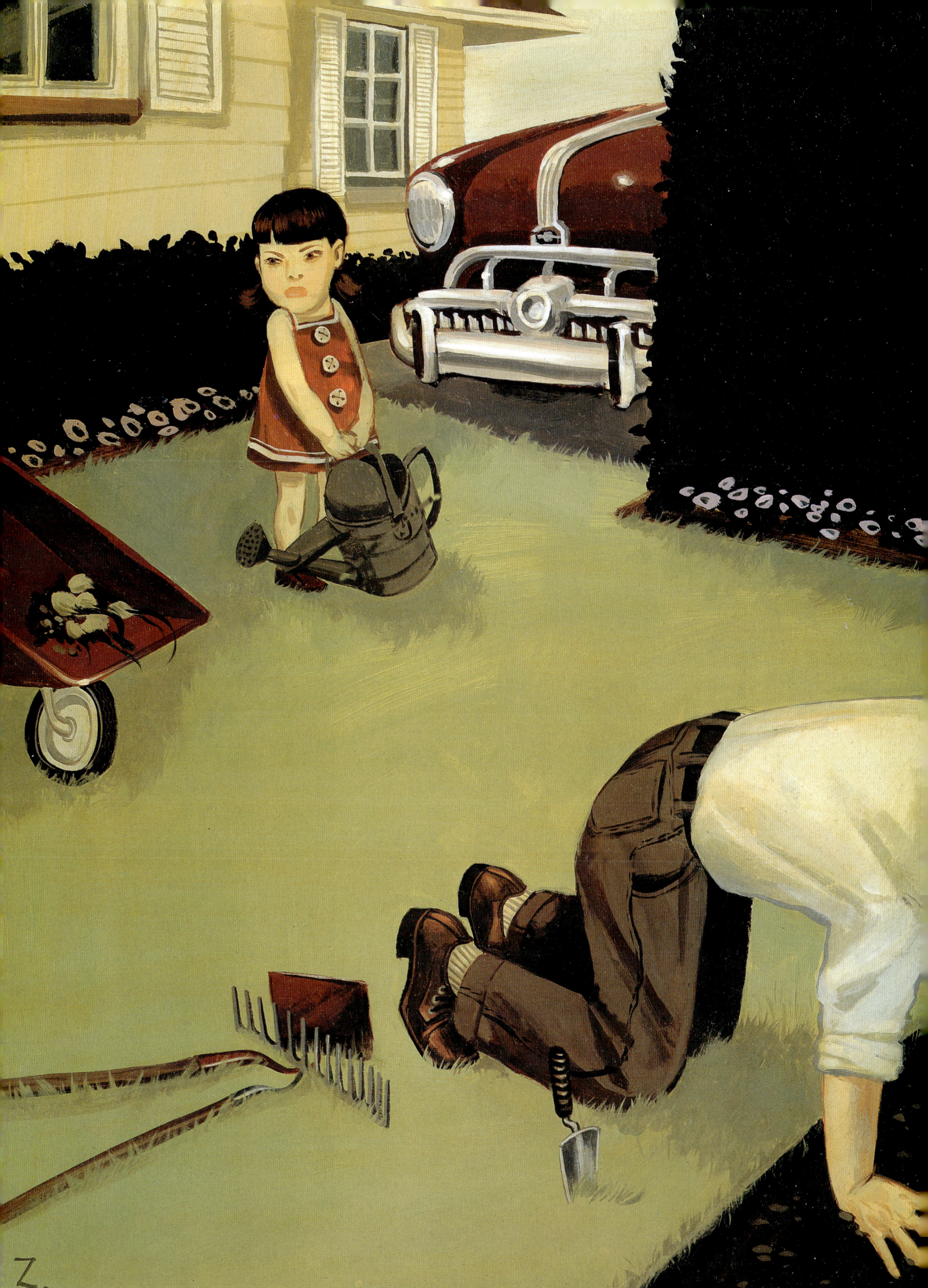

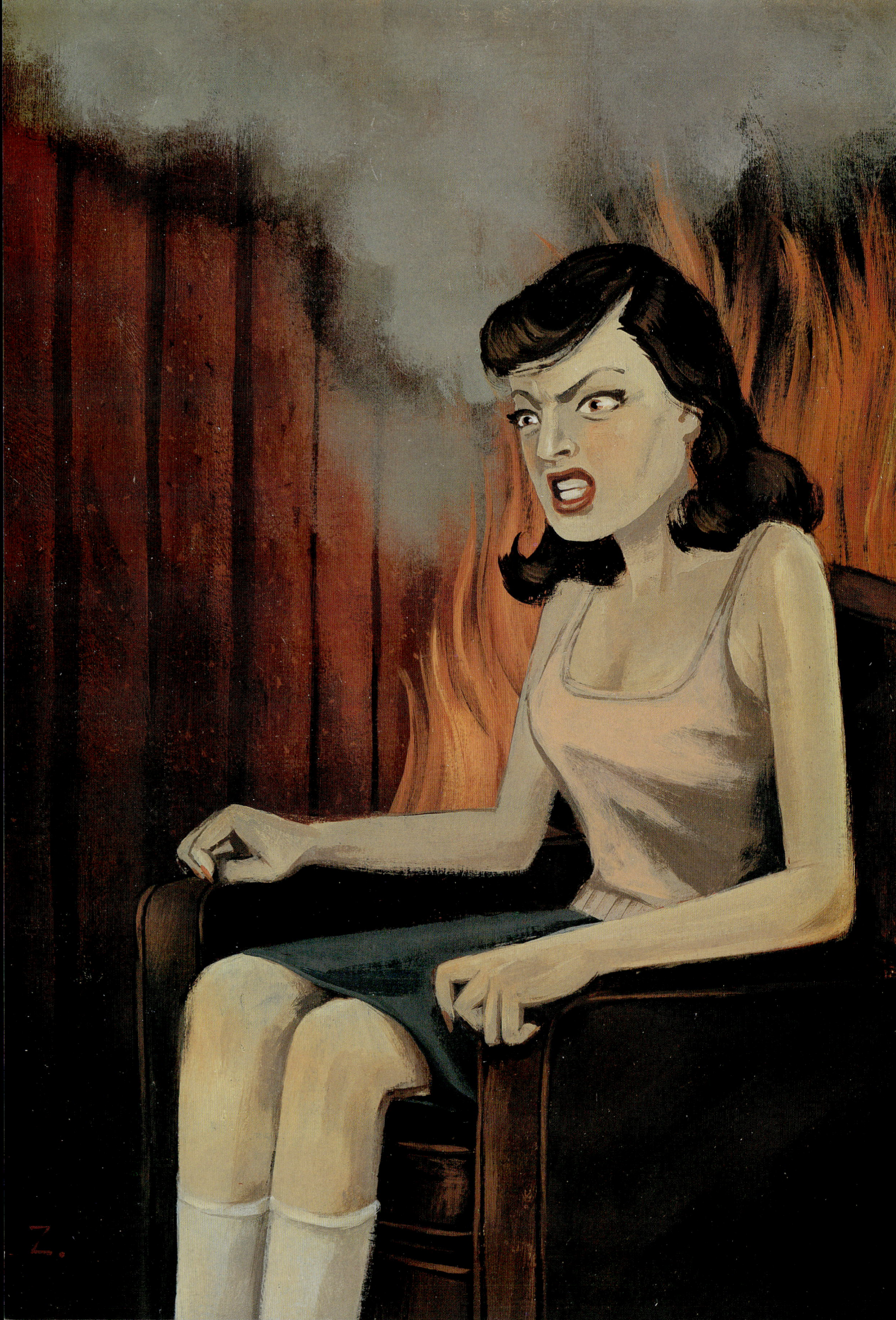

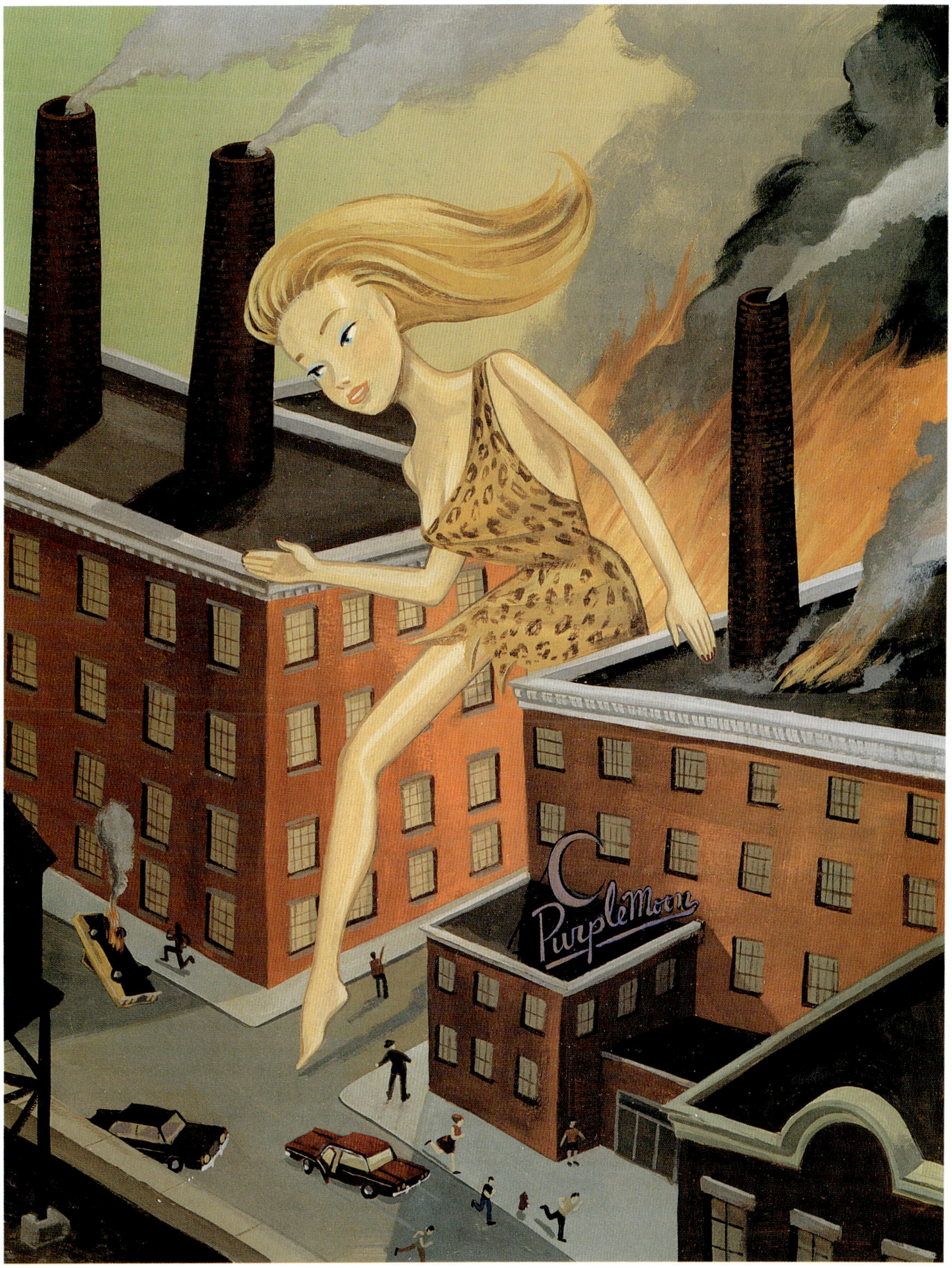

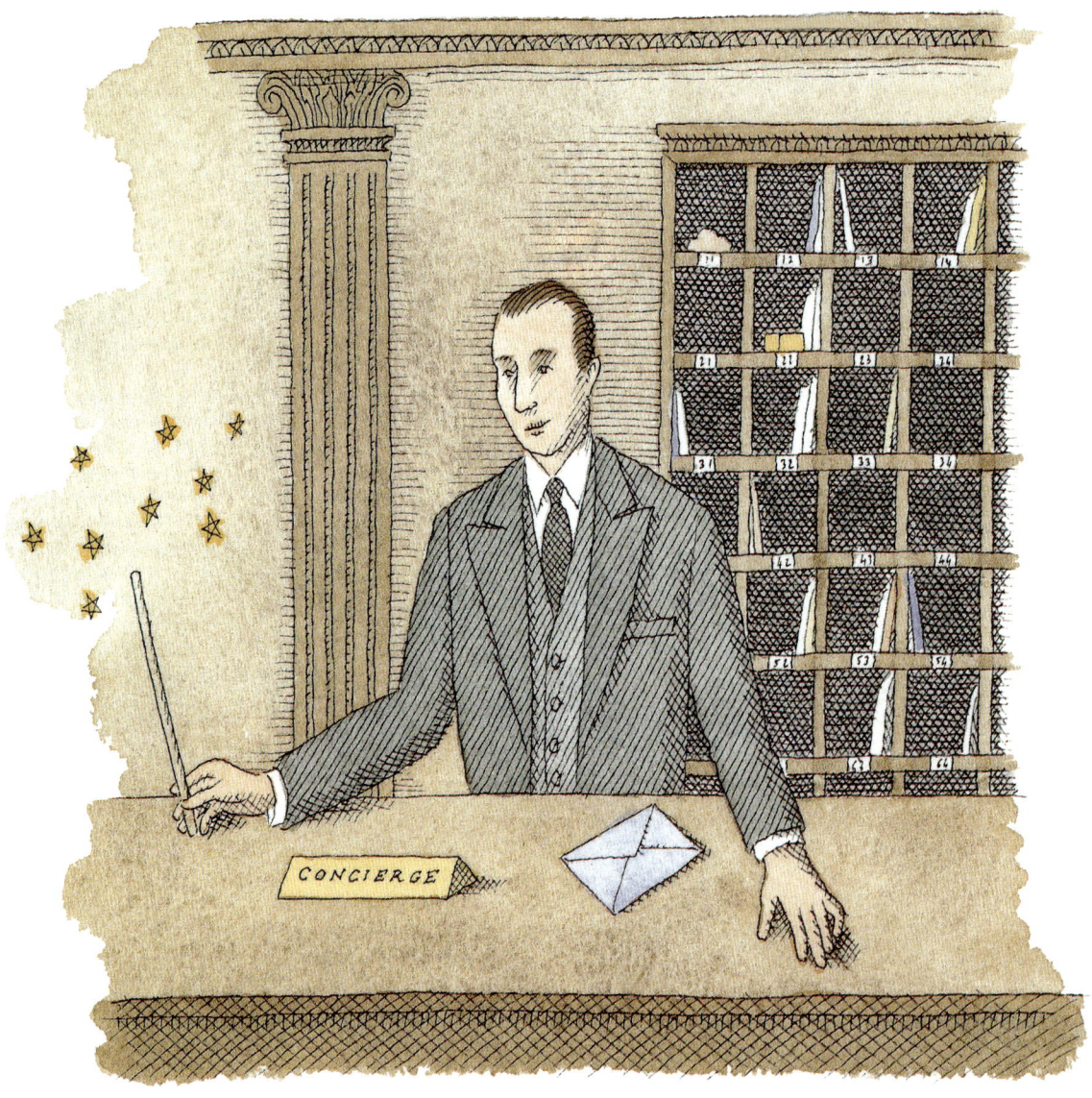

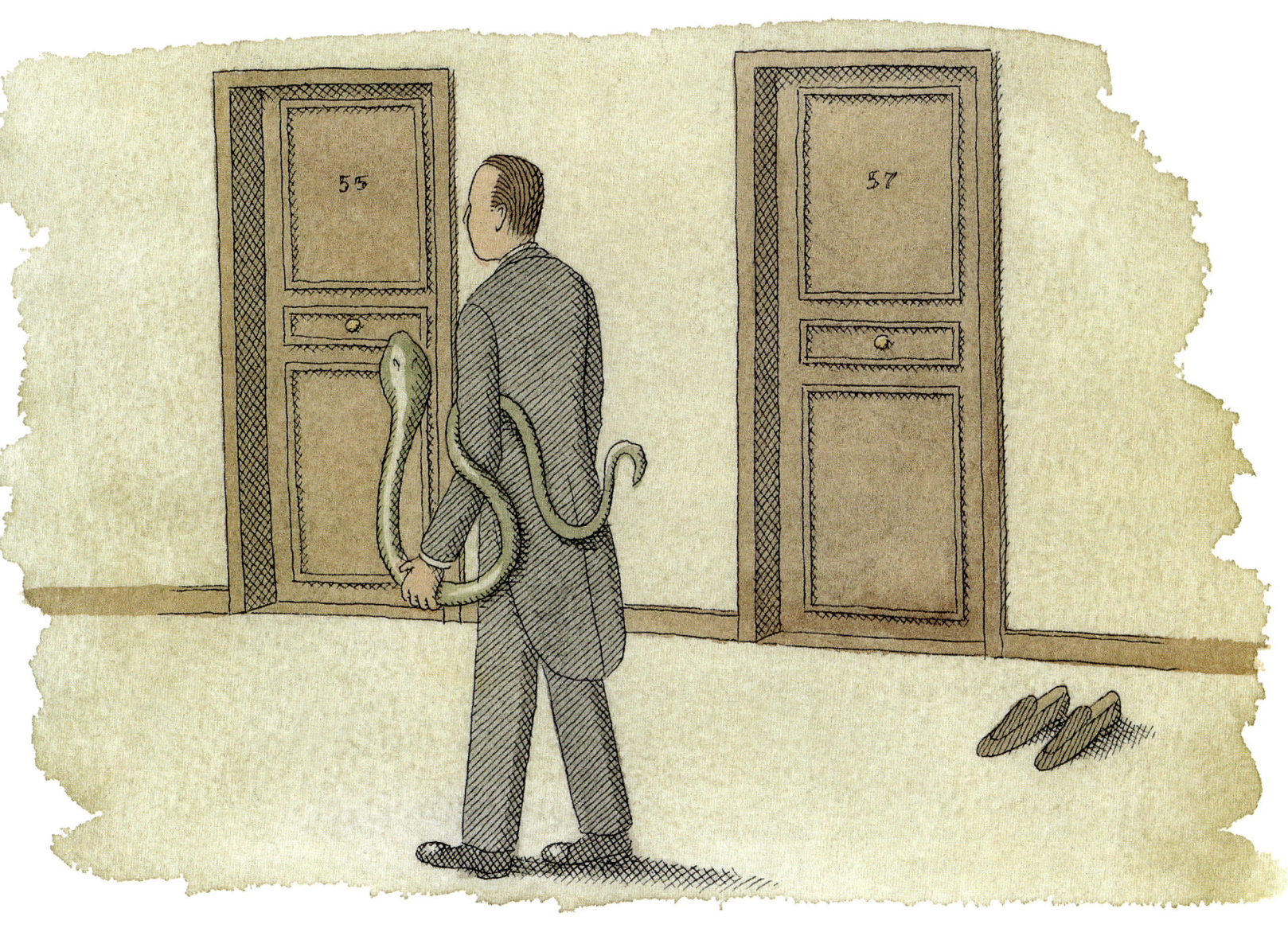

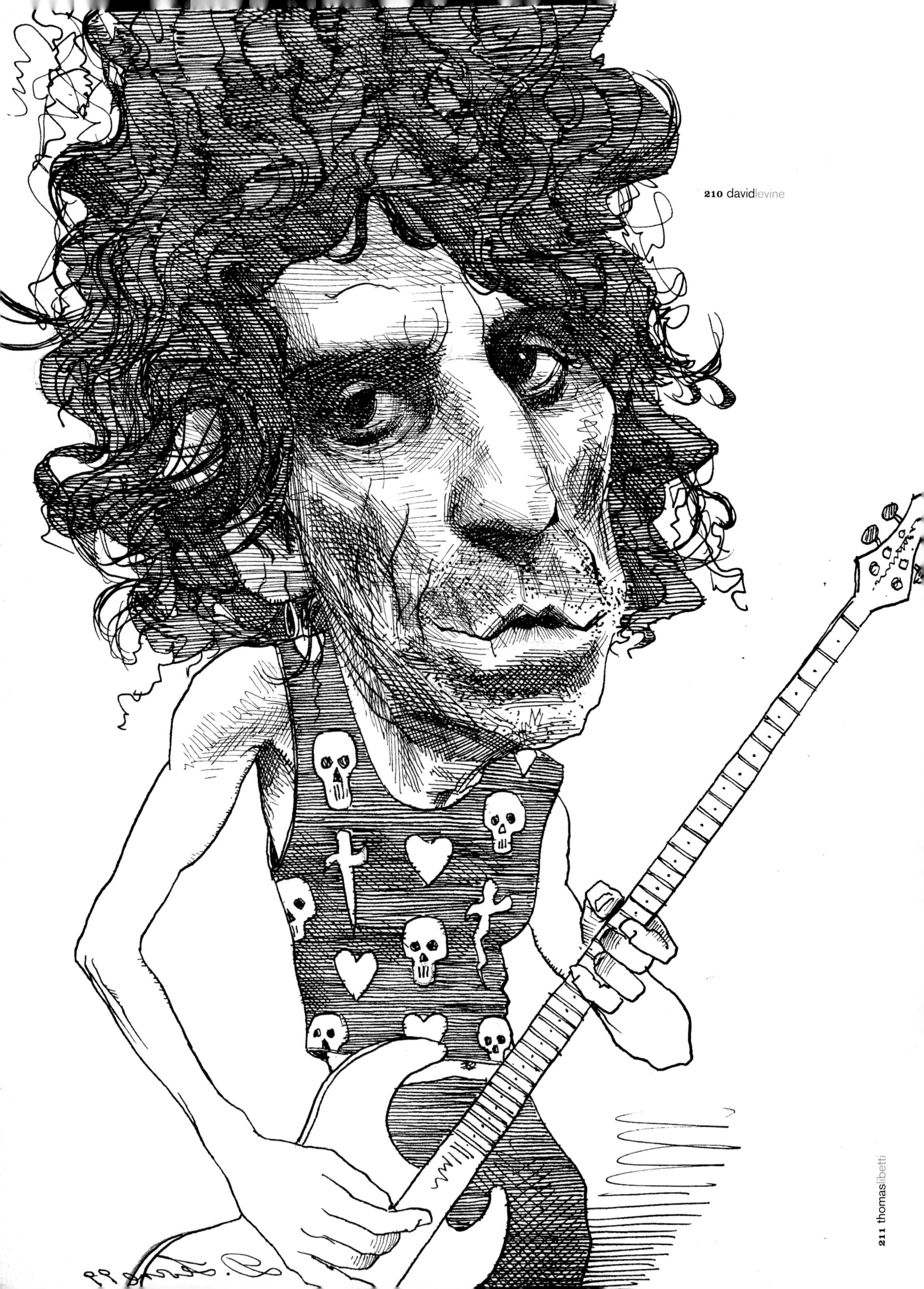

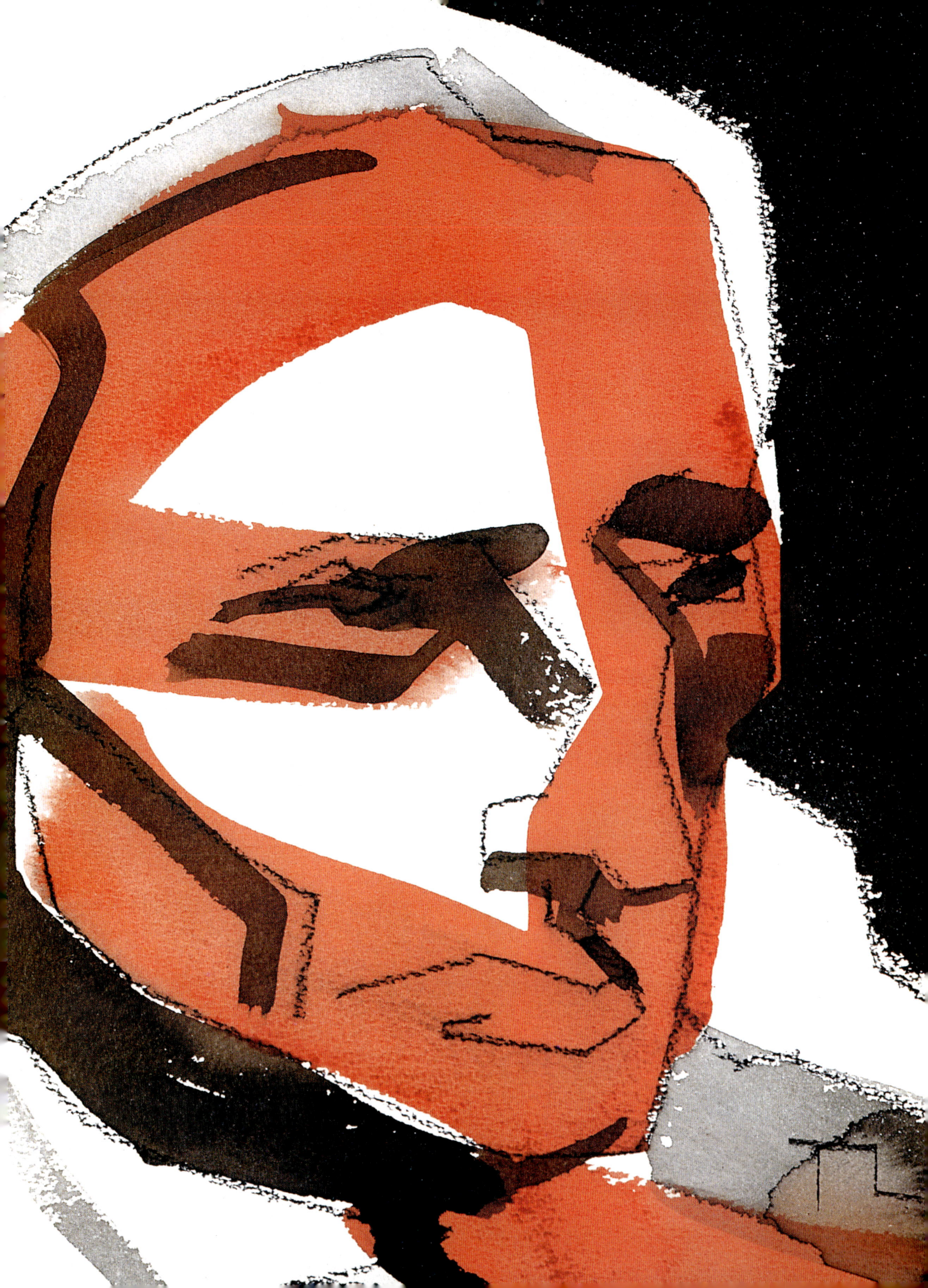

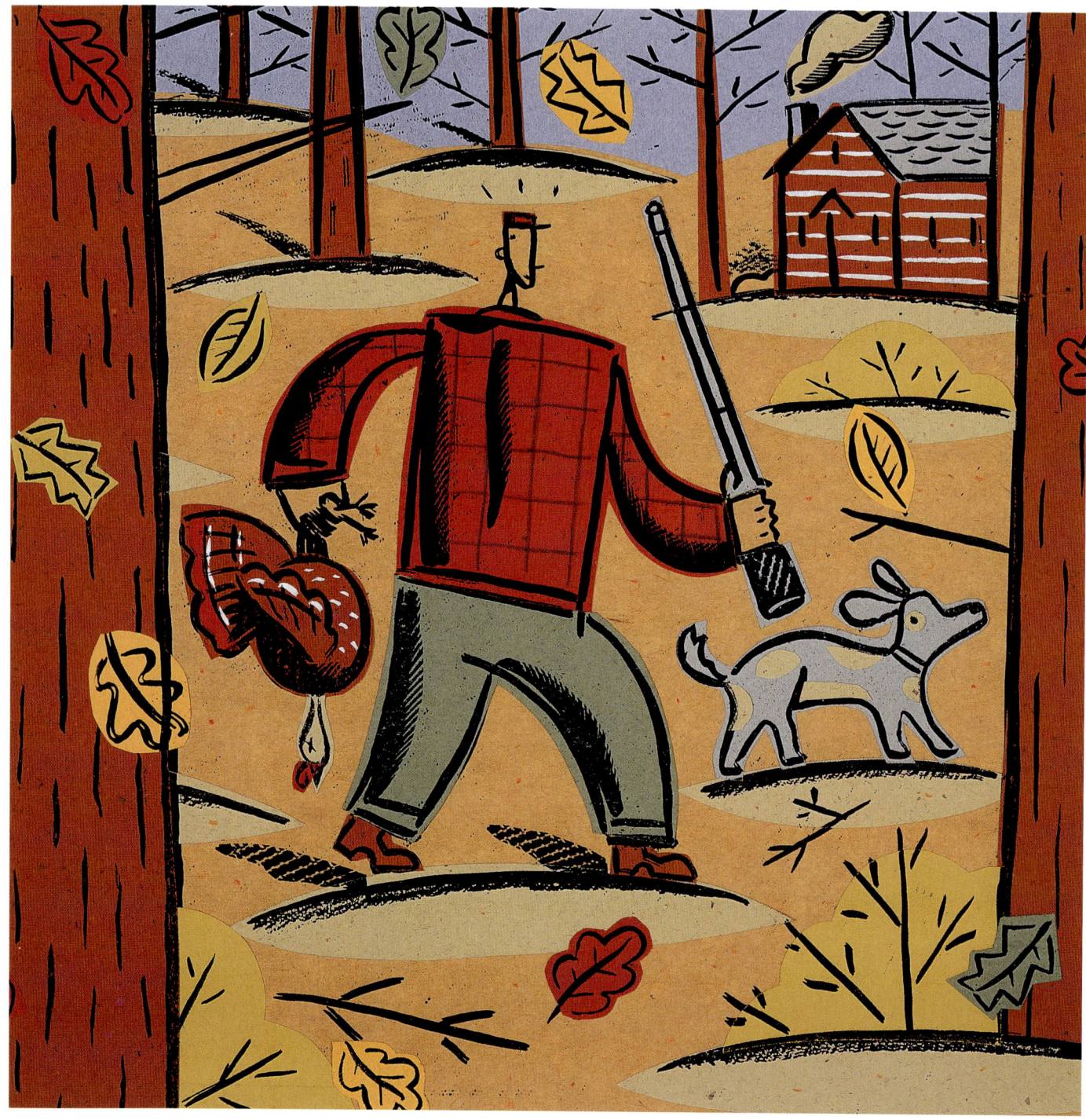

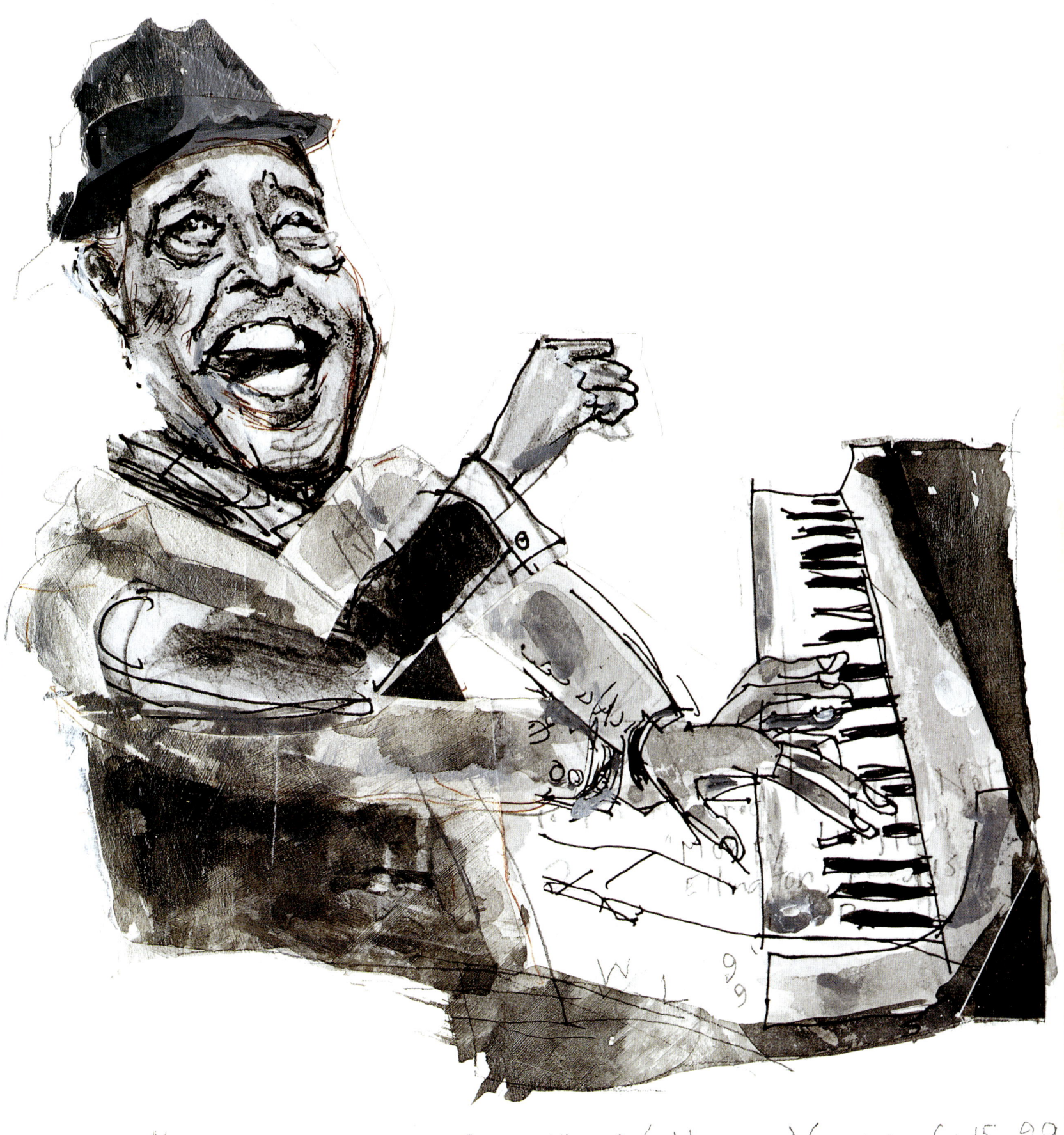

Duke Ellington for The Village Voice 6·15 99

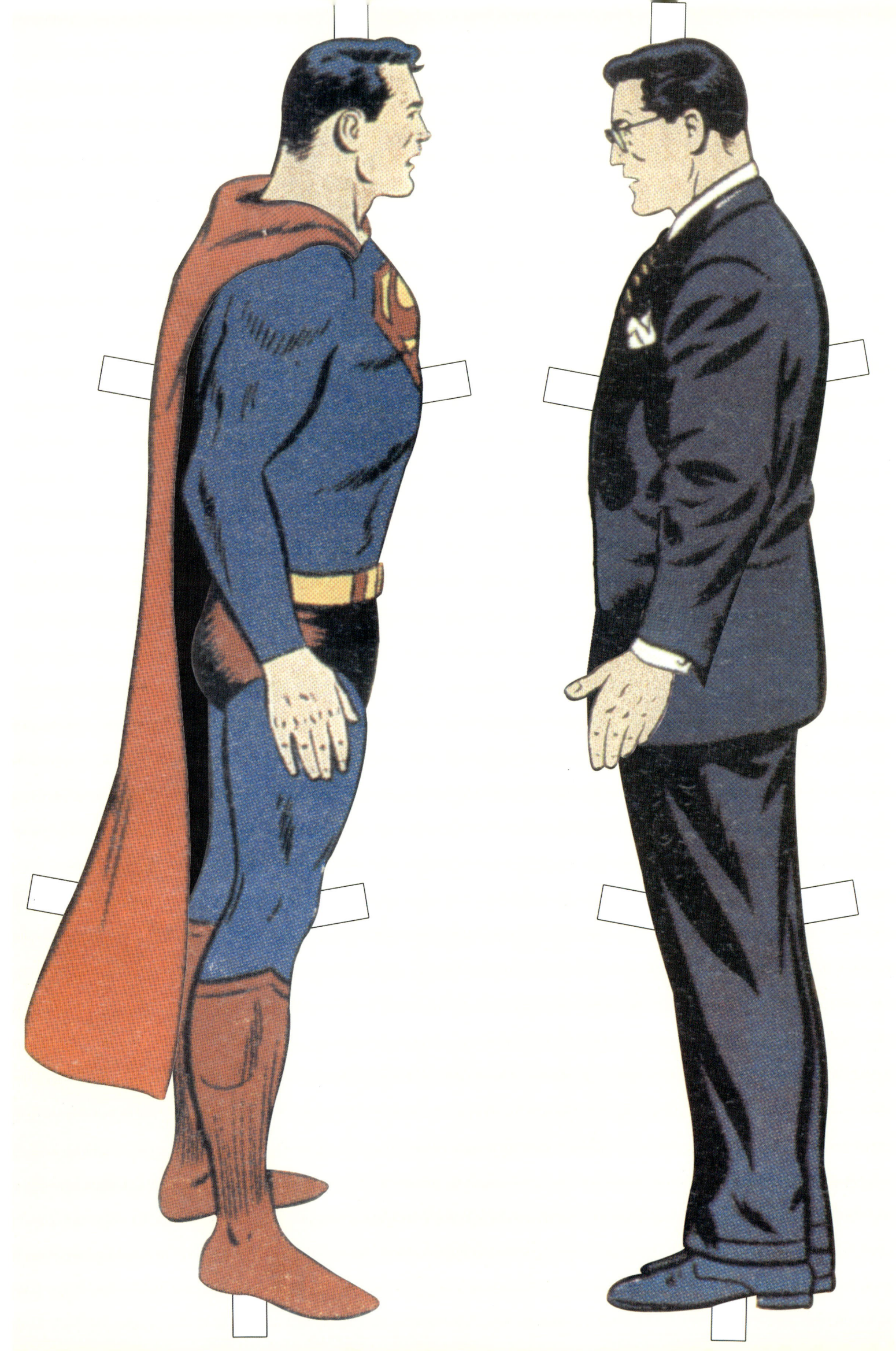

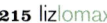

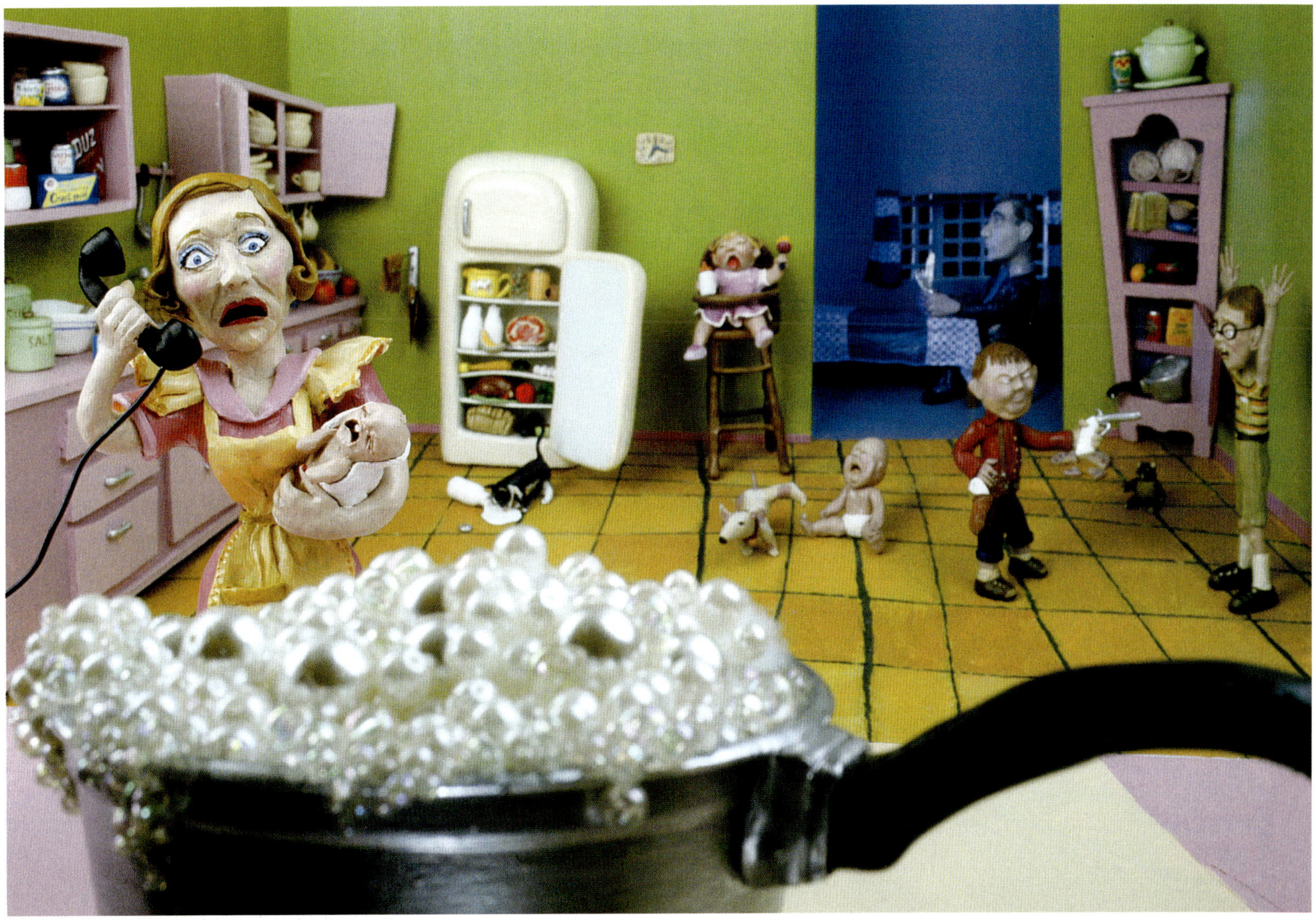

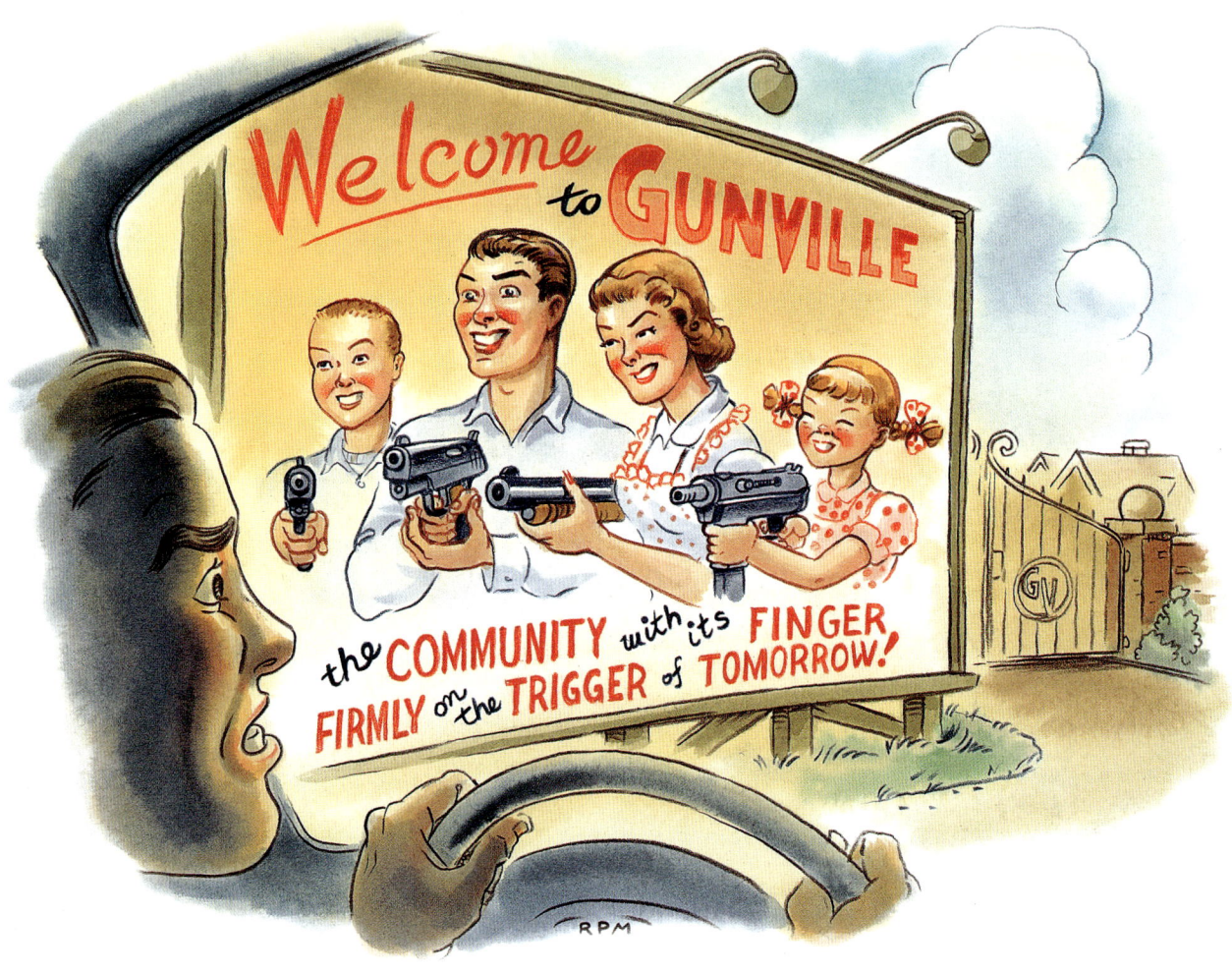

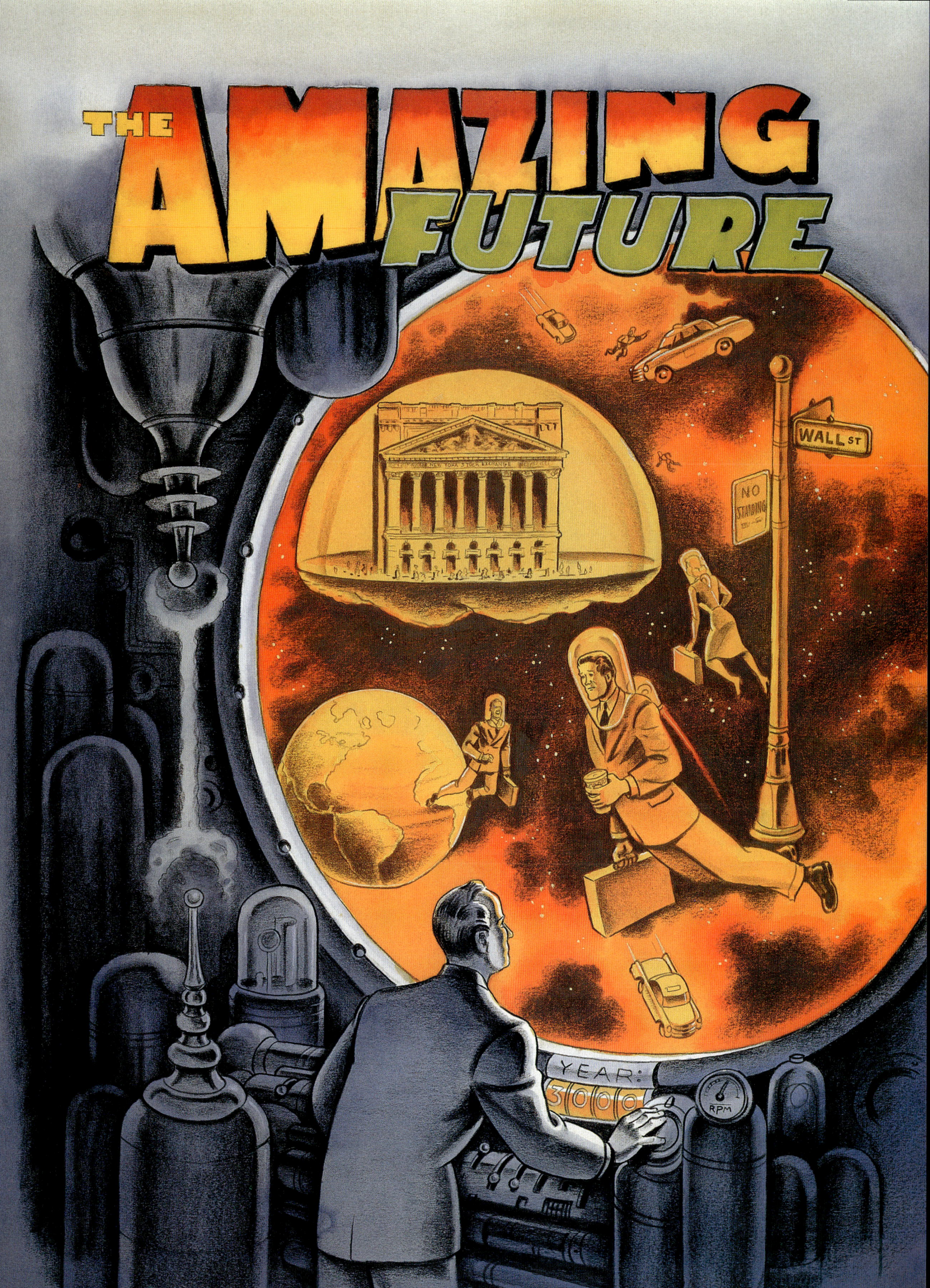

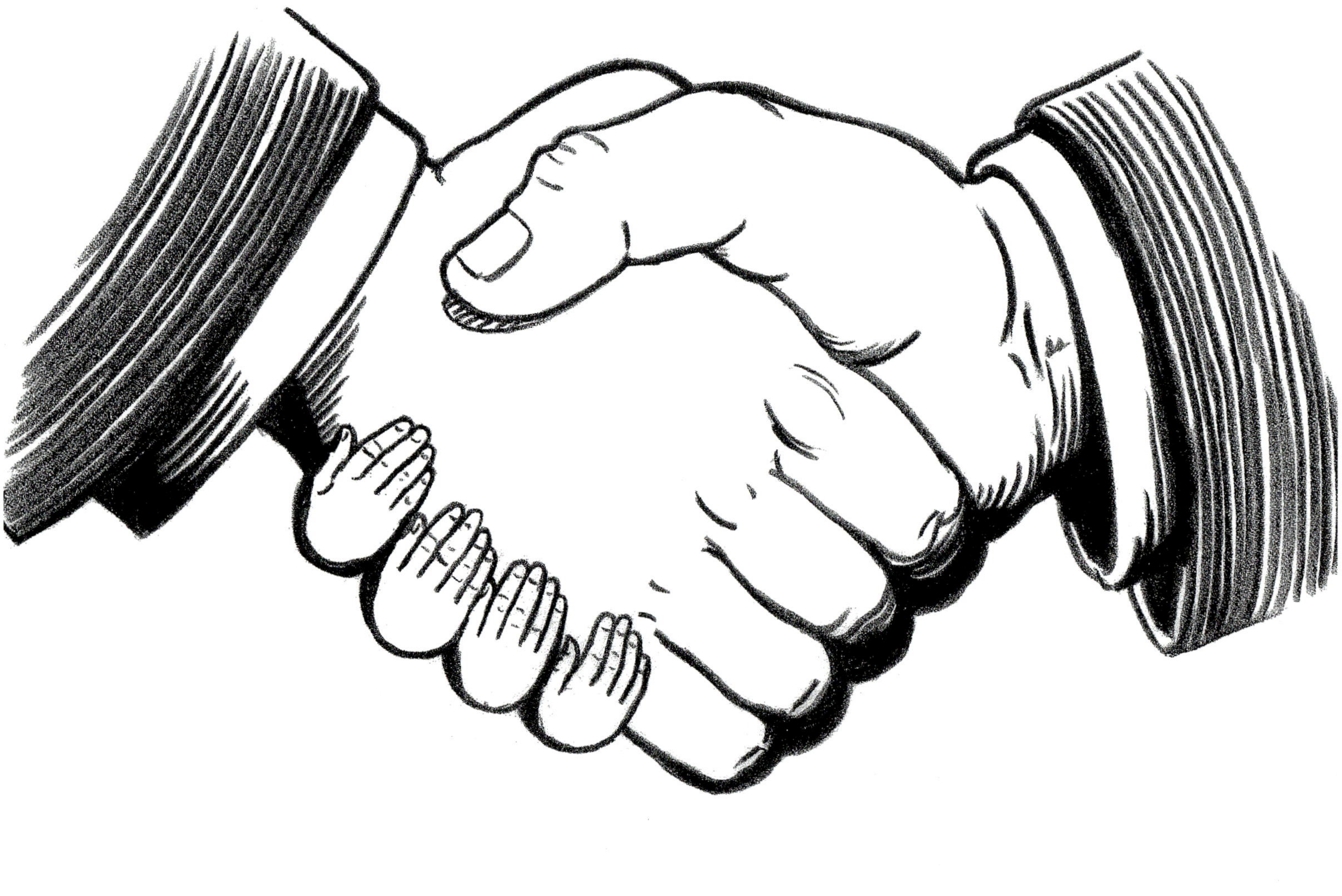

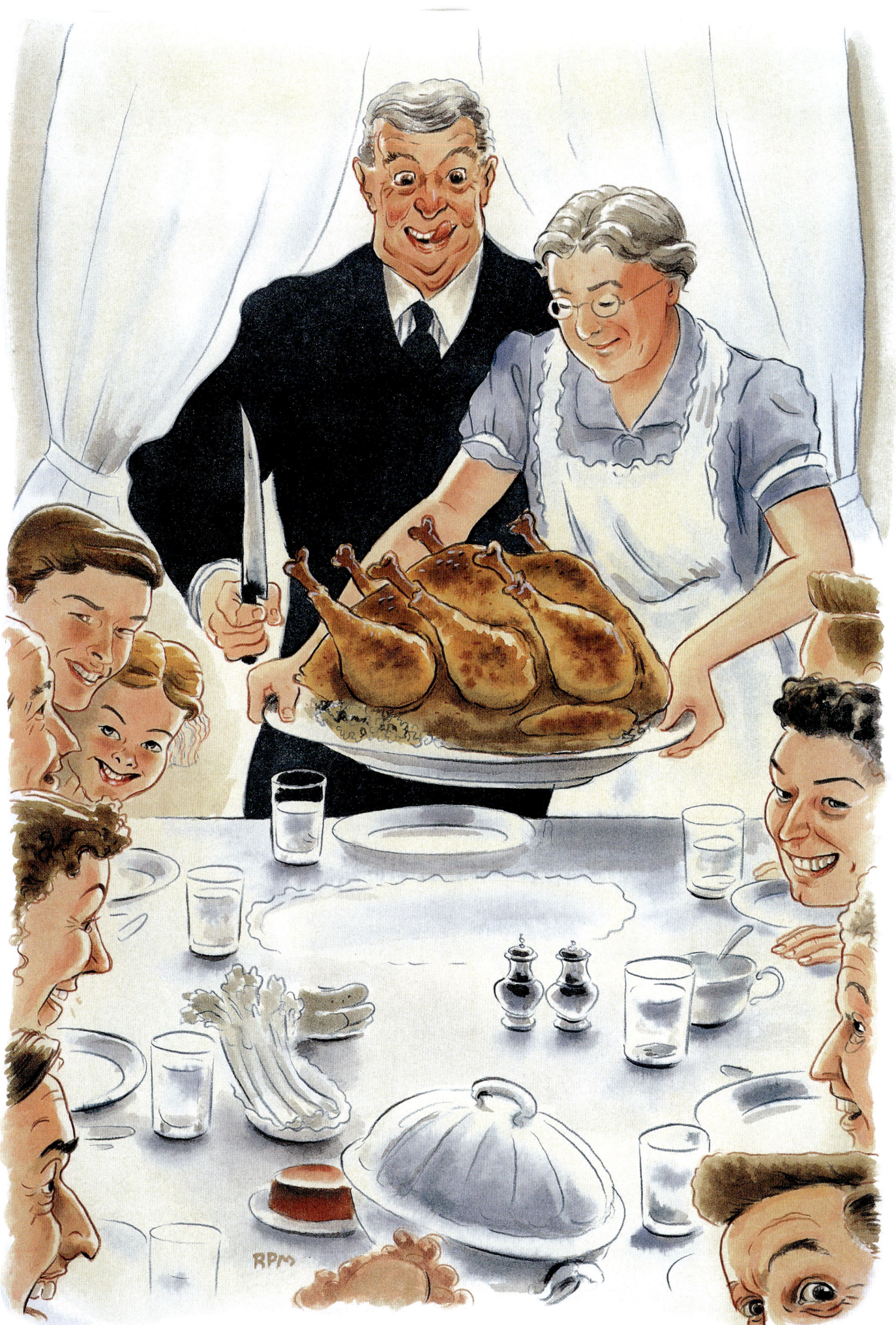

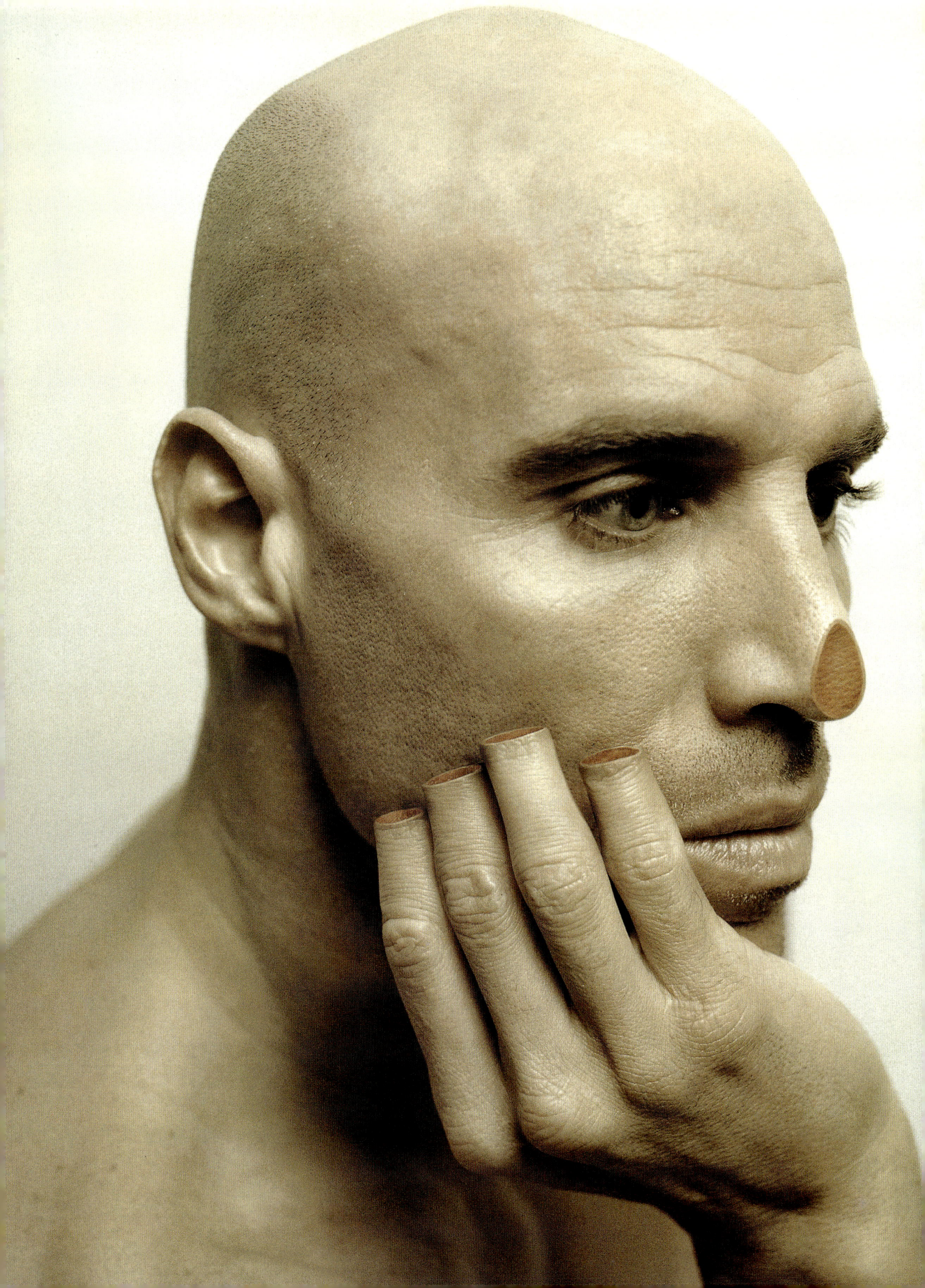

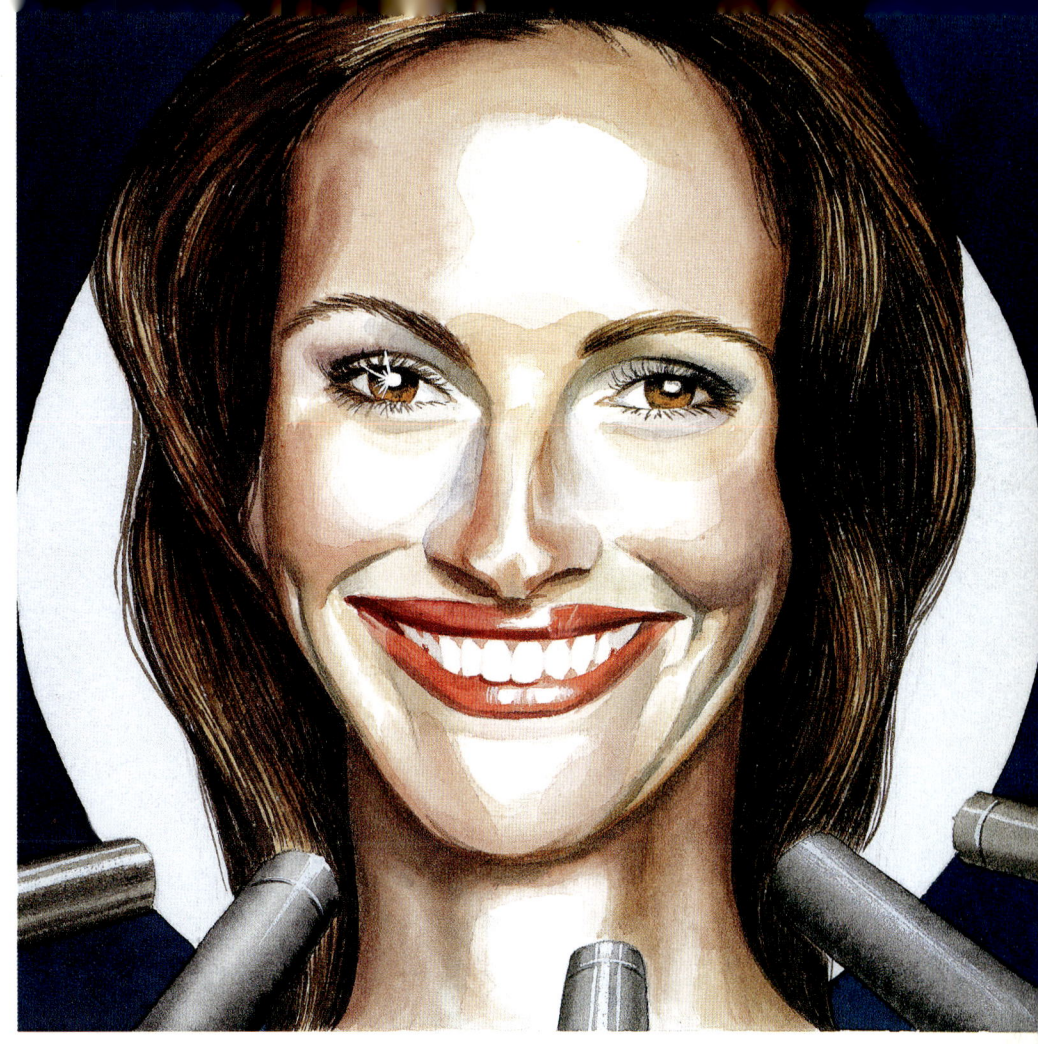

221 ruthmarten

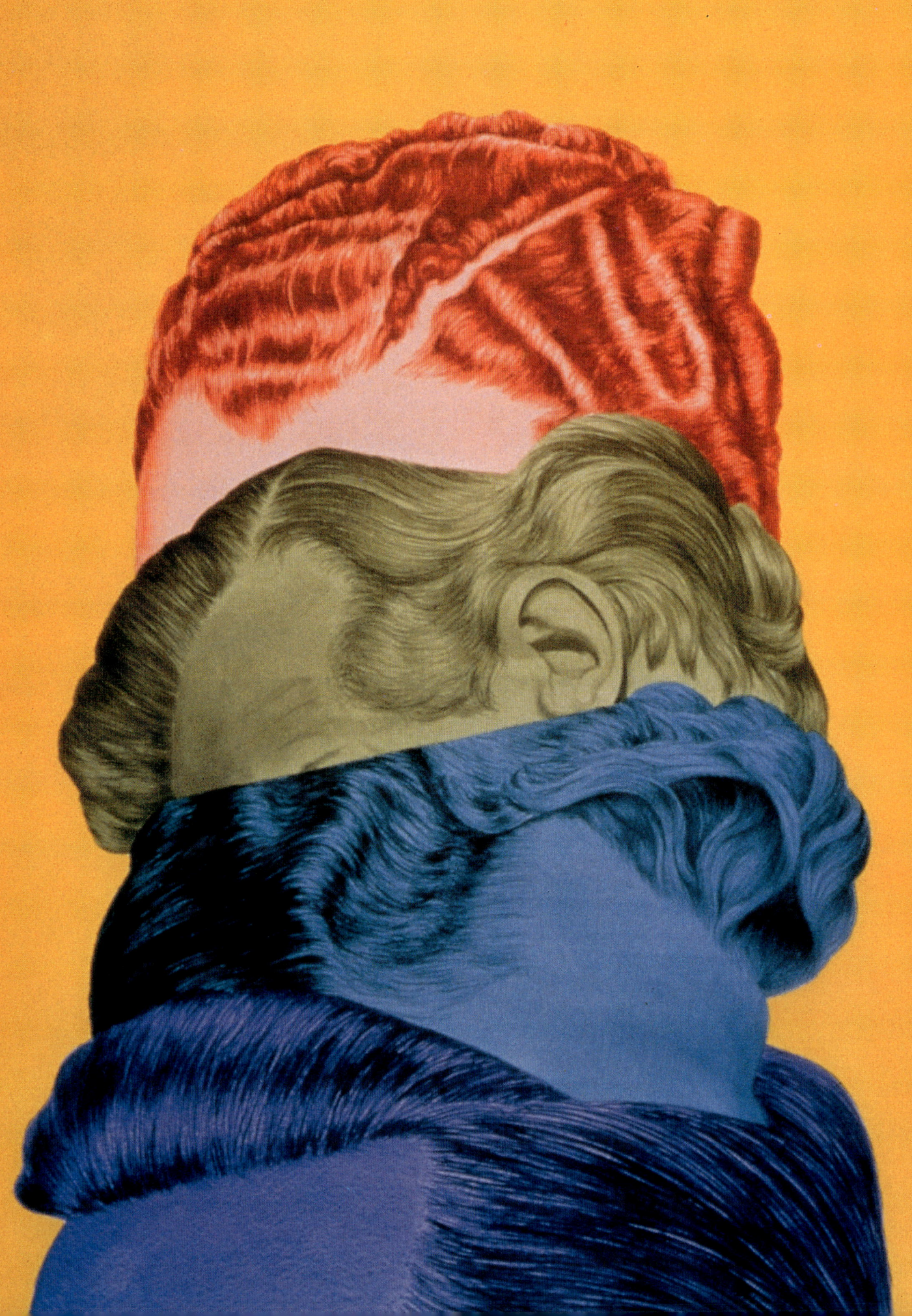

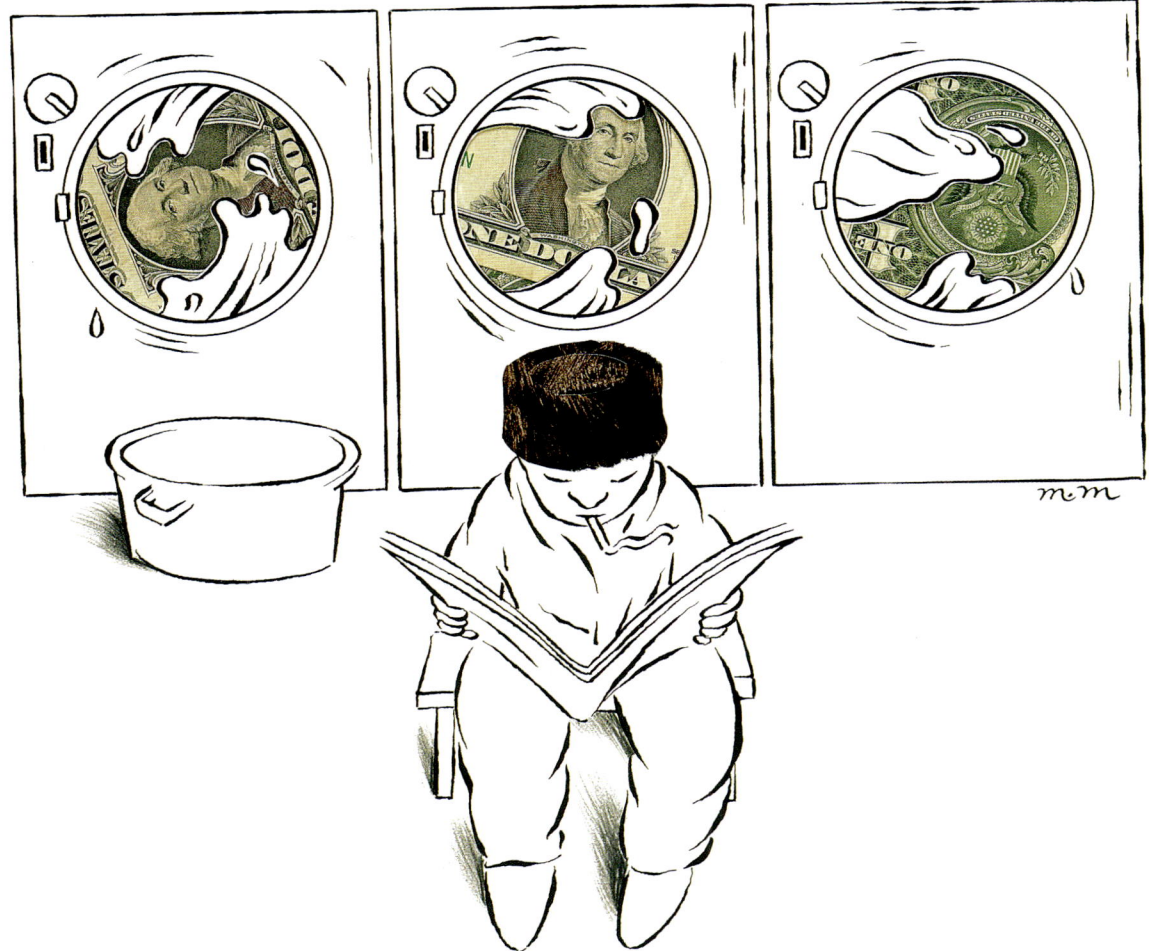

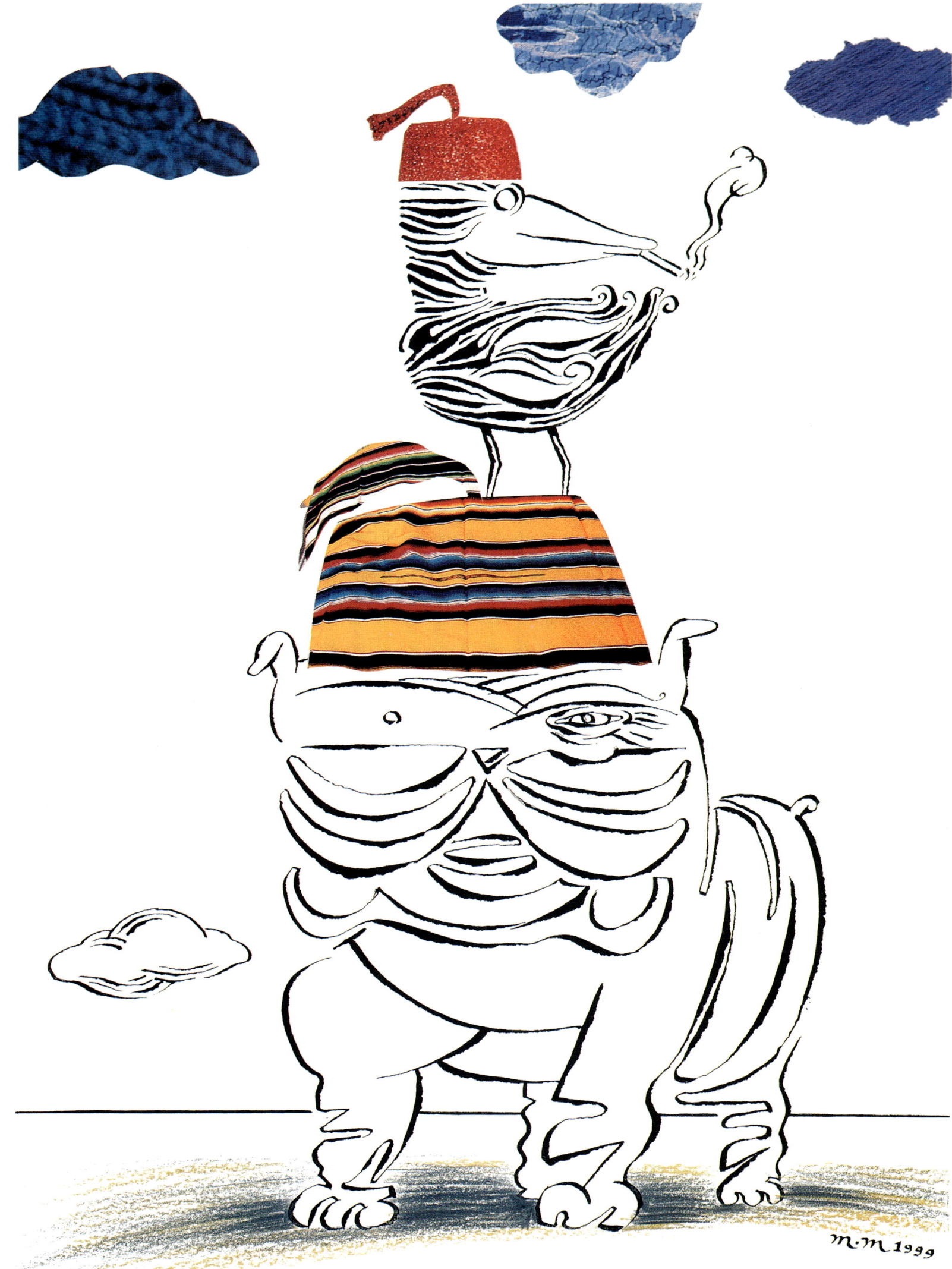

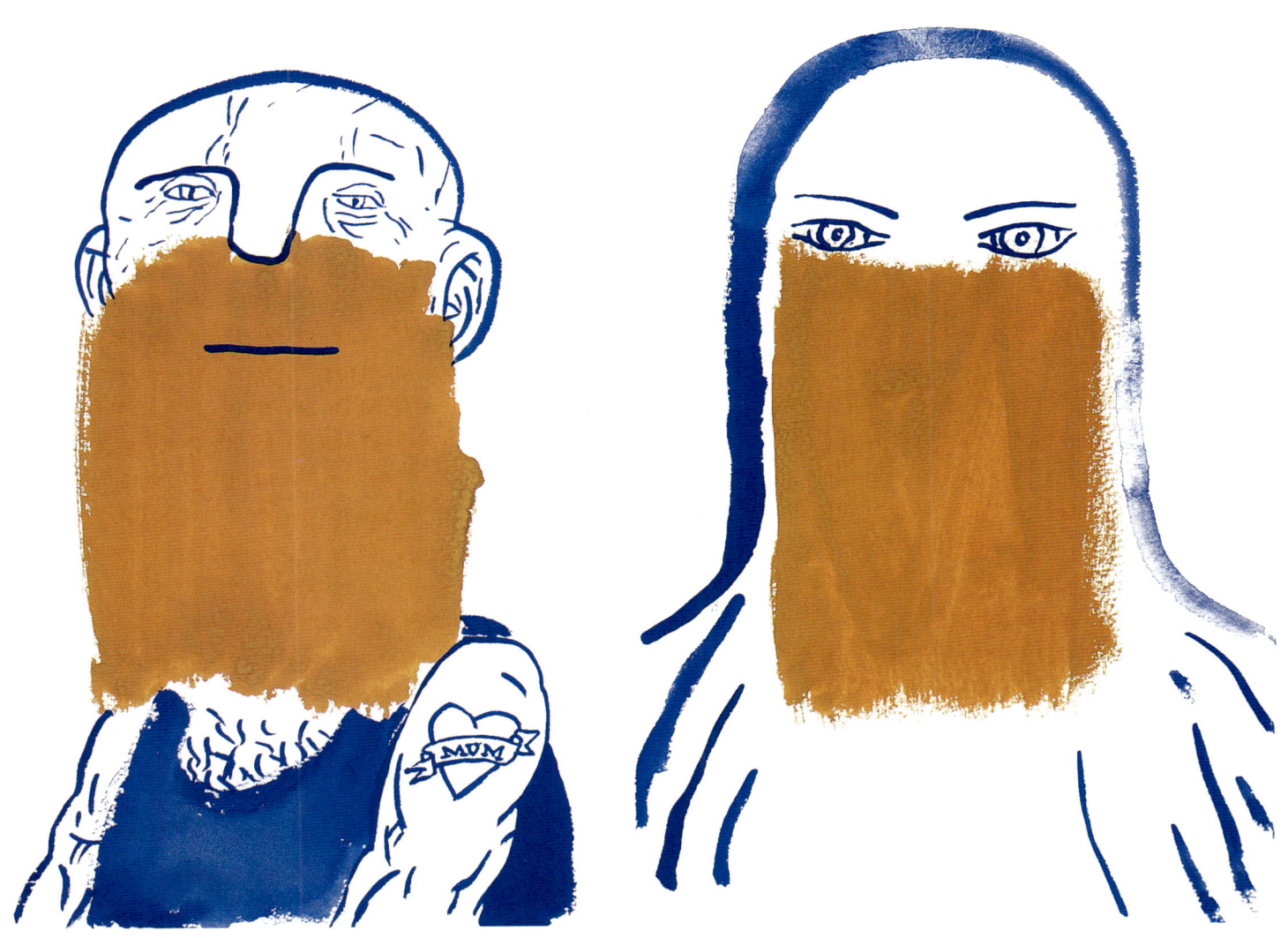

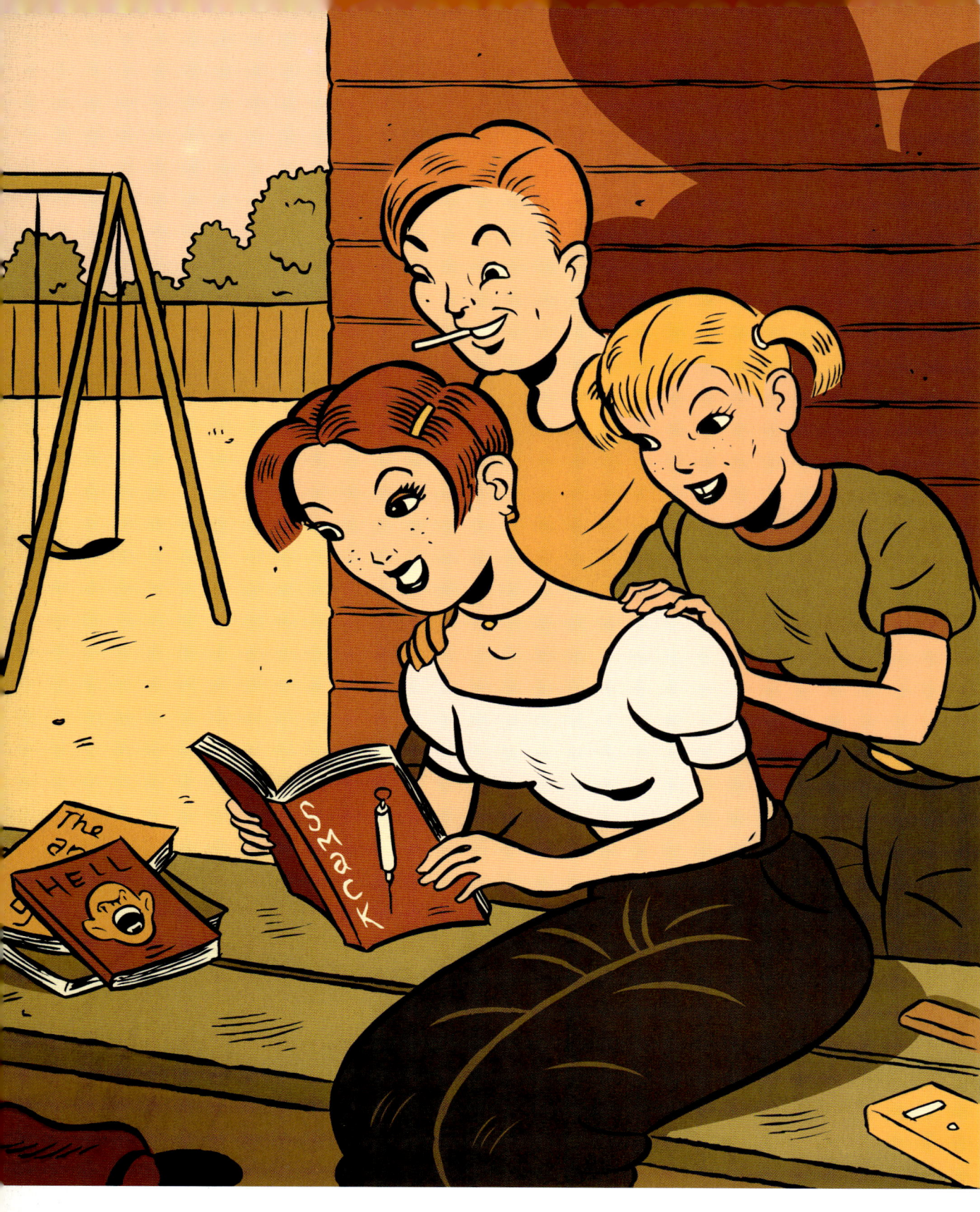

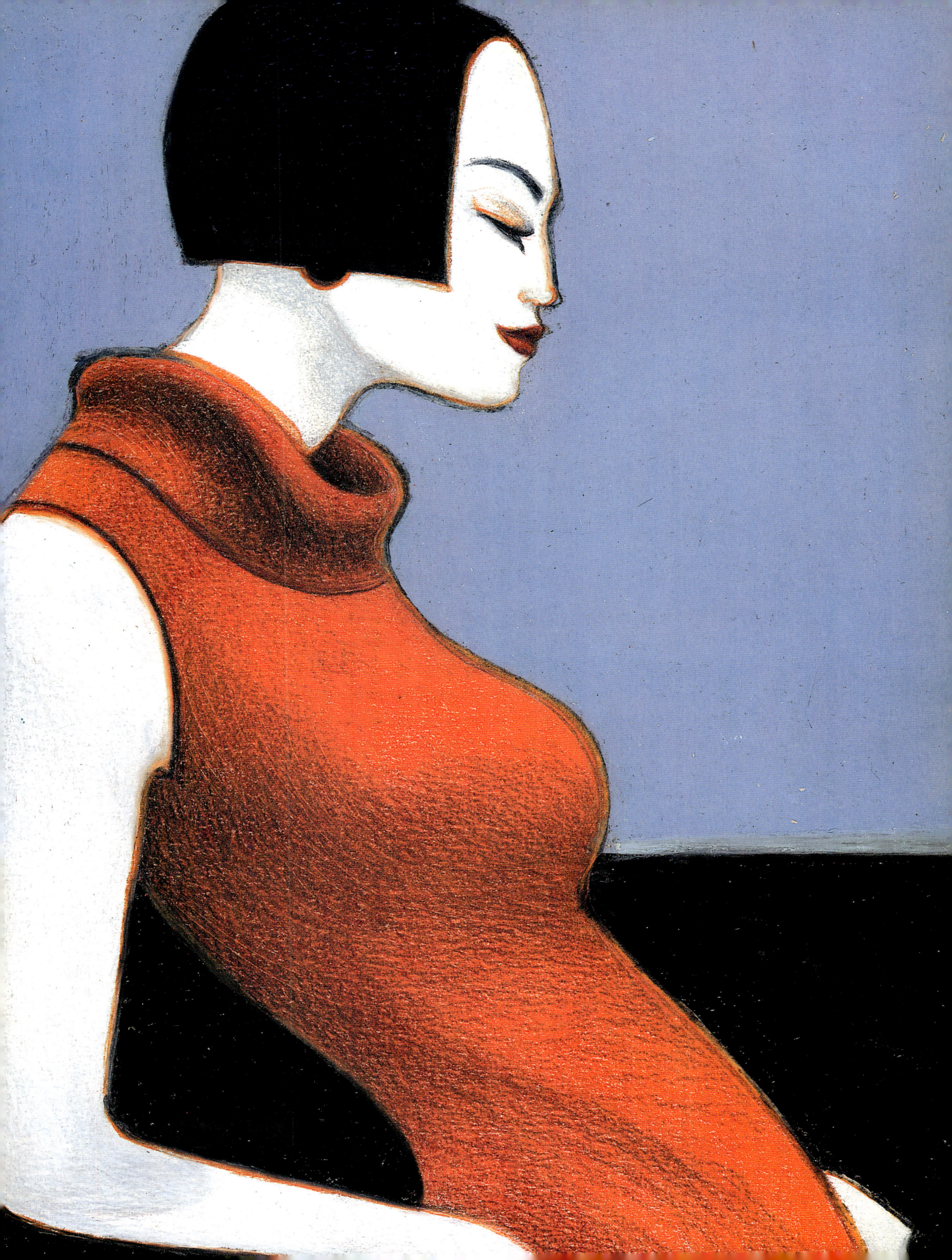

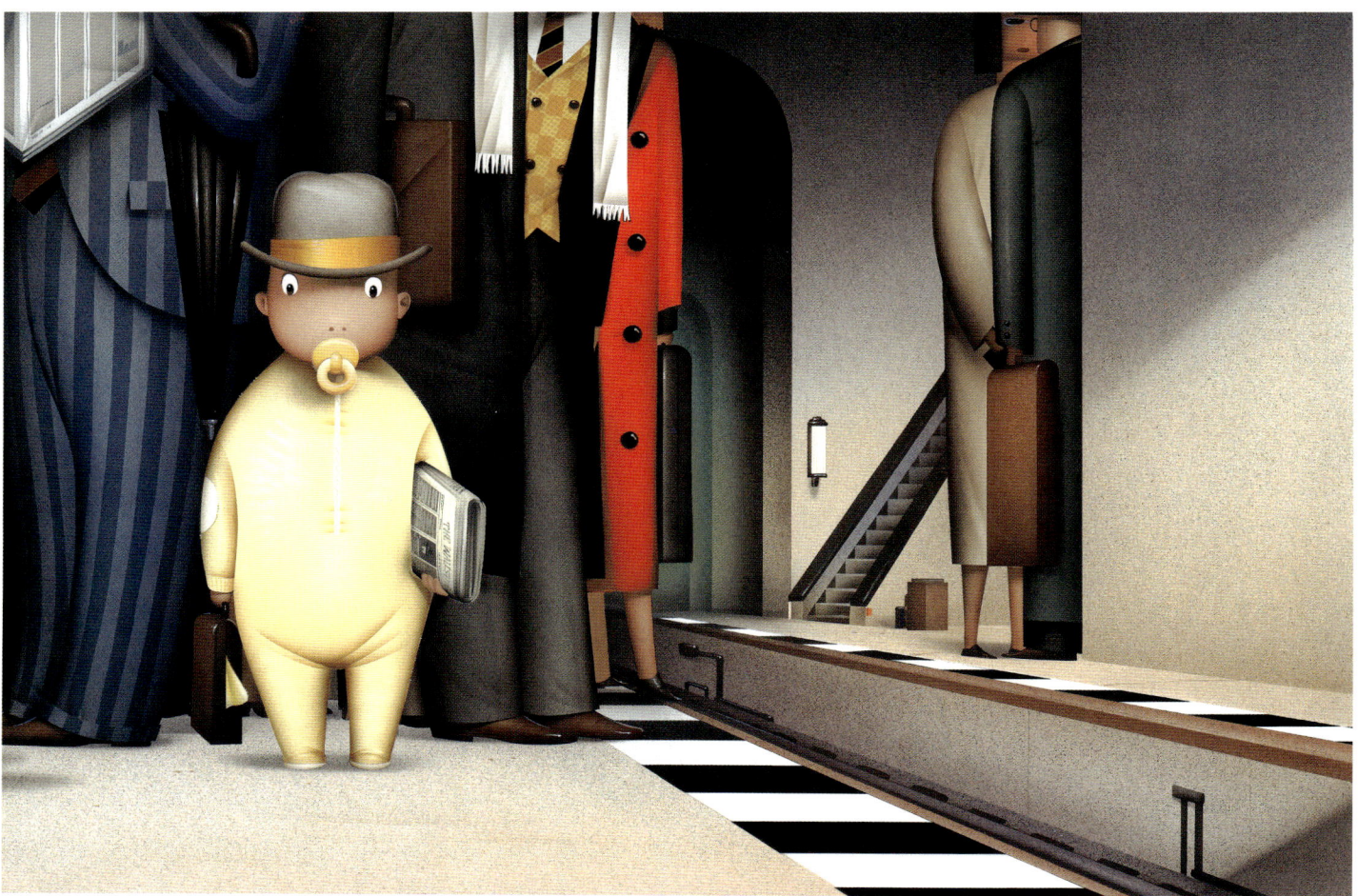

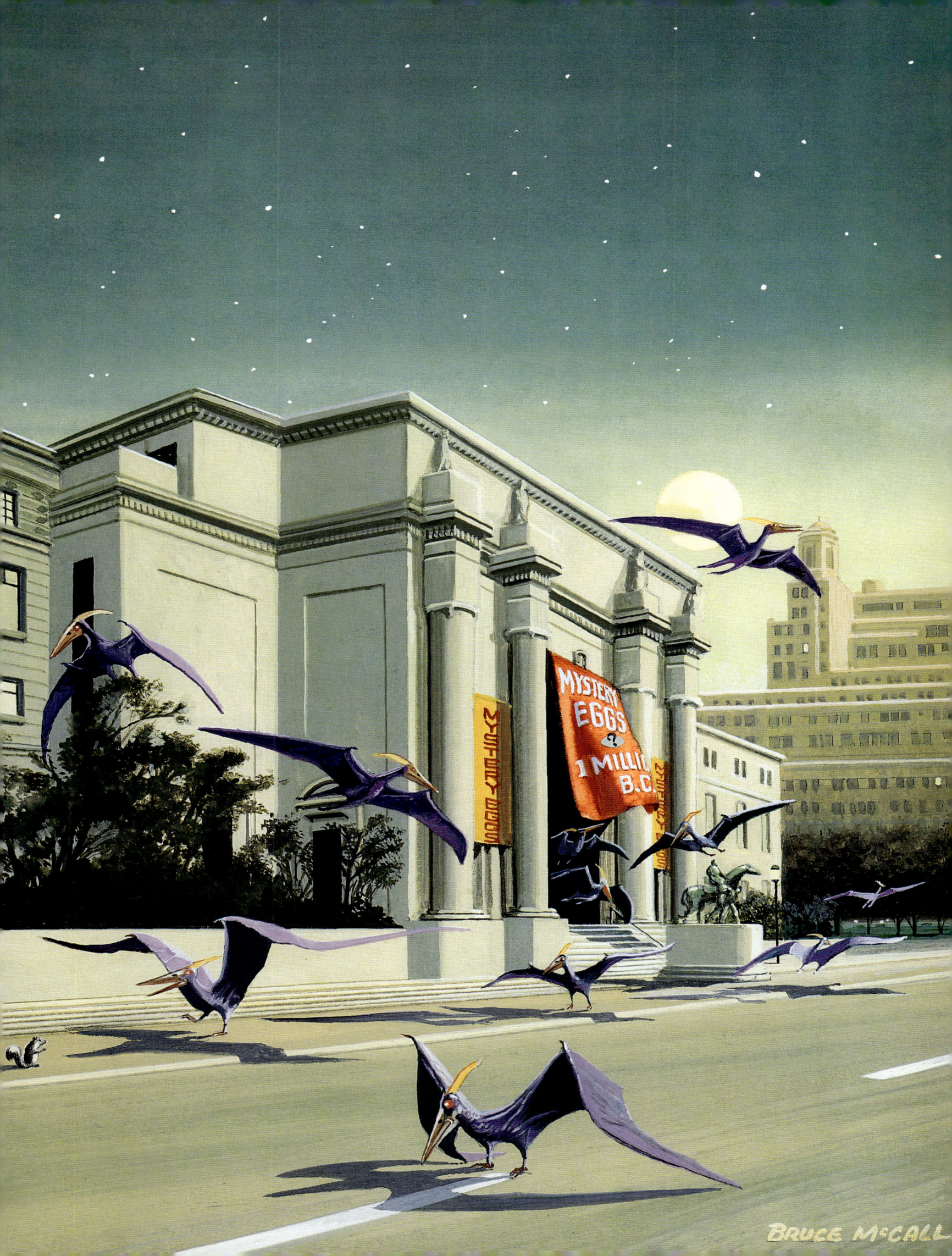

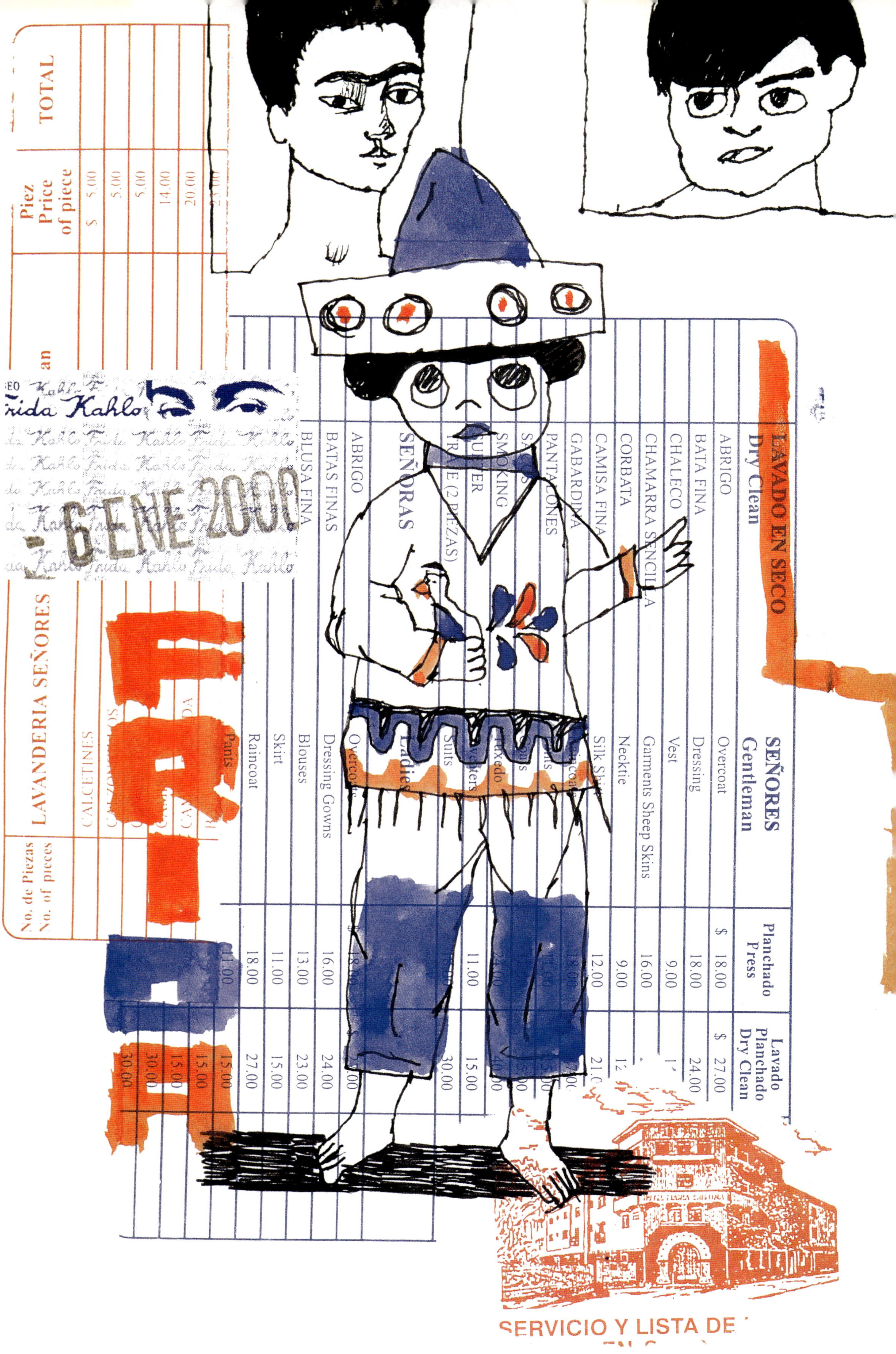
Frida Kahlo
6 ENE 2000
LAVADO EN SECO
Dry Clean
SEÑORES
Gentleman
SEÑORAS
Ladies
LAVANDERIA SEÑORES
TOTAL
Piez
Price
of piece
No. de Piezas
No. of pieces
Planchado
Press
Lavado
Planchado
Dry Clean
FRIDA
SERVICIO Y LISTA DE

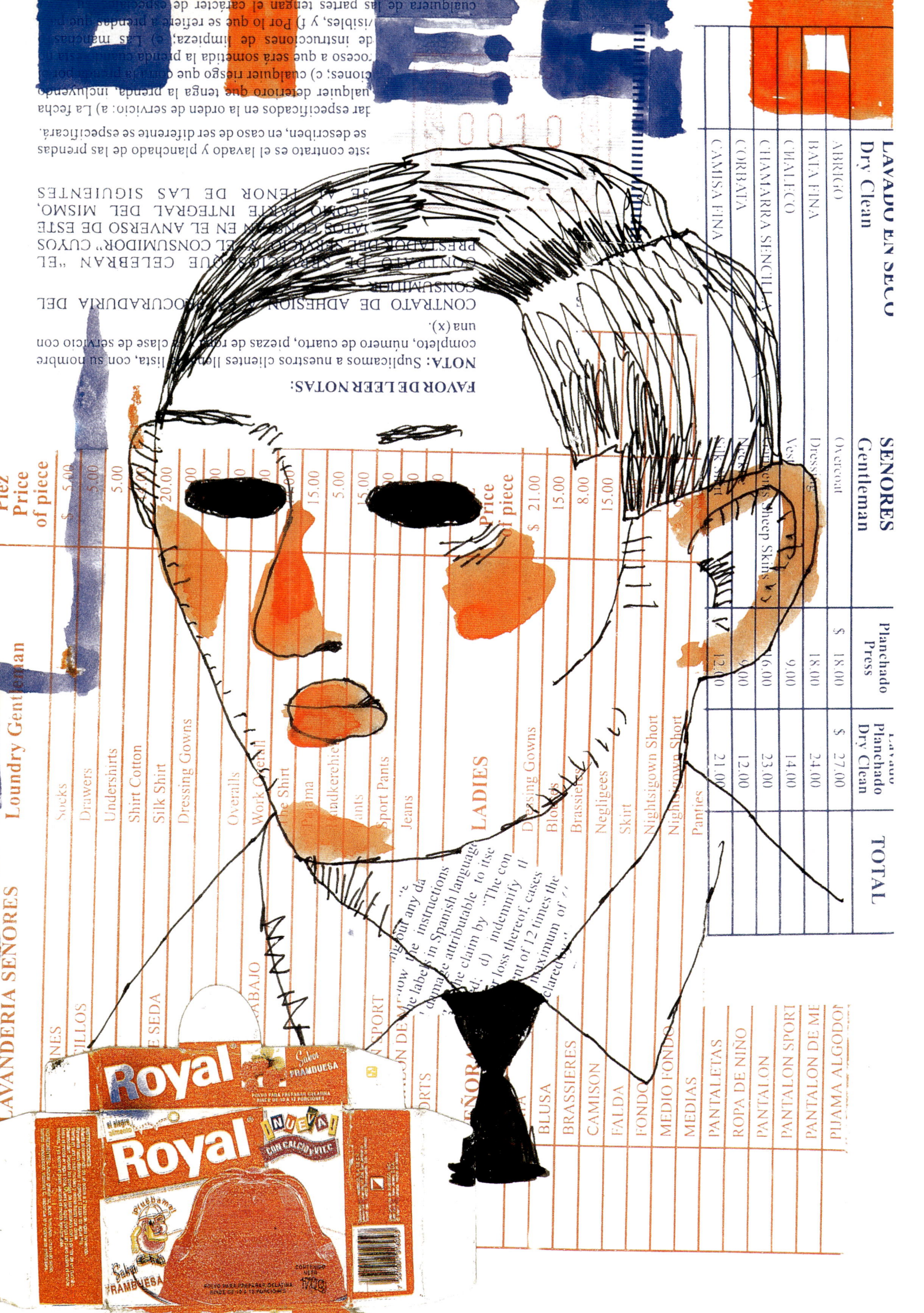

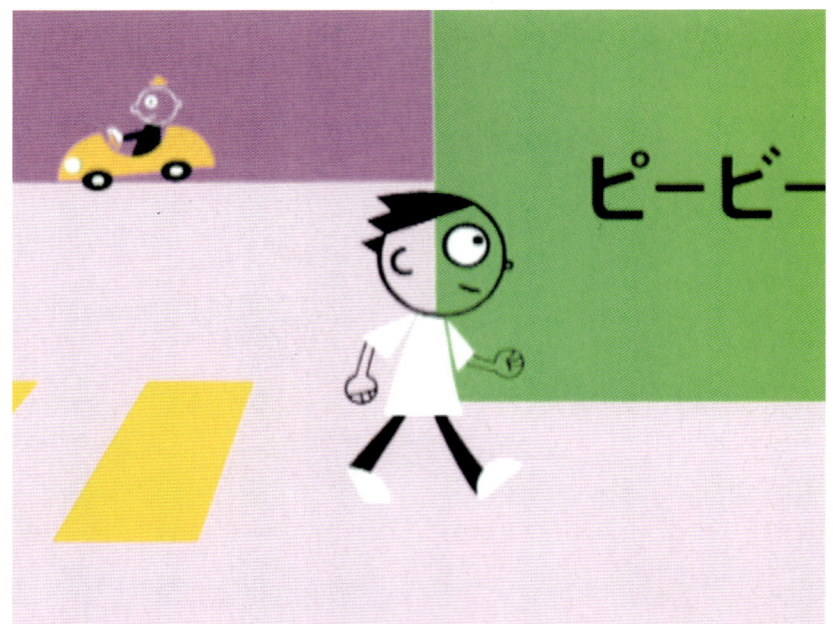

ピービー

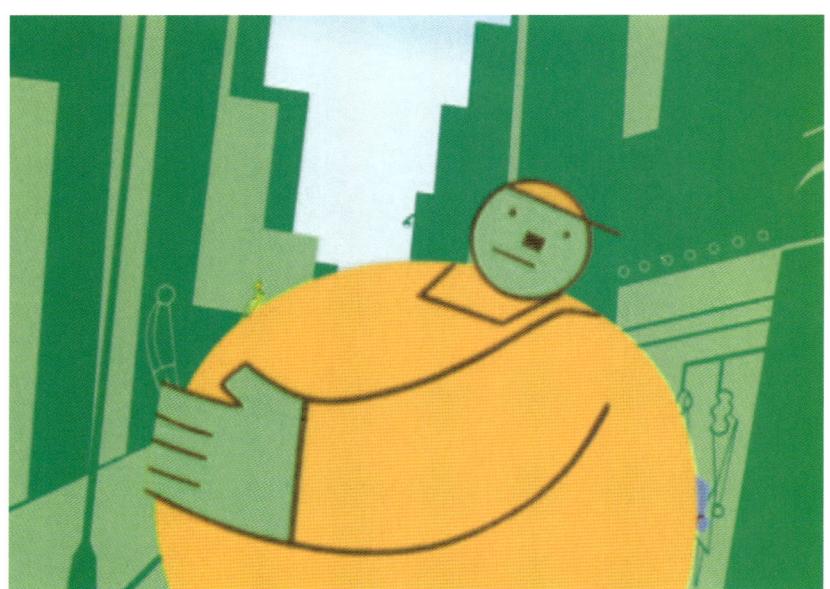

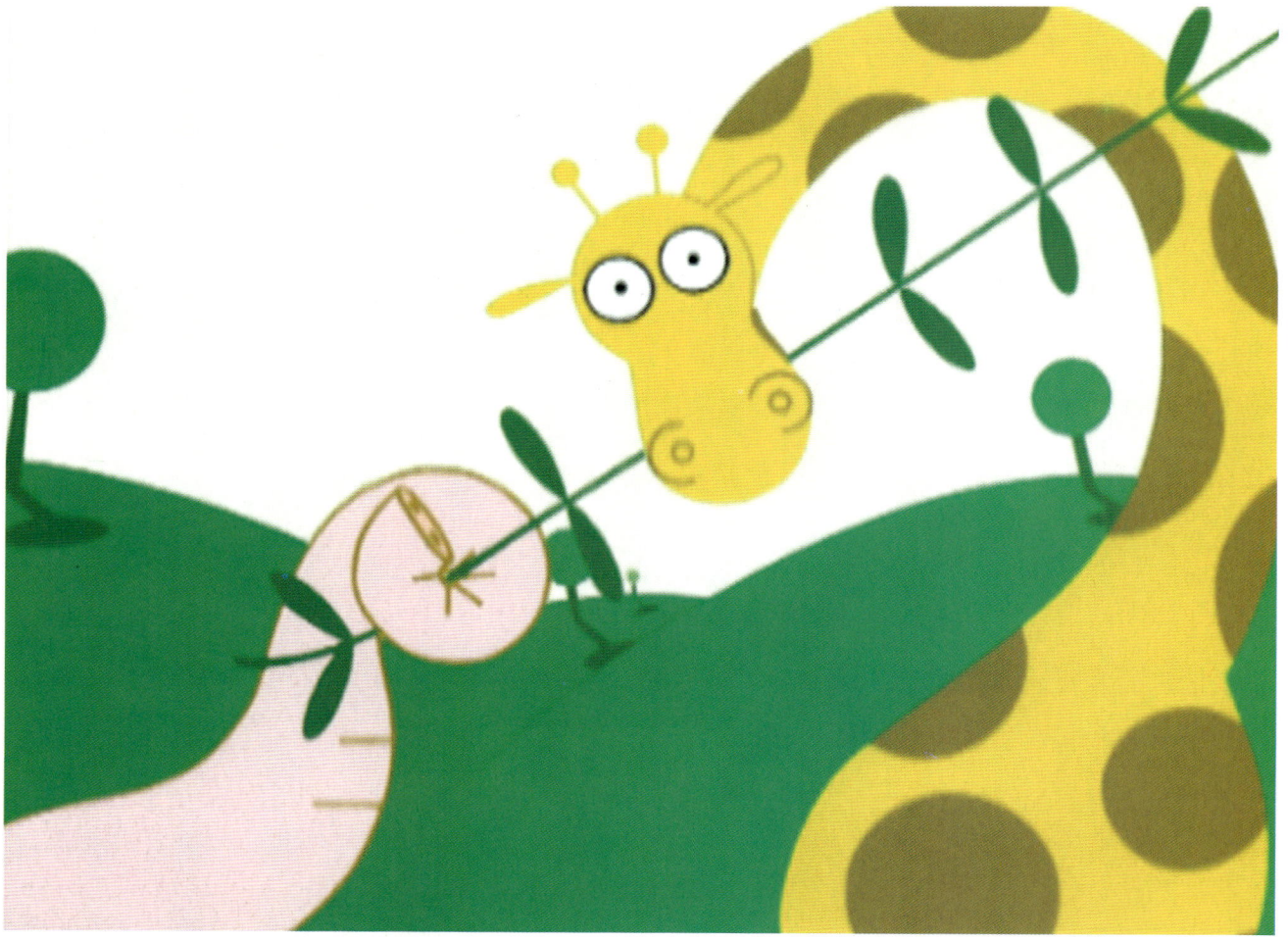

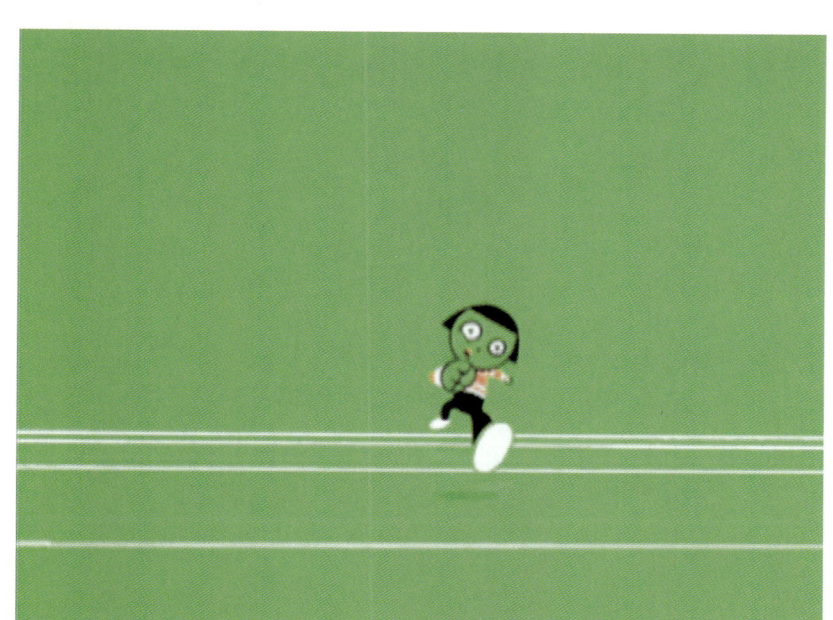

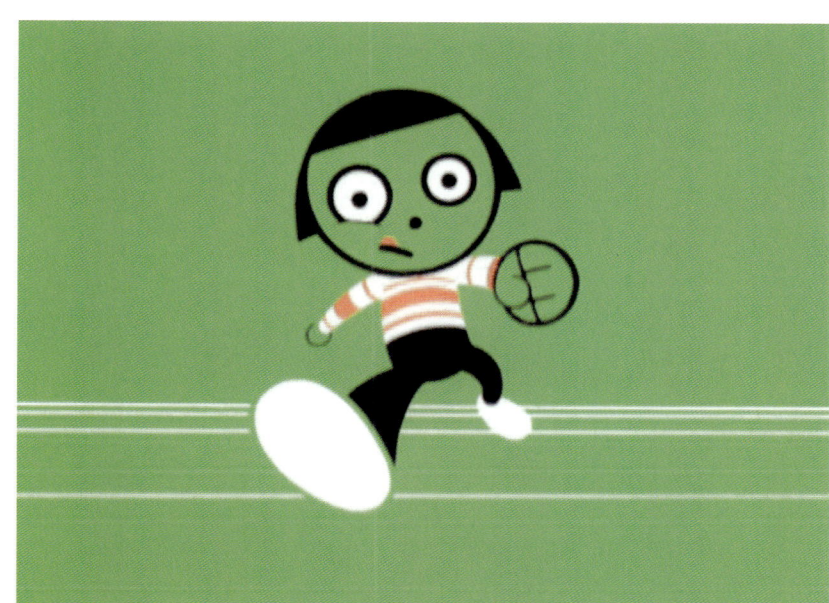

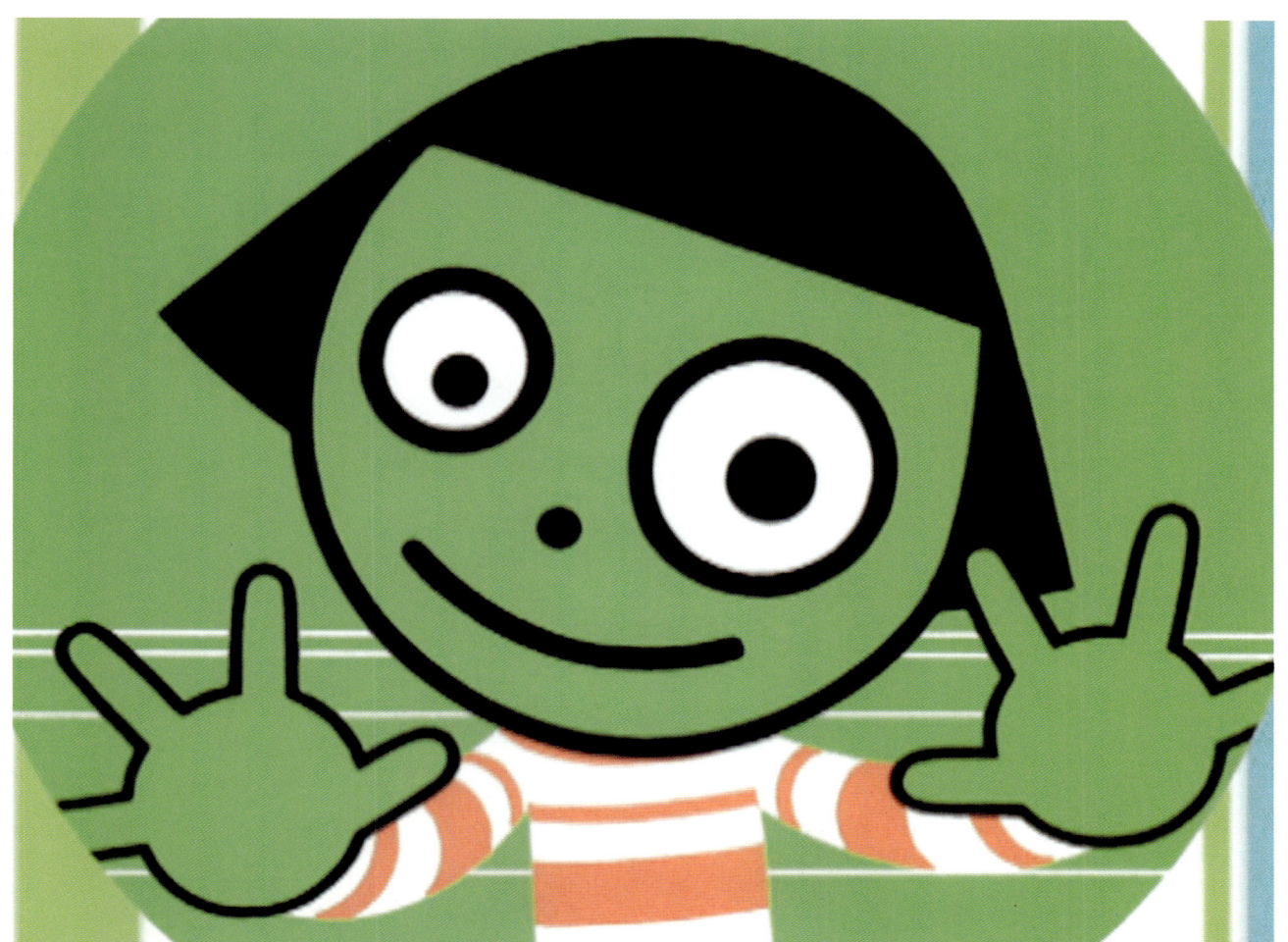

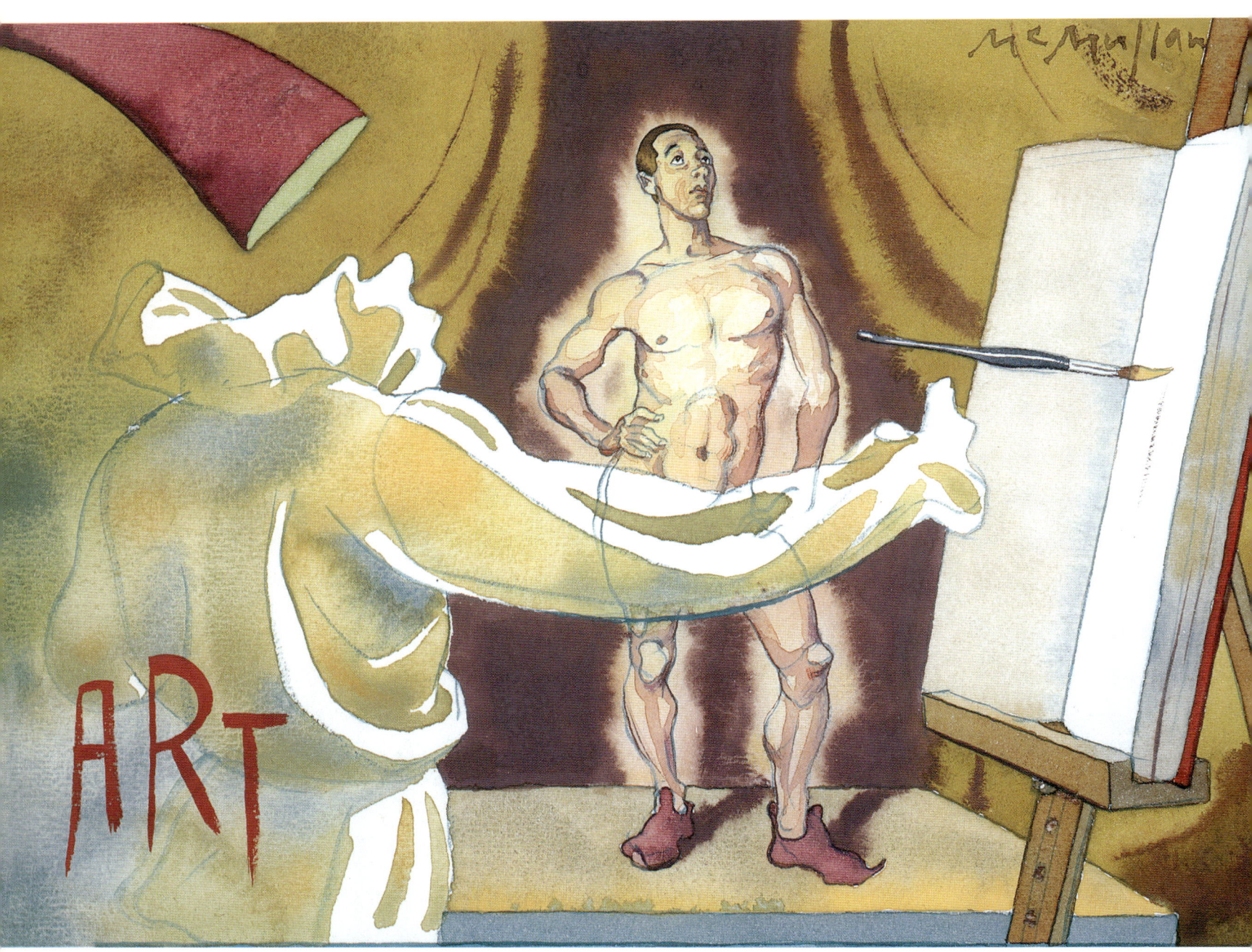

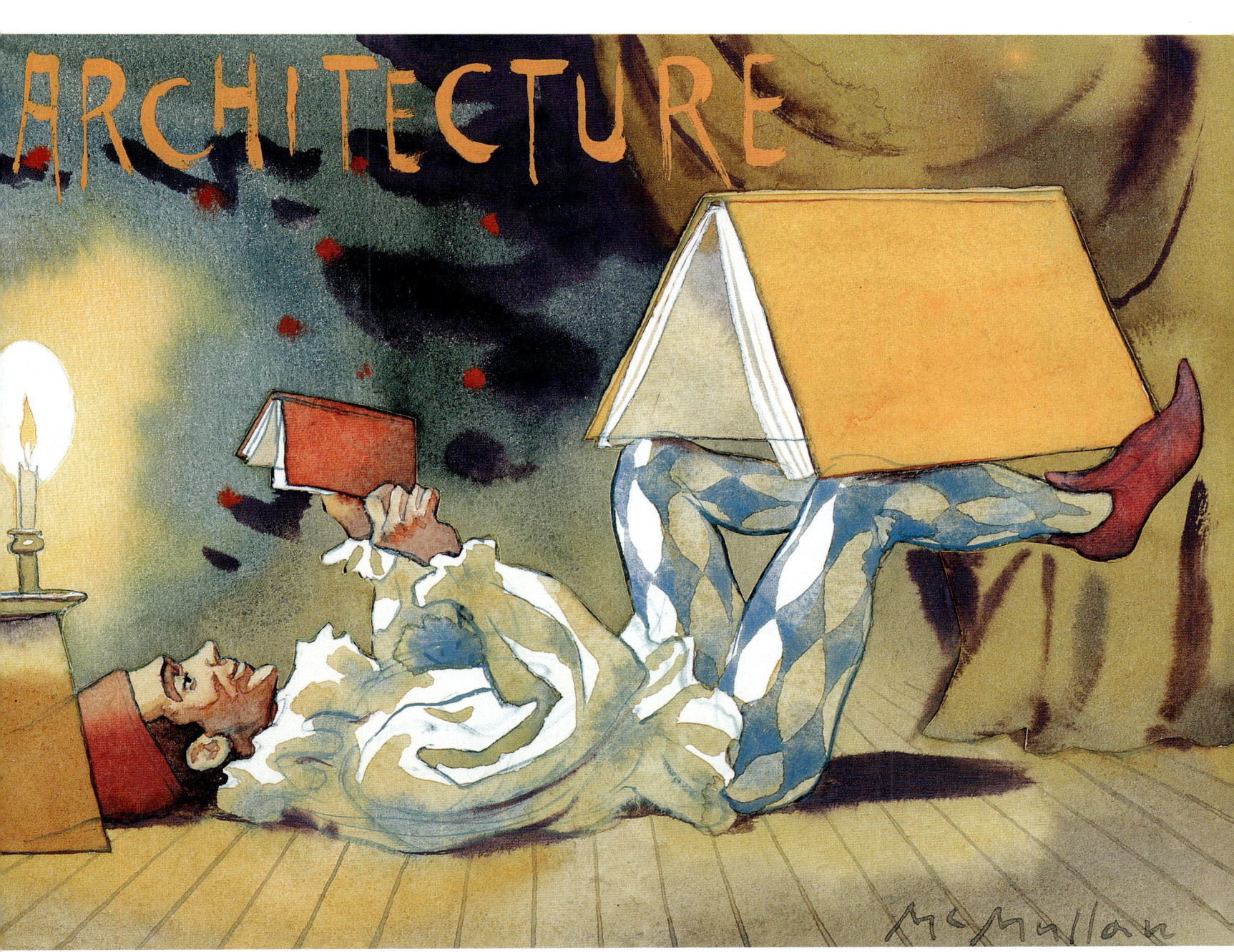

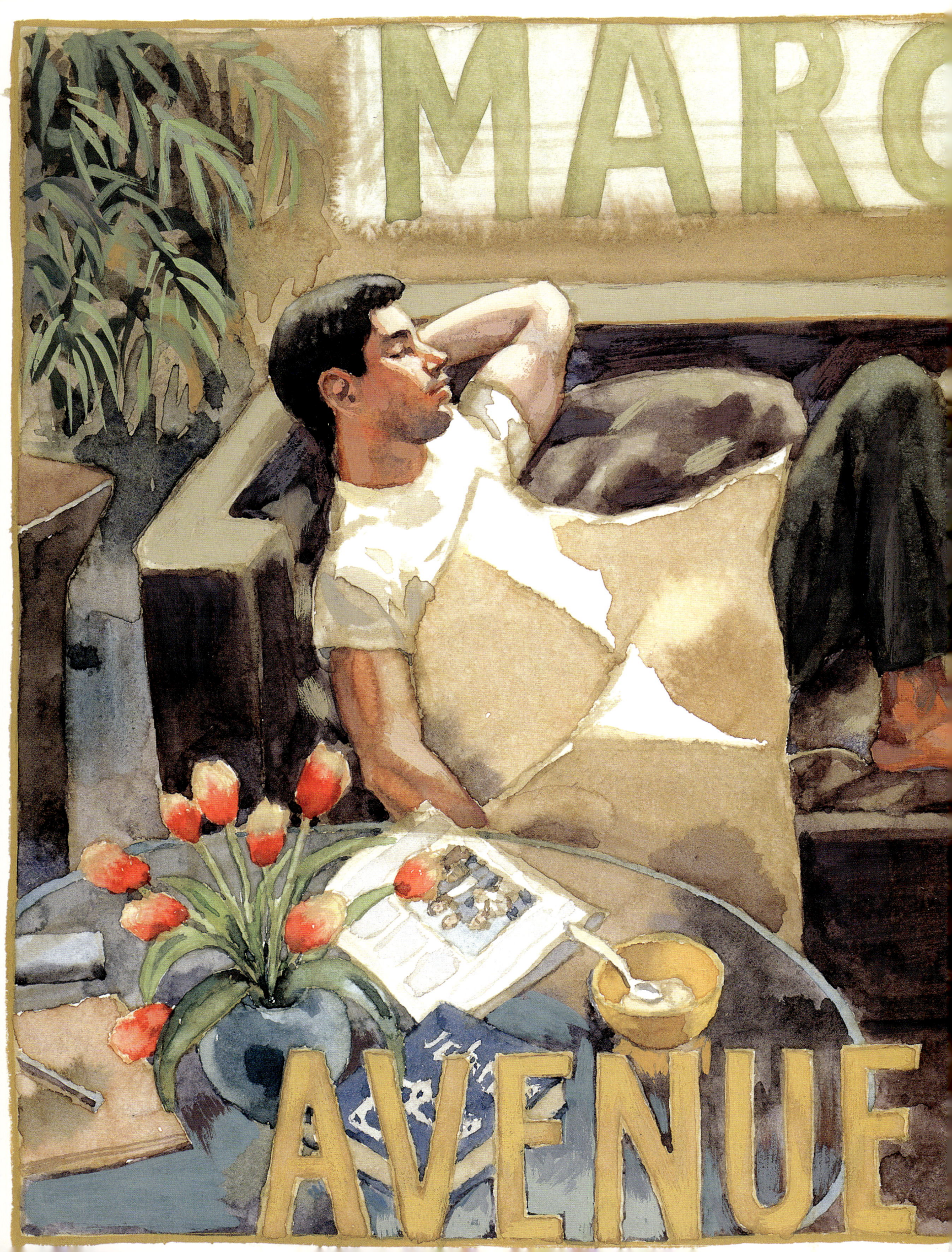

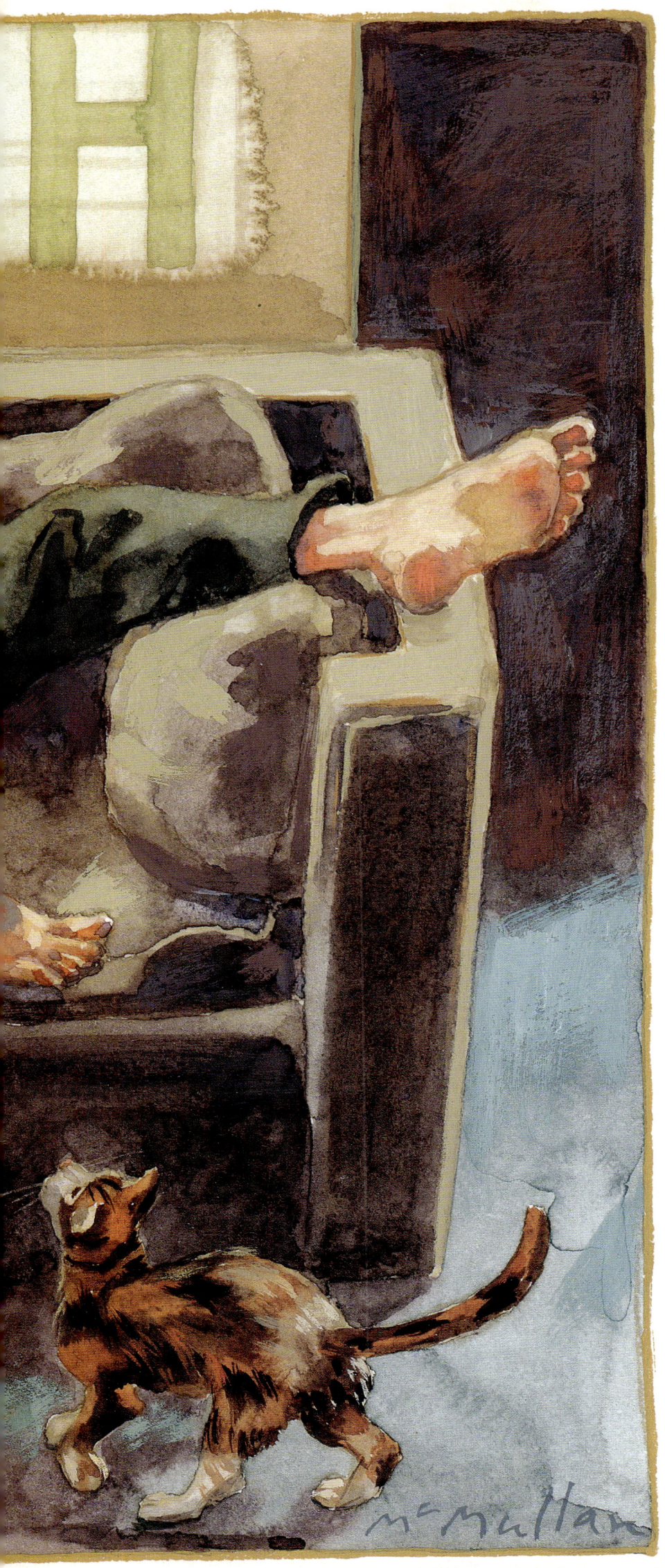

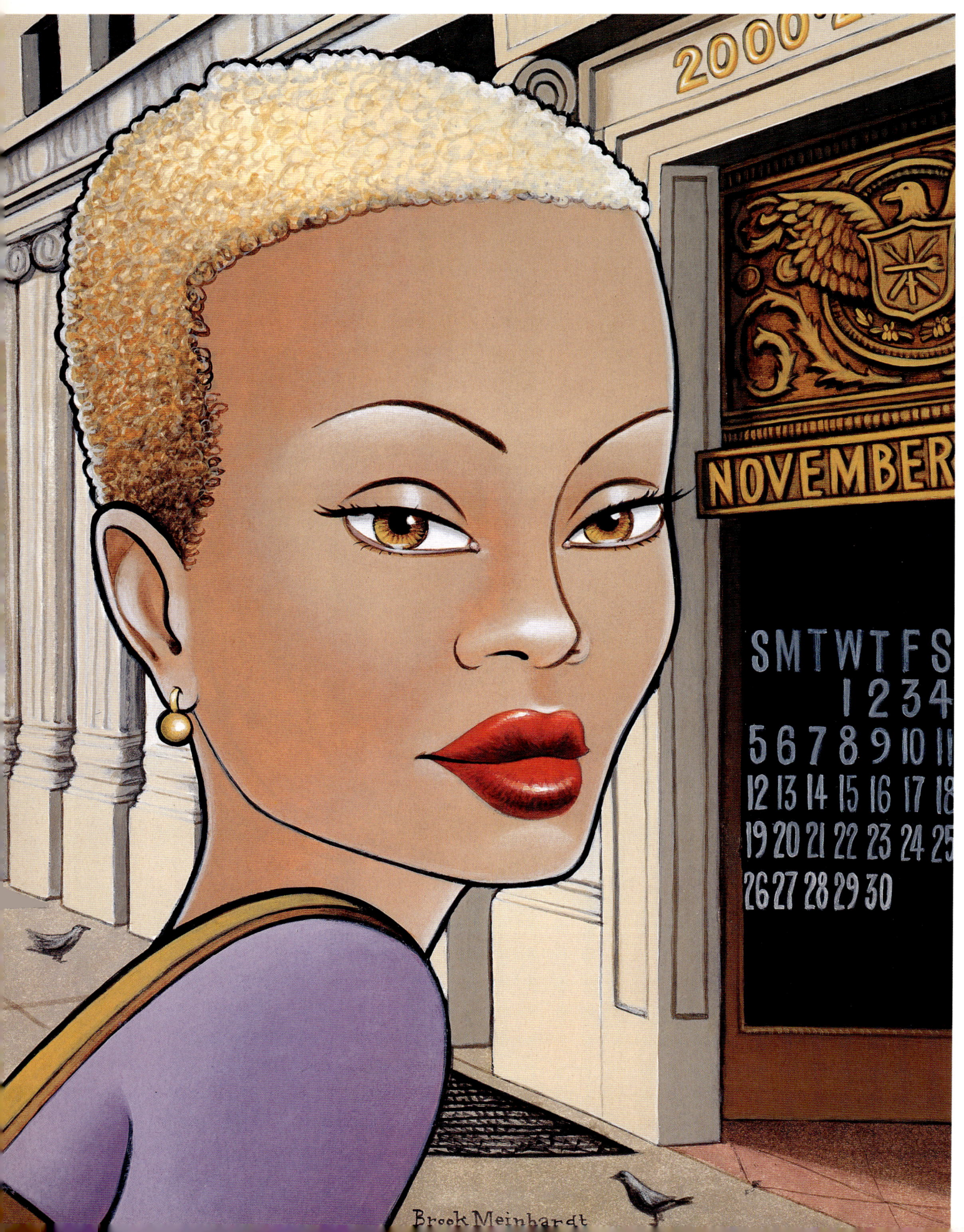

Brook Meinhardt

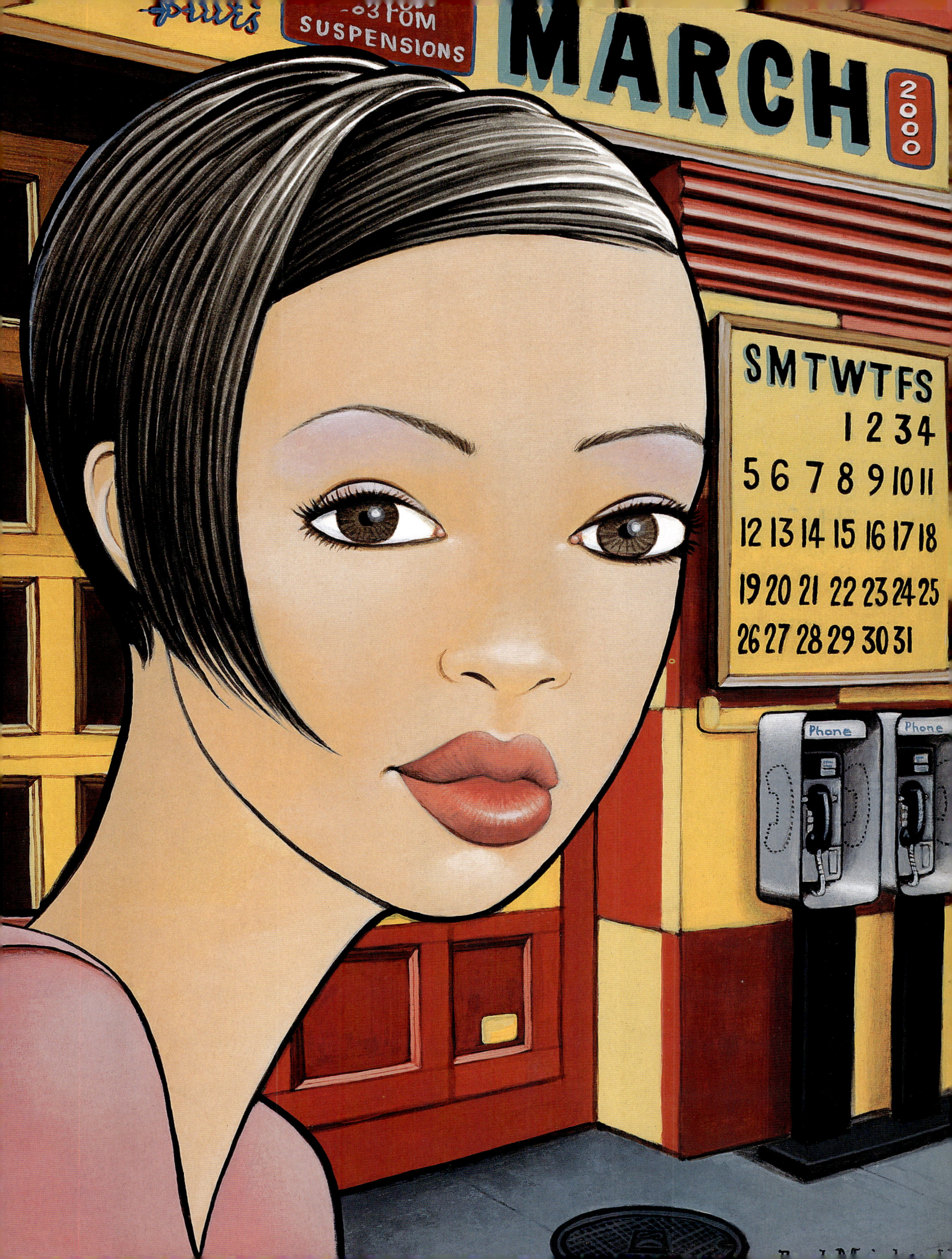

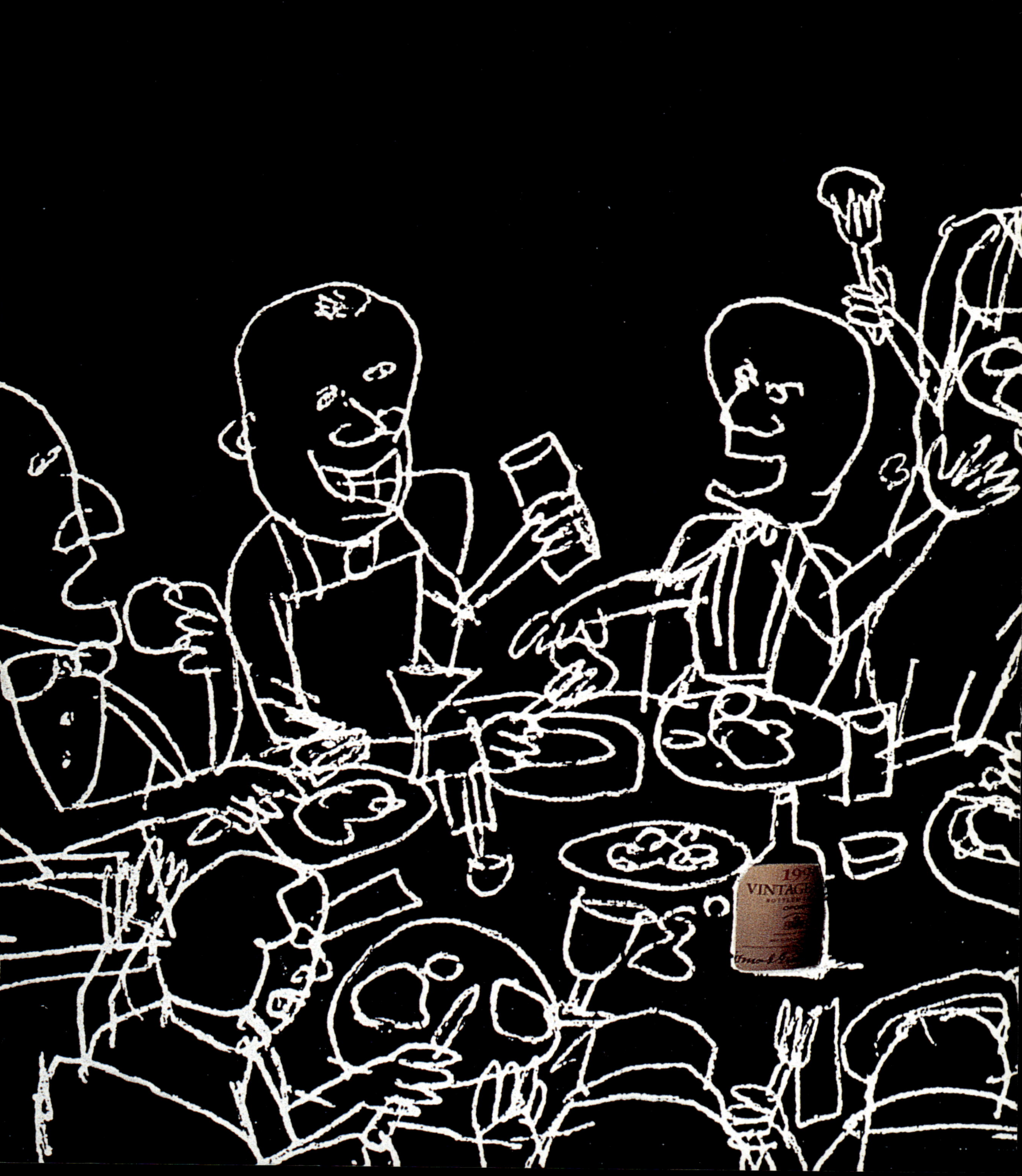

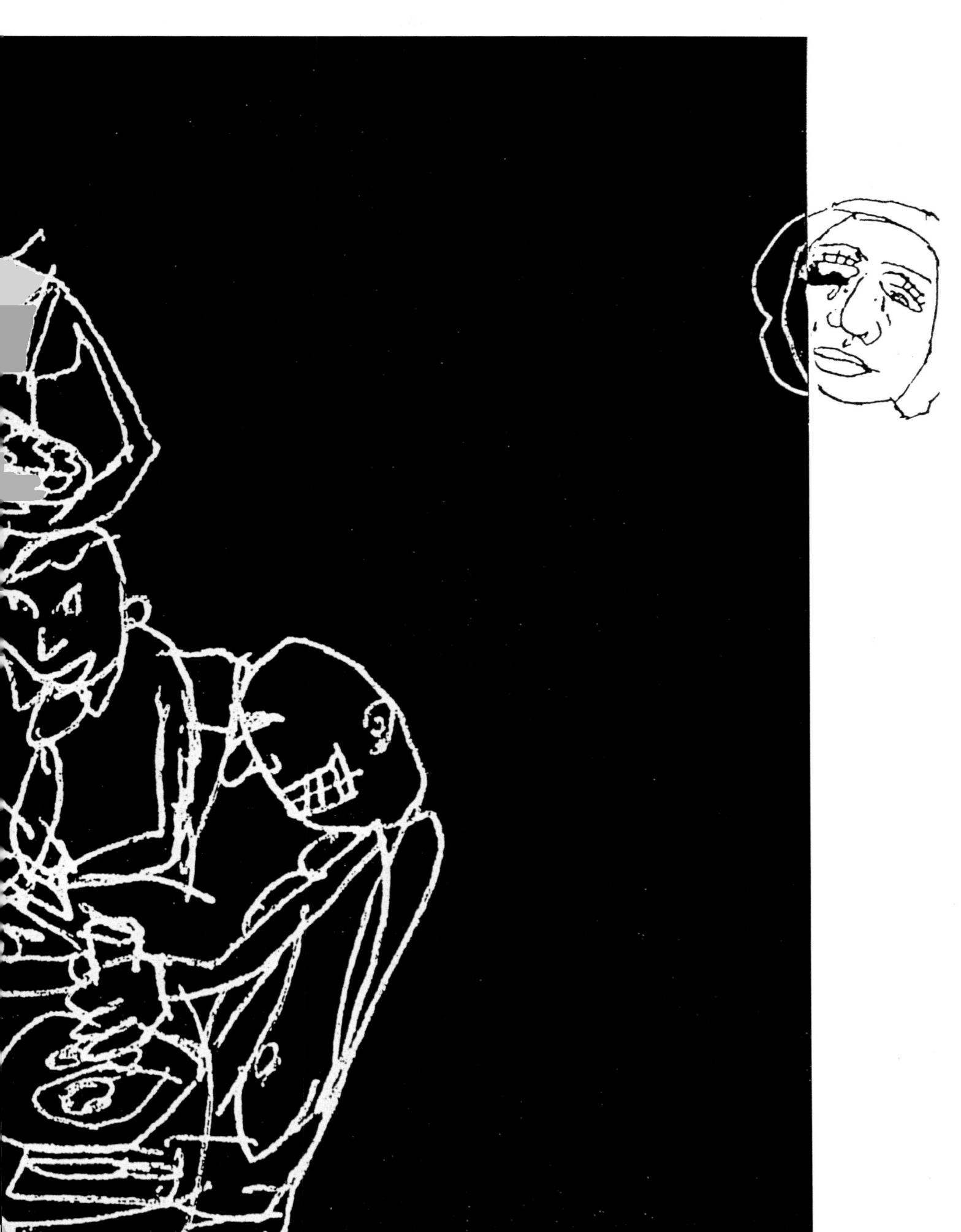

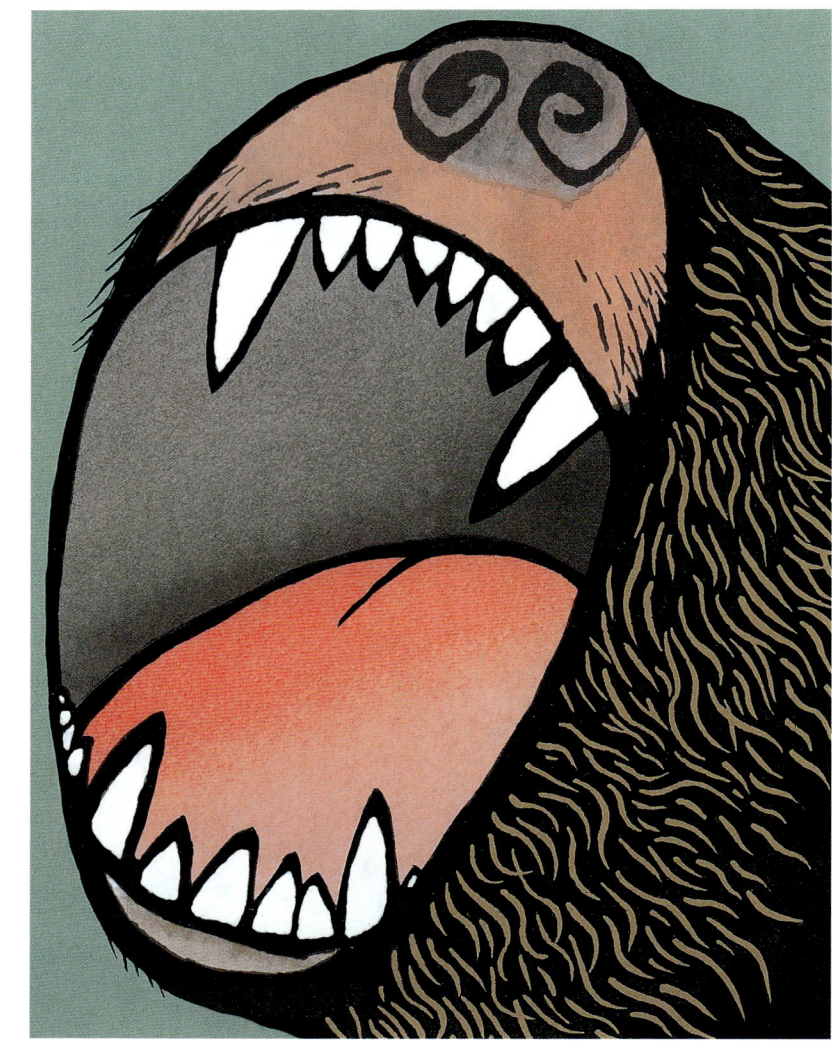

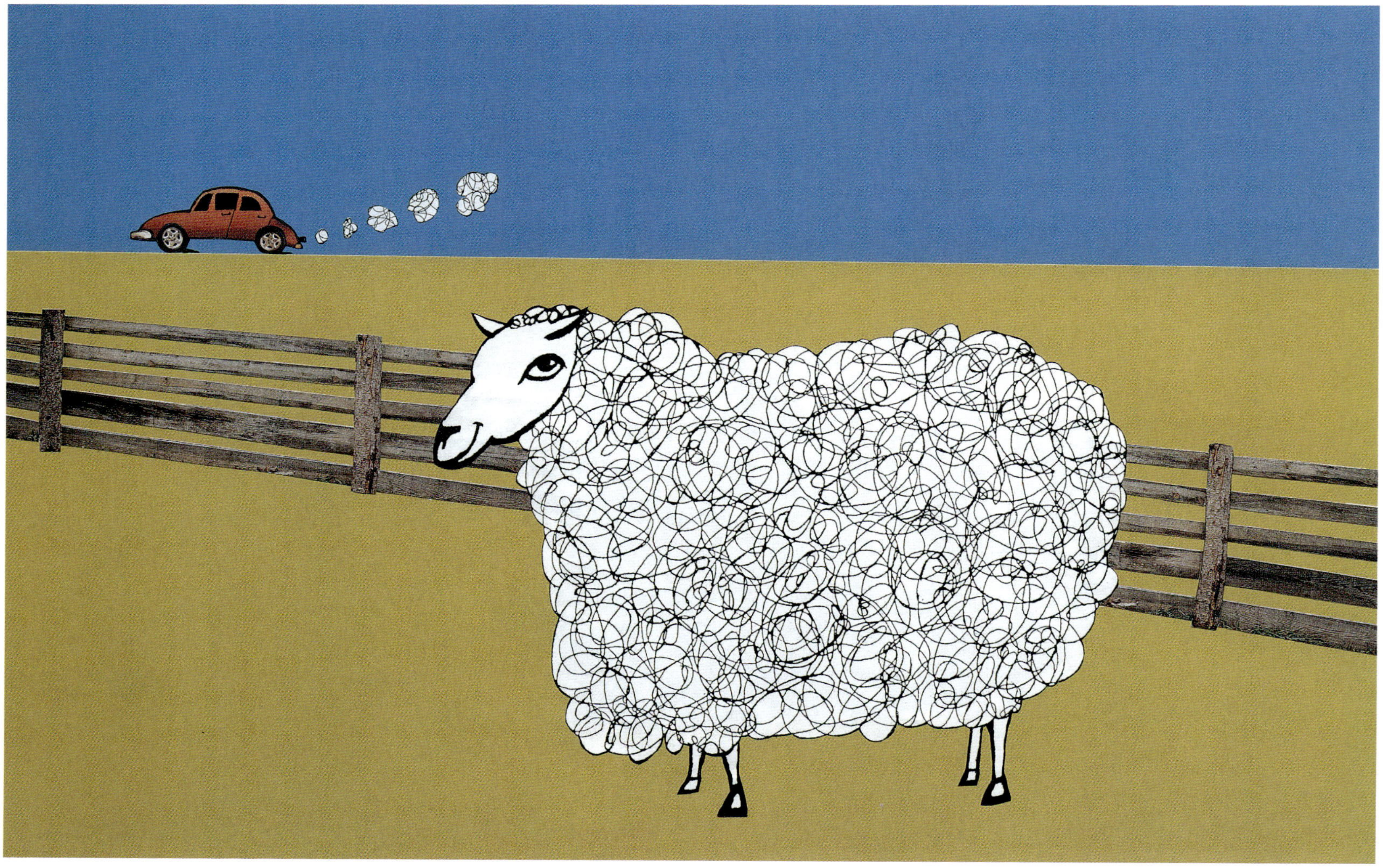

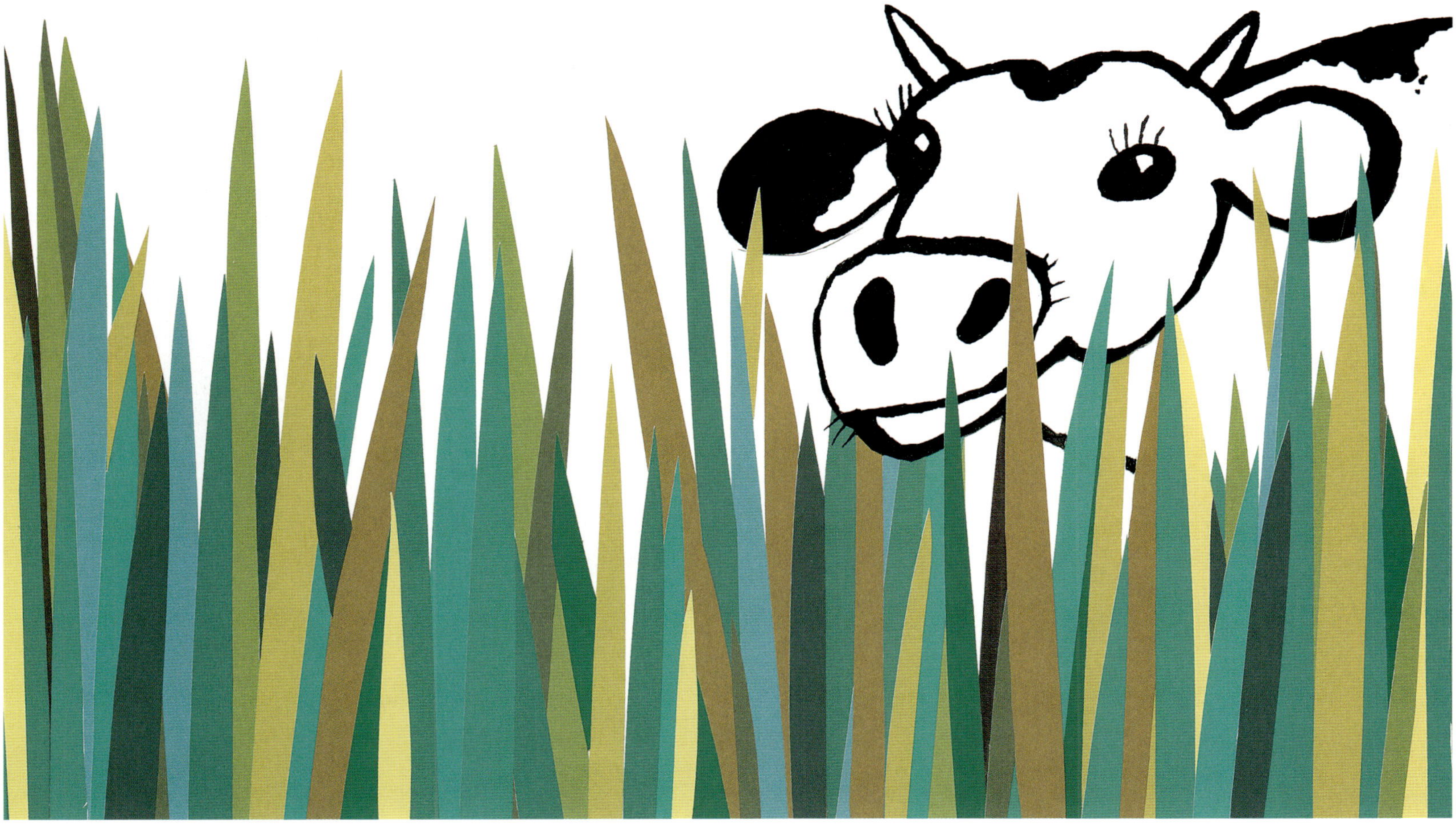

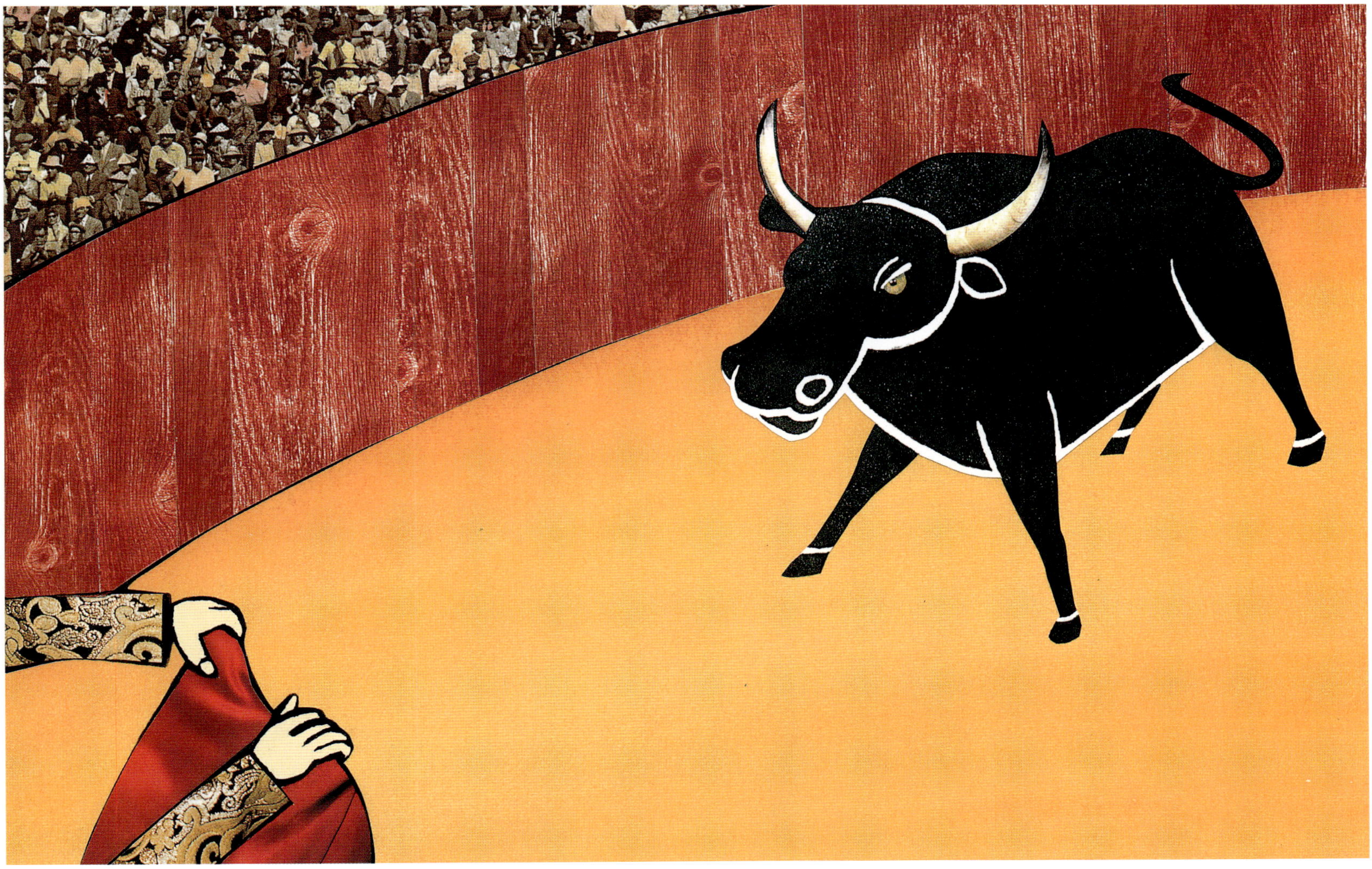

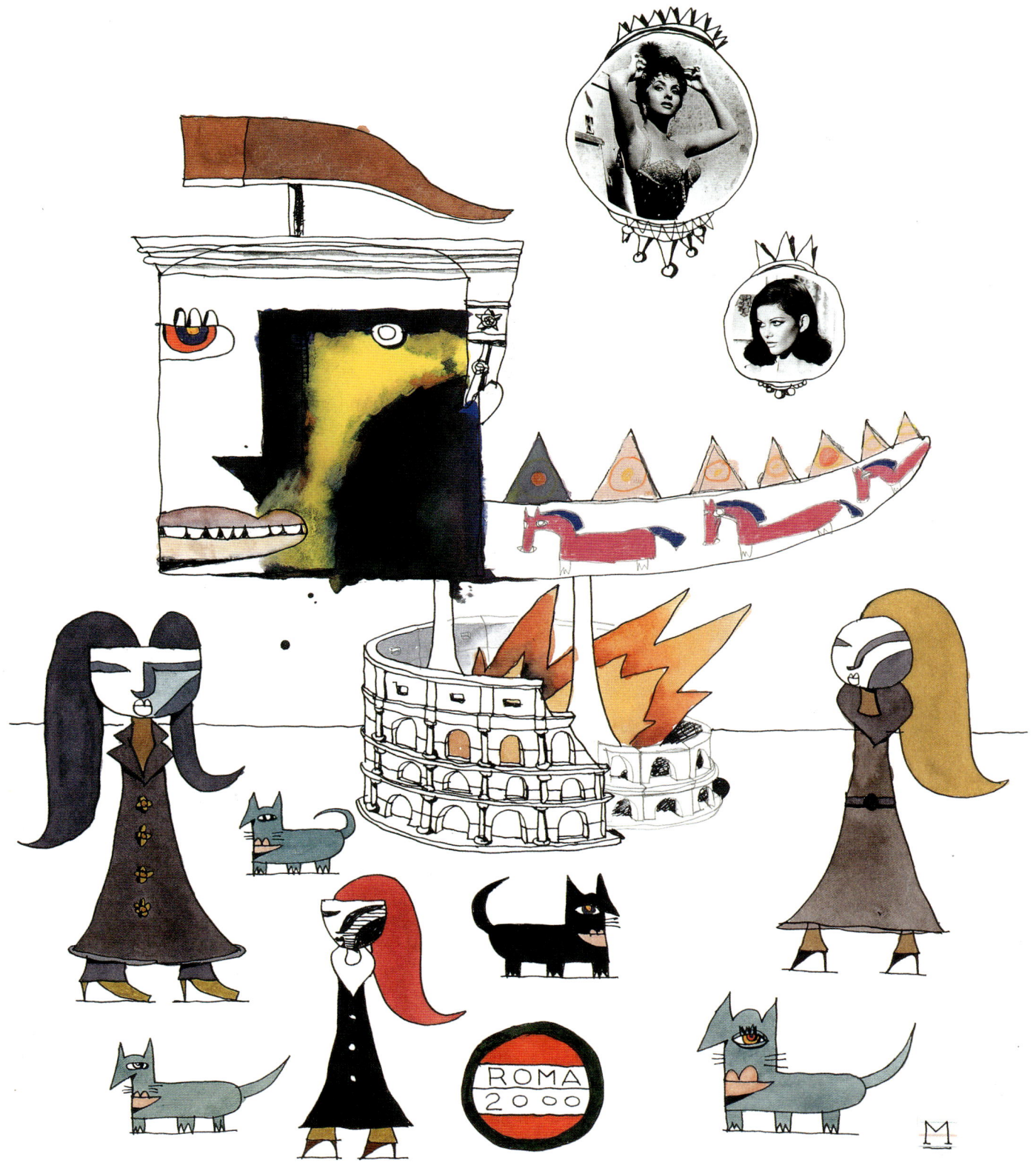

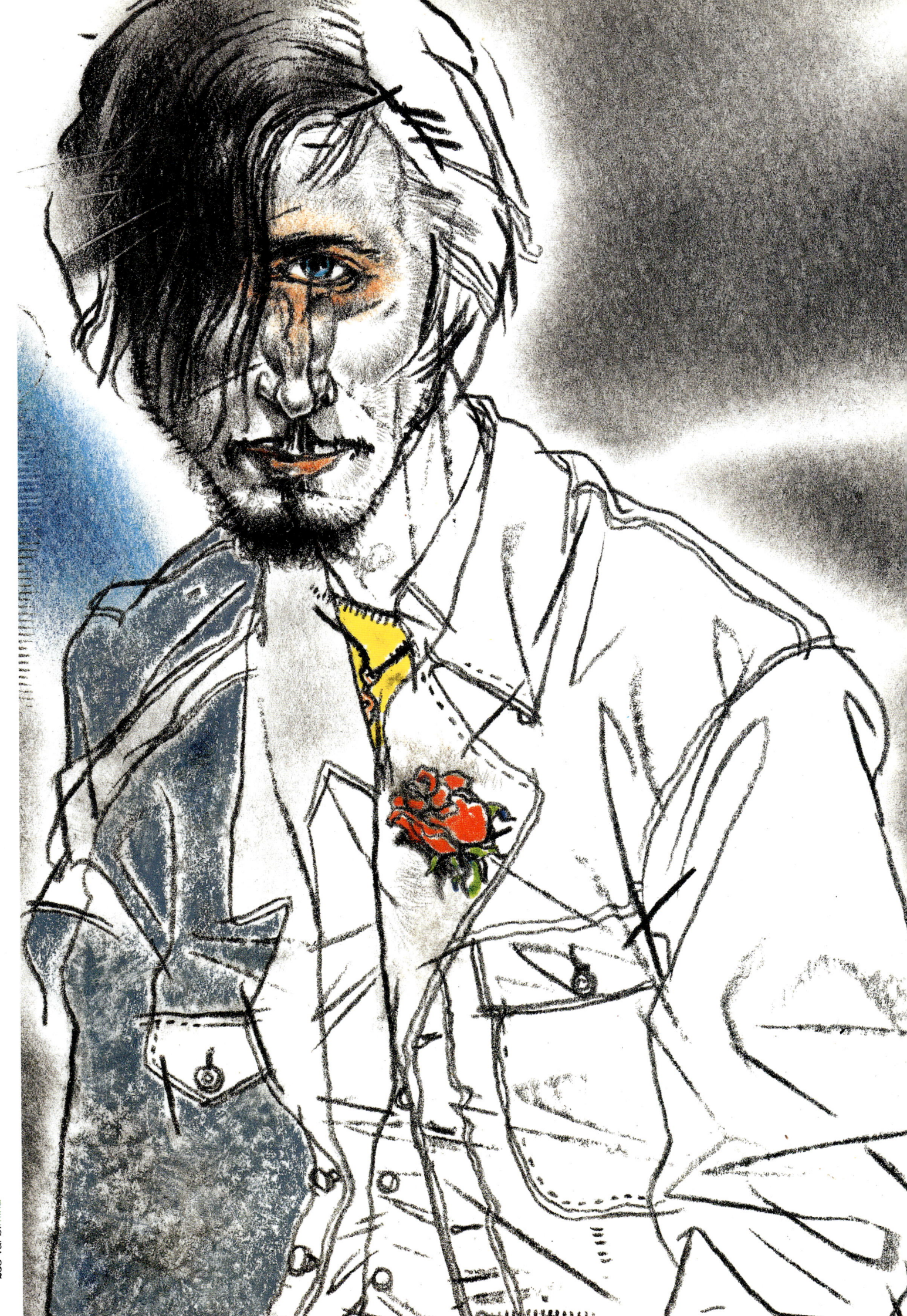

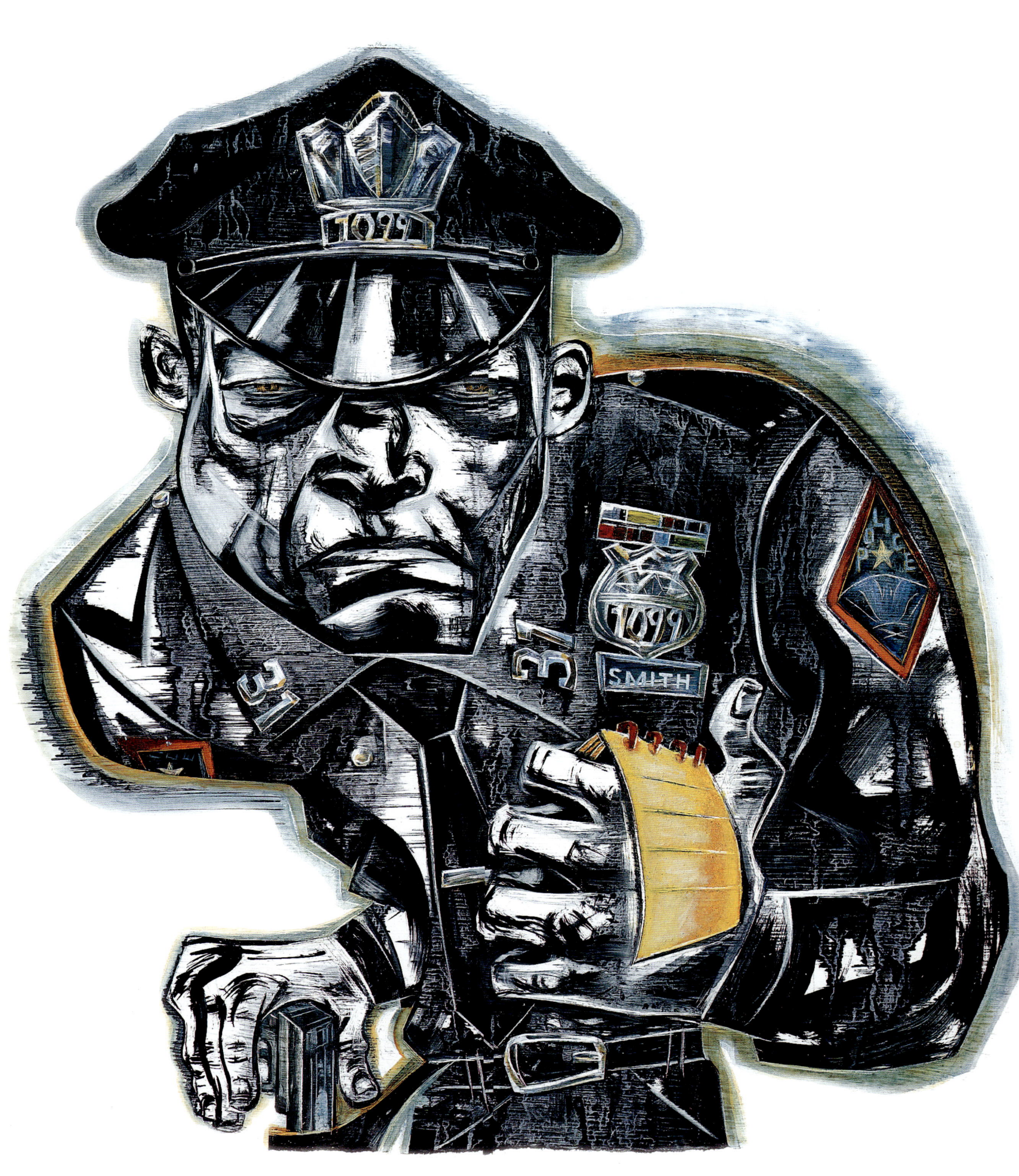

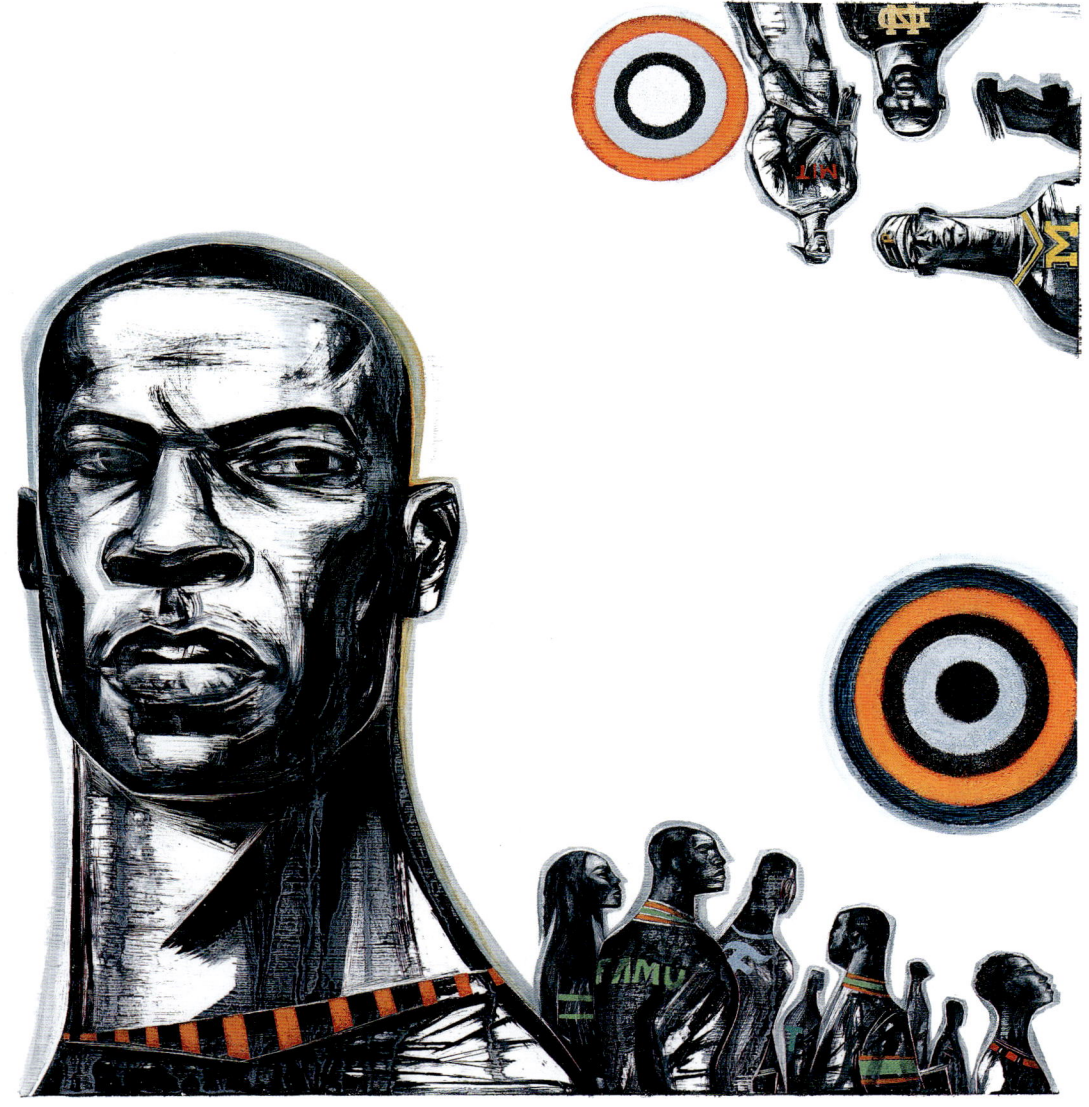

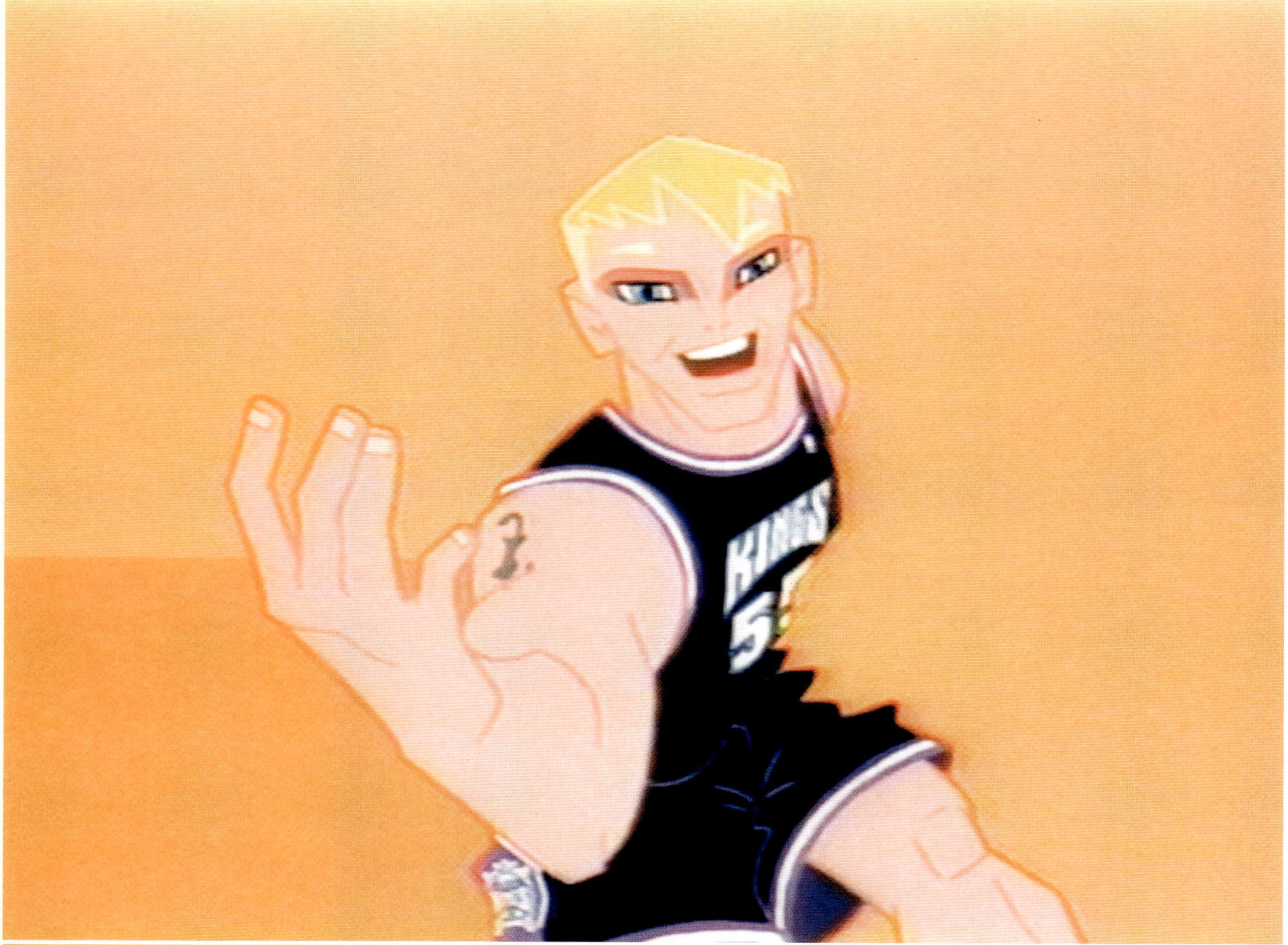
KINGS

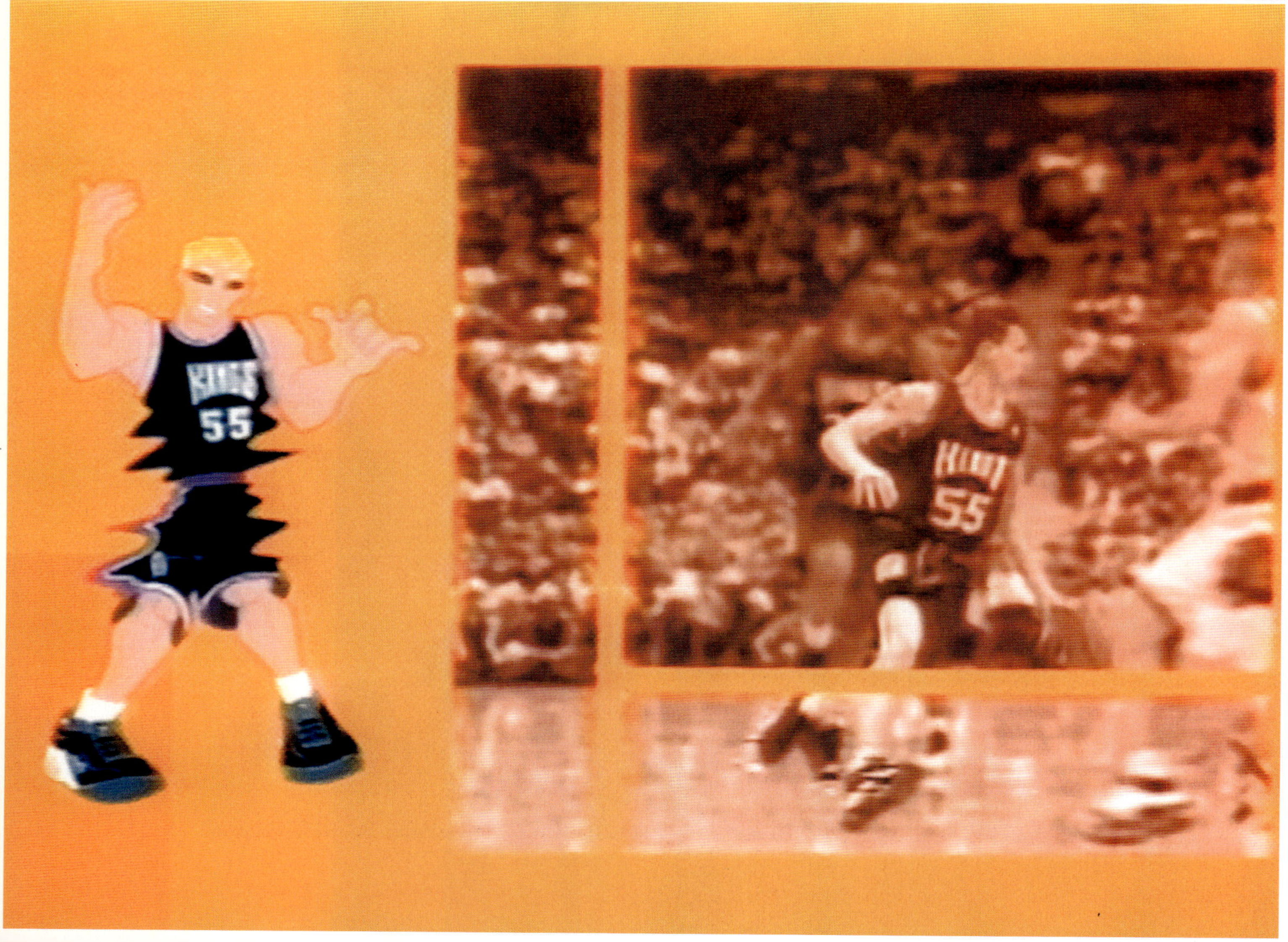
KINGS
55
55

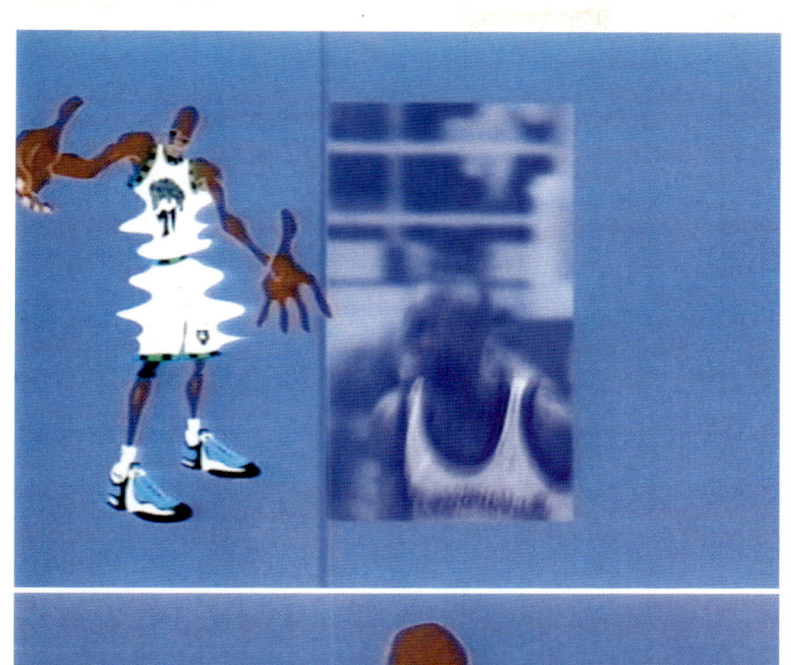

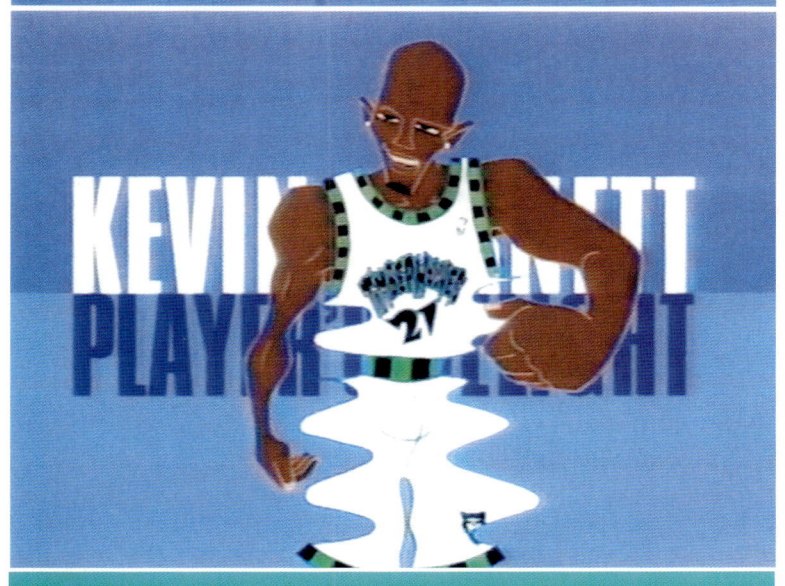

241 katsuramoshino

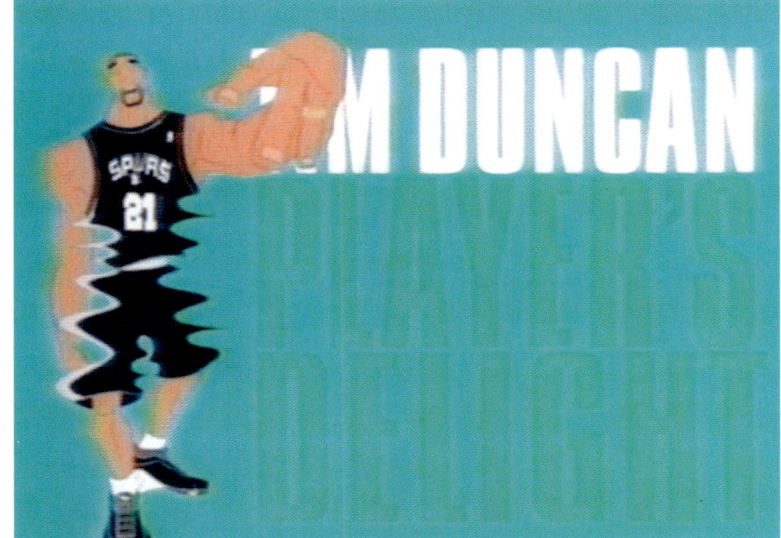

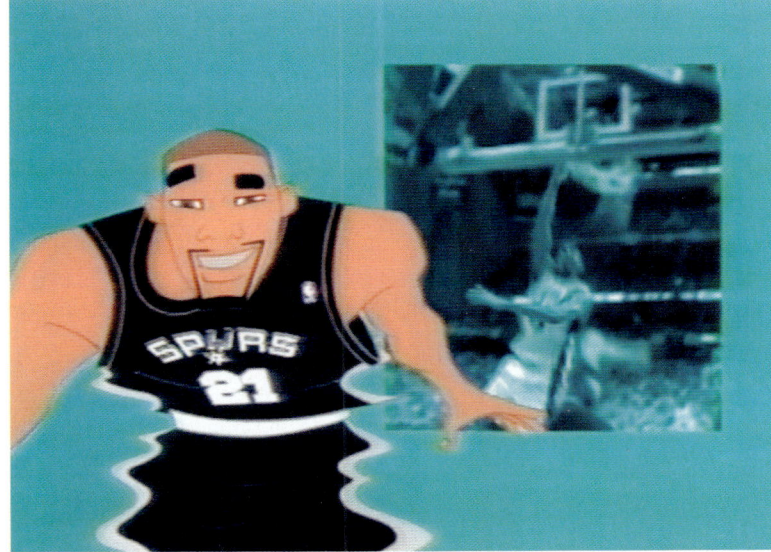

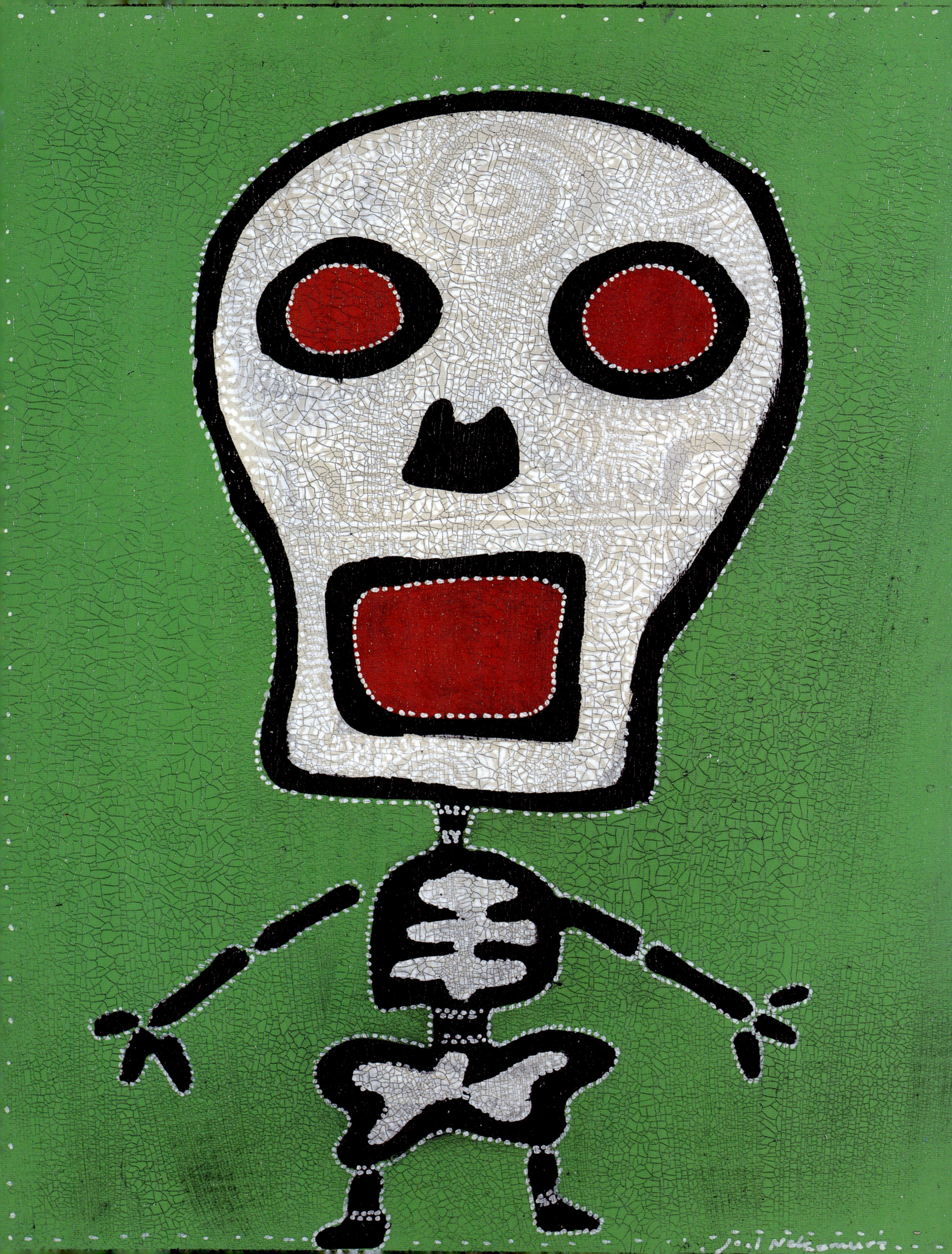

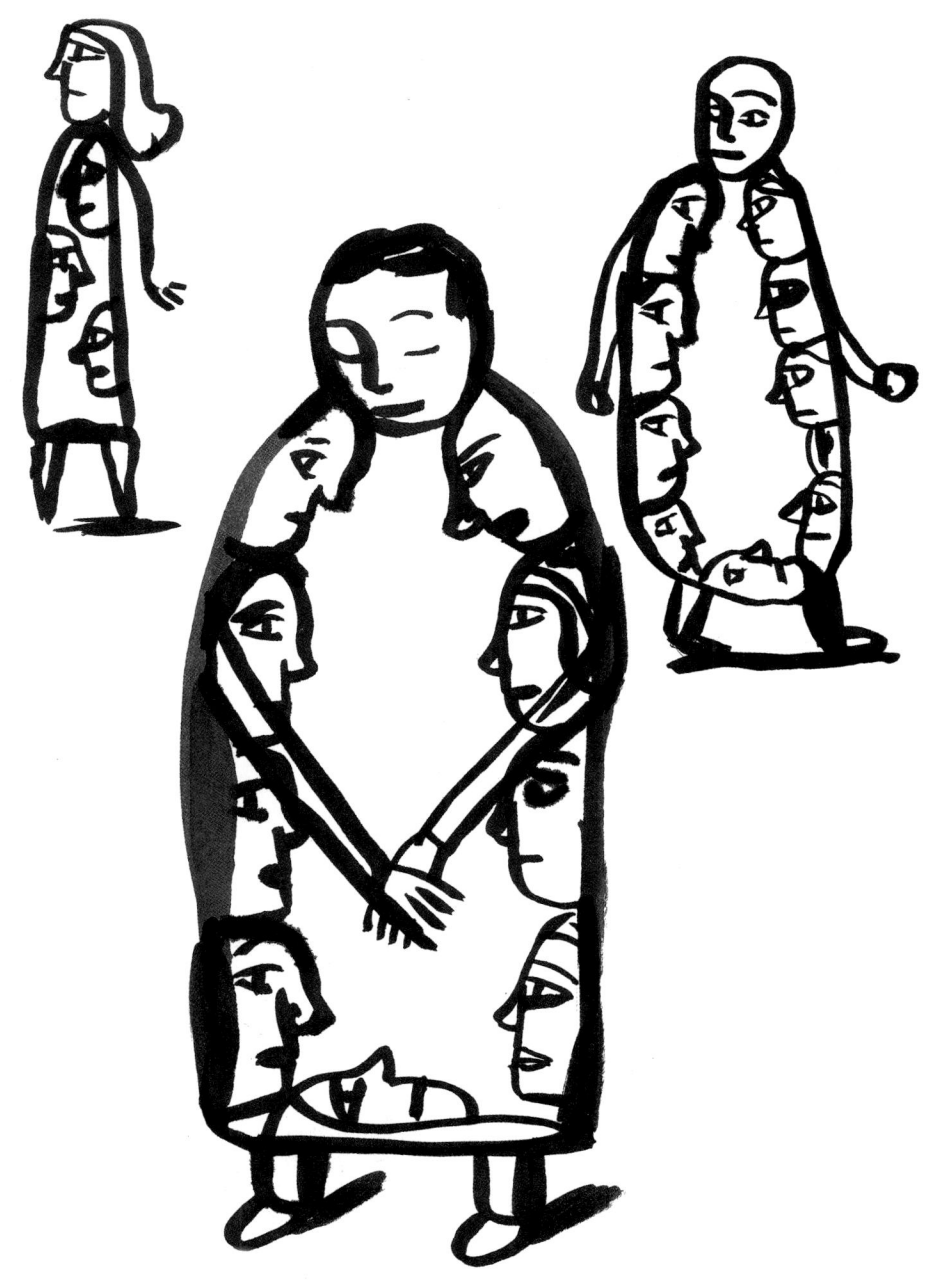

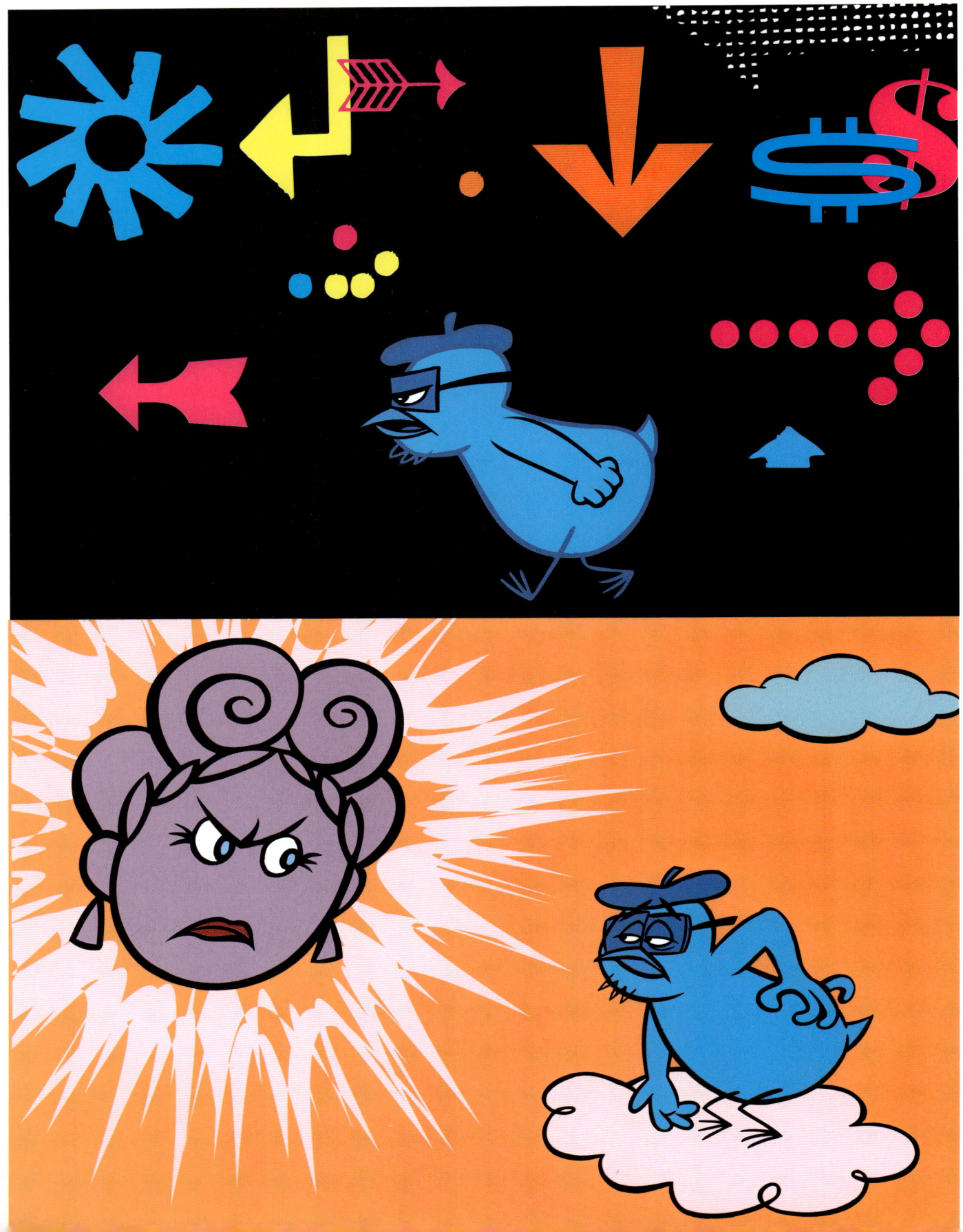

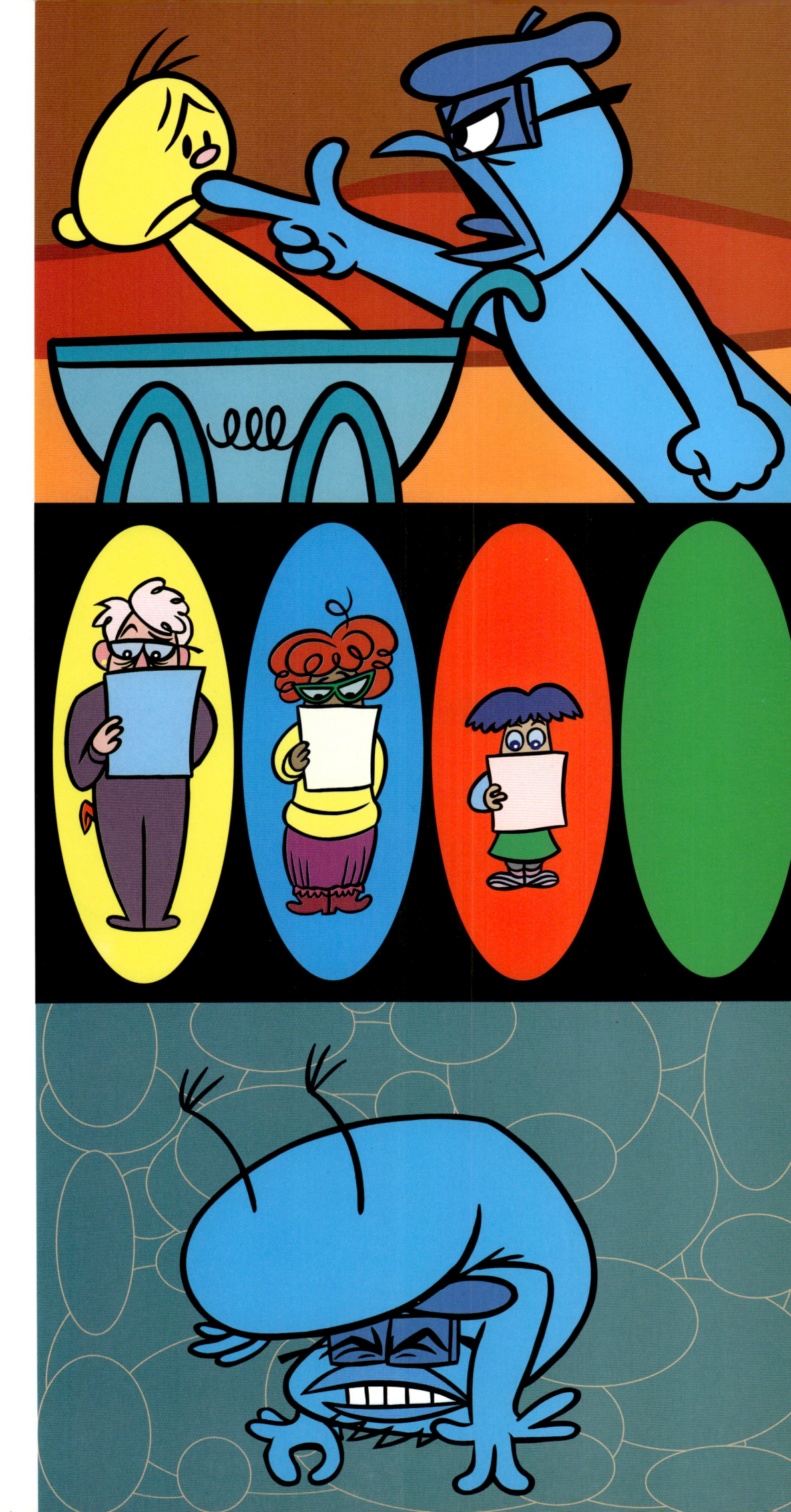

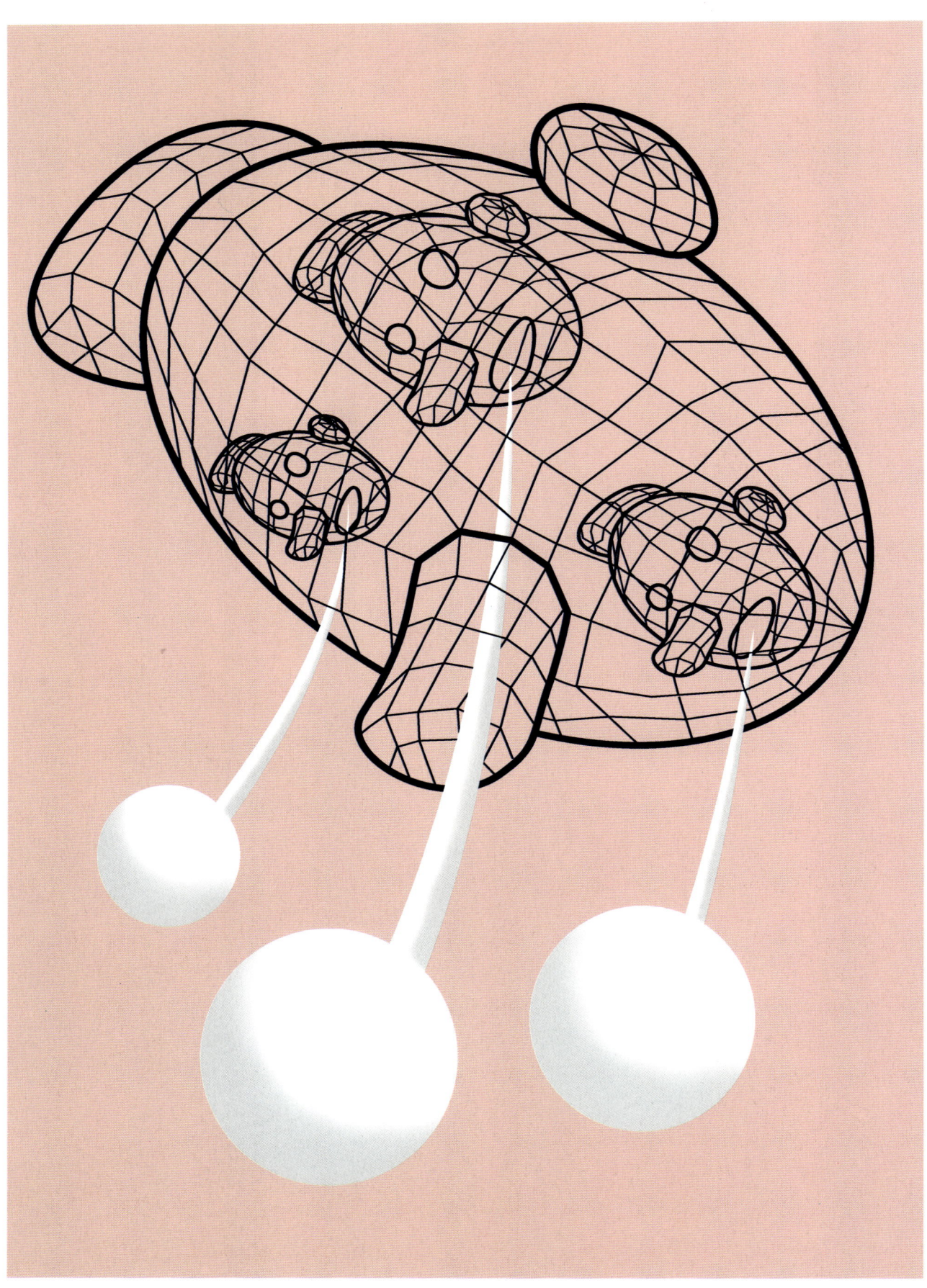

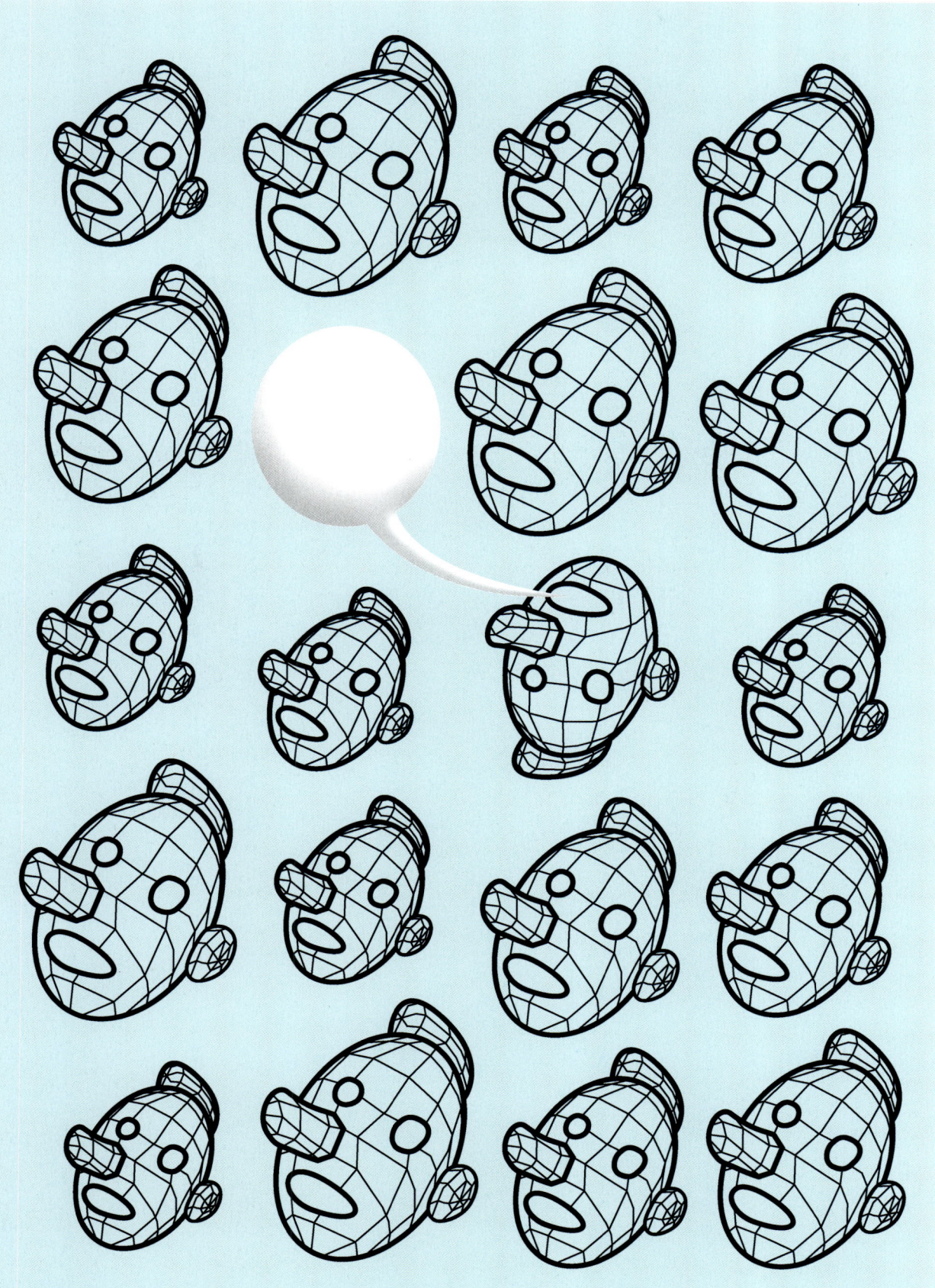

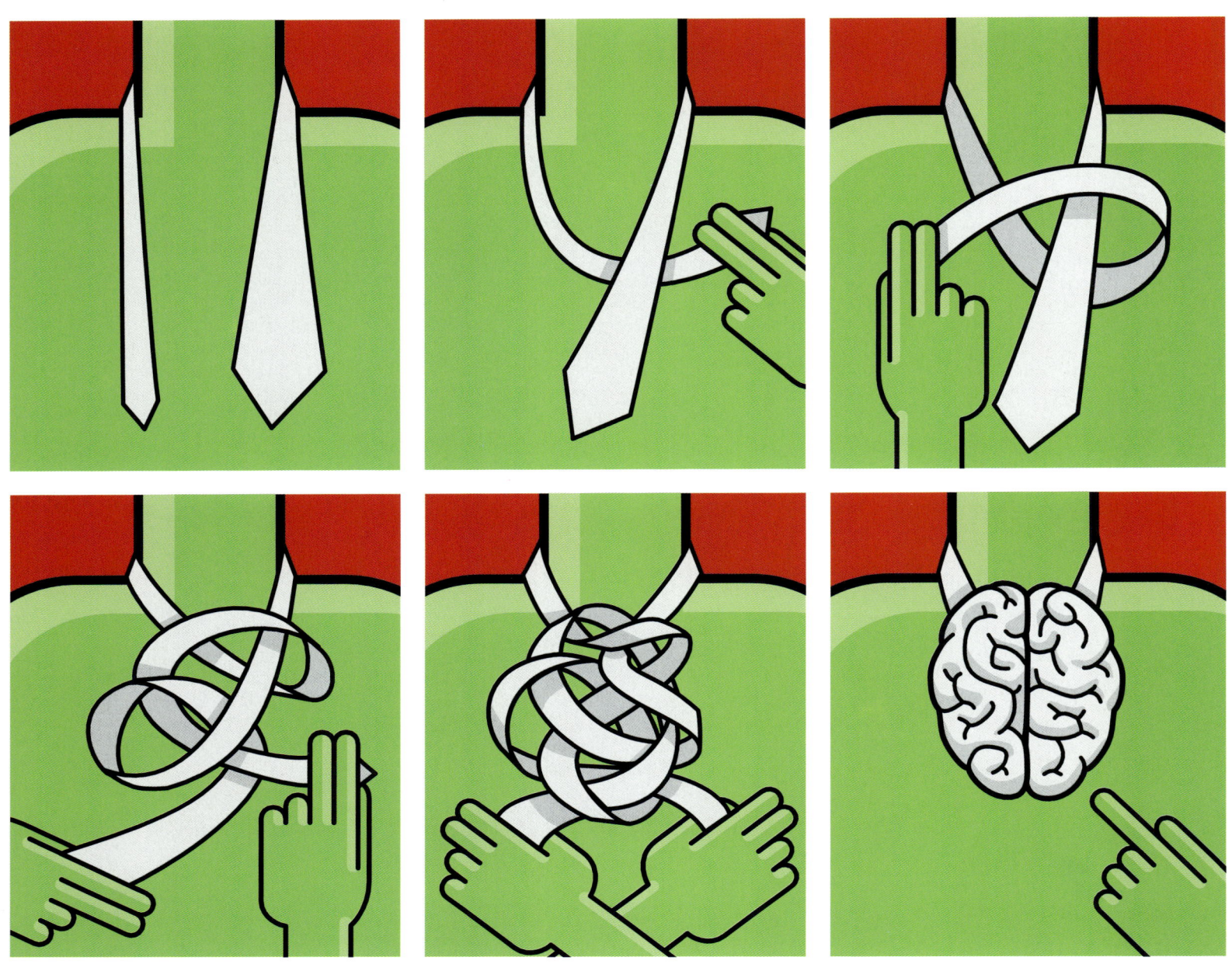

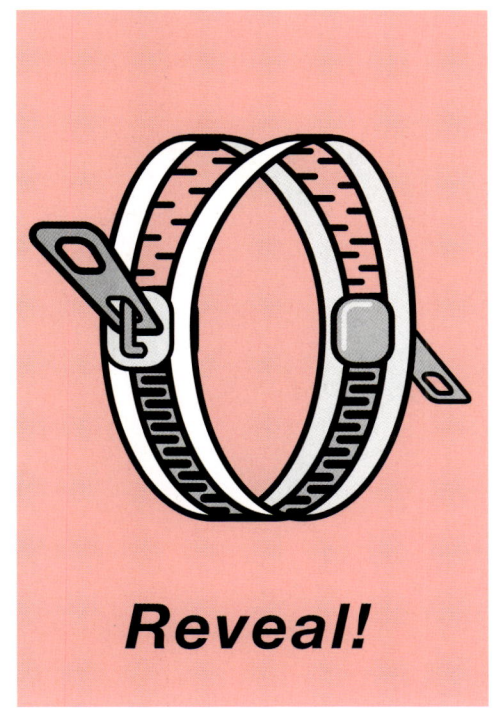

Reveal!

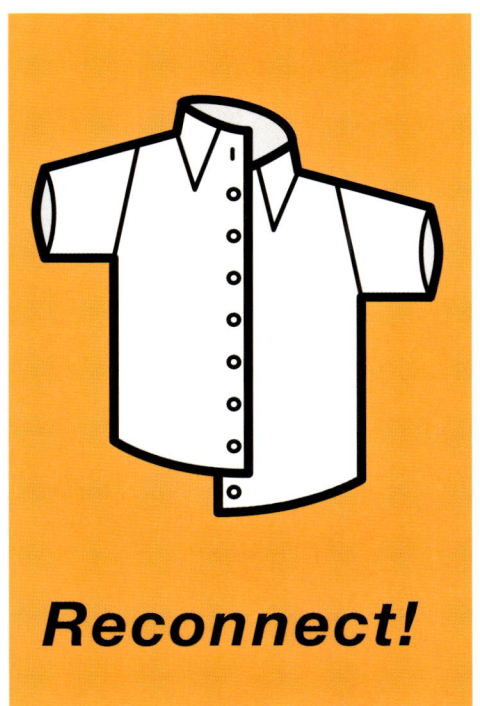

Reconnect!

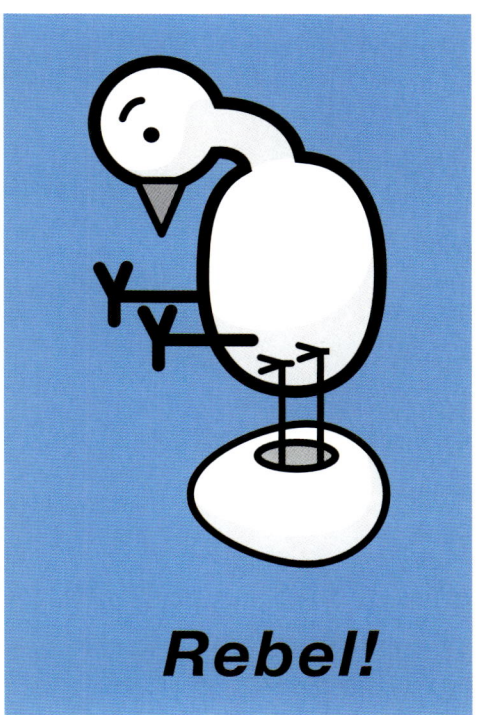

Rebel!

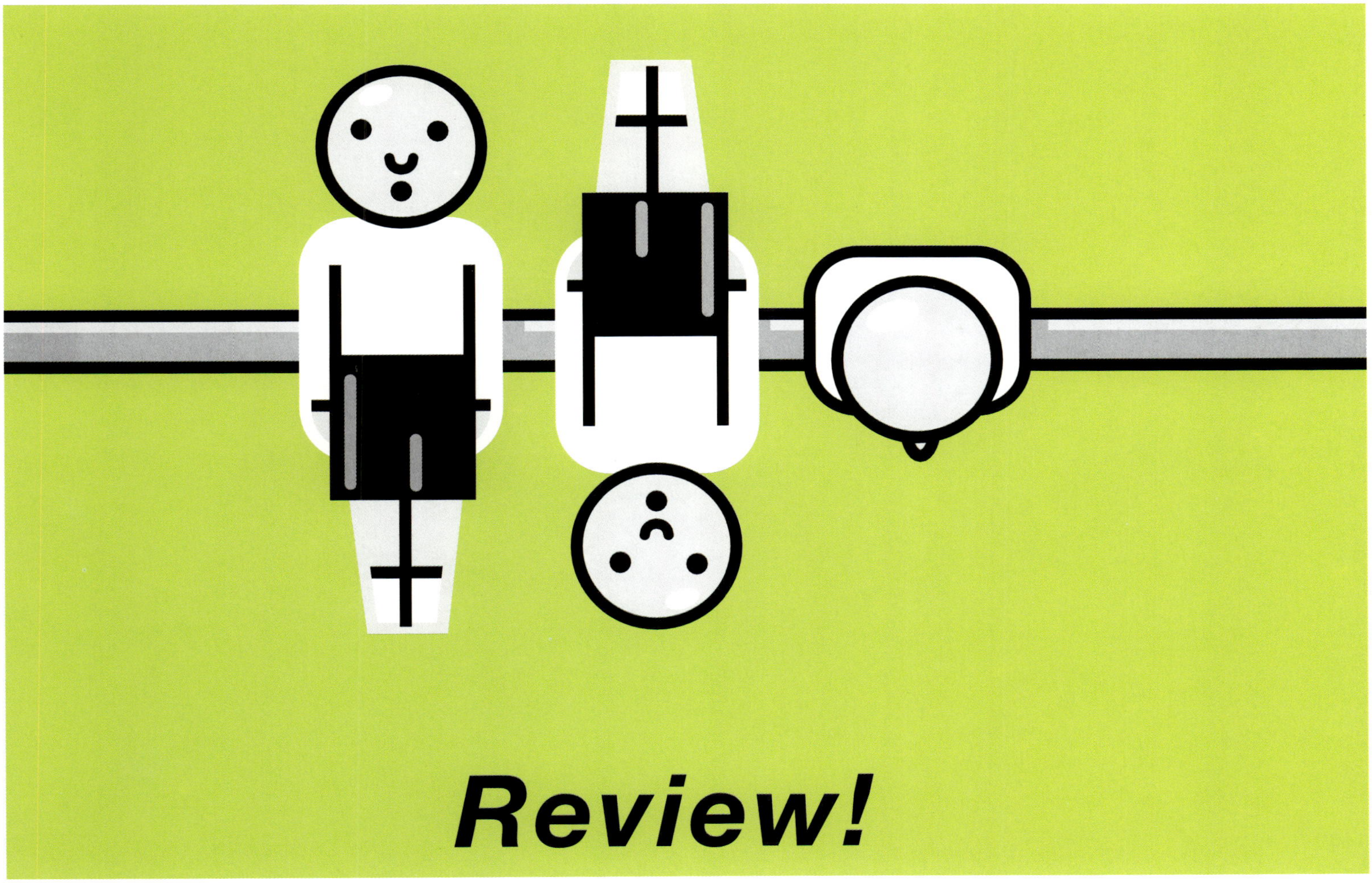

Review!

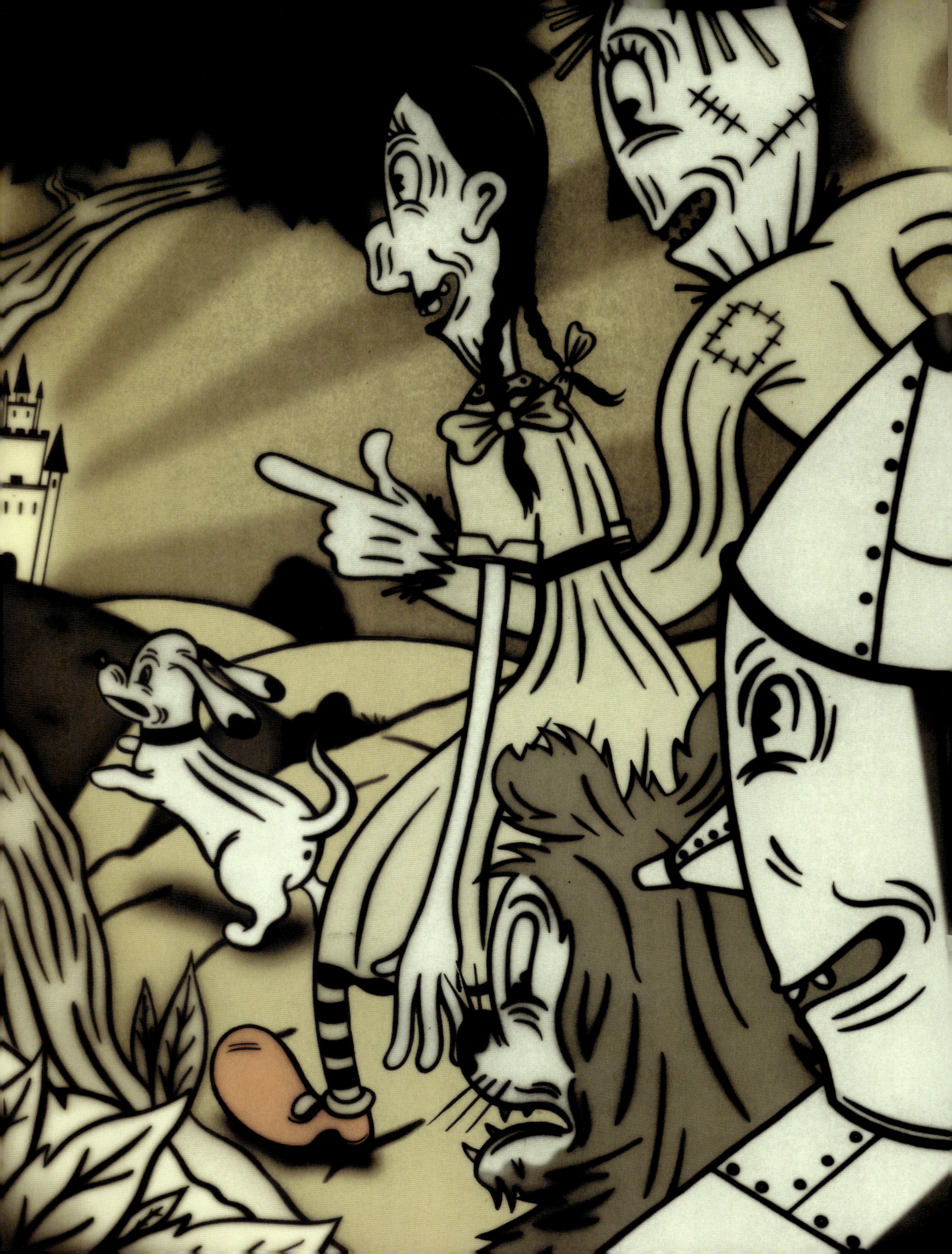

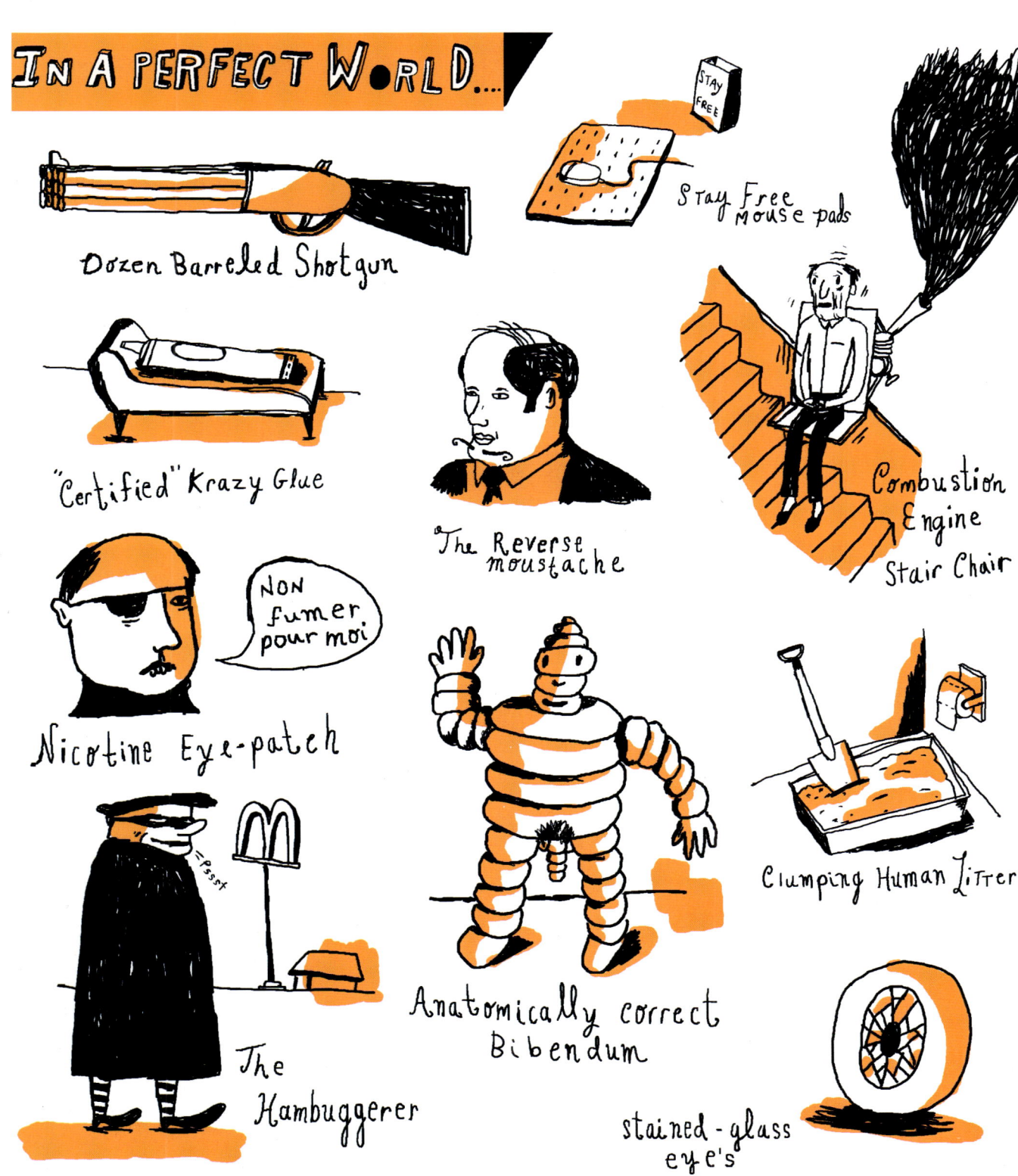

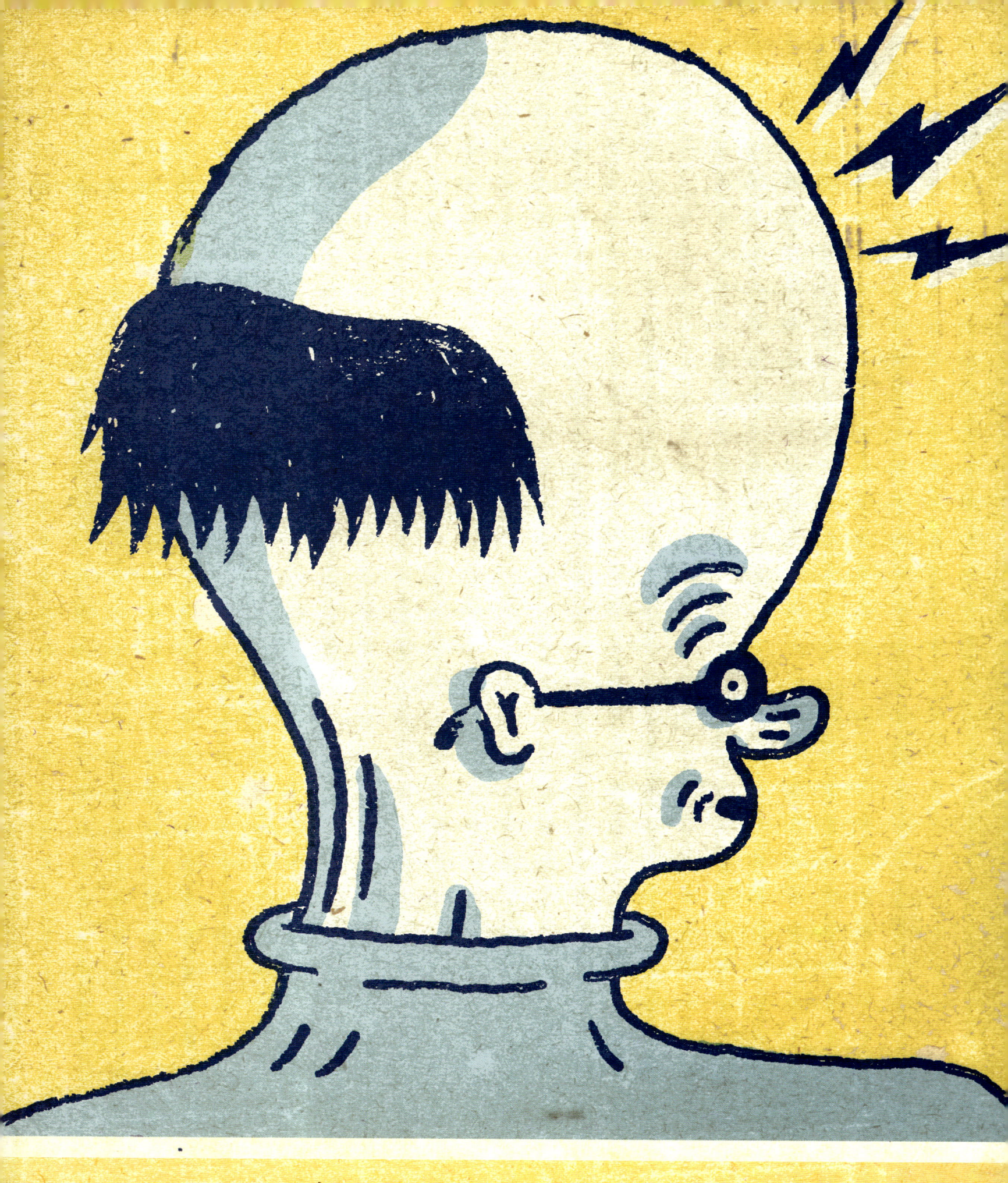

beauty and brain

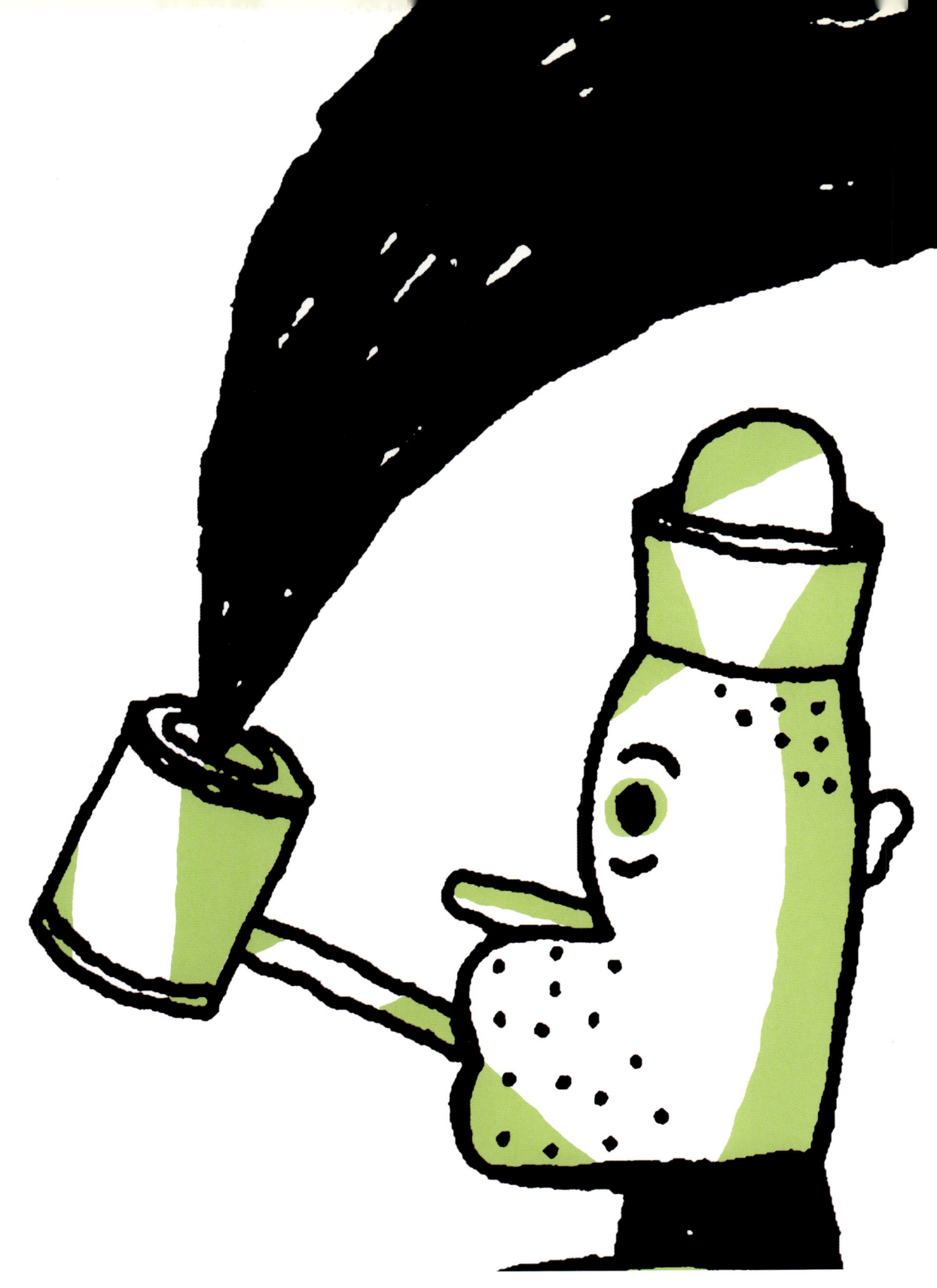

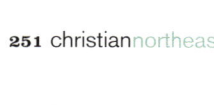

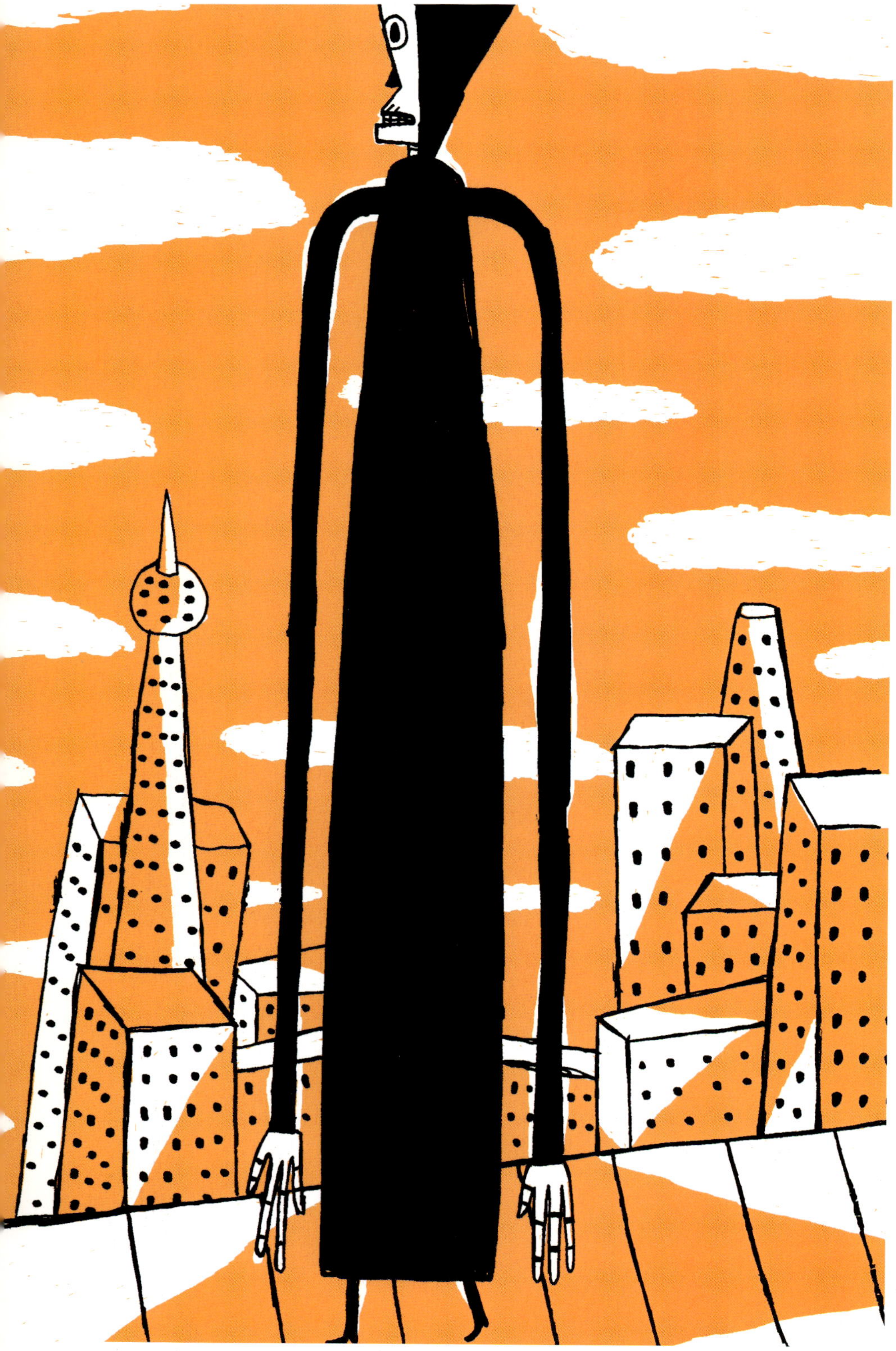

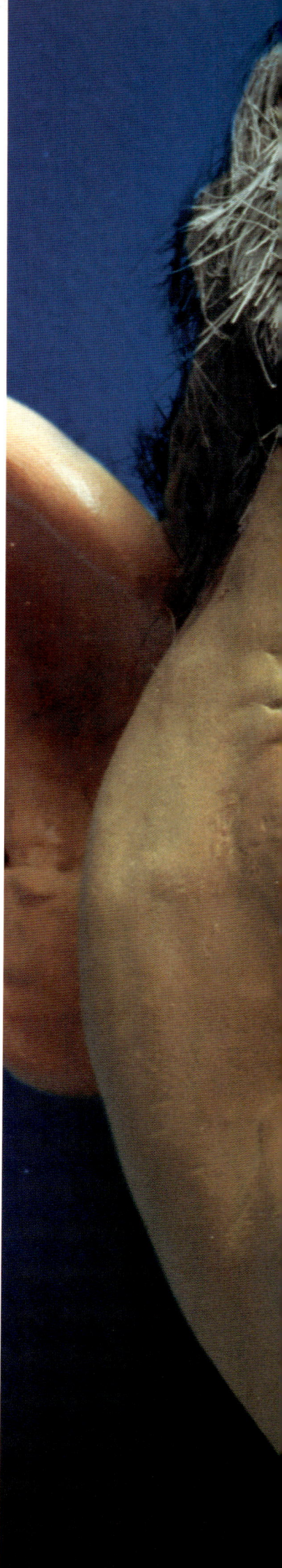

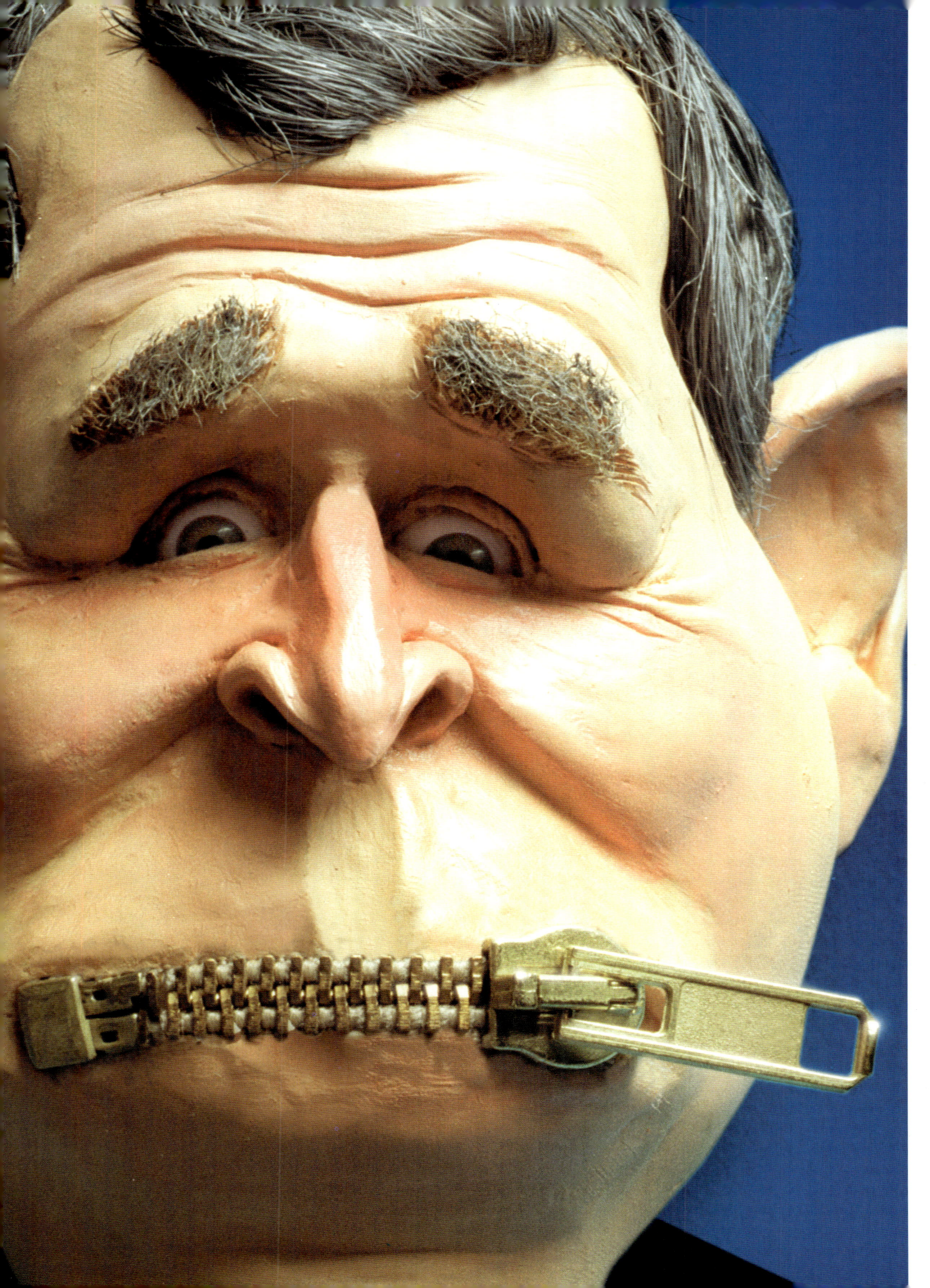

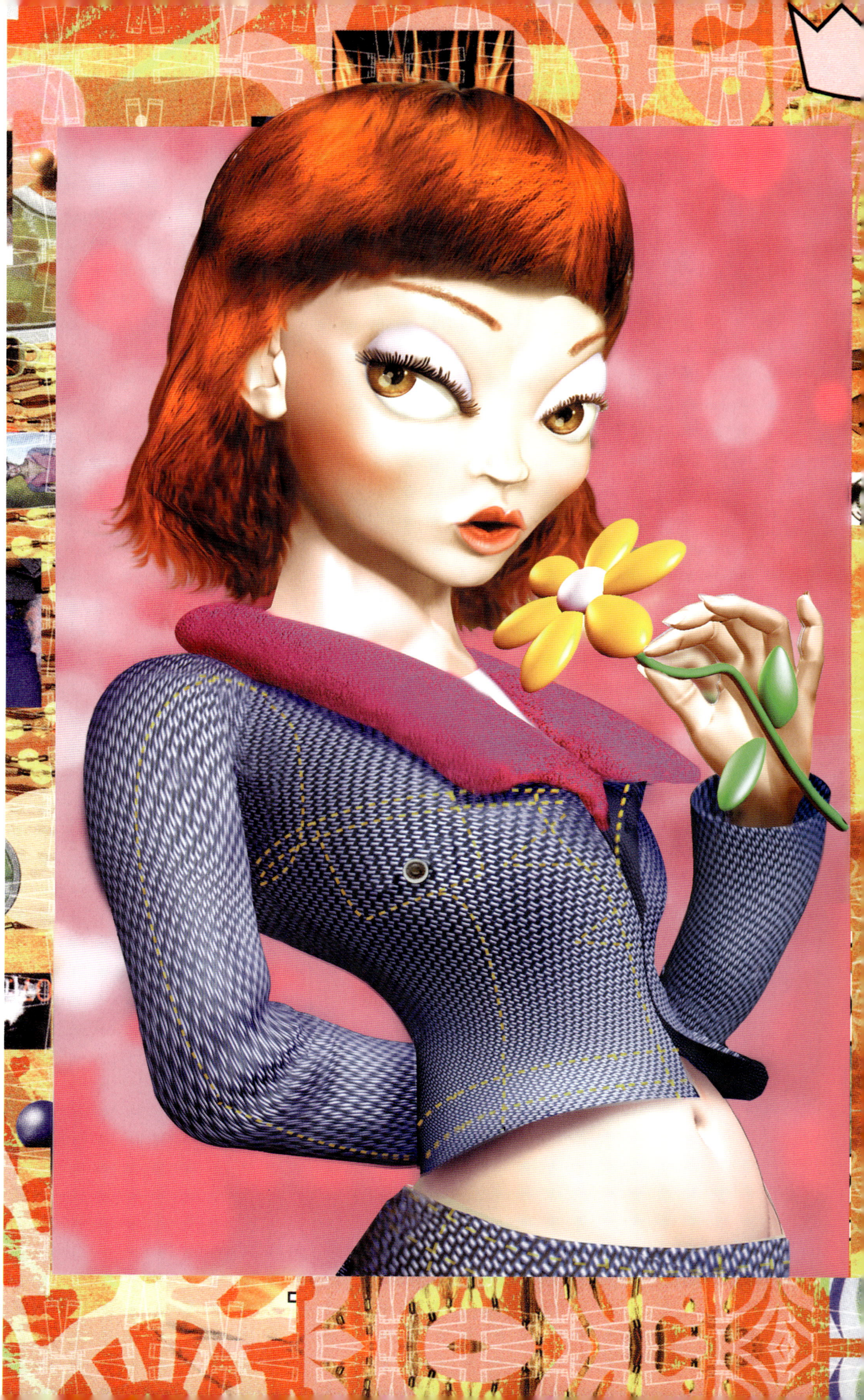

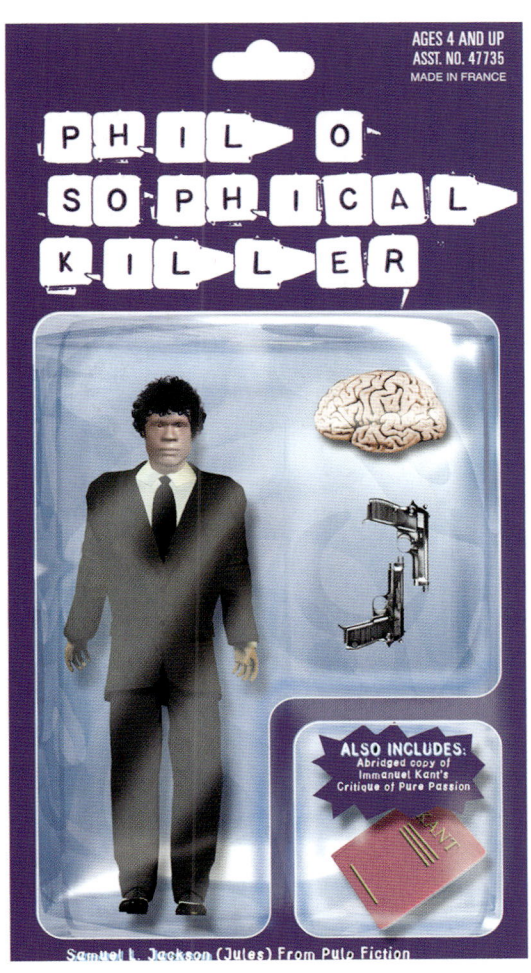

PHILOSOPHICAL KILLER

AGES 4 AND UP
ASST. NO. 47735
MADE IN FRANCE

ALSO INCLUDES:
Abridged copy of
Immanuel Kant's
Critique of Pure Passion

Samuel L. Jackson (Jules) From Pulp Fiction

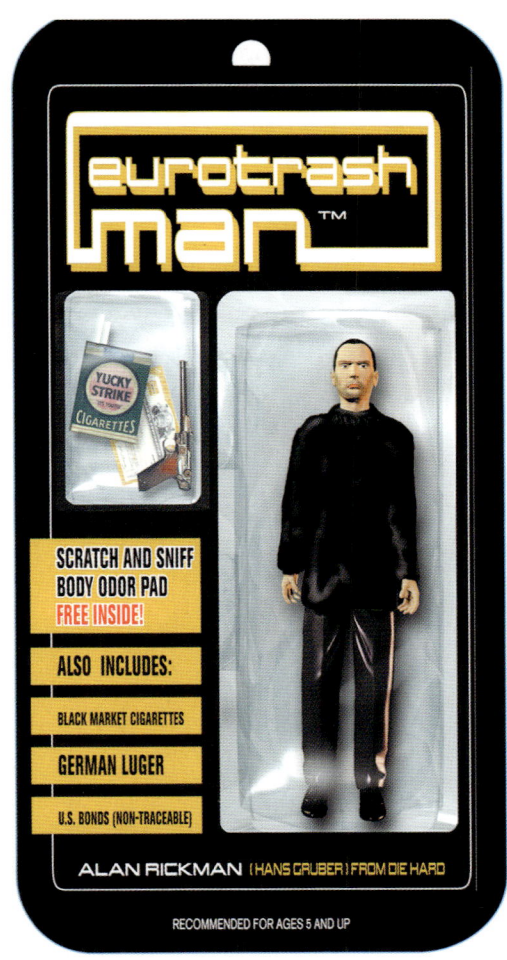

eurotrash man ™

SCRATCH AND SNIFF
BODY ODOR PAD
FREE INSIDE!

ALSO INCLUDES:

BLACK MARKET CIGARETTES

GERMAN LUGER

U.S. BONDS (NON-TRACEABLE)

YUCKY STRIKE CIGARETTES

ALAN RICKMAN (HANS GRUBER) FROM DIE HARD

RECOMMENDED FOR AGES 5 AND UP

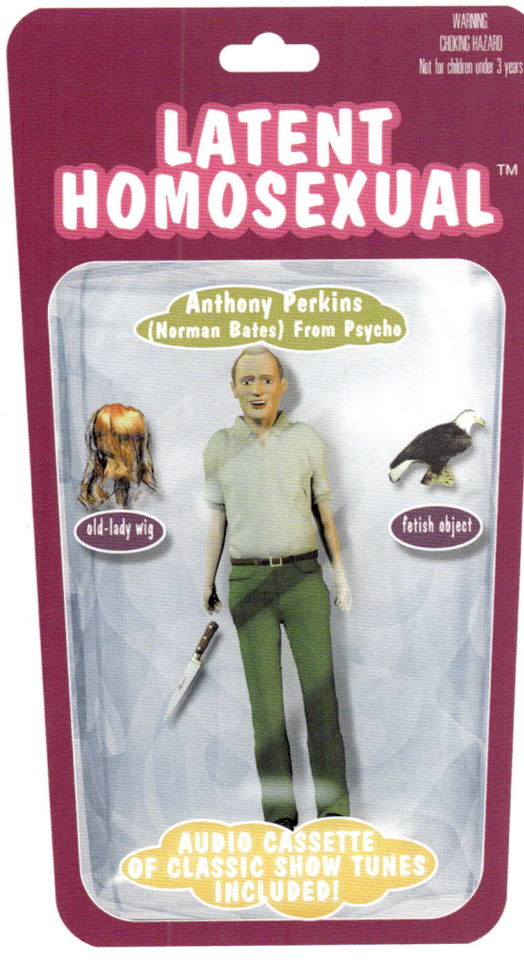

WARNING:
CHOKING HAZARD
Not for children under 3 years

LATENT HOMOSEXUAL ™

Anthony Perkins
(Norman Bates) From Psycho

old-lady wig

fetish object

AUDIO CASSETTE
OF CLASSIC SHOW TUNES
INCLUDED!

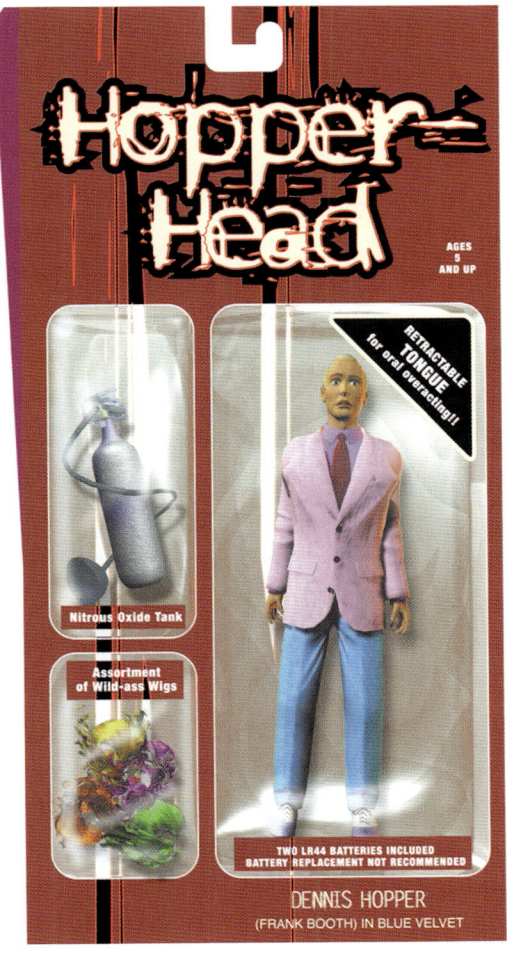

Hopper Head

AGES 5
AND UP

RETRACTABLE
TONGUE
for oral overacting!

Nitrous Oxide Tank

Assortment
of Wild-ass Wigs

TWO LR44 BATTERIES INCLUDED
BATTERY REPLACEMENT NOT RECOMMENDED

DENNIS HOPPER
(FRANK BOOTH) IN BLUE VELVET

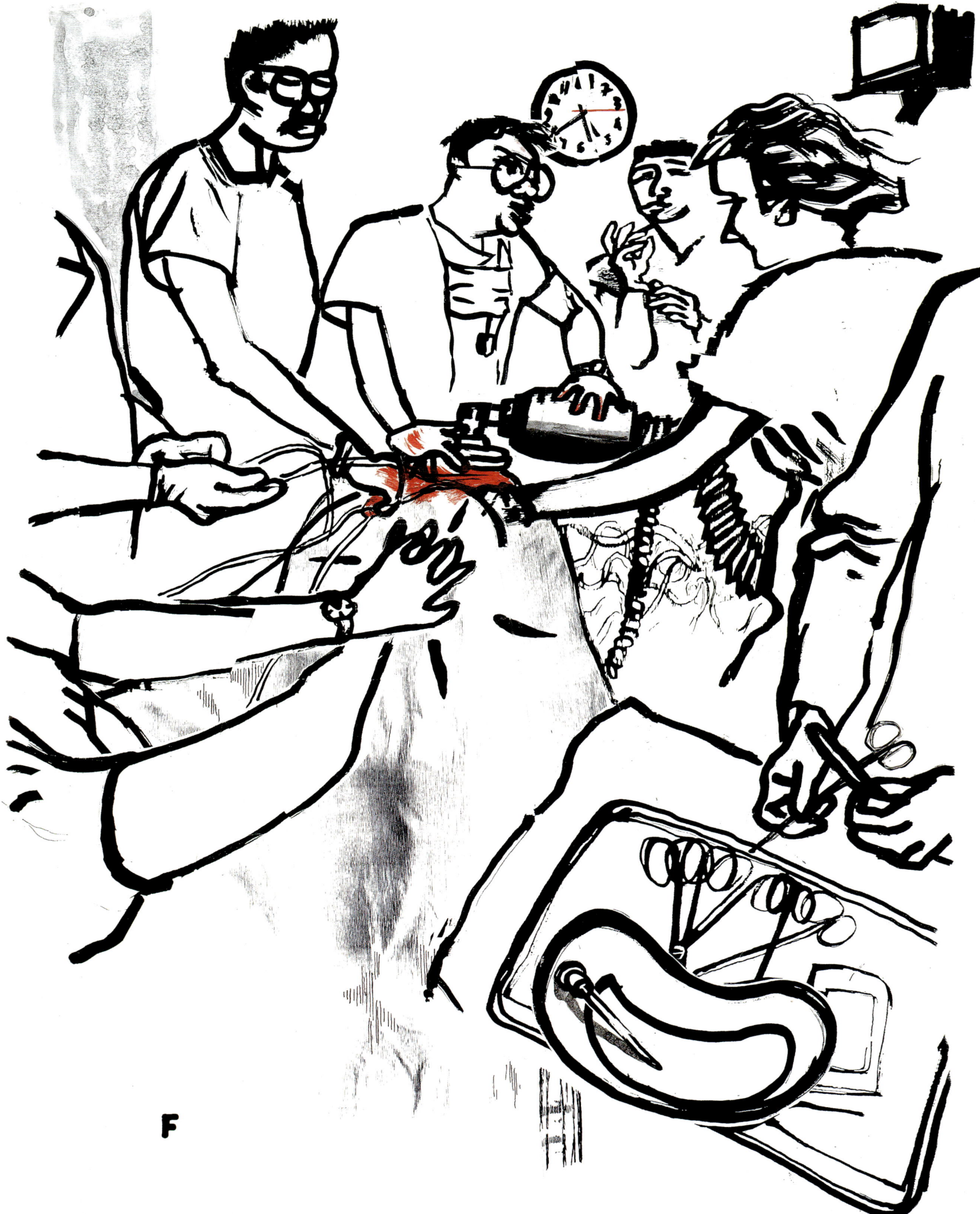

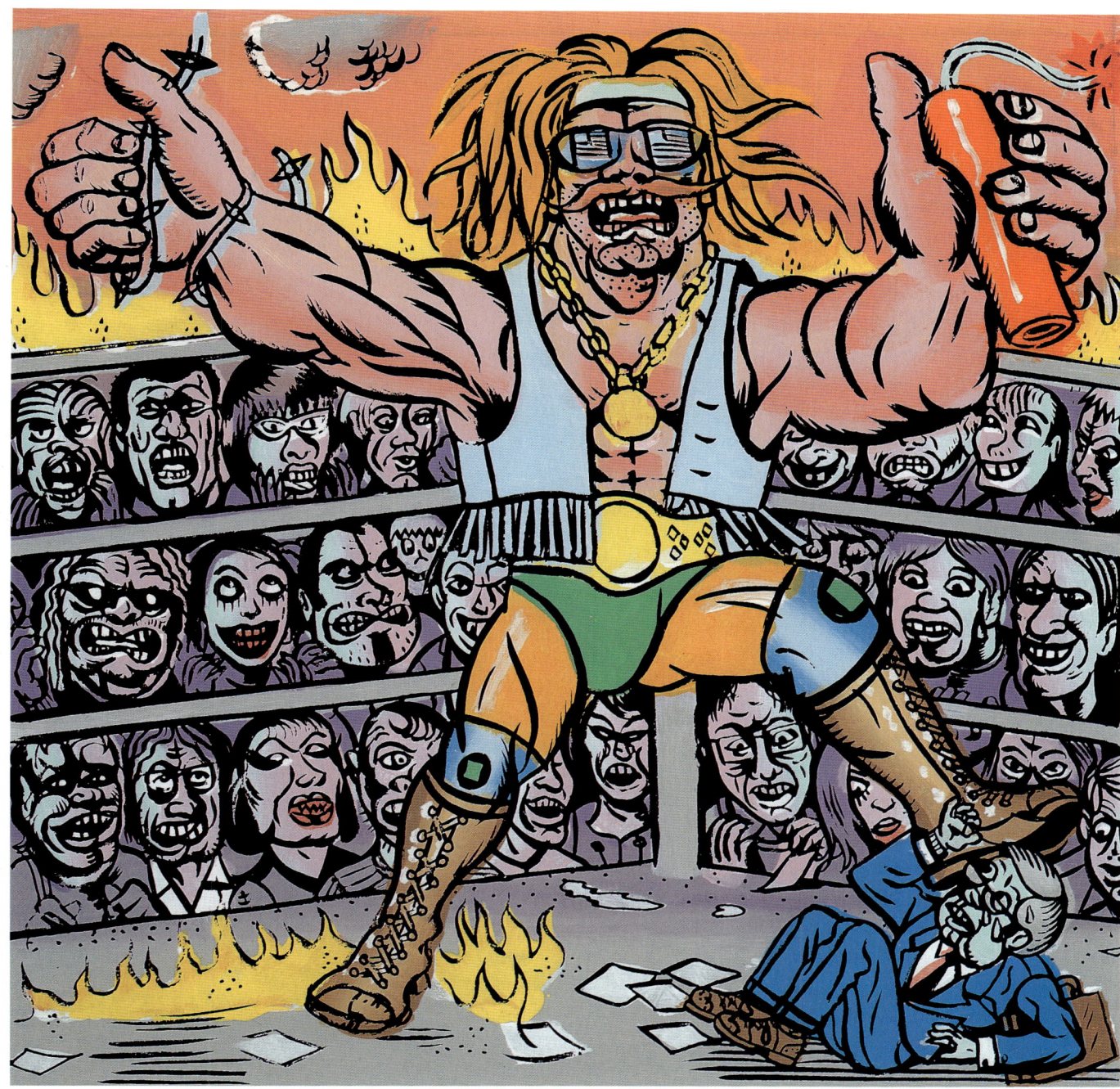

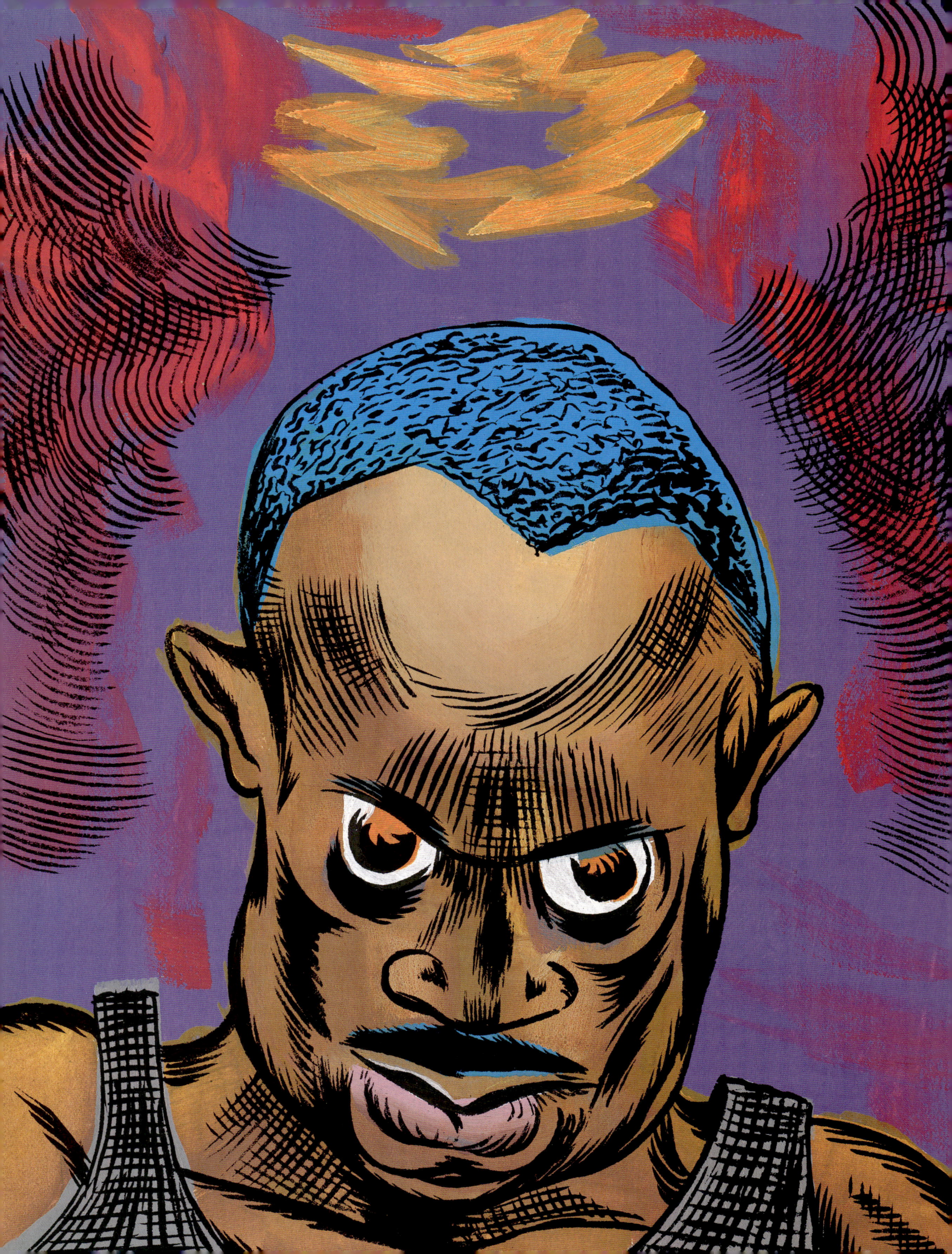

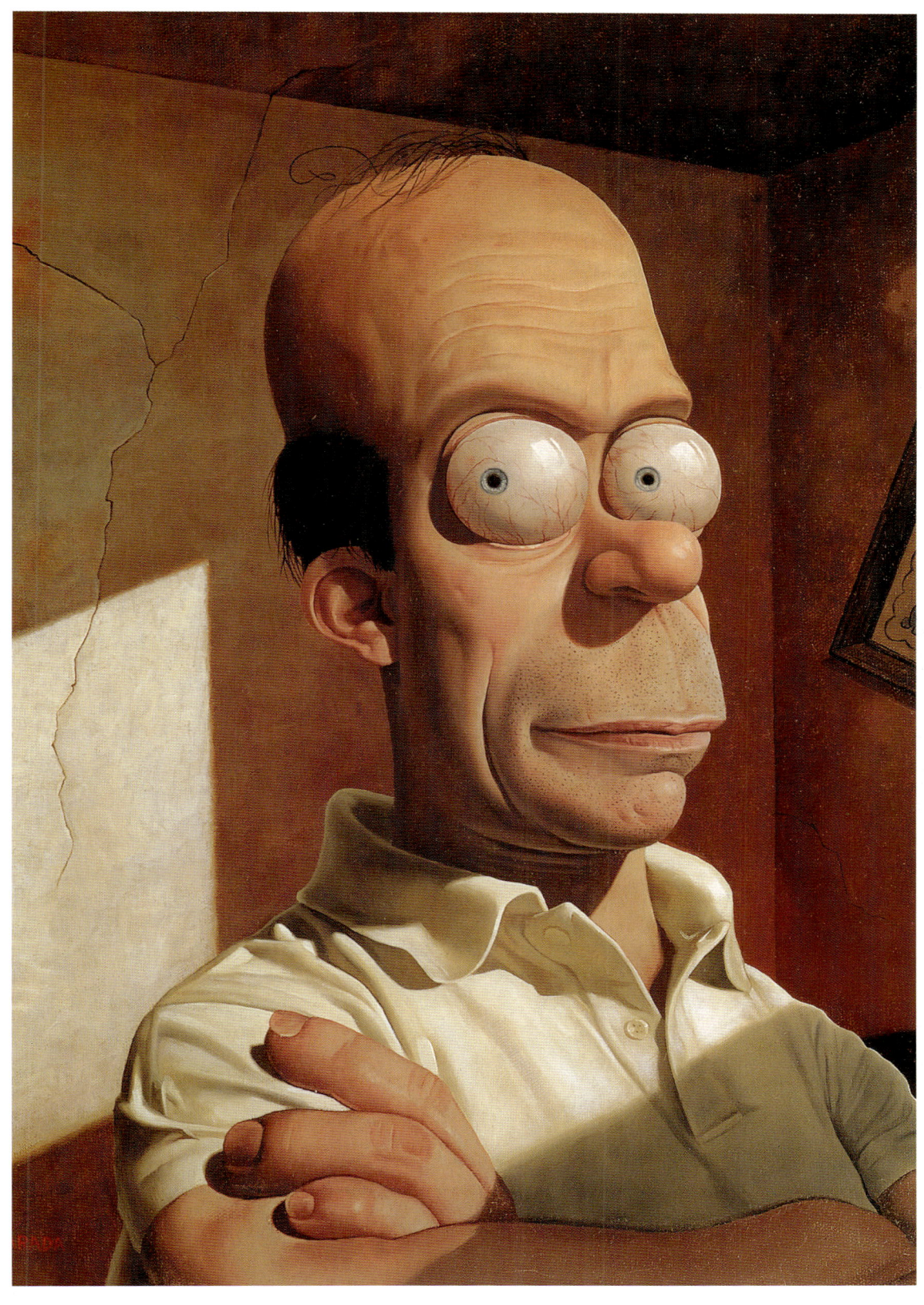

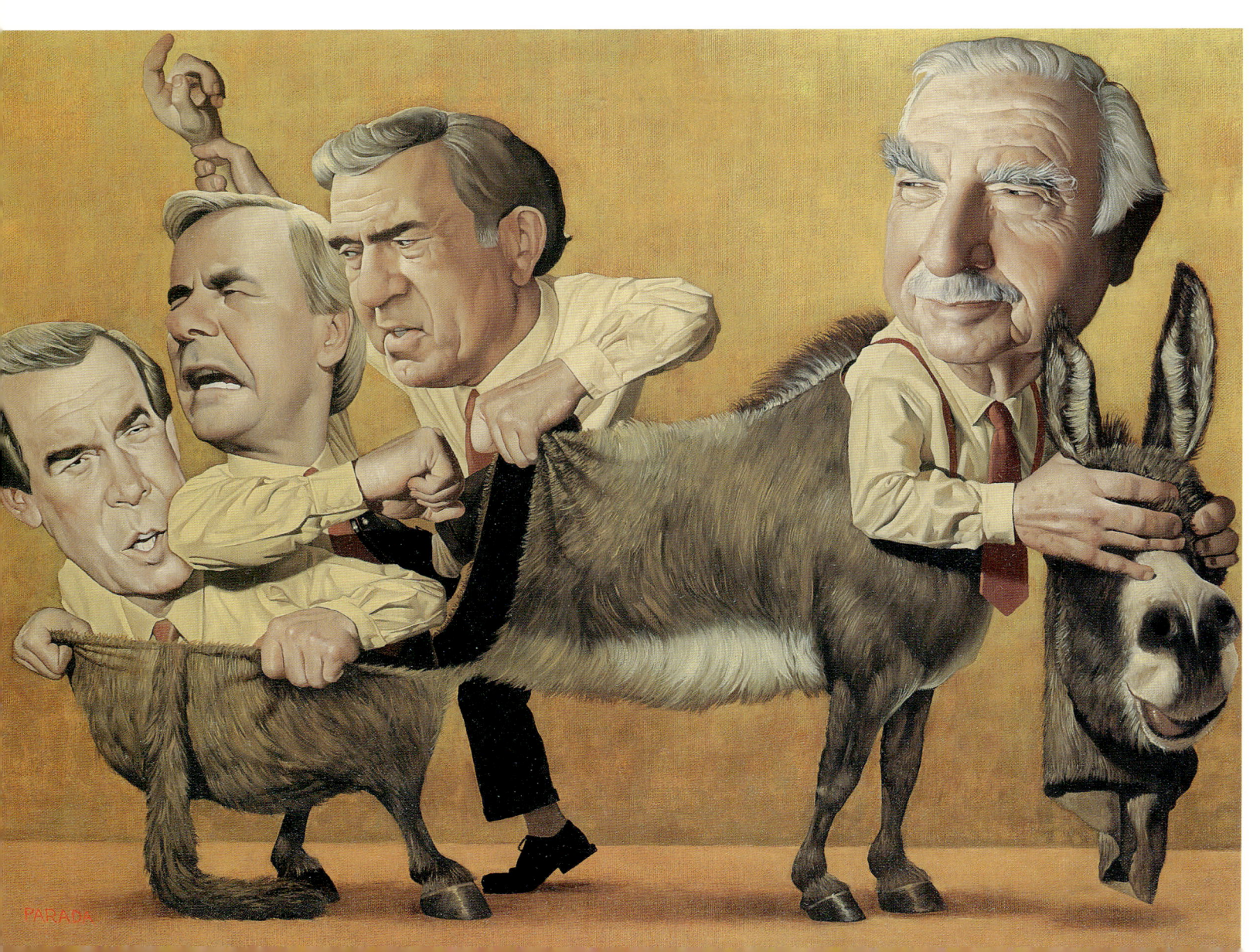

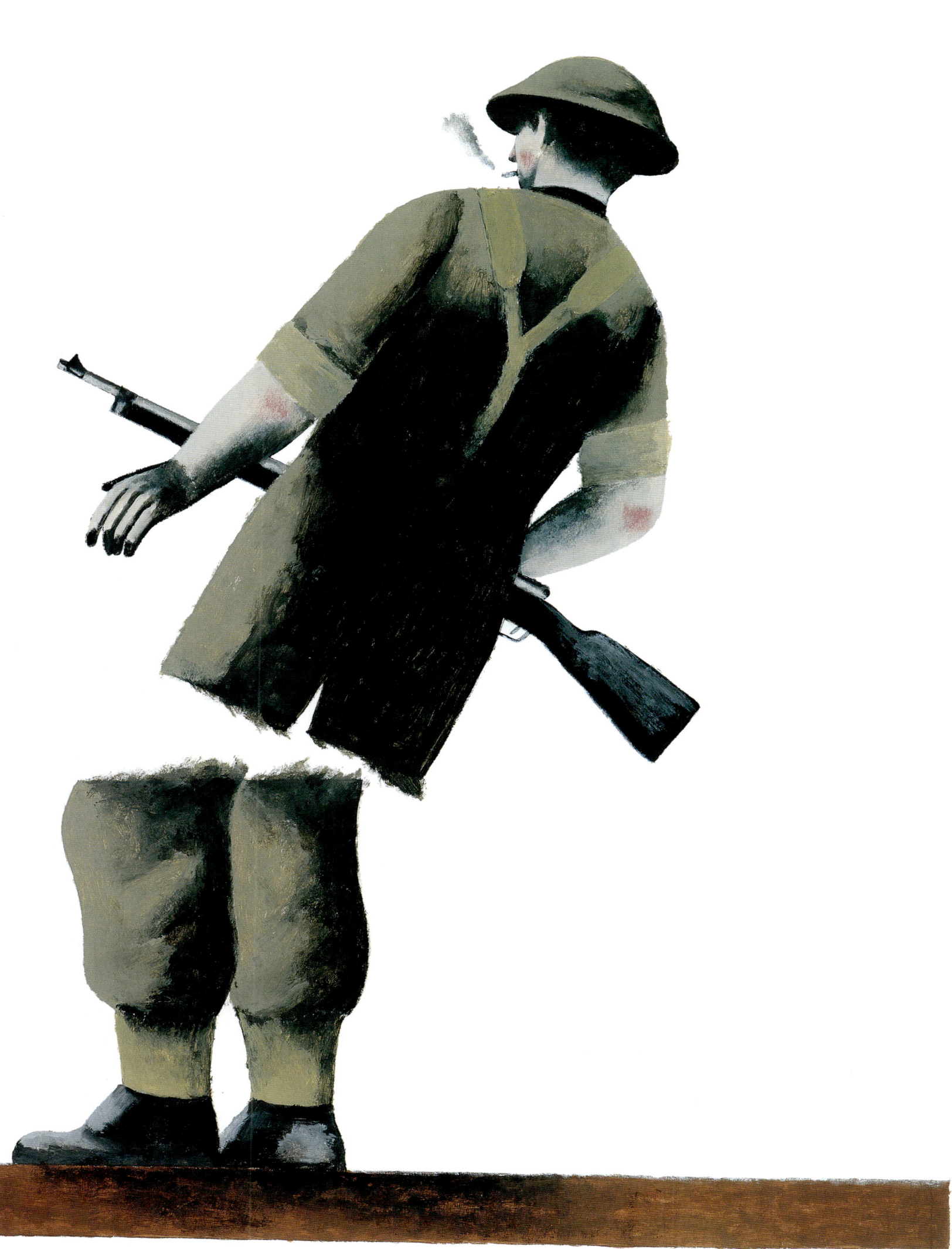

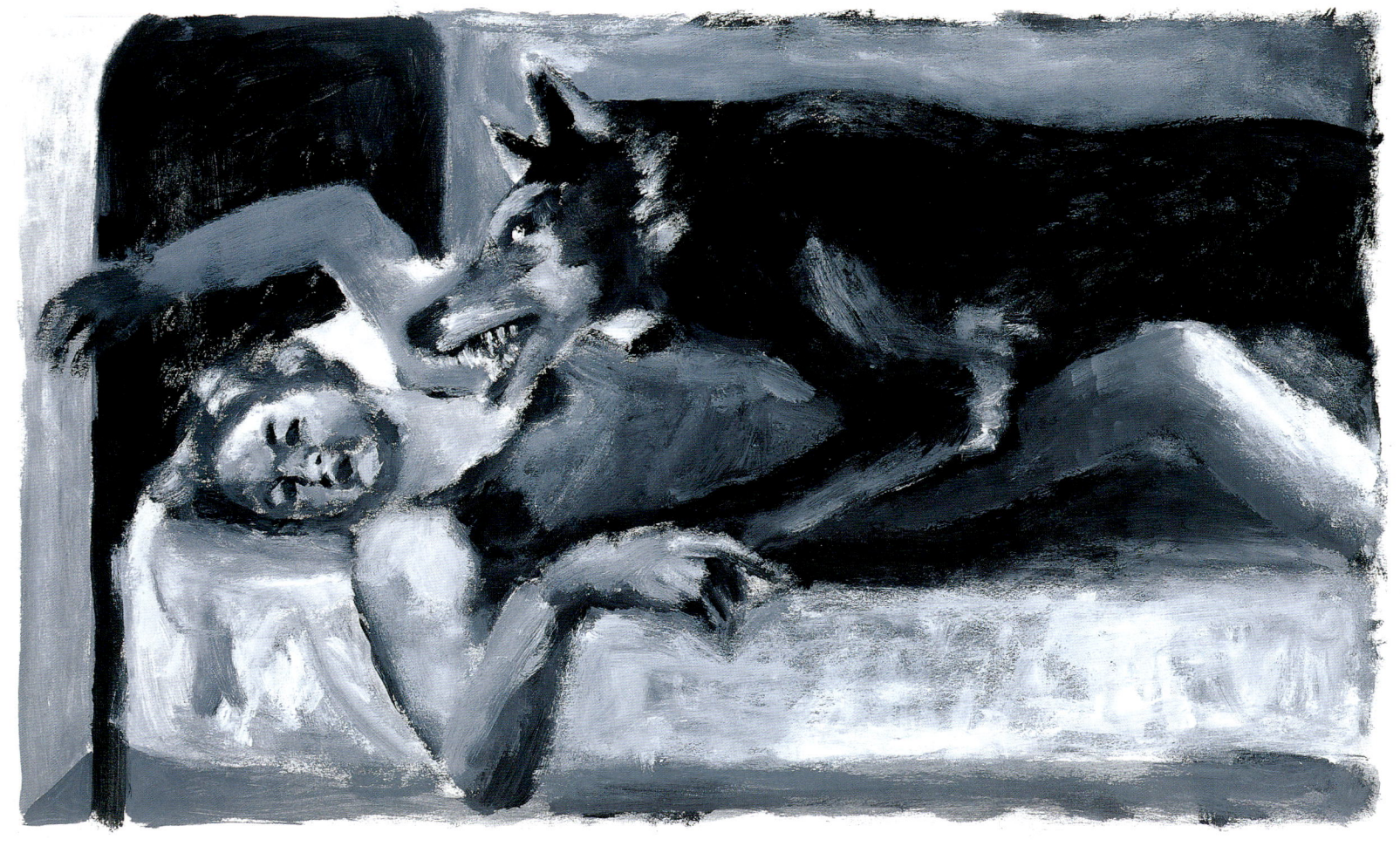

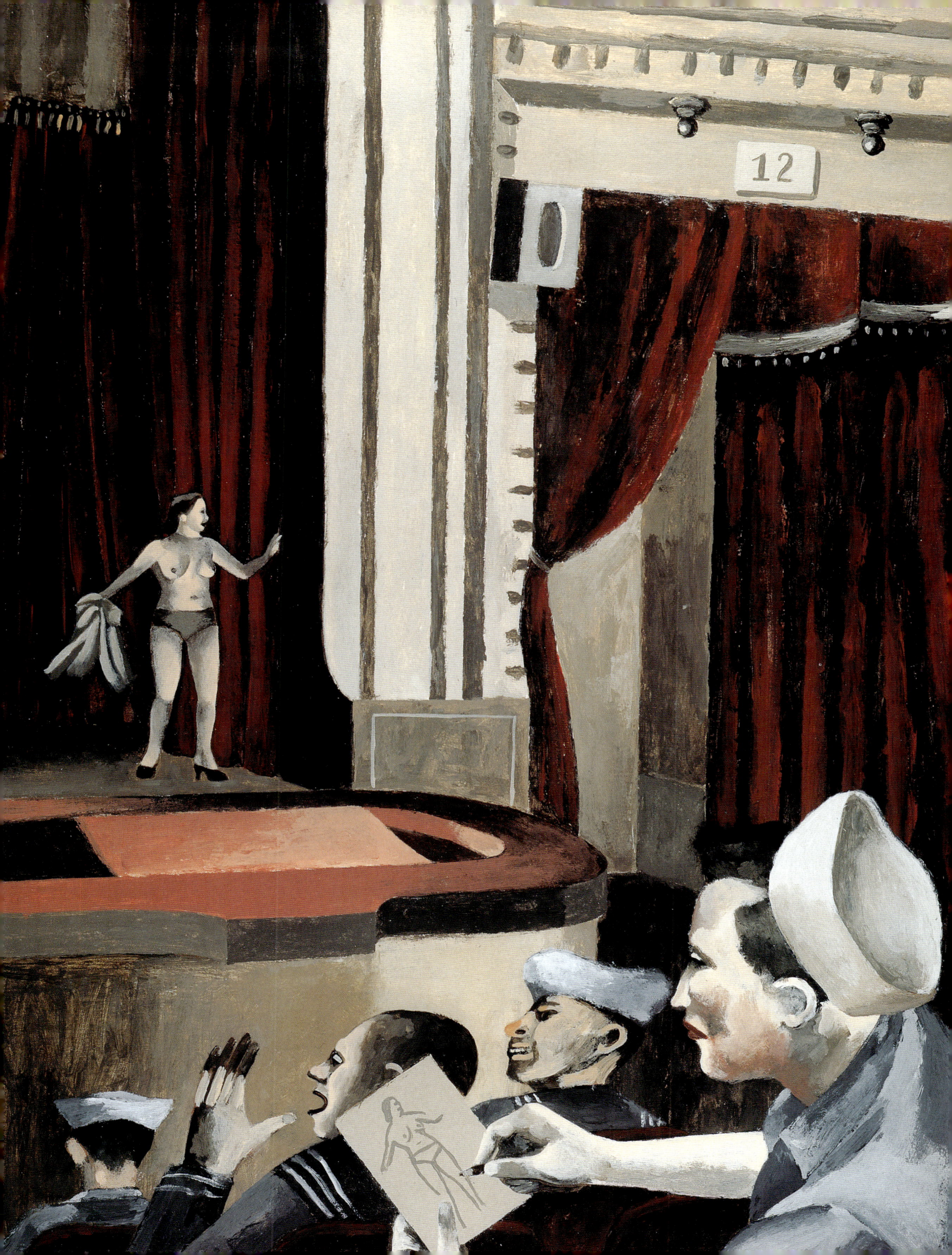

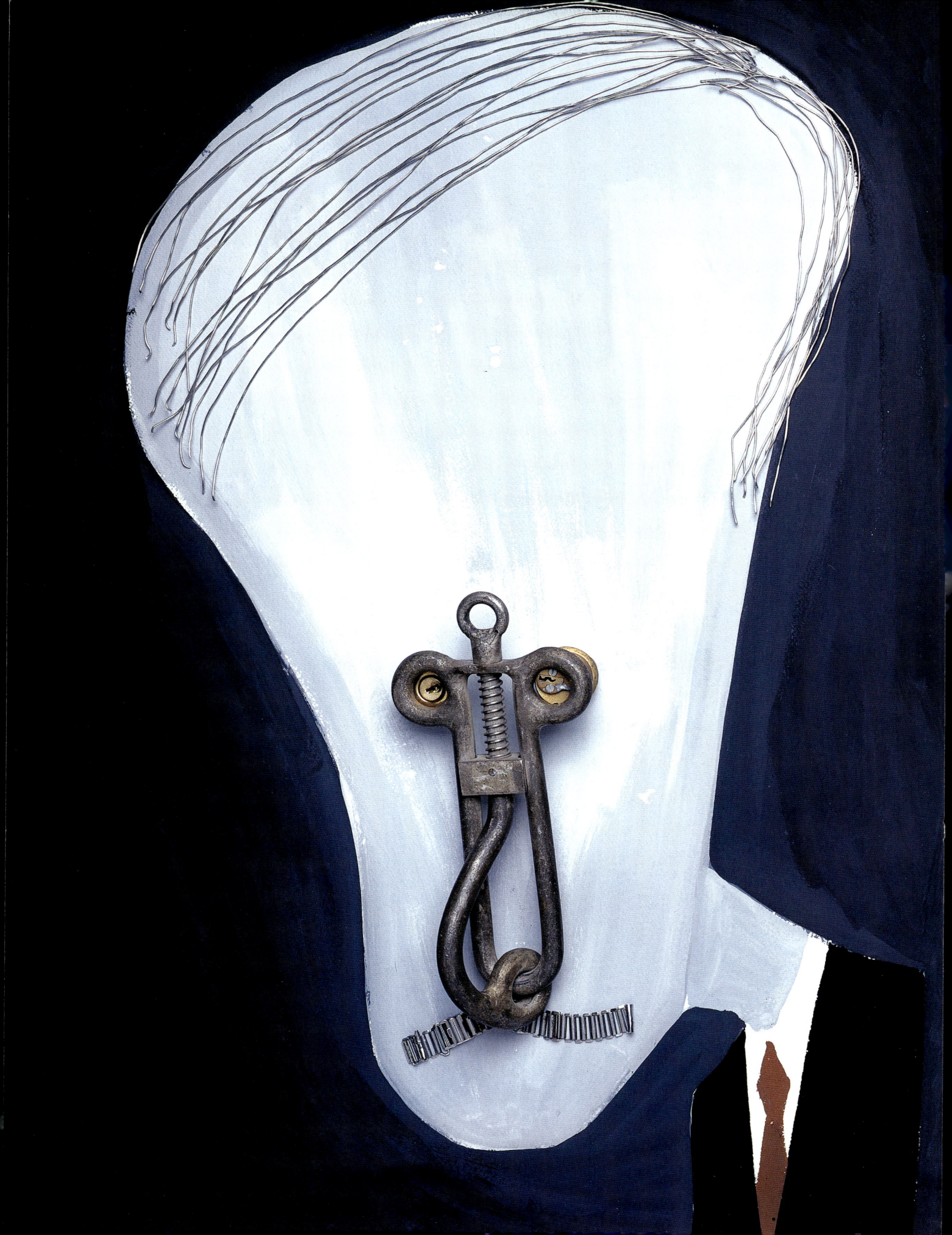

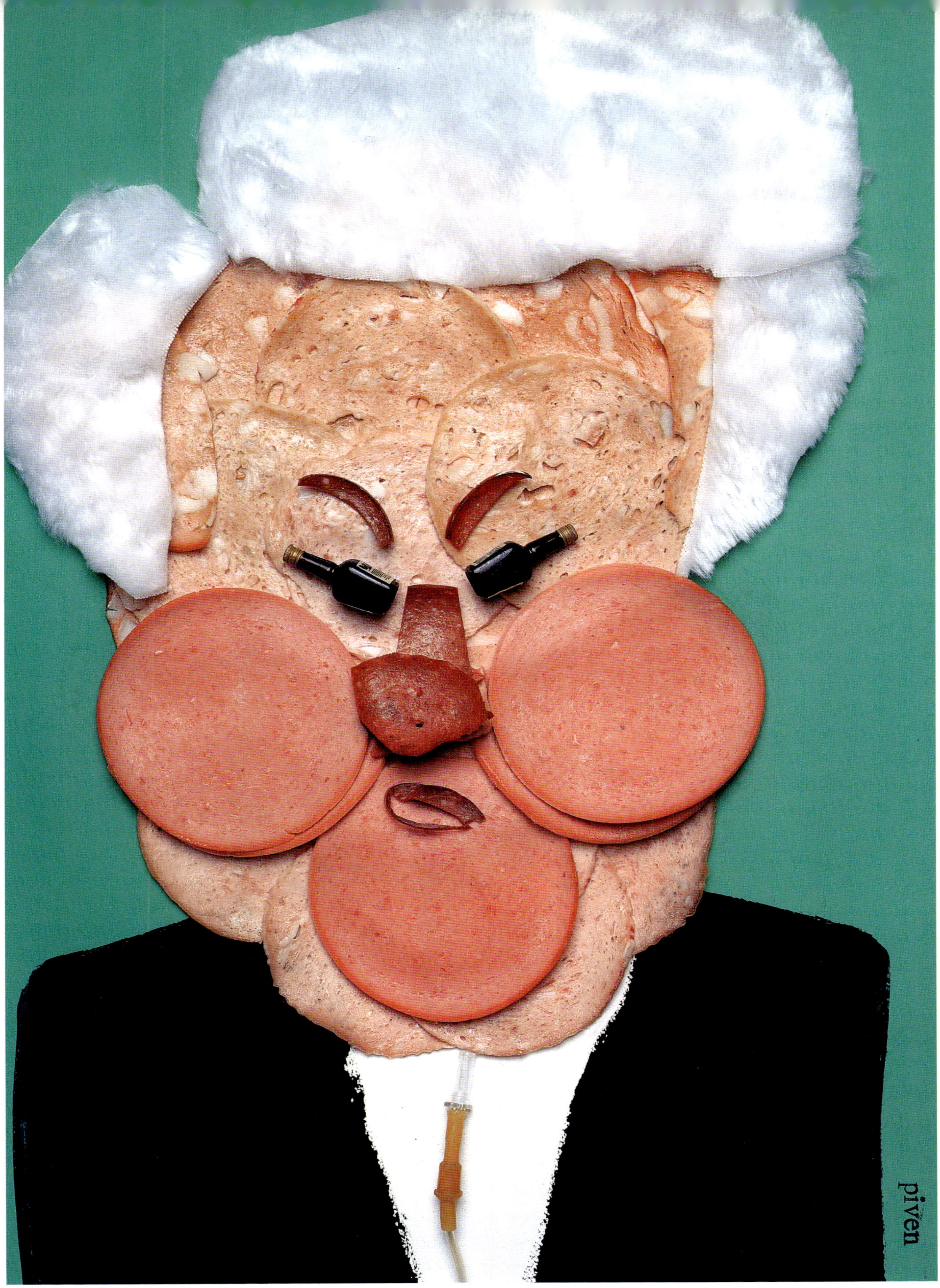

263|264 hanochpiven

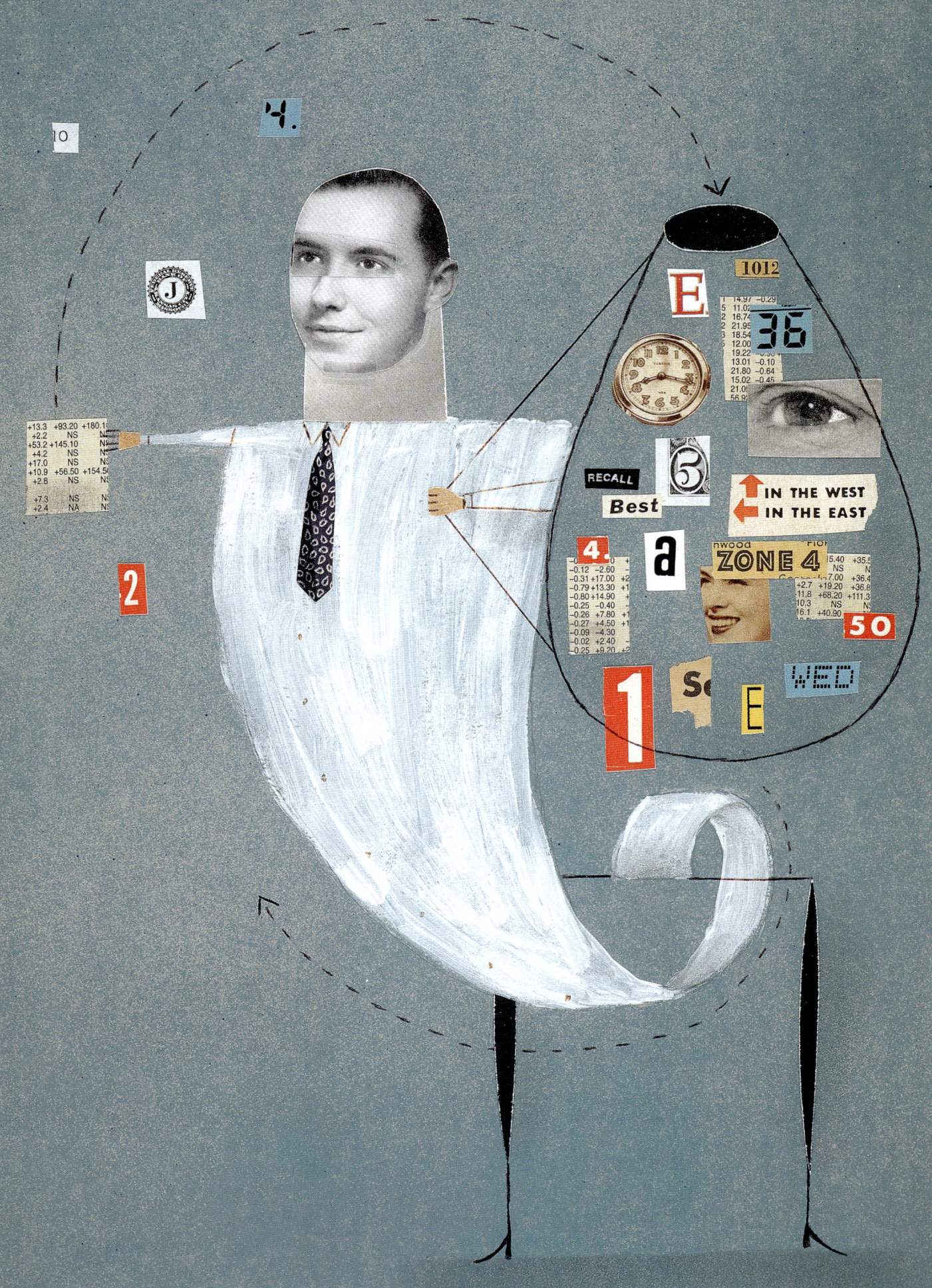

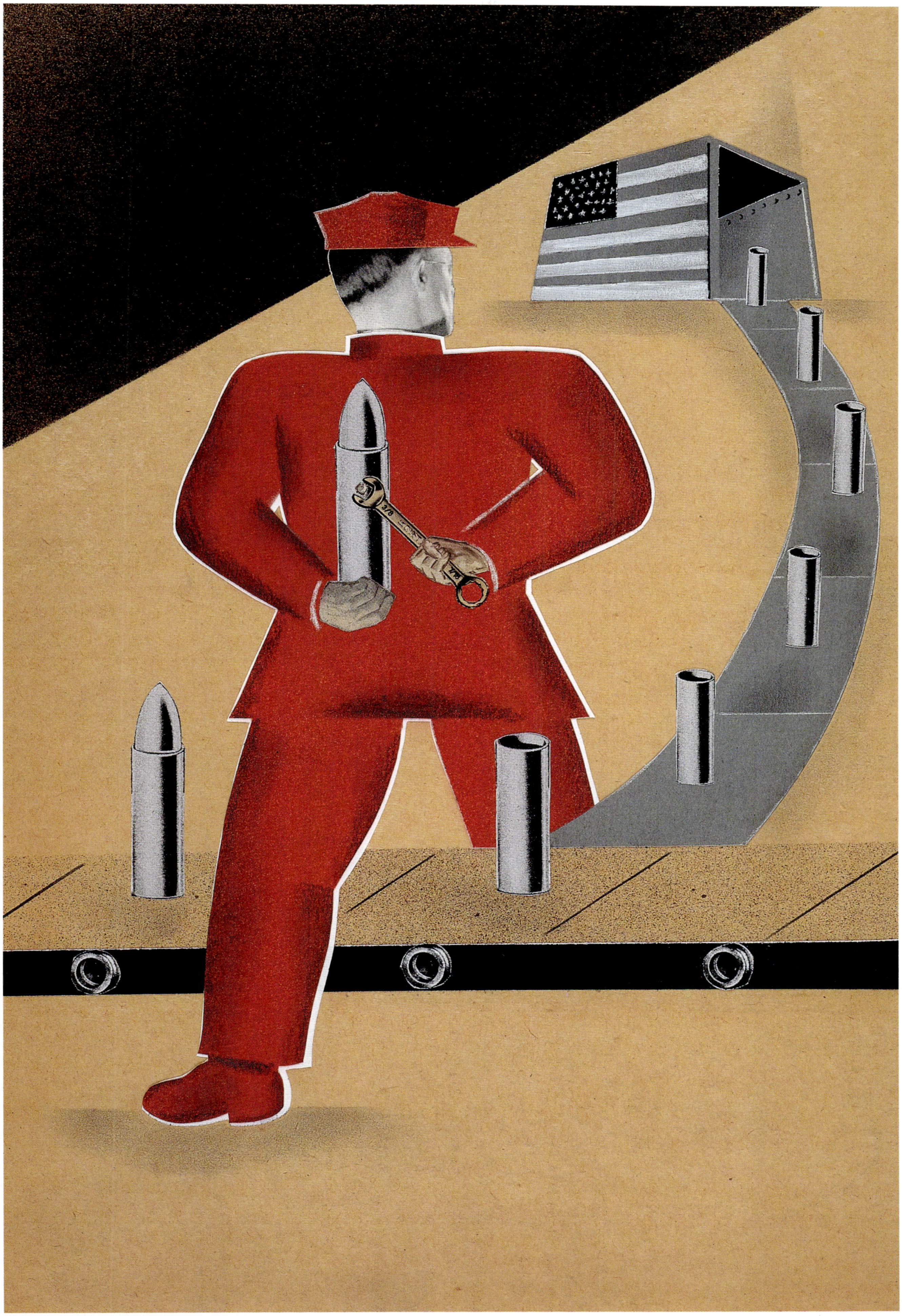

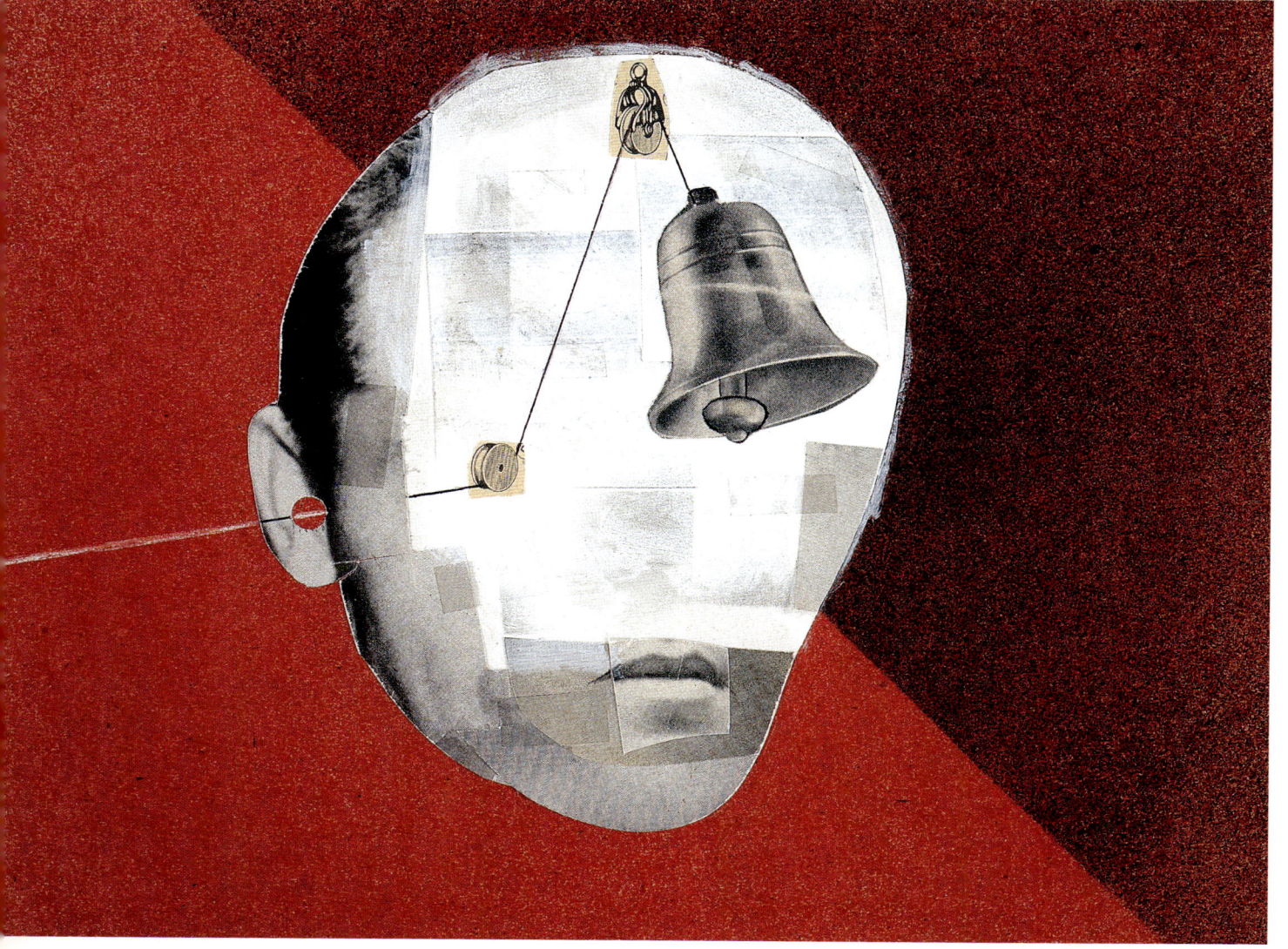

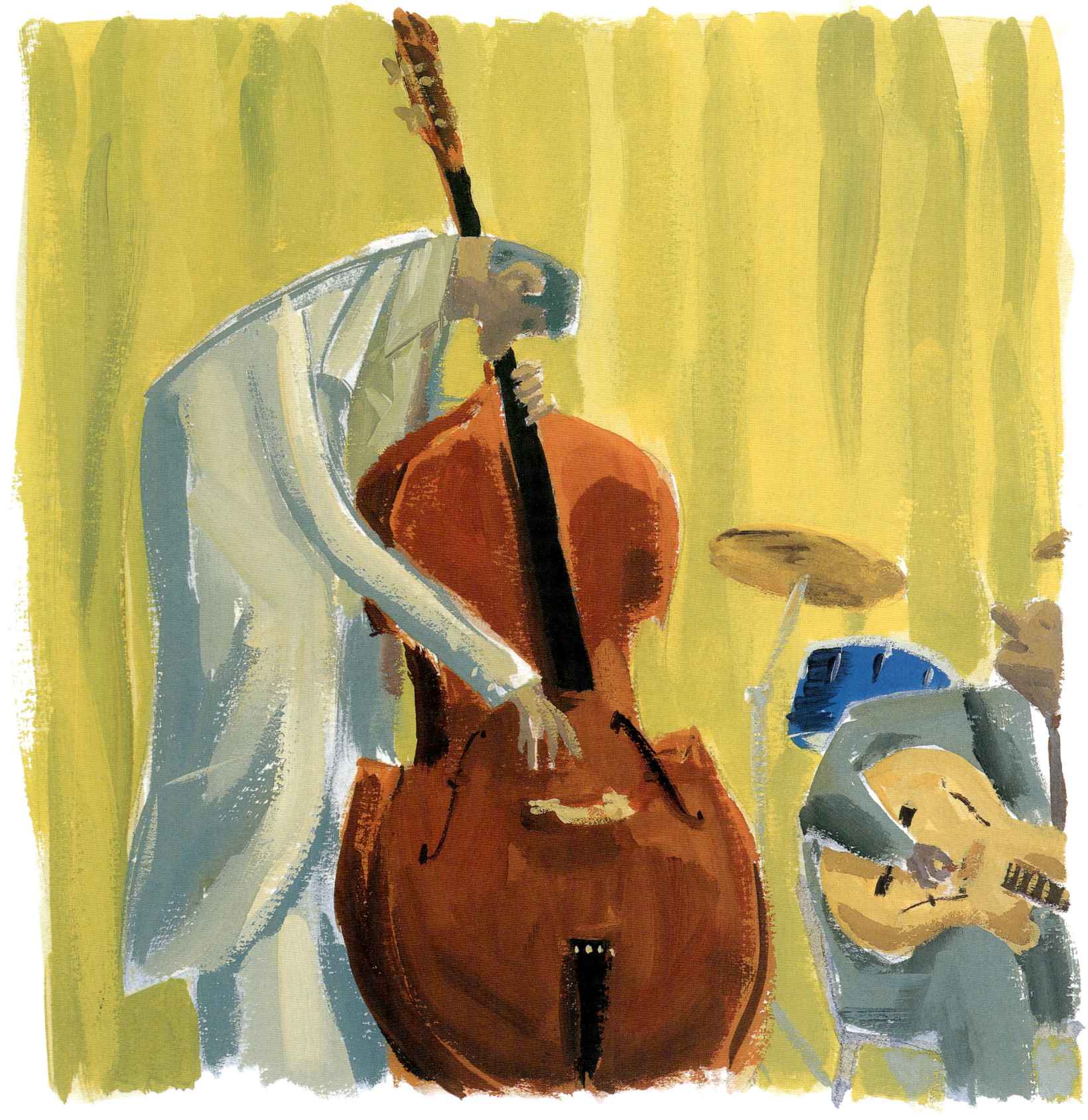

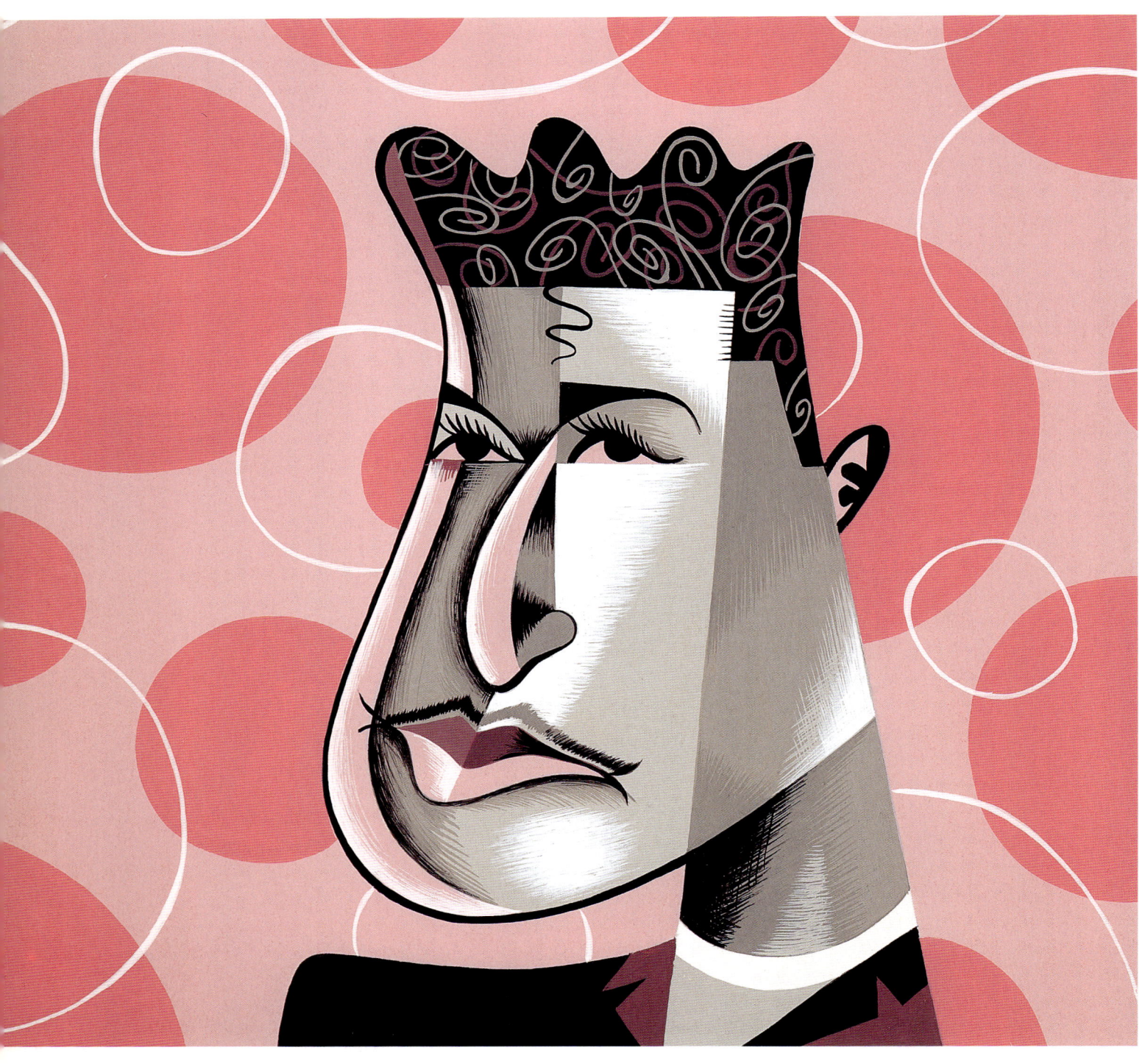

269 chrispyle

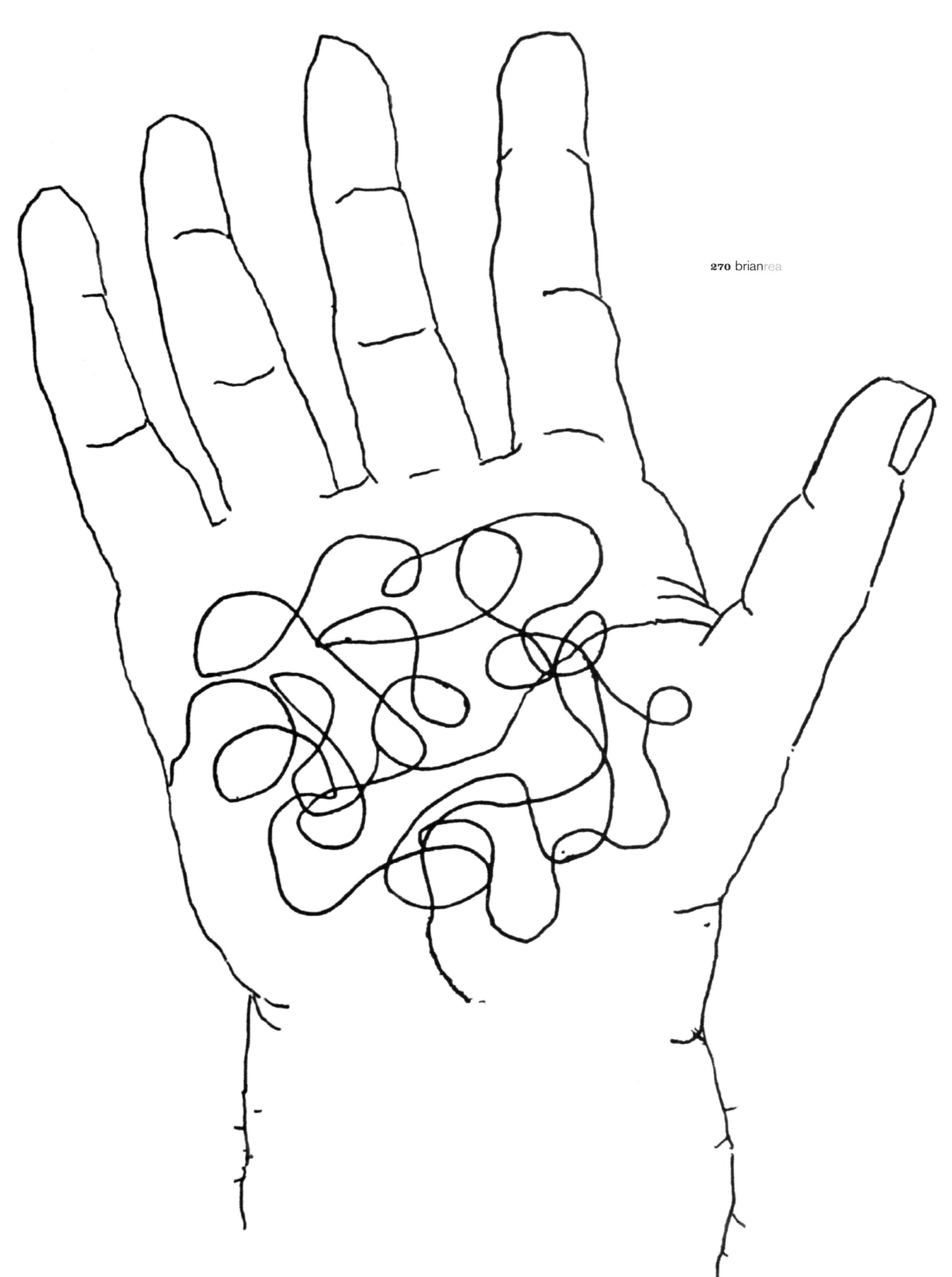

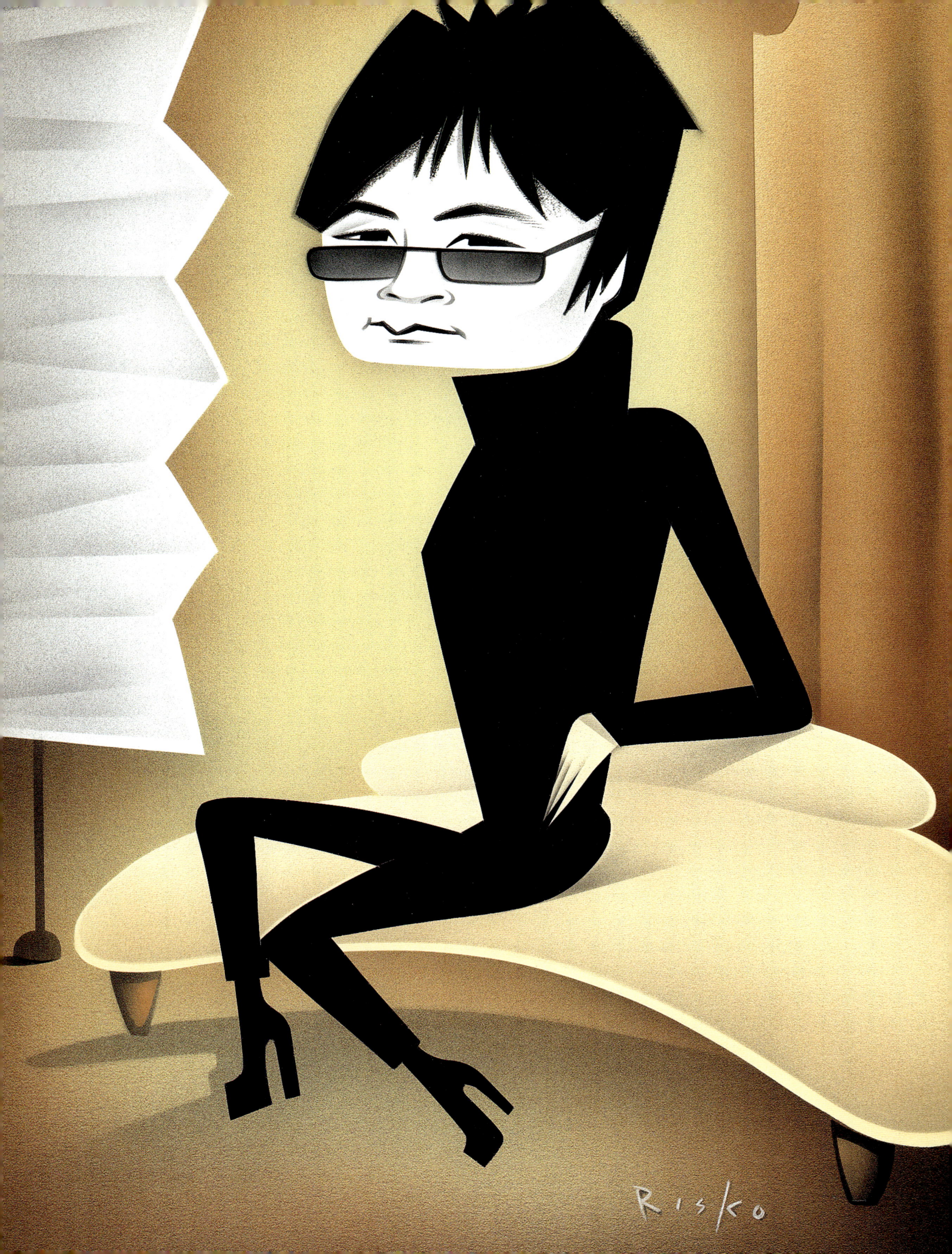

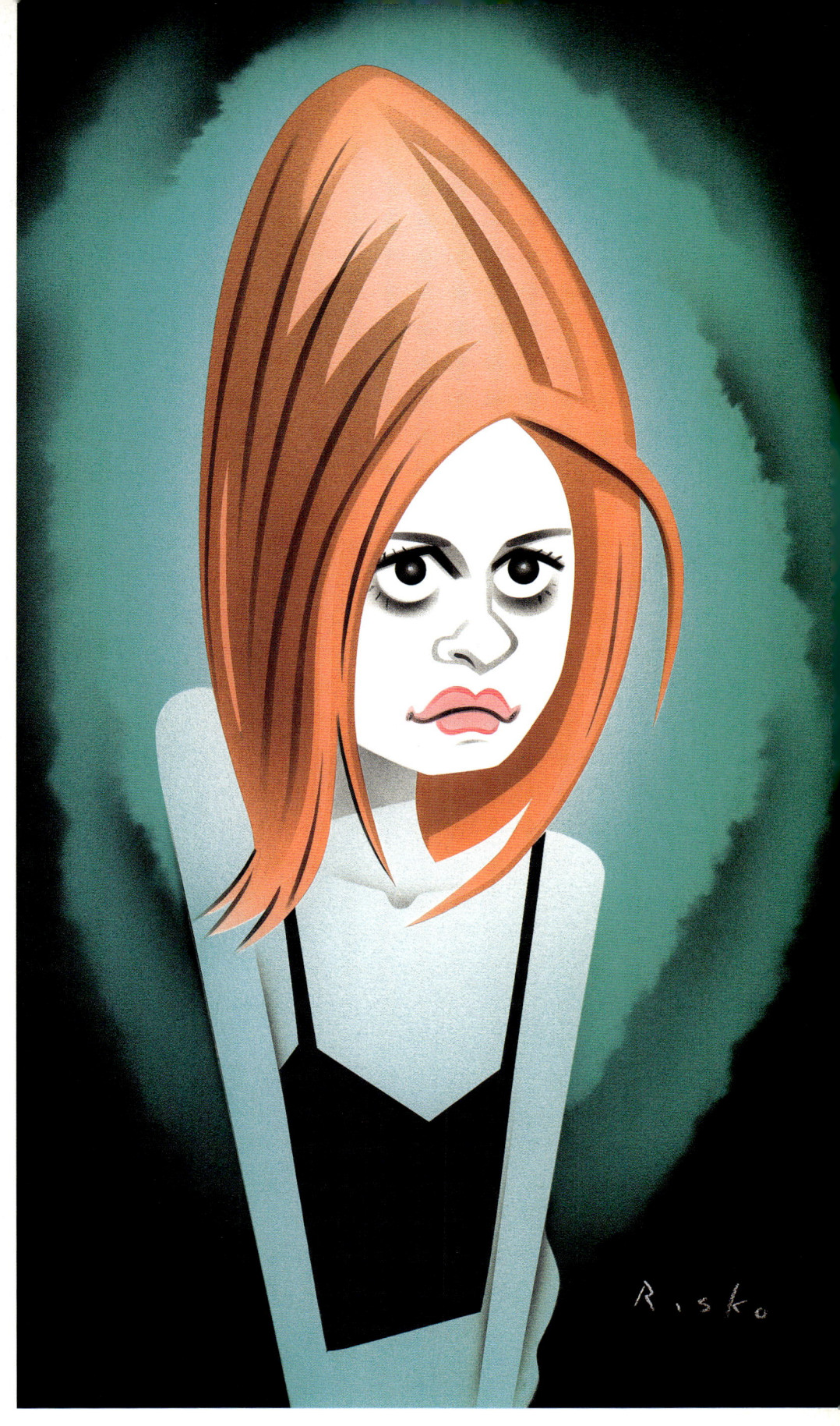

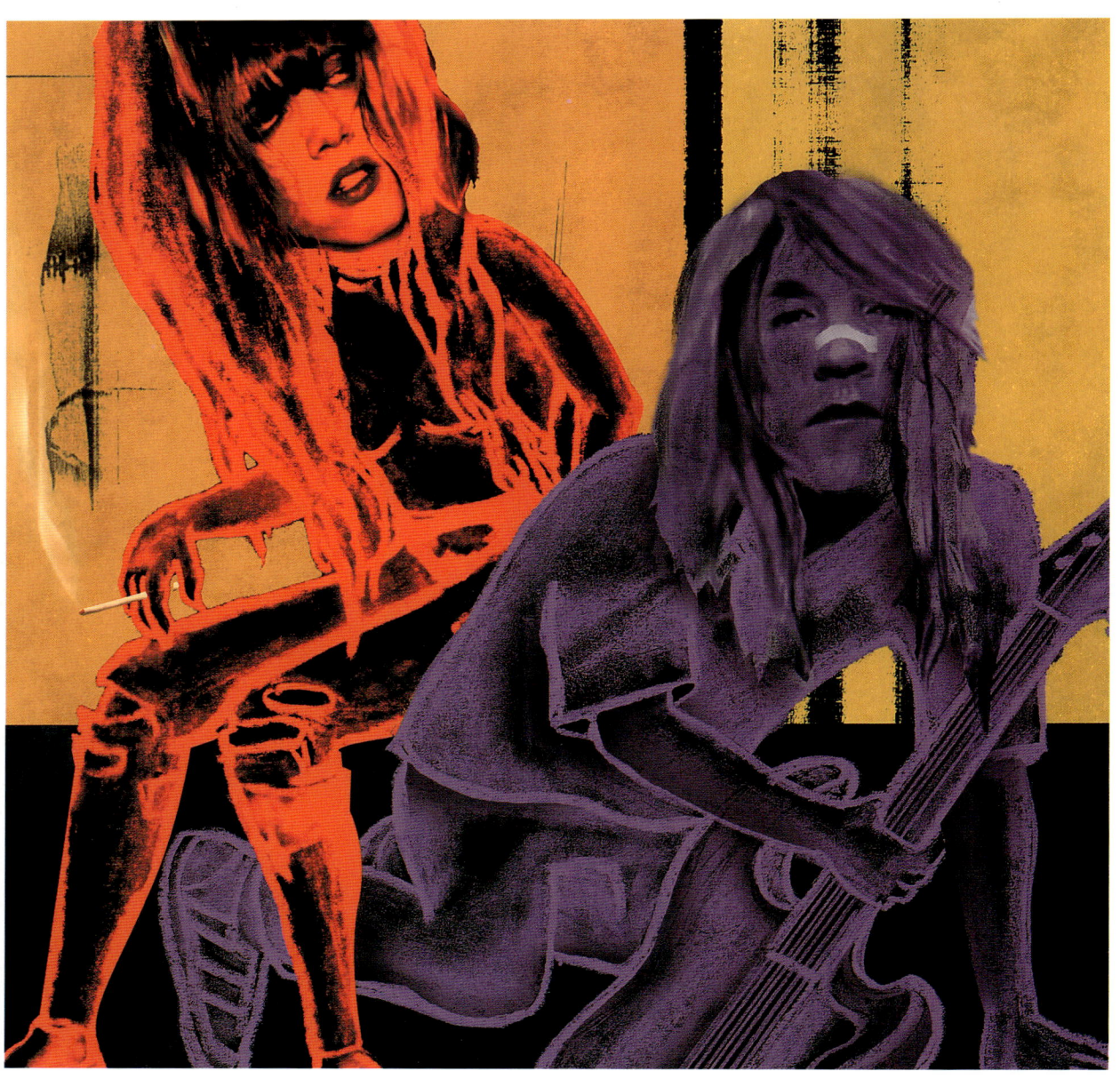

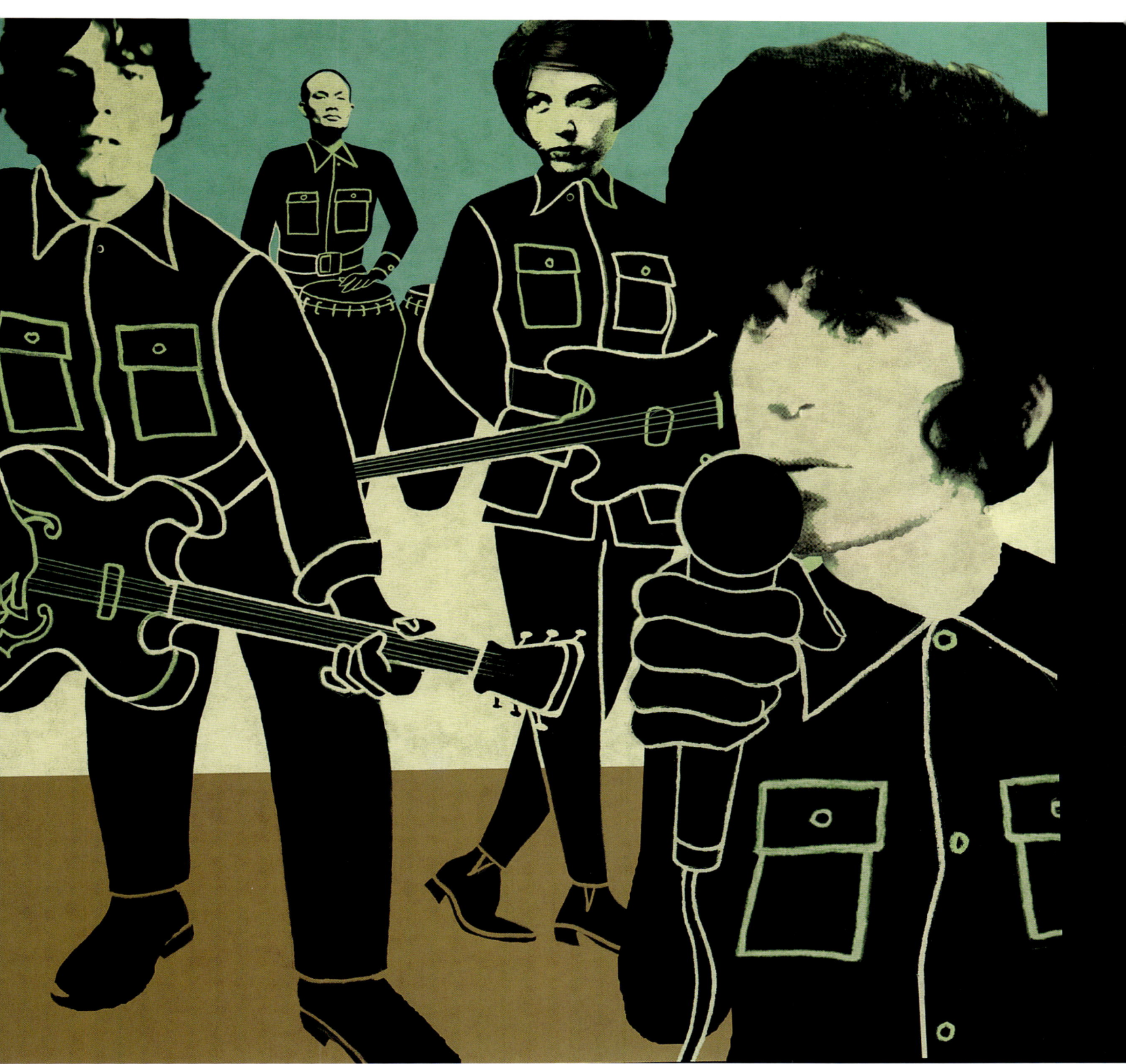

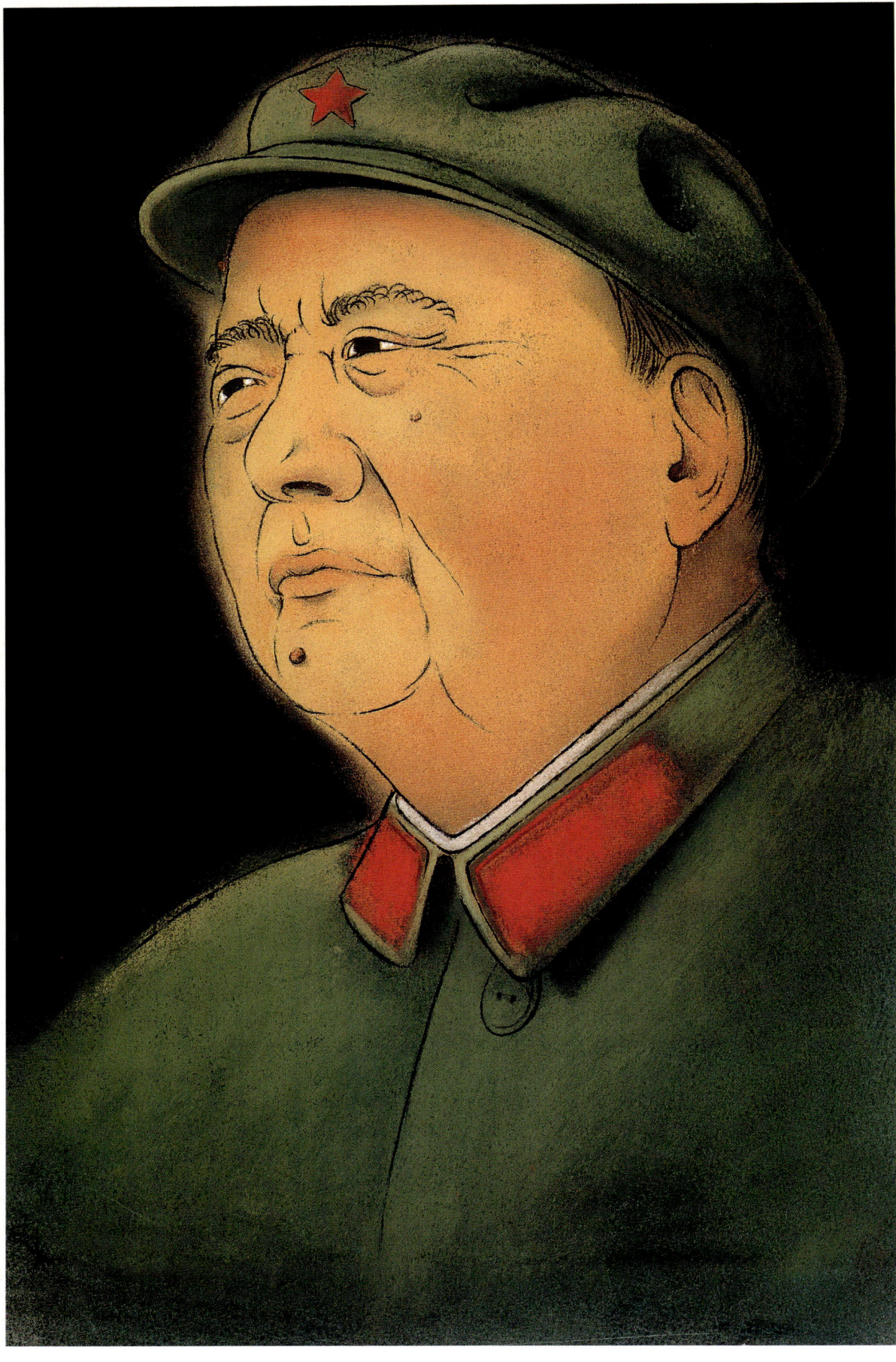

275 edelrodriguez

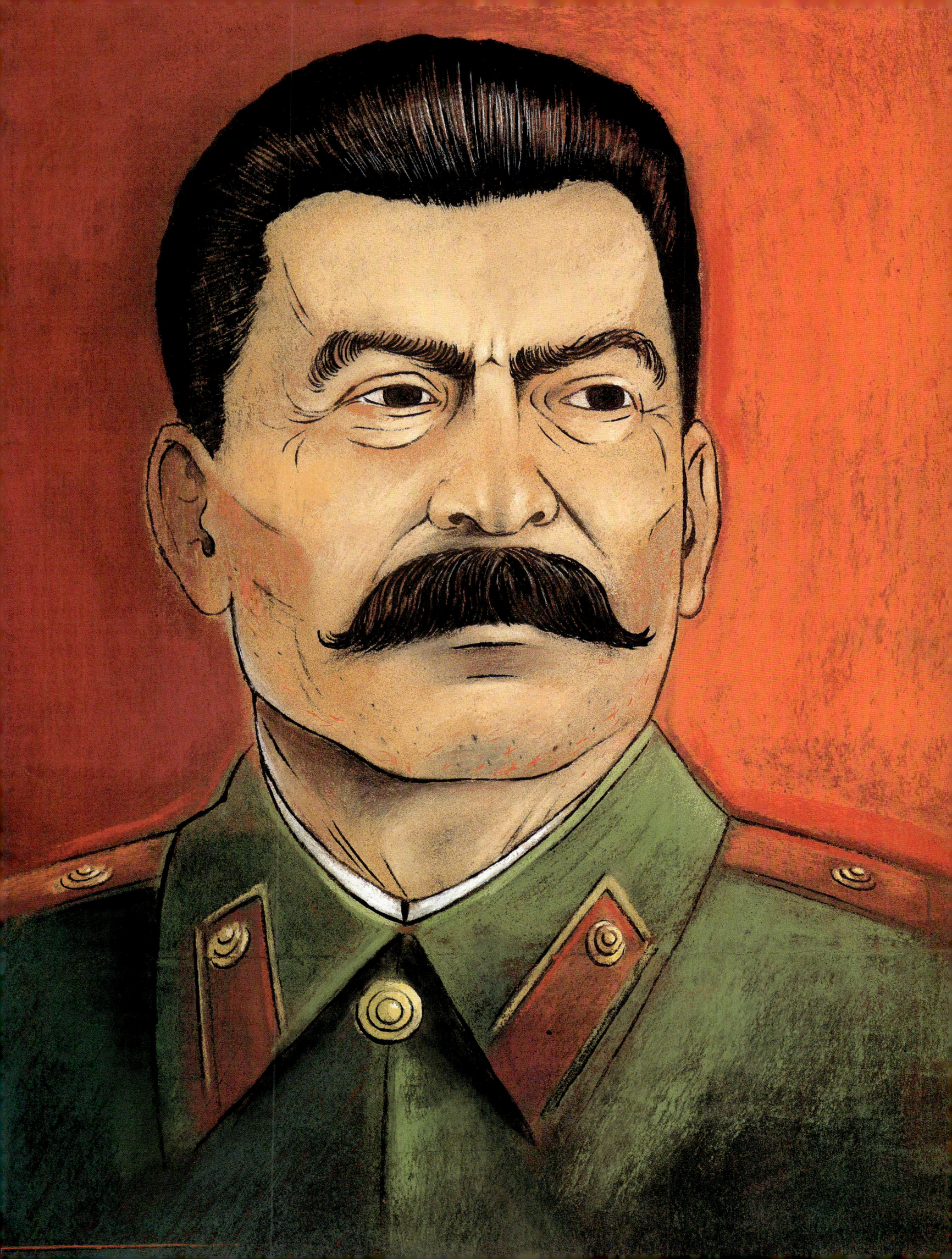

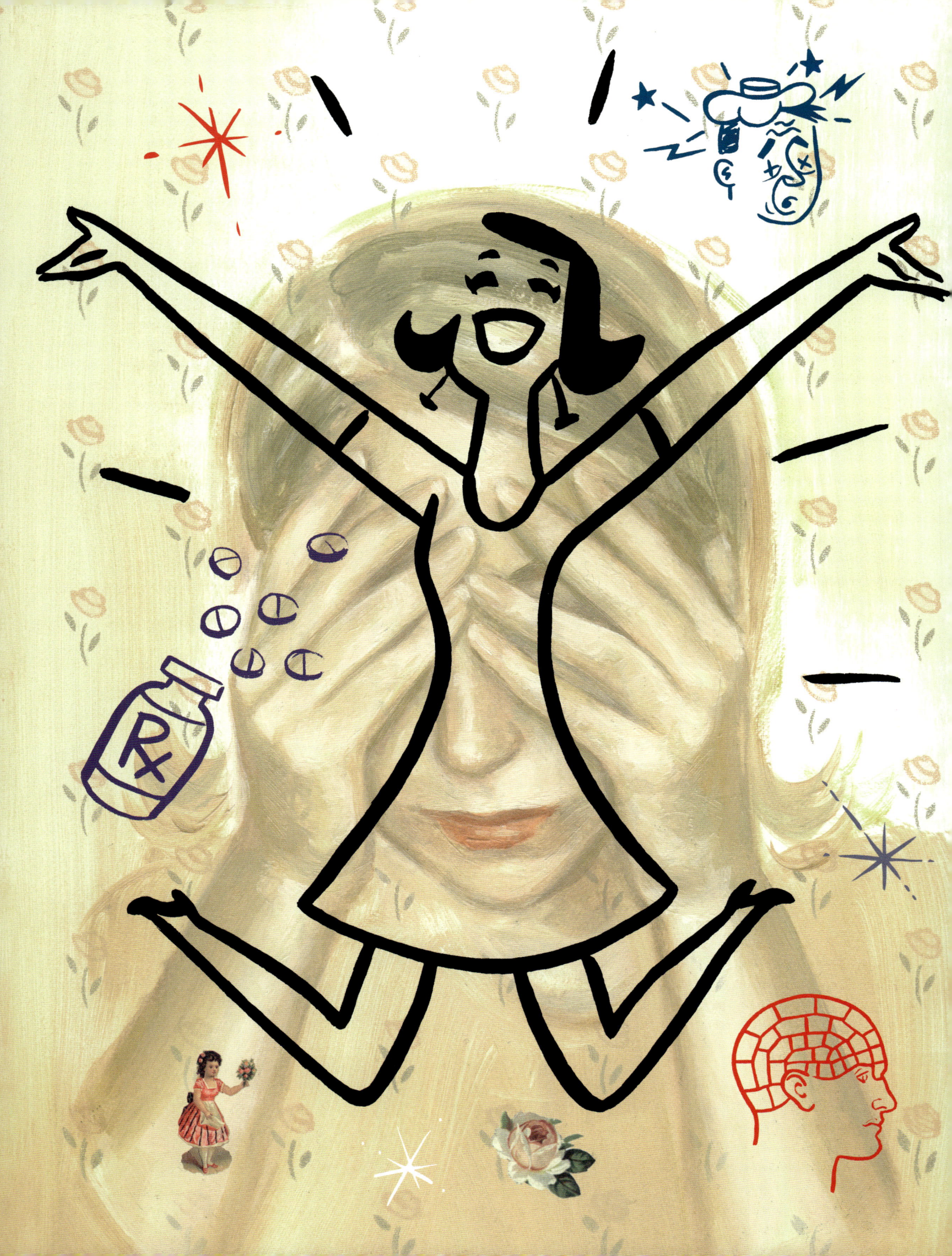

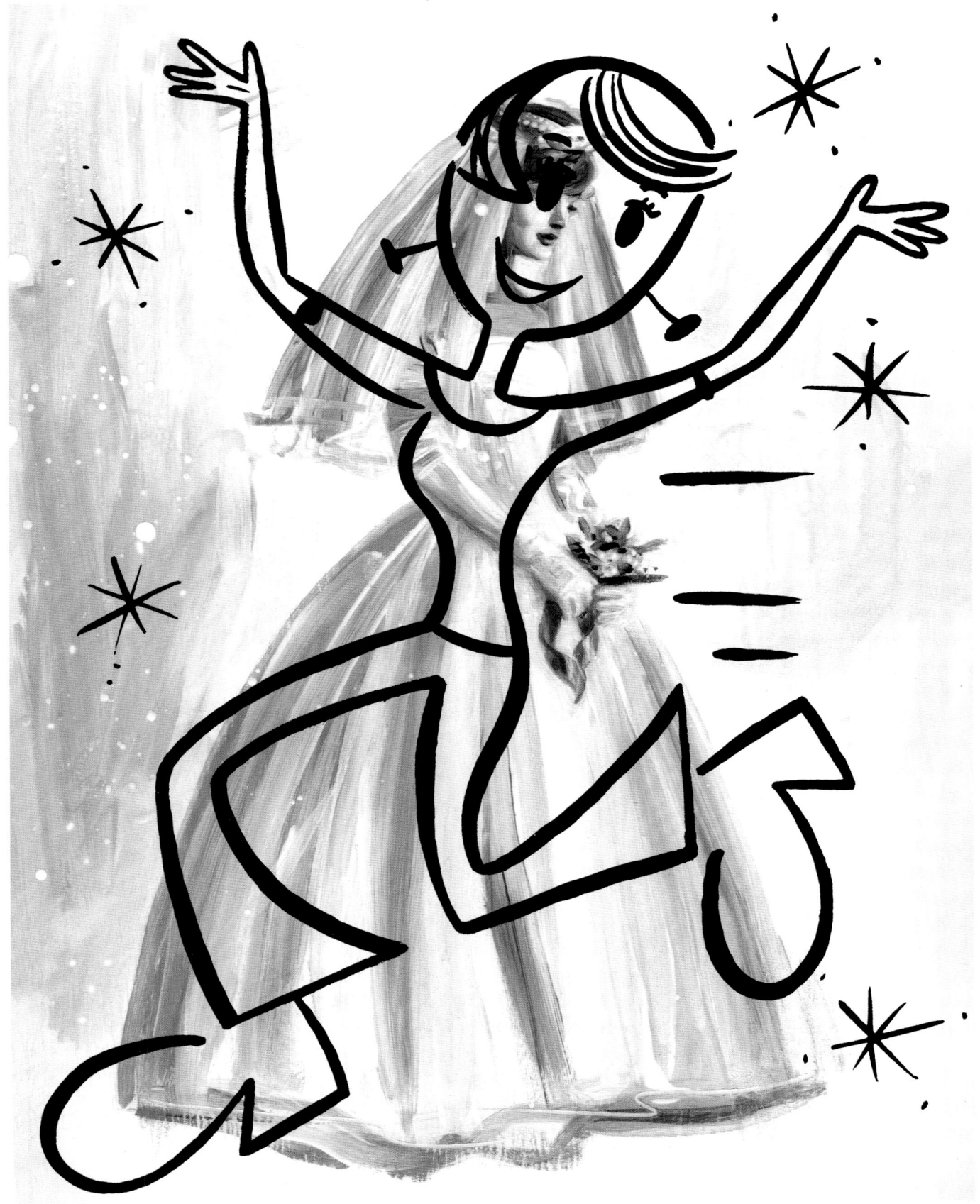

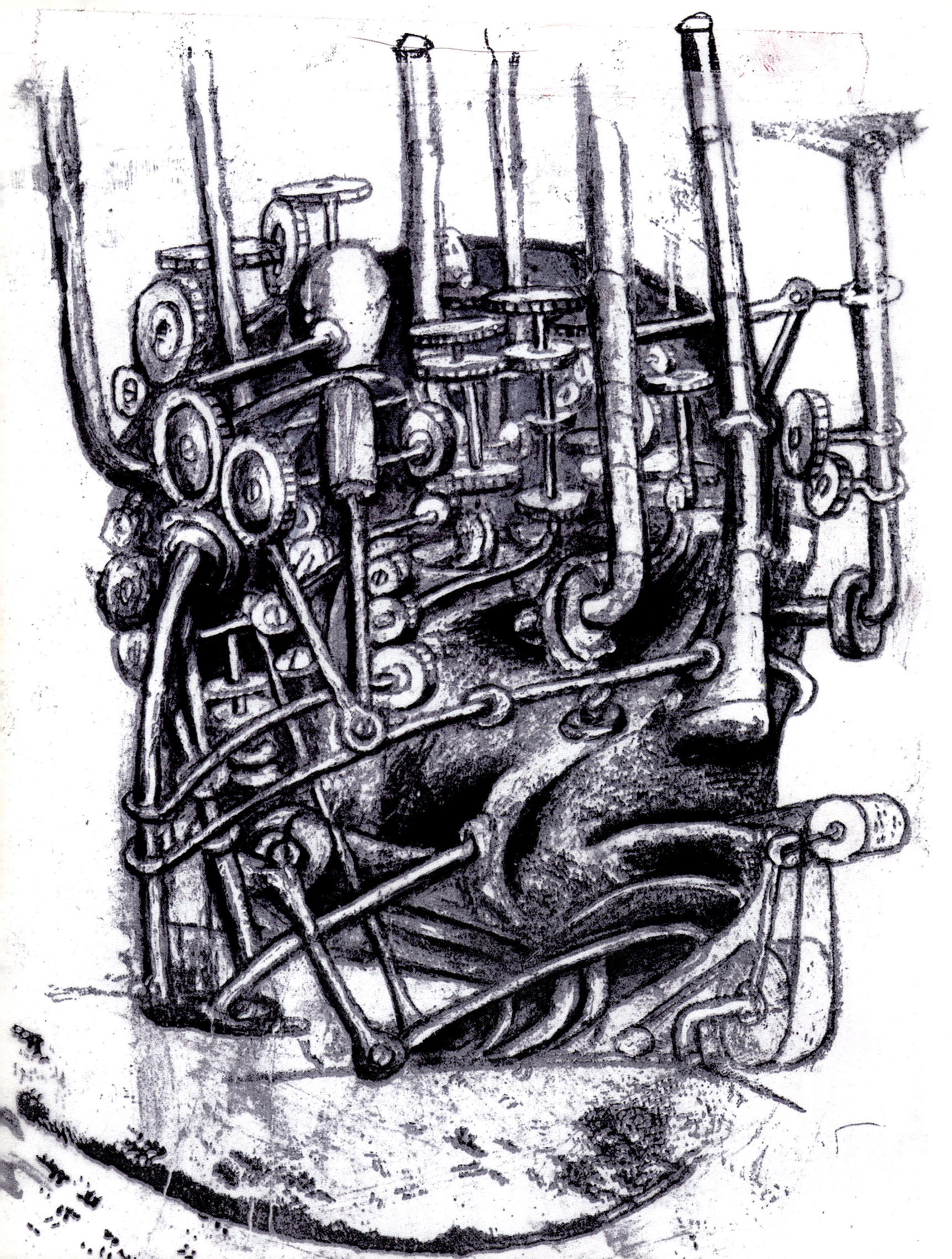

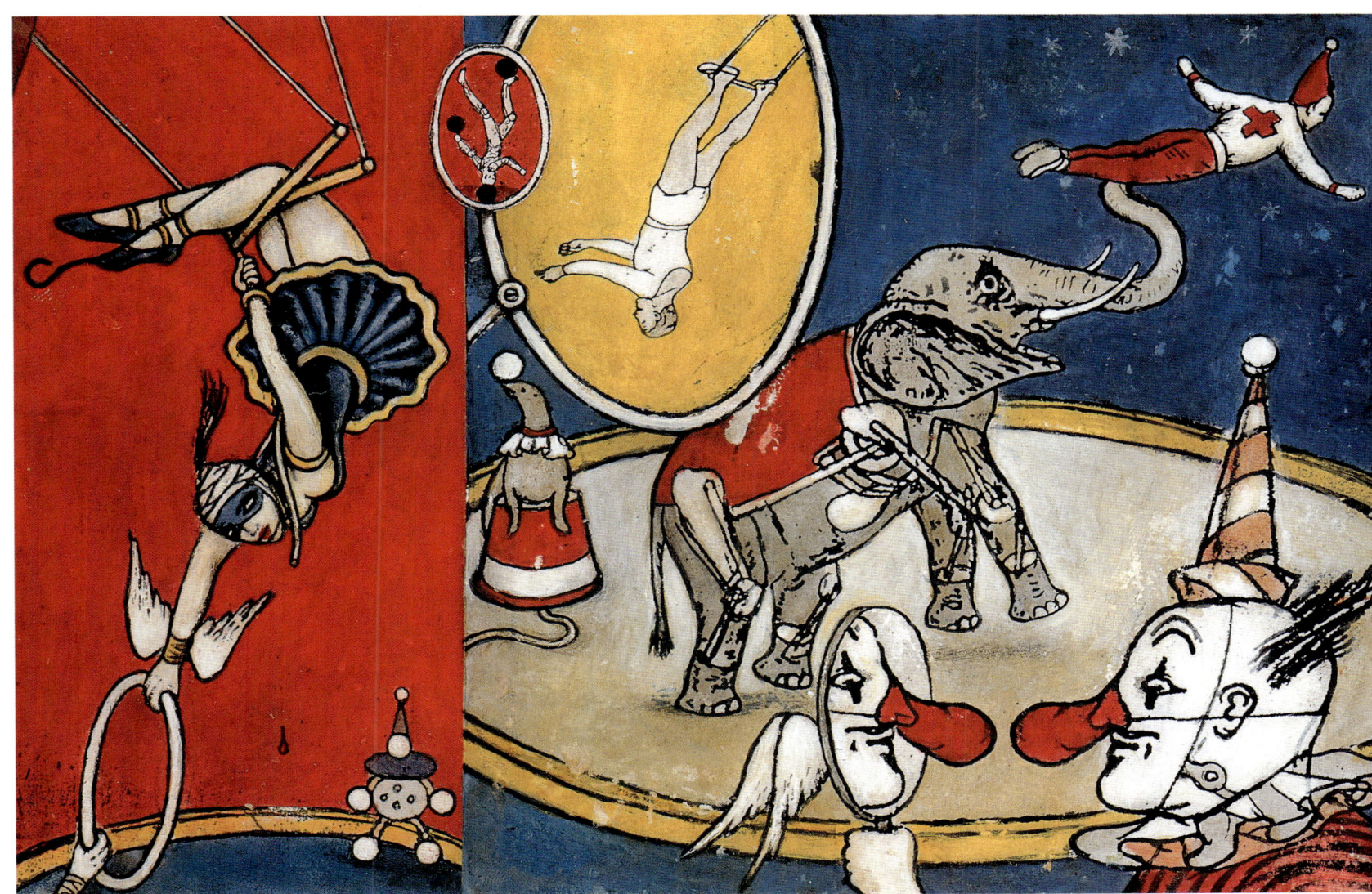

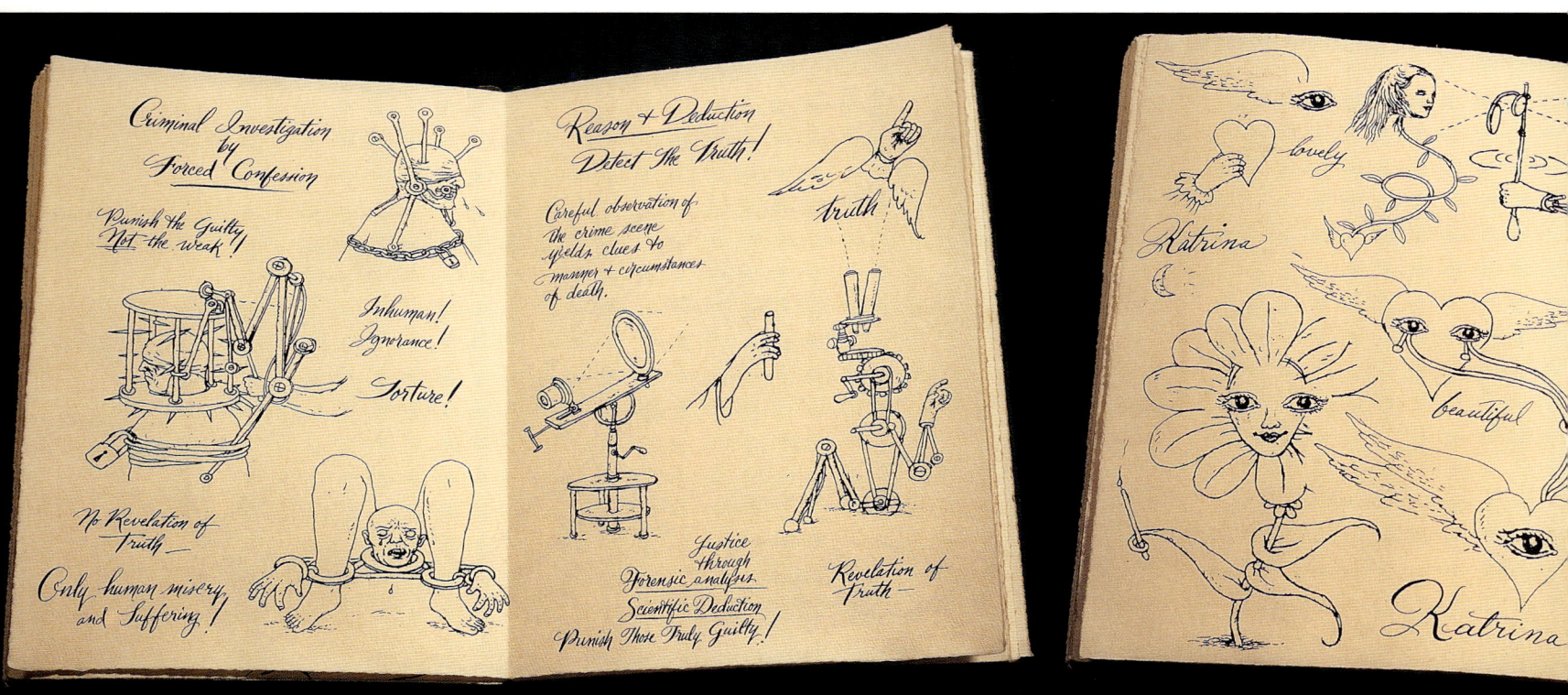

Criminal Investigation
by
Forced Confession

Punish the Guilty
Not the weak!

Inhuman!
Ignorance!

Torture!

No Revelation of
Truth —

Only human misery
and Suffering!

Reason & Deduction
Detect The Truth!

Careful observation of
the crime scene
yields clues to
manner + circumstances
of death.

truth

Justice
through
Forensic analysis
Scientific Deduction
Punish Those Truly Guilty!

Revelation of
Truth

lovely

Katrina

truth

beautiful

Katrina

beautiful

charming

lovely

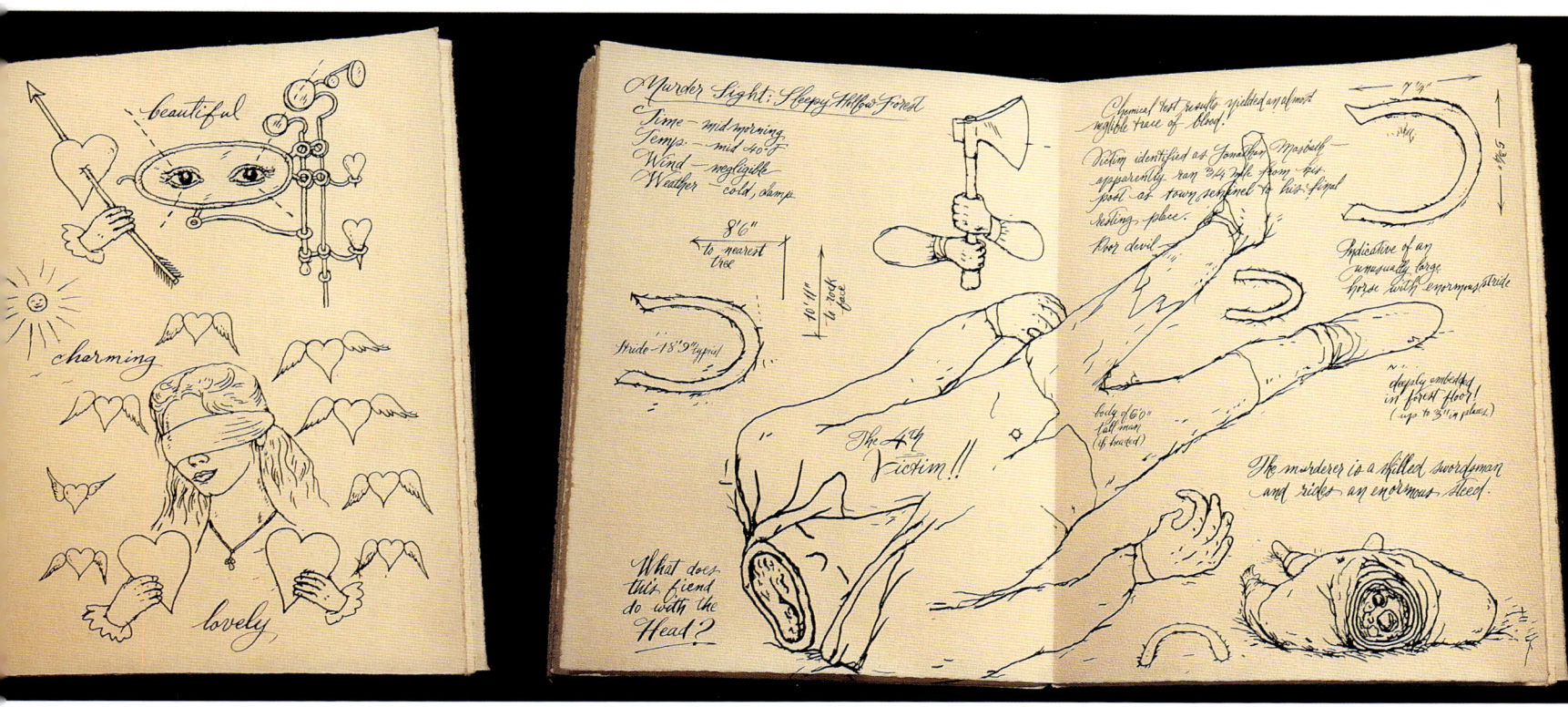

Murder Sight: Sleepy Hollow Forest

Time — mid morning
Temp — mid 40°F
Wind — negligible
Weather — cold, damp

8'6"
to nearest tree

10'11"
to rock face

Stride 15'9" typical

The 4th Victim!!

What does this fiend do with the Head?

Chemical test results yielded an almost negligible trace of blood!

Victim identified as Jonathan Masbeth apparently ran 3/4 mile from his post at town sentinel to his final resting place.

Poor devil

Indicative of an unusually large horse with enormous stride

body of 6'0" tall man (if booted)

deeply embedded in forest floor! (up to 3" in place)

7'4"

The murderer is a skilled swordsman and rides an enormous steed.

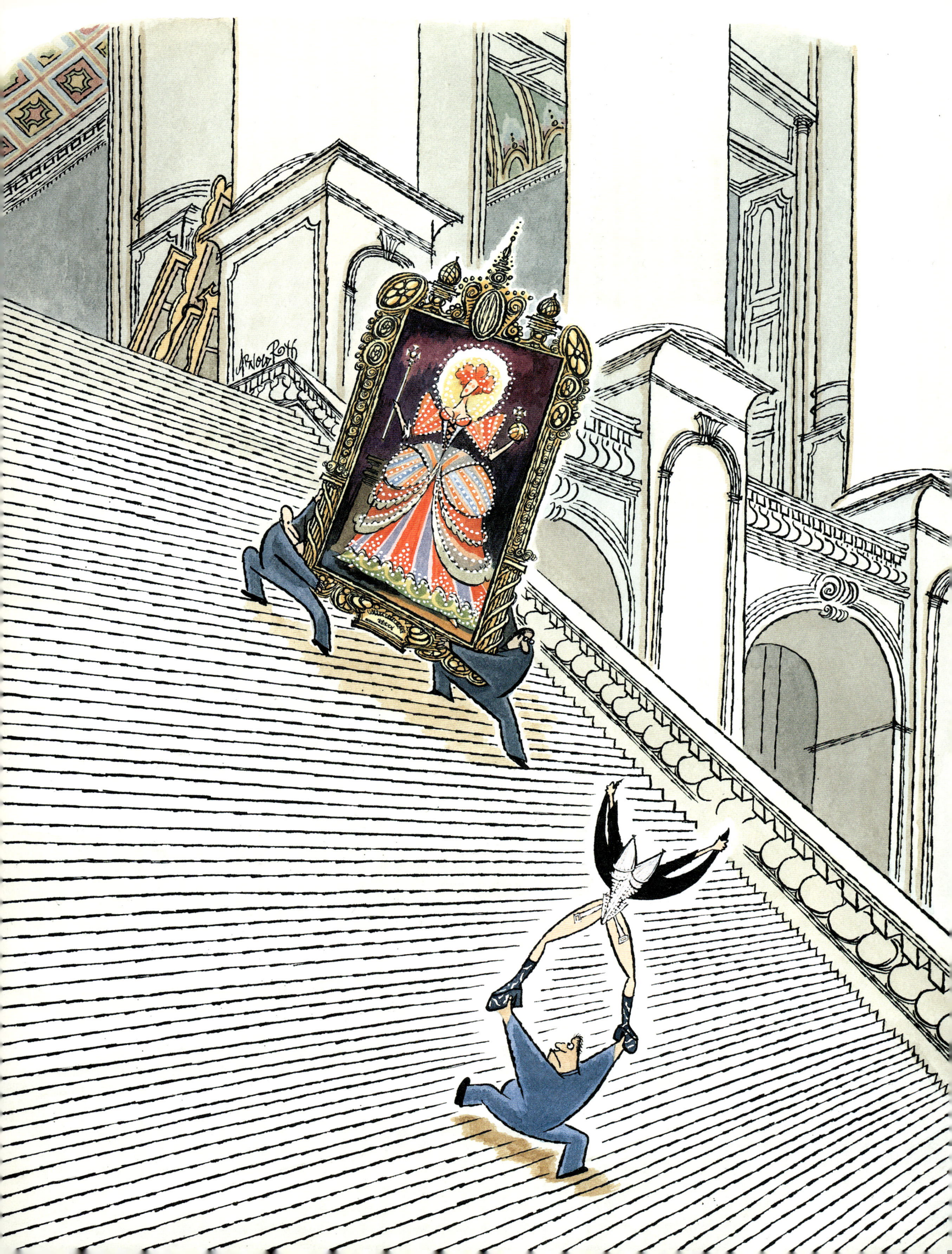

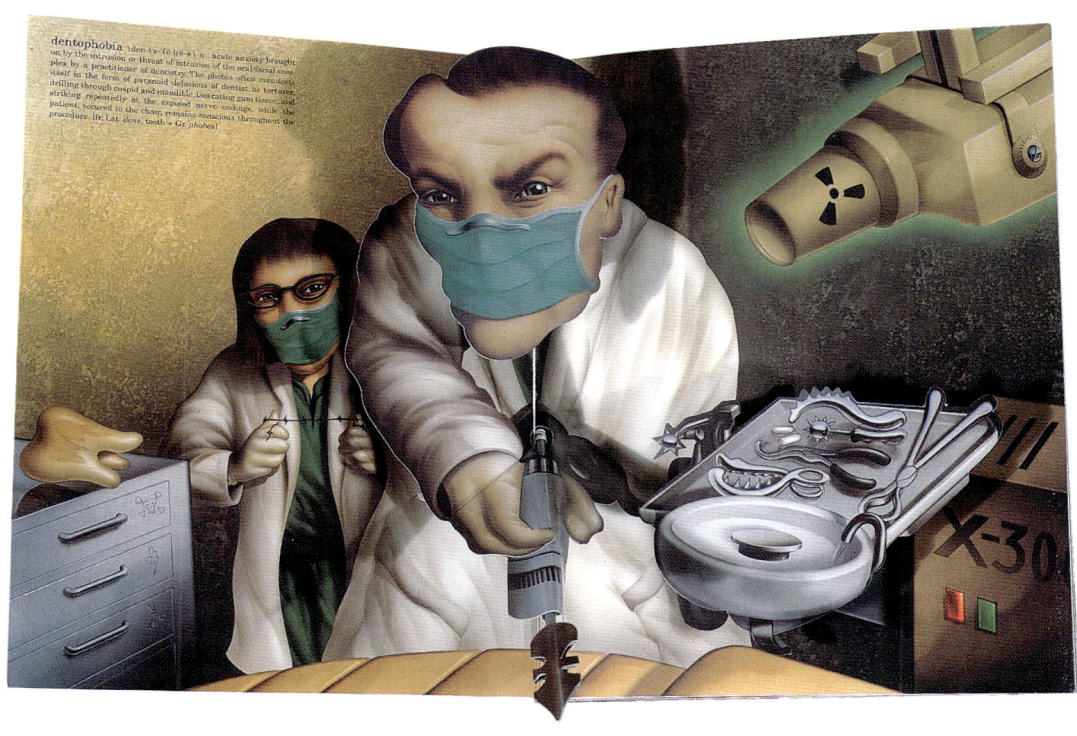

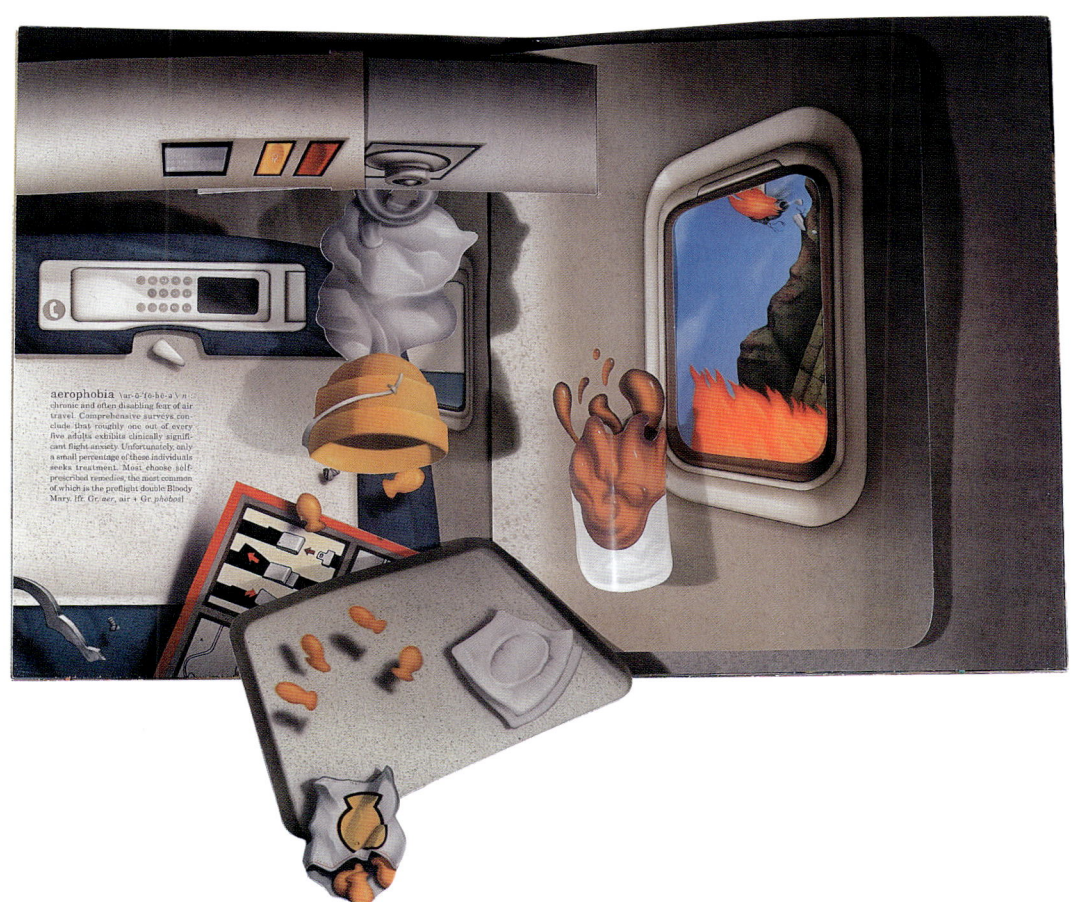

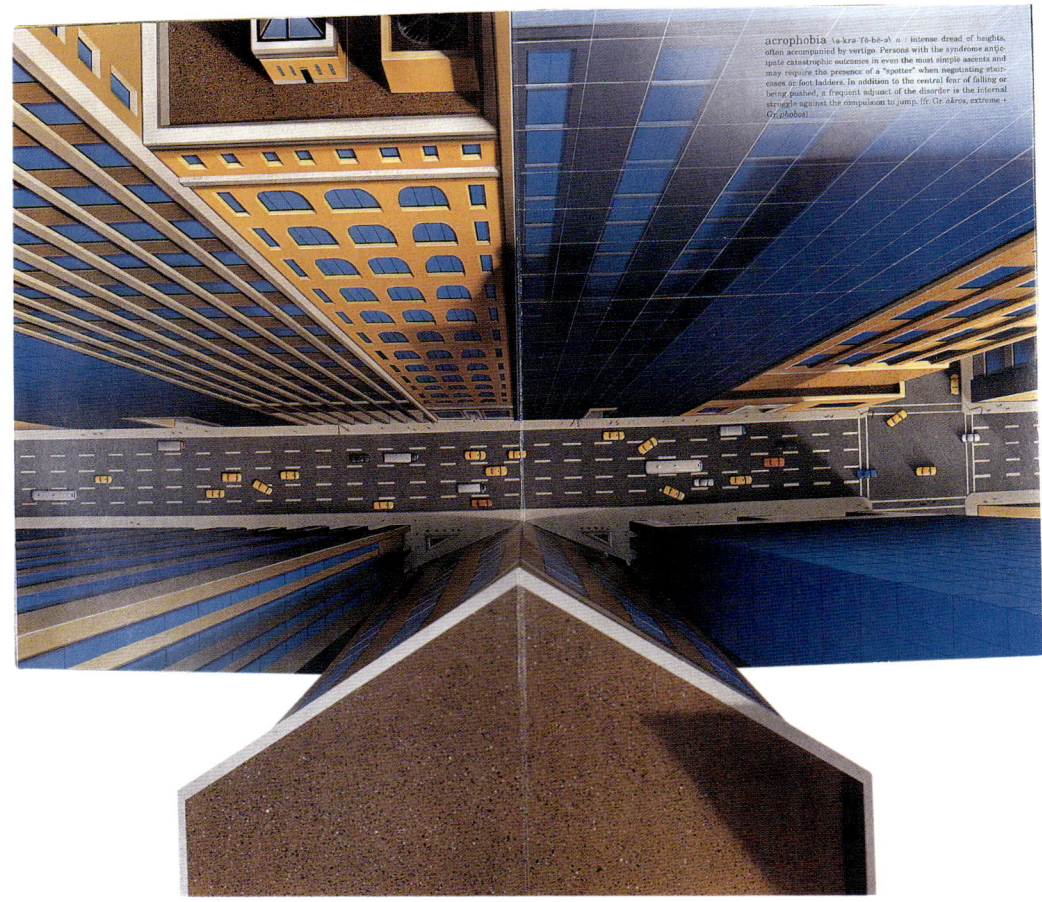

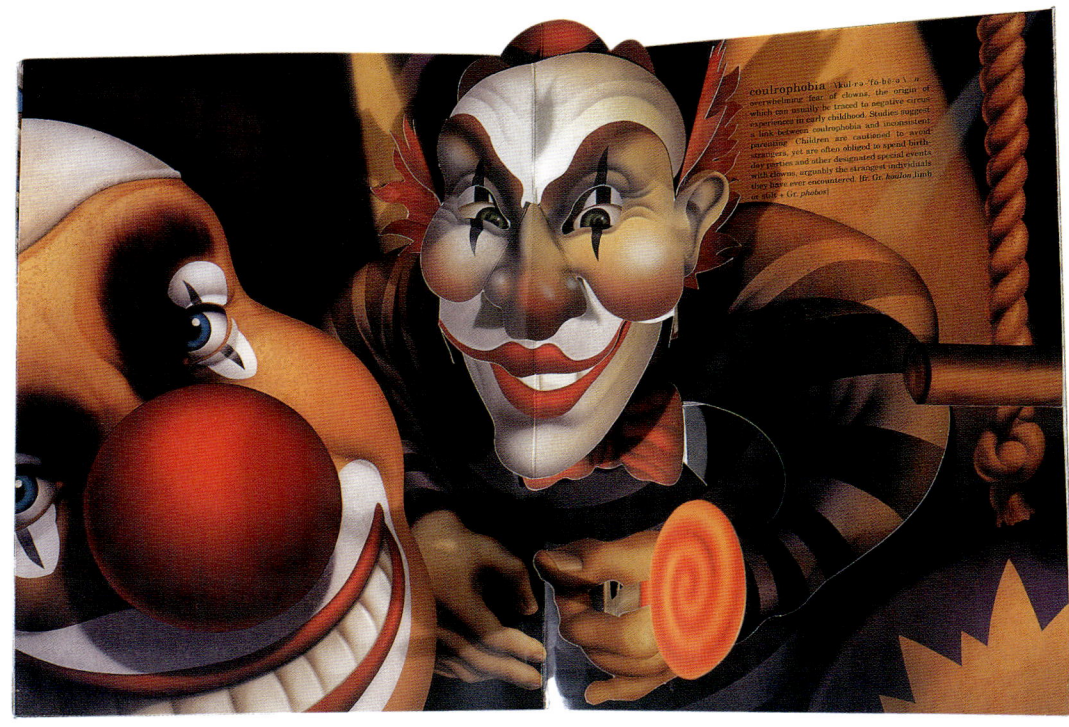

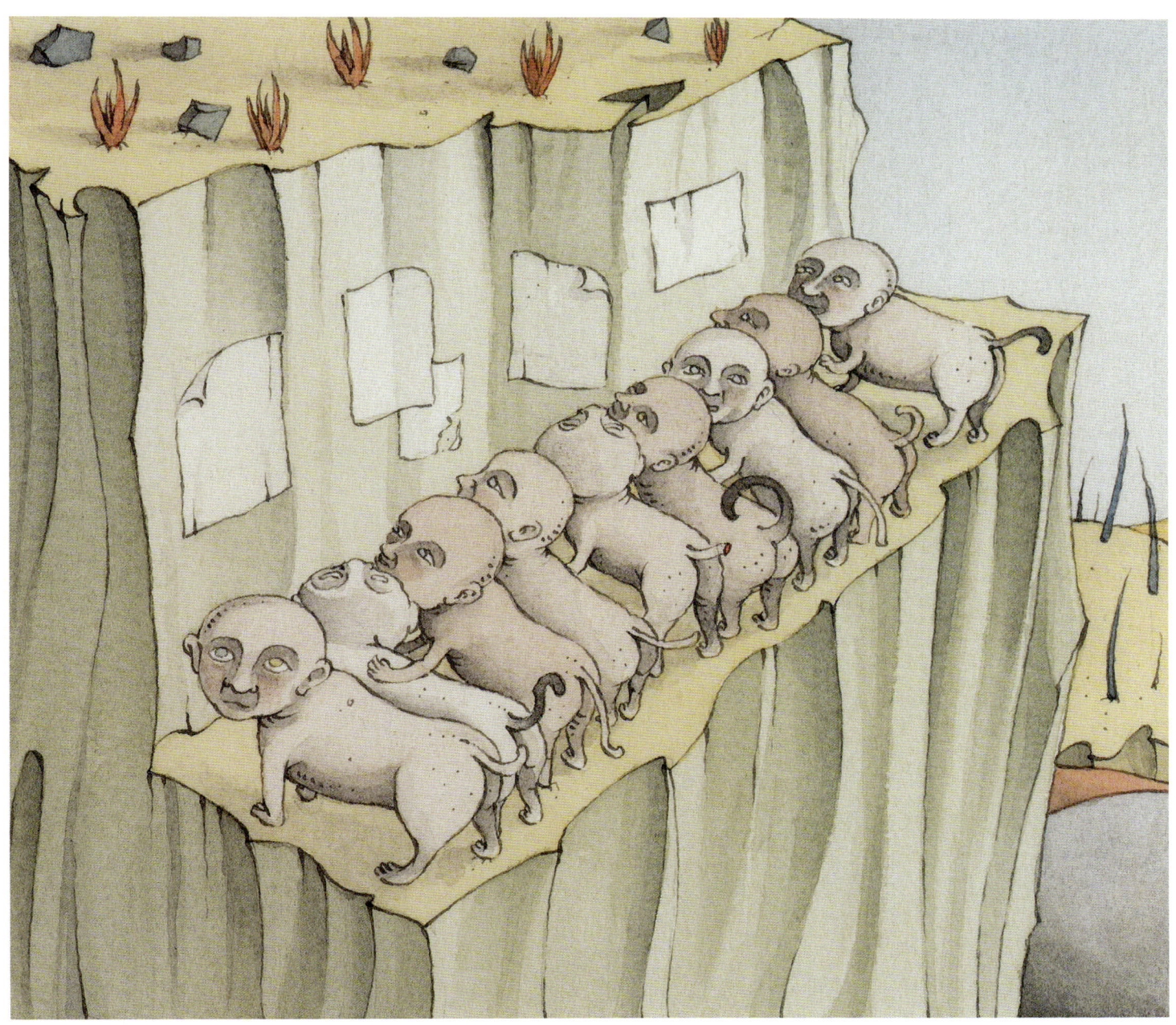

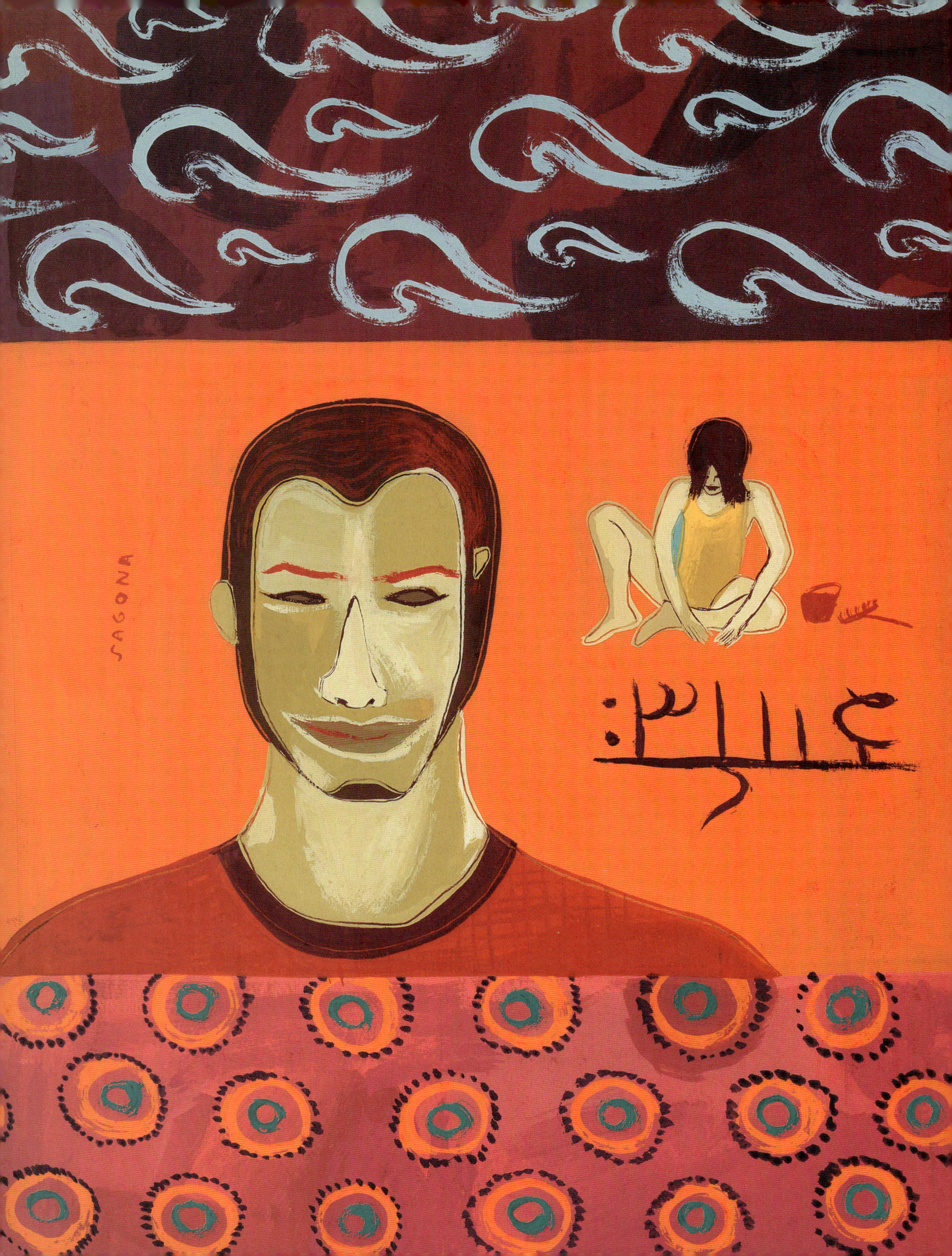

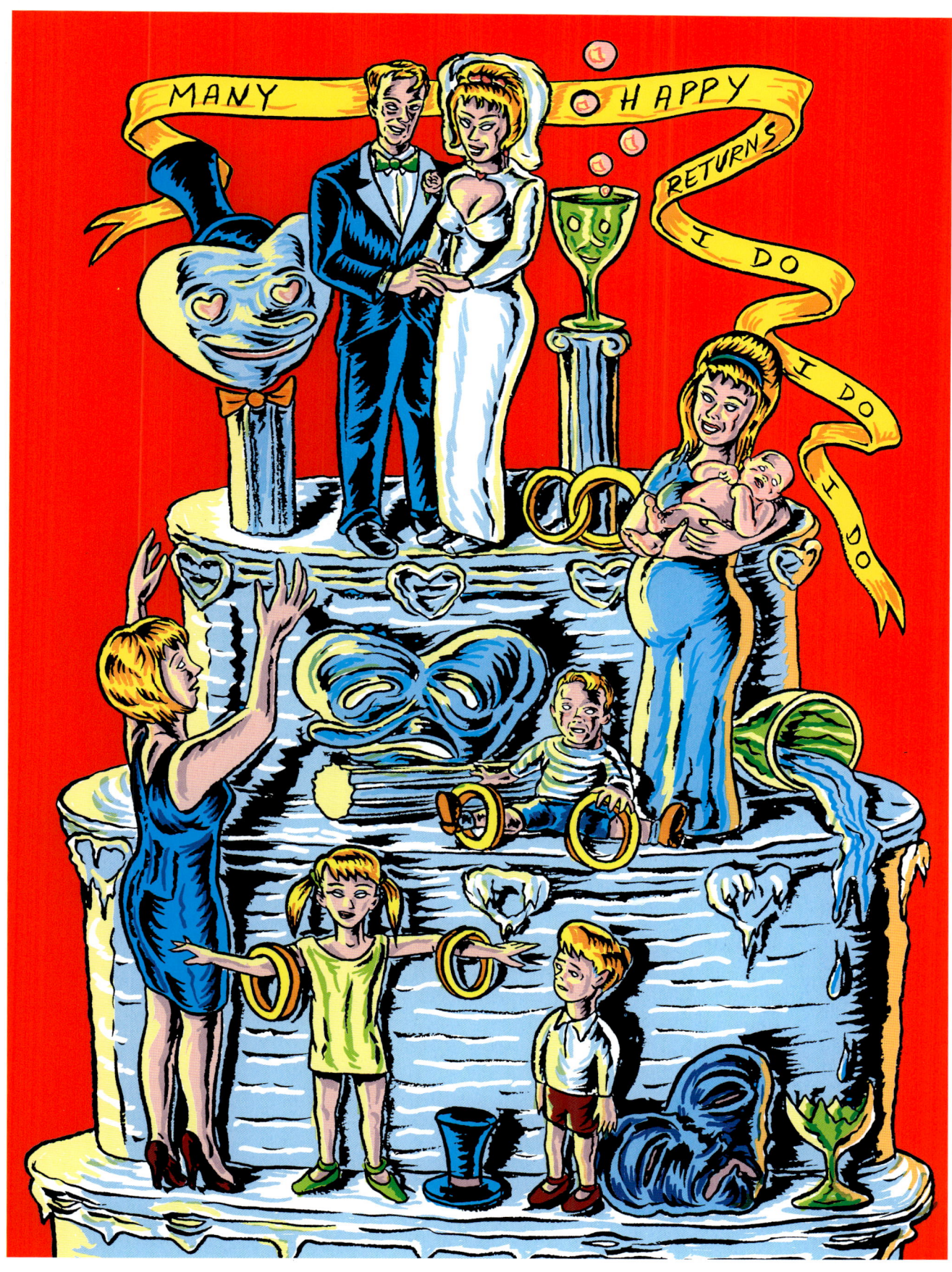

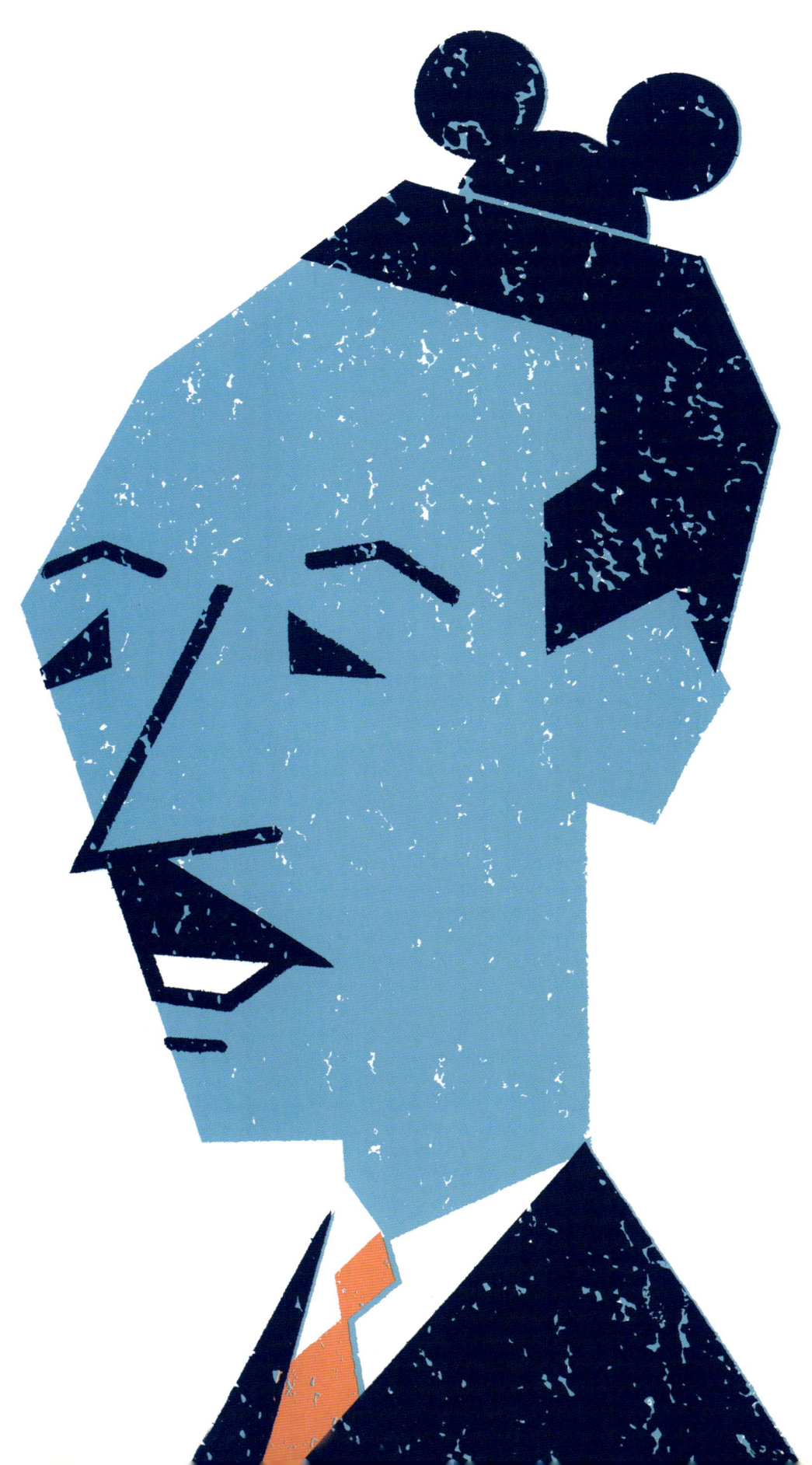

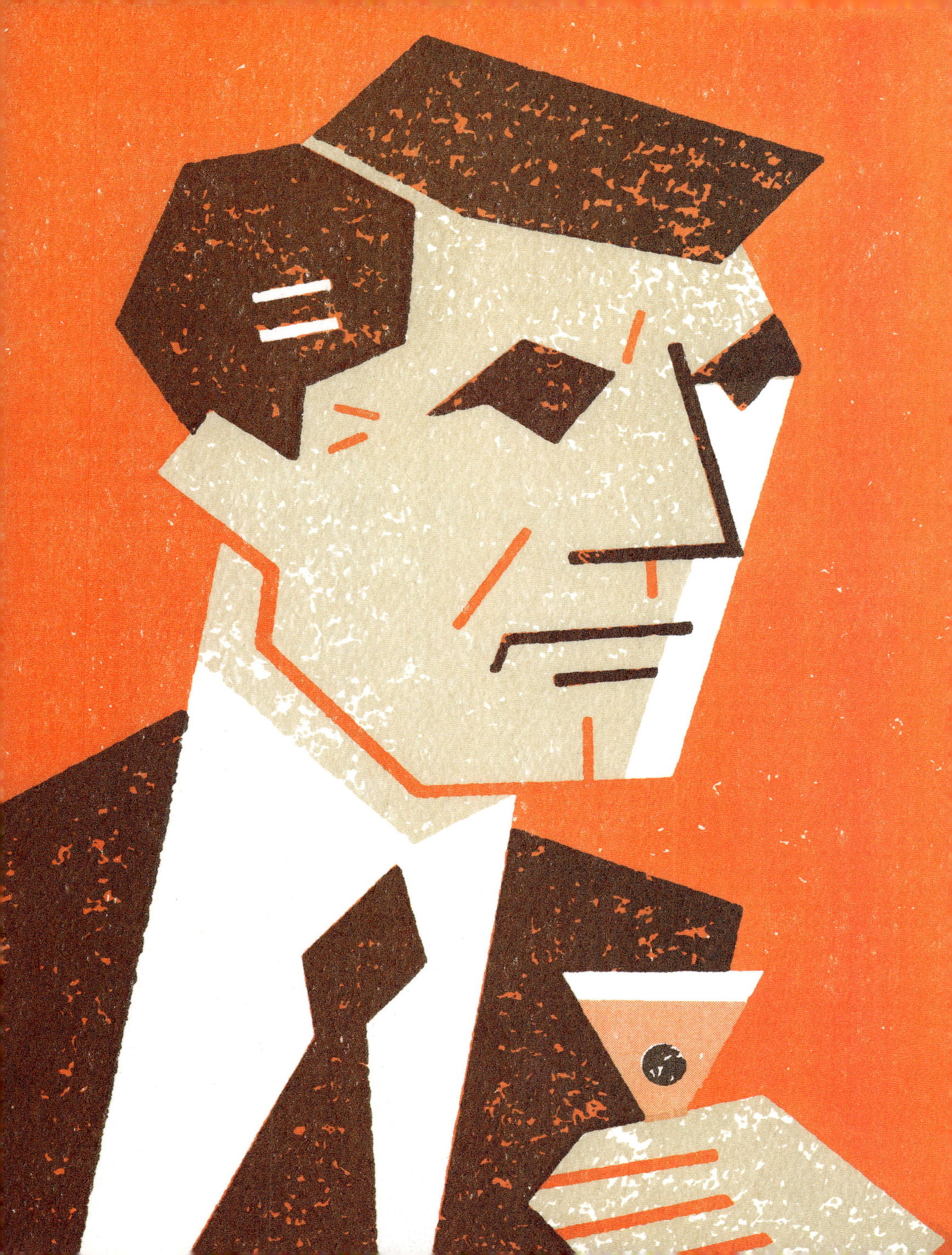

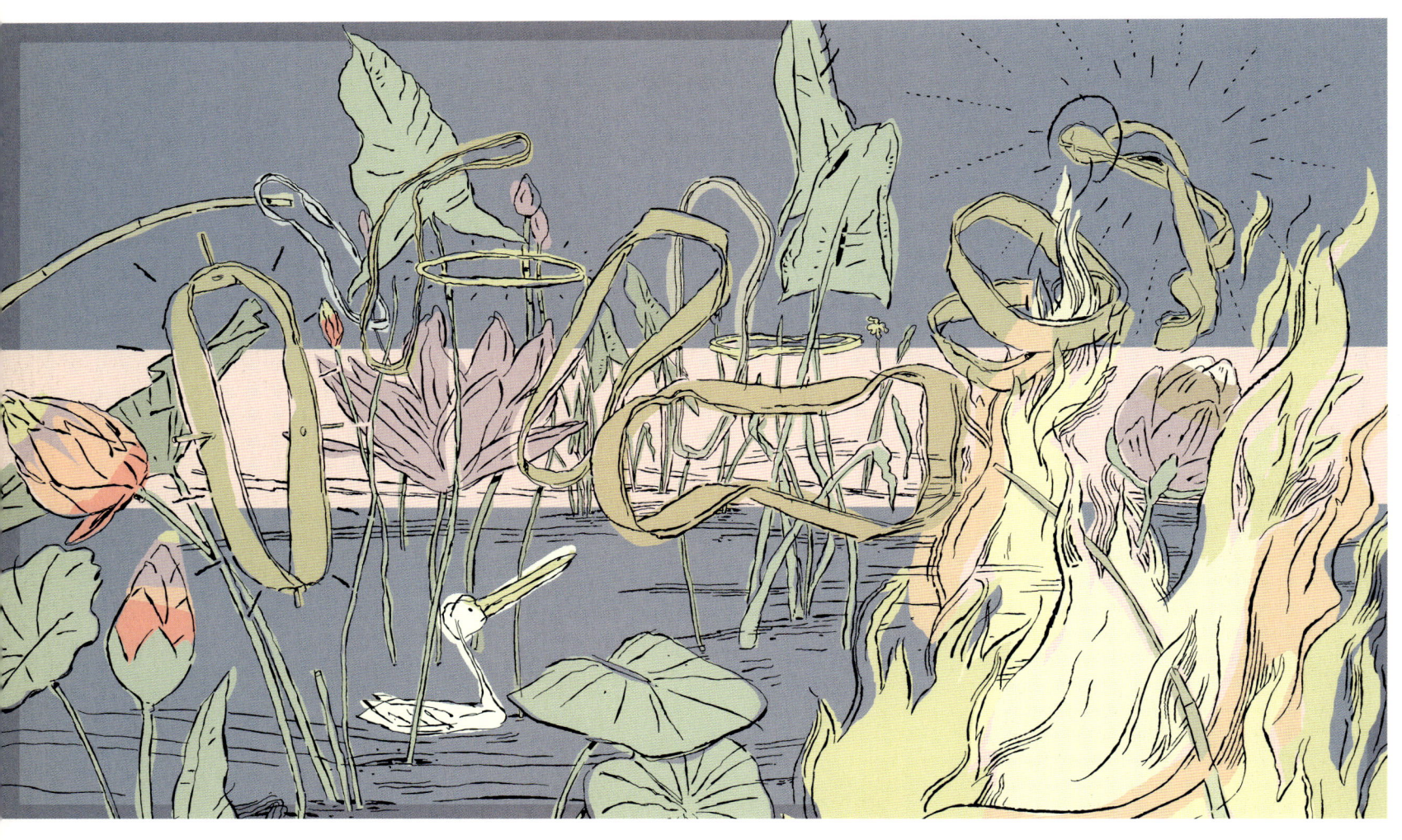

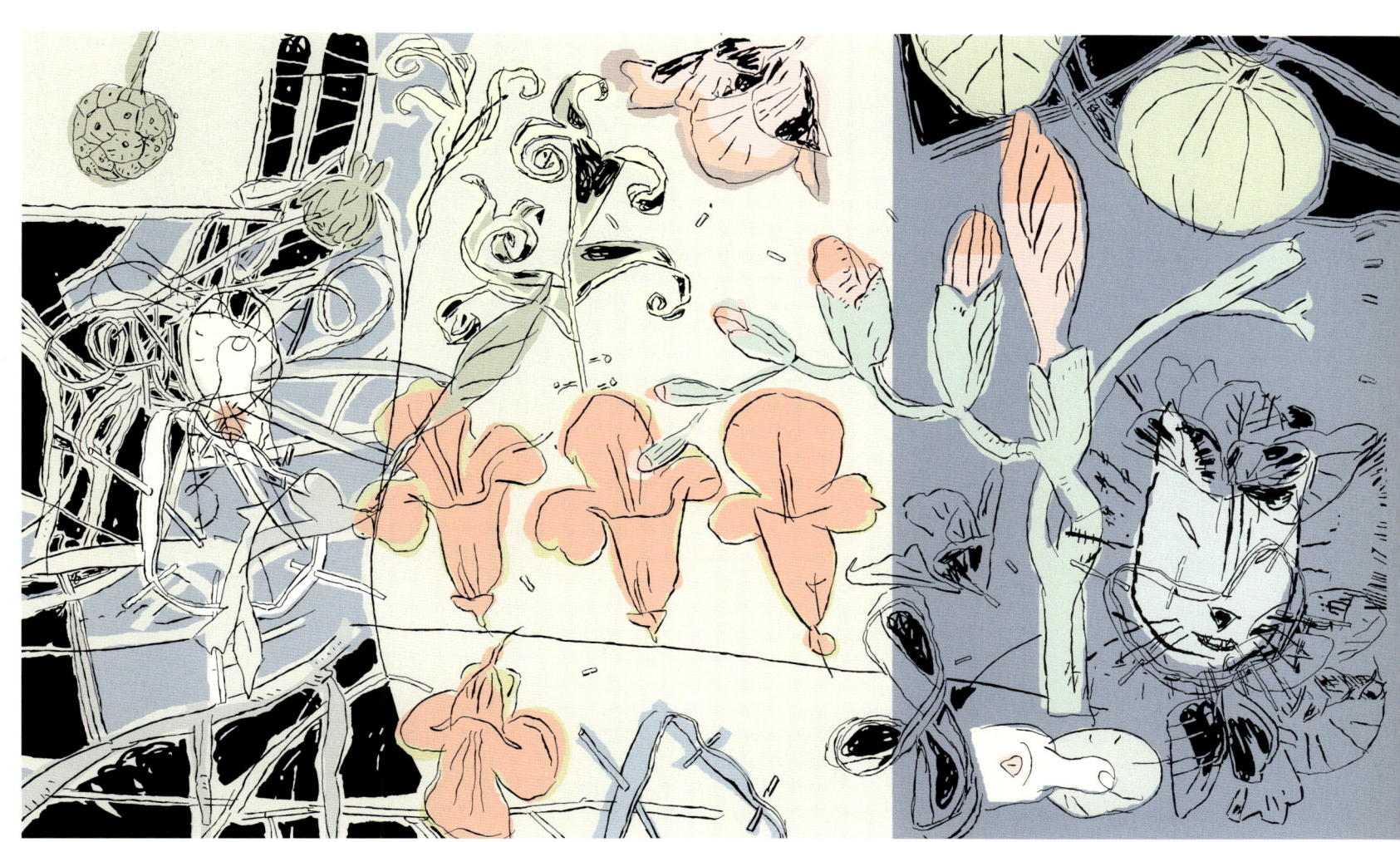

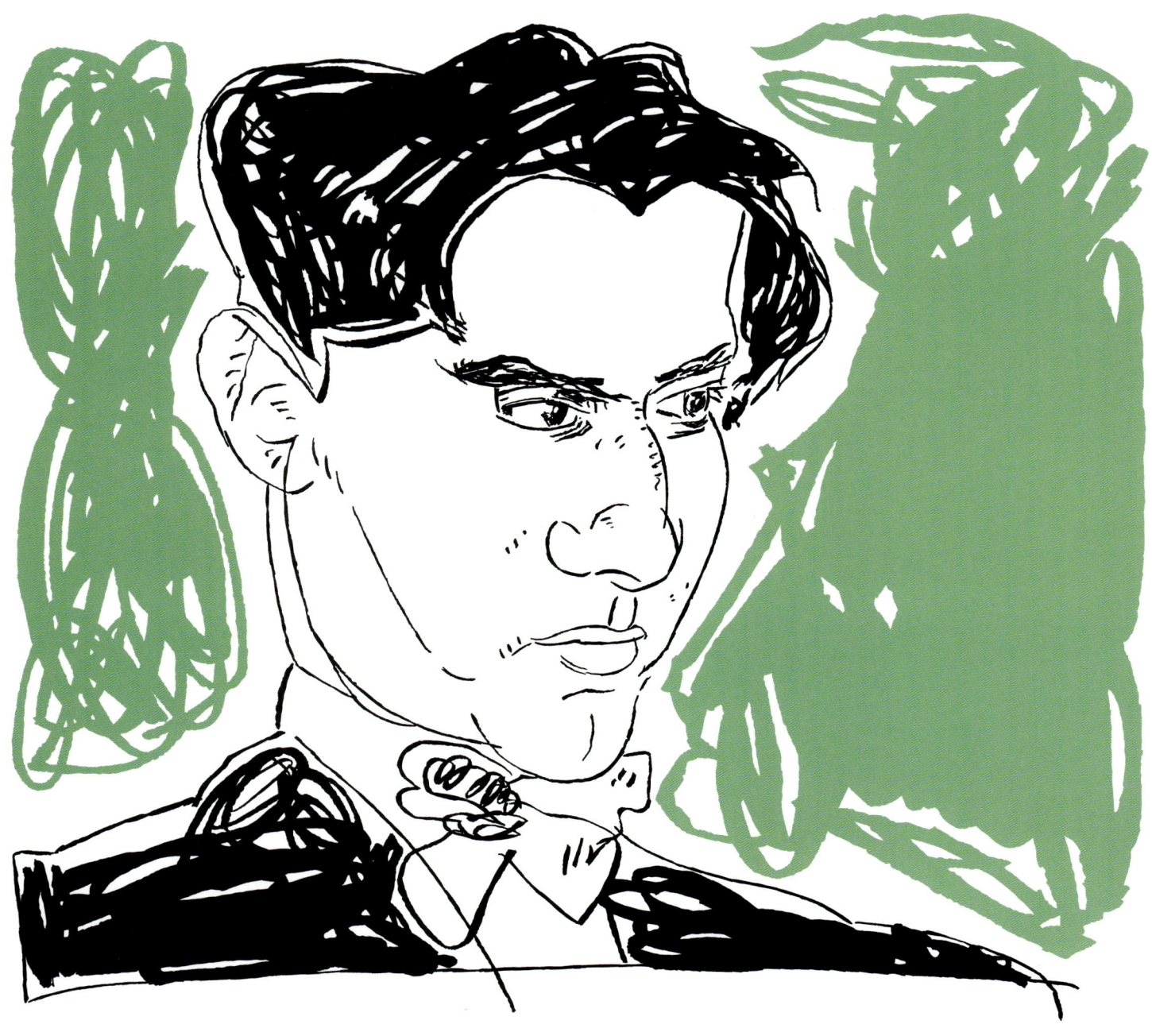

289 wardschumaker

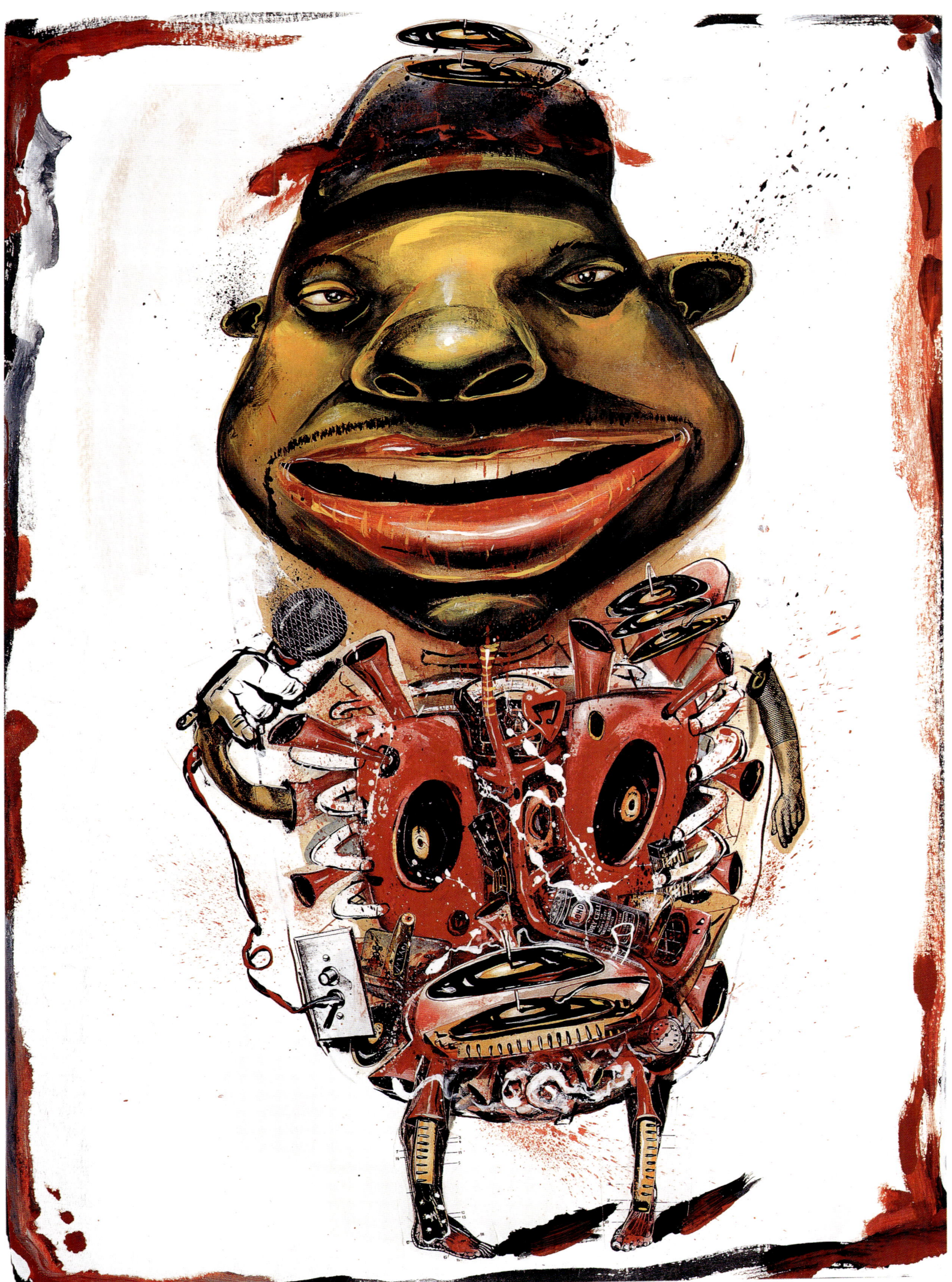

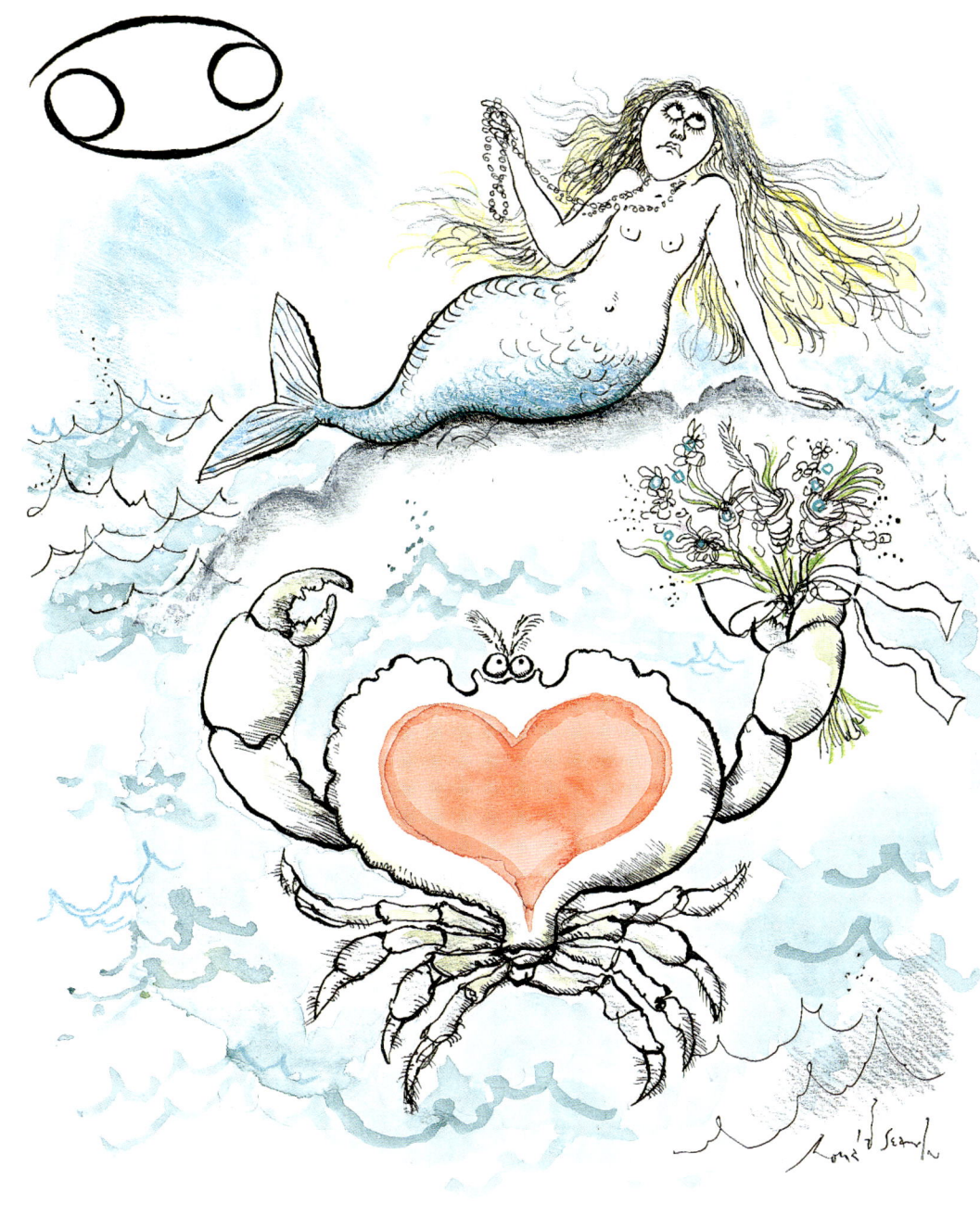

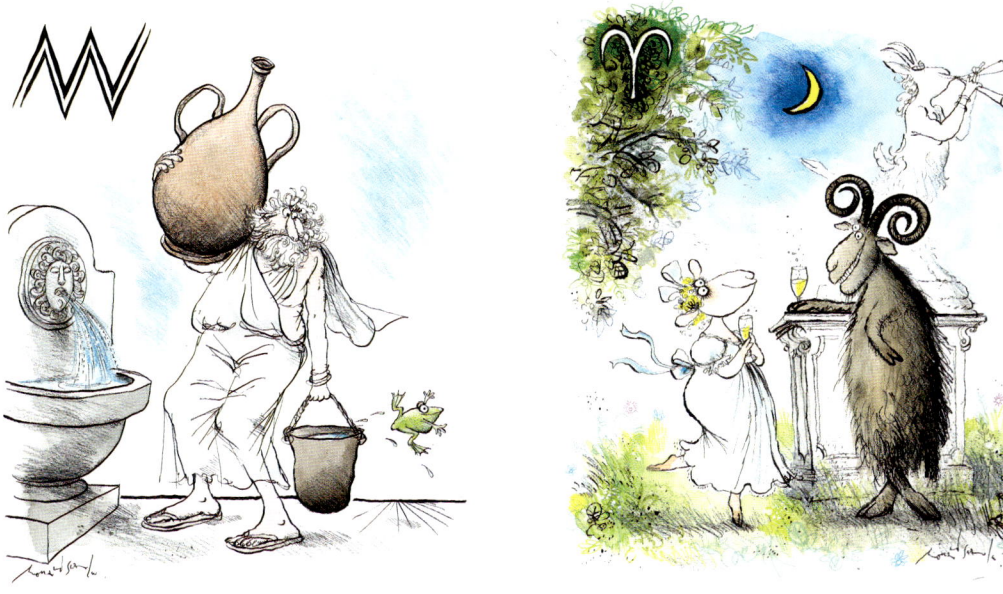

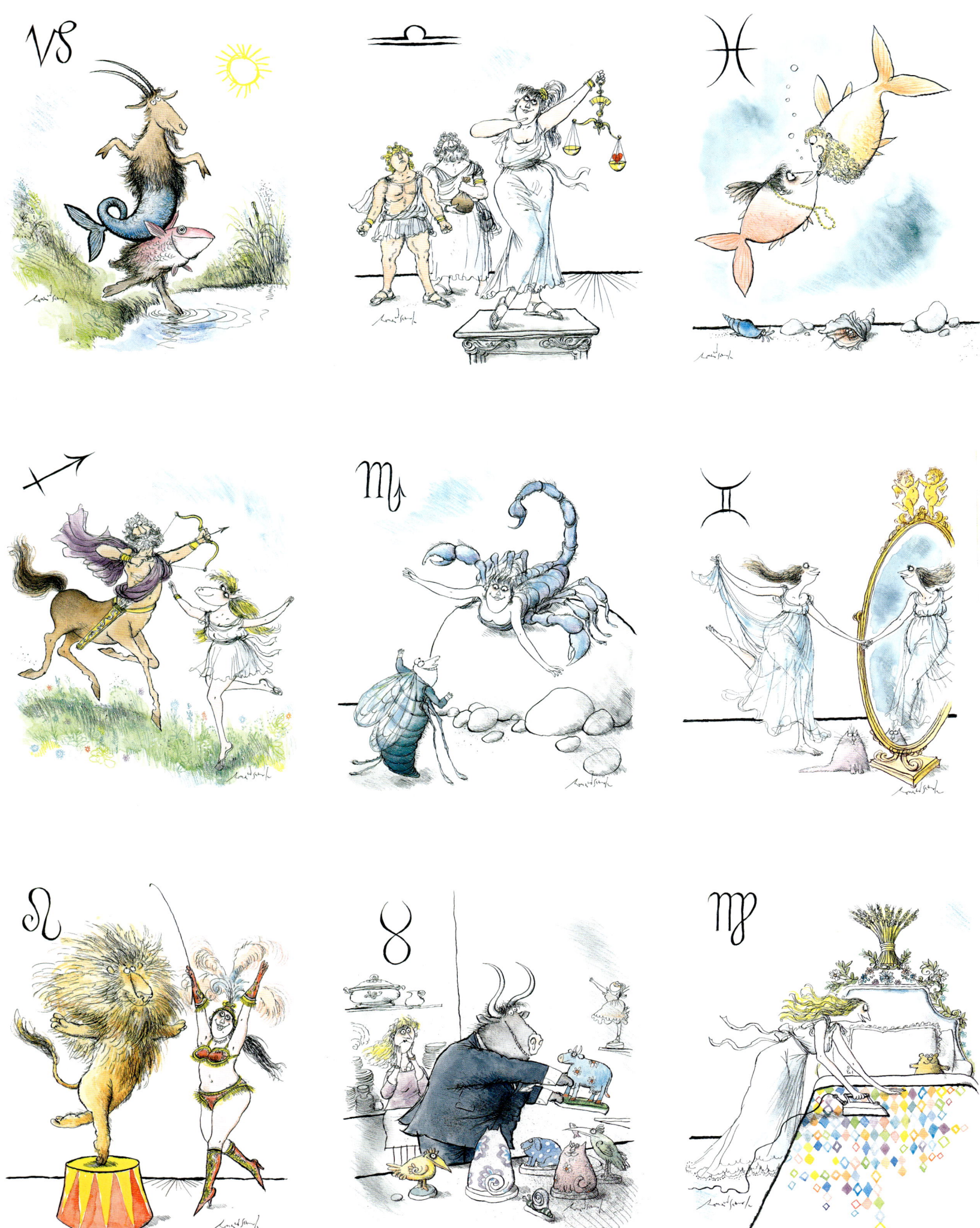

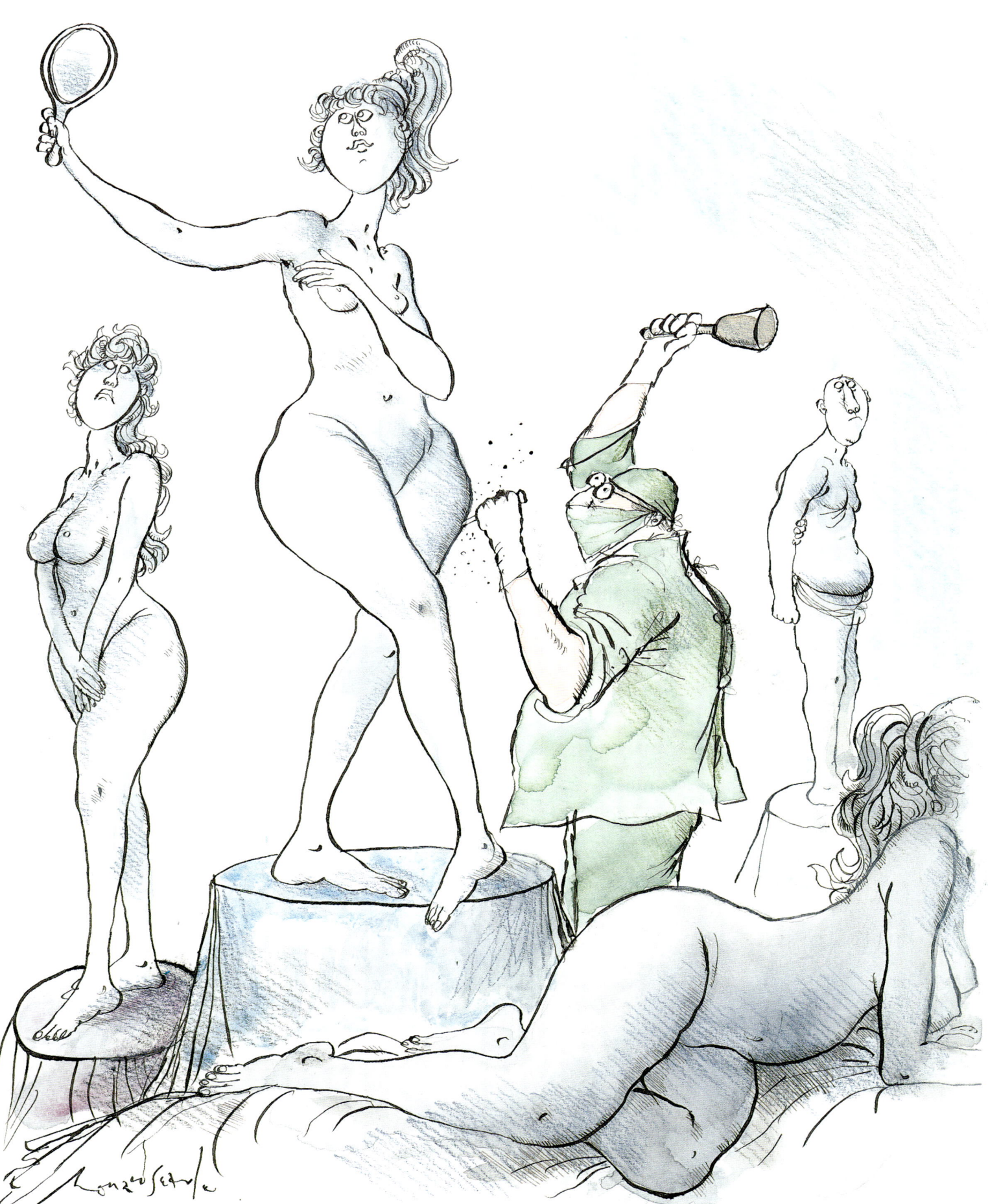

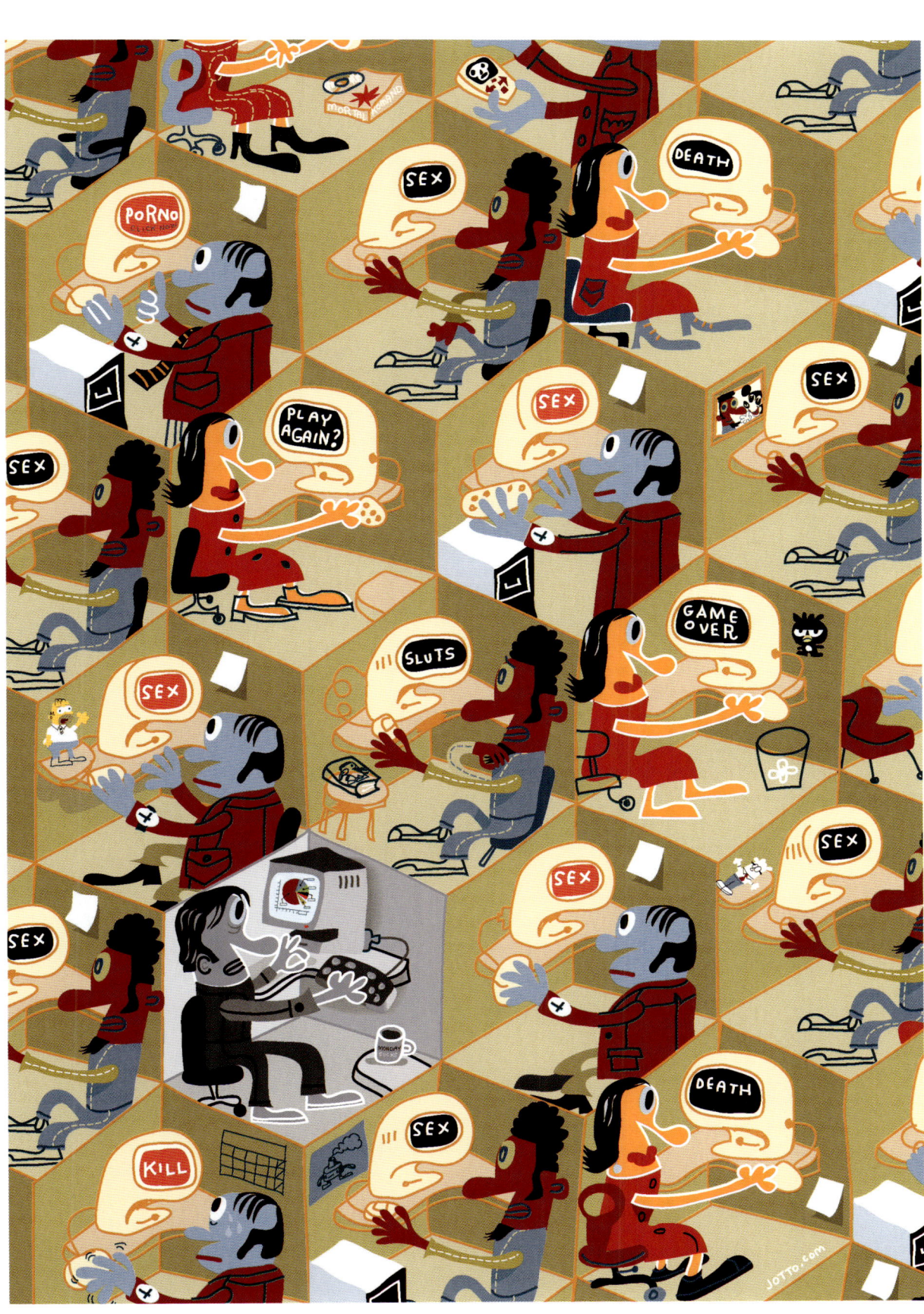

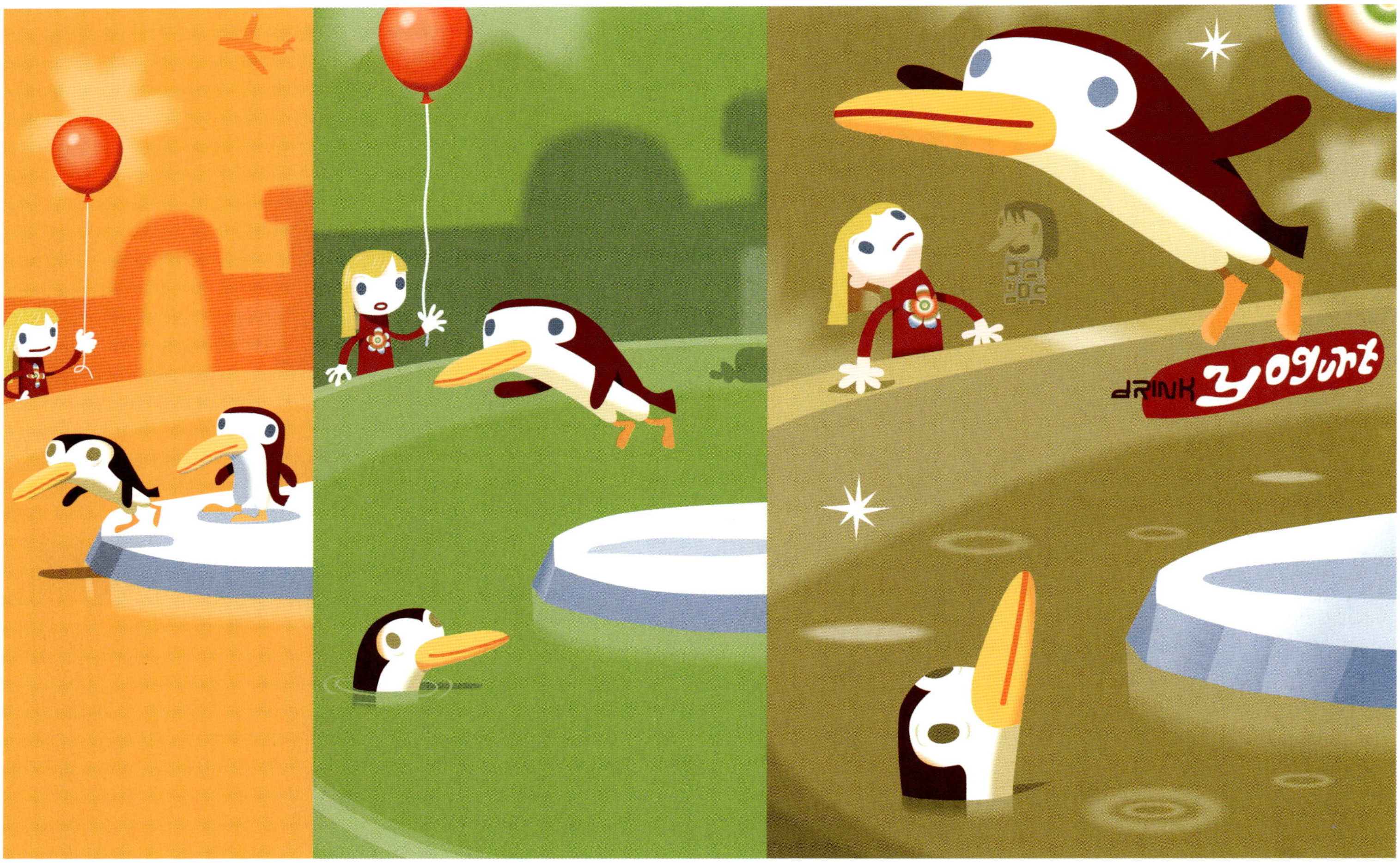
DRINK Yogurt

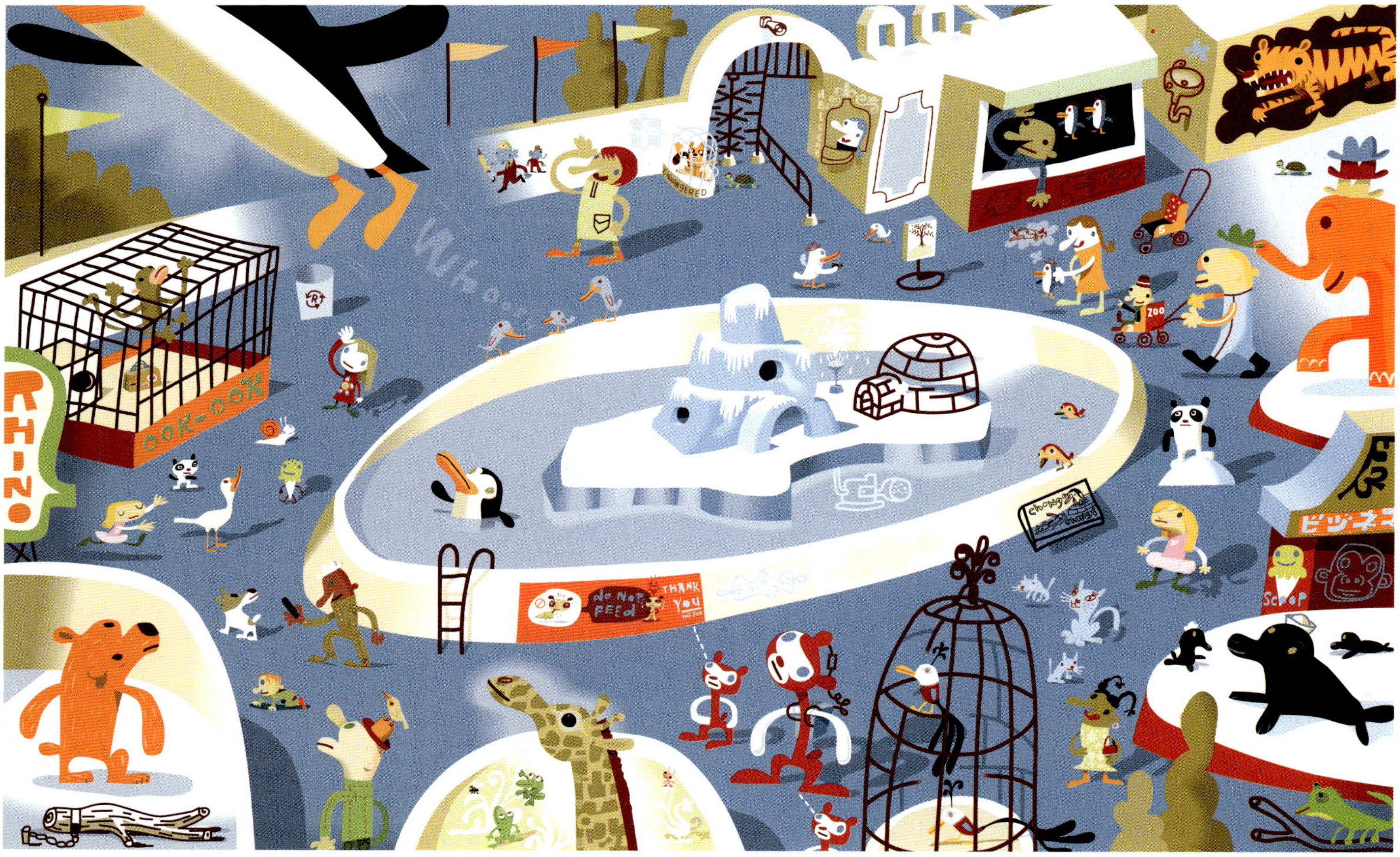
RHINO
OOK-OOK
Whoosh
ZOO
do Not FEEd
THANK YOU
SCOOP
ビッネス

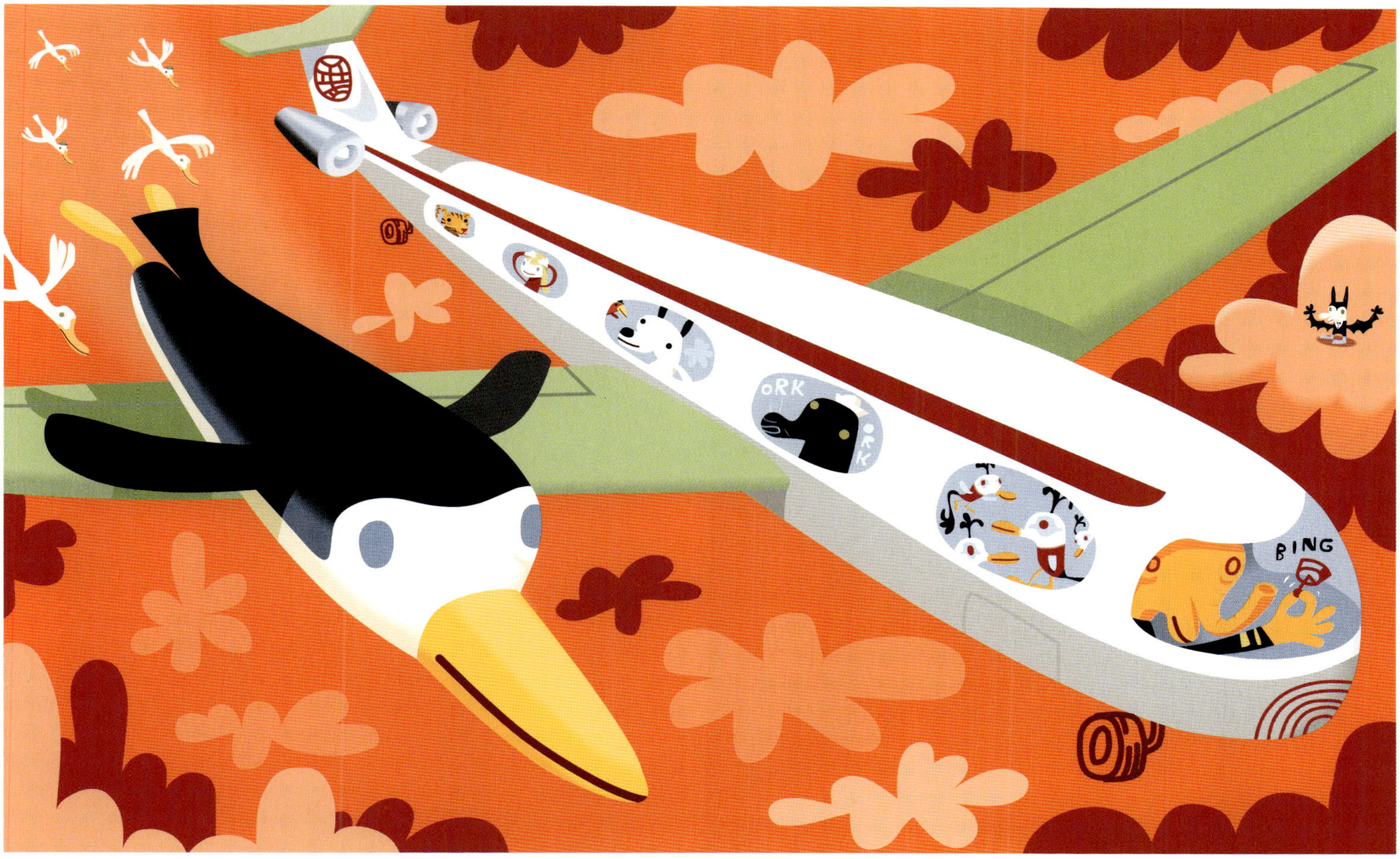
ORK
ORK
BING

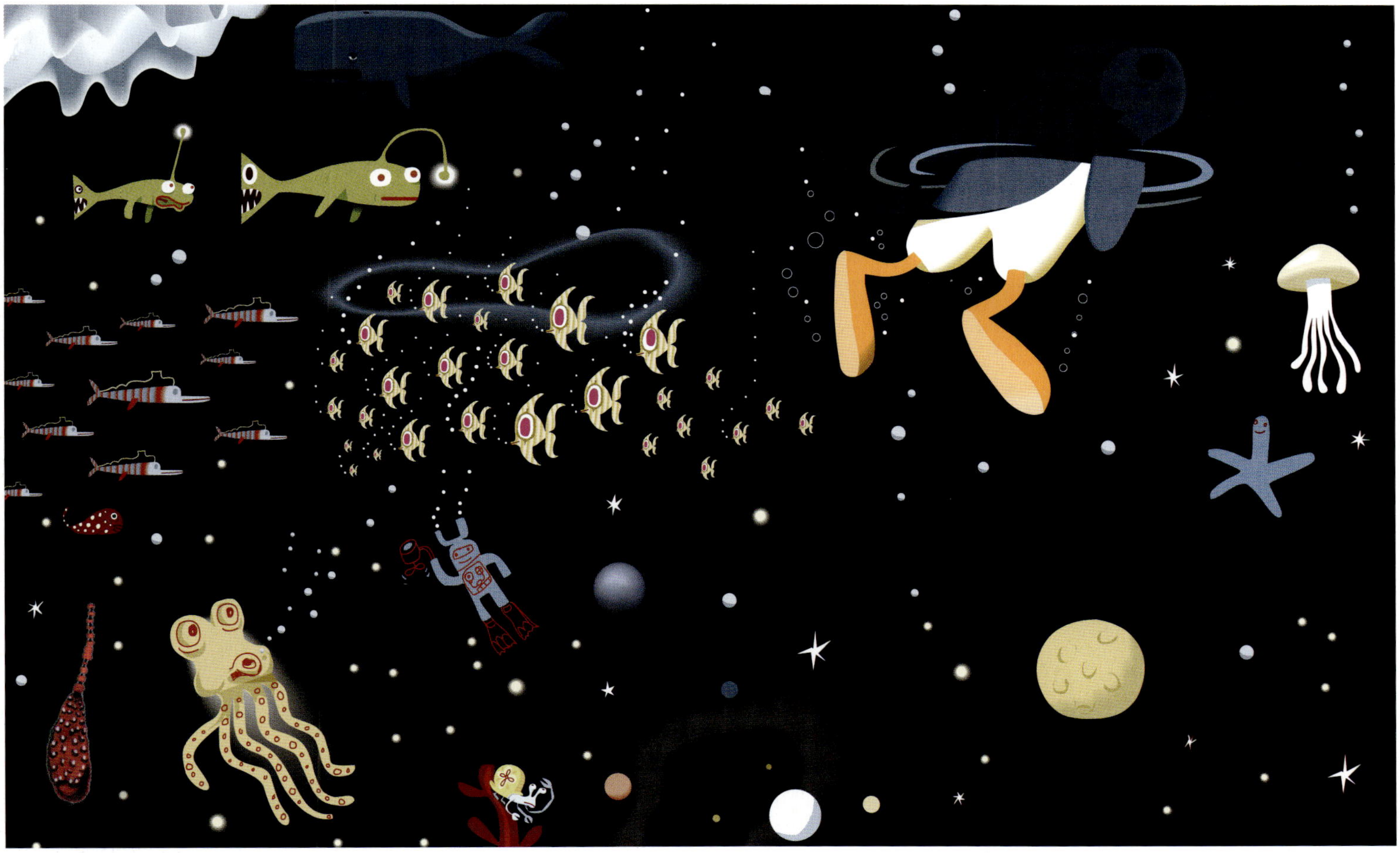

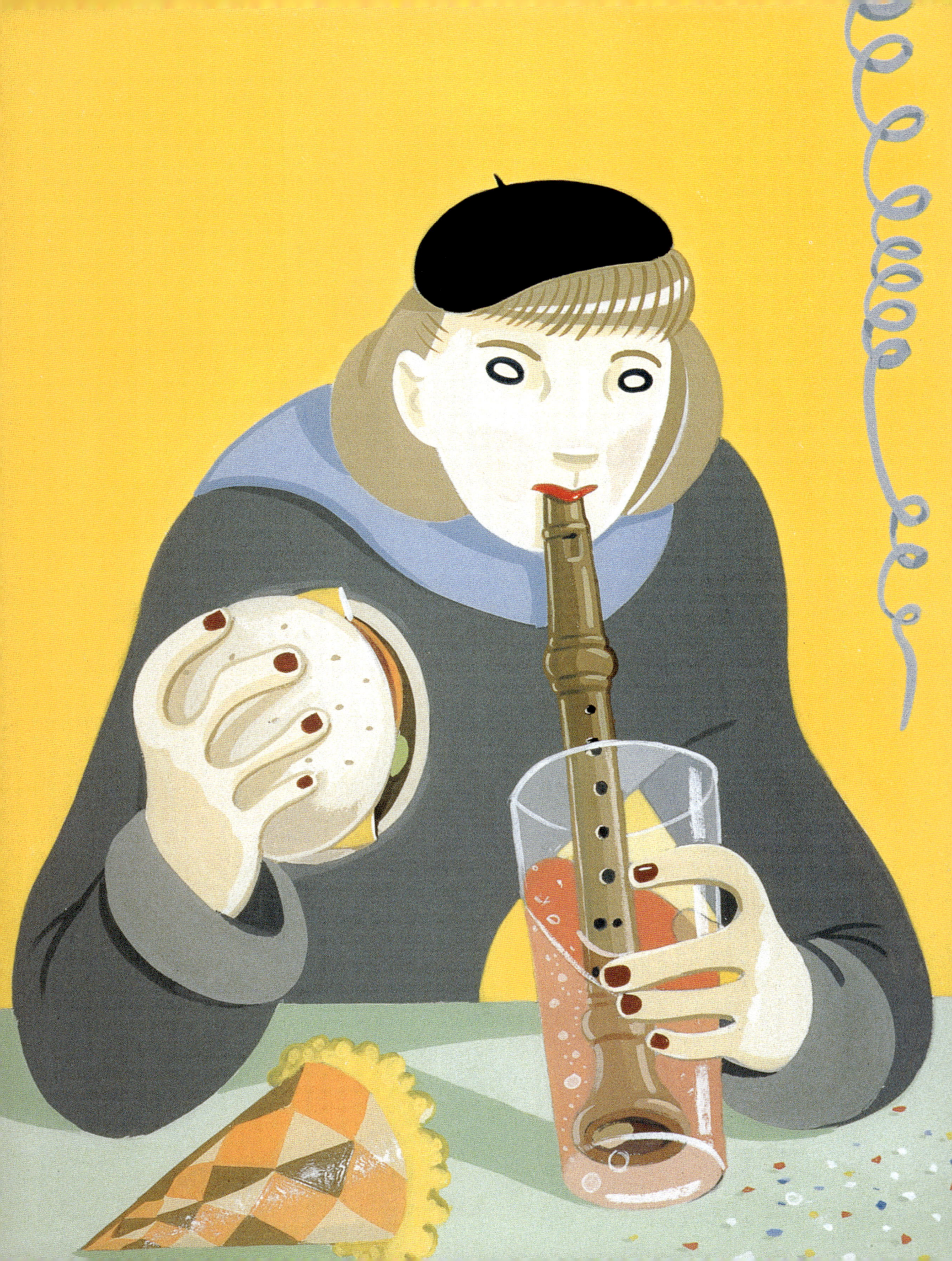

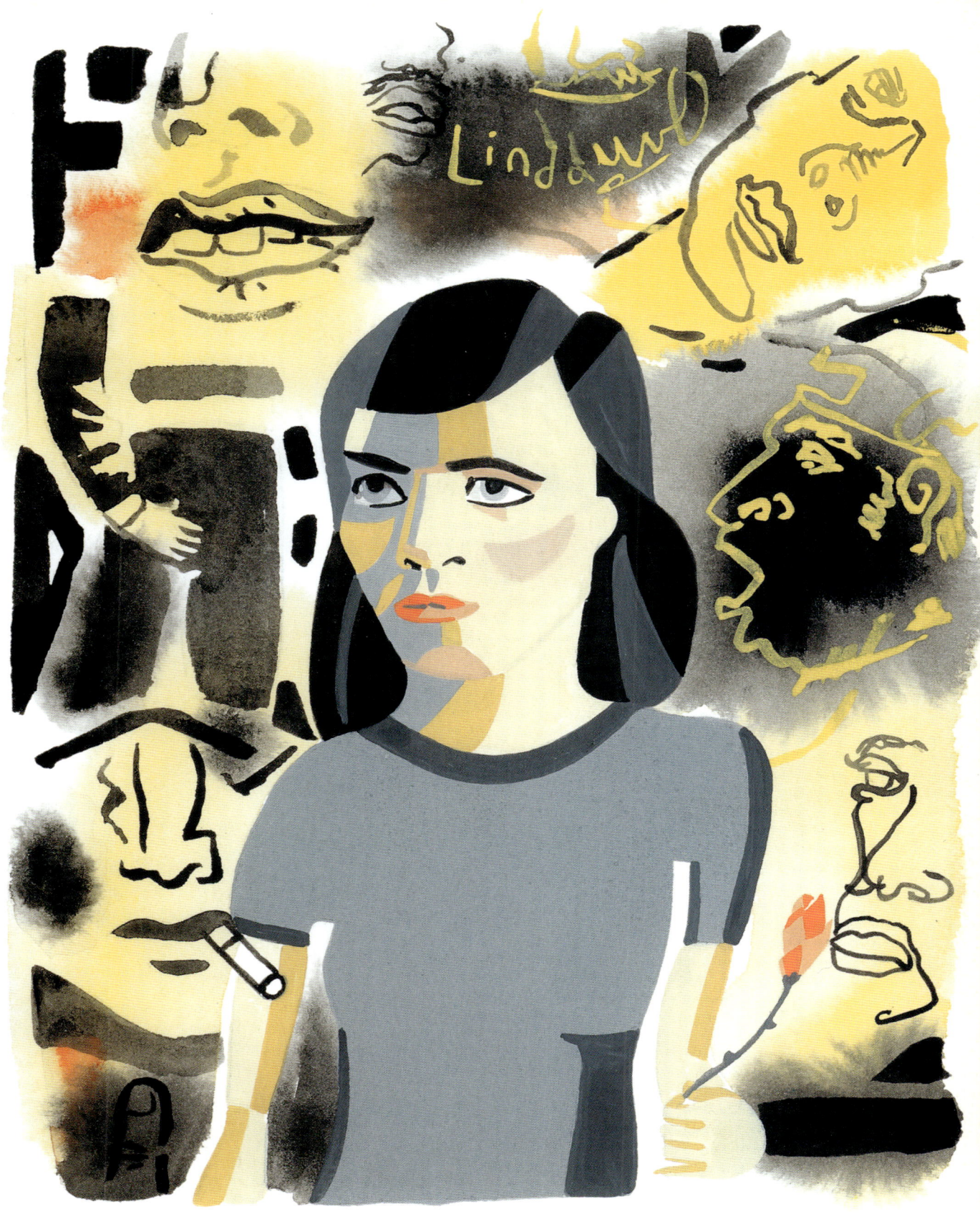

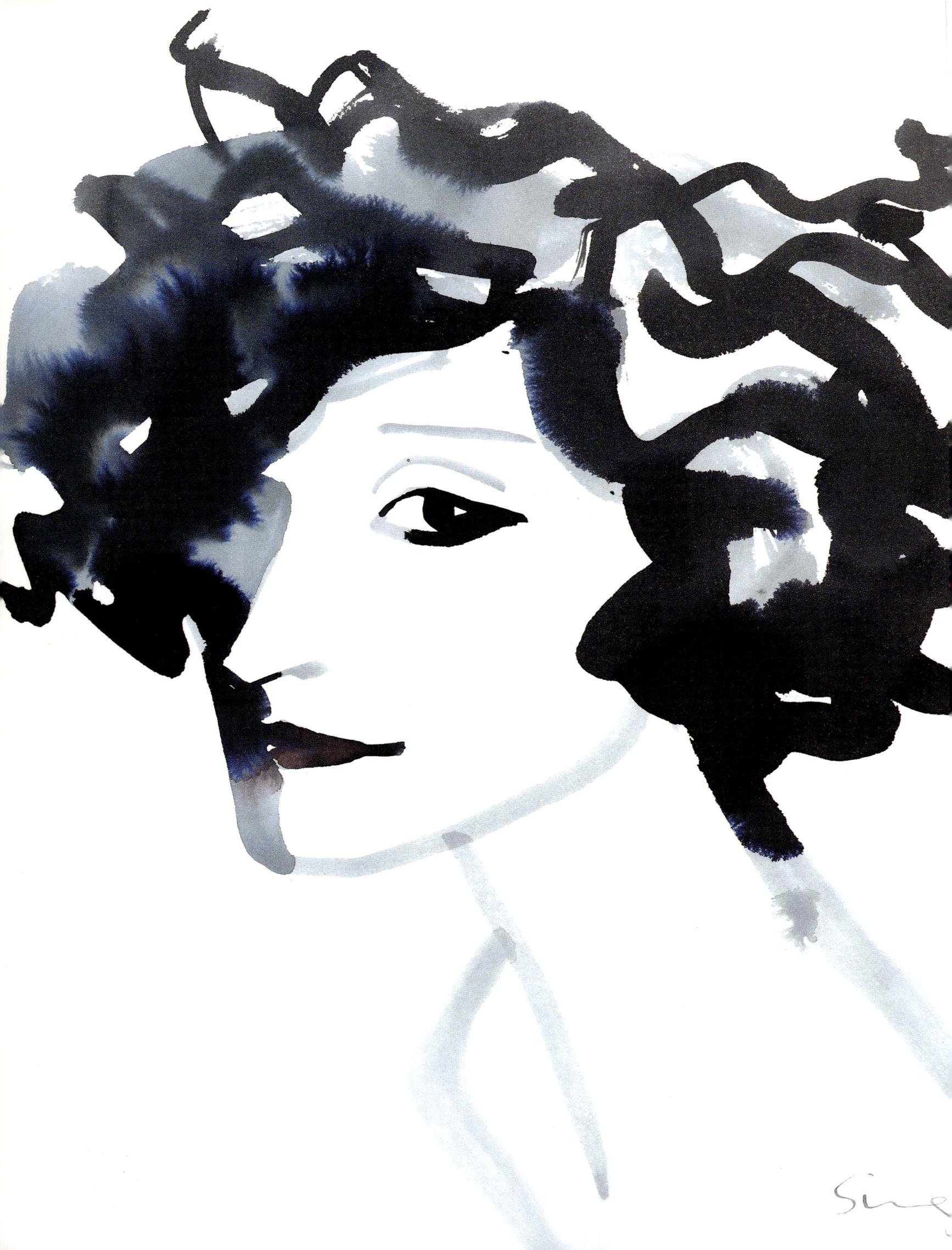

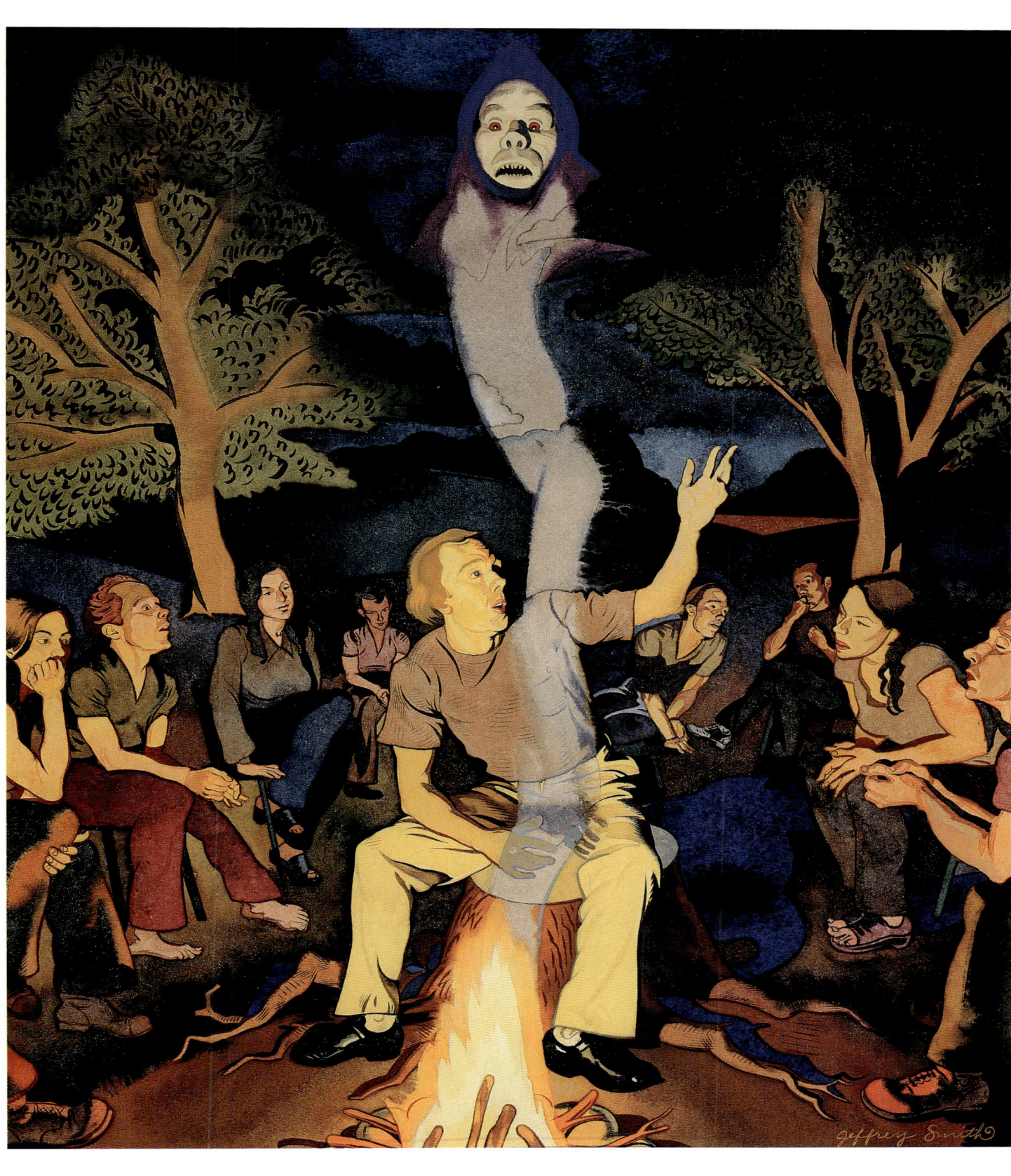

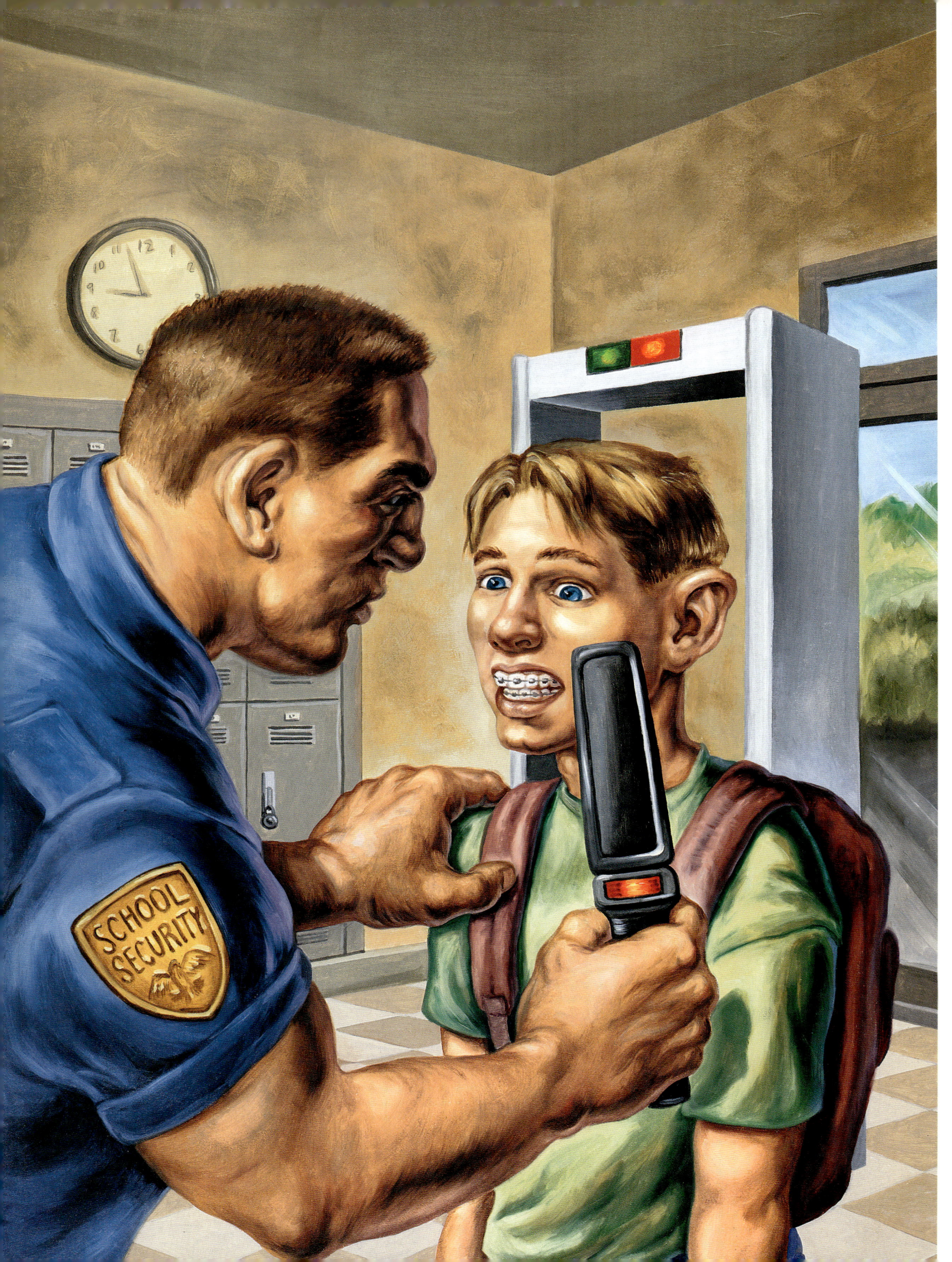

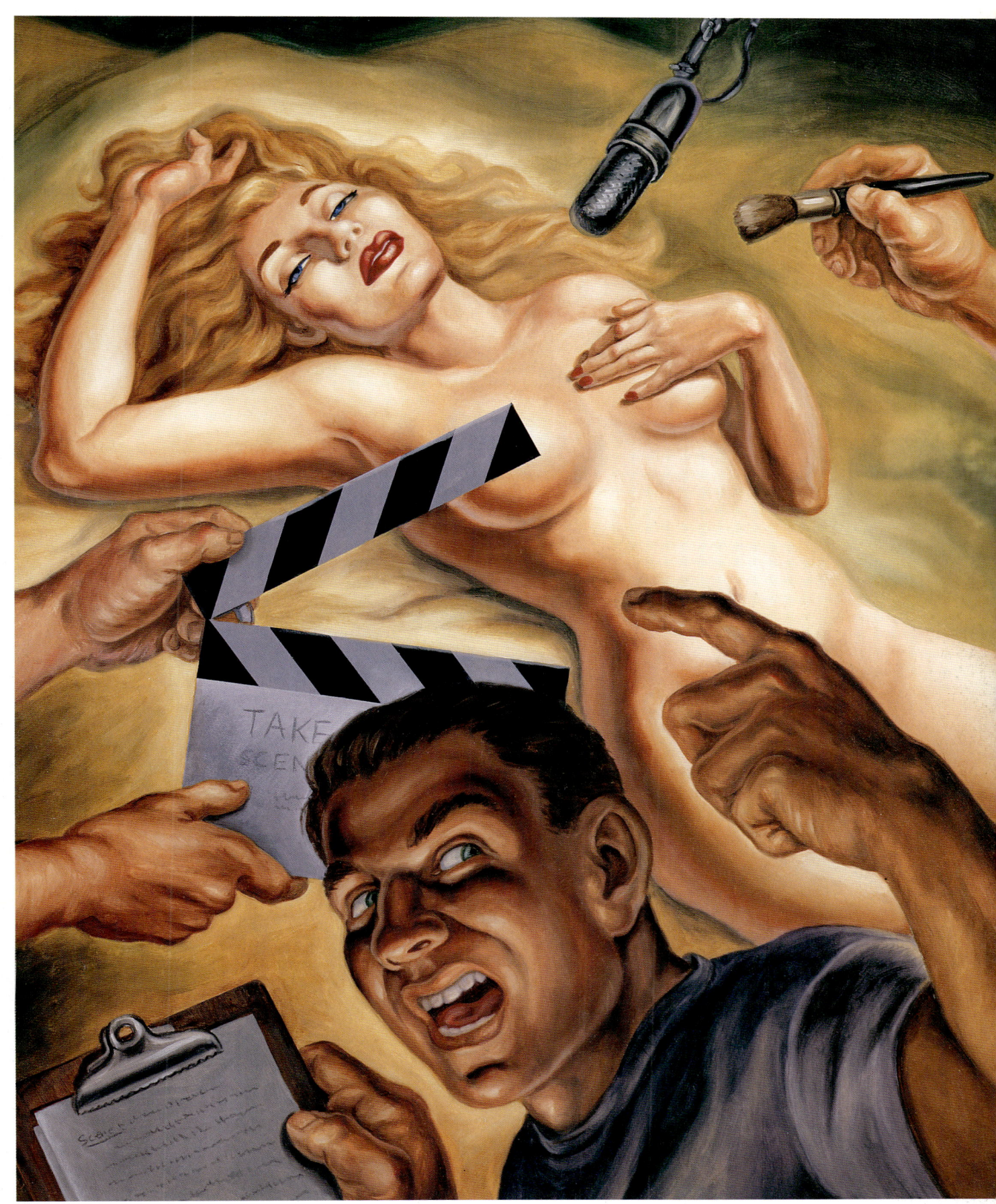

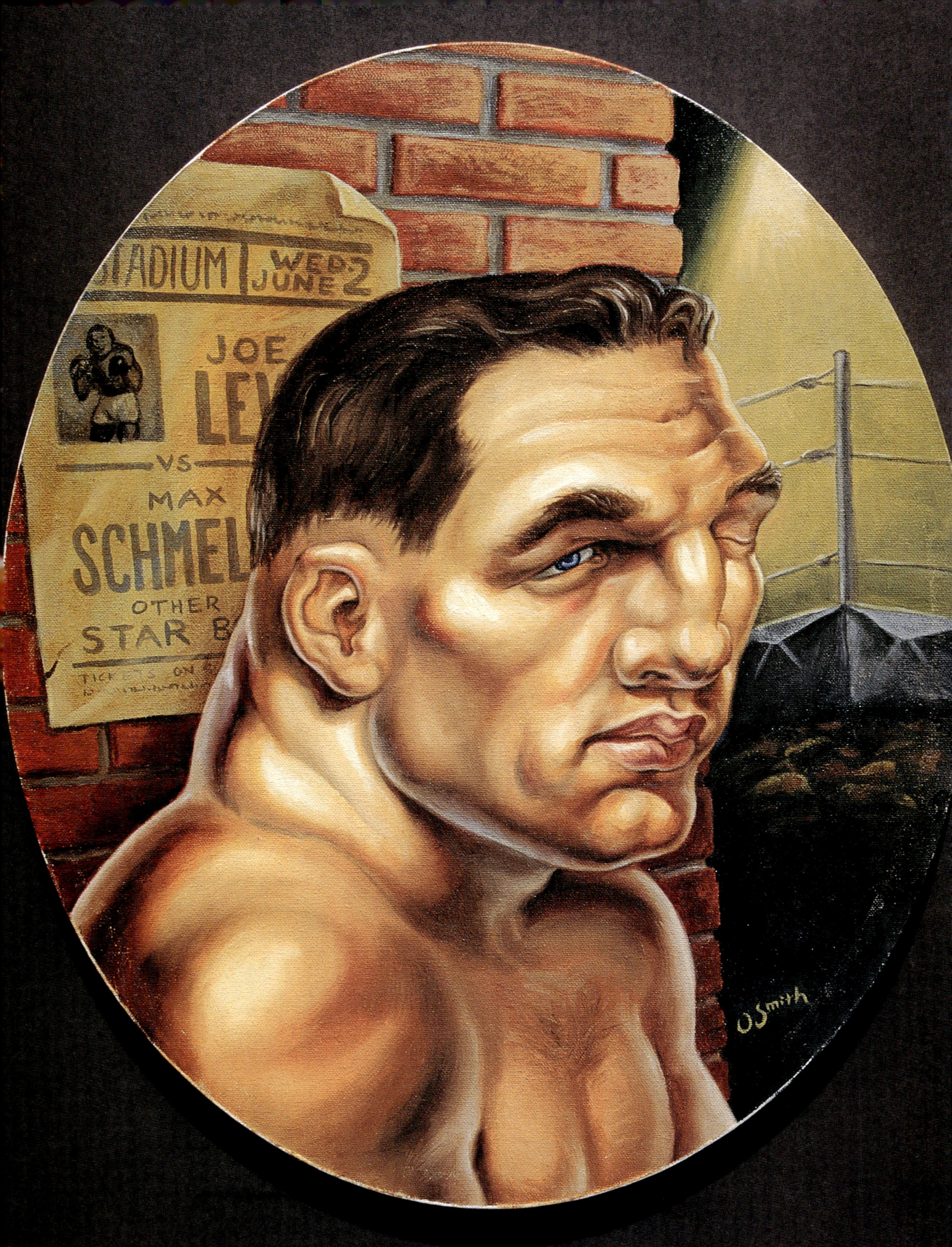

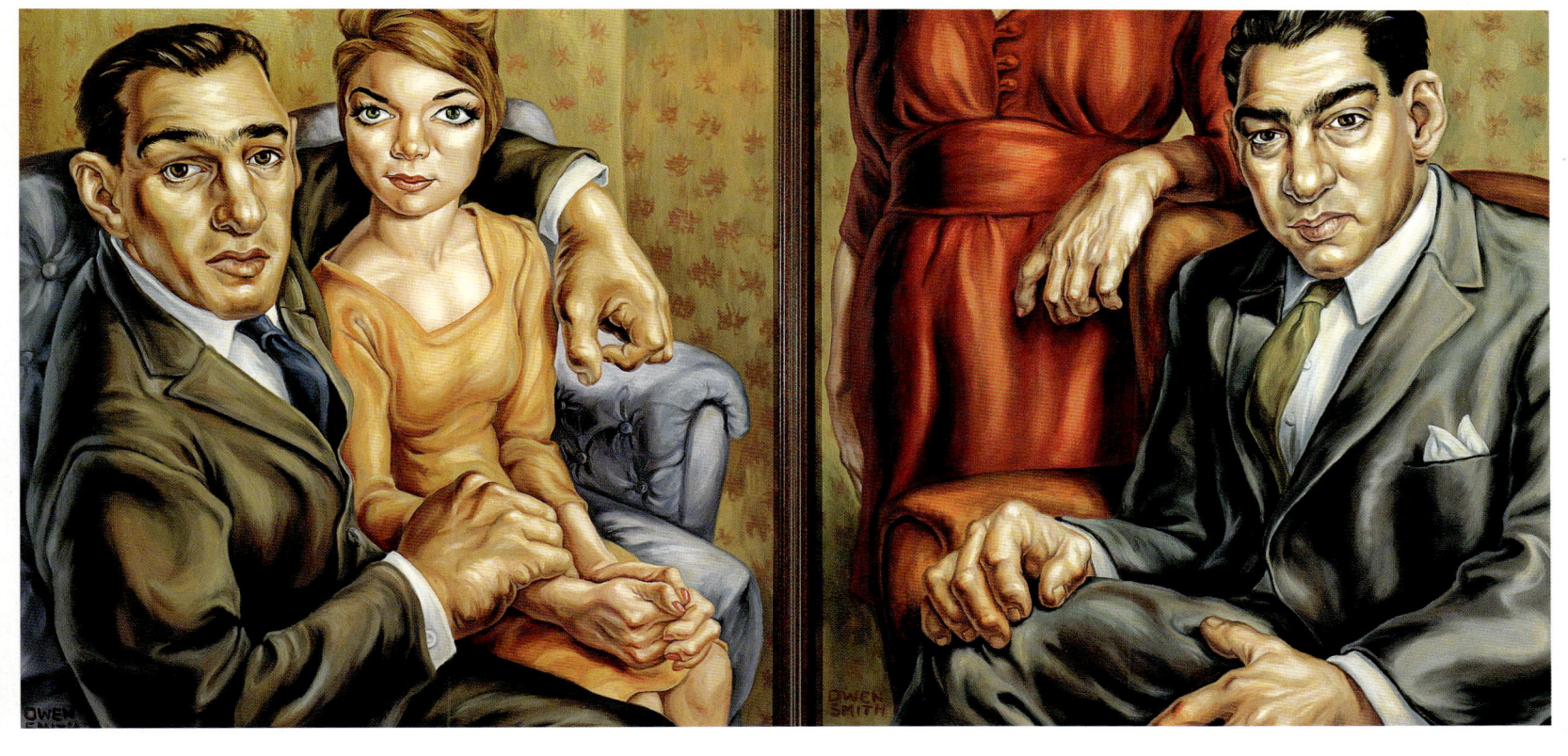

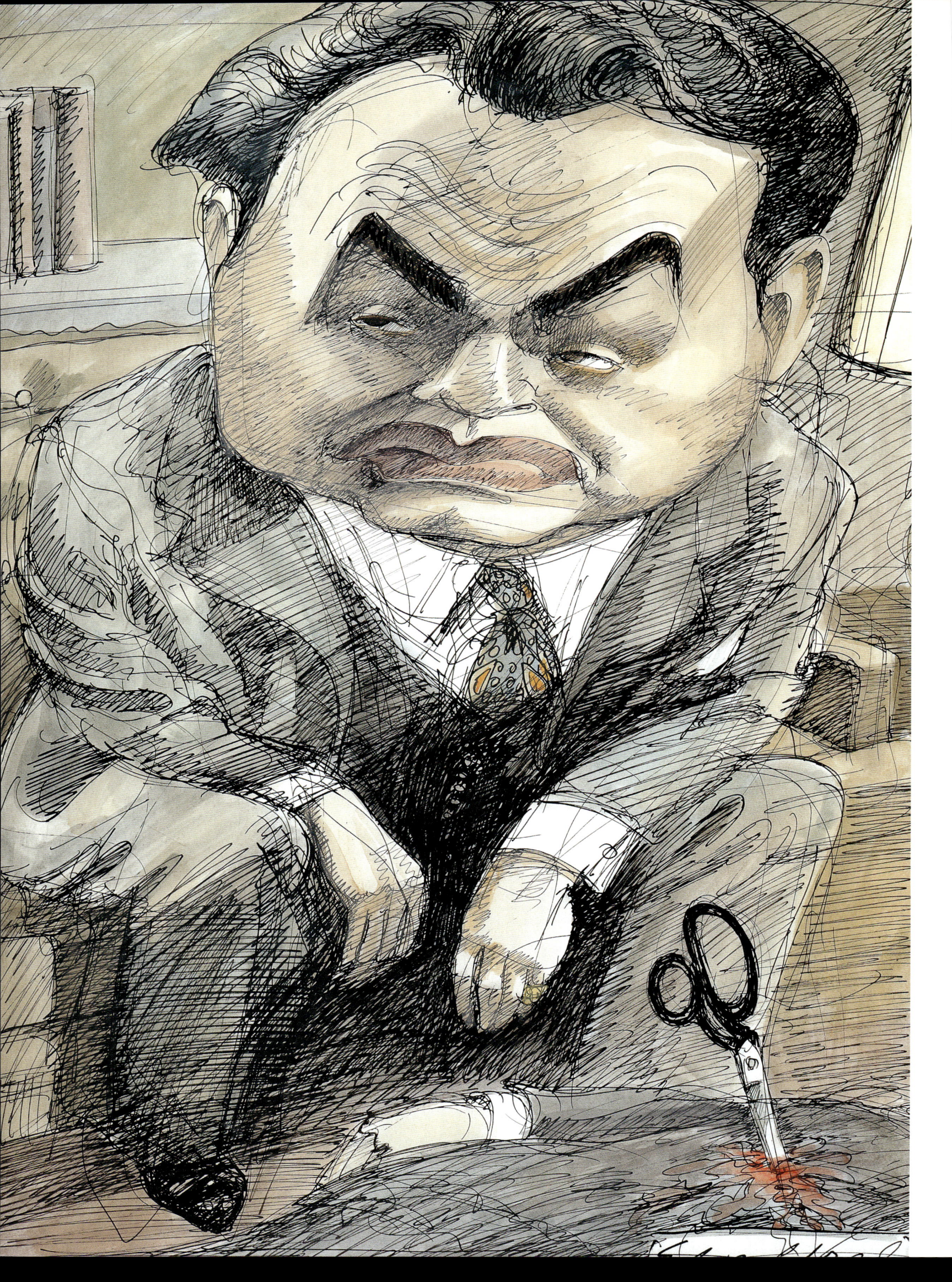

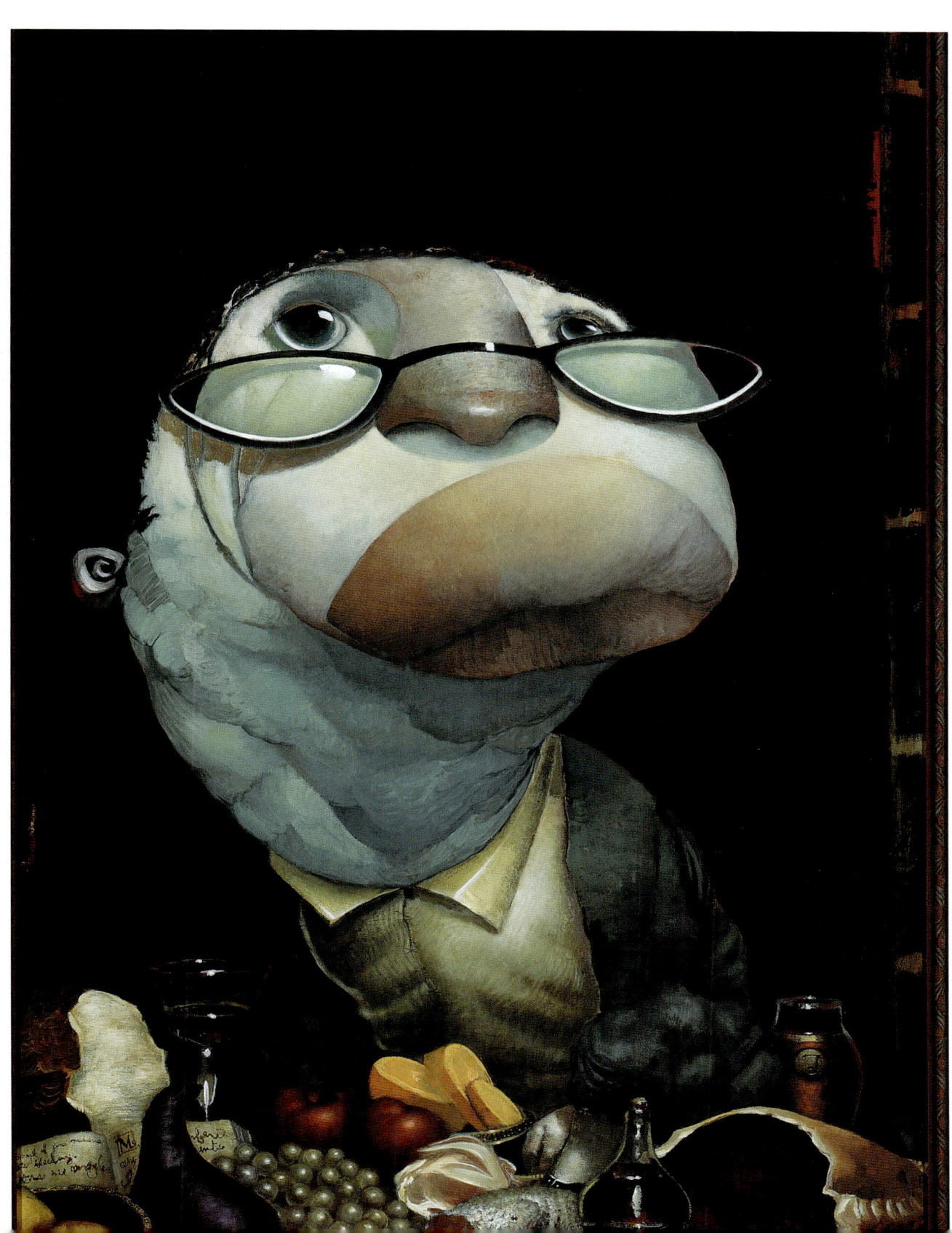

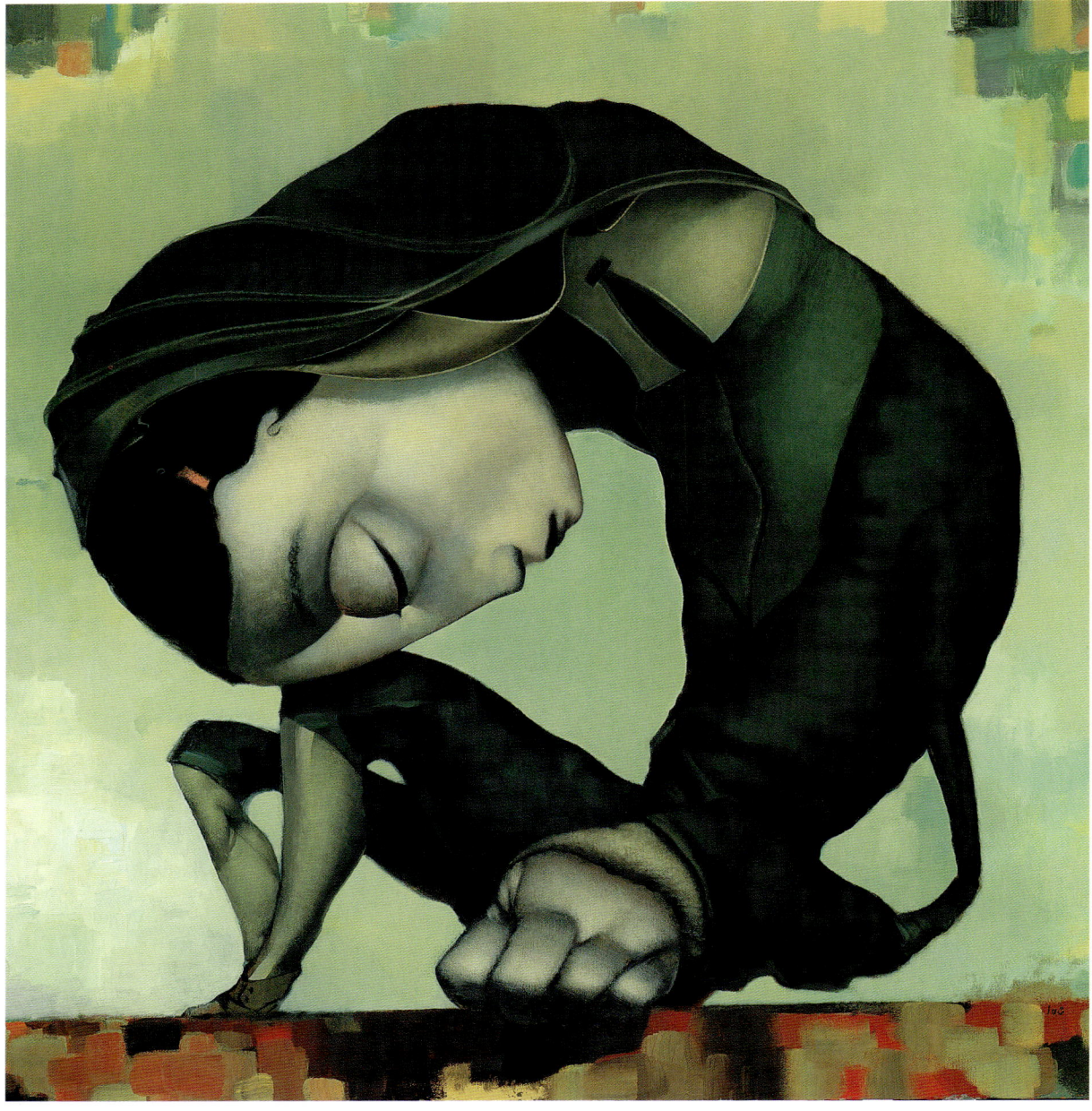

305 joesorren

306 artspiegelman

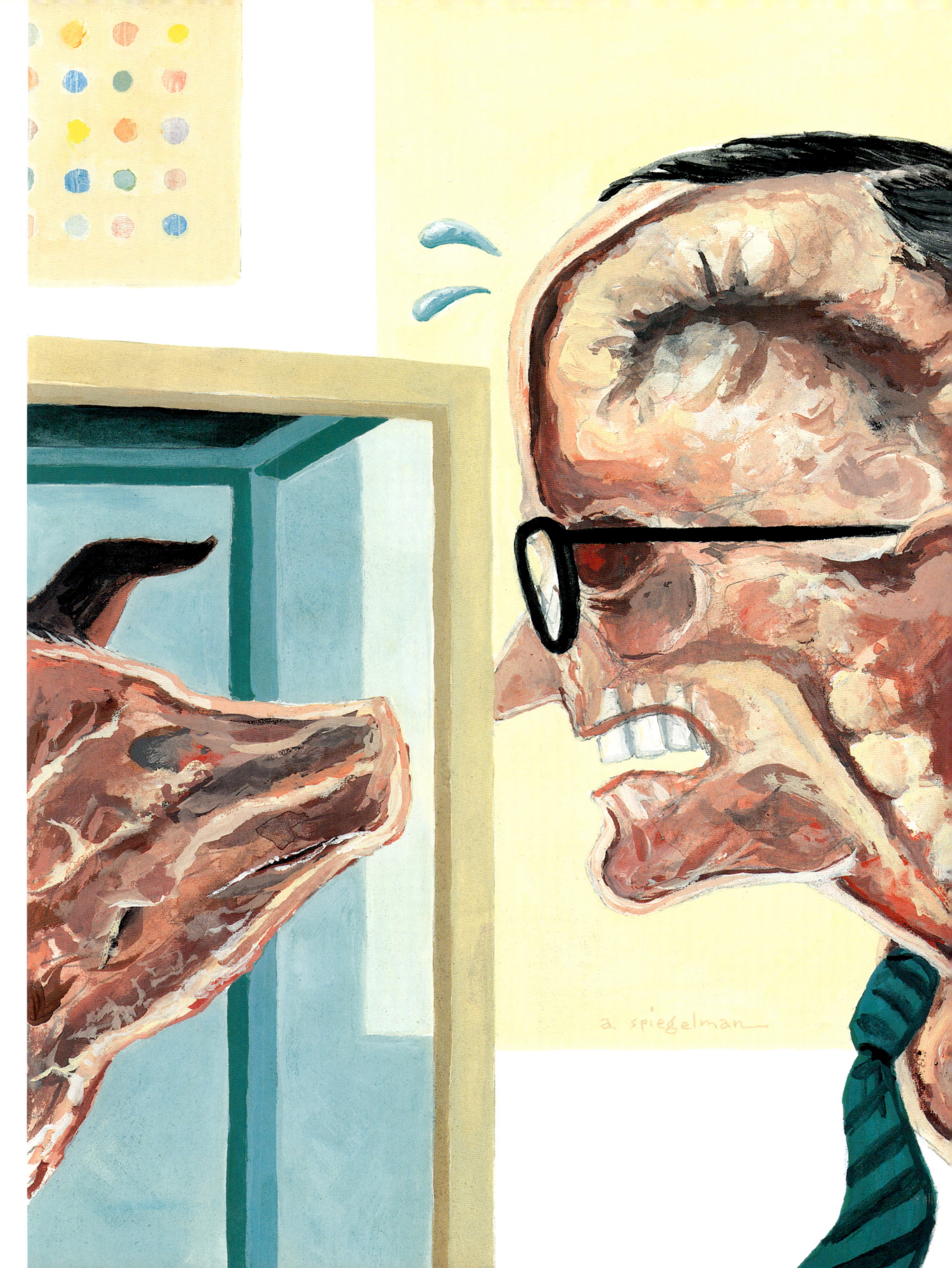

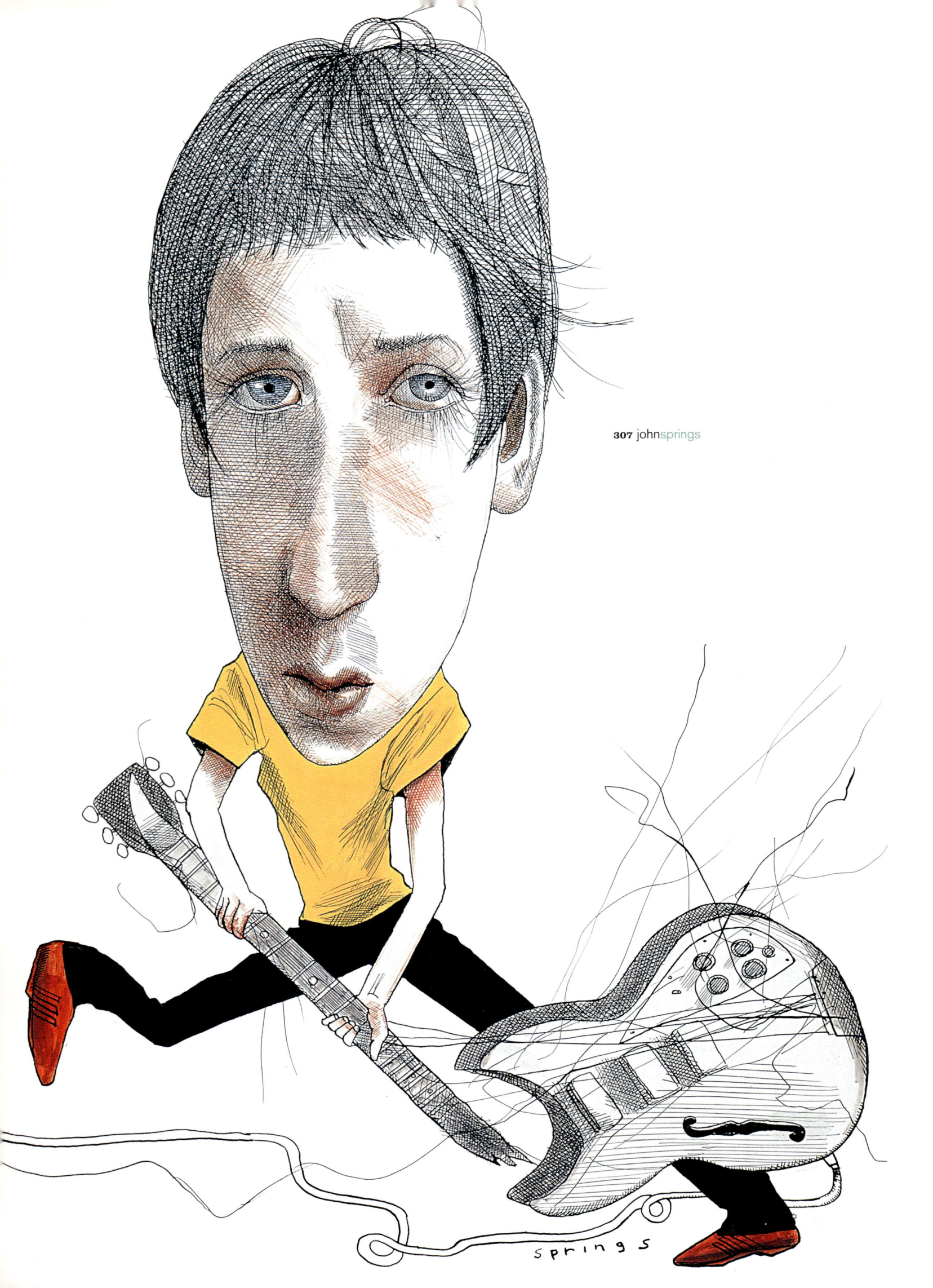

springs

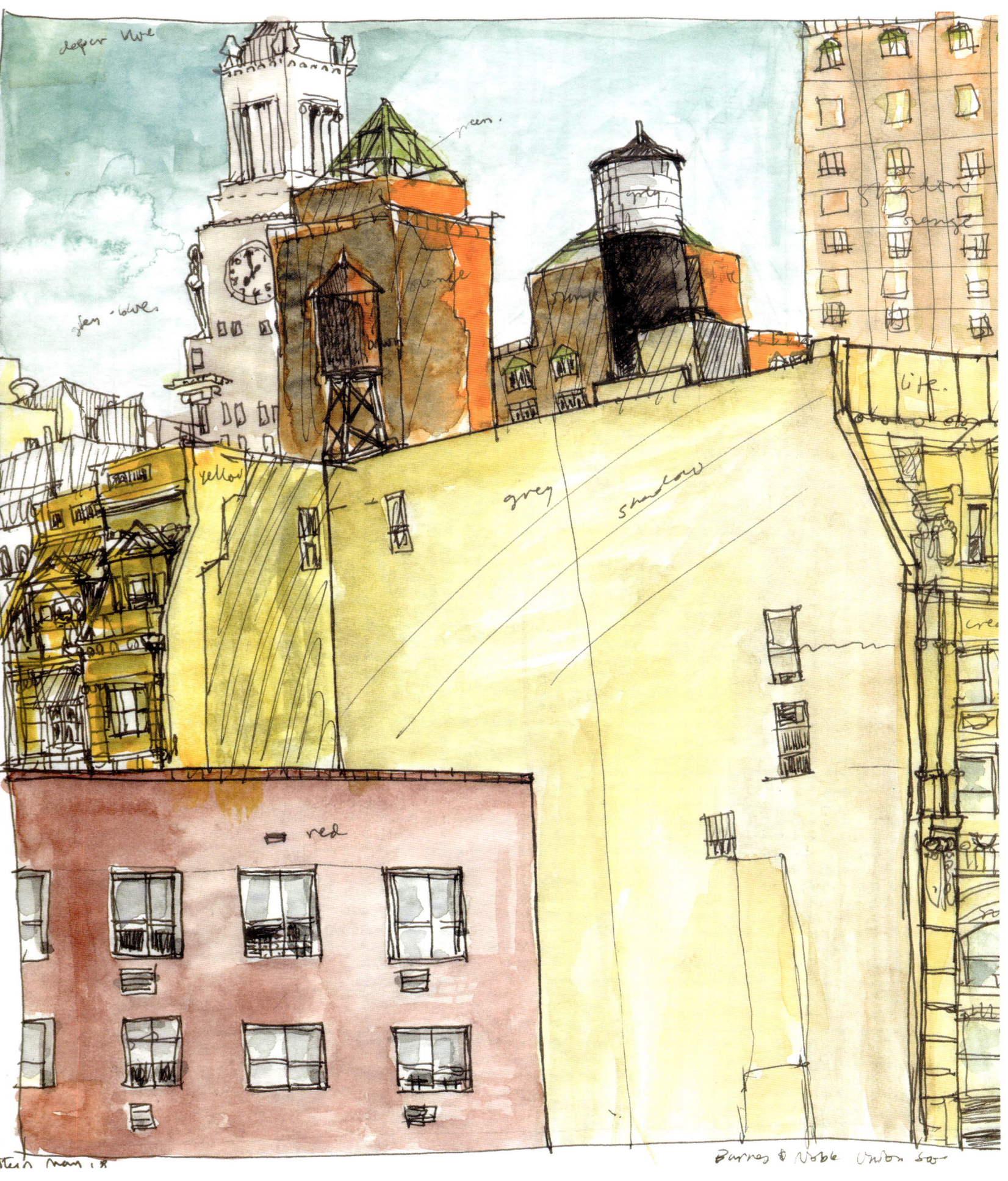

309 david ezrastein

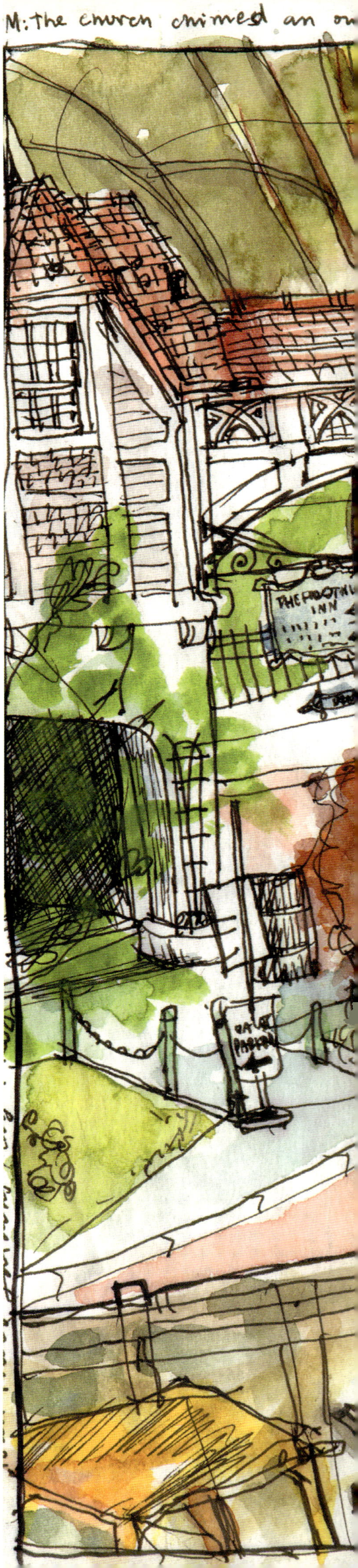

THE FOOTHILL INN

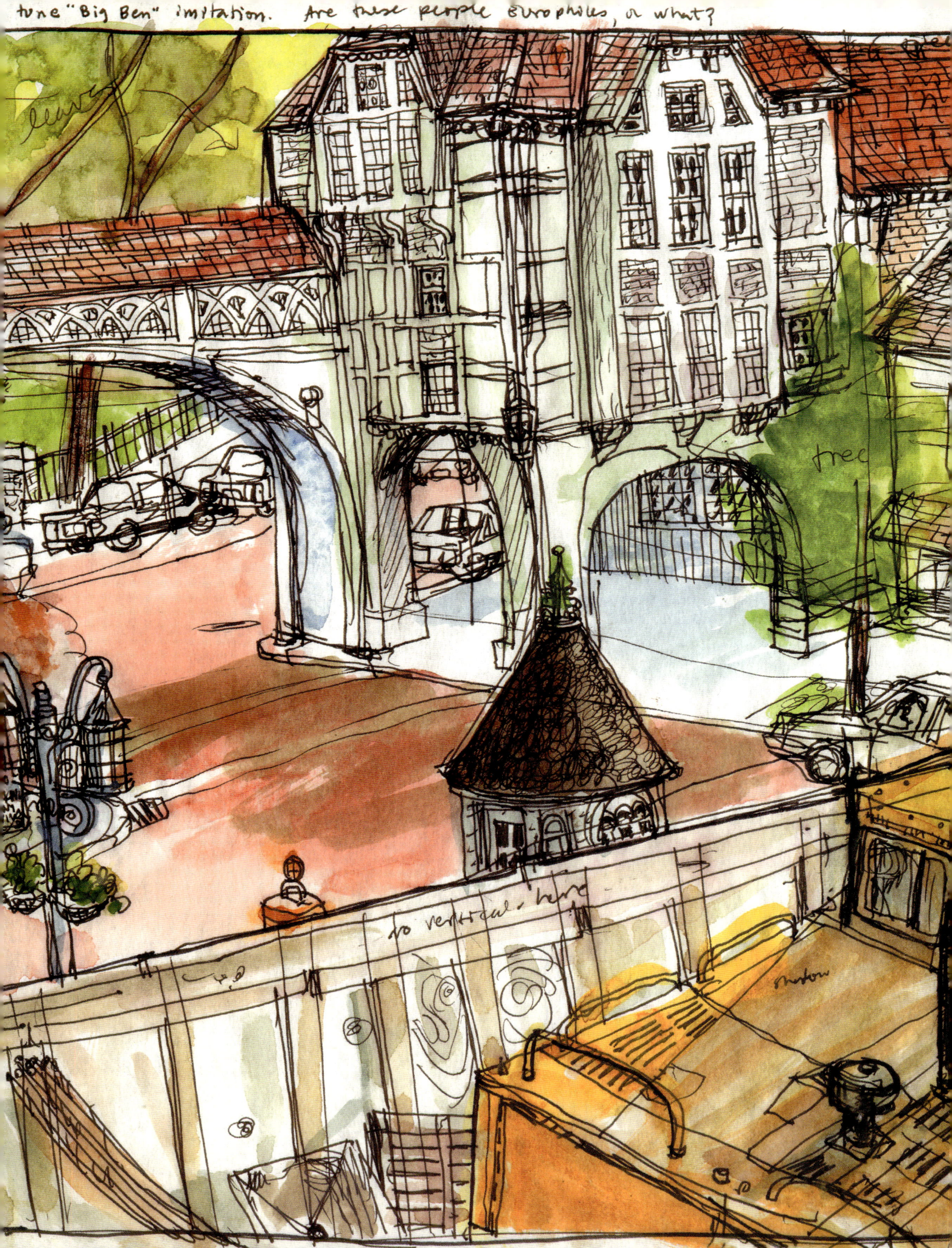

tune "Big Ben" imitation. Are these people Europhiles, or what?

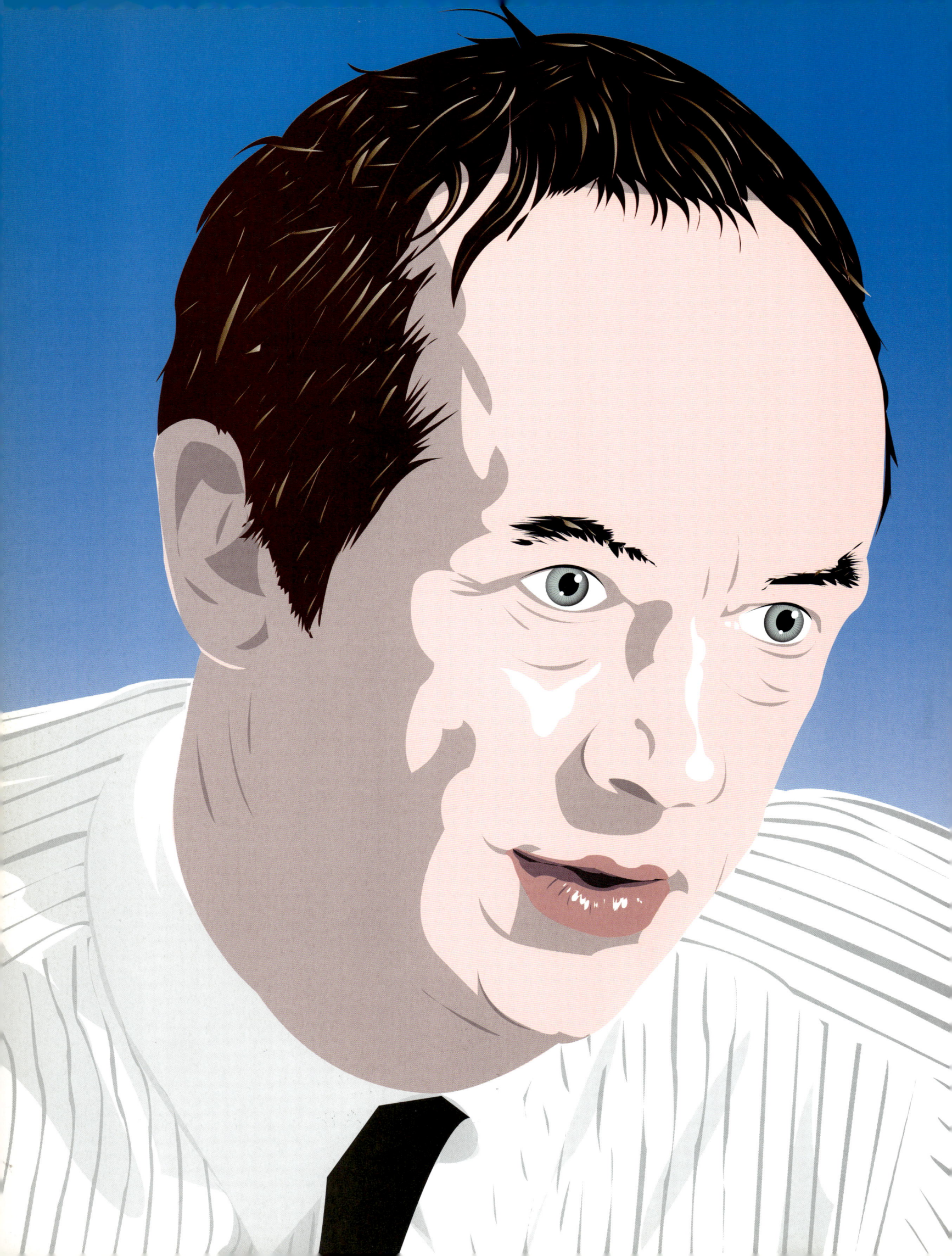

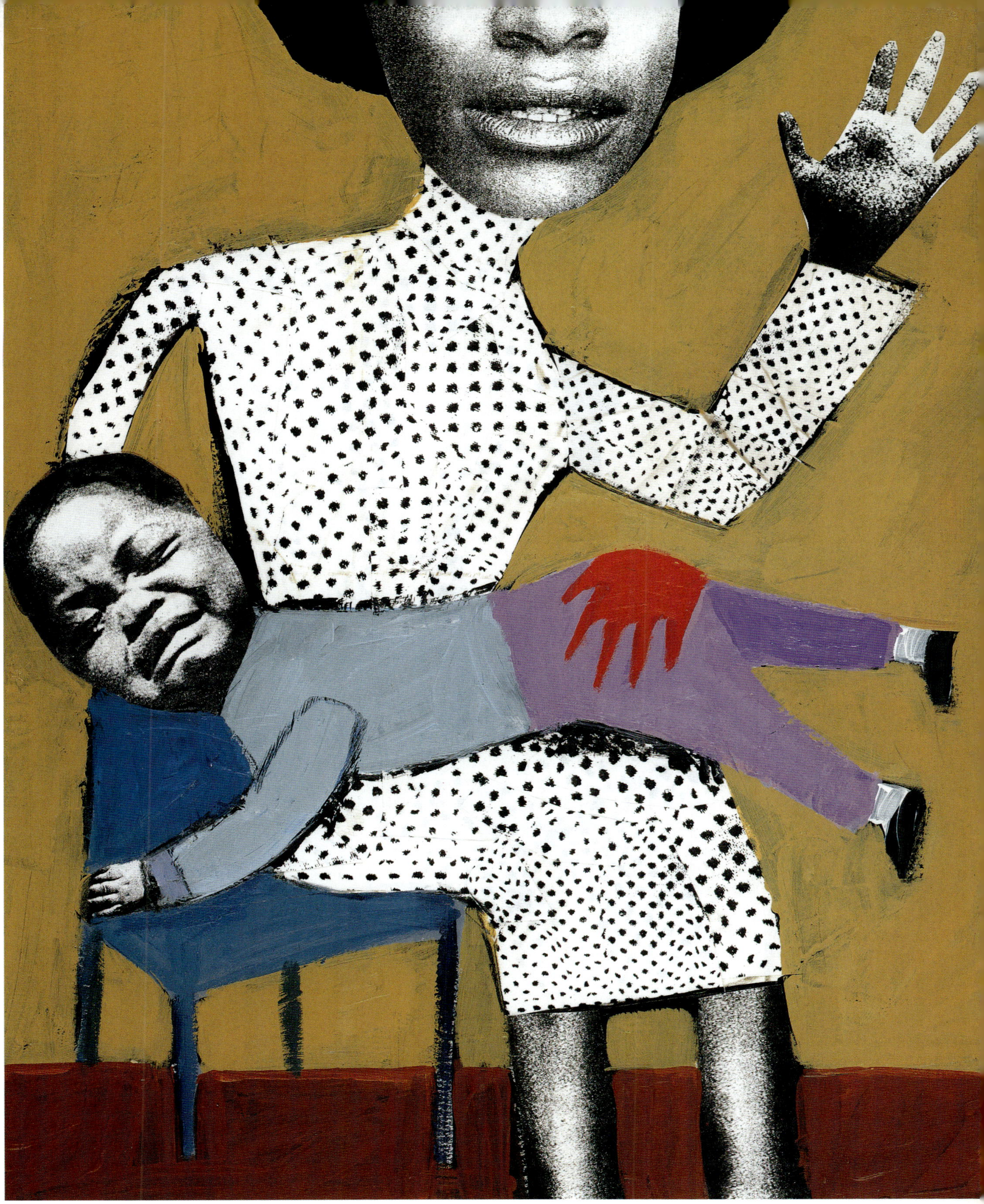

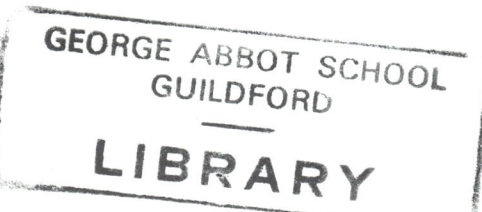

311 katherinestreeter

310 peterstemmler

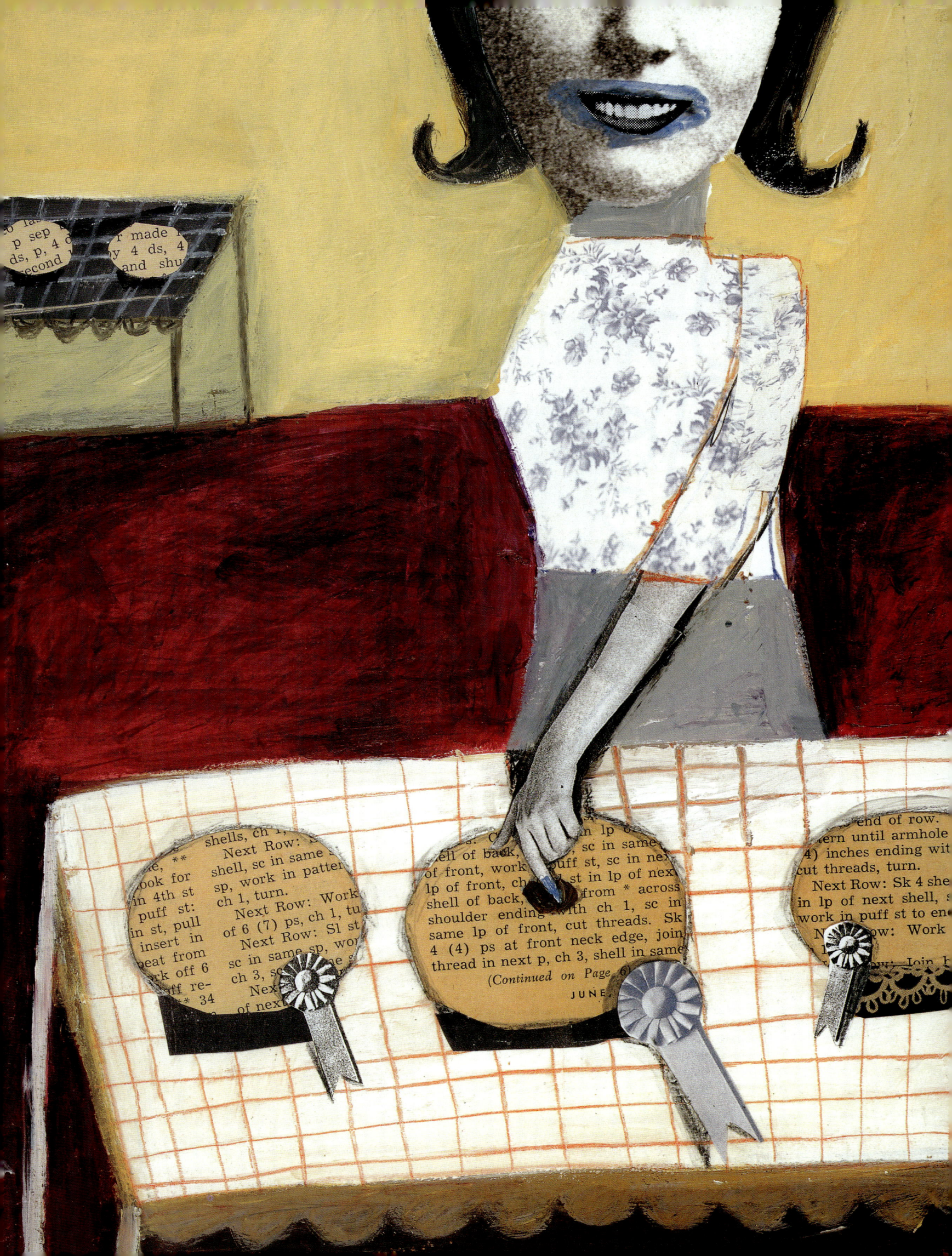

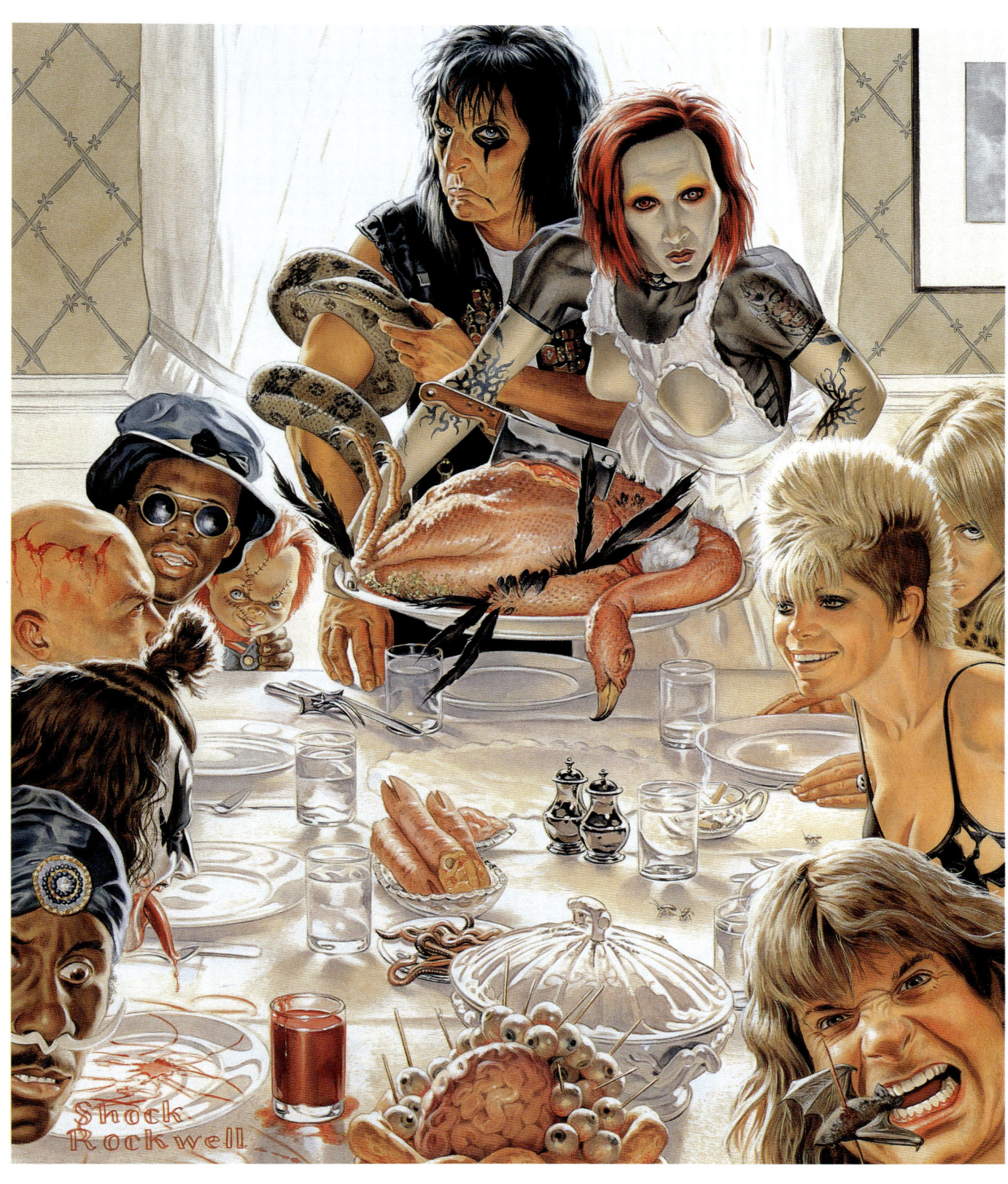

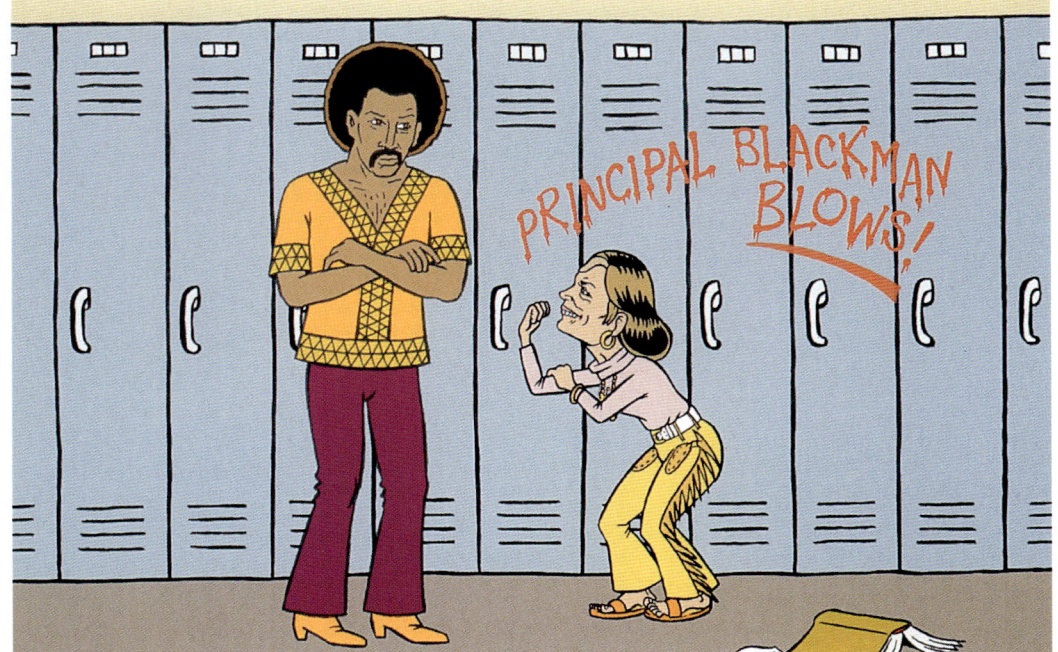

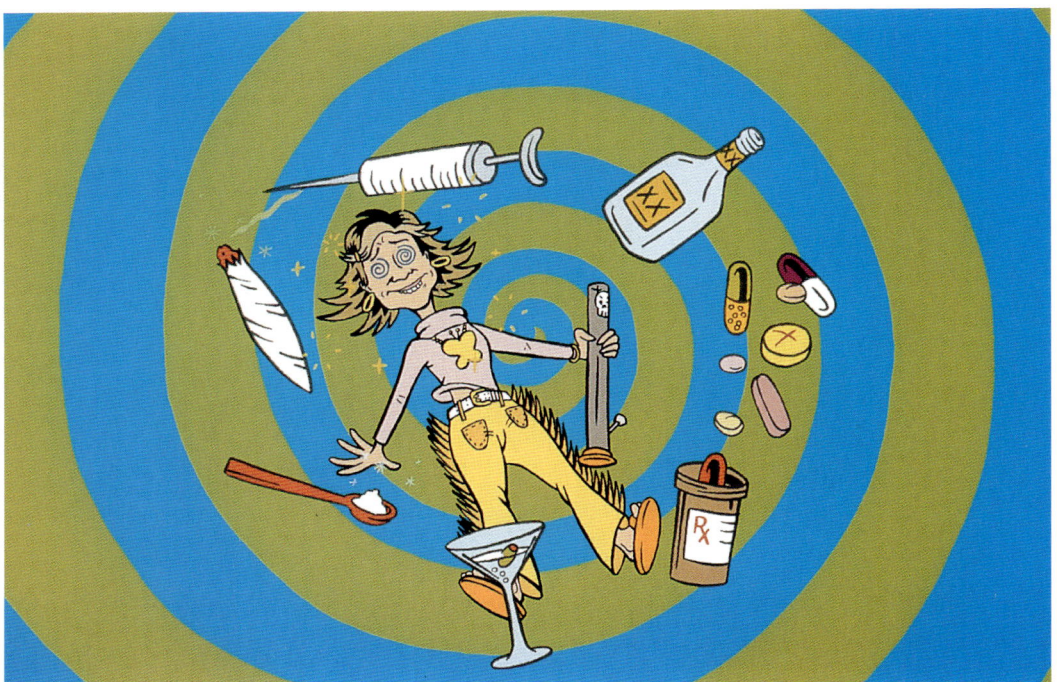

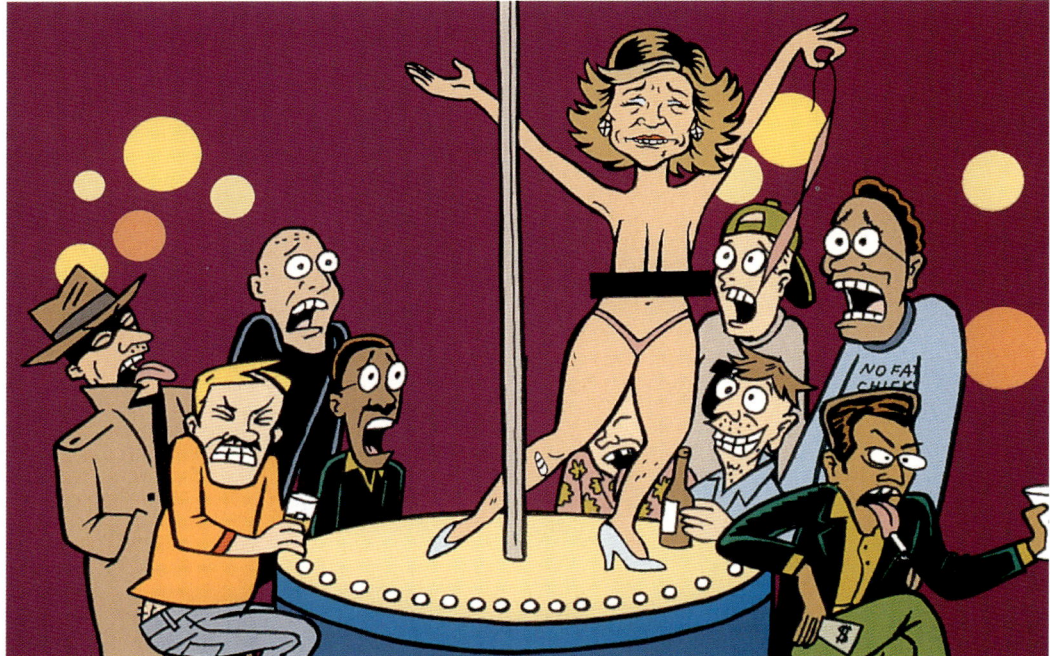

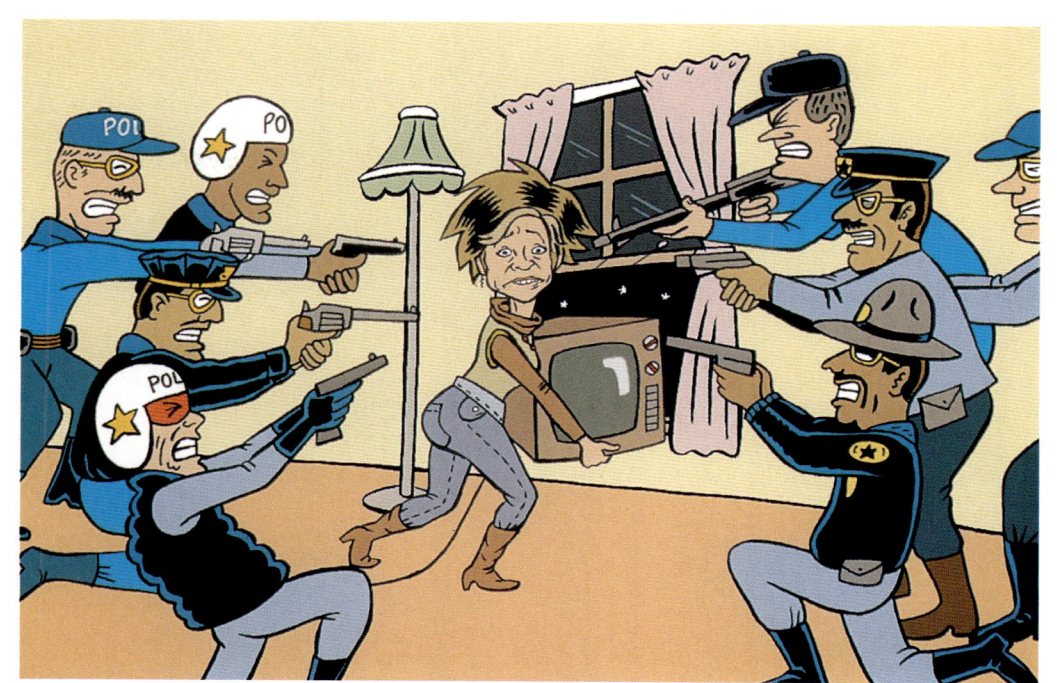

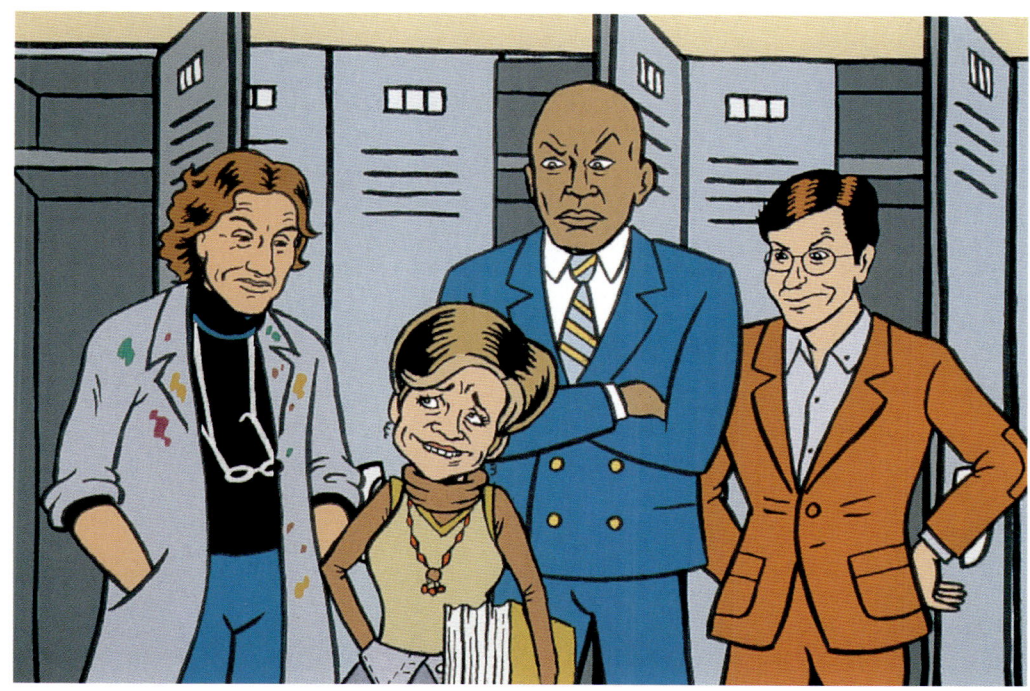

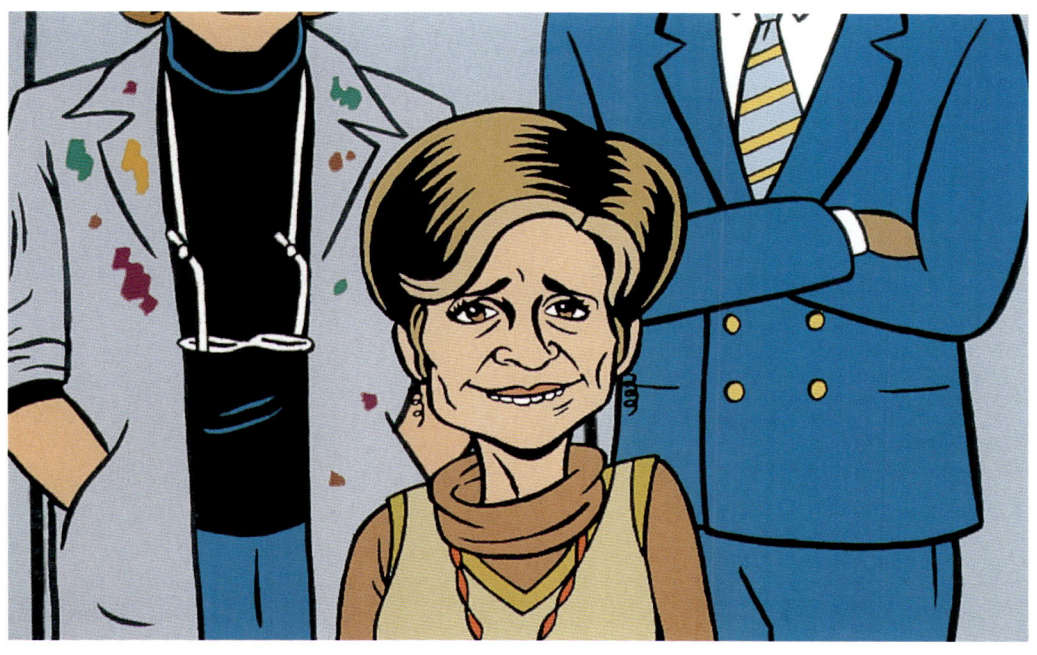

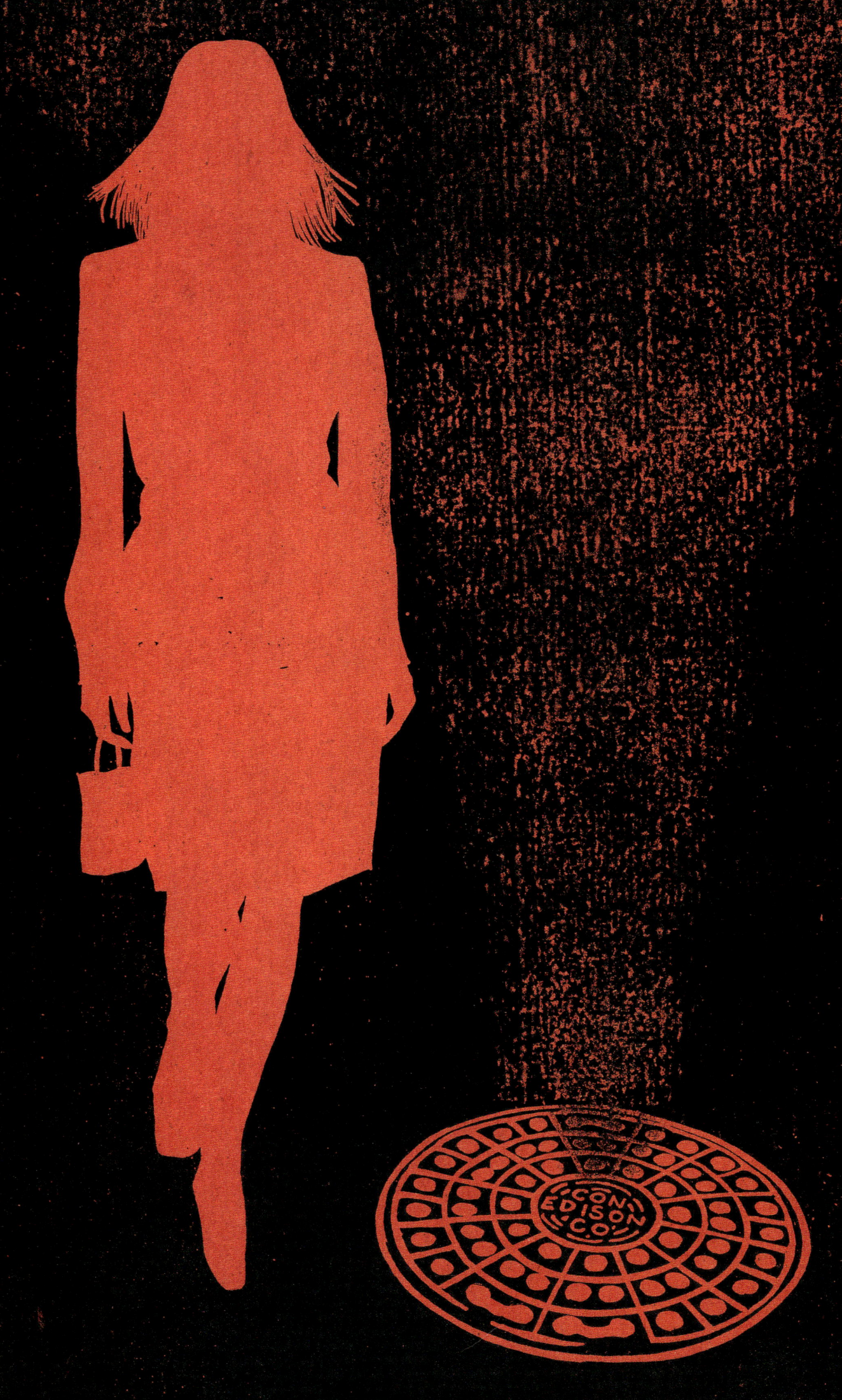

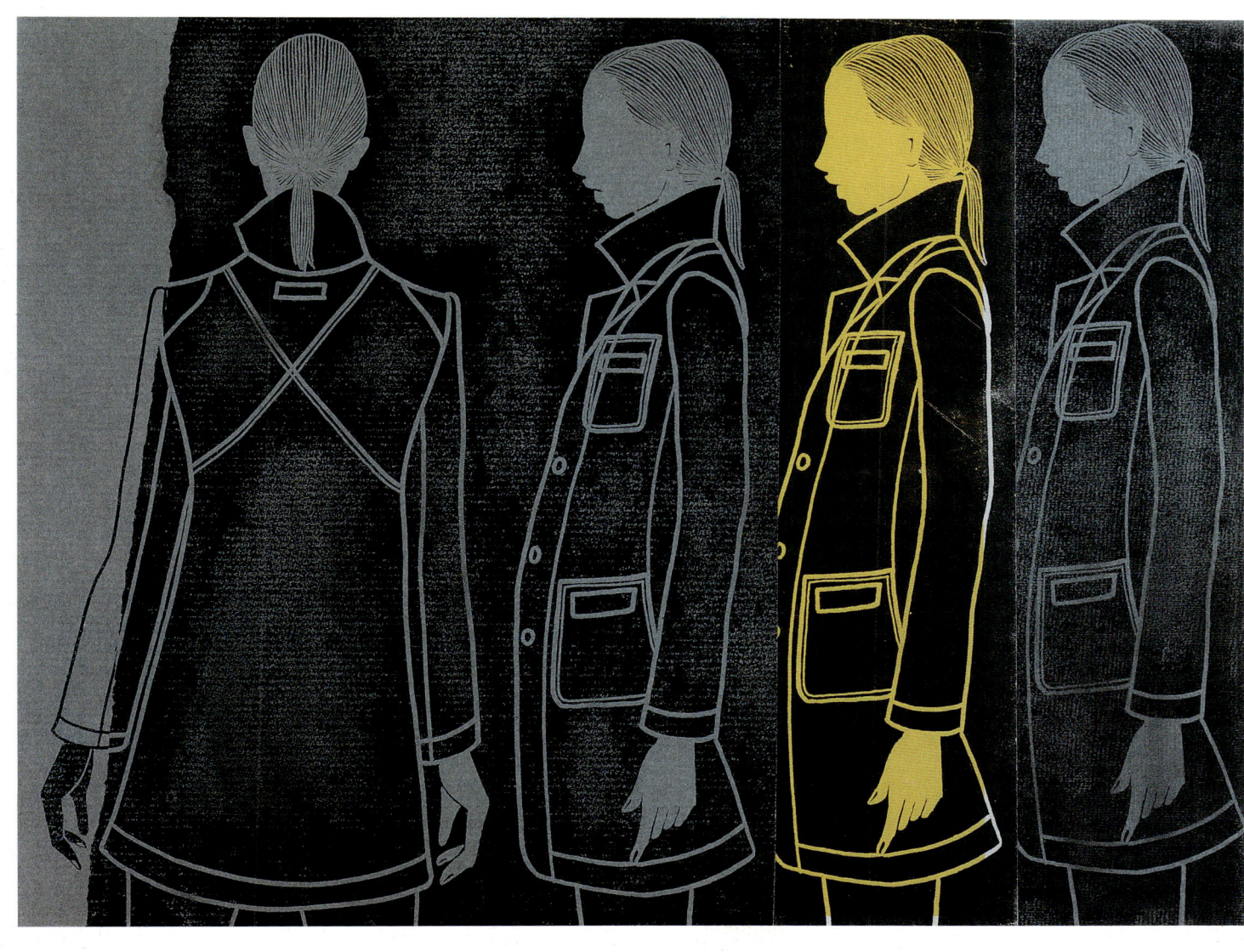

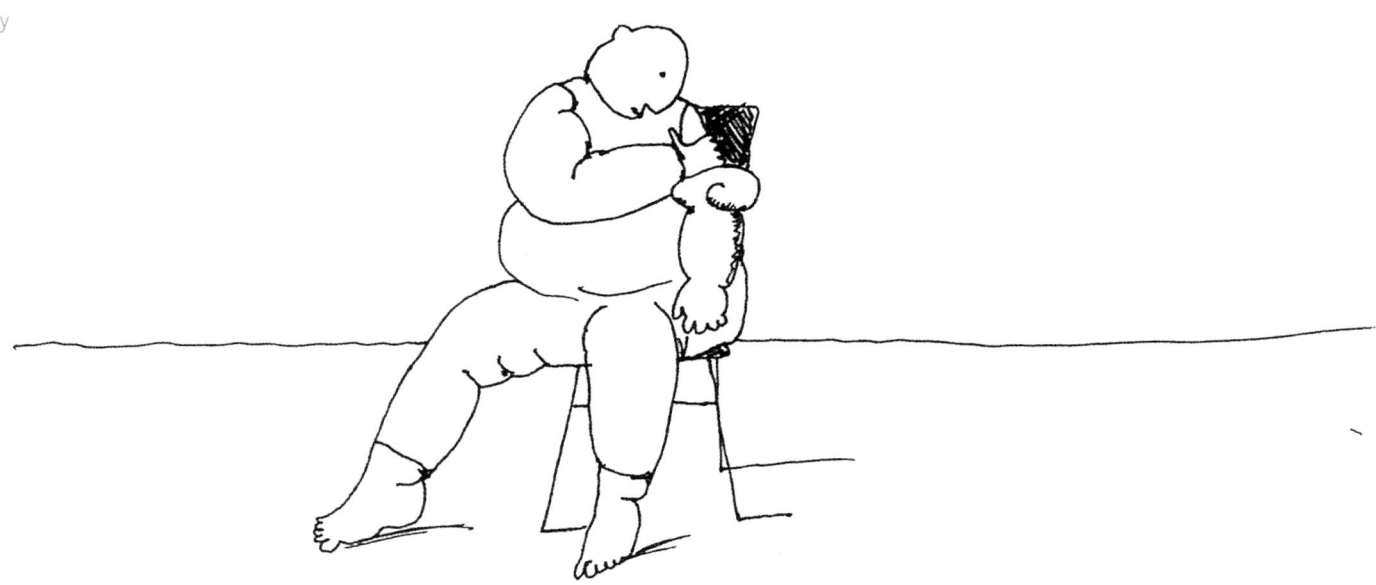

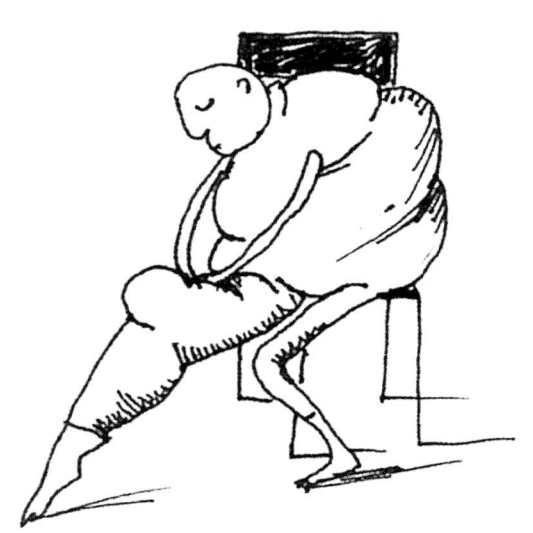

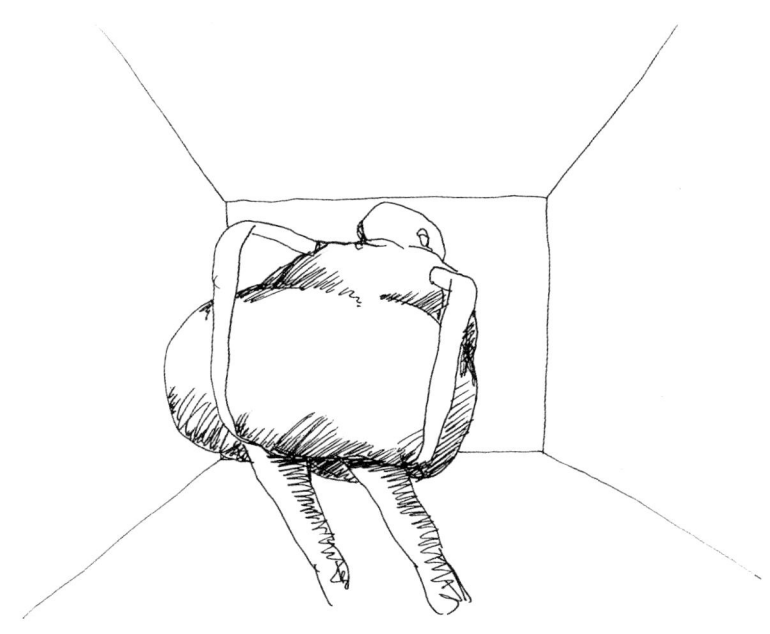

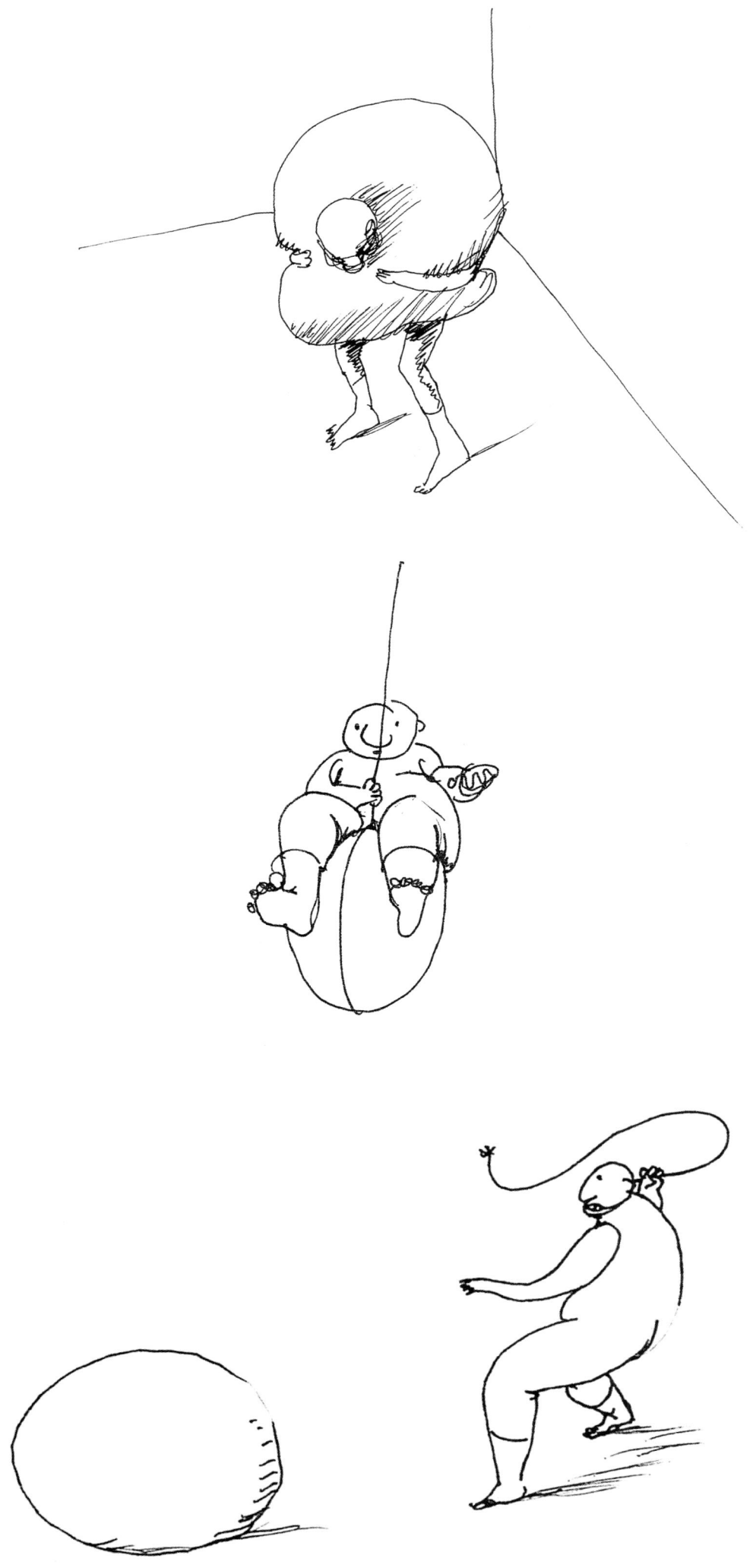

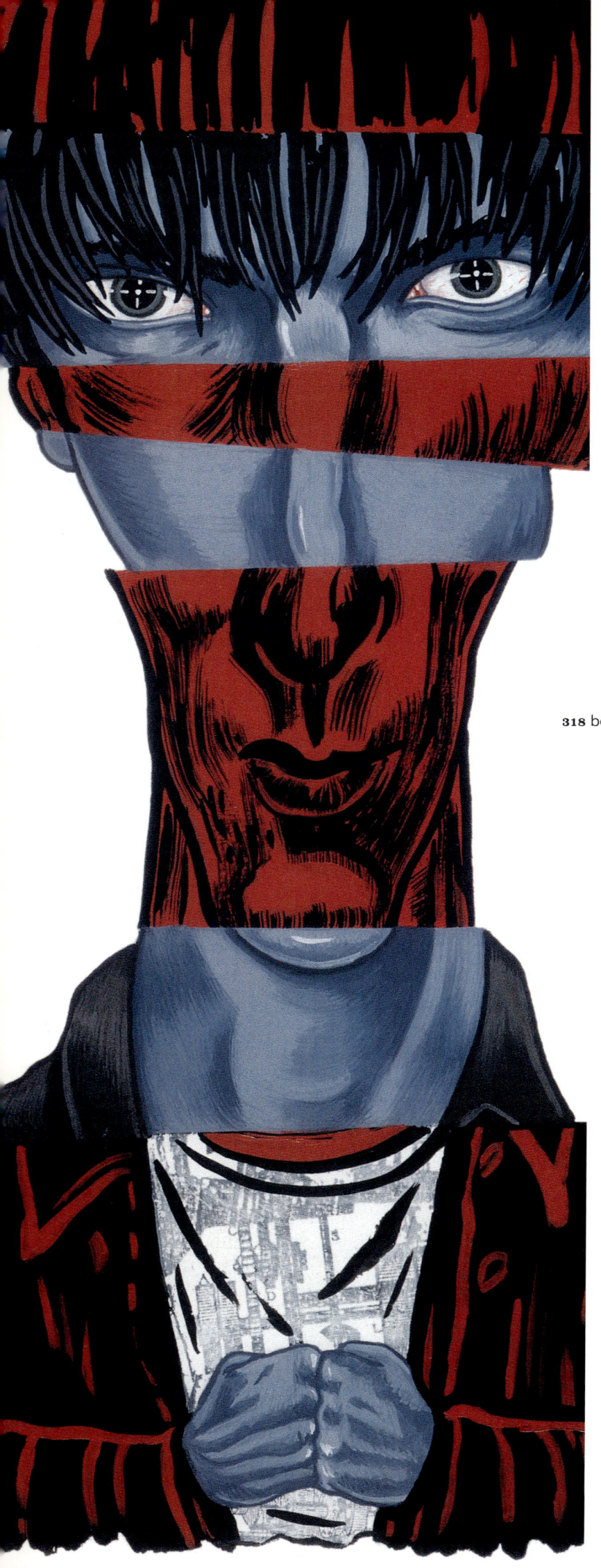

318 bob&val**tillery**-hungry dog studio

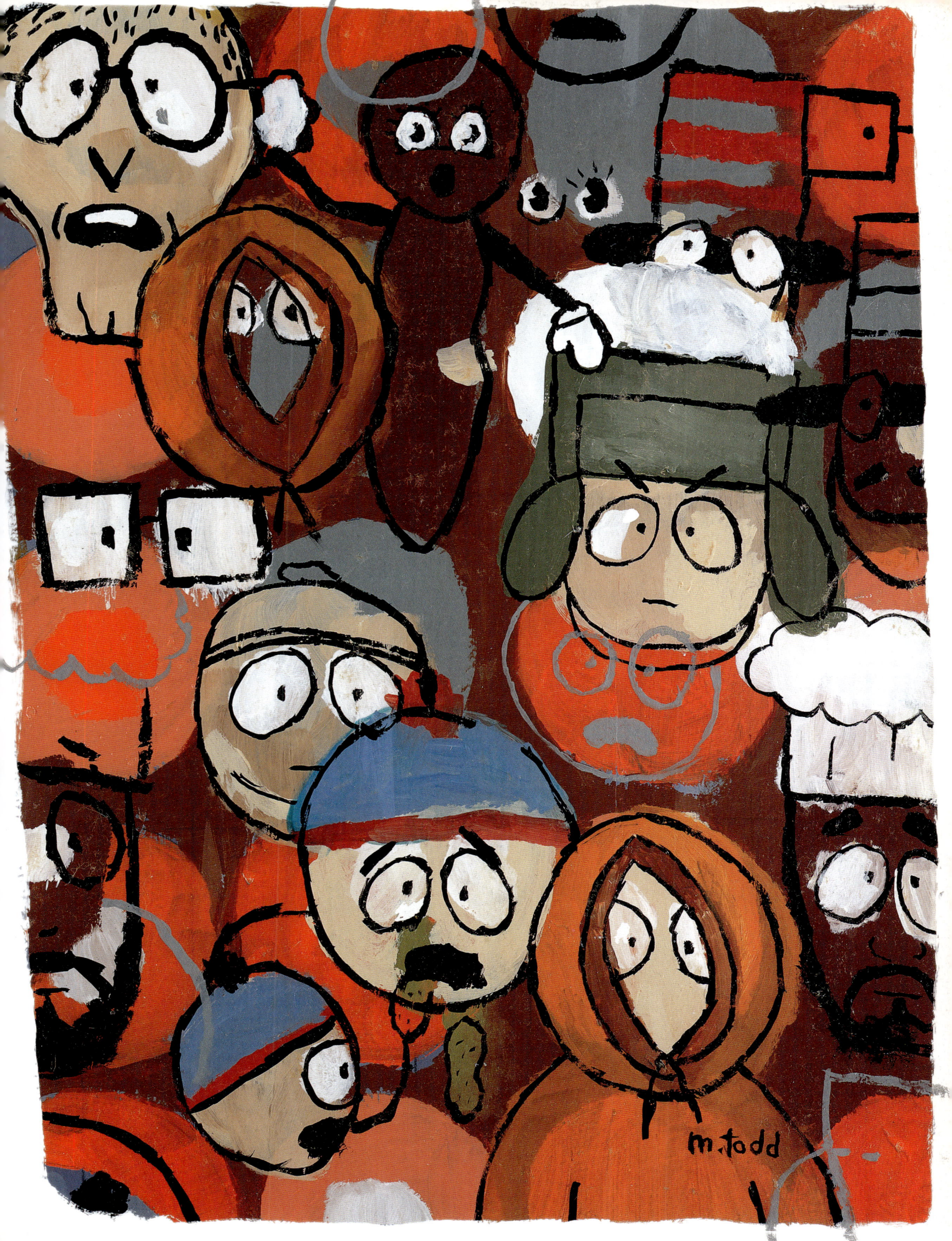

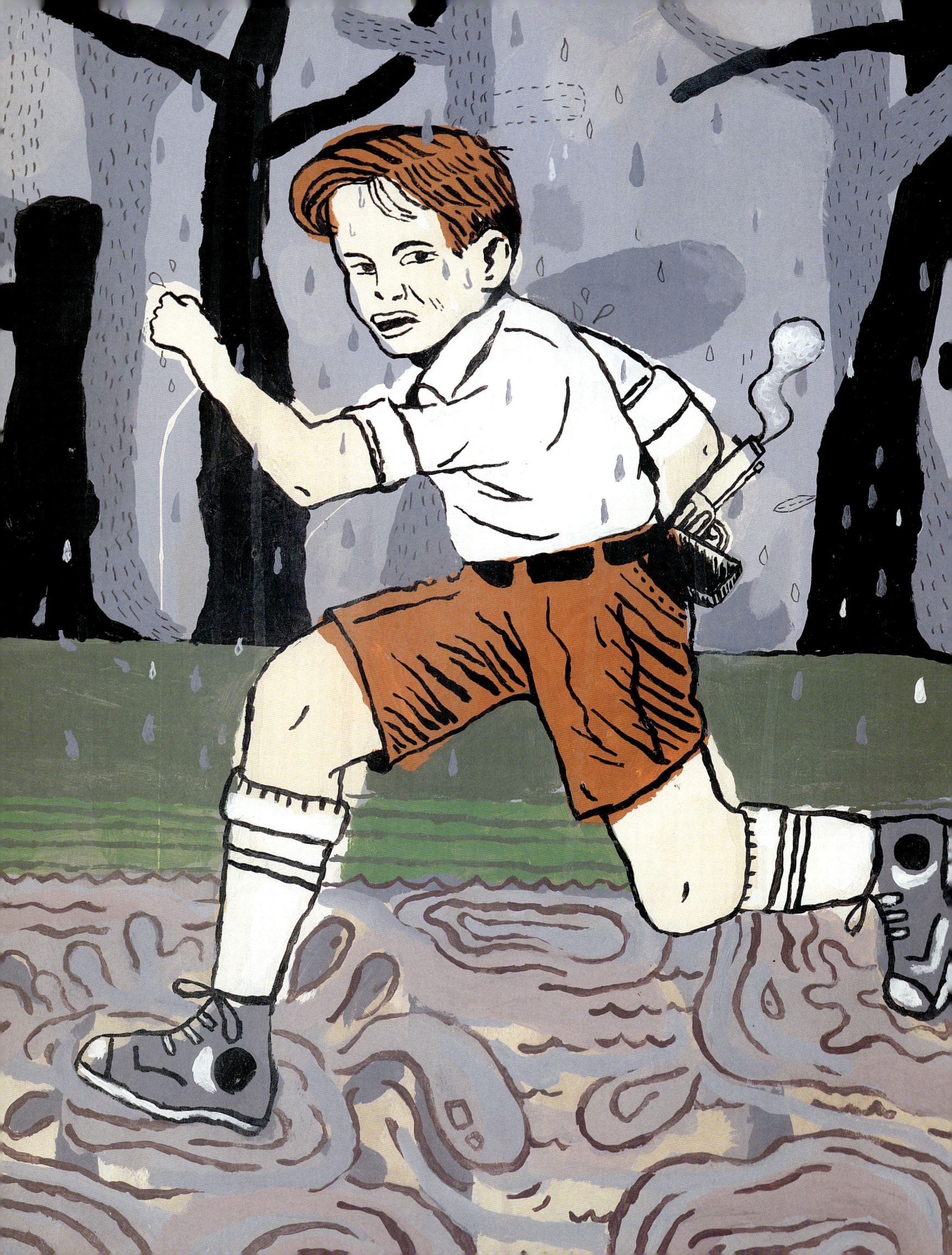

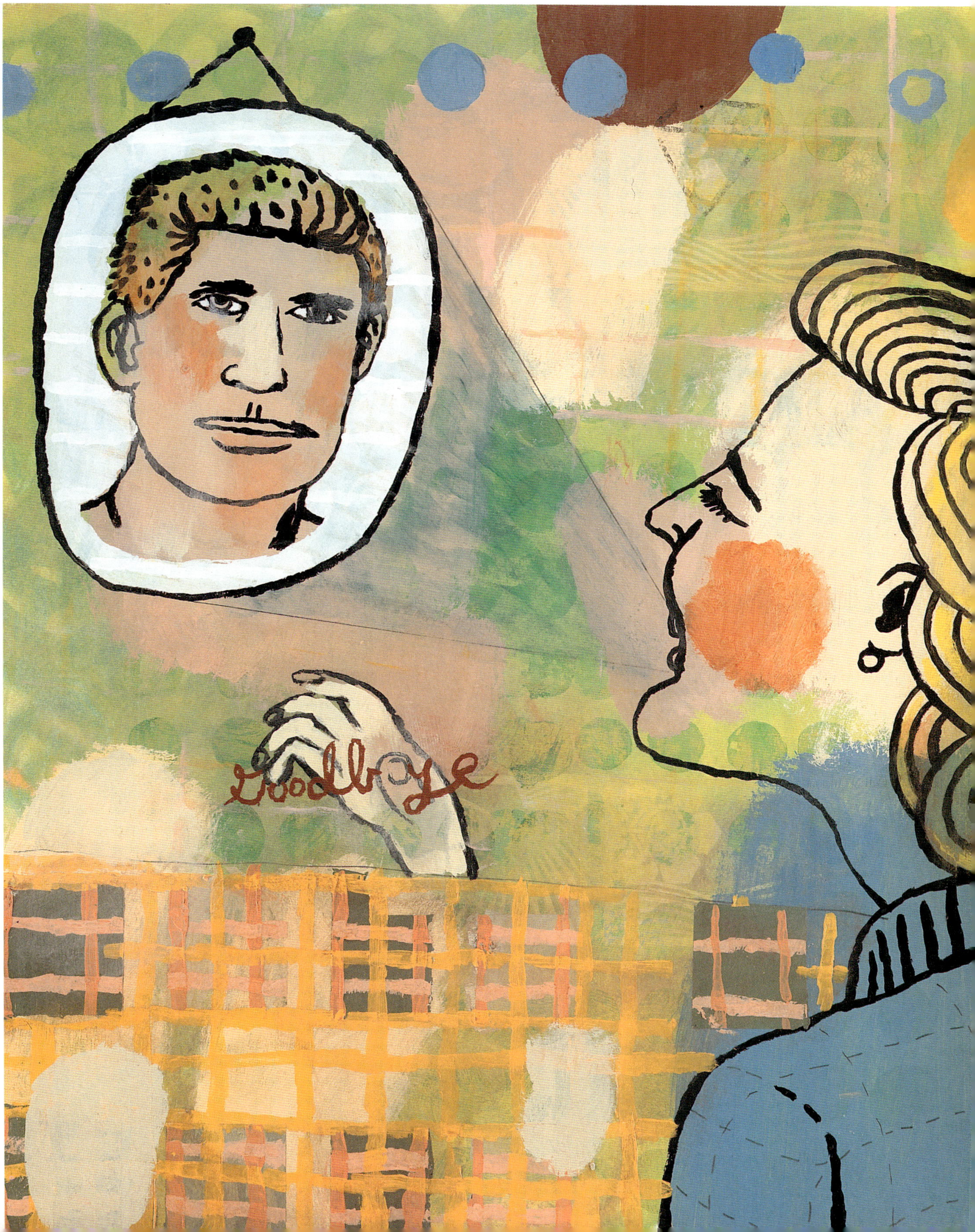
Goodbye

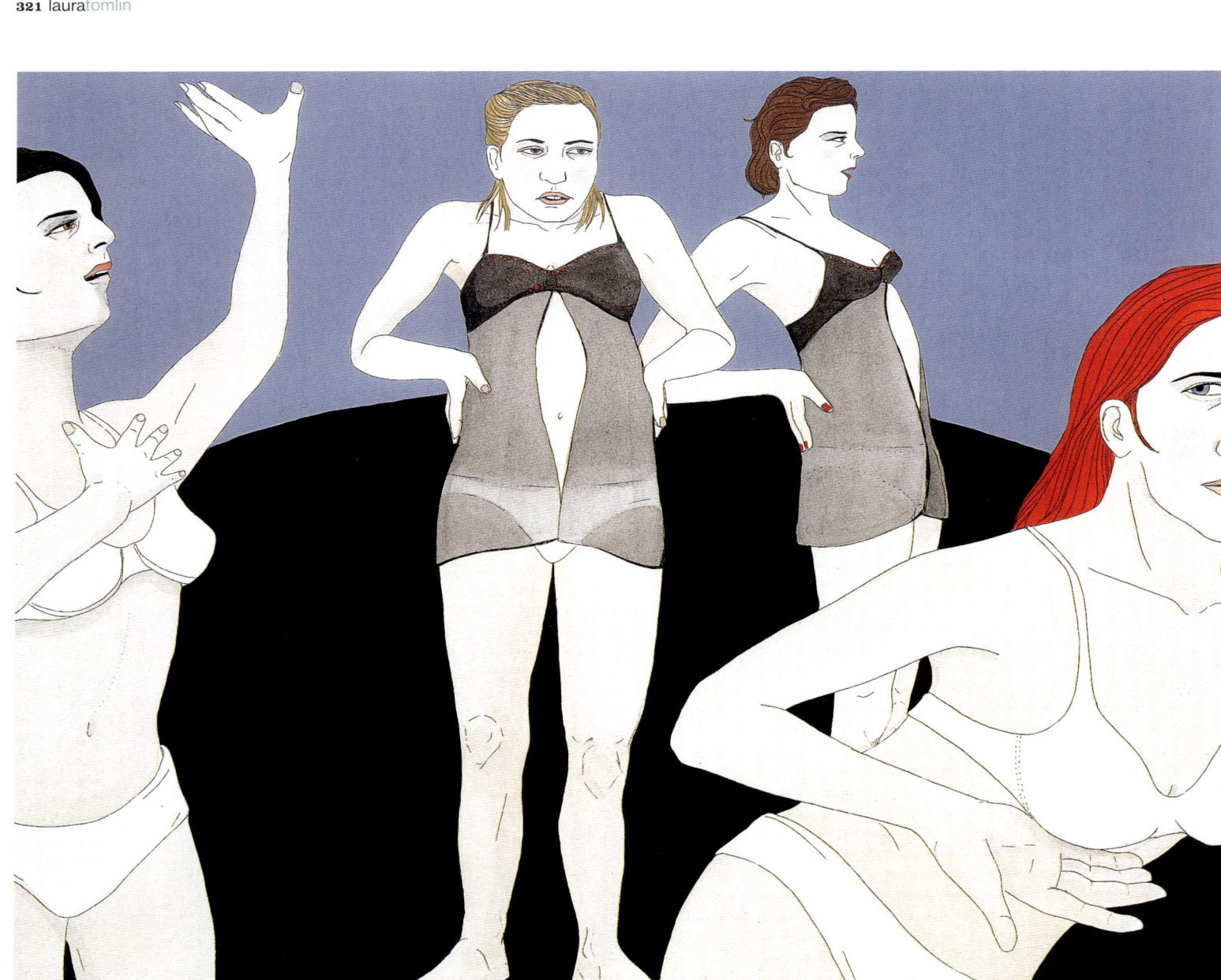

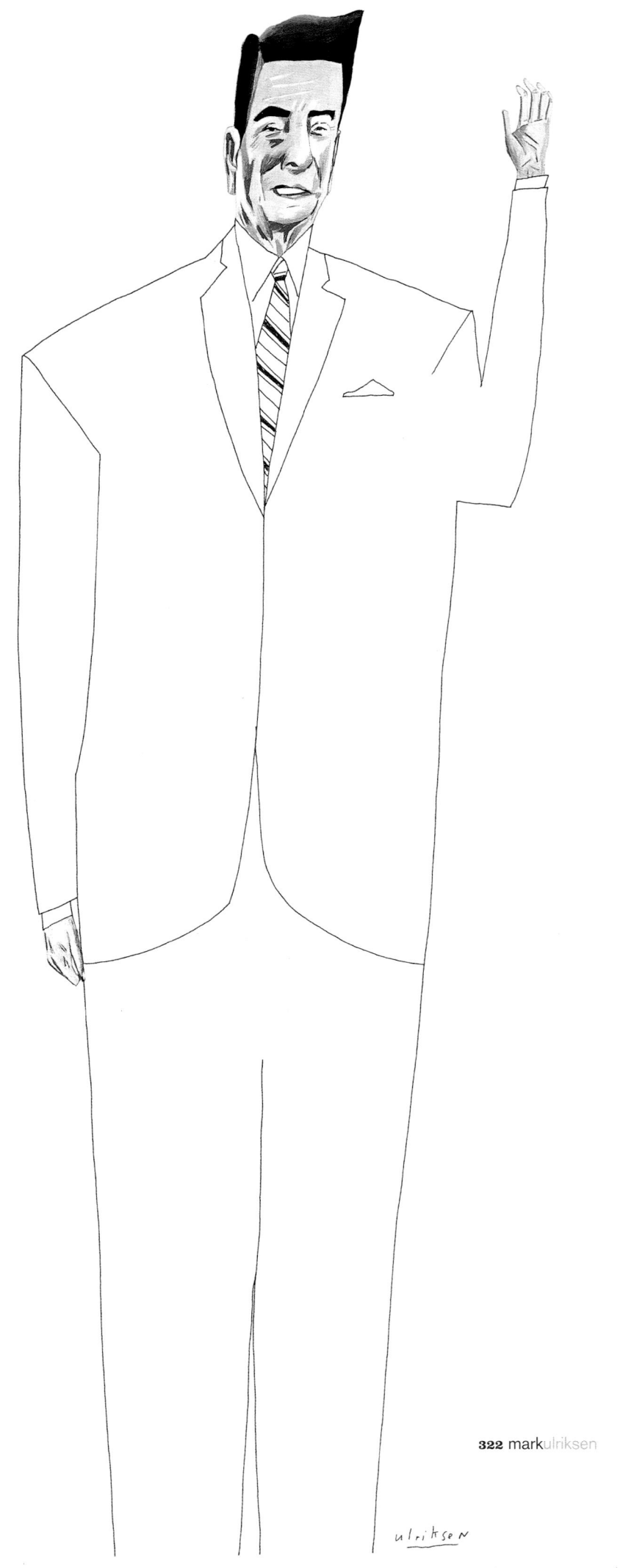

322 markulriksen

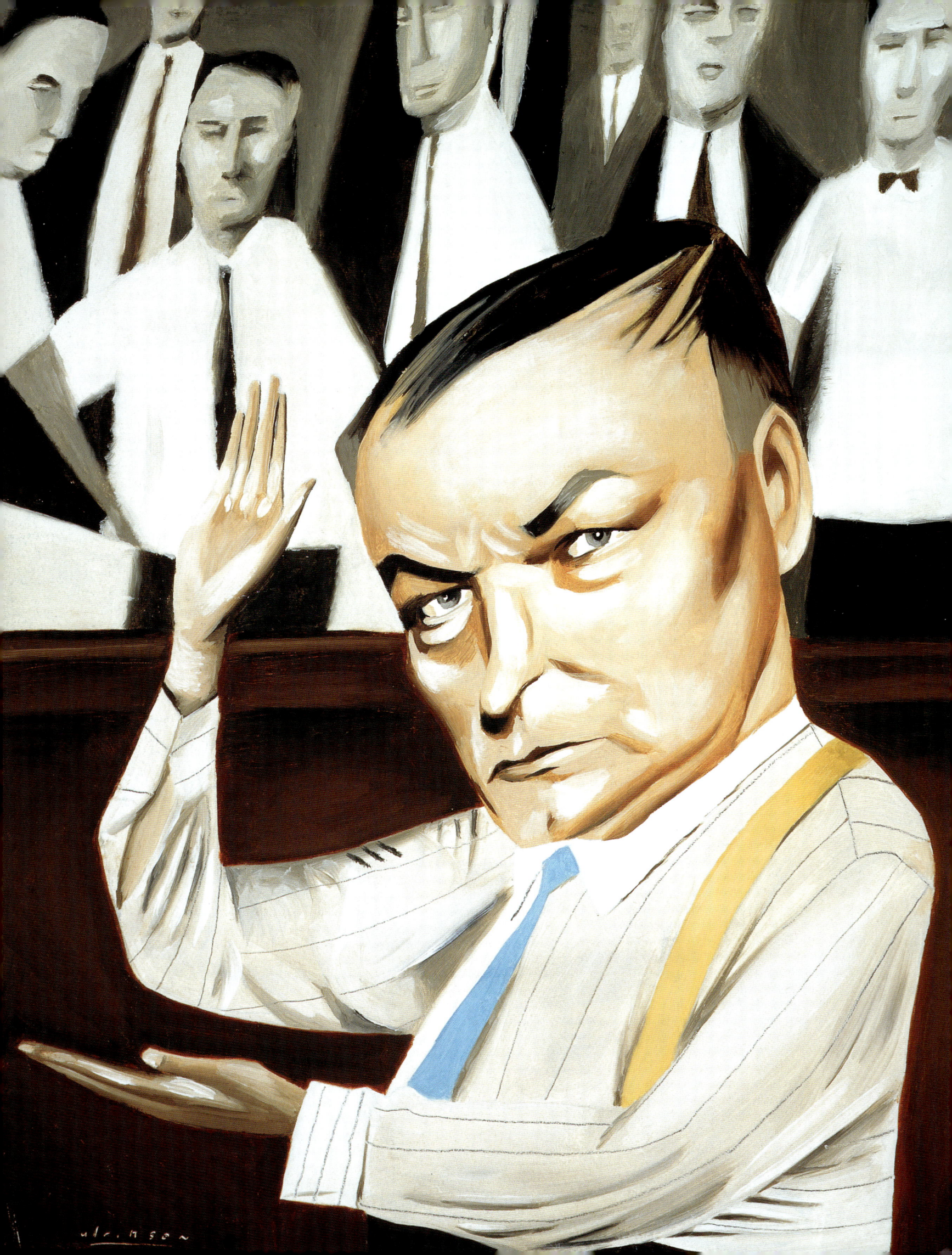

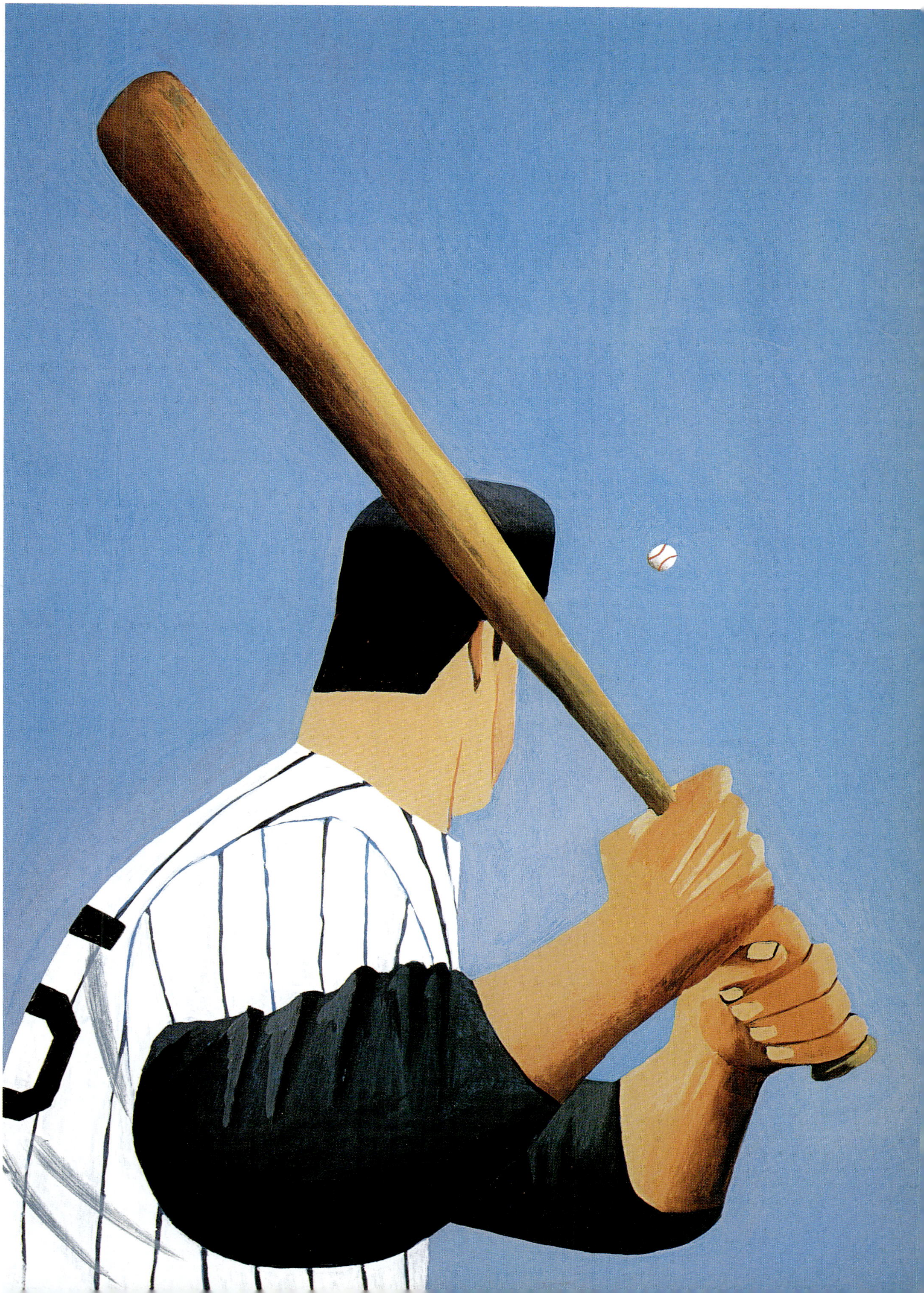

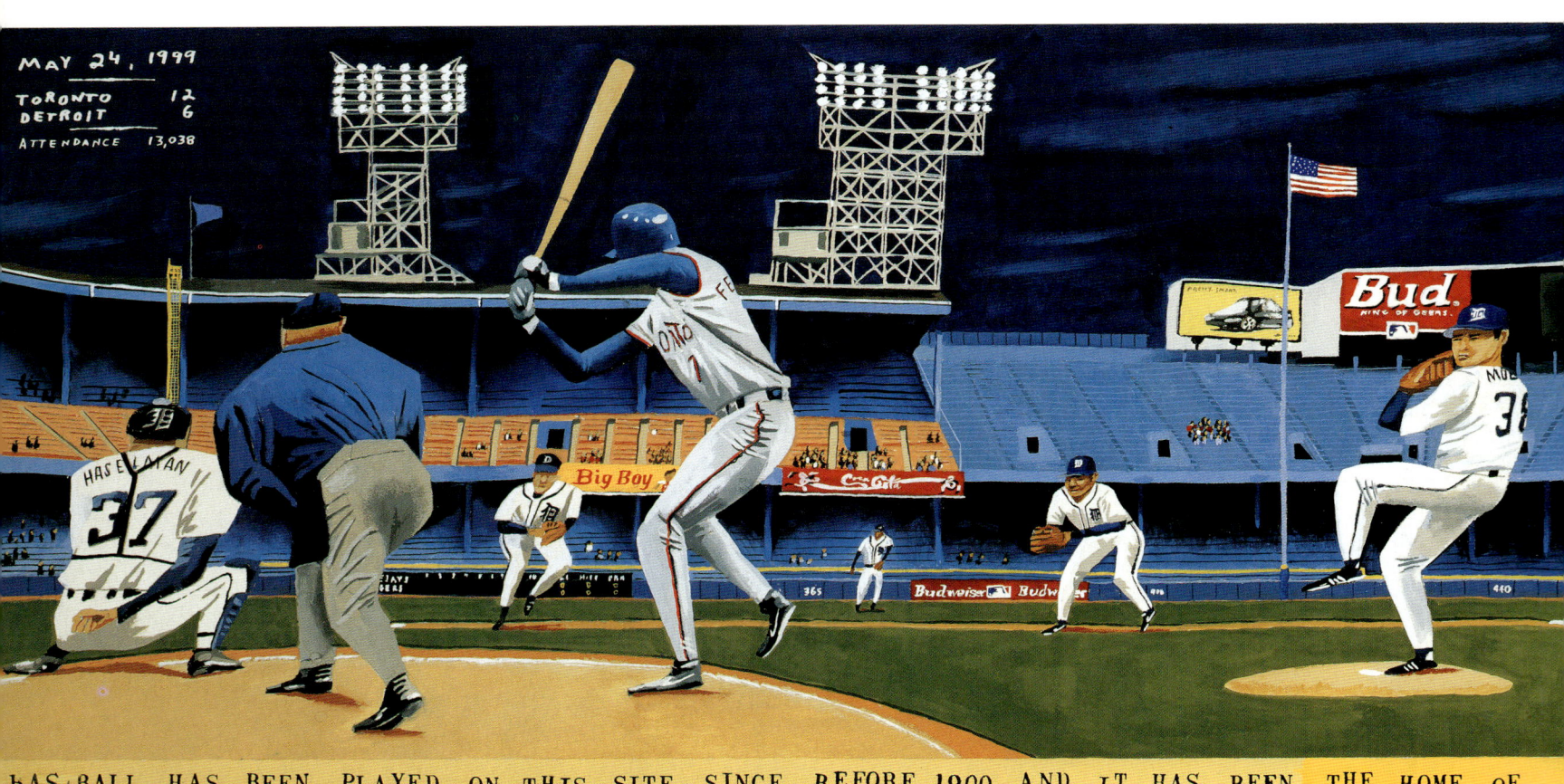

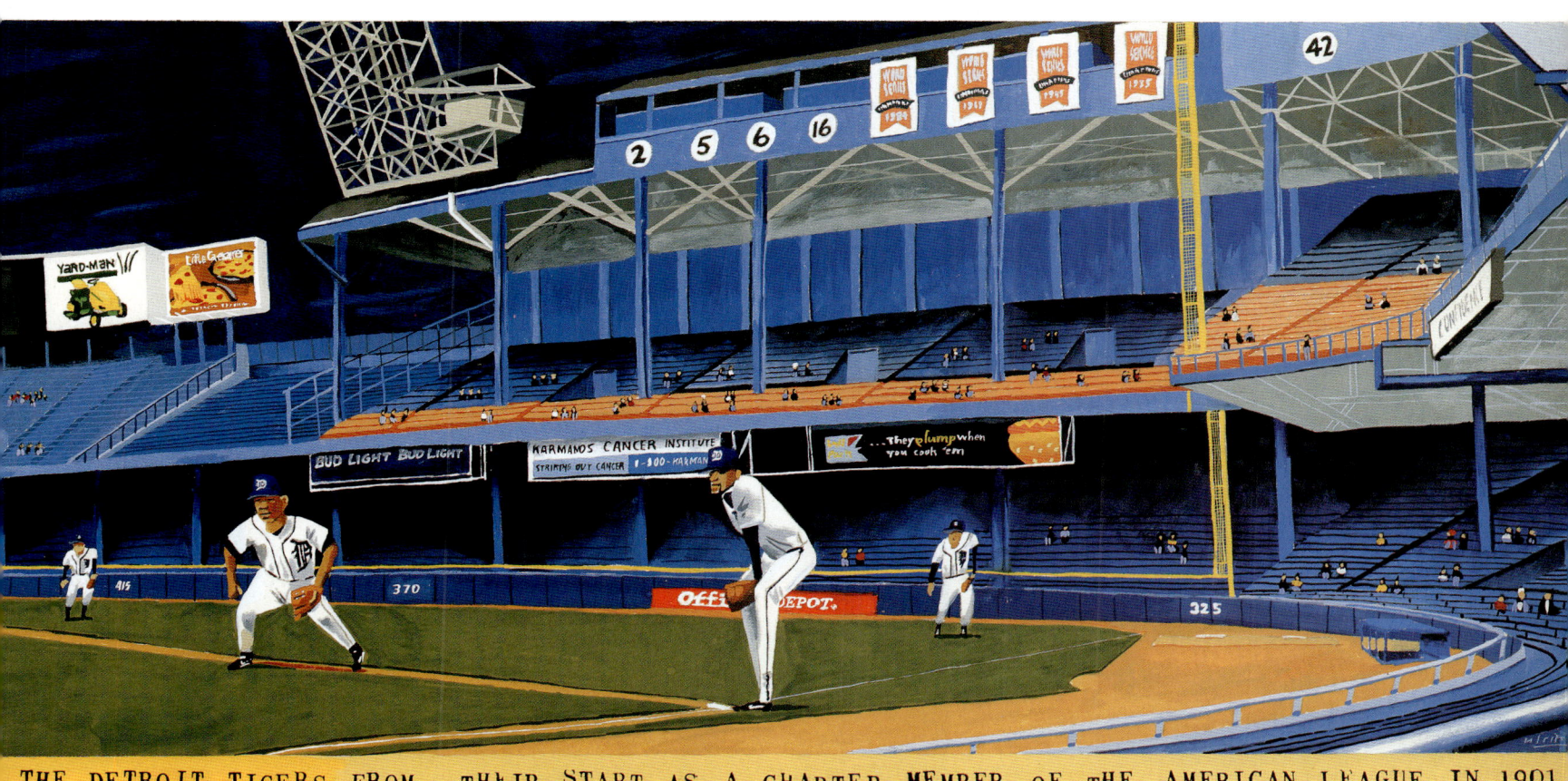

THE DETROIT TIGERS FROM THEIR START AS A CHARTER MEMBER OF THE AMERICAN LEAGUE IN 1901.

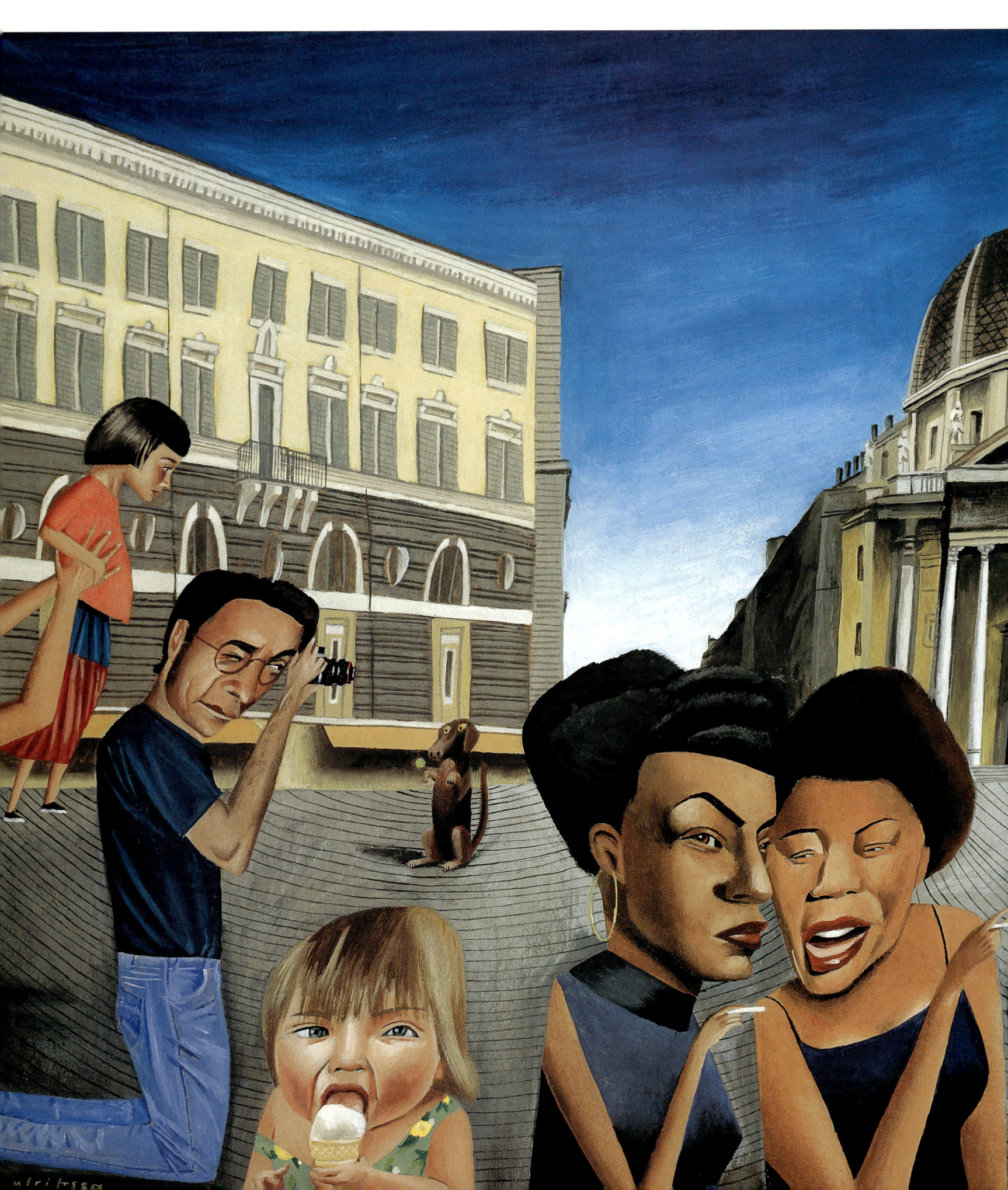

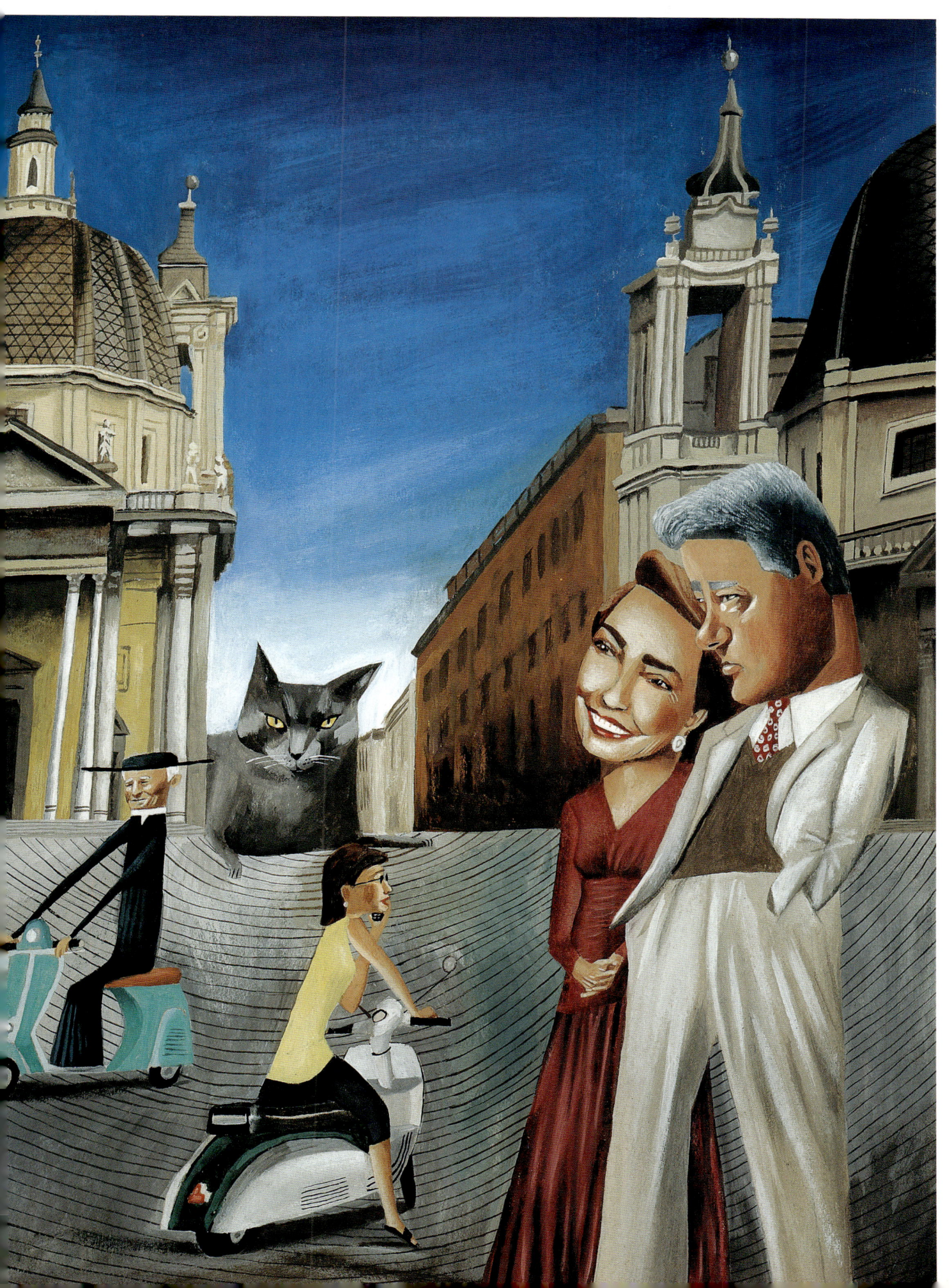

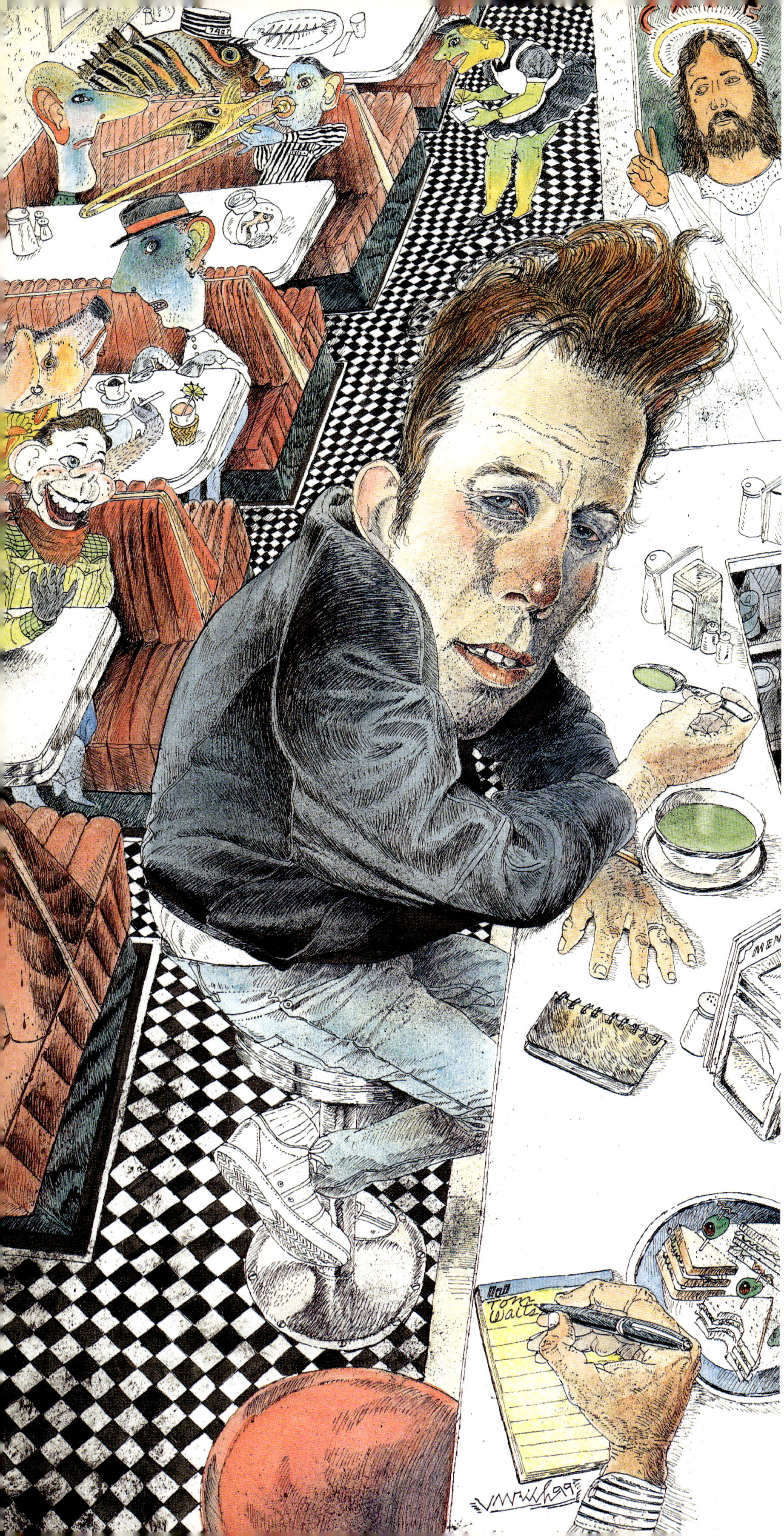

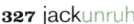

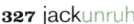

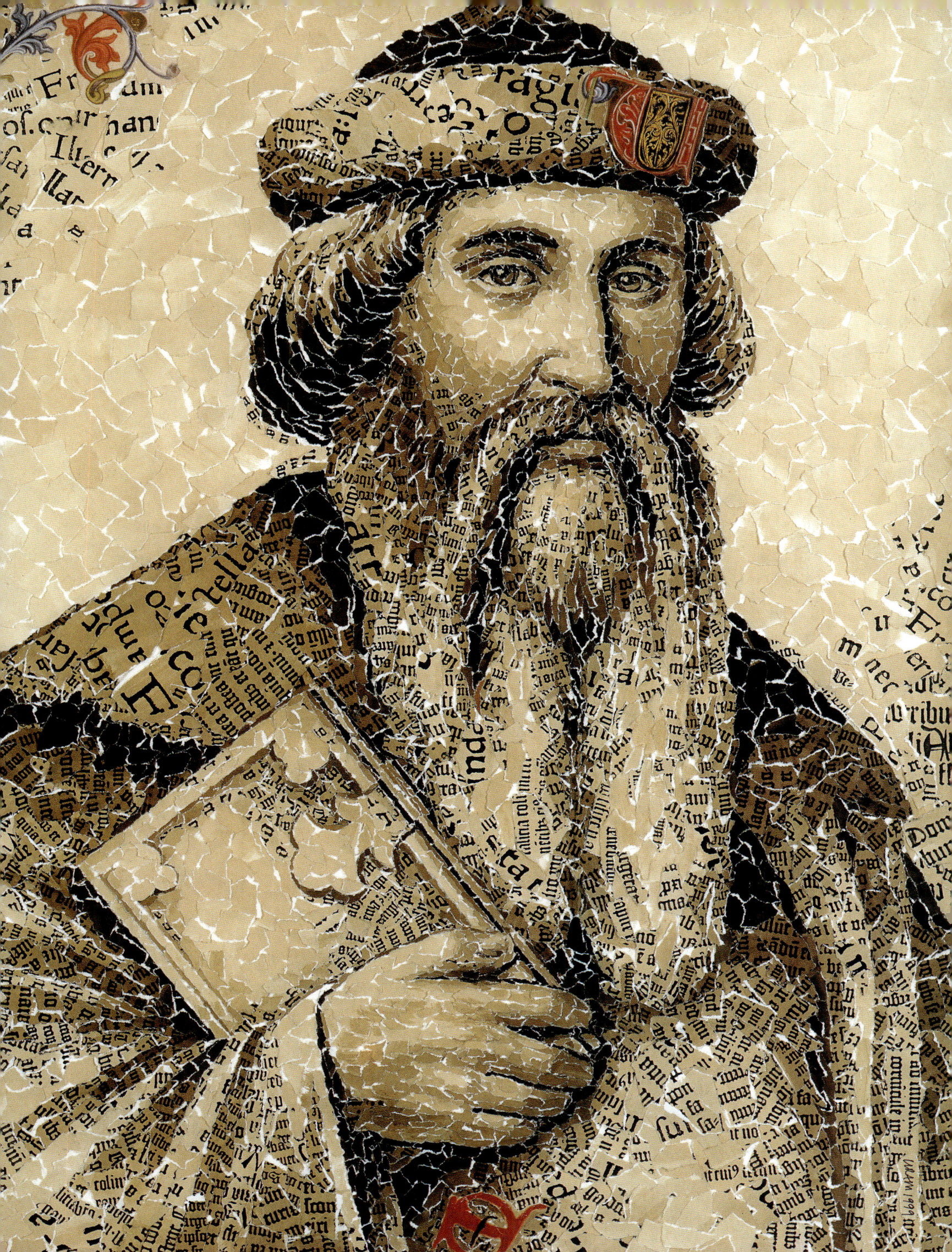

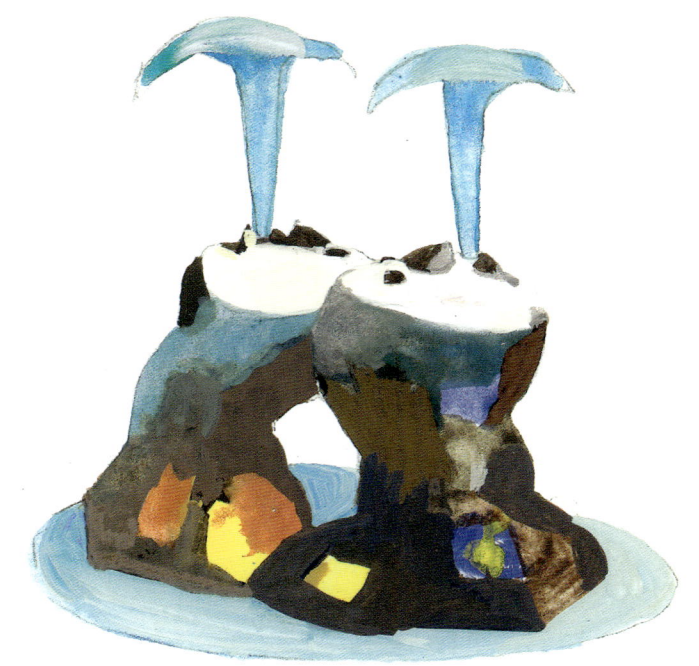

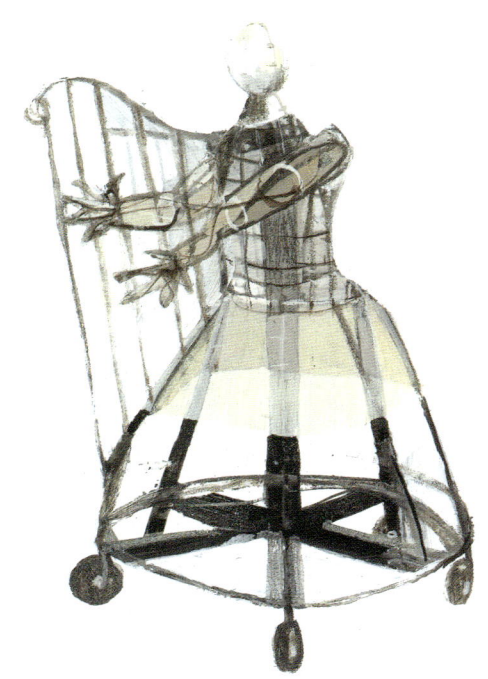

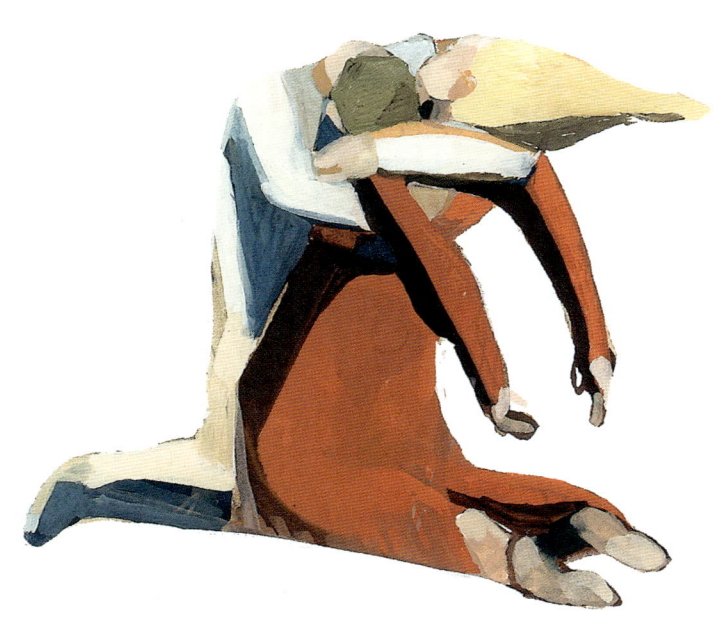

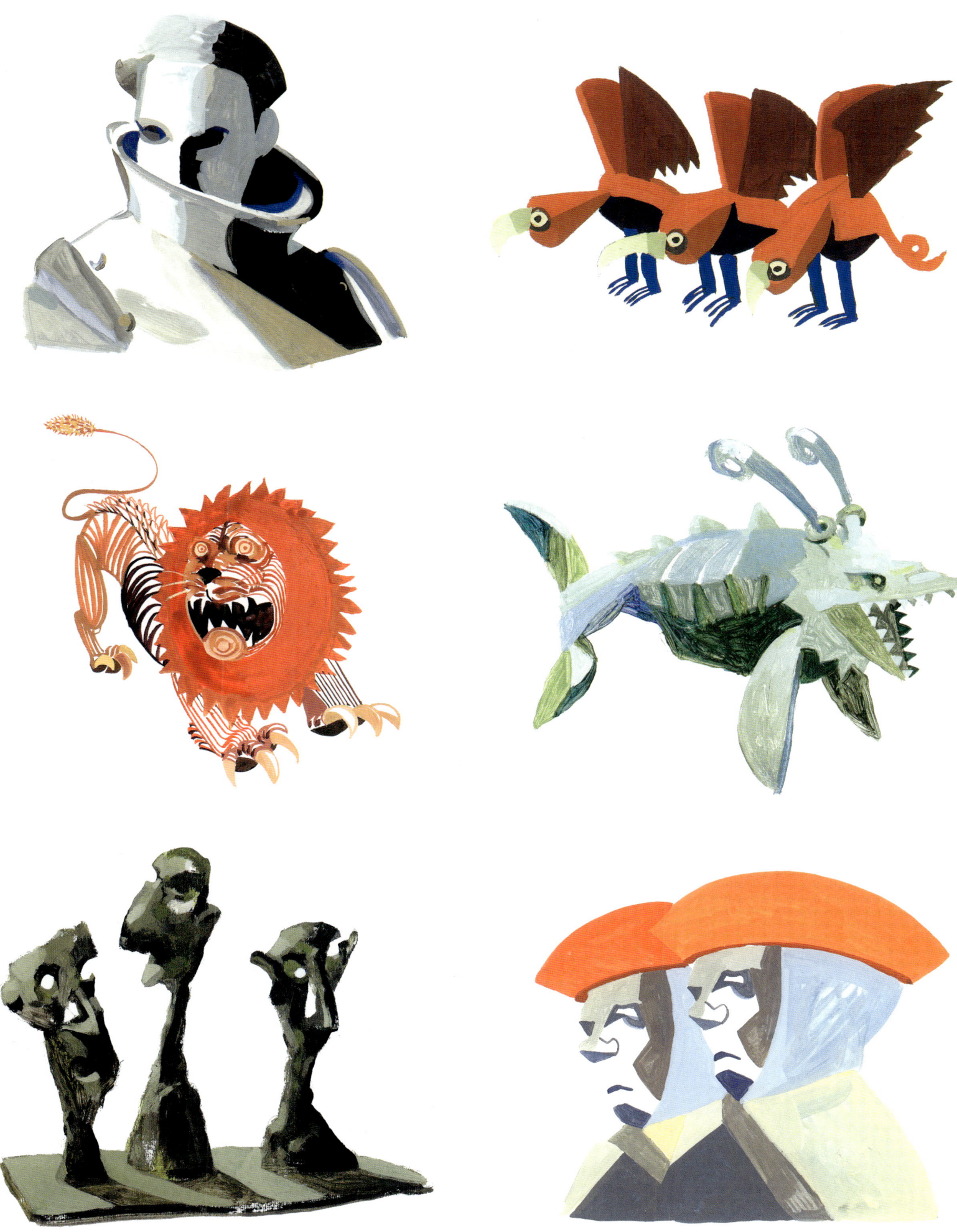

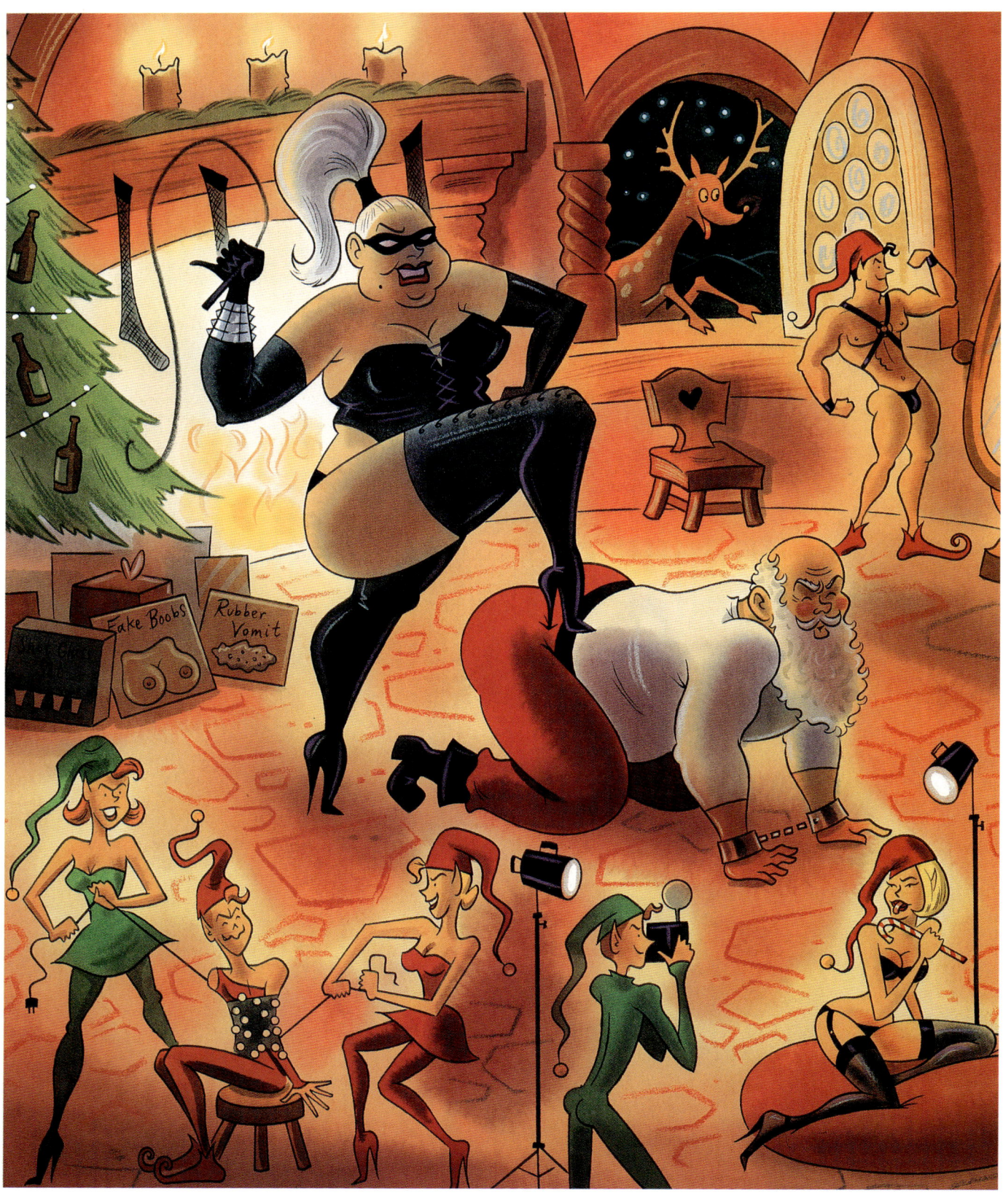

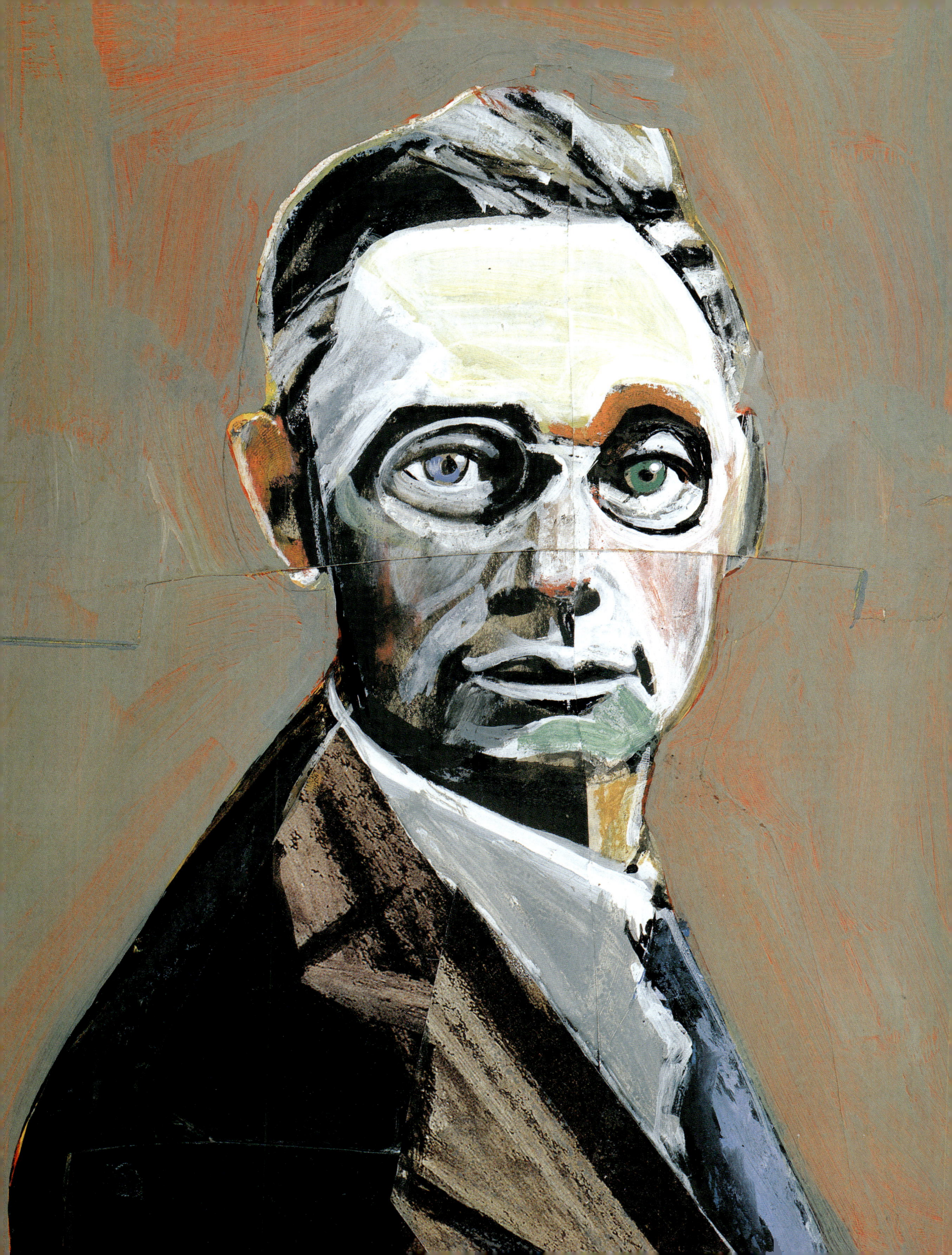

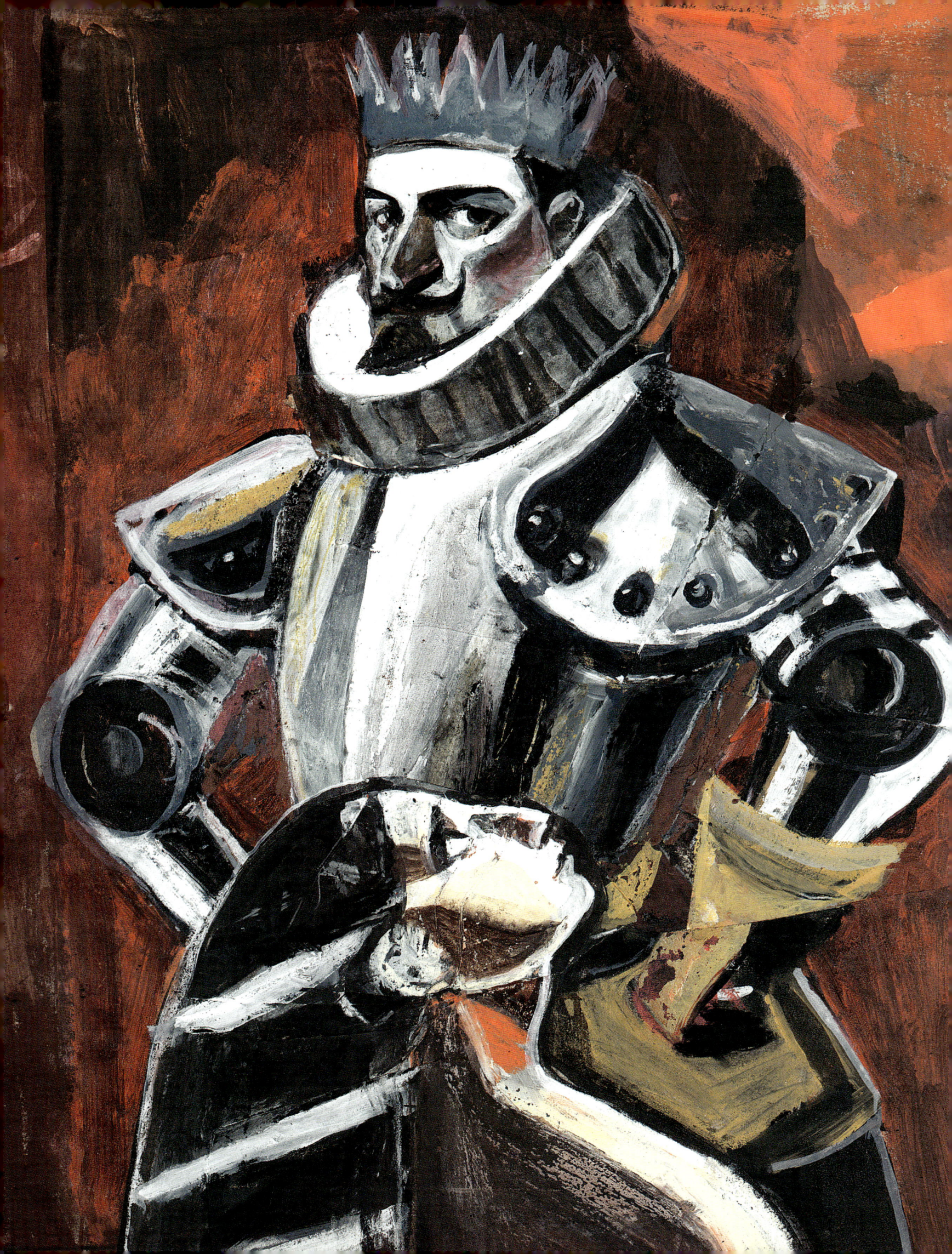

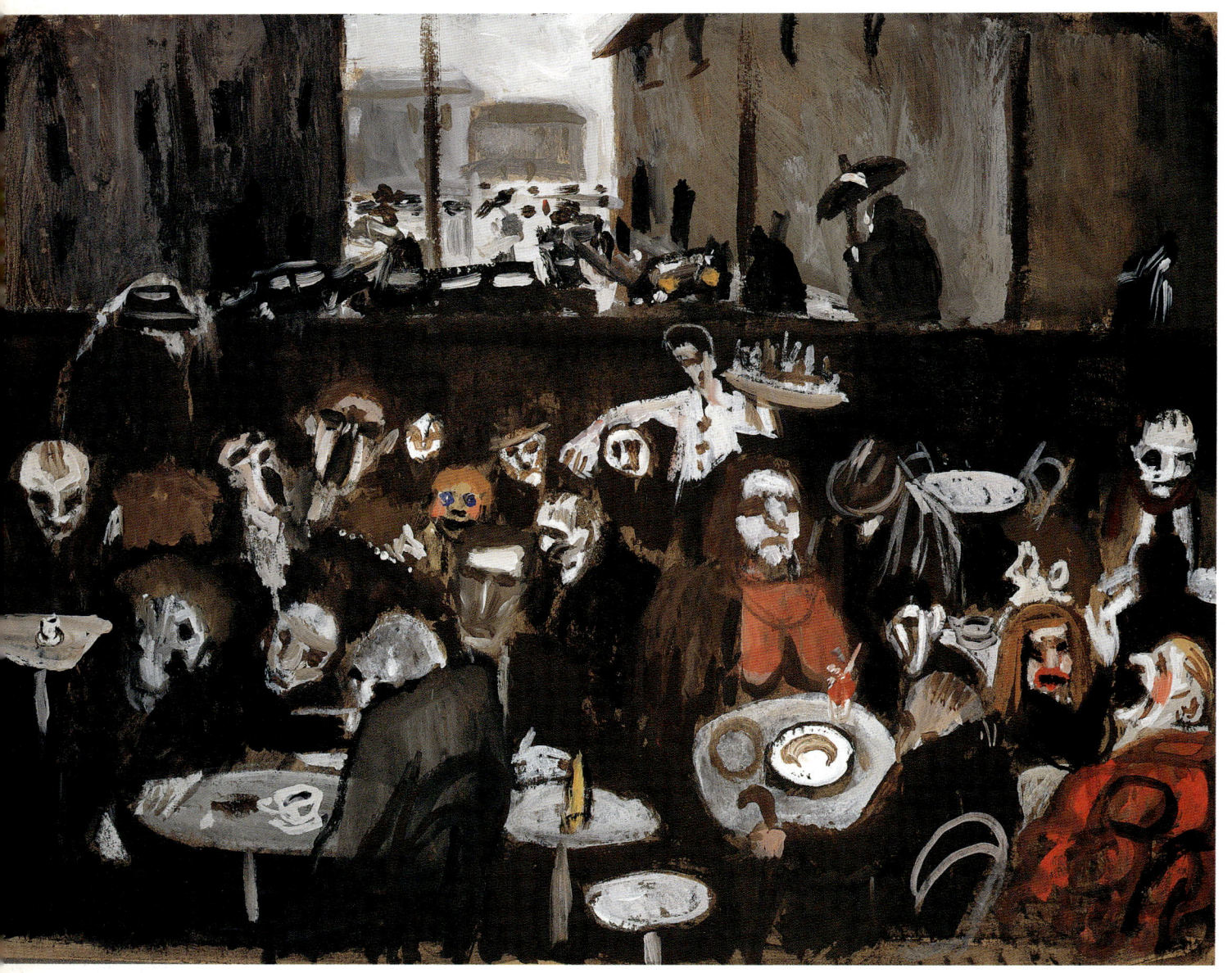

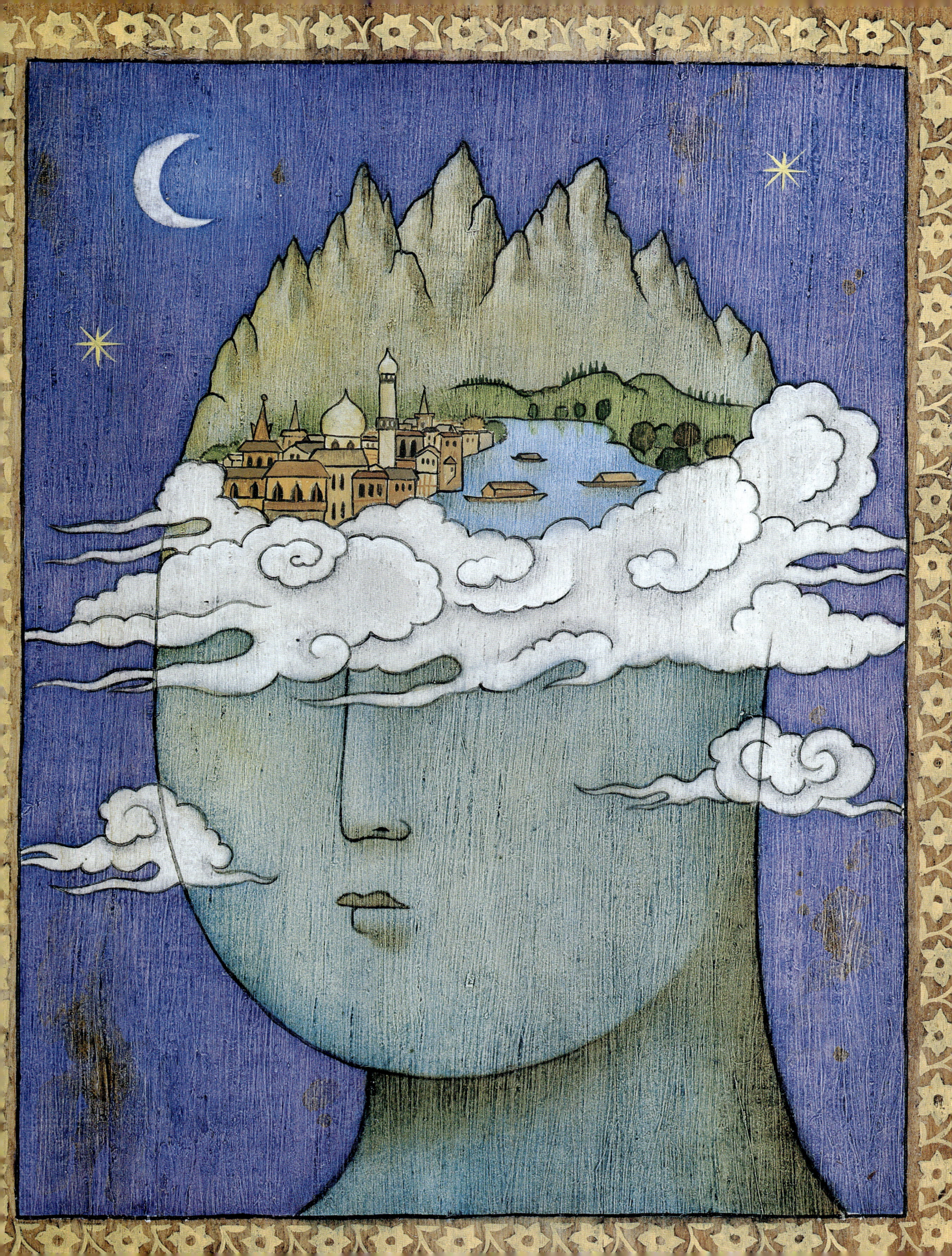

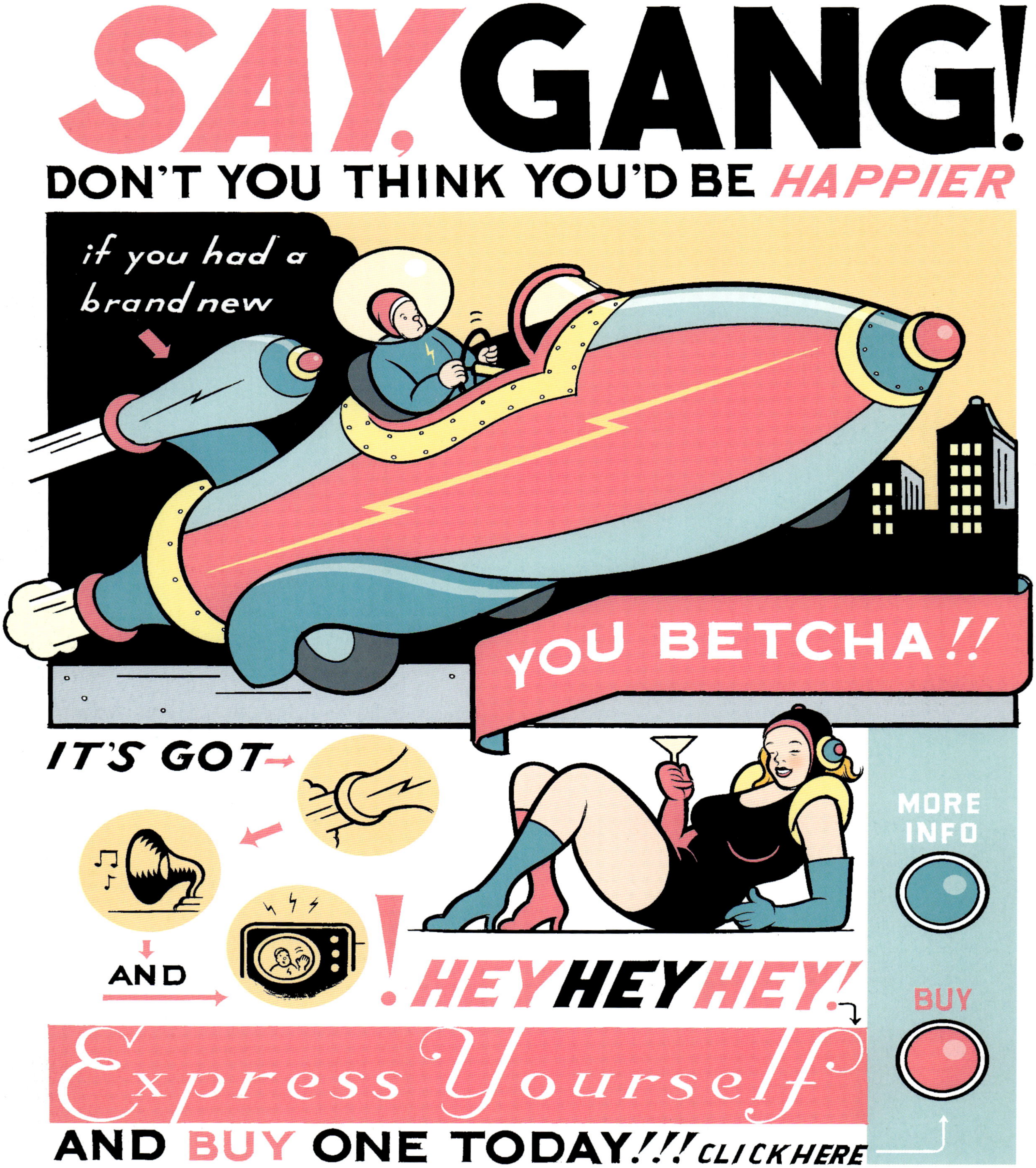

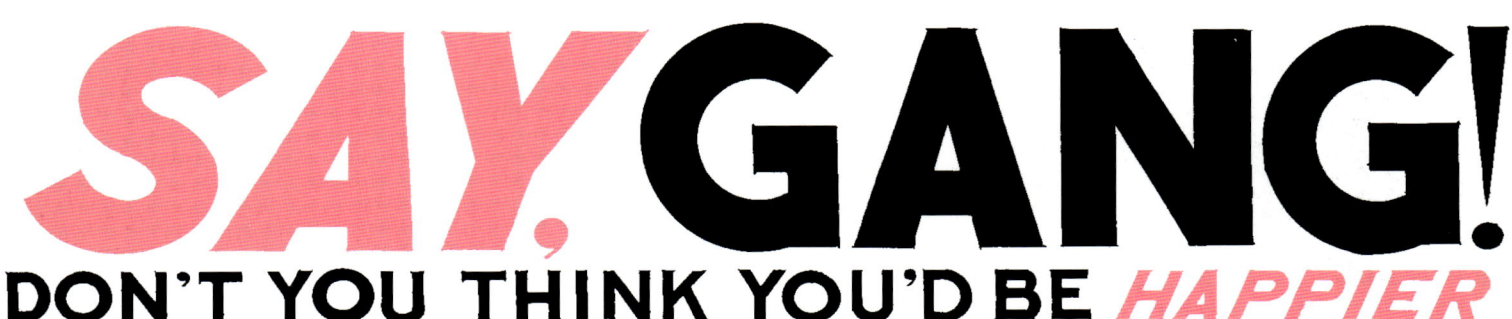

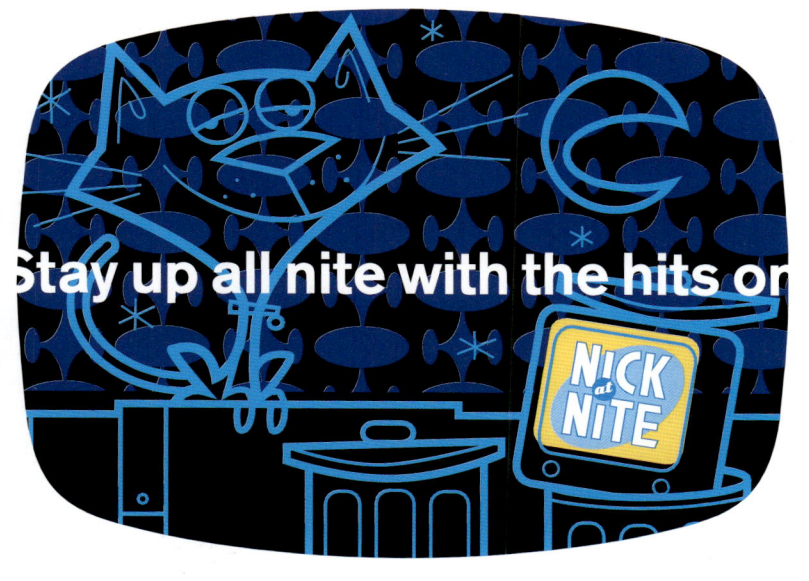

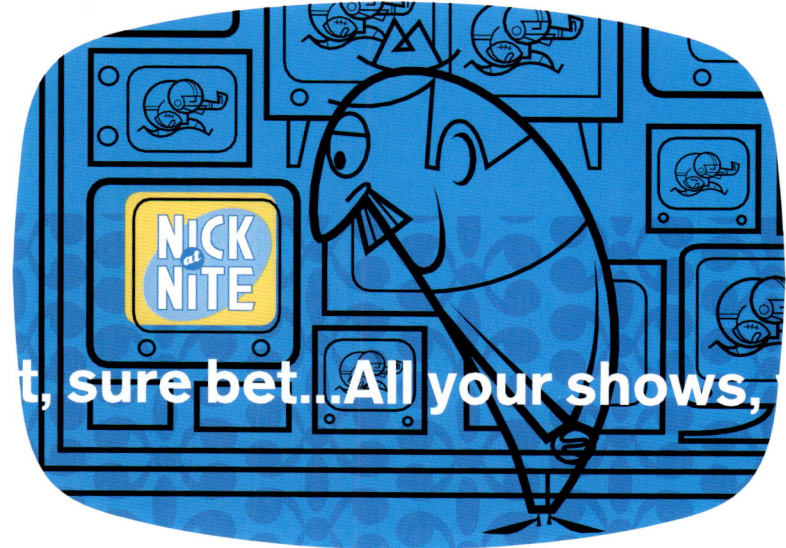

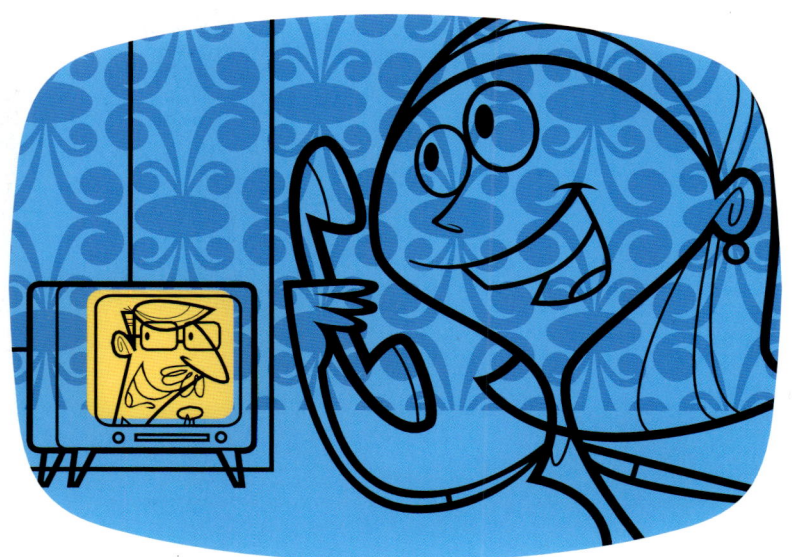

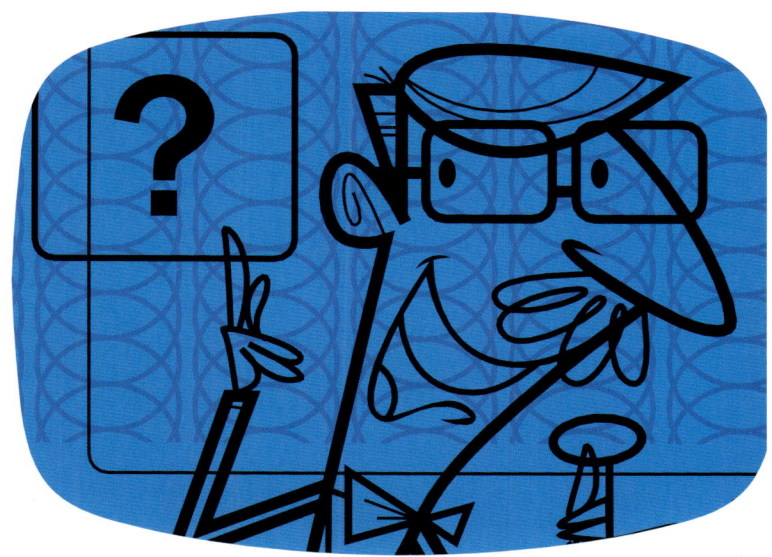

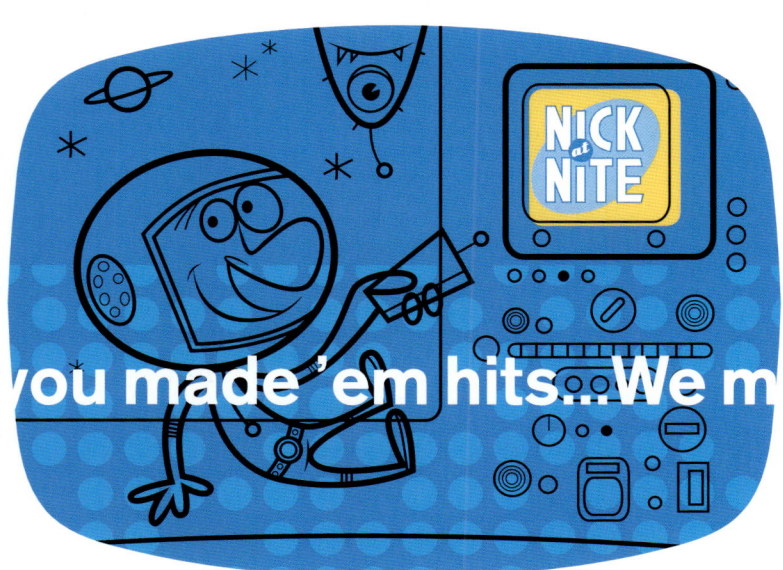

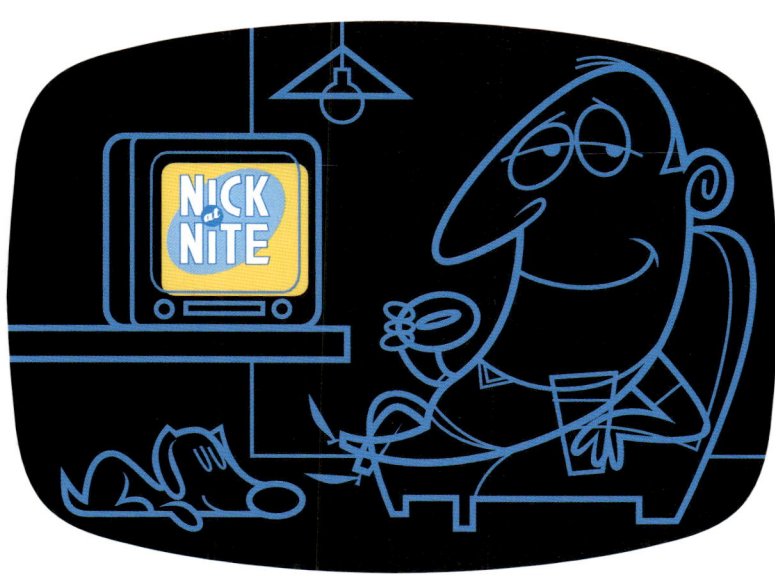

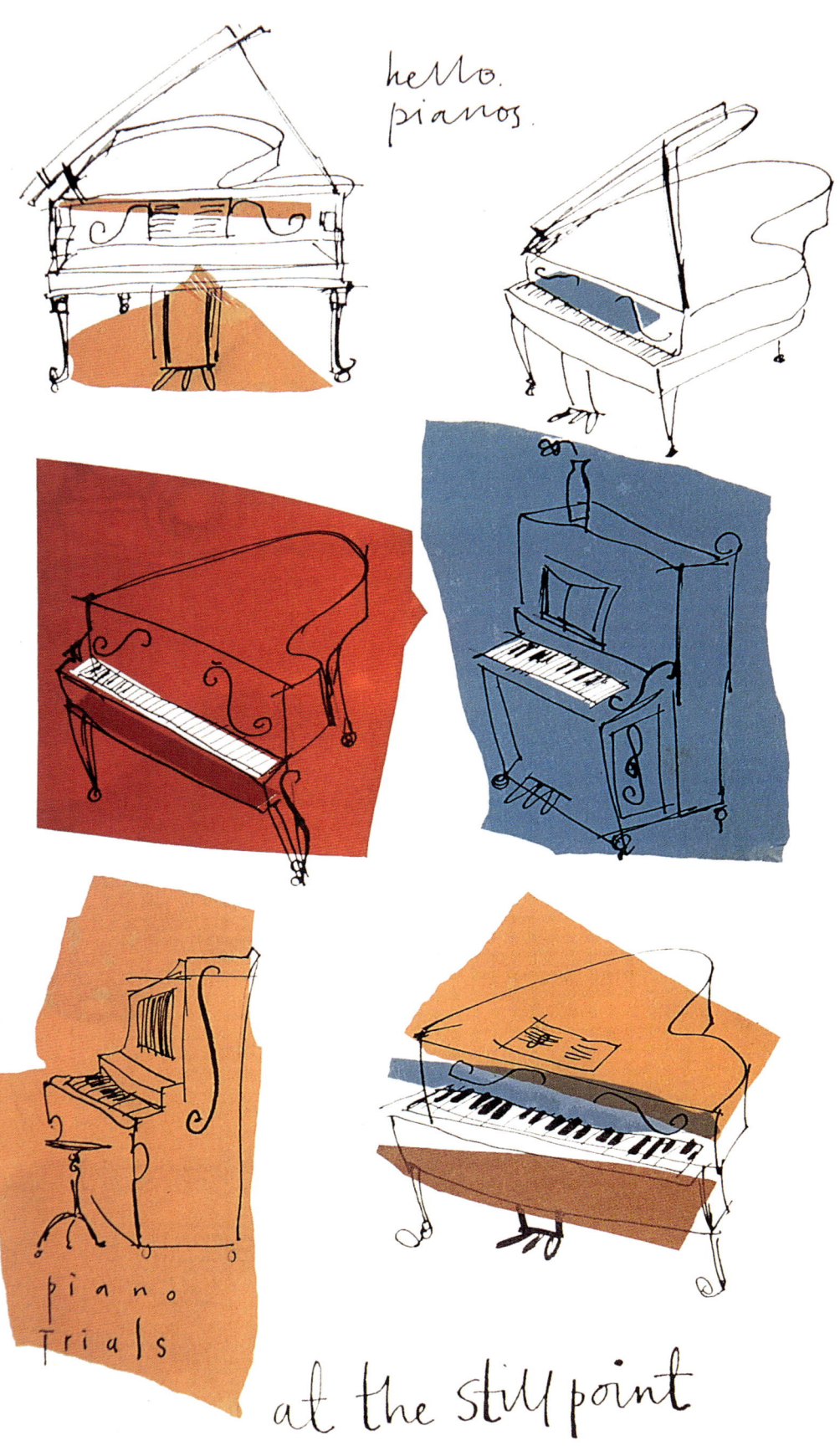

hello.
pianos.

piano
Trials

at the still point

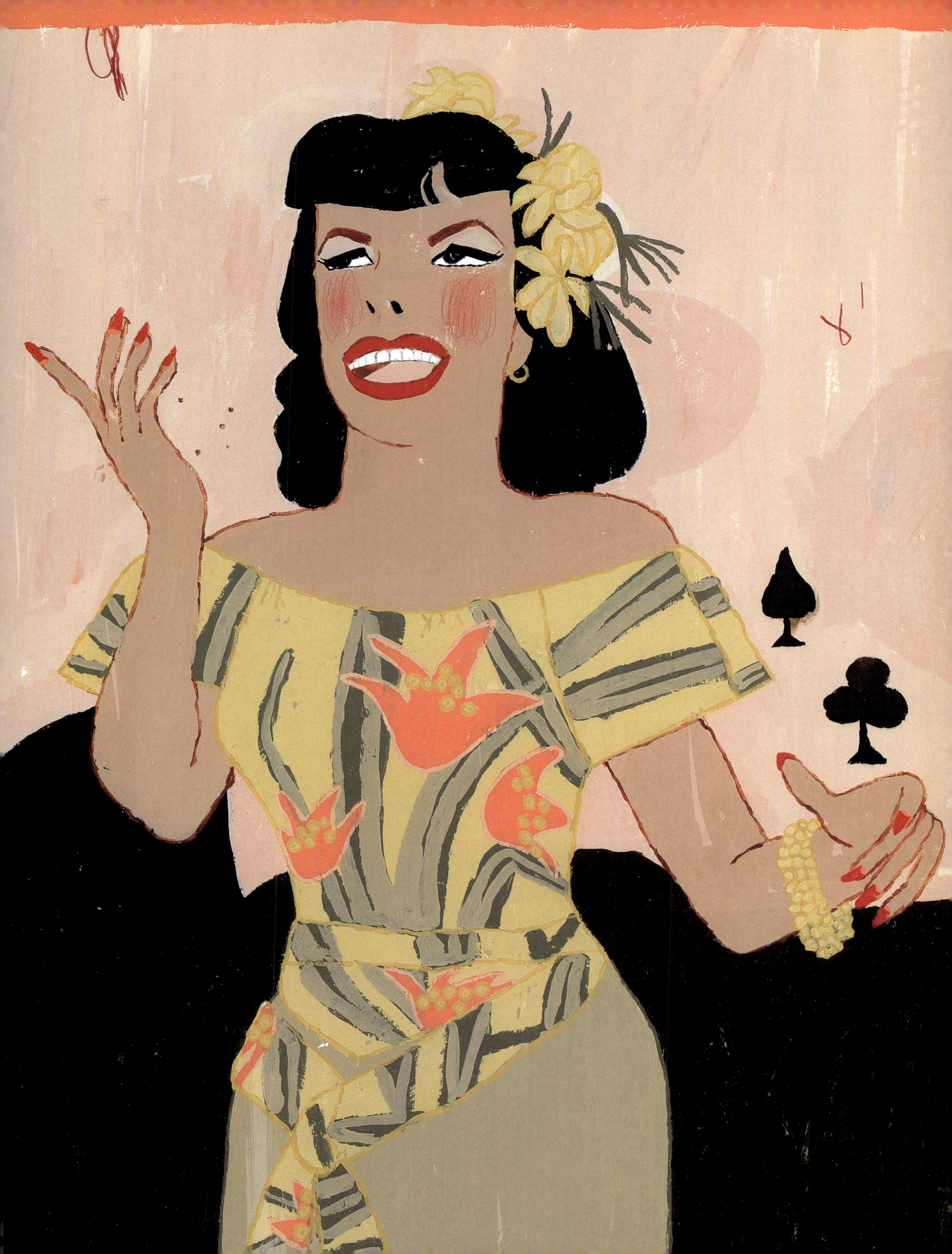

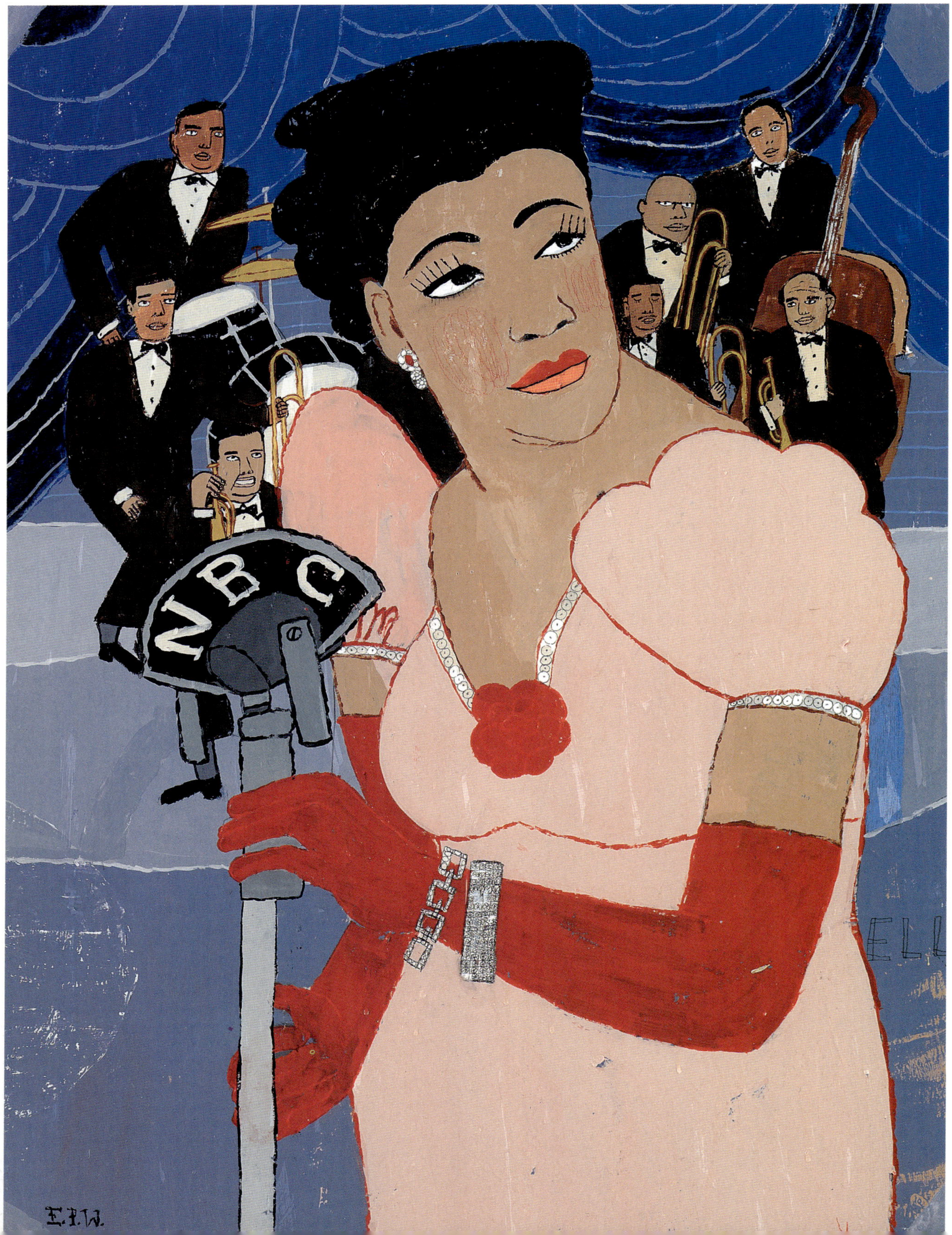
NBC
ELL
E.P.W.

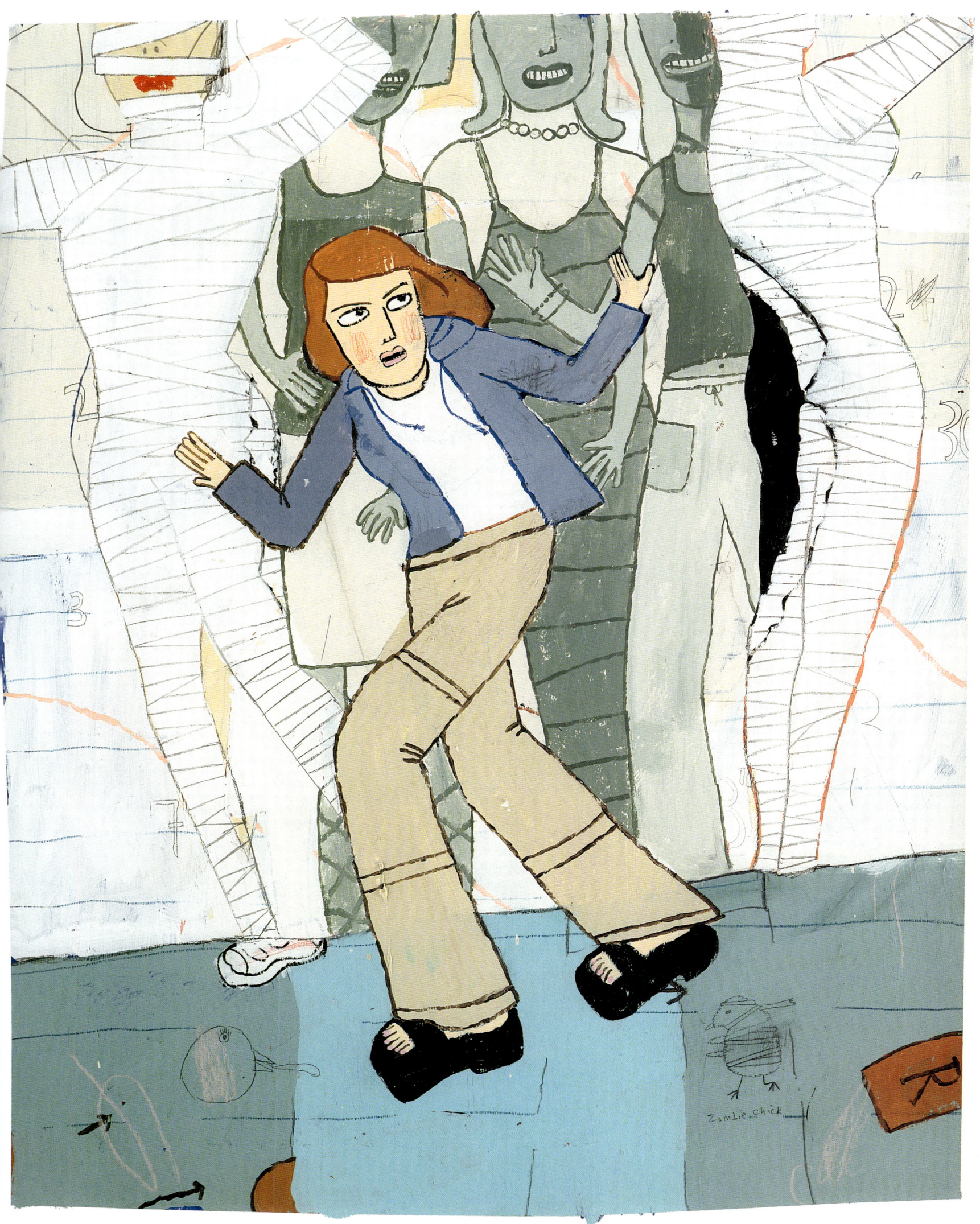

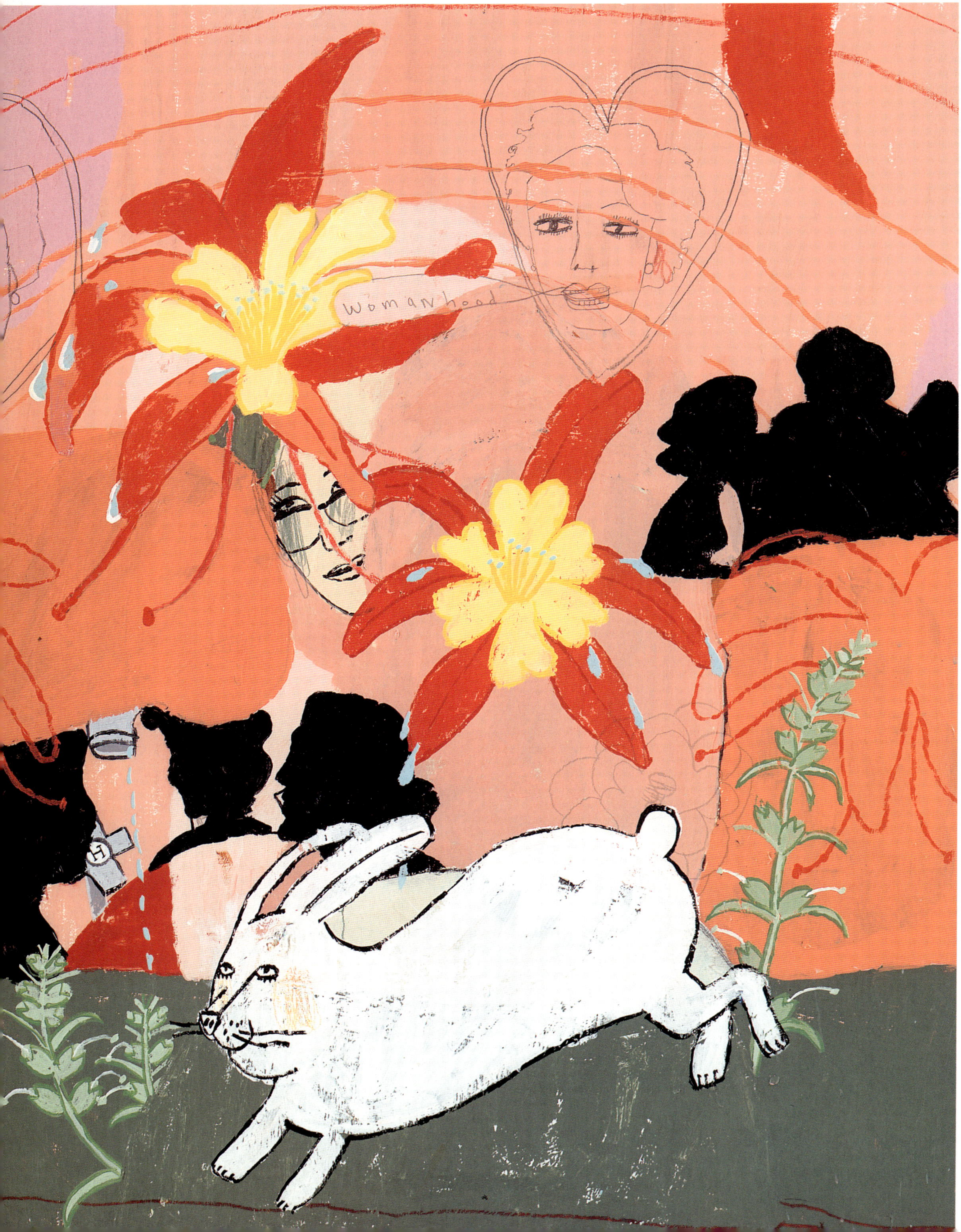
womanhood

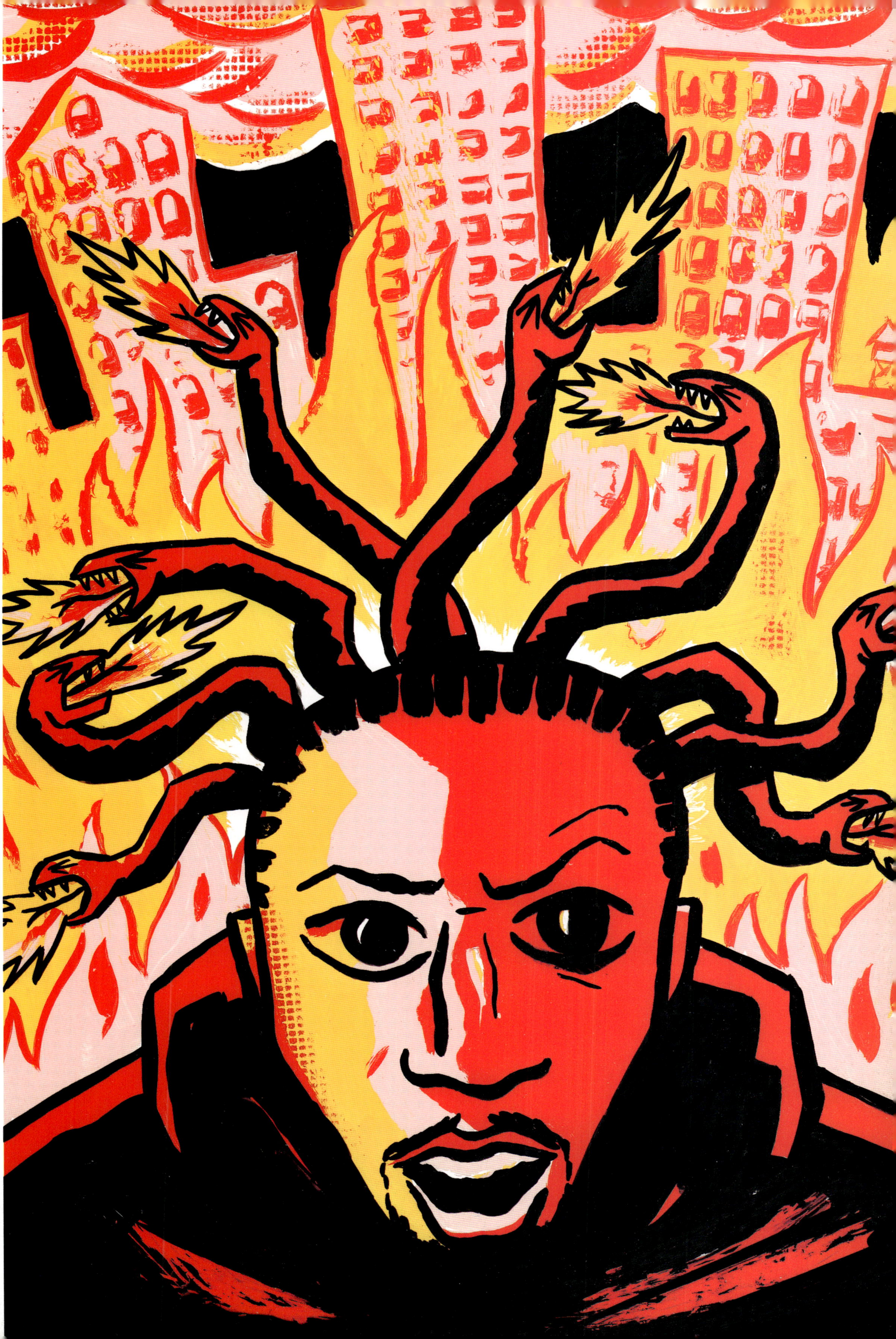

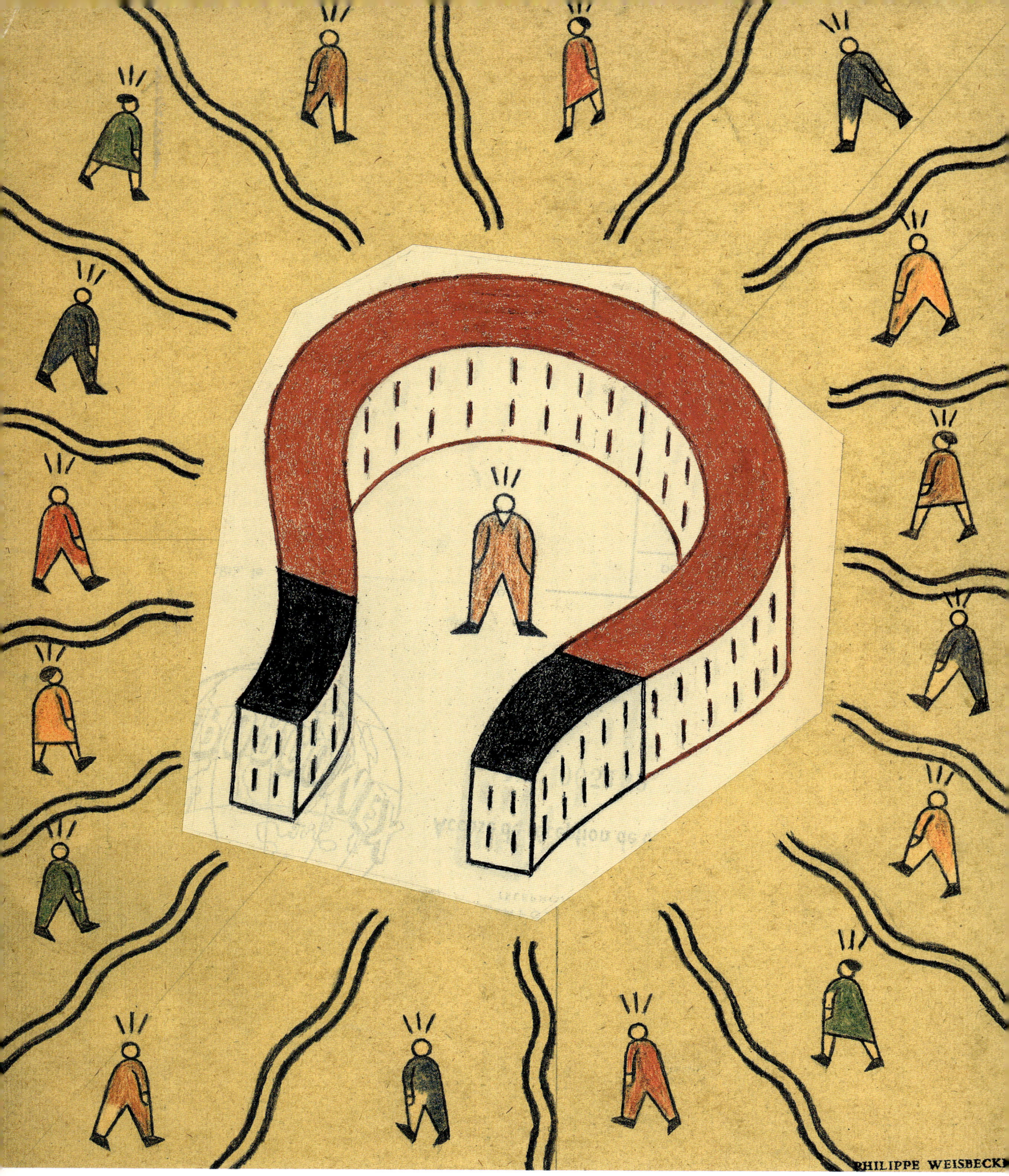

PHILIPPE WEISBECKER

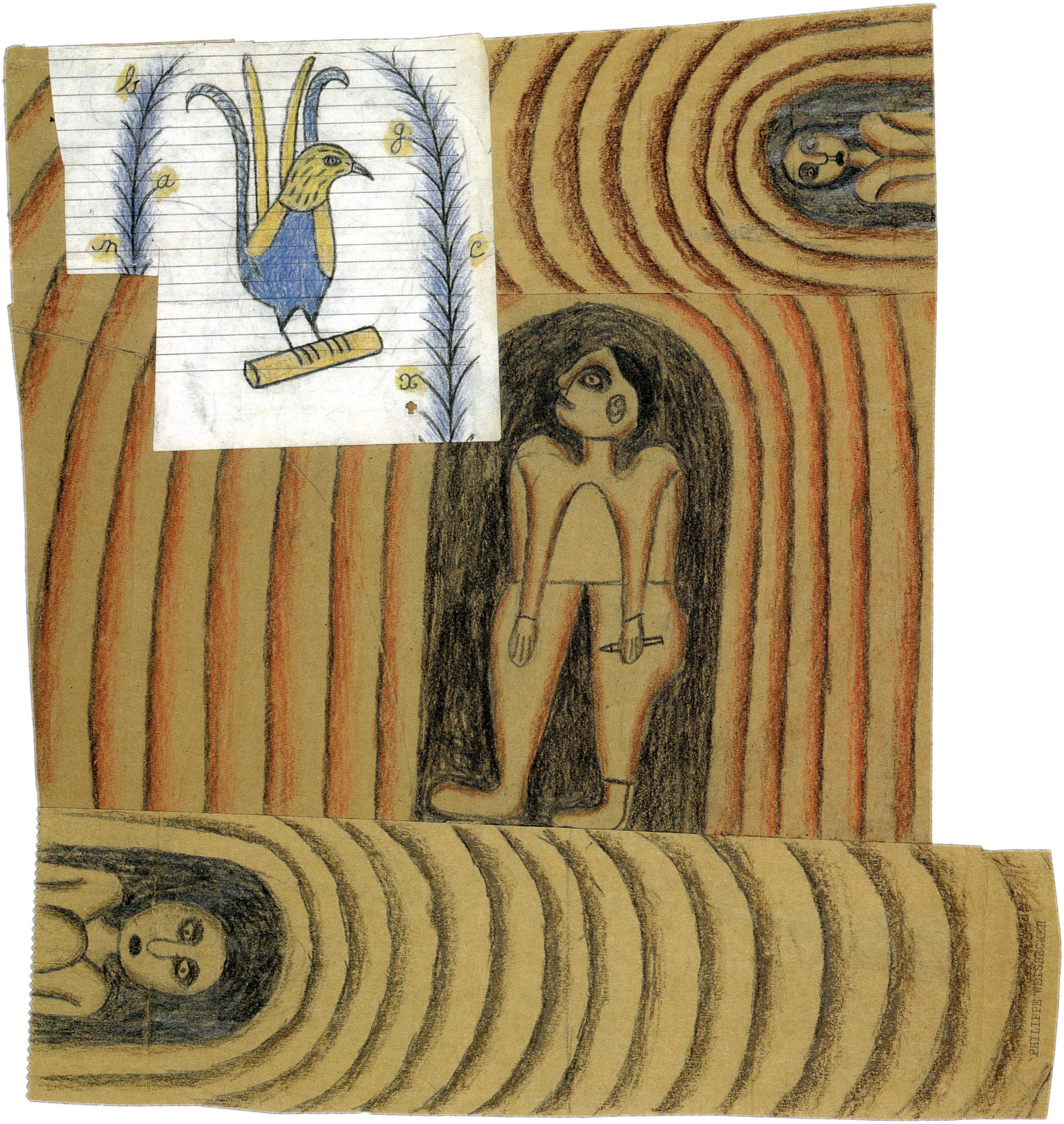
PHILIPPE WEISBECKER

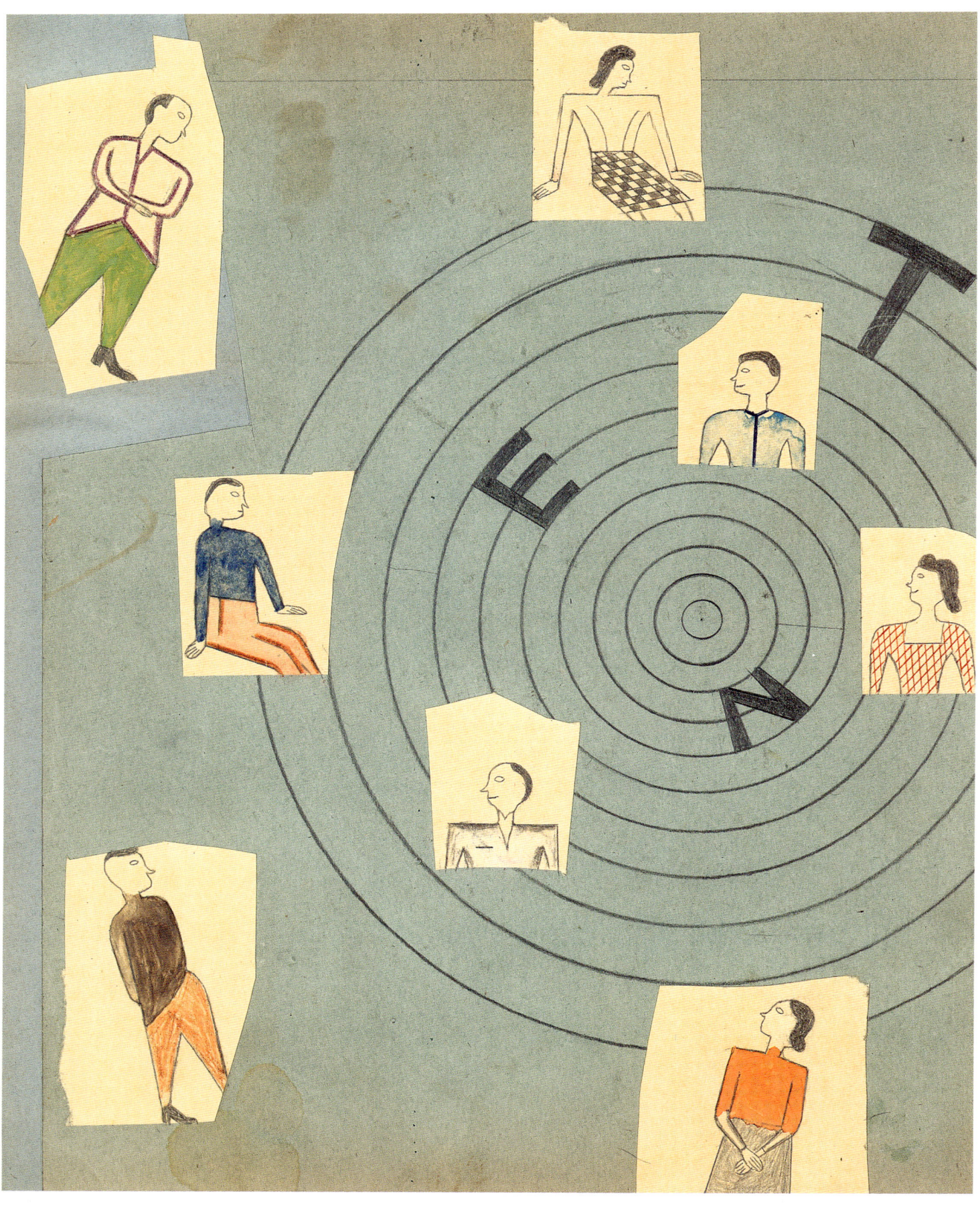

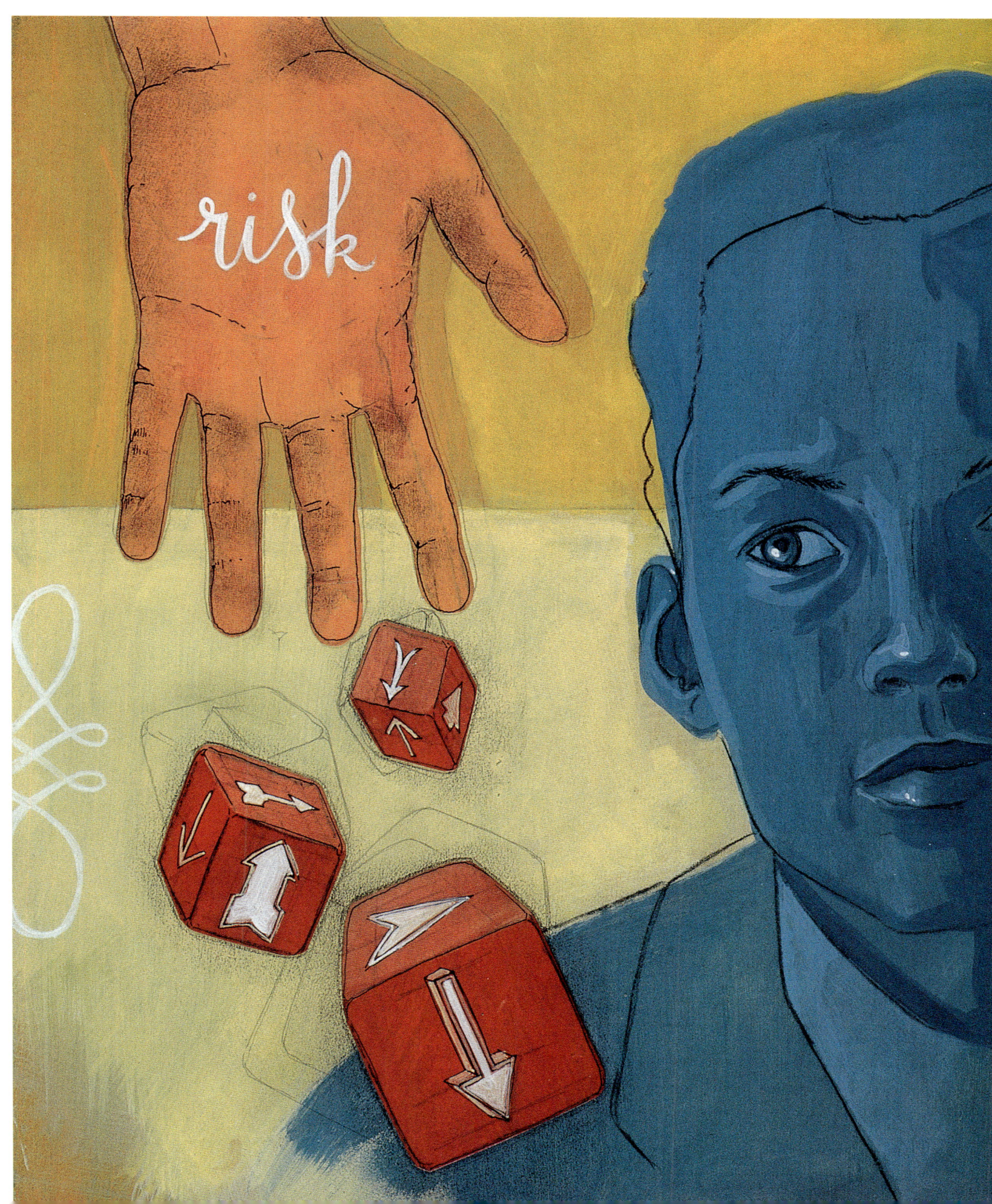

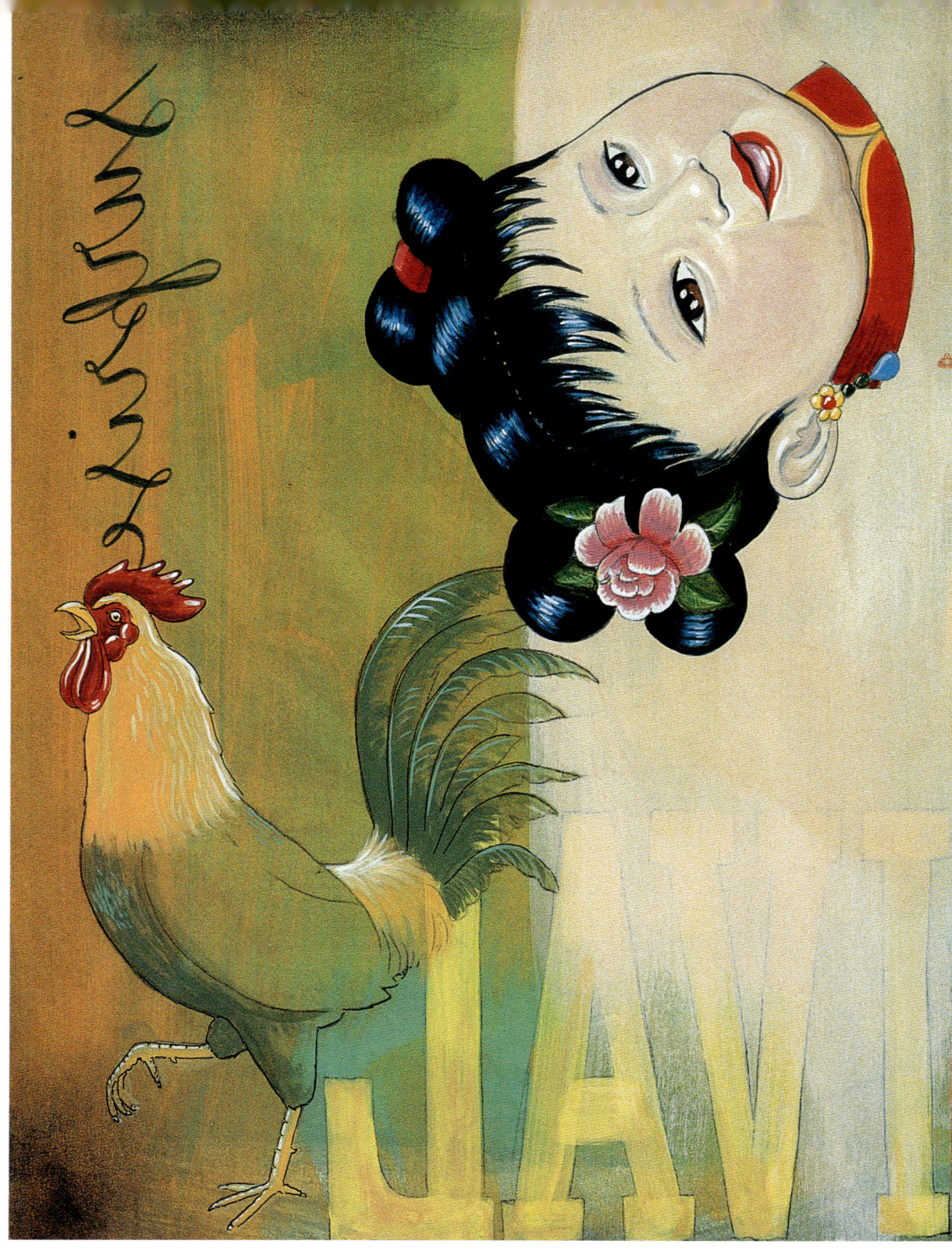

348 leighwells

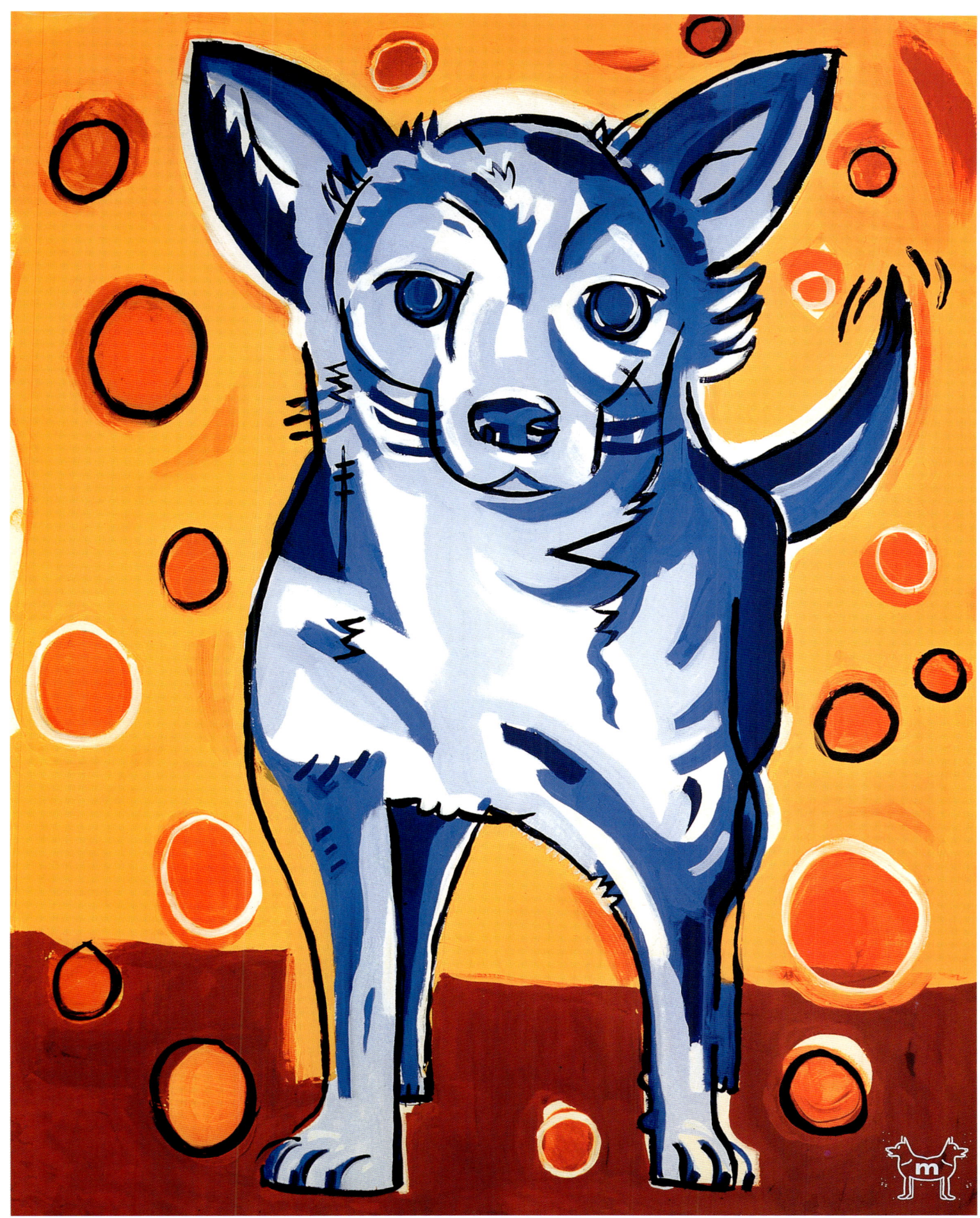

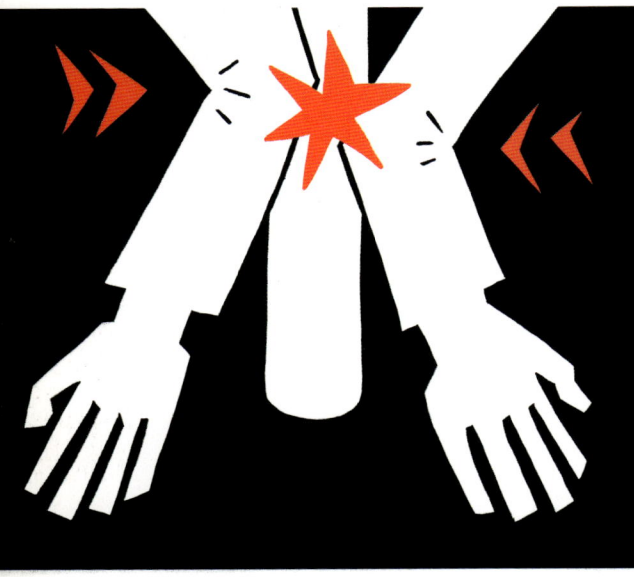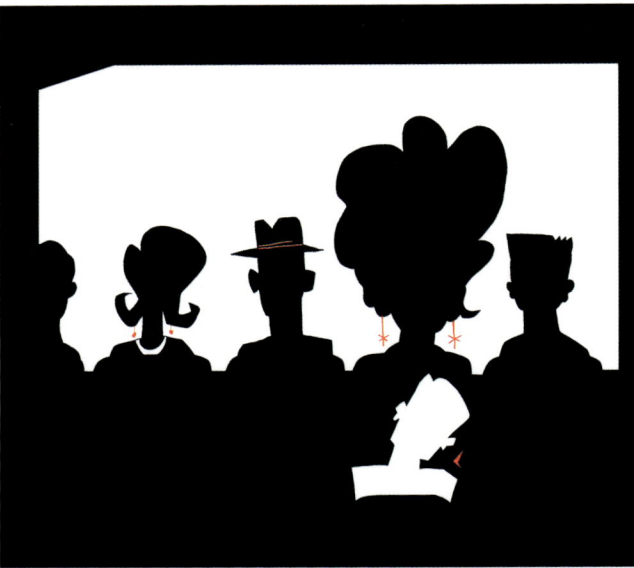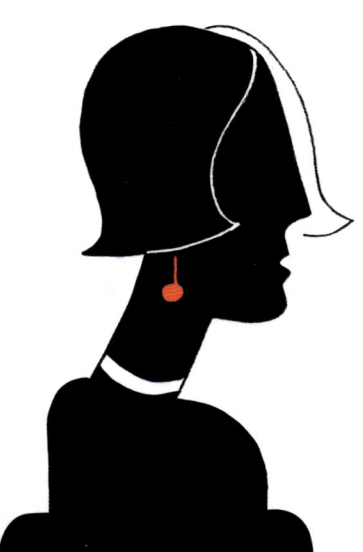

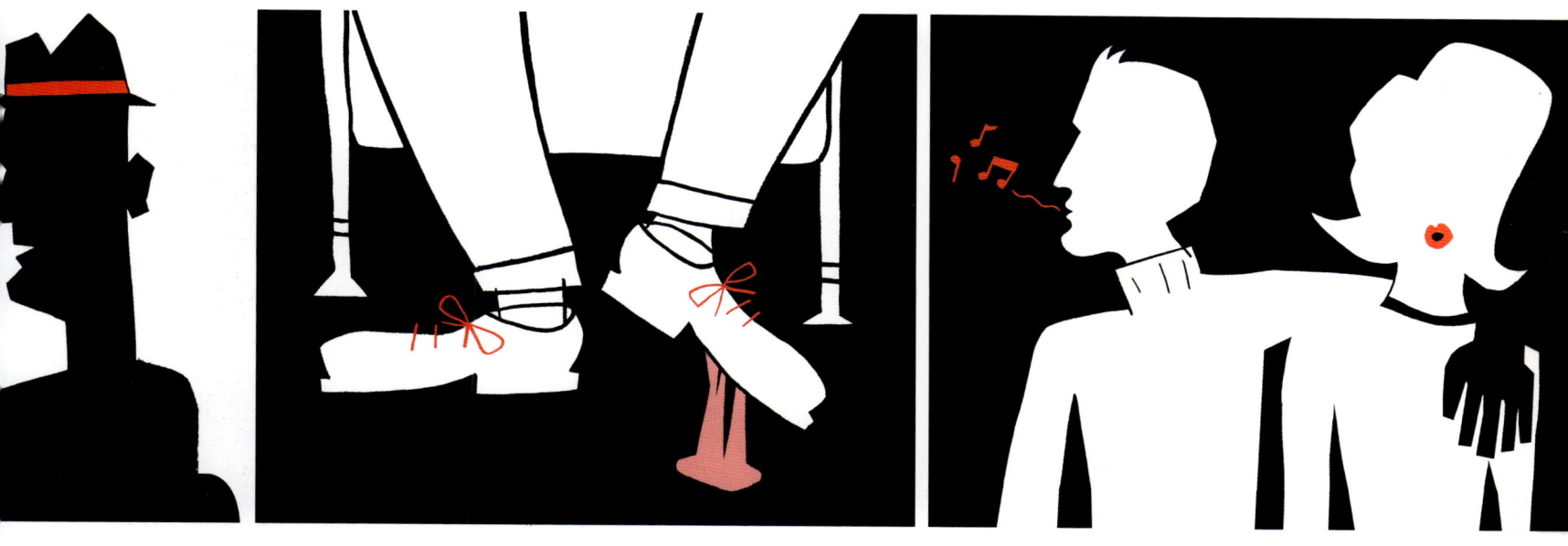

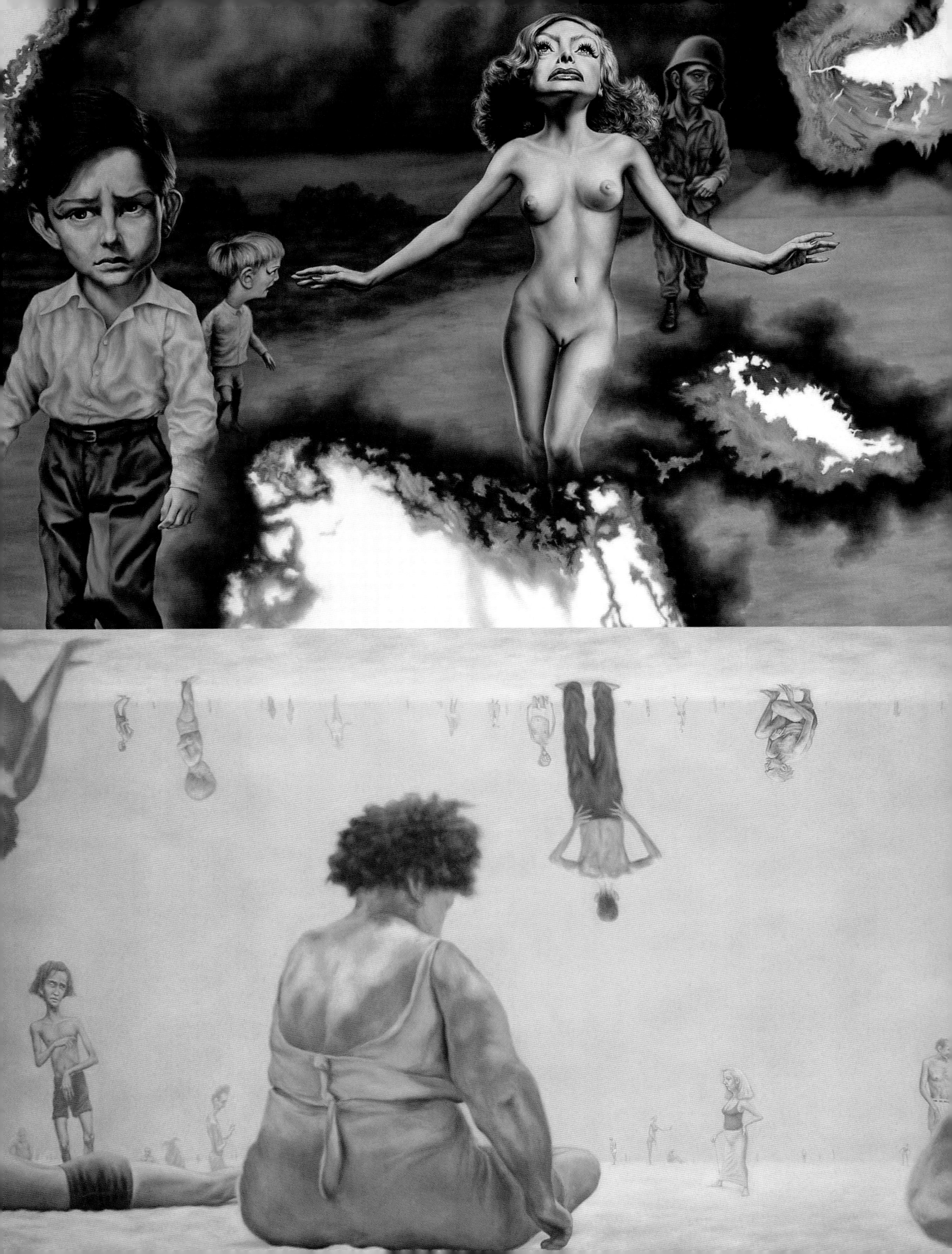

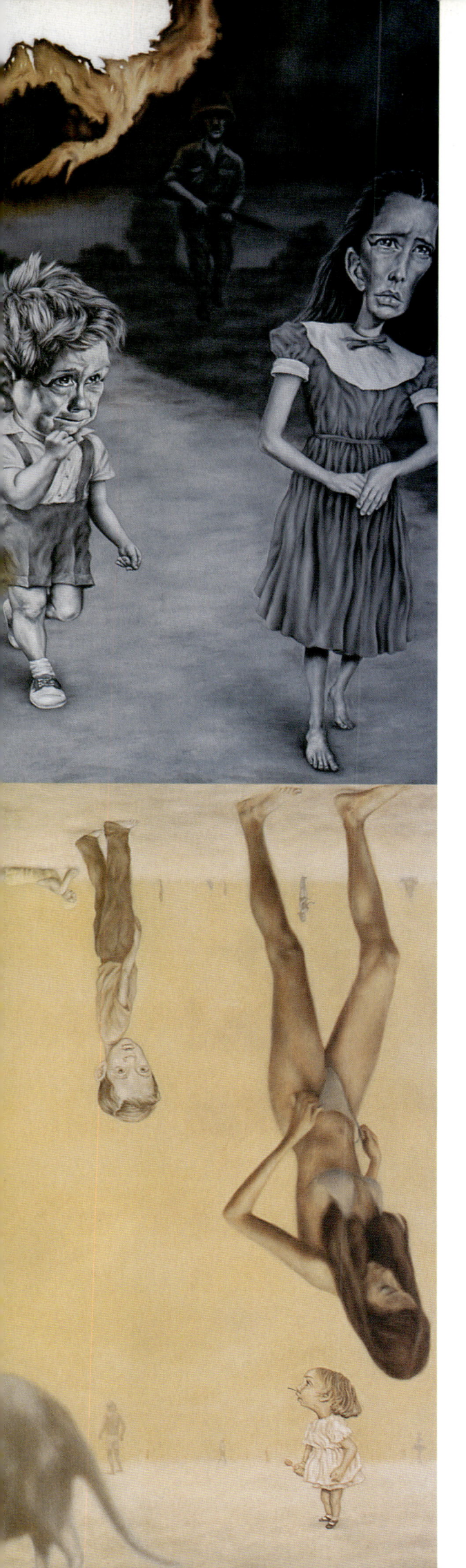

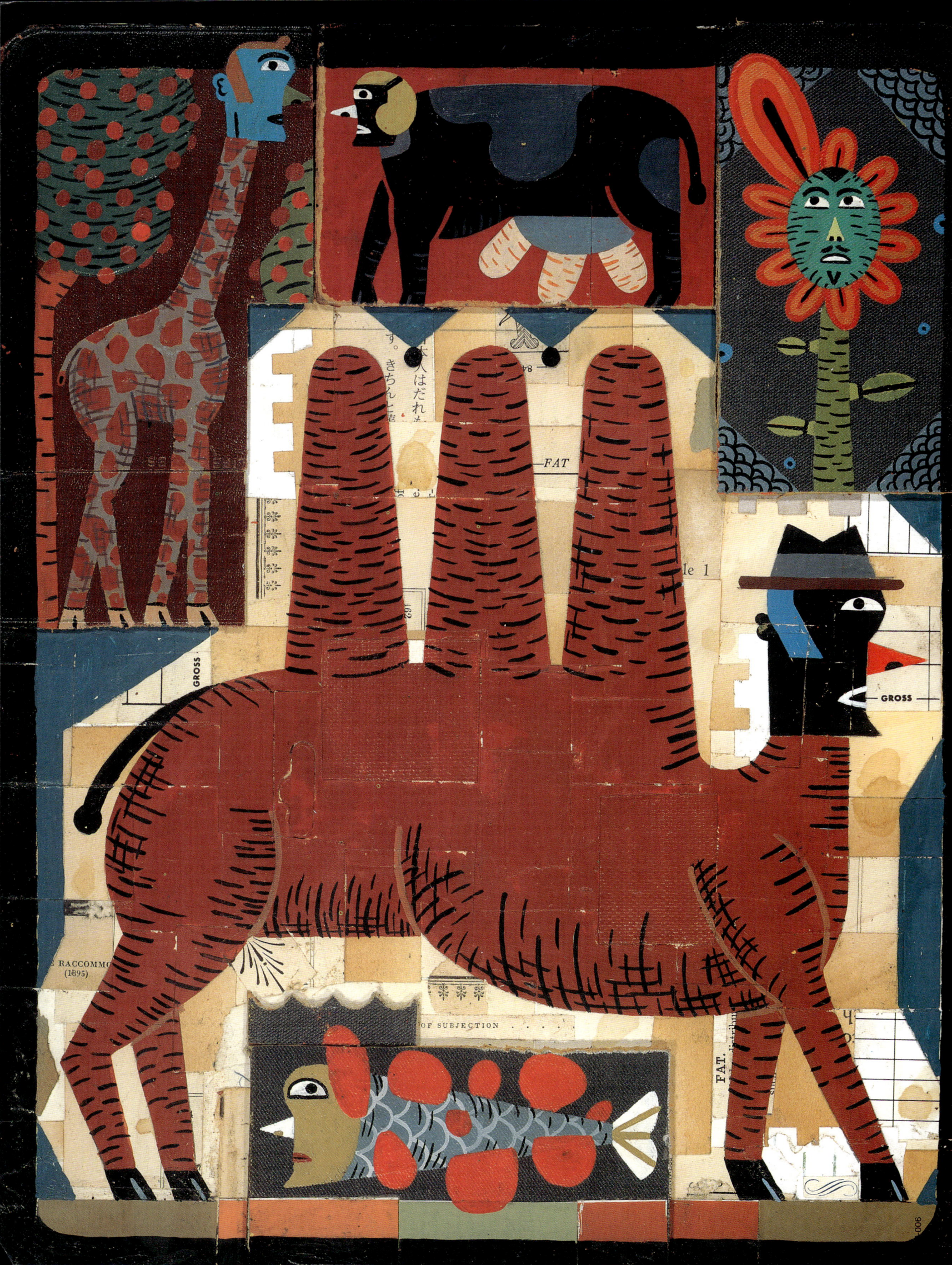

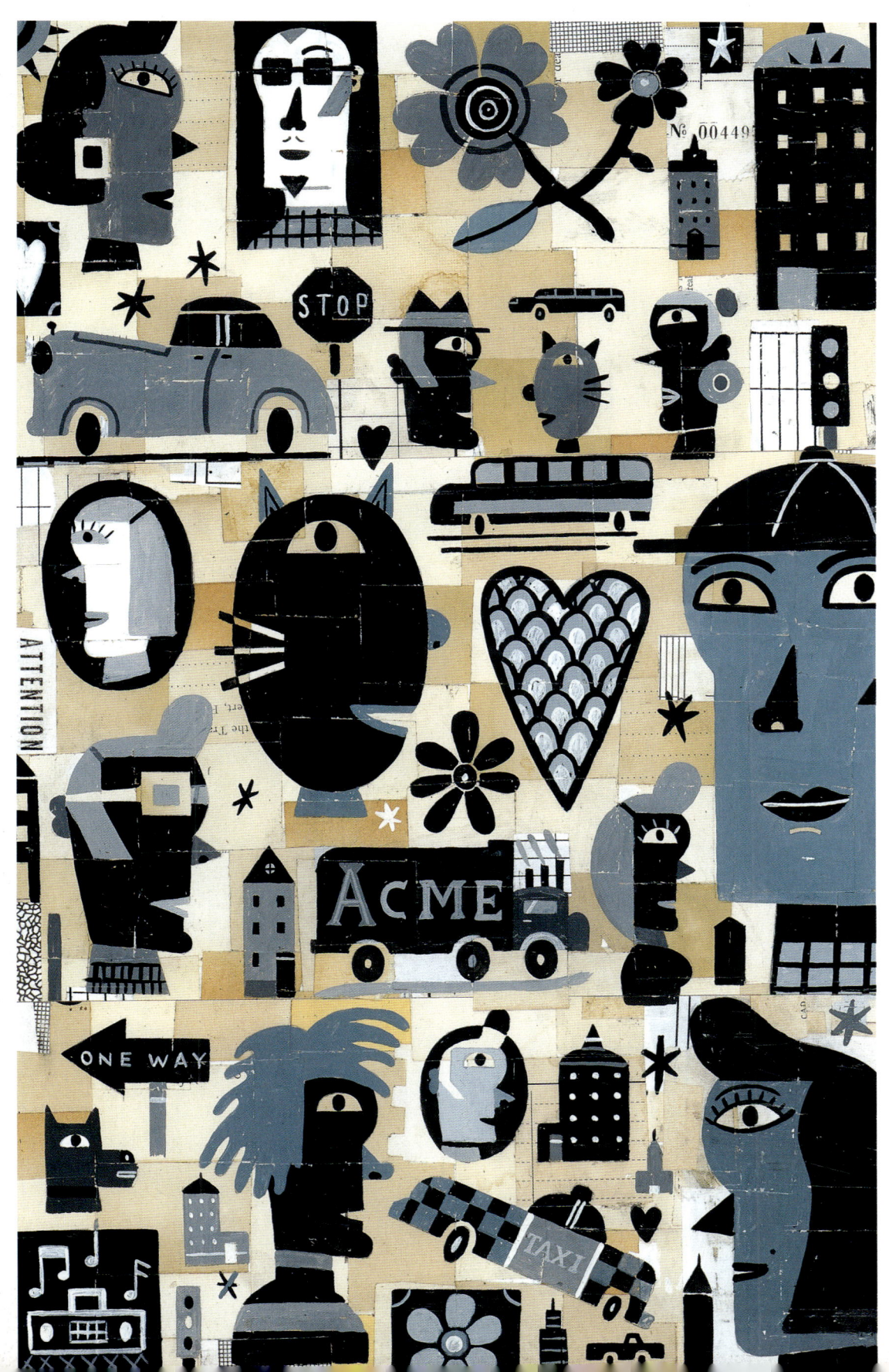

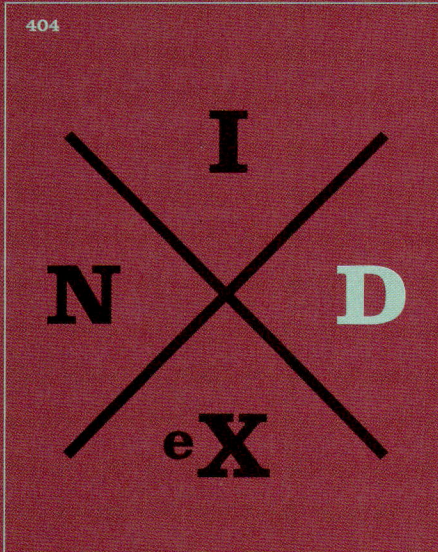

Daniel Adel
56 West 22nd Street, 8th Floor
New York, NY 10010
212-989-6114

001
Design Director: Geraldine Hessler
Publication: Entertainment Weekly
Publishing Company: Time Inc.
Writer: Ty Burr
Medium: Oil
Mike Myers as Austin Powers, for "Austin Taxes," November 19, 1999, a review of his movie "Austin Powers: The Spy Who Shagged Me."

Kari Alberg
11125 Kane Trail
Northfield, MN 55057
507-645-2272
www.studiokari.com

002
Designer: Caroline Ulrich
Design Firm: Caroline Ulrich Design
Client: BMG Classics
Medium: Pastels
CD cover illustration for a re-release of RCA's recording of Puccini's opera "Madama Butterfly."

003
Designer: Caroline Ulrich
Design Firm: Caroline Ulrich Design
Client: BMG Classics
Medium: Pastels
CD cover illustration for a re-release of the Vienna Philharmonic's recording of Bizet's opera "Carmen."

Terry Allen
84 Campfire Road
Chappaqua, NY 10514
914-238-1422

004
Art Director: Janet Froelich
Designer: Paul Jean
Publication: The New York Times Magazine
Publishing Company: The New York Times
Writer: William Safire
Medium: Gouache
Illustration for "Washing Our Dishes," February 21, 1999, for the regular column "On Language."

005
Art Director: Robin Gilmore-Barnes
Designer: Elisabeth Urrico
Publication: The Atlantic Monthly
Publishing Company: The Atlantic Monthly
Writer: Colleen Murphy
Medium: Gouache
Illustration for the article "If The Shoe Fits," April 1999.

Charles S. Anderson
30 North First Street
Minneapolis, MN 55401
612-339-5181

006
Design Director: John Korpics
Publication: Esquire Magazine
Publishing Company: Hearst Magazines
Medium: Collage
Through a survey, it was discovered that Mickey Mouse is "The Most Recognizable Face of the Century." Due to ubiquitous corporate branding Mickey's image is likely to survive a nuclear holocaust (along with the cock roaches).

Marshall Arisman
314 West 100th Street
New York, NY 10025
212-662-2289

007|008
Art Director: Amy Hawk
Publication: How Magazine
Publishing Company: F&W Publications
Medium: Oil on ragboard
Two images from a series for "Fear of Creative Blocks," January 2000, an article that discovered the biggest creative stumbling block is yourself.

N. Ascencios
382 Jefferson Street
Brooklyn, NY 11237
718-386-1240
ascencios@hotmail.com

009
Art Director: Julie Zerbo
Director: Julie Zerbo
Design Firm: J.D'Addario & Co.
Agency: J.D'Addario & Co.
Medium: Oil on canvas
Illustration for an in-store poster based on Moussorgsky's "Night on Bald Mountain" depicting the witching hour in hell.

Tom Bachtell

010
Deputy Illustration Editor: Owen Phillips
Editor: David Remnick
Publication: The New Yorker
Publishing Company: Condé Nast Publications, Inc.
Writer: Roger Angell
Medium: Pen & ink
Portrait of former NYC Mayor Fiorello La Guardia, for "The Talk of the Town" section, February 22-March 1, 1999.

Matthew Bandsuch
497 Prentis #4
Detroit, MI 48201
888-330-7324
bandsuch@earthlink.net

011
Art Director: Ray Stanczak
Editor: Karen Klein
Publication: The Detroit News
Publishing Company: Gannett
Writer: Noreen Seebecher
Medium: Mixed media
Illustration for "How The Home Team Helps You Find Your Home," an article on how real estate agents aid in the process of finding and purchasing a home.

Istvan Banyai
666 Greenwich St., #420
New York, NY 10014
212-627-2953

012
Art Editor: Françoise Mouly
Publication: The New Yorker
Publishing Company: Condé Nast Publications, Inc.
Medium: Pencil and Photoshop
Proposed cover illustration for the Valentines Day issue, February 2000.

013
Illustration Editor: Christine Curry
Publication: The New Yorker
Publishing Company: Condé Nast Publications, Inc.
Writer: Kurt Anderson

Karen Barbour
P.O. Box 1210
Point Reyes Station, CA
94956
415-663-1100

Medium: Pencil and Photoshop
Illustration for the article "Pleasantville/Celebration – Can Disney Reinvent the Burbs?" September 6, 1999.

014
Art Director: Lisa Thackaberry
Designer: Myla Sorensen
Editor: Spencer Beck
Publication: Los Angeles Magazine
Publishing Company: Fairchild Publications
Writer: Dirk Mathison
Medium: Ink and gouache
Illustration depicting the search for the karmic pleasure principle, for the article "Sex – Transcendental Stimulation," June 1999.

015
Art Director: Pamela Berry
Designer: Dan Josephs
Editor: Erik Torkells
Publication: Travel & Leisure Magazine
Publishing Company: American Express Publishing
Writer: Jean Nathan
Medium: Ink and gouache on paper
One image from a series by various artists, for the article "Where Have You Found Romance," February 1999.

016
Medium: Ink, acrylic, gouache on watercolor paper
Unpublished, personal piece.

Deborah Barrett

017
Art Directors: Frank Tagariello and Carol Layton
Designer: Frank Tagariello
Publication: Bloomberg Personal Finance
Publishing Company: Bloomberg LP
Writer: Richard Blerck
Medium: Pencil, collage and gouache
Illustration for "Some Helping Hands," November 1999, an article on how the new philanthropists give their time and expertise in addition to money.

018
Art Director: Gail Anderson
Publication: Rolling Stone
Publishing Company: Wenner Media
Medium: Pencil, gouache and collage
Portrait of Tom Petty for a review of Tom Petty and Heartbreaker's album "Echo," April 29, 1999.

Gary Baseman

019
Art Director: Fred Woodward
Publication: Rolling Stone
Publishing Company: Wenner Media
Medium: Pencil, gouache and collage
Portrait of Fiona Apple, for a review of her album "When the Pawn...," November 25, 1999.

020
Client: Society of Illustrators Los Angeles
Copywriter: Gary Baseman
Medium: Acrylic on canvas
The Society of Illustrators Los Angeles Call For Entry poster entitled "Dare To Enter."

021
Medium: Acrylic on canvas
One painting from a series for the one man show "Dumb Luck," depicting how desperate we are for luck and success.

022
Medium: Acrylic on canvas
One painting entitled "Miss Vassarette," for the one man show "Dumb Luck."

Melinda Beck
536 5th St., #2
Brooklyn, NY 11215
718-499-0985
www.melindabeck.com

023
Art Director: Holger Windfuhr
Designer: Holger Windfuhr
Publication: Impulse
Publishing Company: G&J
Medium: Pen and ink and Photoshop
Illustration for the article "Status Symbols," November 1999.

Polly Becker
258 Shawmut Avenue, #5
Boston, MA 02118
617-426-8284

024
Medium: Assemblage
Personal piece with turning back time as its theme.

025
Art Director: Barbara Dow
Publication: Seattle Weekly
Medium: Assemblage
A re-worked piece, that in its original form ran with an article about how pregnancy feels like something that is taking over your body.

Richard Beckerman
137 East 28th Street, #7B
New York, NY 10016
212-685-7045
rchrdbc@aol.com

026
Medium: Watercolor
Illustration of the artist's old address, for a change-of-address announcement.

Wesley Bedrosian
302 Metropolitan Avenue, #2
Brooklyn, NY 11211
718-782-5018
wesfolio@earthlink.net
www.home.earthlink.net/~wesfolio

027
Art Director: Antonio Deluca
Publication: National Post
Publishing Company: National Post
Writer: Patricia Pearson
Medium: Mixed media
Illustration for "Roman Holiday," July 10, 1999, an article about a couple touring Italy with their toddler.

Lynn Bennett
3180 Carlyle Street
Los Angeles, CA 90065
323-256-2159
lynn@lynnbennett.com
www.lynnbennett.com

028
Medium: Mixed media
One from a personal series on the mythological character Baubo, entitled "Paradise."

029
Medium: Collage
One from a personal series on the mythological character Baubo, entitled "The Witching Hour."

Benoit
c/o Riley Illustration
155 West 15th St., #4C
New York, NY 10011
212-989-8770
www.rileyillustration.com

030
Art Editor: Françoise Mouly
Publication: The New Yorker
Publishing Company: Condé Nast Publications, Inc.
Medium: Oil
Cover illustration, December 20, 1999.

031
Art Director: John Pylypczak
Designer: Claire Dawson
Design Firm: Concrete
Client: Keilhauer
Medium: Oil on paper
One from a series of twelve for a promotional desk calendar entitled "The Best Seat in the House," 2000.

032
Art Director: Dah-Rong Lee
Designer: Miao Moy
Account Executive: Will Carlin
Design Firm: US Web CKS
Client: Pfizer
Medium: Oil
Illustration entitled "Whatever Your Challenge," for an unpublished brochure on patient care solutions.

Jean-M. Benoit
4439 Avenue des Érables
Montréal, Qu. H2H 2C7
Canada
514-522-5572

033
Art Director: Antonio Deluca
Designer: Antonio Deluca
Publication: National Post
Publishing Company: National Post
Writer: Gina Mallet
Medium: Acrylic
Cover illustration for "Holiday Fare With Flair – What is Canadian Thanksgiving?" an article on how Thanksgiving in Canada now includes foods from other cultures.

Guy Billout
380 Rector Place, #4M
New York, NY 10280-1443
212-786-4352

034
Art Directors: Robin Gilmore-Barnes and Judy Garlan
Editor: William Whitworth
Publication: The Atlantic Monthly
Publishing Company: The Atlantic Monthly Group
Writer: Guy Billout
Medium: Watercolor and airbrush
Illustration entitled "Time Line," part of a regular feature where the artist is granted total freedom.

035
Art Directors: Robin Gilmore-Barnes and Judy Garlan
Editor: William Whitworth
Publication: The Atlantic Monthly
Publishing Company: The Atlantic Monthly Group
Writer: Guy Billout
Medium: Watercolor and airbrush
Illustration entitled "Mid-Night," part of a regular feature where the artist is granted total freedom.

Mary Lynn Blasutta
420 Hill St.
Southampton, New York
11968
631-204-1805
www.blasutta.com

036
Medium: Gouache and ink
Unpublished, personal piece entitled "Tito."

R.O. Blechman
2 West 47th St.
New York, NY 10036
212-869-1630

037
Designer: R.O. Blechman
Editor: Lois Rosenthal
Publication: Story Magazine
Publishing Company: F&W Publishing Company
Medium: Pen & ink and photoshop
Cover illustration, Spring 1999.

Cathie Bleck
2270 Chatfield Drive
Cleveland Hts, OH 44106
216-932-4910
cb@cathiebleck.com
www.cathiebleck.com

038
Medium: Scratchboard and collage
Unpublished piece entitled "Emotion #2."

039
Medium: Scratchboard and collage
Unpublished piece entitled "Emotion #1."

Barry Blitt
34 Lincoln Avenue
Greenwich, CT 06830
203-622-2988
barryblitt@aol.com

040
Art Editor: Françoise Mouly
Editor: David Remnick
Publication: The New Yorker
Publishing Company: Condé Nast Publications, Inc.
Writer: B. Blitt
Medium: Pen & ink and watercolor
Cover illustration for Martin Luther King Day, entitled "Hailing Dr. King," January 17, 2000.

041
Art Director: Susan Levin
Design Director: Dan Zedek
Editor: David Mohegan
Publication: The Boston Globe
Publishing Company: The Boston Globe
Writer: Amy Alexander
Medium: Pen & ink and watercolor
Illustration for "Lifting Every Voice," February 14, 1999, an article on Randall Kenan, who traveled the south listening to the stories of African-Americans for his book "Walking on Water."

Juliette Borda
17 Little West 12th St., #310
New York, NY 10014
212-414-2404

042
Deputy Illustration Editor: Owen Phillips
Editor: David Remnick
Publication: The New Yorker
Publishing Company: Condé Nast Publications, Inc.
Medium: Gouache
Illustration for a film review of "Ravenous," a movie about cannibalism, for the "Goings on About Town" section, March 22, 1999.

043
Art Director: Deanna Lowe
Designers: Jorge Colombo and Deanna Lowe
Editor: Jane Berentson
Publication: Equity Magazine
Publishing Company: Worth Media
Writer: Hillary Johnson
Medium: Gouache on paper
One illustration from a series for "Chanel at Home Plate," Fall 1999, a story on the many lives of a Chanel suit.

Tim Bower
61 Pearl Street, #306
Brooklyn, NY 11201
718-834-8974

044
Design Director: Geraldine Hessler
Designer: Ellen Standke
Editor: John McAlley
Publication: Entertainment Weekly
Publishing Company: Time Inc.
Writer: Ty Burr
Medium: Mixed media
Illustration for "The Globe Sessions," July 30, 1999, a review of a CD boxed set of Shakespearean performances from film, radio and LPs.

045
Art Director: Bambi Nicklen
Editor: Mark Robinson
Publication: Stanford Magazine
Publishing Company: Stanford University
Writer: Joan O'C. Hamilton
Medium: Mixed media
Illustration for "Pecking at Crumbs," July/August 1999, an article on the decreasing job market for the increasing number of those graduating with PhDs.

046
Medium: Mixed media
Unpublished, personal piece.

047
Designer: David Armario
Publication: Los Angeles Magazine
Publishing Company: Fairchild Publications
Medium: Mixed media
Portrait of Bob Dylan as he appeared in 1970.

Rebecca Bradley
133 Cypress Street, #D
Brookline, MA 02446
617-970-6067
rebecca30@hotmail.com

048
Professor: Traci Haymans
Medium: Indian ink on color Xerox
Personal piece entitled "Midtown to Downtown," depicting springtime in New York City.

Steve Brodner
711 West 190th St., #5F
New York, NY 10040
212-942-7139
sbrodner@aol.com

049
Art Director: Fred Woodward
Publication: Rolling Stone
Publishing Company: Wenner Media
Medium: Watercolor
Portrait of Marilyn Manson, for the millennium issue feature "The Party 2000," December 30, 1999-January 6, 2000.

050
Art Director: Kelly Doe
Designer: Kelly Doe
Editor: Glenn Frankel
Publication: The Washington Post Magazine
Publishing Company: The Washington Post
Writer: Steve Brodner
Medium: Watercolor
Three political caricatures from the series "The Making of the Caricature 2000," running in different issues from June 1999 - February 2000.

051
Art Editor: Françoise Mouly
Publication: The New Yorker
Publishing Company: Condé Nast Publications, Inc.
Writer: Steve Brodner
Medium: Watercolor
Cover illustration of presidential and senatorial candidates, entitled "Turkey Day," November 29, 1999.

052
Art Director: Janet Froelich
Designer: Claude Martel
Editor: Adam Moss
Publication: The New York Times Magazine
Publishing Company: The New York Times
Writer: Rebecca Johnson
Medium: Watercolor
Portrait of Charlie Rose, for "Rose's Turn," March 21, 1999, an article on his new role as correspondent on "60 Minutes II."

Calef Brown
c/o Lisa Freeman Inc.
317-920-0068
lisa@lisafreeman.com
www.lisafreeman.com

053
Art Director: Karen Simpson
Publication: National Post Business
Medium: Acrylic and oil
Illustration for "Of Mice and (Bronf)Man," September 1999.

Calef Brown   an article on the battles between Disney and Seagrams.

054
Art Director: Megan Wilson
Publication: Solibo Magnificent
Publishing Company: Vintage Books/Randon House
Author: Patrick Chamoiseau
Medium: Acrylic and oil
Cover illustration for the novel "Solibo Magnificent," April 1999, shich takes place in the Antilles and is about the mysterious death of a great storyteller.

Philip Burke
1948 Juron Drive
Niagra Falls, NY 4304
905-894-2760

055
Illustration Editor: Christine Curry
Editor: David Remnick
Publication: The New Yorker
Publishing Company: Condé Nast Publications, Inc.
Writer: John Lahr
Medium: Oil
Writer/director Neil LaBute, center, with actors from his two productions, from top, Ron Eldard, Paul Rudd, Calista Flockhart, Renee Zellweger, Morgan Freeman and Chris Rock, for the article "A Touch of Bad," July 5, 1999.

056
Art Director: Fred Woodward
Publication: Rolling Stone
Publishing Company: Wenner Media
Writer: William Greider
Medium: Oil
Portrait of Senator Trent Lott, appearing on the "Contents Page," for an article in the 'National Affairs' section, February 4, 1999.

Charles Burns

057
Design Director: Geraldine Hessler
Designer: Joe Kimberling
Editor John McAlley
Publication: Entertainment Weekly
Publishing Company: Time Inc.
Writer: Various
Medium: Mixed media
Country music singer Garth Brooks as his alter ego Chris Gaines, for the artilce "Significant Others," September 17, 1999.

058
Design Director: John Korpics
Designer: Erin Whelan
Editor Tina Jordan
Publication: Entertainment Weekly
Publishing Company: Time Inc.
Writer: Lisa Schwarzbaum
Medium: Mixed media
Monica Lewinsky for "Starr-y Eyed," March 19, 1999, a review of Andrew Morton's book "Monica's Story."

Morgan Carver
2420 North Valencia Avenue
Santa Ana, CA 92706
714-541-5957
mismot@msn.com

059
Art Directors: Jane Martin and Catherine Aldrich
Design Director: Lucy Bartholomay
Editor: Ande Zellman
Publication: The Boston Globe Magazine
Publishing Company: The Boston Globe
Writer: David M. Shribman
Medium: Acrylic on panel
Illustration for "A Thousand Years of Deadly Sin: Anger," October 3, 1999.

Saiman Chow
2278 White Street #2
Pasadena, CA 91107
626-792-4754
saimanchow@hotmail.com

060
Art Director: The Clayton Brothers
Medium: Acrylic
Self-promotional piece entitled "Jack Ass."

061
Art Director: The Clayton Brothers
Medium: Acrylic
Self-promotional piece entitled "The Goose Fight."

Seymour Chwast

062
Art Director: Steven Heller
Designer: Seymour Chwast
Design Firm: The Pushpin Group Inc.
Client: The New York Times
Publication: The New York Times
Copywriter: Danté Alighieri
Medium: Pen & ink
Illustration depicting the descent into hell in "Dante's Divine Comedy."

Joe Ciardiello
2182 Clove Road
Staten Island, NY 10305
718-727-4757

063
Art Director: Fred Woodward
Senior Art Director: Gail Anmderson
Publication: Rolling Stone
Publishing Company: Wenner Media
Medium: Pen and ink and watercolor
Portrait of the late Curtis Mayfield appearing on the "Contents Page," February 3, 2000, for a tribute upon his death.

064
Medium: Pen & ink
Portrait of playwright Samuel Beckett, personal piece.

Greg Clarke
214 Twin Falls Court
Thousand Oaks, CA 91320
805-499-8823
Rep: Sally Heflin & Theartworks
212-366-1893

065
Art Director: Gina Manola
Designer: Becky Terhune
Design Firm: Galison
Client: Galison
Publication: Film Journal

Greg Clarke   **Medium:** Watercolor
Cover illustration for a "blank plage" journal for film buffs.

066
Curator: Michael J. Rosen
Writer: Greg Clarke
Medium: Watercolor
Created for an exhibition entitled "Future Dog" at the American Kennel Club Museum of the Dog, St. Louis, MO.

Christian & Rob Clayton
3235 San Fernando Road
Bldg. #1, Unit E
Los Angels, CA 90065
323-478-0210
www.claytonbrothers.com

067
Art Director: Monte Beauchamp
Designer: Monte Beauchamp
Publication: Blab
Writers: Rob and Christian Clayton
Medium: Mixed media
Personal collaborative piece entitled "Carl and His Dog Snowball."

Christian Clayton
3235 San Fernando Road
Bldg. #1, Unit E
Los Angels, CA 90065
323-478-0210
www.claytonbrothers.com

068
Art Director: Dave Allen
Designer Dave Allen
Editor: Hal Espen
Publication: Outside Magazine
Publishing Company: Mariah Media
Writer: Larry Brown
Medium: Mixed media
Illustration for teh article "Thicker Than Blood," August 1999.

069
Medium: Mixed media
Personal piece entitled "Little 'C' Sings."

Rob Clayton
3235 San Fernando Road
Bldg. #1, Unit E
Los Angels, CA 90065
323-478-0210
www.claytonbrothers.com

070
Art Director: Mark Murphy
Design Firm: Murphy Design Inc.
Publication: Future
Medium: Acrylic on board
Personal piece entitled "Future."

071
Medium: Acrylic on wood
Personal piece for a show of the artist's work at the La Luz de Jesus Gallery, Los Angeles.

072
Medium: Acrylic on wood
Personal piece for a show of the artist's work at the La Luz de Jesus Gallery, Los Angeles.

Gary Clement
52 Arlington Avenue
Toronto, Ont. M6K 3K8
Canada
416-657-8975
gclement@nationalpost.com

073
Art Director: Lucy Bartholomay
Publication: The Boston Globe
Publishing Company: The Boston Globe
Writer: Ed Siegel
Medium: Pen & ink, gouache and collage on paper
Illustration for "Ring Out the Noise, Ring Out the Funk: The Arts Go In Search of a 21st Century-ism," March 14, 1999, suggesting that artists in almost every genre must look back in order to look ahead.

Tavis Coburn
1845 Reiter Drive
Pasadena, CA 91106
626-585-1716

074
Art Director: Emily Crawford
Publication: Fast Company
Publishing Company: Fast Company Media Group, LLC
Writer: Charles H. Ferguson
Medium: Silkscreen
Two of three images as part of a series for the article "True Finance," October 1999.

Sue Coe
214 East 8th St., #8
New York, NY 10028
212-767-5450

075
Art Director: Richard Baker
Senior Designer Christine Cucuzza
Editor: Peter Kobel
Publication: Premiere Magazine
Publishing Company: Hachette Filipacchi Magazines
Writer: Christopher Kelly
Medium: Watercolor
Filmmaker Spike Lee for the "Homeguide" section, January 2000, as the movie "Summer of Sam "was released on video.

076
Art Director: Patrick JB Flynn
Designer Patrick JB Flynn
Publication: The Progressive
Publishing Company: The Progressive, Inc.
Writer: Samuel H. Day Jr., Barbara Ehrenreich, Jane Jordan and Catherine Rankovic
Medium: Graphite, ink and acrylic paint
A dove of peace flies over the victims from the Yugoslovian war, for the article "War in Yugoslavia," June 1999.

Jorge Colombo
165 Avenue A, #5
New York, NY 10009
917-653-4089
www.jorgecolombo.com

077
Designer Jorge Colombo
Editor: Marc Weidenbaum
Publication: Fullerton
Publishing Company: Bedeteca de Lisboa/Lisbon's Museum of Illustration and Comics
Author: Jorge Colombo
Essay: João Paulo Cotrim
Medium: Ink and watercolor on paper
Four from "Fullerton," October 1999, a catalogue for an exhibition of ten year's worth of work including both personal and previously published pieces.

Paul Corio

078
Art Director: Florian Bachleda
Senior Art Director Pino Impastato

Paul Corio
263 1st Avenue, #3
New York, NY 10003
212-228-4630

Editor: Randall Lane
Publication: P.O.V. Magazine
Publishing Company: B.Y.O.B. Ventures
Writer: Harmon Leon
Medium: Ink
Illustration for "Licensed to Kill," April 1999, an article on professional bounty hunters.

Christopher Corr
27 Myddelton St.
London EC1R 1VA U.K.
011-44-171-833-5699

079
Art Director: Pamela Berry
Designer: Pamela Berry
Editor: Scott Jolley
Publication: Travel & Leisure Magazine
Publishing Company: American Express Publishing
Writer: Alan Brown
Medium: Gouache
One image from a series for a travel piece entitled "Postcard of Tunisia," November 1999.

Geneviéve Côté
400 de Maisonneuve West
#851
Montréal, Qu. H3A 1L4
Canada
514-282-9399

080
Art Director: Gudrun Gallo
Publication: The Globe and Mail
Medium: Mixed media
Illustration for the article "Why We Crave Hot Stuff," a journalist's view on the growing tabloidization of news.

David Cowles
775 Landing Road North
Rochester, NY 14625
716-381-0910

081
Art Director: Rena Sokolow
Design Director: Dan Zedek
Editor: Scott Powers
Publication: The Boston Globe
Publishing Company: The Boston Globe
Writer: Joan Anderman
Medium: Gouache
Rap/hip-hop artist Lauren Hill, for the article "The New Soul of Hip-Hop," March 21, 1999.

Timothy L. Crawford
1238 Callowhill Street, #405
Philadelphia, PA 19123
215-922-5393

082
Art Director: Paul Kepple
Writer: James English
Medium: Adobe Illustrator
One image from a personal series for a fictitious magazine advertisement geared toward homosexual men using the super-hero Lubri-Lad for the fictitious company Dyna-Rod Condoms.

Brian Cronin
59 West 12th St., #8H
New York, NY 10011
212-727-9539
www.briancronin.com

083
Art Director: Leanne Shapton
Designer: Leanne Shapton
Publication: National Post
Publishing Company: National Post
Medium: India ink and acrylic
Illustration for the "Avenue" section cover, June 1 1999.

084
Designer: Adíd Capeci
Publication: Newsweek
Publishing Company: The Washington Post
Medium: India ink, pencil and acrylic on paper
Commissioned, yet unpublished piece entitled "The New Face of Race in the U.S.A."

085
Art Director: Sue Ng
Publication: Psychology Today
Publishing Company: Sussex Publishers, Inc.
Writer: Jeanne Safer
Medium: Pencil and acrylic on paper
Illustration for the article "Unforgiving."

086
Art Director: Kelly Doe
Designer: Lisa Schreiber
Publication: The Washington Post Magazine
Publishing Company: The Washington Post
Writer: DeNeen L. Brown
Medium: India ink, pencil and acrylic on paper
Illustration for "Her Sister's Keeper," a story about a woman who helped her sister move out of poverty.

087
Design Director: Tom Brown
Art Directors: Dirk Barnett and Todd Albertson
Editor: James R. Gaines
Publication: Travel & Leisure Golf
Publishing Company: American Express Publishing
Writer: Michael M. Thomas
Medium: Acrylic, pencil and felt tip pen on paper
Illustration for "What Fathers Are For," May/June 1999, an article on how golf can be a bonding and healthy experience for a father and son.

088
Art Director: Sue Ng
Publication: Psychology Today
Publishing Company: Sussex Publishers, Inc.
Writer: Jeanne Safer
Medium: India ink and acrylic on paper
Illustration for the article "Perfectionist."

Paul Dallas
54 Rivercrest Road
Toronto, Ont. M6S 4H3
Canada
416-762-5456

089
Art Director: Danielle LeBel
Designers: Denis Paquet and Julie Saindon
Editor: Lise Ravary
Publication: en Route Magazine
Publishing Company: Spafax Canada Inc.
Writer: Austin Clarke
Medium: Watercolor
Illustration for "Privilege," May 1999, which describes the soulful legacy of slave food.

Mark Danielson
914 NW 54th Street
Seattle, WA 98107
206-789-2882
danielson_mark@hotmail.com
www.markdanielson.com

090
Art Director: Patrick Mitchell
Designer: Patrick Mitchell
Editor: Alan Webber
Publication: Fast Company Magazine
Publishing Company: Fast Company Media Group, LLC
Writer: John Ellis
Medium: Acrylic on paper
Illustration for "Digital Matters," January/February 2000, an article on the success of America Online in the1990s and whether it can survive new competition in the new century.

091
Art Director: Nelson Anderson
Design Director: Fabienne Coron
Publication: Detour Magazine
Publishing Company: Detour Magazine, Inc.
Writer: Dawn Brett
Medium: Acrylic
Illustration for "Savage Passions," an article on Dan Savage., America's most popular sex-advice columnist.

Jeffrey Decoster
3530A 22nd Street
San Francisco, CA 94114
415-206-9430

092
Art Director: David Armario
Designer: David Armario
Editor: Rosanne Spector
Publication: Stanford Medicine Magazine
Publishing Company: Stanford University
Writer: Ruthann Richter
Medium: Acrylic
Illustration for "Moving with the Current," Winter 1999/2000, an article that described a treatment for Parkinson's disease where a current of electricity directed in the brain restored fluidity of motion and eliminated tremors.

093
Art Director: James Nelson
Publication: Minneapolis/ST Paul Magazine
Publishing Company: MSP Communications
Writer: William Swanson
Medium: Acrylic
Portrait of convicted murderer Joseph Ture, for the article "How Bad Can Joe Ture Be?" December 1999.

094
Art Director: Rikki Poulos
Design Firm: Rikki Poulos Design
Client: Grammy Awards
Medium: Acrylic
Portrait of the band Garbage, for the 1999 Grammy Awards program.

095
Art Director: Mark Geer
Designer: Mark Geer
Design Firm: Geer Design
Client: Luna Paper Co.
Medium: Acrylic on board
Portrait of Michael Stipe and an interpretation of his song "Man on the Moon," for a paper company promotion, which used the theme of songs about the moon.

Jean-Philippe Delhomme
jpdelhomme@aol.com

096
Art Director: Agnethe Glatved
Designer: Jennifer Bowles
Editor: Melissa Biggs Bradley
Publication: Town & Country Magazine
Publishing Company: Hearst Corporation
Writer: William Sertl
Medium: Acrylic
Opening illustration for the feature "Where To Go in the Year 2000," January 2000, a month-by-month calendar for the "Traveler's Notebook" section.

097
Art Director: Agnethe Glatved
Designer: Agnethe Glatved
Editors: Diane Guernsey and Jim Brosseau
Publication: Town & Country Magazine
Publishing Company: Hearst Corporation
Writer: Charlotte Hays
Medium: Acrylic
Illustration entitled "Losing It," one from a series for "A Guide to Men's Health," which examined the concerns middle-aged men have regarding their physical and emotional well-being.

Isabelle Dervaux
c/o Riley Illustration
155 West 15th St., #4C
New York, NY 10011
212-989-8770
www.rileyillustration.com

098
Self-promotional piece.

Nick Dewar
c/o Kate Larkworthy Artist
Representation, Ltd.
80 Nassau Street
New York, NY 10038
212-964-9141
www.larkworthy.com

099
Art Directors: Janet Froelich and Joele Cuyler
Designer: Ignacio Rodriguez
Editor: Dan Lewis
Publication: The New York Times Magazine
Publishing Company: The New York Times
Writer: Deborah Tannen
Medium: Acrylic on illustration board
Illustration for "Listening to Men, Then and Now," May 16, 1999, an article about how men and women communicate.

100
Art Director: Gary Cook
Designer: Gary Cook

Editor: Michael Watts
Publication: The Business
Publishing Company: Financial Times
Writer: Sir Geoffrey Owen
Medium: Acrylic on illustration board
Illustration for "British Business," January 1, 2000, an article about the resurgence of British Industry.

Don Doe
www.dondoe.com

101
Medium: Oil
Personal piece.

Henrik Drescher
51 Camden Street
Toronto, Ont. M5V 1V2
Canada
800-730-8945
www.reactor.ca

102
Art Director: Patrick JB Flynn
Designer: Patrick JB Flynn
Publication: The Progressive
Publishing Company: The Progressive, Inc.
Medium: Pen, ink, colored pencil and computer
A razor-sharp finger cuts off the tongue of the evil demon, disallowing the voice of its victims, for the article "I For and Eye," July 1999, an homage to a previously published cover by Brad Holland.

103
Designer: Henrik Drescher
Medium: Collage
One from a personal project for a future book entitled "Postal Seance."

Gérard DuBois
c/o Marlena Agency
145 Witherspoon
Princeton, NJ 08542
609-252-9405
www.marlenaagency.com

104
Publication: Rolling Stone
Publishing Company: Wenner Media
Medium: Acrylic
Portrait of comedian Andy Kaufman, for the "Contents Page," December 9, 1999.

105
Art Director: Fred Woodward
Publication: Rolling Stone
Publishing Company: Wenner Media
Medium: Acrylic
Portrait of Carlos Santana, for the "Contents Page," August 19, 1999.

106
Art Director: Sharon Okamoto
Designer: Melany DeForest
Editors: Ben Dickinson and Nelson Aldrich
Publication: Civilization
Publishing Company: Worth Media
Writer: Martha Fay
Medium: Acrylic
Illustration for the article "Sedated by Stuff," August/September 1999.

107
Art Director: Point Five Design
Designers: Alissa Levin and Donald Partyka
Editor: Christy Chapman
Publication: Internal Auditor
Publishing Company: The Institute of Internal Auditor
Writer: R.W. Rudloff
Medium: Acrylic
Illustration for the article "Casino Fraud," June 1999.

108
Art Director: Patricia Kowalczyk
Designer: Patricia Kowalczyk
Client: Marlena Agency/Olver Dunlop Associates
Medium: Acrylic
An illustration of philosopher Lesijek Kolakowski's quotation "Conflict of Values," one from a series by various artists for a promotional calendar.

Carl Dunn

109
Art Director: Jordin Isip
Designer: Vernon Go
Editor: Vernon Go
Publication: Phillipines Yearbook
Publishing Company: Fookien Times
Writer: Marianne Carandang
Medium: Mixed media
Illustration entitled "Oligopoly."

110
Medium: Mixed media
Personal piece.

Marcel Dzama

111
Art Director: Leanne Shapton
Designer: Leanne Shapton
Publication: National Post
Cover illustration for the " Avenue" section, December 1, 1999.

Sara Fanelli
c/o Riley Illustration
155 West 15th St., #4C
New York, NY 10011
212-989-8770
www.rileyillustration.com

112
Publication: Dear Diary
Publishing Company: Candlewick Press
Author: Sara Fanelli
Medium: Collage
Four illustrations from "Dear Diary," February 2000, which describes the events of one day through the diaries of 7 different characters.

Ingo Fast
25 Broadway
Brooklyn, NY 11211
718-387-9570
www.ingofast.com

113
Medium: Pen & ink and watercolors on watercolor paper
Untitled, personal piece.

Ivetta Fedorova

114
Art Directors: Frank Tagariello and Carol Layton

Ivetta Fedorova
640 Broadway, #3E
New York, NY 10012
212-673-5363

Designer: Frank Tagariello
Editor: Bill Inman
Publication: Bloomberg Personal Finance
Publishing Company: Bloomberg L.P.
Writer: Jonathan Burton
Medium: Collage
Illustration for "A Cut Above," May 1999, an article on how investors can earn big discounts from financial advisers when they buy in "bulk."

Jeffrey Fisher
c/o Riley Illustration
155 West 15th St., #4C
New York, NY 10011
212-989-8770
www.rileyillustration.com

115
Medium: Acrylic
Personal piece, one from a series for a one-man show in London, U.K., June 13, 2000.

116
Designer: Susan Hochbaum
Design Firm: Susan Hochbaum Design
Medium: Acrylic
Commissioned, yet unpublished illustration for a marketing service company's brochure.

117
Art Directors: Lynn Trickett and Brian Webb
Designers: Lynn Trickett and Brian Webb
Medium: Acrylic
Unpublished piece.

Vivienne Flesher

118
Art Director: Fred Woodward
Publication: Rolling Stone
Publishing Company: Wenner Media
Medium: Pastel
Portrait of Johnny Rzeznik, for the "Contents Page," November 11, 1999.

Edwin Fotheringham
206-624-3699
efotheringham@uswest.net

119
Deputy Illustration Editor: Owen Phillips
Editor: David Remnick
Publication: The New Yorker
Publishing Company: Condé Nast Publications, Inc.
Medium: Mixed media
Illustration of Keannu Reeves in the movie "The Matrix," for the "Goings On About Town" section, April 5, 1999.

Douglas Fraser
3613 6th Street SW
Calgary, AB T2S 2M6
Canada
403-287-7337
doug@fraserart.com
www.fraserart.com

120
Medium: Alkyds on canvas
Unpublished personal piece entitled "17B," depicting this passenger's whirling thoughts as the other passengers descend into their prescribed distractions.

121
Medium: Alkyds on canvas
Unpublished personal piece entitled "3:35," which illustrates insomnia, anxiety and isolation for the contemporary urban dweller.

Craig Frazier
90 Throckmorton Ave., #28
Mill Valley, CA 94941
415-389-1475

122
Art Director: Gary Barden
Designers: Tom Michlig and Jennie Stueber
Design Firm: Tamzen Media
Client: Wausau Paper
Medium: Cut/Digital
Illustration for a promotional poster and swatchbook cover for Wausau Paper's Royal Silk.

123
Designer: Conrad Jorgensen
Design Firm: Conrad Jorgensen Studio
Client: Redwood Residential Funding
Copywriter: Steven Goldstein
Medium: Cut/Digital
Illustration depicting the benefits of collaboration.

Anthony Freda
284 Mott Street #5G
New York, NY 10012
212-966-7330

124
Art Directors: Frank Tagariello and Carol Layton
Designer: Frank Tagariello
Editor: Bill Inman
Publication: Bloomberg Personal Finance
Publishing Company: Bloomberg L.P.
Writer: Timothy Middleton
Medium: Mixed media
Illustration for "A Nice Fit," an article showing the value of investing in midcap stocks as opposed to small or largecap stocks.

Drew Friedman
388 Bush Road
Cresco, PA 18326
570-620-1875

125
Art Director: Fred Woodward
Designer: Gail Anderson
Publication: Rolling Stone
Publishing Company: Wenner Media
Writer: Various
Medium: Watercolor
Gatefold illustration, for the millennium special feature "The Party 2000," December 1999/January 2000.

Dagmar Frinta
248-594-5934

126
Art Director: Kelly Doe
Designer: Lisa Schreiber
Publication: The Washington Post Magazine
Publishing Company: The Washington Post
Medium: Watercolor and gouache
Illustration for the article "13 Ways of Looking at a Daughter," January 24, 1999.

Arthur E. Giron Jr.
501 West Lime Street, #B
Monrovia, CA 91016 (cont.)

127
Medium: Oil on wood
Personal piece for a project involving movement.

Arthur E. Giron Jr.
626-358-2039
AEGillustration@excite.com

128
Medium: Oil on wood
Untitled, personal piece.

Milton Glaser

129
Art Director: Cristina Taverna
Publication: La Divina Commedia Purgatorio
Publishing Company: Nuages
Author: Dante Alighieri
Medium: Mixed media
One of four illustrations from a series for the Italian publication "La Divina Commedia Purgatorio," October 1999

David Goldin
111 4th Avenue
New York, NY 10003
221-529-5195

130
Untitled personal piece.

Josh Gosfield
200 Varick St., #508
New York, NY 10014
212-645-8826
joshgosfield.com

131
Art Director: Antonio De Luca
Publication: National Post
Publishing Company: National Post
Medium: Watercolor
Illustration for the article "Murder."

132
Medium: Photography
Unpublished, personal piece entitled "High John the Conqueror."

133
Medium: Photography
Unpublished, personal piece, entitled "White Girl Doll."

Geoffrey Grahn
4054 Madison Avenue, #E
Culver City, CA 90232
310-838-7824
geoffgrahn@earthlink.net

134
Art Director: Patrick Mitchell
Designer: Rebecca Rees
Publication: Fast Company Magazine
Publishing Company: Fast Company Media Group, LLC
Medium: Gel pen and computer
Illustration of Whirlpool's training program modeled after MTV's "Real World."

135
Art Director: Fred Woodward
Sr. Art Director: Gail Anderson
Publication: Rolling Stone
Publishing Company: Wenner Media
Medium: Mixed media
Illustration for the "Best of the 90s" Table of Contents page, a composite of Keith Flint, Missy Elliot, Alanis Morissette, Beck, Bob Dylan, P.J. Harvey, Adam Yauch, Notorious B.I.G., Adam Horovitz, Eddie Vedder, Tupac Shakur and Mike D.

136
Art Directors: James McMullan and Hannu Laakso
Publication: Reader's Digest
Publishing Company: Reader's Digest
Writer: Salley Shannon
Medium: Scratchboard and computer
Four illustrations from a series for the article "Teach Your Child Temper Control," May 1999.

Alex Gross
1708 LaSenda Place
South Pasadena, CA 91030
626-799-4014

137
Art Director: Alan Wiesner
Designer: Alex Gross
Publication: Hyper Hobby Magazine
Writer: Masaaki Kawakubo
Medium: Oil
Illustration for "Reminiscences," September 1999, a fiction piece about a war-mongering general who discovers the ability to travel in time.

138
Art Director: Bruce Frisch
Designers: Morgan Slade and Alex Gross
Agency: Frisch Ideas, Inc.
Client: Koga Entertainment International
Copywriter: Bruce Frisch
Writer: Masaaki Kawakubo
Medium: Oil
Illustration for a print ad and poster for an upcoming web site that will feature vintage science-fiction movie memorabilia, particularly from Japan.

Robert Grossman
19 Crosby St.
New York, NY 10013
212-925-1965
robertgrossman@earthlink.net

139
Art Director: Fred Woodward
Publication: Rolling Stone
Publishing Company: Wenner Media
Medium: India ink and watercolor on bristol board
Presidential hopeful George W. Bush with his father, for the "Contents Page," August 5, 1999.

140
Medium: Painted clay
Unpublished bust of Milton Glaser.

Steven Guarnaccia
31 Fairfield Street
Montclair, NJ 07042
973-746-9785
sguarnaccia@hotmail.com

141
Art Director: Gretchen Smelter
Publication: Fast Company
Publishing Company: Fast Company Media Group LLC
Medium: Pen, ink and watercolor
Illustration for "Crisis in the New Economy-Limits of Miniaturization," November 1999, a monthly feature commenting on new technology and the economy.

142
Art Director: Jean Beinart

Publication: Boston Magazine
Publishing Company: Metrocorp
Medium: Pen, ink and watercolor
Commissioned, yet unpublished piece for an article on the future of the internet.

Amy Guip
91 East 4th St., 6th Floor
New York, NY 10003
212-674-8166

143
Art Director: Edel Rodriguez
Designer: Edel Rodriguez
Editor: George Russell
Publication: Time Latin America
Publishing Company: Time Inc.
Writer: Ariel Dorfman
Medium: Digital
Illustration for "The Spirit of the Future," May 24, 1999, an article on the "duendes," a mythological Latin American creature who inhabits the wisdom of experience, part of the Latin American Leaders issue.

Mats Gustafson
c/o Art + Commerce
755 Washington Street
New York, NY 10014

144
Illustration Editor: Christine Curry
Editor: David Remnick
Publication: The New Yorker
Publishing Company: Condé Nast Publications, Inc.
Writer: Joan Acocelle
Medium: Ink
Portrait of Penelope Fitzgerald, February 7, 2000, for a feature on the eighty-three year old novelist.

Eddie Guy
309 Race Track Road
Hohokus, NJ 07423
201-251-7660

145
Art Director: David Matt
Designer: David Matt
Editor: Anne Thompson
Publication: Premiere Magazine
Publishing Company: Hachette Filipacchi Magazines
Writer: George Lucas
Medium: Collage
Portrait of filmmaker George Lucas for "Movies Are An Illusion," February 1999, an essay on digital effects and advances in filmmaking.

146
Art Director: Robert Newman
Designer: Brandon Kavulla
Publication: Vibe Magazine
Publishing Company: Miller Publishing Group
Writer: Sacha Jenkins
Medium: Collage
Portrait of rap artist Ol' Dirty Bastard, for the article "Looking For Jesus," December 1999.

147
Art Director: Sonya Ives
Design Firm: Island Records Inc.
Client: Island/Def Jam
Medium: Collage
Illustration entitled "Gen X Girl," created for a record label and also used on a self-promotional card.

Olaf Hajek
c/o Kate Larkworthy Artist
Representation, Ltd.
80 Nassau Street
New York, NY 10038
212-964-9141
www.larkworthy.com

148
Deputy Illustration Editor: Owen Phillips
Publication: The New Yorker
Publishing Company: Condé Nast Publications, Inc.
Medium: Acrylic on cardboard
Illustration announcing the Ingres show at the Metropolitan Museum of Art, for the "Goings On About Town" section.

Marcellus Hall
174 Delancey St., #8R
New York, NY 10002
212-477-4620
marcellushall@earthlink.net

149
Deputy Illustration Editor: Owen Phillips
Publication: The New Yorker
Publishing Company: Condé Nast Publications, Inc.
Medium: Ink, watercolor and gouache
Illustration of two Japanese comedians, for the "Goings On About Town" section.

Eric Hanson
4444 Upton Anenue South
Minneapolis, MN 55410
612-927-9054
www.joaniebrep.com

150
Art Director: Diana LaGuardia
Designer: Flavia Schepmans
Editor: Dominique Browning
Publication: House & Garden
Publishing Company: Condé Nast Publications, Inc.
Writer: Eric Hanson
Medium: Watercolor
Four from a series for "Literary Furniture," a humorous take on the current popularity of naming furniture collections after famous (and often dead) authors.

151
Medium: Watercolor and collage
Unpublished illustration entitled "Naiad."

152
Medium: Watercolor and collage
Unpublished illustration entitled "Liberté."

Tomer Hanuka
449 Grand Street, #2L
Brooklyn, NY 11211
718-963-3383
tomer@thanuka.com
www.tomerhanuka.com

153
Medium: Mixed media on wood
Portrait of the first African American ring master in The Ringling Bros. Circus.

Jim Heimann
8522 National Blvd., #108
Culver City, CA 90230
310-204-0749

154
Medium: Collage
One from the "American Nude Series for Collectors of the Finest Art" entitled "Whoopee! – Ping Pong."

Jim Heimann

155
Medium: Collage
One from the "American Nude Series for Collectors of the Finest Art" entitled "Family Fascination."

156
Medium: Enamel on tin
One from a series of paintings exploring Mexican bars in Los Angeles.

Suzy Helme
45-26 39th Place, #3C
Sunnyside, NY 11104
suzy_helme@hotmail.com

157
Medium: Mixed media
Personal piece based on a review of the movie "Addams Family Values."

Linda Helton
c/o Marlena Agency
145 Witherspoon St.
Princeton, NJ 08542
609-252-9405
www.marlenaagency.com

158
Designer: Patricia Kowalczyk
Design Firm: Olver Dunlop Associates
Client: Marlena Agency/Olver Dunlop Associates
Copywriters: Leszek Kolakowski and Marlena Torzecka
Medium: Acrylic
One from a promotional calendar, which illustrates the quote "We do not assent to our moral beliefs by admitting 'This is true,' but by feeling guilty if we fail to comply with them."

John Hersey
546B Magnolia Avenue
Larkspur, CA 94939
415-927-2091

159
Art Director: Patrick Mitchell
Designer: Gretchen Smelter
Publication: Fast Company
Publishing Company: Fast Company Media Group, LLC
Writer: Chuck Salter
Medium: Digital
One from a series for the article "Ideas.com," September 1999, based on the illustrator's idea: "The main thing about great ideas is great brains."

Jody Hewgill
260 Brunswick Avenue
Toronto, Ont. M5S 2M7
Canada
416-924-4200
hewgill@home.com
Rep: Sally Heflin &
Theartworks
212-366-1893

160
Art Director: Shauna Wolf Narciso
Publication: Amazing Stories
Publishing Company: Wizards of the Coast, Inc.
Writer: Elizabeth Braswell
Medium: Acrylic
Illustration for "The Bride," Winter 2000, a short story based on the novel "Frankenstein," where the bride discovers her own unusual appearance and thirst for knowledge and freedom while under the constant surveillance by the doctor and her husband.

Malcolm Hill
127 West 15th St., #2R
New York, NY 10011
212-206-3937
Rep: Art Department
212-925-4222

161
Client: Veuve Clicquot
Publishing Company: Assouline
Medium: Gouache and latex house paint on canvas
One illustration from a series for a promotional book.

Arthur Hochstein
74 5th Avenue, #10B
New York, NY 10011
212-243-4165

162
Design Director: Arthur Hochstein
Art Director: Ken Smith
Publication: Time Magazine
Publishing Company: Time Inc.
Medium: Digital
Portrait of Federal Reserve Chairman Alan Greenspan.

Peter & Maria Hoey
1534 Waller St.
San Francisco, CA 94117
415-431-1069
hoeyart@earthlink.net
www.peterhoey.com

163
Art Director: Monte Beauchamp
Designer: Monte Beauchamp
Publication: Blab Magazine
Publishing Company: Fantagraphics
Medium: Digital
One of four from a series for the story "50 Times Brighter Than the Brightest Star," January 2000.

Brad Holland

164
Art Director: Dottie Jones
Publication: Dow Jones Investment Advisor
Medium: Ink and acrylic on board
Cover illustration for the feature "Last Tango," May 1999.

165
Art Director: Patrick JB Flynn
Designer: Patrick JB Flynn
Publication: The Progressive
Publishing Company: The Progressive, Inc.
Writer: Ariel Dorfman
Medium: Oil paint on wood panel
Cover portrait of Augusto Pinochet for the feature "The Chile Files, Pinochet, the Lincoln Brigade, and Me," May 1999. The image, originally rejected by the editor, was ultimately published. The art director, refusing to replace the image, was fired.

166
Art Director: Fred Woodward
Publication: Rolling Stone
Publishing Company: Wenner Media
Medium: Pen and ink
Portrait of David Bowie, for the millennium issue feature "The Party 2000," December 30, 1999-January 6, 2000.

Jason Holley
391 West Grandview Avenue
Sierra Madre, CA 91024
626-403-0152

167
Design Director: Tom Brown
Art Directors: Dirk Barnett and Todd Albertson
Editor: James R. Gaines
Publication: Travel & Leisure Golf
Publishing Company: American Express Publishing
Writer: William Kittredge
Medium: Mixed media

Jason Holley

Map for "Holes in the Sky," June 1999, an article for a travel/golf feature on Montana.

168
Design Director: Tom Brown
Art Directors: Dirk Barnett and Todd Albertson
Editor: James R. Gaines
Publication: Travel & Leisure Golf
Publishing Company: American Express Publishing
Writer: Geoffrey Norman
Medium: Mixed media
Map for "Pilgrimage to the Panhandle," an article on travel/golf in the Redneck Riviera.

169
Art Director: Patrick Mitchell
Designer: Patrick Mitchell
Editor: Alan Webber
Publication: Fast Company
Publishing Company: Fast Company Media Group, LLC
Medium: Mixed media
Illustration for the feature "Digital Matters," December 1999, which examined the difficulties advertisers will have reaching consumers due to new technologies that can block broadcast ads.

170
Art Director: David Armario
Designer: David Armario
Editor: Rosanne Spector
Publication: Stanford Medicine
Publishing Company: Stanford University
Medium: Mixed media
Illustration for "Branching Out," Summer 1999, an article on how researchers are learning to control angiogenesis - the body's natural way of growing blood vessels.

171
Art Director: Fred Woodward
Publication: Rolling Stone
Publishing Company: Wenner Media
Medium: Mixed media
Portrait of Don Van Vliet, a.k.a. Beefheart, for a review of Captain Beefheart's album "Grow Fins," August 5, 1999.

172
Design Director: Tom Brown
Publication: Global
Publishing Company: Deloitte & Touche LLP
Medium: Mixed media
Illustration for "Other Euros, Other Countries," an article that explored the concept of a unified currency for Asia & Central America.

173
Art Director: Keith Campbell
Publication: Details
Publishing Company: Condé Nast Publications, Inc.
Medium: Mixed media
Map for "Somebody Find Me a Kidnapper," a story about a writer who goes to Yemen just to be kidnapped because he heard it was fun.

John H. Howard
115 West 23rd St., #43A
New York, NY 10011
212-989-4600

174
Medium: Acrylic on paper
Personal, promotional piece, one of ten from a series for a show in London entitled "A Repeat Offender Exiled In Excess," June 1999, referring to the observations and experiences of an expatriate in New York.

David Hughes

175
Art Director: Kelly Doe
Publication: The Washington Post Magazine
Publishing Company: The Washington Post
Medium: Ink and watercolor
Portrait of Minnesota Governor Jesse "The Body" Ventura, for the article "Barbarian at the Gate," May 9, 1999, which examined how his rise to power parallels to the rise of pro wrestling.

176
Illustration Editor: Christine Curry
Editor: David Remnick
Publication: The New Yorker
Publishing Company: Condé Nast Publications, Inc.
Writer: Susannah Clap
Medium: Ink, watercolor and collage on paper
Portrait of Patricia Highsmith, author of "The Talented Mr. Ripley," as the movie based on her book opened, for the article "The Simple Act of Murder," December 20, 1999.

Phung Huynh
c/o Frank Sturges
142 West Winter St.
Delaware, OH 43015
212-472-6542
www.sturgesreps.com

177
Medium: Oil paint and mixed media
Personal piece based on the subject of Chinese feet-binding.

Mirko Ilić
207 East 32nd Street
New York, NY 10016
212-481-9737

178
Art Director: Minh Uong
Publication: The Village Voice
Publishing Company: V.V. Publishing Corporation
Medium: Computer
Cover illustration for "Suddenly Not Susan," November 1999, a feature on transgendered persons.

179
Art Director: Steven Heller
Publication: The New York Times Book Review
Publishing Company: The New York Times
Medium: Computer

Cover illustration for the feature "Breaking the Test Barrier," October 1999.

Donna Ingemanson
82 Central Avenue
Braintree, MA 02184
781-848-2012
ingemanson@earthlink.net
www.lillarogers.com

180
Art Director: Armand Eisen
Designer: Diane Hobbing
Publication: The Secret Life of Cats
Publishing Company: Andrews McMeel Publishing Co.
Medium: Paint and pastels
One from a series for the book "The Secret Life of Cats," Fall 1999.

Jordin Isip
536 5th St., #2
Brooklyn, NY 11215
718-499-0985
www.jordinisip.com

181
Art Director: Vernon Go
Editor: Vernon Go
Publication: Philippines Yearbook
Publishing Company: Fookien Times
Writer: Melinda Quintos de Jesus
Medium: Mixed media on paper
Portrait of dictator Ferdinand Marcos, for the article "The 20th Century's Most Influential 20 in the Philippines," July 1999.

182
Art Director: Patrick JB Flynn
Designer: Patrick JB Flynn
Publication: The Progressive
Publishing Company: The Progressive Inc,
Writer: Samuel H. Day Jr.
Medium: Acrylic paint and collage
A feeble bird of peace navigates through heavy fog on its quest for compassion and reason, for the article "America at Its Worst," June 1999.

Jeff Jackson
92 Bedford Road
Toronto Ont. M5R 2K2
Canada
416-972-6468

183
Art Director: Neville Smith
Designer: Neville Smith
Publication: Canada A Portrait
Publishing Company: Statistics Canada
Medium: Chalk pastels
Cover illustration for "Canada A Portrait," a book on Canada's cultural diversity.

184
Art Director: Bill Grigsby
Designer: Sonya Julia Franko
Design Firm: Reactor Art & Design
Client: Rolland Papers
Publication: Visi
Medium: Chalk pastels and gold leaf paint
Illustration for a paper promotion calendar entitled "Visi."

Erik Johnson

185
Art Director: Fred Woodward
Publication: Rolling Stone
Publishing Company: Wenner Media
Medium: Mixed media
Illustration for a review of Sugar Ray's album "14:59," February 4, 1999.

Ted Jouflas
1000 First Ave. West, #504
Seattle, WA 98119
206-282-9803

186
Art Director: Patrick JB Flynn
Designer: Patrick JB Flynn
Editor: Matthew Rothschild
Publication: The Progressive
Publishing Company: The Progressive, Inc.
Writer: Bill Mesler
Medium: Montage
Illustration for "The Mess NATO Left Behind," August 1999, an article on unexploded bombs in Yugoslavia and the dangers their toy-like appearance pose to children.

187
Art Director: Ted Jouflas
Designer: Ted Jouflas
Editor: Gary Groth
Publication: Filthy
Publishing Company: Fantagraphics
Writer: Ted Jouflas
Medium: Montage
Cover illustration for the graphic novel "Filthy," July 1999.

William Joyce
3302 Centenary Boulevard
Shreveport, LO 71104
318-869-0180

188
Art Editor: Françoise Mouly
Publication: The New Yorker
Publishing Company: Condé Nast Publications, Inc.
Medium: Oil
Cover illustration entitled "Reap What You Sew," May 17, 1999.

Maira Kalman
30 West 21st St., 9th Floor
New York, NY 10010
212-414-1459

189
Art Editor: Françoise Mouly
Publication: The New Yorker
Publishing Company: Condé Nast Publications, Inc.
Medium: Gouache
Cover illustration entitled "Dog Reads Book," February 1, 1999.

Margaret Keane
c/o Keane Eyes Gallery
3036 Larkin St.
San Francisco, CA 94109
415-922-9309
www.keane-eyes.com

190
Art Director: Janet Froelich
Designer: Claude Martel
Editor: Adam Moss
Publication: The New York Times Magazine
Publishing Company: The New York Times
Medium: Oil on canvas
Two from a series for the fashion story "Peachy Keane," May 23, 1999.

Gary Kelley

191
Art Director: Robin Gilmore-Barnes

Gary Kelley
226 1/2 Main Street
Cedar Falls, IA 50613
319-277-2330

Publication: The Atlantic Monthly
Publishing Company: The Atlantic Monthly Group
Writer: David M. Kennedy
Medium: Pastel
Cover illustration for "Victory At Sea," March 1999, an article on how the U.S. won WWII .

192
Art Director: Fred Woodward
Publication: Rolling Stone
Publishing Company: Wenner Media
Medium: Pastel
Portrait of Joni Mitchell, for the millennium issue feature "The Party 2000," December 30, 1999-January 6, 2000.

Michael Klein
22 Edgewood Road
Madison, NJ 07940
973-765-0623
mk-illustration.com

193
Design Director: Florian Bachleda
Sr. Art Director: Pino Impastato
Editor: Randall Lane
Publication: P.O.V. Magazine
Publishing Company: B.Y.O.B. Ventures
Writer: Marc Herman
Medium: Ink and watercolor
Illustration for "Spies Like Us," October 1999, a feature on the booming, high-stakes business of corporate espionage.

Trisha Krauss
58 Gansevoort Street
New York, NY 10014
212-243-2134

194
Medium: Acrylic on plywood
Personal piece entitled "Man Eater."

Anja Kroencke
c/o Kate Larkworthy Artist
Representation, Ltd.
80 Nassau Street
New York, NY 10038
212-964-9141
www.larkworthy.com

195
Art Director: James Pyott
Design Firm: Pyott Design
Client: British Airways
Medium: Mixed media
One from a series for "Shopping The World," a duty-free shopping catalogue for British Airways.

196
Art Director: Heidi Fener
Designer: Heidi Fener
Design Firm: Studio Tangerine
Client: New York City Opera
Copywriter: Natalie Warady
Medium: Mixed media
Two poster illustrations for the Fall 1999 season of the New York City Opera.

Stephen Kroninger
303 Mercer St., #B304
New York, NY 10003
212-505-9150
www.stephenkroninger.com

197
Art Director: Steve Diamond
Design Firm: Steve Diamond Inc.
Client: ESPN Zone
Medium: Collage
Ali/Frazier Fight 1971, for a mural at the ESPN Zone theme restaurant in New York City.

198
Art Director: Stephen Kroninger
Designer: Stephen Kroninger
Director: Steven Dovas
Animators: Nick Digital/Joel Krasnove and Jason Strougo
Digital Artists: Marco Vukovic, Jeremy Butler, Josh Cordes and Joel Sevilla
Production Manager: Ashley Oliver
Executive Producers: Ka-Blam!/Bob Mittenthal, Will McRobb and Chris Viscardi
Supervising Producer: Irene Sherman
Co-Producer: Mike Rubiner
Consulting Producer: Jay Martle
Executive Producer: Albie Hecht
Co-Executive Producer: Kevin Kay
Executive In Charge: Cricket Benevento
Client: Nickelodeon
Story By: Stephen Kroninger
Written By: Andy Rheingold
Music Composition: Jared Faber
Sound Design: Dig It Audio
Voices: Craig Lee Thomas, Billy Kay, Doug Preis, Kel J. Vann, Shelagh Ratner, Katelyn Zakrzewski and Stanley Belt
Six key frames from the Nickelodeon series "Garbage Boy."

199
Art Director: David Armario
Designer: David Armario
Editor: Rosanne Spector
Publication: Stanford Medicine Magazine
Publishing Company: Stanford University
Writer: Kristin Weidenbach
Medium: Mixed media
Illustration for "Plotting For Clotting," Winter 1999/2000, an article on how a new gene therapy technique can control hemophilia.

Anita Kunz
218 Ontario Street
Toronto Ont. M5A 2V5
Canada
416-364-3846
www.anitakunz.com

200
Art Directors: Rockwell Harwood and Robert Priest
Designers: Rockwell Harwood and Robert Priest
Publication: Esquire Magazine
Publishing Company: Hearst Corporation
Medium: Mixed media
Illustration for the article "The Birds and the Bees," February 1999, a father's explanation about sex to his son.

Peter Kuper
235 West 102nd St., #16U
New York, NY 10025
212-932-1722
kuperart@aol.com
www.peterkuper.com

201
Art Director: Amid Capeci
Publication: Newsweek Magazine
Publishing Company: The Washington Post
Writers: Anne Underwood and Pat Wingert
Medium: Enamel, watercolor, colored pencil and

Peter Kuper

collage on paper
Illustration for the article "Stress in the Skies," November 29, 1999.

202
Art Director: Patrick JB Flynn
Publication: The Progressive
Publishing Company: The Progressive, Inc.
Writer: Boris Kagarlitsky
Medium: Enamel, pencil and collage on paper
Illustration for the article "Rumblings in Russia," about the state of President Boris Yeltsin, July 1999.

Philippe Lardy
135 West 70th Street
New York, NY 10023
212-219-0324
philippe@lardy.com
www.lardy.com

203
Designer: Suzy Preston
Publication: Outside Magazine
Publishing Company: Mariah Media
Writer: Bill Vaughn
Medium: Mixed media
Illustration for "Skating Home Backward," January 2000, a story about a man who transformed a polluted little swamp into a glassy ice pond.

Scott Laumann
2653 Orange Avenue, #A
Costa Mesa, CA 92627
949-548-8046

204
Art Director: Dwayne Shaw
Designer: Brandon Kavulla
Publication: Vibe Magazine
Publishing Company: Miller Publishing Group
Writer: Danyel Smith
Medium: Mixed media
Illustration for "Girls II Women," May 1999, a commentary on the new breed of R&B singers.

Zohar Lazar
102 Luquer St., #1L
Brooklyn, NY 11231
718-852-2293

205
Art Director: Leslie Vinson
Illustration Consultant: Teresa Fernandez
Editor: Tina Brown
Publication: Talk Magazine
Publishing Company: Miramax/Hearst Corporation
Writer: Cheryl Mendelson
Medium: Acrylic
Illustration for "In Praise of Housekeeping (My Secret Life)," October 1999, an article about modern women who keep house in a traditional way.

206
Art Director: Kelly Doe
Publication: The Washington Post Magazine
Publishing Company: The Washington Post
Writer: Jennifer Moses
Medium: Acrylic
Illustration for "In My Father's Garden," the author reminisces about spending time with her father in his garden.

207
Art Director: Sabrina Weberstetter
Deputy Art Director: Laura Gharrity
Editor: Miriam Arond
Publication: American Health
Publishing Company: Reader's Digest
Writer: Stacey Colino
Medium: Acrylic
Illustration for "Getting Over Getting Angry," September 1999, an article on women and their anger.

208
Design Director: John Korpics
Designer: Jennifer Procopio
Editor: Ty Burr
Publication: Entertainment Weekly
Publishing Company: Time Inc.
Writer: Noah Robischon
Medium: Acrylic
Illustration for "Rocket Attack," April 1999, an article about Mattle and how it is putting smaller toy companies out of business.

Pierre Le-Tan
c/o Riley Illustration
155 West 15th St., #4C
New York, NY 10011
212-989-8770
www.rileyillustration.com

209
Art Director: Teresa Fernandez
Editor: Tina Brown and Armin Harris
Publication: Talk Magazine
Publishing Company: Miramax/Hearst Corporation
Writer: Mimi Swartz
Medium: Ink and watercolor
Two illustrations from a series for the article "The Rich Are Different."

David Levine

210
Art Director: Fred Woodward
Designer: Gail Anderson
Publication: Rolling Stone
Publishing Company: Wenner Media
Medium: Pen and ink
Portrait of Keith Richards, for the millennium issue feature "The Party 2000," December 30, 1999-January 6, 2000.

Thomas Libetti
251 Water St., #2C
Brooklyn, NY 11201
718-643-7152

211
Art Director: Rike Gauss
Publication: National Post
Publishing Company: National Post
Medium: Watercolor, sumi ink and marker on paper
Portrait of Ta-Shunka-Witco, the real name of the Sioux Indian leader Crazy Horse, for a review of the biography "Crazy Horse," April 3, 1999.

Rich Lillash
c/o Frank Sturges Artist
Representative
142 West Winter St.
Delaware, OH 43015
740-369-9702
www.sturgesreps.com

212
Design Director: Steve Gabor
Design Firm: Salvato Coe & Gabor
Client: Salvato Coe & Gabor / Frank Sturges Artist Rep
Medium: Cut paper
Illustration entitled "Cold Turkey," for a promotional calendar.

Warren Linn
c/o Riley Illustration
155 West 15th Street, #4C
New York, NY 10011
212-989-8770
www.rileyillustration.com

213
Art Director: Jesus Diaz
Publication: Village Voice
Publishing Company: V.V. Publishing Corporation
Medium: Mixed media and collage
Cover illustration for the "Jazz Supplement," June 15, 1999.

Rico Lins
R. Campevas, 617
S. Paulo SP 05016-010
Brazil
55 11 36753507
ricolins@yahoo.com

214
Design Director: Dan Zedek
Art Director: Susan Levin
Editor: David Mehegan
Publication: The Boston Globe
Publishing Company: The Boston Globe
Writer: E.J. Graff
Medium: Digital collage
Illustration of the ordinary man confronting the extraordinary man, for "Male Models," October 3, 1999, a review of the book "Stiffed: The Betrayal of The American Man."

Liz Lomax
320 8th Avenue, #4A
Brooklyn, NY 11215
718-965-4570
lizalomax@aol.com

215
Medium: Acrylic paint on foamcore, wire, sculpture
Self-promotional piece entitled "A View From the Edge."

Ross MacDonald
56 Castle Meadow Road
Newtown, CT 06438
203-270-6438

216
Art Director: Dale Hrabi
Designer: Alden Wallace
Publication: Details
Publishing Company: Condé Nast Publications, Inc.
Writer: Mason Brown
Medium: Watercolor
Illustration for "Home on the Range," October 1999, an article on a gated residential community for gun enthusiasts.

217
Art Directors: Greg Leeds, Joe Dizney and Tony Vecchione
Designer: Tony Vecchione
Editors: Thomas Petzinger Jr. and Larry Rout
Publication: The Wall Street. Journal
Publishing Company: Dow Jones
Medium: Watercolor, pencil and crayon
Cover illustration, the first in the paper's history, for the first issue of the year 2000.

218
Art Director: Nicholas Blechman
Editor: Katy Roberts
Publication: The New York Times
Publishing Company: The New York Times
Writer: Robert M. Gates
Medium: Pencil
Illustration for the Op-Ed piece "One Treaty Doesn't Fit All," October 13, 1999, about the difficulties of modern test ban treaties which are ratified by dozens of countries.

219
Art Director: Michael Valenti
Editor: John Rockwell and Ann Kolson
Publication: The New York Times
Publishing Company: The New York Times
Writers: Jamie Malanowski and Stuart Klawans
Medium: Watercolor
Parody of Norman Rockwell's painting for "The Ghosts of Hollywood Past," November 14, 1999, a special Thanksgiving section.

Matt Mahurin
212-691-5115

220
Publication: GQ Magazine
Publishing Company: Condé Nast Publications, Inc.
Medium: Digital
Illustration for an article on circumcision, February 2000.

Ruth Marten
8 West 13th Street
New York, NY 10011
212-645-0233

221
Design Director: Geraldine Hessler
Designer: Liliane Vilmenay
Editor: Mark Bernardin
Publication: Entertainment Weekly
Publishing Company: Time Inc.
Writer: Rebecca Ascher-Walsh
Medium: Watercolor
Portrait of actress Julia Roberts for the article "Star Struck," November 12, 1999, as her video of "Notting Hill" was released.

222
Medium: Watercolor and acrylic ink
Personal piece entitled "Dax" from a series thematically focused on hair called "The Hurricane Series."

Matthew Martin
19 Prince Street, #4
New York, NY 10012
212-431-5033

223
Art Director: Wesley Bedrosian
Editor: Katy Roberts
Publication: The New York Times
Publishing Company: The New York Times
Writer: James A. Leach
Medium: Ink, pencil and collage
Illustration for an Op-Ed piece entitled "The New Russian Menace," September 9, 1999, about the new corruption in Russia exemplified by the money laundering scandal involving a New York bank.

224
Art Director: Luc Levy
Client: Café Aitane
Medium: Ink, pencil and collage
One from a series of two illustrations created for menu covers.

225
Medium: Gouache
Personal piece.

Mark Matcho
70 Harkness Avenue, #9
Pasadena, CA 91106
626-796-6906

226
Art Direction: Erin Whelan
Publication: Entertainment Weekly
Publishing Company: Time Inc.
Medium: Brush and ink
Illustration for "What Your Kids Are Reading," October 1999, an article on the changing face of books for teens.

Lorenzo Mattotti
55 Rue des Petites Ecuries
Paris 75010 France
331 4247 1492

227
Illustration Editor: Christine Curry
Editor: David Remnick
Publication: The New Yorker
Publishing Company: Condé Nast Publications, Inc.
Writer: Rebecca Mead
Medium: Pencil and pastels
Illustration for the article "The Crisis In Cashmere," February 1, 1999, about how the wool reflects a revolution in the global economy.

Bill Mayer
240 Forkner Drive
Decatur, GA 30030
404-378-0686

228
Art Director: Patrick Mitchell
Designer: Patrick Mitchell
Publication: Fast Company
Publishing Company: Fast Company Media Group, LLC
Writer: Ron Lieber
Medium: Airbrush and gouache
Illustration for the article "First Jobs Aren't Child's Play," June 1999, about how companies get the most from their youngest employees.

Bruce McCall
327 Central Park West, #7B
New York, NY 10025
212-749-1392

229
Art Editor: Françoise Mouly
Publication: The New Yorker
Publishing Company: Condé Nast Publications, Inc.
Medium: Gouache
Cover illustration entitled "Easter Surprise," April 5, 1999.

Adam McCauley

230
Medium: Mixed media
Sketchbook piece drawn at Frida Kahlo's studio in Coyoacan, Mexico, January 2000.

Richard McGuire
45 Carmine St., #3B
New York, NY 10014
212-627-9464
rmcguire@thing.net

231
Creative Director: Juan Delcan
Art Director: Bob Shea
Agency: RazorFish
Client: PBS
Production Company: Passion Pictures
Medium: Gouache
Series of six key frames used as branding and openings for the PBS program "Kids Block."

James McMullan
207 East 32nd St.
New York, NY 10016
212-689-5527

232
Art Director: Steven Heller
Designer: Steven Heller
Editor: Charles McGrath
Publication: The New York Times Book Review
Publishing Company: The New York Times
Medium: Watercolor and gouache
Two from a series created for the reviews of several books on art and architecture, December 5, 1999.

233
Art Director: Leanne Shapton
Designer: Leanne Shapton
Publication: The National Post
Publishing Company: National Post
Medium: Mixed media
Cover illustration for the "Avenue" section, March 1, 1999.

Brook Meinhardt
26 Boylston St., #1
Boston, MA 02130
617-983-0412

234
Two from a series for a self-promotional calendar.

Scott Menchin
640 Broadway
New York, NY 10012
212-673-5363

235
Art Director: Andy Kner
Editor: Martin Fox
Publication: Scenario Magazine
Publishing Company: RC Publications
Writer: Charles Burnett
Medium: Pen and ink and collage
Illustration of an abused wife serving her husband and his friends, accompanied the screenplay "To Sleep With Anger," Spring 1999.

236
Art Director: Ivetta Fedorova
Publication: Man Gave Names to all the Animals
Publishing Company: Harcourt Brace
Writer: Bob Dylan
Medium: Pen and ink and collage
Four illustrations from a series for the book "Man Gave Names to all the Animals," Fall 1999.

David Miller
195 Chrystie Street, #803C
New York, NY 10002
212-477-4576
917-568-5318
www.illustrationmarket.com

237
Curators: Oddo de Grandis and Maria Ida Gaeta
Painting commissioned for the exhibit "Rome 2000," a collection of existing and new American illustration at the Galleria Comuanale d'Arte Moderna e Contemporanea, Rome, Italy.

Val B. Mina

238
Art Director: Fred Woodward

Joe Morse
217 Indian Grove
Toronto, Ont. M6P 2H4
Canada
416-516-2835
Rep: Sally Heflin &
Theartworks
212-366-1893

Katsura Moshino

Joel Nakamura

Robert Neubecker
505 East 3rd Avenue
Salt Lake City, UT 84103
212-219-8435
robert@neubecker.com
www.neubecker.com

Mark Newgarden
Laffpix Inc.
18 Havemeyer Street.
Brooklyn, NY 11211
718-387-2286
mark@laffpix.com

Christoph Niemann
www.christophniemann.com

Christian Northeast
336 Rusholme Road, Top Fl.
Toronto, Ont. M6H 2Z5
Canada
416-538-0400
www.christiannortheast.com

Publication: Rolling Stone
Publishing Company: Wenner Media
Medium: Colored pencil
Portrait of Chris Cornell for a review of his album "Euphoria Morning," September 30, 1999.

239
Art Director: David Curcurito
Designer: Brian Martino
Publication: The Source
Writer: Steve Walker
Medium: Oil and acrylic
Illustration for "Cop Stop Survival Guide," June 1999, an article on how to react when a police officer pulls you over.

240
Art Director: Jenny Leigh Thompson
Designers: Jenny Leigh Thompson and Jessica Ellis
Publication: Link
Publishing Company: College Television Network
Writer: Jeff Howe
Medium: Oil and acrylic
Illustration for "Still Black and Proud," March 1999, an article on black colleges and funding.

241
Creative Director: John C. Jay
Art Director: Philip Lord
Producers: Ted Yukawa and Bruce D. Ikeda
Agency: Wieden and Kennedy Tokyo
Client: Nike Japan
Production Company: Wieden and Kennedy Tokyo
Six key frames from the promotional video "Player's Delight."

242
Medium: Mixed media on panel
Personal piece.

243
Art Director: Wesley Bedrosian
Designer: Tom Bodkin
Editor: Howell Raines
Publication: The New York Times
Publishing Company: The New York Times
Writer: Nathan Black
Medium: Ink on paper
Illustration for the Op-Ed piece entitled "Yes, I'm in a Clique," April 29, 1999, an article on cliques at Columbine High School.

244
Director: Mark Newgarden
Designer: Mark Newgarden
Title Design: Peter Girardi
Animators: Devin Flynn, Jonathan S. Brzyski, Dave Redl, Veronique Brossier and Xeth Fineberg
Producers: Denise Rottina and Kristin Ellington
Agency: Cartoon Network
Client: Turner Broadcasting System
Production Company: Funny Garbage Inc.
Copywriter: Mark Newgarden
Music Composition: Brian Dewan
Six key frames from the video "B. Happy," a cartoonnetwork.com World Premiere Toon, featuring an irritable bluebird of happiness whose job is to redress all personal misery, one wretched individual at a time.

245
Art Director: Hans-Georg Pospischil
Editor: Peter Hintereder
Publication: Deutschland Magazine
Publishing Company: Frankfurter Societäts Druckerei
Medium: Computer
Two illustrations from a series for the article "Freedom of Speech."

246
Art Director: Janet Levy
Designer: Christoph Niemann
Client: Parsons School of Design
Copywriter: Christoph Niemann
Medium: Computer
Series for subway and catalogue advertisement campaign for Parsons School of Design.

247
Art Director: Patrick Mitchell
Designer: Patrick Mitchell
Editor: Alan Webber
Publication: Fast Company
Publishing Company: Fast Company Media Group, LLC
Writer: Harriet Rubin
Medium: Digital
Illustration for "Living Dangerously," December 1999, a feature on a new theme park in Kansas based on "The Wizard of Oz."

248
Medium: Ink and computer
Personal, self-promotional piece entitled "In a Perfect World."

249
Medium: Ink and computer
Personal, self-promotional piece entitled "Beauty and Brains."

250
Medium: Ink and computer
Personal, self-promotional piece entitled "Sailor."

251
Medium: Ink and computer

Personal, self-promotional piece entitled "Reaper."

David O'Keefe
3520 Buckboard Lane
Brandon, FL 33511
813-684-4099

252
Design Director: Arthur Hochstein
Art Director: Ken Smith
Publication: Time Magazine
Publishing Company: Time Inc.
Medium: Clay sculpture
Caricature of presidential candidate George W. Bush, who refused to answer questions on whether or not he used cocaine in his youth, for the "Notebook" section, August 30, 1999.

Alex Ostroy
227 East 12th St., #2C
New York, NY 10003
212-995-2692
alex@ostroy.com

253
Art Director: Naoto Ono
Designer: Naoto Ono
Agency: RDA
Client: Todd Oldham
Publication: Summer '99
Copywriter: Colin Kerr
Medium: Computer
Character named Petunia created for a TO2 Jeans ad campaign.

254
Art Director: Alex Ostroy
Editor: David Gaston
Publication: Ikon Magazine
Publishing Company: Ikon LLP
Medium: Computer
Villain dolls portraying fictitious movie bad guys, for the article "Usual Suspects," June 1999.

Filip Pagowski
17-19 West 108th St., #111
New York, NY 10025
212-665-7553

255
Art Directors: Teresa Fernandes and Leslie Vinson
Publication: Talk Magazine
Publishing Company: Miramax/Hearst Corporation
Writer: Tony Dajer
Medium: Ink on paper
One illustration from a series for "ER Diary II," February 2000, a doctor's journal of his experiences from the emergency room.

Gary Panter
153 Roebling Street
Brooklyn, NY 11211
718-782-5420

256
Art Director: Janet Froelich
Designer: Nancy Harris
Editor: Adam Moss
Publication: The New York Times Magazine
Publishing Company: The New York Times
Writer: Garrison Keillor
Medium: Acrylic on paper
Politicized strongman takes down a bureaucrat before a crowd of rowdy voters, for "How I Won The Minnesota Statehouse," February 14, 1999, an adaptation of a book inspired by the election of Jesse (The Body) Ventura as governor of Minnesota.

257
Design Director: Robert Newman
Designer: Alden Wallace
Publication: Details
Publishing Company: Condé Nast Publications, Inc.
Medium: Paint
Portrait of troubled comedian Martin Lawrence, for the article "He's So Crazy," April 1999.

Roberto Parada
c/o Levy Creative
Management, LLC
300 East 46th St., #4G
New York, NY 10017
212-687-6463

258
Design Director: John Korpics
Art Director: Rockwell Harwood
Editor: David Granger
Publication: Esquire
Publishing Company: Hearst Corporation
Writer: Tom Carson
Medium: Oil on canvas
Portrait of Homer Simpson for the article "The Gospel According to Homer," which claimed that the current crop of television cartoons is the best place to find an accurate account of contemporary America.

259
Design Director: John Korpics
Art Director: Rockwell Harwood
Editor: David Granger
Publication: Esquire
Publishing Company: Hearst Corporation
Writer: Tom Carson
Medium: Oil on canvas
Portrait of news anchors Tom Brokaw, Peter Jennings and Dan Rather, all jockeying for Walter Cronkite's position, for the article "Bray Without Ceasing."

Alain Pilon
c/o Wanda Nowak
231 East 76th St., #5D
New York, NY 10021
212-535-0438

260
Art Director: Gianni Caccia
Editor: Editions Fides
Publication: Nine Days of Hatred
Publishing Company: Bibliothèque Québècoise
Author: Jean-Jules Richard
Medium: Acrylic
Cover illustration for "Nine Days of Hatred," a book about a Canadian soldier during W.W. II.

261
Art Director: Stéphane Jorisch
Designer: Andrée Lavzon
Client: Les 400 Coups
Publication: The Little Red Riding Hood
Copywriter: Philippe A. Poloni
Medium: Acrylic
Unused sketch for the book "The Little Red Riding Hood."

262
Art Director: Alain Massicotte

Designer: Louis Désilets
Design Firm: Studio D Design Inc.
Client: The Association des Illustrateurs et Illustratrices du Quebec
Publication: Directory 1999-2000
Copywriter: Philippe A. Poloni
Medium: Acrylic
Back cover illustration for a directory of Canadian illustration.

Hanoch Piven
c/o Sally Heflin &
Theartworks
455 West 23rd St., #8D
New York, NY 10011
212-366-1893

263
Designer: Orna Oshry
Editors: Udi Asheri and Avner Abrahamy
Publication: Haaretz
Medium: Collage
Portrait of Syrian President Haffez Assad, for a regular column by the artist, July 30, 1999.

264
Designer: Orna Oshry
Editors: Udi Asheri and Avner Abrahamy
Publication: Haaretz
Medium: Collage
Portrait of former Russian President Boris Yeltsin, for a regular column by the artist, July 30, 1999.

David Plunkert
c/o Spur
3504 Ash Street
Baltimore, MD 21211
410-235-7803
dave@spurdesign.com
www.spurdesign.com

265
Art Director: Dennis McLeod
Designer: Dennis McLeod
Publication: Informix Magazine
Publishing Company: Informix Corporation
Writer: Talia Baron
Medium: Collage
Illustration for the article "Putting Digital Data to Work," Winter 2000, about Media 360, a program that allows access, management, storage and retrieval of all types of digital files.

266
Art Director: Hannu Laakso
Editor: Christopher Wilcox
Publication: Reader's Digest
Publishing Company: Reader's Digest
Writer: Kenneth R. Timmerman
Medium: Collage
Illustration for "Our Secrets on Sale," December 1999 , an article about China stealing U.S. technology. David Plunkert

267
Art Director: Kelly McMurray
Editor: John Benditt
Publication: Technology Review
Publishing Company: The Association of Alumni & Alumnae of The Massachusetts Institute of Technology
Writer: Victor D. Chase
Medium: Collage
Illustration for "The Implant Heard 'Round the World," May/June 1999, an article describing the latest hearing implants.

Pierre Pratt
c/o Wanda Nowak
231 East 76th Street, # 5D
New York, NY10021
212-535-0438

268
Art Director: Dominic Champagne
Agency: Sogestalt 2001
Client: Sogestalt 2001
Publication: A Jazz Song for Anne
Copywriter: Pierre Pratt
Medium: Gouache
Illustration for the television show "A Jazz Song For Anne," created as a background poster accompanying the singer.

Chris Pyle
c/o Lisa Freeman
770 East 73rd Street
Indianapolis, IN 46240
317-920-0068

269
Design Director: Geraldine Hessler
Designer: Joe Kimberling
Editor: John McAlley
Publication: Entertainment Weekly
Publishing Company: Time Inc.
Writer: Various
Medium: Mixed media
R&B record producer/performer Baby Face for "Significant Others," September 17, 1999, a Fall preview feature of upcoming music.

Brian Rea
180 Varick St., 8th Floor
New York, NY 10014
646-486-3512
b.rea@erols.com

270
Art Director: Nicholas Blechman
Designer: Paul Sahre
Publication: The New York Times
Publishing Company: The New York Times
Medium: Papermate fine point pen
Illustration for the Op-Ed piece "The Line on Life," an article on how scientists are attempting to alter human genetics in order to increase the length of a person's life.

Robert Risko

271
Publication: Rolling Stone
Publishing Company: Wenner Media
Medium: Gouache
Portrait of Yoko Ono, for the millennium issue feature "The Party 2000," December 30, 1999-January 6, 2000.

272
Art Director: Fred Woodward
Designer: Gail Anderson
Publication: Rolling Stone
Publishing Company: Wenner Media
Medium: Gouache
Portrait of Sarah Michelle Gellar, appearing on the "Contents Page," March 18, 1999, for a review of her movie "Cruel Intentions."

John Ritter

273
Associate Illustration Editor: Owen Phillips

John Ritter
4300 Butler Street
Pittsburgh, PA 15201
412-802-0800
jrill@earthlink.net

Editor: David Remnick
Publication: The New Yorker
Publishing Company: Condé Nast Publications, Inc.
Medium: Mixed media
Illustration for an announcement of a live performance by the group Royal Trux, for the "Goings On About Town" section, October 4, 1999.

274
Associate Illustration Editor: Owen Phillips
Editor: David Remnick
Publication: The New Yorker
Publishing Company: Condé Nast Publications, Inc.
Medium: Mixed media
Illustration for an announcement of a concert by the group the Make-Up, for the "Goings On About Town" section, December 6, 1999.

Edel Rodriguez
16 Ridgewood Avenue, #102
Mount Tabor, NJ 07878
973-983-7776
www.theispot.com/artist/
erodriguez

275
Art Director: Sharon Okamoto
Editor: Walter Isaacson
Publication: Time Magazine
Publishing Company: Time Inc.
Writer: Walter Isaacson
Medium: Pastel, oil base ink and gouache on paper
Portrait of Mao and Stalin, two of the nominees for Person of the Century, from a series for "Who Mattered and Why," December 31, 1999.

Irene Rofheart
P.O. Box 420
Garrison, NY 10524
914-424-8304
irene@highlands.com

276
Art Director: Dorothy Marschall
Designer: Jane Palecek
Publication: Health Magazine
Publishing Company: Time Inc.
Writer: Alice Kelly
Medium: Mixed media on computer
Illustration for "Break Free From Headaches," April 1999, an article on finding headache relief.

277
Art Director: Donna Agajanian
Publication: Barnard Magazine
Publishing Company: Barnard
Writer: Amanda Beesley
Medium: Mixed media on computer
Illustration for "On Love and Companionship," February 2000, an article on the first year of marriage.

Jonathon Rosen
612 Degraw Street, #2
Brooklyn, NY 11217
718-855-6599
gryluss@walrus.com
www.walrus.com/~gryllus

278
Art Directors: Jonathon Rosen and Giorgio Camuffo
Client: Studio Camuffo/Giorgio Camuffo
Medium: Mixed media on paper
Announcement card for "Immagini Cerebroviscerali" (Pictures of the Brain's Passion) an exhibition of the artist's artwork and animation in Venice, Italy.

279
Art Director: Jonathon Rosen
Designer: Jonathon Rosen
Client: Adam Baumgold Fine Art
Medium: Mixed media
Announcement card for "Medical, Mechanical & Carnivalesque" an exhibition of the artist's work at Adam Baumgold Fine Art Gallery.

280
Production Designer: Rik Heinrichs
Director: Tim Burton
Calligrapher: Sweetbryar
Film Title: Sleepy Hollow
Production Company: Paramount Pictures
Screenplay: Andrew Kevin Walker
Medium: Mixed media on paper
Series of drawings from Ichabod Craines' journal, as seen in the movie "Sleepy Hollow," November 1999, based on the Washington Irving novel "The Legend of Sleepy Hollow." (Courtesy of Paramount Pictures and Mandalay Pictures LLC.)

Arnold Roth
157 West 57th St., #904
New York, NY 10019
212-333-7606

281
Illustration Editor: Christine Curry
Editor: David Remnick
Publication: The New Yorker
Publishing Company: Condé Nast Publications, Inc.
Medium: Pen and ink and watercolor
Illustration for the opening of the Metropolitan Museum of Art's exhibit "Rock Style," December 13, 1999, depicting Madonna's peach bustier and pin-striped jacket and George Clinton's platform boots.

Balvis Rubess
260 Brunswick Avenue
Toronto, Ont. M5S 2M7
Canada
416-927-7071
blavi@home.com
www.headinabox.com

282
Art Director: Balvis Rubess
Senior Editor: Duncan Bock/Melcher Media
Director of Production: Andrea Hirsh
Publication: The Pop-Up Book of Phobias
Publishing Company: Rob Weisbach Books/
William Morrow
Author: Gary Greenberg
Medium: Hybrid digital/analog
Four illustrations from a series for the book "The Pop-Up Book of Phobias," November 1999. Included here: aerophobi, acrophobia, coulrophobia and dentophobia.

Sergio Ruzzier
c/o Wanda Nowak
231 East 76th St., #5D
New York, NY 10021
212-535-0438

283
Designer: Giacomo Spazio
Publication: The Empty Cradle
Publishing Company: Cane Andaluso
Author: Sergio Ruzzier
Medium: Pen and ink and watercolor

One illustration from a series for the book "The Empty Cradle," 1999.

Marina Sagona
c/o Riley Illustration
155 West 15th St., #4C
New York, NY 10011
212-989-8770
www.rileyillustration.com

284
Art Director: Johan Svensson
Designer: Amy Demas
Publication: Jane Magazine
Publishing Company: Fairchild Publications, Inc.
Medium: Acrylic
Illustration for the article "Shanti," February 2000.

David Sandlin
58 East 1st St., #5C
New York, NY 10003
212-388-1558

285
Art Director: Leanne Shapton
Designer: Leanne Shapton
Publication: National Post
Publishing Company: National Post
Medium: Mixed media
Illustration for the article "Home and Away," July 5, 1999, about how with the computer database, it's becoming more difficult for the migrating bigamists to hide.

Stephen Savage
444 Sackett Street
Brooklyn, NY 11231
718-624-5435

286
Art Director: Richard Baker
Designer: Richard Baker
Publication: Premiere Magazine
Publishing Company: Hachette Filipacchi Magazines
Writers: Howard Karren and Glenn Kenny
Medium: Linocut
Portrait of Walt Disney for the article "Hall of Fame," October 1999.

287
Medium: Linocut
Portrait of Cary Grant for a self-promotional mailer.

Ward Schumaker
466 Green Street
San Francisco, CA 94133
415-398-1060
www.warddraw.com

288
Designer: Ward Schumaker
Publication: Land of Knives
Medium: Pen and ink and Photoshop
Two personal illustrations for the, as yet, unpublished book "Land of Knives," based on experiences and encounters during the artist's youth.

289
Art Director: Steven Heller
Publication: The New York Times Book Review
Publishing Company: The New York Times
Writer: Roberto González Echevarría
Medium: Pen and ink and Photoshop
Portrait of Garcia Lorca for "Lorca, A Dream of Life," September 1999, a review of a new biography on the Spanish writer.

Rick Sealock
P.O. Box 98
Milo AB T0L 1L0 Canada
403-276-5428
www.ricksealock.com

290
Art Director: Mark Shaw
Designer: Mark Shaw
Editors: Mimi Valdés and O.J. Lima
Publication: Blaze Magazine
Publishing Company: Vibe Ventures LLC
Writer: Jon Caramanica
Medium: Mixed media
Portrait of hip-hop beatboxer Rahzel, for "Vinyl Exams," August 1999, a review of his album "Make the Music 2000."

Ronald Searle
c/o Eileen McMahon & Co.
201-436-4362

291
Art Director: Margot Frankel
Designer: Jennifer Bowles
Editor: Diane Guernsey
Publication: Town & Country Magazine
Publishing Company: Hearst Corporation
Writer: Katharine Merlin
Medium: Watercolor
Series for "Town & Country's Heavenly Horoscopes," January 1999.

292
Art Director: Agnethe Glatved
Designer: Agnethe Glatved
Editors: Janet Carlson Freed and Diane Guernsey
Publication: Town & Country Magazine
Publishing Company: Hearst Corporation
Writer: Leslie Laurence and Beth Weinhouse
Medium: Watercolor
Opening illustration for "Town & Country's Comprehensive Guide to Cosmetic Surgery," March 1999.

J. Otto Seibold
1261 Howard, #3
San Francisco, CA 94114
415-558-9115

293
Art Editor: Françoise Mouly
Publication: The New Yorker
Publishing Company: Condé Nast Publications, Inc.
Medium: Digital
Cover illustration, December 6, 1999

294
Art Director: J. Otto Seibold
Designer: J. Otto Seibold
Editor: Victoria Rock
Publication: Penguin Dreams
Publishing Company: Chronicle Books
Authors: J. Otto Seibold and Vivian Walsh
Medium: Digital
Four illustrations from the book "Penguin Dreams."

Alison Seiffer
7 Deforest Road
Montauk, NY 11954
631-668-0326

295
Art Director: Emily Crawford
Designer: Emily Crawford
Publication: American Recorder

Publishing Company: American Recorder Society
Medium: Gouache
Cover illustration for "American Recorder" magazine,
January 2000.

Chris Sharp
17 Little West 12th St., #310
New York, NY 10014
212-647-9368

296
Art Director: Tim Hussey
Designer: Tim Hussey
Publication: Troika
Publishing Company: Lone Tout Publications, Inc.
Writer: Julie Kruger
Medium: Gouache
Illustration for "The Art of the Piropo", December 1999, an
article on the Latin American custom of men who make
"amorous compliments," "flirtatious remarks" or "cat calls"
to women.

Sara Singh
c/o Unit
25 Cedar Street
New York, NY 10006
212-766-4117

297
Art Director: Pamela Berry
Designer: Pamela Berry
Editor: Sheila Glaser
Publication: Travel & Leisure
Publishing Company: American Express Publishing
Writer: Judith Thurman
Medium: Watercolor and ink
Portrait of author Colette, for "Colette's Riviera," May 1999, a
story on her romance with the French Riviera in the early 1900s.

Jeffrey Smith
642 Moulton Avenue, #E22
Los Angeles, CA 90031
323-224-8317

298
Art Director: Martin Colyer
Publication: Reader's Digest
Publishing Company: Reader's Digest Association, Inc.
Writer: Andro Linklater
Medium: Watercolor
Illustration for "Let Me Tell You a Story," January 1999, an article
on America's regained interest in the art of storytelling.

Owen Smith
1608 Fernside Boulevard
Alameda, CA 94501
510-865-1911
lizowen@home.com

299
Art Editor: Françoise Mouly
Publication: The New Yorker
Publishing Company: Condé Nast Publications, Inc.
Medium: Oil
Cover illustration entitled "Brace Yourself," September 13, 1999.

300
Art Director: Richard Baker
Designer: Richard Baker
Editor: Glenn Kenny
Publication: Premiere Magazine
Publishing Company: Hachette Filipacchi
Writer: Jewel Shepard
Medium: Oil on board
Illustration for the article "Shy, But Barely," November 1999,
about a film actress' experience auditioning for and doing
nude scenes.

301
Art Director: Greg Evans
Editor: Timothy Rhys
Publication: Movie Maker
Publishing Company: Movie Maker Publishing Co. Inc.
Medium: Oil on canvas
Illustration for "Boxing's Back," January/February 1999, an
article on the slew of new boxing movies with a discussion on
boxing films of the past.

302
Medium: Oil on canvas
Two portraits of twin gangsters Reggie and Ronnie Kray who
dominated London's East End in the 1950s and 1960s. Reggie,
left, with his wife Frances Shea who committed suicide, died in
1995; Ronnie, right, with loyal mother Violet, has served 31
years in prison.

Edward Sorel
156 Franklin Street
New York, NY 10013
212-966-3949

303
Illustration Editor: Christine Curry
Publication: The New Yorker
Publishing Company: Condé Nast Publications, Inc.
Medium: Pen, ink and watercolor
Caricature of Edward G. Robinson for an announcement of
a festival of his films.

Joe Sorren
520-214-9980
www.joesorren.com

304
Art Director: Ei Ming
Client: Minna St. Gallery
Publication: Juxapox Magazine
Medium: Acrylic on canvas
Promotional piece for a show at the Minna St. Gallery.

305
Art Directors: Rich Brown and Jane Williams
Client: Universalia Jane
Medium: Acrylic on canvas
CD cover for "In Her Silent Way" by singer/songwriter
Jane Williams.

Art Spiegelman
c/o Raw Books
27 Greene Street
New York, NY 10013
212-226-0146

306
Art Editor: Françoise Mouly
Publication: The New Yorker
Publishing Company: Condé Nast Publications, Inc.
Medium: Acrylic
Cover illustration, "Open Minded Mayor," October 11, 1999.

John Springs

307
Design Director: John Korpics
Designers: Geraldine Hessler and Jennifer Procopio
Editor: John McAlley

David Ezra Stein
113 82nd Road
Kew Gardens, NY 11415
718-261-6225
monsieurtiger@hotmail.com

Peter Stemmler
325 West 38th St., #903
New York, NY 10018
212-244-6059

Katherine Streeter
17 Little West 12th St., #310
New York, NY 10014
212-924-7966
www.streeterart.com

Mark Stutzman

Ward Sutton
799 Greenwich St., #4S
New York, NY 10014
212-924-4992
wardsutton@aol.com

Hiroshi Tanabe
c/o Kate Larkworthy Artist
Representation, Ltd.
80 Nassau Street
New York, NY 10038
212-964-9141
www.larkworthy.com

Blair Thornley
1251 University Avenue
San Diego, CA 92103
619-299-3874

Bob & Val Tillery
Hungry Dog Studio
239 Riverside Drive
Nashville, TN 37206-1958
615-262-8654

Mark Todd

Publication: Entertainment Weekly
Publishing Company: Time Inc.
Medium: Mixed media
Portrait of Pete Townshend smashing his first guitar, for the
feature "100 Greatest Moments in Rock," May 28, 1999.

308
Medium: Watercolor and ink
Personal piece entitled "Union Square."

309
Medium: Watercolor and ink
Personal piece entitled "Forest Hills."

310
Art Director: Robert Newman
Designer: Brandon Kavulla
Publication: Vibe Magazine
Publishing Company: Miller Publishing Group
Writer: Carter Harris
Medium: Digital
Democratic presidential hopeful Bill Bradley, for the article "He
Has a Dream," March 2000.

311
Art Director: Debra Moore
Publication: Heart & Soul Magazine
Writer: Monica V. Utsey
Medium: Acrylic
Illustration for the article "Taming Your Tot," January 2000,
about the controversy over spanking your child".

312
Art Directors: Elizabeth Kairys and Mignon Khargie
Web Site: Salon.com
Medium: Acrylic and mixed media
Web site cover for Salon.com's Book Awards, the editor's picks
of the best books of 1999.

313
Design Director: John Korpics
Designers: Geraldine Hessler and Jennifer Procopio
Editor: John McAlley
Publication: Entertainment Weekly
Publishing Company: Time Inc.
Medium: Mixed media
Illustration entitled "Appall in the Family," which sets various
shock-rock stars in the famous Rockwellian setting, for the
feature "100 Greatest Moments in Rock," May 28, 1999

314
Art & Animation Director: J.J. Sedelmaier
Designers: Ward Sutton and J.J. Sedelmaier
Animators: Tony Eastman and Sean Lattrell
Producer: J.J. Sedelmaier
Agency: Central Productions
Client: Comedy Central
Production Company: J.J. Sedelmaier Productions, Inc.
Copywriters: Paul Dinello, Amy Sedaris and David Wain
Music Composition: Bob Golden
Six key frames from the opening title sequence for the
Comedy Central show "Strangers with Candy," which
chronicles the main character's life between leaving and
returning to high school.

315
Art Director: Debbie Smith
Designer: Aoi Hirai
Publication: Nippon Vogue
Publishing Company: Nikkei Condé Nast
Publications, Inc.
Medium: Mixed media
One illustration from a series of three for a story about
New York City.

316
Creative Director: Kazuyoshi Minamimagoe
Designer: Madoka Iwabuchi
Client: Gentosha Publishing Inc.
Publication: Blink
Medium: Mixed media
Illustration of fashions from the clothing line Under Cover, for
"Blink," a hardcover book of collaborations between illustrators,
fashion designers and manufacturers.

317
Art Director: Wolfgang Hastert
Animator: Blair Thornley
Producer: Wolfgang Hastert
Agency: Z.D.F.-Arte (German Public Television Station)
Production Company: Wolfgang Hastert Productions
Music Composition: Saint-Saens, The Aquarium
Six frames from the film "Mr. Lou," about a man who is trying to
lose weight and the problems he faces in his struggle to do so.

318
Art Director: George McCalman
Publication: Entertainment Weekly
Publishing Company: Time Inc.
Writer: Rob Brunnek
Medium: Mixed media
Portrait of Nine Inch Nail's Trent Reznor, for an interview as his
new album "Fragile" was released, Fall 1999.

319
Deputy Illustration Editor: Owen Phillips

Mark Todd
123 Prospect Place, #1
Brooklyn, NY 11217
718-783-1488
www.mtodd.net

Editor: David Remnick
Publication: The New Yorker
Publishing Company: Condé Nast Publications, Inc.
Medium: Acrylic on paper
The characters from "South Park," as their movie" Bigger, Longer, Uncut" opens, for the "Goings on About Town" section, July 5, 1999.

320
Art Director: Margaret Raymo
Designer: Bob Kosturko
Editor: Margaret Raymo
Publication: The Pain Tree
Publishing Company: Houghton Mifflin
Writer: Various
Medium: Acrylic on paper
Two illustrations from "The Pain Tree," Spring 2000, an illustrated book of poems written by and for teenagers.

Lara Tomlin
543 55th Street
Brooklyn, NY 11220
718-439-1671

321
Deputy Illustration Editor: Owen Phillips
Editor: David Remnick
Publication: The New Yorker
Publishing Company: Condé Nast Publications, Inc.
Medium: Mixed media
The Nicholas Leichter Dance performing "Breakdown," at the Flea Theater, for the "Goings On About Town" section, November 1999.

Mark Ulriksen
841 Shrader Street
San Francisco, CA 94117
415-387-0170
www.mulriksen.com
theispot.com

322
Art Director: Nicholas Blechman
Publication: The New York Times
Publishing Company: The New York Times
Writer: Michael Deaver
Medium: Pen, ink and gouache
Portrait of Ronald Reagan, for the Op-Ed piece "The Elusive Ronald Reagan," September 29, 1999.

323
Art Director: Joan Ferrell
Designer: Joan Ferrell
Editor: Amy Singer
Publication: The American Lawyer
Publishing Company: American Lawyer Media
Writer: Geoffrey Cowan
Medium: Oil on paper
Portrait of attorney Clarence Darrow, circa 1925, during the Scopes Monkey Trial, for "A Man for Some Seasons," December 1999, in a special issue on the lawyers of the century.

324
Art Editor: Françoise Mouly
Editor: David Remnick
Publication: The New Yorker
Publishing Company: Condé Nast Publications, Inc.
Medium: Acrylic on paper
Cover illustration entitled "Opening Day," April 2, 1999.

325
Illustration Editor: Christine Curry
Editor: David Remnick
Publication: The New Yorker
Publishing Company: Condé Nast Publications, Inc.
Medium: Gouache on board
One illustration from a series for "Haunted Houses," September 13, 1999, a portrait of closing baseball stadiums.

326
Curators: Oddo de Grandis and Maria Ida Gaeta
Painting entitled "The Time We Met Bill & Hillary in the Piazza del Popolo," commissioned for the exhibit "Rome 2000" a collection of existing and new American illustration at the Galleria Comunale d'Arte Moderna e Contemporanea, Rome, Italy.

Jack Unruh
8138 Santa Clara Drive
Dallas, TX 75218
214-327-6211
www.jackunruh.com

327
Art Director: Fred Woodward
Publication: Rolling Stone
Publishing Company: Wenner Media
Medium: Mixed media
Portrait of Tom Waits, appearing on the "Contents Page," March 18, 1999, for an article on his album "Mule Variations."

Lauren Uram
224 Lincoln Road
Brooklyn, NY 11225
718-469-2695

328
Design Director: Arthur Hochstein
Art Director: Sharon Okamoto
Publication: Time Magazine
Publishing Company: Time Inc.
Medium: Paper and ink
Portrait of Johann Gutenberg made from the text of the Gutenberg Bible, for the article "The Most Important People of the Millennium," December 31, 1999.

Riccardo Vecchio
260 Norman Avenue, #6
Brooklyn, NY 11222
718-389-5728

329
Art Directors: Gail Belenson and Marc Melnick
Publication: The Pelican Shakespeare
Publishing Company: Penguin Putnam
Medium: Gouache on paper
Series of cover illustrations for a collection of Shakespeare plays.

Maurice Vellekoop
c/o Reactor Art & Design
51 Camden Street
Toronto, Ont. M5V 1V2
Canada
800-730-8945
www.reactor.ca

330
Designer: Savas Abadsidis
Publication: Abercrombie & Fitch Catalogue
Client: Abercrombie & Fitch
Medium: Watercolor
Illustration entitled "Naughty or Nice," for the Abercrombie & Fitch 1999 Christmas catalogue.

Andrea Ventura

331
Art Director: Joan Ferrell

Andrea Ventura
346 Leonard St., #2
Brooklyn, NY 11211
718-349-3131

Designer: Joan Ferrell
Editor: Amy Singer
Publication: The American Lawyer
Publishing Company: American Lawyer Media
Writer: Geoffrey Cowan
Medium: Acrylic and charcoal on paper
Portrait of Attorney and Judge Louis Brandeis, for the article "The Unlikely Radical," December 1999, in a special issue on the lawyers of the century.

332
Art Director: Patrick Mitchell
Designer: Patrick Mitchell
Editor: Alan Webber
Publication: Fast Company
Publishing Company: Fast Company Media Group LLC
Writer: Harriet Rubin
Medium: Acrylic and charcoal on paper
Illustration for the feature " Living Dangerously" November 1999, about how we mythologize, criticize and misunderstand our leaders.

333
Medium: Ink and watercolor on paper
Personal peice, street scene in Milan, Italy.

334
Medium: Gouache on board
Personal piece, bar scene.

Stefano Vitale
49 Sandy Hill Road
Oyster Bay Cove, NY 11771
516-922-7130

335
Art Director: Gerard Sealy
Deputy Art Director: Leigh Borghesani
Editor: Keith Bellows
Publication: National Geographic Traveler
Publishing Company: National Geographic Society
Writer: Anthony Weller
Medium: Oil on wood
Illustration for the article "Dreaming of Kashmir," January/February 2000, a region that is currently closed to tourists, so at this point, only dreaming is possible.

Chris Ware

336
Art Director: Cynthia Currie
Senior Designer: Daniel Kohan
Editor: Theodore J. Miller
Publication: Kiplinger's Personal Finance
Publishing Company: Kiplinger's Washington Editors
Writer: Ed Henry
Medium: Digital
Illustration for the article "Wired Wheels," January 2000, a look at the car of the future.

Chip Wass
180 Varick Street, 8th Floor
New York, NY 10014
212-741-2550
www.worldofwassco.com

337
Art Directors: Scott Stowell and Chip Wass
Designer: Scott Stowell/Open
Animator: Sam Dewitt/Spontaneous Combustion
Producer: Simone Pillinger
Client: Nick at Nite
Music Composition: Pomposello Productions
Six frames from the Nick at Nite on-air redesign, 1999.

Susy Pilgrim Waters
11 Eden Avenue
West Newton, MA 02465
617-965-4954
pilgrimwaters@mediaone.net
www.lillarogers.com

338
Medium: Mixed media
Warm-up sketchbook drawing for a piece on pianos.

Esther Pearl Watson
123 Prospect Place, #1
Brooklyn, NY 11217
718-783-1488
www.estherwatson.com

339
Medium: Acrylic on paper
Personal piece, portrait of Lena Horne.

340
Medium: Acrylic on paper
Personal piece, portrait of Ella Fitzgerald.

341|342
Art Director: Margaret Raymo
Designer: Bob Kosturko
Editor: Margaret Raymo
Publication: The Pain Tree
Publishing Company: Houghton Mifflin
Writer: Various
Medium: Acrylic on paper
Two illustrations from "The Pain Tree," Spring 2000, an illustrated book of poems written by and for teenagers.

Mark Weber

343
Art Director: Fred Woodward
Publication: Rolling Stone
Publishing Company: Wenner Media
Medium: Mixed media
Portrait of Ol' Dirty Bastard, for a review of his album "Nigga Please," October 14, 1999.

Philippe Weisbecker
c/o Riley Illustration
155 West 15th St., #4C
New York, NY 10011
212-989-8770
www.rileyillustration.com

344
Art Director: Lloyd Ziff
Designer: Charles Wallace
Editor: Jennnifer Sucov
Publication: Winning Team
Publishing Company: Time Inc. Custom Publishing
Writer: Thomas A. Stewart
Medium: Mixed media
One from "The Employee as Investor," Fall 1999, about how employers get better employees by treating them like investors.

345
Art Director: Leanne Shapton

Philippe Weisbecker

Designer: Roland Yves Carignan
Publication: National Post
Publishing Company: National Post
Medium: Graphite, colored pencil and paper
Illustration for "Inner Voices," April 29, 1999, an article that ran during National Poetry Month and featured poetry by people with schizophrenia.

346
Art Director: Patrick Mitchell
Designer: Patrick Mitchell
Editor: Jennnifer Sucov
Publication: Fast Company
Publishing Company: Fast Company Media Group, LLC
Medium: Collage
Illustration for "Where Are You On the Web?" October 1999, an article on the different types of web users: fanatics, skeptics and the great middle.

Leigh Wells
17 Little West 12th St., #310
New York, NY 10014
212-627-8518
leigh@leighwells.com
www.leighwells.com

347
Medium: Acrylic and mixed media
Self-promotional piece about the risks of investing.

348
Medium: Acrylic and mixed media
Personal piece inspired by imagery associated with the Chinese New Year.

Michael S. Wertz
385 1/2 Jersey Street
San Francisco, CA 94114
415-824-5542
michael@wertzateria.com
www.wertzateria.com

349
Medium: Acrylic on paper
Personal piece entitled "Yoda," a portrait of the deceased.

350
Art Director: Dennis Crowe
Designer: Margaret Blatchford
Animator: Gordon Clark/Wild Brain
Producer: Kaye Robinson
Agency: Zimmerman Crowe Design
Client: San Francisco Film Society
Production Company: Wild Brain
Music Composition: Zack Smith/Dustpan
Six key frames from the 1999 San Francisco International Film Festival trailer.

Eric White
718-399-2997
ewhite@firstworld.net
www.ewhite.com

351
Medium: Oil on canvas
Personal piece entitled "Nam! 1949 RKO Radio Pictures."

352
Medium: Oil on canvas
Personal piece entitled "Swims."

Noah Woods
c/o Gerald & Cullen Rapp
108 East 35th Street
New York, NY 10016
212-889-3337
www.theispot.com/artist/nwoods

353
Art Director: Clara Huang
Designer: Noah Woods
Publication: Poz Magazine
Publishing Company: Poz Publications
Writer: Linda Grinberg
Medium: Mixed media
Illustration for "Honeymoon to Heartache," May 1999, an article about how some AIDS patients on protease inhibitors experience bizarre side effects of changes in body shape.

354
Art Director: David Plunkert
Designers: Noah Woods and David Plunkert
Design Firm: Spur
Client: A.I.R.S. (AIDS Interfaith Residential Services)
Medium: Mixed media
Cover illustration for a brochure describing the many services provided by A.I.R.S., an organization that provides care to low-income persons living with HIV/AIDS.

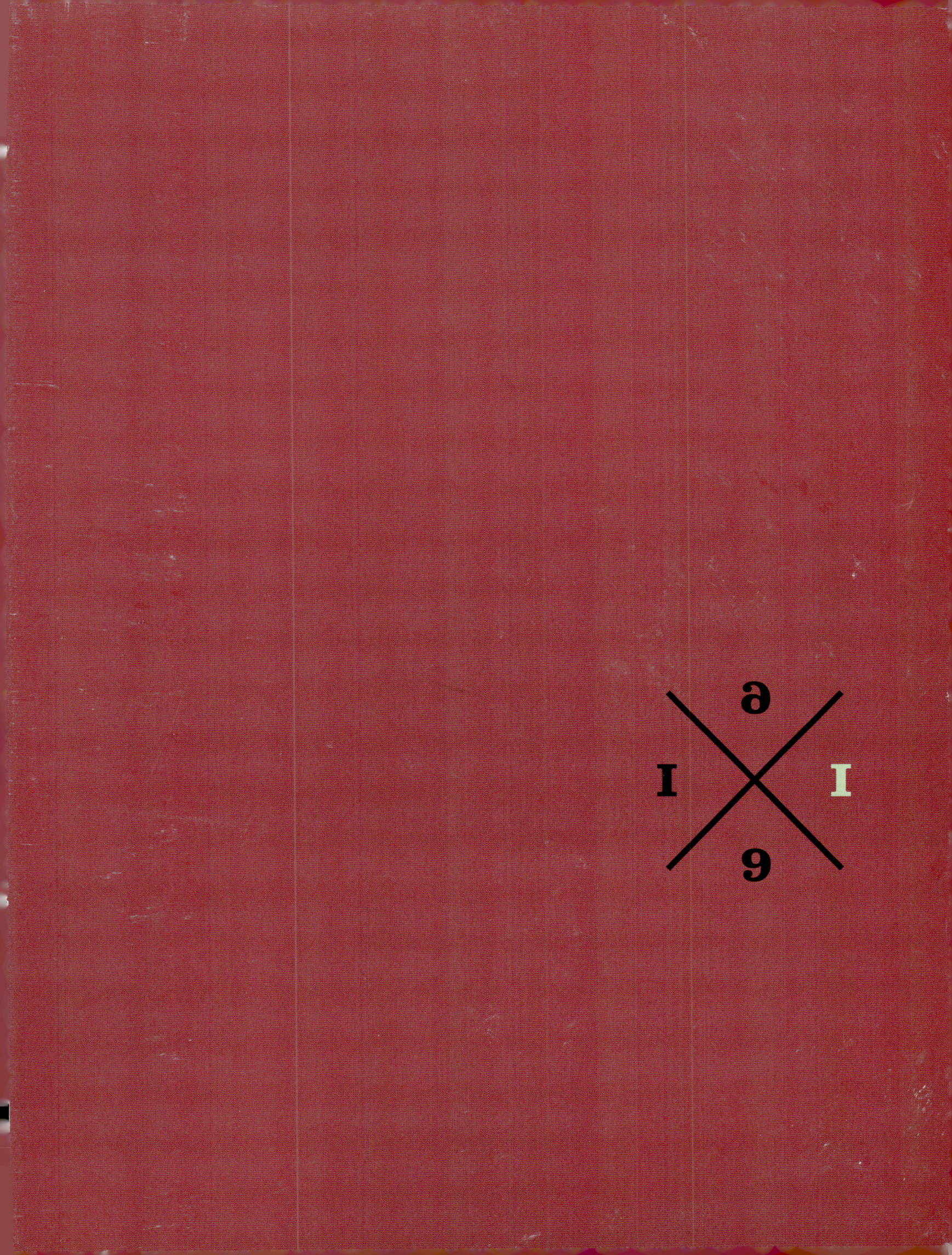

424

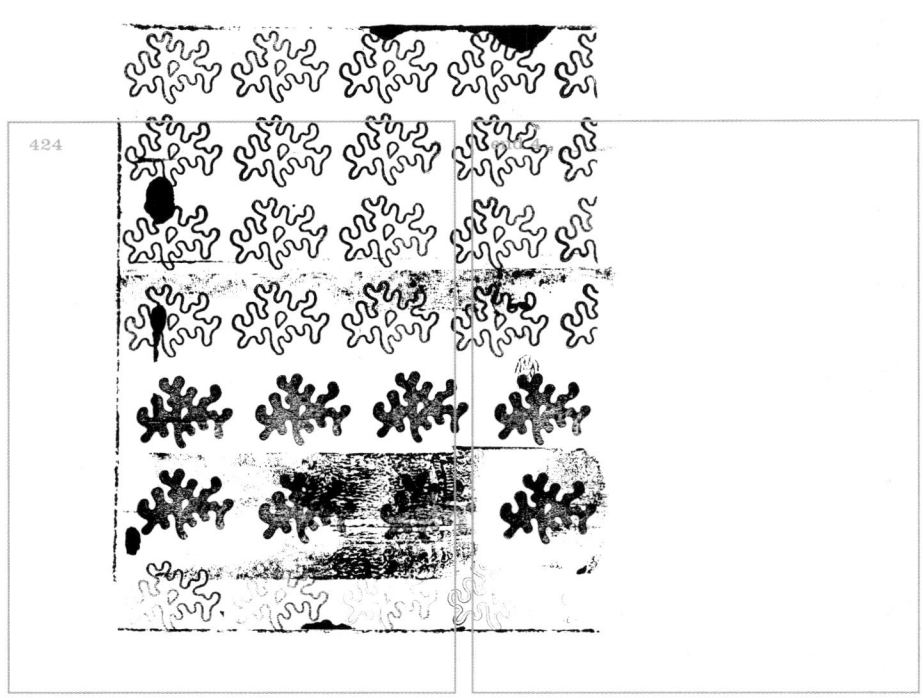

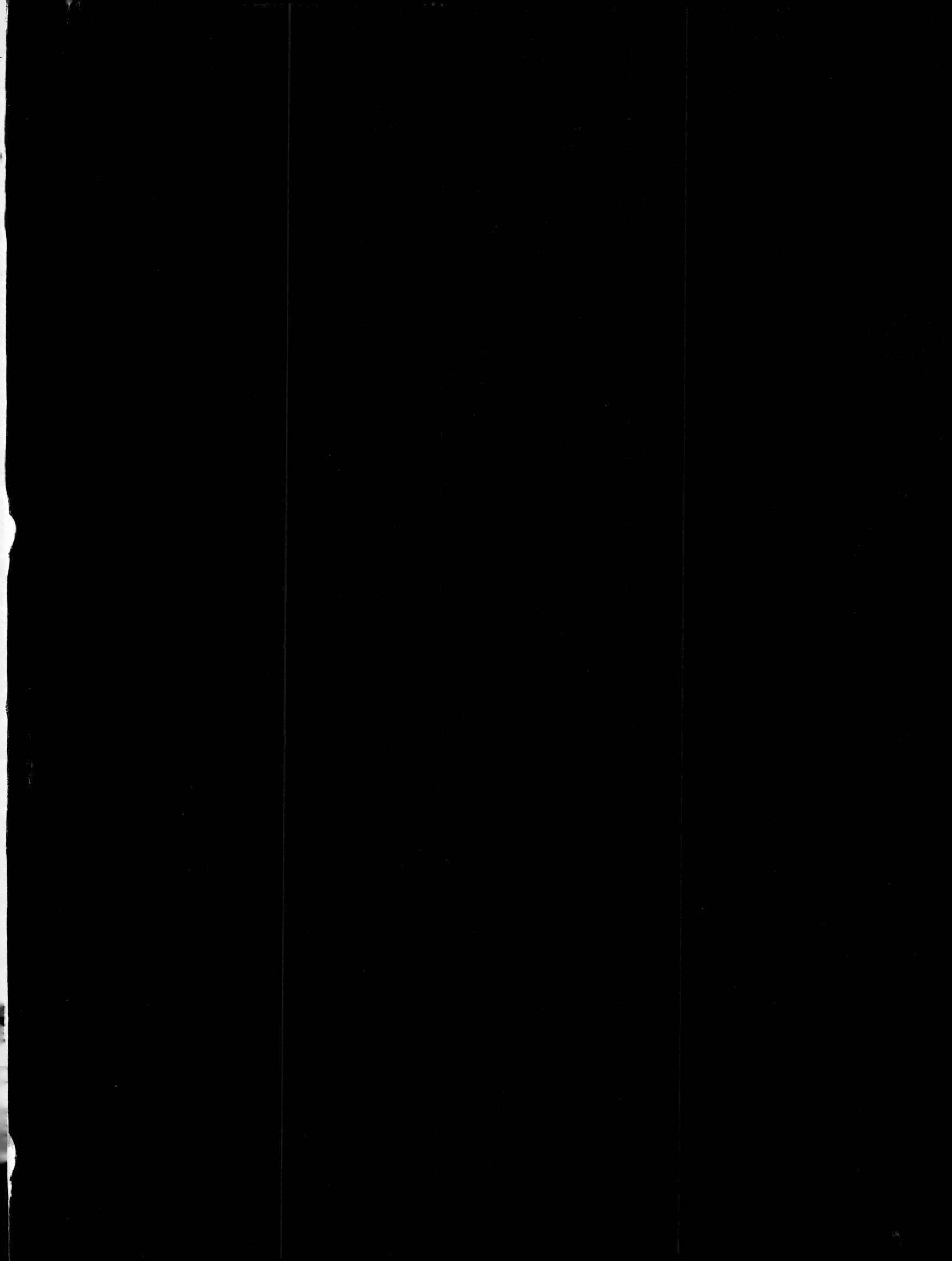

end 5

end 6

BOOK DESIGN: Tom Brown TBA+D
ASSISTANT DESIGNER: Jenn Roberts
COVER/BOOK ILLUSTRATION: Brian Cronin
~~CHAIRMAN: Fred Woodward~~
PUBLISHER: Kenneth Fadner
DIRECTOR: Mark Heflin

PRINTER: Dai Nippon, Hong Kong